THE DESIGNED WORLD

THE DESIGNED

WORLD

Images, Objects, Environments

Richard Buchanan, Dennis Doordan, and Victor Margolin

Oxford • New York

English edition
First published in 2010 by
Berg
Editorial offices:
First Floor, Angel Court, 81 St Clements Street, Oxford OX4 1AW, UK
175 Fifth Avenue, New York, NY 10010, USA

Berg is the imprint of Oxford International Publishers Ltd.

Library of Congress Cataloging-in-Publication Data

The designed world : images, objects, environments / [edited by] Victor Margolin, Dennis Doordan, and Richard Buchanan. — English ed.
p. cm.
ISBN 978-1-84788-585-2 (pbk.) — ISBN 978-1-84788-586-9 (cloth)
1. Design. 2. Architectural design. 3. Industrial design. I. Margolin, Victor, 1941- II. Doordan, Dennis P. III. Buchanan, Richard. IV. Design issues.
NK1520.D467 2010
745.2—dc22

2010029807

British Library Cataloguing-in-Publication Data

A catalogue record for this book is available from the British Library.

ISBN 978 1 84788 586 9 (Cloth)
978 1 84788 585 2 (Paper)

Typeset by JS Typesetting Ltd, Porthcawl, Mid Glamorgan
Printed in the UK by the MPG Books Group

www.bergpublishers.com

CONTENTS

PART II: FABRICATION

PART III: EVALUATION

EDITORS' BIOGRAPHIES

Richard Buchanan is Professor of Design, Management, and Information Systems in the Weatherhead School of Management, Case Western Reserve University. He has extended the application of design into new areas of theory and practice, writing and teaching, as well as practicing with the concepts and methods of Interaction Design. At the Weatherhead School, he has turned his work toward "collective interactions," focusing on problems of organizational change and a reform of management education around the concept of "managing by design." He served for two terms as President of the Design Research Society. His numerous publications include the edited volumes *Discovering Design: Explorations in Design Studies*, *The Idea of Design*, and *Pluralism in Theory and Practice*.

Dennis Doordan is a design educator, historian, critic, museum consultant, co-editor of *Design Issues* and a faculty member at the University of Notre Dame. He has published books and articles on a wide variety of topics dealing with twentieth-century architecture and design including political design, the impact of new materials, and the evolution of exhibition design techniques.

Victor Margolin is Professor Emeritus of Design History at the University of Illinois, Chicago. He is a founding editor of, and now co-editor of, *Design Issues*. Books which he has written, edited, or co-edited include *Propaganda: The Art of Persuasion, World War II*; *The Struggle for Utopia: Rodchenko, Lissitzky, Moholy-Nagy, 1917–1946*; *Design Discourse*; *Discovering Design*; *The Idea of Design*; *and The Politics of the Artificial: Essays on Design and Design Studies.* He is currently working on a world history of design.

AUTHORS' BIOGRAPHIES

Giovanni Anceschi is an artist and designer, design historian and theorist, organizer of design culture and design research. He is a Professor of Communication Design, of Information Design and of Basic Design, and he is coordinator of the doctoral research program in design sciences at the Università IUAV di Venezia, Italy. Recently: Inaugural lecture at the international congress ("Multiple Ways to Design Research") at the SUPSI University of Lugano (February 11, 2009) and "Combinatoire et Somatique" at Umberto Eco's Colloque "Oeuvres Ouverte/Vertige de la Liste," Louvre Contemporain (February 14, 2009).

Paul Betts is Associate Professor of Modern German History at the University of Sussex in Brighton, UK. He is the author of *The Authority of Everyday Objects: A Cultural History of West German Industrial Design* (Berkeley, 2004), and is completing a book on the history of private life in the German Democratic Republic, to be published by Oxford University Press in 2010.

Albert Borgmann is Regents Professor of Philosophy at the University of Montana, where he has taught since 1970. His special area is philosophy of society and culture. His most recent book is *Real American Ethics* (2006).

Jerry Busby currently works in the Department of Management Science at Lancaster University, UK. His research interests are in risk analysis and risk management, systemic failure, human and organizational error, design organizations and design processes. He has formerly worked at Bath University, Cranfield University, and a number of engineering firms.

Medardo Chiapponi is Full Professor of Industrial Design, Dean of the Faculty of Design and Arts at the Università IUAV di Venezia. Previously, he was a professor at the Politecnico di Milano and Politecnico di Torino (Italy) and at the Hochschule für Gestaltung Schwäbisch Gmünd (Germany). He has published books, essays, and papers in different countries.

Alain Findeli is Honorary Professor of the School of Industrial Design of the University of Montreal and currently Full Professor at the University of Nîmes in France, where he co-founded *Les Ateliers de la recherche en design*, a French and Francophone design research community. His research interests and recent publications address general issues in the theory and practice of design (logics, aesthetics, ethics), and more specifically pedagogical aspects of design research education (Ph.D).

Dr. Tony Golsby-Smith is the founder and CEO of Second Road Pty Ltd., as well as the architect of the tools and methods at the heart of firm. A regular speaker on innovation in Australia and North America, he is among the world's leading innovators in pioneering the power of visualization and conversation to solve complex organizational problems for business and government agencies. Primarily an advisor to senior leadership teams, he has worked with a wide range of clients including Suncorp, AMP, The ATO, Leighton Holdings, Customs, ADF, PwC and the CBA.

John Hirst graduated from the University of Sussex, UK with a master's degree in philosophy. He taught design education in polytechnics in the UK, and then from 1976 in the Hong Kong Polytechnic University. Returning to the United Kingdom in 1995, he set up a private practice in hypnotherapy and counseling. He continues teaching part-time with the East Sussex Flexible Learning Educational Support Service.

Wolfgang Jonas studied naval architecture and earned his Ph.D. on the computer-aided optimization of streamlined shapes. He worked as a consulting engineer for companies in the automobile industry and the German standardization institute. Since 1988, he has been teaching CAD and industrial design, and doing design research on system theory and design theory; 1994 lecturing qualification (Habilitation) in design theory. Since 1994, he has been professor at several German design schools, currently Professor of System Design at the School of Art and Design, University of Kassel. His focus of interest is design theory as meta-theory, design methods in a systemic perspective, and scenario planning.

Barry Katz is Professor of Design at the California College of the Arts, Consulting Professor of Design at Stanford University, and Fellow at IDEO, Inc., the global design and innovation consultancy. His most recent book, co-authored with Tim Brown, is *Change by Design: How Design Thinking Can Transform Organizations and Inspire Innovation.* A new book, *Tectonic Shift: The Unstable History of Silicon Valley Design*, will be published by MIT Press.

Peter Lloyd is Head of the Design Group at The Open University, UK and associate editor of *Design Studies* journal. His research is focused on the process and discourse of designing in all fields, with a recent emphasis on ethics in the design process. He has taught courses in design thinking, design methodology, and design ethics.

Petran Kockelkoren is Professor of Art and Technology at the University of Twente (The Netherlands). He also teaches philosophy at Artez Institue of the Arts. His work focuses on the relations between technology and art, and makes connections with cultural anthropology, industrial design, and media theory. He is the author of *Technology: Art, Fairground and Theatre* (Rotterdam: NAi, 2003) and *Mediated Vision* (Rotterdam: Veenman, 2007).

John V. Maciuika is an Associate Professor of Art and Architectural History at the City University of New York, Baruch College, and the CUNY Graduate Center Ph.D. program in art history. His research interests include modern architecture and cultural identity in Central Europe, notably Germany, Austria, and the Baltic states. He is the author of *Before the Bauhaus: Architecture, Politics, and the German State, 1890–1920* (Cambridge: Cambridge University Press, 2005), and is currently completing a book entitled: *Global Forces, Local Modernities: Modern Architecture in Cultural Context.*

Pauline Madge has training and teaching in the history of modern architecture and design. In the late 1980s and 1990s, she specialized in the theory and history of ecodesign. Since 1996, she has been practicing modern homesteading in Wales.

Ezio Manzini is Professor of Design at the Politecnico di Milano, Honorary Doctor at The New School of New York (2006) and at Goldsmiths' College, University of London (2008), and Honorary Professor at the Glasgow School of Art (2009). Presently, his main interests are toward design for social innovation, and he is promoter and coordinator of DESIS Network, an international network on Design for Social Innovation and Sustainability (www.desis-network.org). His recent publications include *Collaborative Services: Social Innovation and Design for Sustainability* (Milan: Polidesign, 2008), "Service Design in the Age of Networks and Sustainability" in S. Miettinen and M. Koivisto (eds.), *Designing Services with Innovative Methods* (Helsinki: University of Arts and Design, 2009), and "Small, Local, Open and Connected: Design Research Topics in the Age of Networks and Sustainability," in *Journal of Design Strategies*, 4:1 (Spring 2010).

Massimo Negrotti has been Full Professor of Sociology of Knowledge and Methodology of Human Sciences at the Universities of Parma and Genoa since 1980, and is now with the LCA (Lab for the Culture of the Artificial) at the University of Urbino. His main areas of interest are methodology and the culture of the artificial. Since 1980, he has carried out theoretical and empirical studies related to AI in Europe and in the USA. He has reported on both of the above subjects at several conferences and lectures in Europe, the USA, and Japan, and in many Italian and international books and journals. He is now working on the sociocultural and techno-methodological premises and regularities of "naturoids," conceived as a general area of research within which technology tries to reproduce natural exemplars.

Mika Pantzar, Ph.D., is acting as a Research Professor in the National Consumer Research Center, Helsinki, Finland. His current project, "Co-Production of Innovations – Toward an Integrative Theory of Practice," is financed by the Academy of Finland and Aalto University (Helsinki). The final outcome of this project is a book, co-authored with Elizabeth Shove and Matt Watson, *Everyday Life: The Dynamics of Social Practice* (SAGE Publications), which will be published in 2011.

Michael Punt is Professor of Art and Technology in the Faculty of Technology at the University of Plymouth, UK and is editor-in-chief of *Leonardo Reviews*. He is the Director of Transtechnology Research, which conducts research in to how technologies acquire meaning in the public domain. A full list of his publications, films and exhibitions can be found at: www.trans-techresearch.net.

Raimonda Riccini is a Professor at the Faculty of Design and Arts of the Università IUAV di Venezia, Italy, where she is director of the graduate program in Industrial Design and is a member of the faculty board of Doctorate Studies in Design Sciences. Also, she is assistant director of the magazine *DIID – Disegno Industriale*, and a charter member of AIS.Design (Italian Association of Historians of Design), June 2009. Her most recent writings include "Diseño y teorías de los objectos," in *Historia del diseño en America Latina y el Caribe*, eds. S. Fernandez and G. Bonsiepe (São Paulo: Editora Blucher, 2008), "Cultures for Teaching Design," in *Made in IUAV: From Research to Project at a Design University*, eds. R. Riccini and M. Chiapponi (Tavagnacco: Graphic Linea, 2008) and "Cultura de la técnica y teoria del diseño," in *Tomás Maldonado: Un moderno en acción*, ed. M. H. Gradowczyk (Buenos Aires: EDUNTREF, 2008).

Sara K. Schneider, Ph.D., is a Chicago-based performance anthropologist, National-Louis University professor, yoga teacher, and author of three books on the expressive body. She conducts workshops on comparative somatic-spiritual practices at the Esalen Institute and directs the Center for Bodylore and Learning, linking education about global cultures with the professional development of educators, healthcare professionals, and clergy. Her monthly e-zine, *Skin in the Game*, treats the role of the body in culture, learning, work, and spiritual practice. She can be reached at sks@thinkingdr.com.

David Stairs coordinates the Graphic Design program at Central Michigan University, where he has taught since 1994. He founded Designers Without Borders (www.designerswithoutborders.org) in 2001 and has worked extensively in Africa. Since the launch of his Design-Altruism-Project (http://design-altruism-project.org) in 2006, Mr. Stairs has been actively involved in the expanding discussion about shifting paradigms of professional practice in design.

Loretta Staples has over twenty-five years of experience in visual literacy and communication, spanning traditional and digital technologies. She has worked as an art historian and design educator, as a designer of graphics, exhibits, and computer interfaces, and as a painter and cultural critic. Loretta lives and works in Connecticut, USA.

Tamiko Thiel (www.mission-base.com/tamiko) received her bachelor's degree from Stanford University in Product Design Engineering and a master's in Mechanical Engineering from Massachusetts Institute of Technology. Writing this article made her realize that the Connection Machines CM-1/CM-2 were to be her last engineering job and her first work of fine art. Since then she has been developing the dramatic and narrative capabilities of interactive 3D virtual reality as an artistic medium for addressing social and cultural issues.

Ellen Mazur Thomson is an independent scholar. She is the author of *The Origins of Graphic Design in America, 1880–1920* and has written on various subjects in design history.

Ann Tyler is Professor of Visual Communication at the School of the Art Institute of Chicago. Her design work has received numerous national awards and is included in the Library of Congress Prints and Photographs Collection. Her artist books are in many private collections including that of the Getty, Los Angeles, and the Tate Library, London.

Peter-Paul Verbeek is Professor of Philosophy of Technology at the University of Twente (the Netherlands) and part-time Extraordinary Professor of Philosophy at Delft University of Technology (Socrates chair). His work focuses on the ethical and anthropological aspects of human-technology relations, with a focus on issues of design and human enhancement. He is the author of *What Things Do: Philosophical Reflections on Technology, Agency, and Design* (Penn State University Press, 2005).

Nigel Whiteley is Professor of Visual Arts in the Lancaster Institute for the Contemporary Arts at Lancaster University, UK. He is the author of, among others, *Reyner Banham: Historian of the Immediate Future*; *Design For Society* (Cambridge, MA: MIT Press, 2002); and *Pop Design: From Modernism to Mod* (London: Design Council, 1987).

GENERAL INTRODUCTION

The question, "What will design be like in the future?" is frequently posed at design conferences, based on the premise that the world is moving in a certain direction and designers need to understand how they can respond to it. Experts on the future are frequently invited to such conferences to tell designers what the world will be like in the coming years, so the designers can then project their own practices forward to adapt to new sets of conditions and situations.

This is a problematic scenario. First, it assumes that the world is given, not only to designers but to most people, and not made by them. Second, it characterizes design as a reactive rather than a proactive practice and it denies designers the agency to participate in the primary world-making that determines how we live. Third, it does not take into account that design activity itself is embedded in a much larger web of discourse. Design is a professional practice, a topic of research, a subject of debate, and an object of evaluation. And fourth, it does not recognize that the conception and planning of projects is a complex process that is not always easy to manage, and consequently the products that result are often different from those that are conceived.

The essays selected for this anthology address some of the complicated questions that challenge the simplified scenarios about how design functions in world-making. They come from an important ten-year period of the journal *Design Issues*, a period that represents the beginnings of a new stage of maturity in the study and practice of design, a period when the seeds of a new way of thinking about design became evident.[1] Since the beginning of a design research culture in the early 1960s, theorists, historians, and others who comprise the design research community have become active participants in the discourse about design's role in society and how the diverse participants in the design process might fulfill that role. Within design research, there are two major strands. One is research that is pragmatically directed to making a product. The other is research that is directed to reflecting on how products are made and used both in the present and in the past. This second strand is frequently referred to as design studies and includes design history, criticism, and theoretical inquiries as well as research that focuses more on the philosophical, anthropological, psychological, and social meanings and consequence of products.[2]

The first stage of design studies focused on the objects and artifacts created by designers. From early writers such as Adolf Loos, Walter Gropius, and Lázsló Moholy-Nagy, to rationalist writers of the 1950s and 1960s such as Tomás Maldonado and Gui Bonsiepe, to the reactions against formalist theories that emerged around new-wave typography and industrial design in the 1970s and early 1980s, the center of attention in design studies was on the exploration of the formal qualities of products – and reactions against such qualities if they hindered personal expression and aesthetic sensibility.

The second stage of design studies found writers who shifted attention toward the psychological, social, and cultural context of products and of the discipline of design itself. Writers did not entirely break with the earlier stage, but they broadened the scope of design to address problems that had seldom been developed in depth. This stage is marked by the ways that products are situated in human experience.

By the mid- and late 1990s and the beginning years of the twenty-first century, however, three new trends began to emerge, signaling a new stage of maturity in the design community and influencing the direction of design studies, the education of designers, and even the professional practice of design. The first trend is a blurring of the boundaries that have separated history, theory, and criticism in the study of design. This is reflected in the organization of the present volume. Instead of separate sections that treat the traditional branches of design studies, the book is organized around the process or the activity of designing: conceptualization, fabrication, and evaluation. *Conceptualization* focuses on the formation of ideas about design and the place of design in the world. This section is about the pluralism of approaches to design and ways of thinking about design, whether those ideas come from historical analysis, theoretical speculation, philosophy, critical analysis, or from other disciplines that in the past may have seemed remote from the central issues of designing. How we conceive of design has implications for how we study it, teach its discipline, and practice it in professional life. Only now are design educators starting to recognize that the earlier pedagogical models that focused primarily on the production of artifacts are no longer adequate and that the new direction in design education requires a much greater emphasis on the complexities of how designs are conceived, which means a much stronger preparation in the humanistic and social sciences, not as ancillary subjects but as integral parts of the design curriculum. The growing awareness that these new subjects are important to design is reflected in the proliferation, in recent years, of Ph.D. programs that concentrate on research which may become useful for understanding and charting new directions for designers.

In turn, *fabrication* focuses on the work of designing: the making of products of all kinds, ranging from graphic and information design to industrial design and engineering, to computers and software, to management and organizational change. Although designers and design commentators have long acknowledged the importance of the process of making in the translation of abstract ideas, personal visions, and communal goals into concrete and effective presences in lives, fabrication remains a fertile field for investigation. The division of labor characteristic of modern economic systems and the celebration of creative individualism that are characteristic of modern cultural criticism together have tended to privilege treatments of designers as form-givers delivering inspired concepts to be executed by others. Far less attention has been paid to their (the designer's) role in *form-making*.

The articles collected in this section portray a more nuanced and complex picture of fabrication. In this portrait, designers promote dialogue with multiple stakeholders, integrate diverse skill sets and negotiate the resolution of competing demands. Rather than marking the simple and unavoidable interval between conceptualization and a product's arrival in the marketplace, in this anthology fabrication emerges as a constituent part of the generative process. In situations where materials, tools, techniques, and vested interests impede the process of making, designers bring their distinctive abilities to bear to reconfigure problems as possibilities and extend the creative process deep into the life cycle of products, services, and environments.

This section points toward the blurring and repositioning of design problems among the "four orders" of design. The four orders offer a conceptual framework for identifying the central problems of design and design thinking. First-order problems focus on issues of communication and the delivery of information through images and symbols. Second-order problems focus on the issues surrounding the construction of tangible artifacts of any scale. Third-order problems focus on the planning and implementation of actions, interactions, processes, and services. Finally, fourth-order problems focus on the issues of how we organize the complex wholes that surround us and provide the systems and environments of human culture.

Fabrication is about how design conceptions are brought forward in concrete expression, often blending different forms or disciplines of traditional professional practice. It includes case studies that demonstrate how older models of practice were revised to address the demands of new situations. As design problems change, so do the ways of fostering collaboration between teams of professionals. The growing complexity of design projects has called for cooperation among experts such as software designers, product designers, sociologists, anthropologists, psychologists, graphic designers, and engineers. Because these forms of working together are relatively new, they lack precedents for developing design protocols and consequently depend on intense and spontaneous conversations among the practitioners about how to develop the projects. Once again, history, theory, and criticism blur in the study and practice of design, and research makes use of schema and techniques that reflect the pluralism of design work. Case studies are of particular importance in providing examples of how the collaborative process works.

Finally, *evaluation* focuses on the values of practice, both in determining what might be designed as well as assessing the consequences of what has been done. Evaluation is about how we understand the human purposes that lie behind design and about how we bring forward a new discourse that draws out the values that are actually embodied in products, whether or not they correspond to the intended purpose and values of the designer and his or her client. John Dewey provides the direction for understanding what we mean by evaluation. Just as "ex-pression" is the pressing out of emotion from raw materials through form, so too is "e-valuation" the drawing out of values through the consequences of design. As one may expect, evaluation is more than an assessment of functionality. It is also a matter of ethics and politics, with the understanding that, as Aristotle observes, these do not address different subject matters but the same subject matter from different perspectives. Here too, however, criticism, theory, and history work together in the new discourse of evaluation.

Along with the blurring of design history, theory, and criticism, the reader will also find in these essays signs that some of the traditional categories for the study of design have reached a limit as conceptual tools. There is little attention given here to "ism's" or "styles." "Post-modernism" and "post-structuralism" do not figure decisively in the arguments, and if they do appear it is so that they may be put aside in favor of new issues and concerns. Artistic biography, the stock-in-trade of traditional art and design history, is little evident. Rather than focusing on aesthetics and idealist notions of design, products are discussed in terms of their social existence. All of these are signs of the first trend reflected in this volume – the blurring of boundaries and traditional concepts of design studies.

The second trend is the migration of new ideas and new writers into the design community from discourse communities that have, in the past, been considered outside the traditional domain of design. Of course, there are precursors of this trend throughout the past century as the study of design began to take on substantial shape, but the movement has become more pronounced in the first decade of the twenty-first century. The effect has been to confirm the significance and legitimacy of design and design studies as a serious area of research and inquiry. Philosophy, economics, the social and human sciences, technical communication and communication studies, management and organization studies, computer science, information systems, and the history and philosophy of technology: these are some of the areas where attention to design has emerged and where contributions to the study of design may now be found. The seeds of this trend are evident in many of the essays in this volume, including, for example, works by Albert Borgmann, Peter Paul Verbeek and Petran Kockelkoren, Mika Pantzar, Michael Punt, and Massimo Negrotti.

The third trend is only hinted at in the essays of this volume, but it is a trend that should be noted by students and design educators. It presents a challenge to the design community. This trend is the recent engagement with design in many other fields and disciplines without direct reference to the existing literature of design and design studies. For many fields, design has emerged as a topic of interest that offers a new perspective on past research and practice. Design is a way of bringing knowledge into action. In philosophy, it addresses the relation between being as an internal state and as a way to engage with the artificial world. In psychology, attention to design recognizes that products such as cell phones, televisions, and computers are closely related with the human psyche and may have a bearing on how well that psyche is adjusted to manageable norms of social life. In anthropology, designed objects are part of human culture and play the same role in defining cultural values today as pottery and iron tools did in earlier times. As design becomes a greater tool for the creation of organizational structures, it has attracted interest from the discipline of management and is now beginning to play a role in the curricula of some management schools. Historians too are recognizing that the study of the designed world can make an important contribution to the broader understanding of how societies and civilizations have developed over time.

In essence, design is changing in significant and powerful ways and the individual essays in this volume herald some of those changes. Consolidated into a single collection, they enable us to recognize ways that design is now a far more pervasive practice than it once was. They also enable us to analyze specific instances of conception, fabrication, and evaluation that expand our understanding of how those three categories characterize the process of design as we know it and how they might help us to anticipate design in the future.

NOTES

1. See the three earlier *Design Issues* anthologies: Victor Margolin (ed.), *Design Discourse: History, Theory, Criticism* (Chicago and London: The University of Chicago Press, 1989); Victor Margolin and Richard Buchanan (eds.), *The Idea of Design* (Cambridge, MA: MIT Press, 1995); and Dennis Doordan (ed.), *Design History: An Anthology* (Cambridge, MA: MIT Press, 1995).
2. On design studies, see Victor Margolin, "Design History and Design Studies," (218–33) and "The Multiple Tasks of Design Studies," (234–43) in Victor Margolin, *The Politics of the Artificial: Essays on Design and Design Studies* (Chicago and London: The University of Chicago Press, 2002). See also Hazel Clark and David Brody (eds.), *Design Studies: A Reader* (Oxford and New York: Berg, 2009).

PART I

CONCEPTUALIZATION

INTRODUCTION

The growing popularity of design in public consciousness belies many difficult, unanswered questions about the nature of design and its proper place in the world. There are, in fact, many writers who have recognized the growing interest in design and have quickly sought to capitalize on the surge by offering books and articles that "slim down" the fundamental problems of design until they look simple and may be resolved into catchy, trendy terms such as "integration," "innovation," and "creativity." Behind these enthusiastic but thin books, however, there is a growing literature of sophisticated discussions that explore the conceptual roots of the field and its diverse forms of practice. This literature introduces new concepts and arguments that help us to question and understand the direction of design as a field of study as well as a discipline of practice.

One feature of the new conceptualizations of design is the blurring of boundaries between history, theory, and criticism, revealing the deeper interconnections that explain the importance of design as a social and cultural influence. The guiding idea of such work is that design is the location of a new exploration of culture that combines theory (ideas about the nature of the world) with practice (the skills and purposes of practical action that have an impact on the lives of individuals and communities). The meeting ground of theory and practice in the twenty-first century is the designed world of images, objects, activities, and environments. In short, the meeting ground is the making and remaking of our world in products of the imagination. This is a new understanding of the nature of imagination, and design is one of the disciplines where this understanding takes concrete form. In the nineteenth century, imagination was considered a faculty of the mind, operating between reason and will. In the twenty-first century, the discussion of imagination and the productivity that follows from the power of imagination is placed not in the context of faculties of the mind but in the context of experience and expression – the context of productive action. Imagination is the ability of human beings to visualize and create images that interpret reality, shape our understanding of the world, and help us to act more fully as human beings. The ability to visualize and to bring visions into concrete experience is the ability of design. Despite much confusion and disagreement over the meaning of "design thinking," our understanding of this phrase would benefit by considering this observation by the philosopher Richard McKeon: "The mind which is actively thinking is the objects which it thinks." We understand the activity of thinking in design by understanding the objects that we create in the imagination and that we often bring to concrete form in the world around us. How else can one identify the mind of the actively thinking designer than by the visions and objects of thought that he or she creates through the activity of imagination?

The articles in this first section of the book offer objects of thought for reflection and discussion. Instead of "honing down" the problems of design until they appear simple, the authors confront the difficulties of design and lead us down different pathways of exploration. They encourage the reader to begin actively thinking about design in new ways. In short, they help to reveal the unfinished work of understanding design.

This section begins with an article by Richard Buchanan on the problem of identity and moral purpose in design. Using an article by the designer Andrea Branzi as a point of departure, he discusses a dilemma faced by designers and by design itself in the turbulent times of cultural change that mark our historical period. Without a unifying ideology – such as provided in general terms by earlier forms of modernism – where is the designer to turn for new vision and values? He argues that in the emerging pluralism of contemporary culture we do not have to retreat into the tribalism of individual camps and sects, each guided by a powerful leader. Instead, we should recognize that vision and values are precisely the proper subjects for discussion, often reflected in the repositioning of design in new places of engagement such as strategic planning and organizational change – the new third and fourth orders of design. He argues that we may begin to think about the problem in a new way if we change our commonplace idea of culture as merely an ideology and think of it instead as a human activity of cultivation, with continual ordering, disordering, and reordering through responsible discussion, supported by new tools that are beginning to emerge in the work of design.

Massimo Negrotti reopens one of the fundamental problems of design that many writers have regarded as a settled matter: the relationship between the natural and the artificial. By introducing a new distinction in what we regard as the artificial, he takes design into a new sphere of work, seeking to clarify the complex relationship of design and natural science. He argues that earlier writers, including Herbert Simon, have neglected the teleological difference between artificial objects such as cathode tubes and artificial hearts. To explain this, he points toward two constructive ambitions that have characterized human culture and civilization from its earliest period. One he calls the Prometheus syndrome, focused on inventing objects that can dominate nature and that are adapted to natural laws. The other may be called the Icarus syndrome, focused on reproducing natural objects and processes through different strategies than those that nature, itself, employs. This is the difference, he argues, between "conventional technology" and what could be termed "the technology of the artificial." By tracing out the implications of this distinction in areas such as biology and ecology, he introduces the idea of "exemplars" which are selected by designers to guide their work. What follows is an intriguing exploration that culminates in a proposed "third reality," midway between natural reality and the reality of conventional technology.

Though more and more people recognize that design is a discipline in its own right, the issue is not settled. Wolfgang Jonas takes up the problem of explaining design as a discipline through an exploration of earlier efforts to move design toward adequate theory in the major design schools of the twentieth century, the Design Methods Movement, and contemporary issues of epistemology. Notably, he then turns toward Niklas Luhmann's theory of social systems and the concepts of autonomous systems and autopoiesis – the concept of living systems. Jonas argues that design must become an autonomous system if it is to fulfill its proper function in society. "The guiding idea is that design, if it intends to act generatively, has to become an autonomous system itself (theory)." In essence, if design is reduced to other autonomous systems – i.e. other disciplines – it loses its identity and its functional purpose. What follows is a useful discussion of systems theory and its relevance to understanding design and the work of designing. However, a systems approach to the autonomy of design stands in need of an appropriate methodology that serves to characterize the design process. That methodology, for Jonas, lies in a scenario-based activity, addressing issues of Analysis, Synthesis, and Projection. Indeed, for Jonas, scenario-building is one of the central concepts of design, developed through a variety of types or kinds of scenarios that work together in the process of designing. The remainder of the article is a discussion of the various implications of scenarios for designing and, ultimately, for design research.

The scenario-guided design process offered by Jonas stands in need of information, and information is the theme of the next essay by Albert Borgmann, known for his work in the philosophy of technology. His contribution to this volume is a clear, easily accessible discussion of one of the important ideas of the twentieth century, which has set the stage for the development of technology in the twenty-first century. After discussing the semiotic meaning of information as the interplay of messenger, recipient, and message, he proceeds to introduce a set of distinctions that bear on the pragmatic dimension of communication. The core meaning of information, he argues, is *information about reality*. However, information illuminates not only "what is distant in time and space, but also what is remote in conception and imagination; and what would remain a distant possibility without the aid of conventional signs." The illumination of conception and imagination through all of the carriers of information in culture – all of the images, objects, and environments created by design – leads to another meaning of information: *information for reality*. While these two meanings of information serve to mediate the relationship between humanity and reality, Borgmann then argues that the development of this mediation through technology has led to a third meaning of information: *information as reality*. The remainder of the article develops the implications of this third meaning, leading to a brief and stark conclusion: information in the twenty-first century "tends to enfeeble people and attenuate things," calling for a new counter-balance to bring us back to the relationship of people and things.

The problem with which Borgmann ends his article, a problem of the twenty-first century and its new forms of digital technologies, may be contrasted with benefit in the next article, Ellen Mazur Thomson's study of Thorstein Veblen, the University of Chicago, and the socialization of aesthetics. Writing at the turn of the nineteenth century, Veblen produced a classic of economic and sociological thought, but also a key text in the unfolding story of material culture and design aesthetics. The *Theory of the Leisure Class* is one of a number of books that brought our understanding of the fine arts and design into the context of human experience, culminating perhaps in John Dewey's *Art As Experience*, a key text used by Moholy-Nagy at the New Bauhaus in Chicago. Thomson's study is an important guide to the importance of Veblen and other scholars at the University of Chicago for the development of design in the twentieth century and the gathering influence of technology on culture. "Veblen's understanding of design and the industrial arts derives, in large measure, from his belief that history, by which he meant cultural evolution, is driven by technological advances. Technology remakes culture, but that does not necessarily mean that cultural institutions immediately change to accommodate it." As Thomson explains, Veblen was interested in how aesthetic appreciation and issues of value and beauty were distorted by the monetary value of goods. However, she also shows how the sociological and economic analysis of Veblen and others did not reduce aesthetic values to purely social concerns. The trend toward exploring the social dimension of design that emerged at the end of the twentieth century and continues in the twenty-first century was prefigured at the beginning of the twentieth century, and Thompson's article makes clear the attitude at that time toward the "benign potential of technology" – a strong contrast to the closing concerns of Borgmann. More than this, however, one should note the conclusion that Thomson reaches: "By defining aesthetics within culture, as the University of Chicago scholars did, they were able to identify the politics underlying hierarchical schemes that relegates design to a lesser position within the artistic canon."

The complex issue of design, technology, and human experience raised by Bergmann and Thomson continues in "The Things That Matter," by Peter-Paul Verbeek and Petran Kockelkoren. They begin by observing the turn from ideas to things in the philosophy of technology, a turn that has brought discussions of science and technology into closer relationship with industrial design. (As Verbeek notes, this is a turn originally guided by philosopher Albert Borgmann and developed by Don Ihde.) The point of departure, then, is a discussion of Eternally Yours, the foundation and its subsequent books on sustainable design and product development. Verbeek and Kockelkoren offer a provocative argument that will be controversial among designers and many others. They argue that while the ideas expressed in the book – notably the idea of extending the lifespan of products by focusing on the psychological bond between users and products – are important and illuminating, the reduction of products to something immaterial is not entirely adequate in addressing the problems of consumption. They argue that Eternally Yours, as well as industrial design, are Platonic in their orientation, primarily concerned with ideas rather than things:

> In short, industrial design has always been a Platonic discipline, concerned primarily with ideas and only in the second instance with things. The same goes for Eternally Yours. Attempts to realize "durable design" should not only focus on signs, shapes, surfaces, sales, and services. However important they are, all of these items – we deliberately did not mention "scripts," which will become clear later – fail to take the materiality of products into account. They understand products as elements of all kinds of *languages:* languages of form, of product meaning, and of relationships between company and customer. But when we strip all nonmaterial aspects of products, something remains that is more than language; more than symbol, meaning, function, or icon. What remains is the thing as *thing.*

Whatever position one takes on these matters, the article serves a useful role in forcing the reader to think about the problem of sustainability in the context of design – and to question the nature of industrial design.

Whether design and technology are primarily concerned with ideas or things, the study of products would be incomplete without consideration of consumers and the social histories of products. This is what Mika Pantzar takes up in the next article. Pantzar is an economist who has focused on consumer research, and his article, "Domestication of Everyday Life Technologies," focuses on the lack of general theories for the integration of technology, needs, and human beings. What makes this a problem, he argues, is that in the past, social development was seen in one or another of two simple perspectives. It was either a result of social determinism or the result of human needs and preferences. Neither is entirely adequate, and to help correct the deficiency he begins with an overview of some of the central ideas of consumption and consumer research, including "consumption rituals." He then discusses four perspectives that are common in the literature of social science and technology studies and could provide the kind of general theory that is needed. The four perspectives are: the biography of things, the social shaping of technology, actor network theory, and the ecology of goods. In addition to characterizing each perspective in a concise review, he also identifies leading proponents, including figures such as Bruno Latour, Kenneth Boulding, Thomas Hughes, and John Law. The discussion is a useful introduction for designers, students of design, and the general reader who wants to better understand some of the reasons for the success or failure of products in the twenty-first century.

The final article in this section returns to the central practices of design, focused on how we may integrate environmental design and industrial design to address the urgent problem faced by twenty-first-century social and cultural life. Medardo Chiapponi acknowledges that most people recognize that environmental and industrial design are now connected, but he argues that the connection requires refinement and elaboration if it is to be fruitful. This is needed precisely because of the difference of disciplinary practices in each branch of design. He begins with a characterization of industrial design and the changes that are taking place in that practice. He then discusses environmental design and some of the central concepts of that discipline, giving special emphasis to the idea of an environmental *system*. The main body of the article is a discussion of many of the central themes of the new form of practice that is emerging, including the process of design and the distributed agency that is now called for in the growing complexity of environmental system problems and the need to integrate the different forms of knowledge that must be in dialogue if we hope to reach acceptable solutions. Like the other articles in this section, Chiapponi presents another conceptualization of design that leads us to further questions and discussion.

1

BRANZI'S DILEMMA: DESIGN IN CONTEMPORARY CULTURE

Richard Buchanan

This article was originally presented as a keynote address at "Design: Pleasure or Responsibility," an international conference held at the University of Art and Design Helsinki in June 1994. The address was subsequently printed in *Design: Pleasure or Responsibility?* edited by Päivi Tahkokallio and Susann Vihma, University of Art and Design Helsinki, 1995. The author is grateful for the innovative work at UIAH and for the encouragement of Yrjo Sotamaa, President of UIAH.

INTRODUCTION

My subject today is a challenge faced by many individuals and groups in the new circumstances of contemporary culture: how to find identity and moral purpose when central values are *essentially contested.* I call this challenge Branzi's dilemma because the problem was stated with elegance and clarity by Andrea Branzi in a 1985 essay called "We Are the Primitives."[1] I cite this essay neither because I agree with Branzi's way of solving the problem nor because I intend to discuss his philosophy of design in detail. Rather, it provides a useful way to focus attention on one of the fundamental changes that have taken place in design over the last two decades, a change that continues to unfold with gathering force in directions that few people can anticipate and no one can entirely comprehend. The occasion that draws us together, a conference on pleasure and responsibility in design, is a sign of that change.[2] Whether by accident or forethought, the organizers have selected one of the variations of Branzi's dilemma as our theme, and we will address this theme from a variety of perspectives. However, I want to raise a cautionary note before we begin. We should be concerned that unless the deeper dilemma that stands behind our discussions is well understood, we may simply repeat old doctrines or propound new dogmas, contributing little to the advance of design at a time when its disciplines and professions require thoughtful reconsideration that goes beyond ideology.

Perhaps the current situation would not present difficulty if the direction of design rested entirely in the hands of designers. In such a case, where we *would* go, we *shall* go in addressing the issue of pleasure and responsibility. Indeed, this is how some designers prefer to see the current situation, and they act accordingly. But the direction of design is not entirely in the hands of designers, no matter how much we cling to the old mythic idea of the designer as a heroic cultural figure leading the avant-garde. No doubt, there will always be an avant-garde. This is what sustains confidence among some people that the heroic model of design will remain adequate to new challenges – and there is a tincture of truth in this confidence. However, the fate of design does not lie entirely within the framework of design culture or in the hands of a few gifted individuals. It lies within the framework of culture as a whole.

This framework is changing before our eyes, altering the attitudes of the public, the environment of corporations, and the way we understand all of the professions with which we must collaborate in developing new products. I do not mean the constantly changing surface of culture, the ever-new, ever-shifting fads and styles that emerge and are discarded in the pursuit of novelty. This aspect of twentieth-century culture is what art critic Harold Rosenberg calls the "tradition of the new."[3] Surface changes will go on continuously because it is in human nature to seek out new experiences and expressions. Instead, what I am referring to is the philosophic engine that stands behind culture: the fundamental issues, problems, and ideas that are shared with varying degrees of understanding by all participants.

This engine is what Branzi perceives in his essay, and his perception is strengthened precisely because he is uncomfortable with the form that the new engine has taken. I believe he understands, at least in principle, that the cultural and philosophic revolution that began in the early decades of the twentieth century has taken another turn and continues to move forward with unabated force to the present. Indeed, Branzi deserves credit for the courage to engage the new cultural issues. Unlike Paul Rand, who fought bitter rear-guard skirmishes and then retreated to lofty silence, Branzi attempts to understand the philosophy of design in the context of current problems, despite the attacks to which he has been subjected by some members of the old guard and by many of the new guard. His voice has remained a presence in the pluralism of contemporary design, emphasizing the continued importance of aesthetics and artistic experimentation.

However, I do not intend this to be a paean to Andrea Branzi. Branzi is a participant in the new culture, but his response is idiosyncratic. His idea of a "second modernity" evades the deeper problem which design confronts in the contemporary world. We need Branzi and his artistic vision, but we do not know exactly why – and I am not convinced that he can adequately explain why. There is danger for design in a retreat to aesthetic self-expression, and there is hopelessness if the elegance of art is not included in its new visions.

THE DILEMMA OF IDENTITY AND MORAL PURPOSE

The circumstances of Branzi's dilemma are quite familiar by now, heralded in what some people refer to as the collapse of modernism. As he explains in his essay, the ideals of modernism no longer provide the unifying ideology of design and world culture. Those ideals, expressed in a variety of ways among the many forms of modernism, pointed towards the continual improvement of the human condition – in some minds perhaps even the perfection of humanity – through progress in art, design, and technology. However, the "ideological parachute" of modernism, Branzi says, no longer works.

> Culture and design no longer are forces that slowly but heroically move the world toward salvation through logical and ethical radicalism. They are mechanisms of emotions and adaptations of changes that fail to drag the world toward a horizon; they only transform it into many diffuse diversities. Progress no longer seems to be valued; instead, the unexpected is valued. The grand unitarian theorems no longer exist, nor do the leading models of the rational theologies. What exists is modernism without illuminism. We are witnessing a definitive and extreme secularization of design, within which design represents itself and no longer is a metaphor for a possible unity of technologies and languages.[4]

Whether we agree with the accuracy of Branzi's account is not the issue. It is an adequate account for present purposes, because it enables us to focus on one of the central problems of contemporary culture: if there is no unifying ideology shared by the design community and world culture as a whole, where does the individual find identity and moral purpose?

This problem immediately leads to what I have called Branzi's dilemma. It is a dilemma because both of the obvious alternatives to the contemporary problem of finding identity are either distasteful or dangerous. One alternative is to substitute a new general ideology for the old ideology, perhaps resuscitating a modified form of "modernism." I believe this is eventually what Branzi attempted to do three years later with the publication of *Learning from Milan*, particularly in the chapter "Toward the Second Modernity." After a brief and very insightful discussion of the changing nature of materials and technology, he explains the nature of his proposed second modernity: "What I mean by this term is an acceptance of Modernity as an artificial cultural system based neither on the principle of necessity nor on the principle of identity but on a set of conventional cultural and linguistic values that somehow make it possible for us to go on making choices and designing."[5]

Recognizing the Eurocentric origins of modernism, Branzi in effect capitulates to theorists of the postmodern by repudiating any substantial value in the various forms of modernism. He turns away from the value and integrity of identity to embrace conventional values. Furthermore, he proposes for the second modernity an agenda that amounts to a retreat to the themes of power and control in design. These are the themes which many of the leaders of design in the earlier decades of the twentieth century sought to oppose in public and corporate culture, too often without success. They are expressed in the destructive sophistry of the idea of art for art's sake and in the original version of this idea in economics: business for business's sake.

> Modernity represents the point of aggregation around which the European nations have attained the maximum of their potential, both industrial and humanistic. All in all it is the product of a range of technological and linguistic imagery, highly recognizable and acknowledged as the child of this continent. What is needed is to apply a strategy of international communication to it, converting Modernity into a commercial and political system. Culture is a great added value. It should be regarded not as indispensable and necessary but as the best sauce with which to season the development of postindustrial society. So it will be an enthusiastic Second Modernity, made up of new European sensations to be distributed round the world. It could be very good business.[6]

I cannot conceal the bitterness I feel about this proposal. From someone of less accomplishment than Branzi, it would be no more than a cynical gesture, born of a failure of imagination and ingenuity. Yet, we must take it seriously and examine its implications.

The steps leading to this proposal were prepared three years earlier in the essay we are discussing. In this essay, Branzi details his initial alternative to the dilemma of identity in the contemporary world, an alternative that is strikingly different from substituting a new general ideology for the old ideology of modernism. He suggests that without a unifying ideology in the culture around us, each individual must look within himself or herself for the original key – the language and code – of personal identity. There is no longer a world culture; there are only individuals, each grappling to make personal order and sense out of an increasingly complex world. Indeed, in 1985 Branzi suggests that this is the only viable alternative, and he embraces this side of the dilemma, expressing only mild regret and disappointment – something more than nostalgia but less than determined and well-argued resistance. An optimist, he tries to direct attention toward the positive features of the new cultural climate.

> Complexity, real and theoretical, is spreading. Lacking in the postindustrial society is that unified symbolic universe capable of integrating various institutional environments and the

> individuals in them. Symbolic worlds proliferate and become differentiated. The very process that multiplies the integrity and the plausibility of that person's familiar world, also enormously widen the field of various possibilities perceived by individuals.[7]

However, he recognizes, and has the courage to express, the fate of individual identity in these circumstances.

> The range of choices becomes wider and more fluid. There occurs not only the disintegration of the strong type of identity, but also the development of a new weak identity, which is flexible, open to change, intimately differentiated, and reflexive. The weak identity considers every choice as temporary and reversible and becomes the object of "different biographies," at the border, but only at the border, of pathological dissociation.[8]

I doubt whether diversity is actually greater today than in earlier decades of the twentieth century – in fact, if anything, I suspect it is less. But the *idea* of diversity and of pluralism is clearly a prominent feature of the new cultural climate. Instinctively, however, Branzi understands where diversity may lead in the absence of a unifying vision outside the individual. It may lead to faction and tribalism, as some individuals emerge with greater power than others and exert subtle or overt control over their colleagues.

> The design panorama that awaits us in that extreme secularization of design consists of an ensemble of linguistic families grouped around ever more numerous family heads who will assemble around their own expressive minor archetypes and aggressive followers. That tribalization of cultural society is at once a result of the neo-primitive condition and awaiting the fall of the old cultural tinsels in front of a new and different civilization. Similar to the good savage, we are naked while awaiting the worse or the better.[9]

From this perspective, the idea of a second modernity proposed in *Learning from Milan* is something less than the substitution of a new general ideology for the old – as if one could will a new ideology into existence by the force of personality. Instead, the second modernity is merely Branzi's personal code, projected as his own tribal rallying cry, which some will heed and others ignore. I prefer his aesthetic vision, not his weak rationalization of the value of Eurocentric aesthetics.

As a radical pluralist – someone who values intellectual, artistic, and cultural diversity on grounds of principle, not merely out of vague tolerance or benign neglect of others – I am not entirely distressed by the initial alternative of Branzi's dilemma. No one possesses all of the knowledge and wisdom required to understand and act responsibly in this world. We need diversity and alternative perspectives to keep alive the ongoing inquiry into ordering, disordering, and reordering that is the central enterprise of human culture. We need the diversity of many personal visions to avoid entrapment in narrow thinking.

In the past, I have tried to survey the alternative approaches to design that have helped to form the discipline and professions of design in the twentieth century and whose energies continue to expand the understanding and influence of design in the contemporary world.[10] The approaches are endless in their subtle differences, but they may be grouped in four areas, each based on a rhetorical commonplace which has been made fundamental in design practice and speculation. This is illustrated in Figure 1.1.

It is not necessary to elaborate these approaches for present purposes, but we may suggest a tentative mapping of some of the most prominent individuals and schools of design in the twentieth century. This is illustrated in Figure 1.2. Without the diversity suggested in this map, design would be in a poorer state than it is today.

What concerns me about Branzi's alternative of personal codes is the danger for designers of arrogance and entrapment in narrow-minded and

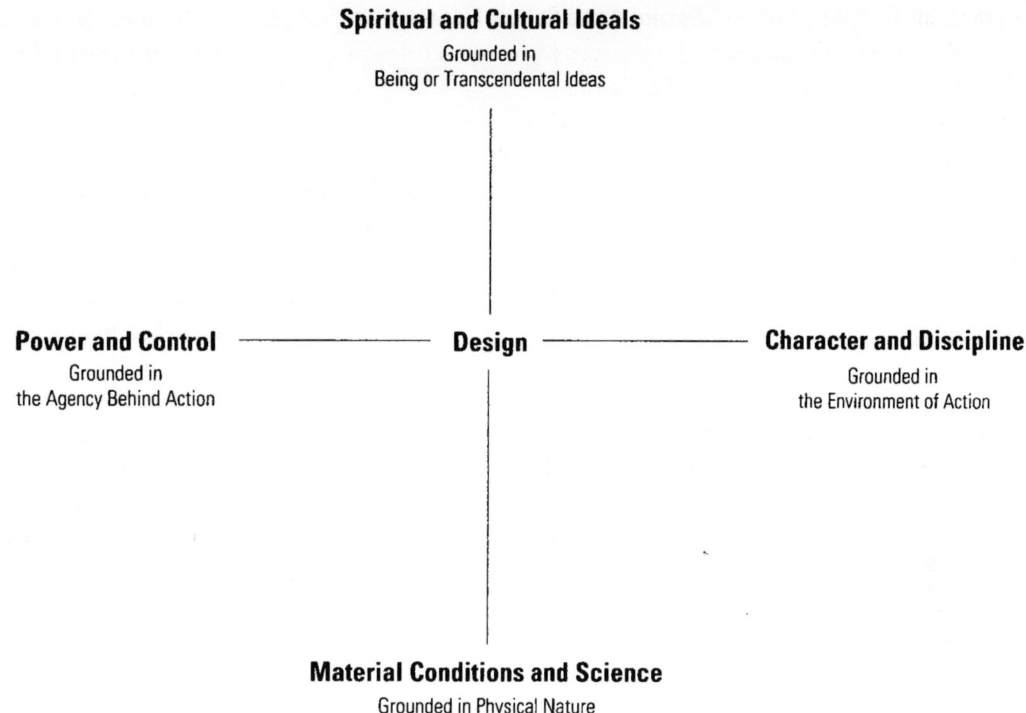

Figure 1.1 Commonplaces of Design Theory and Practice.

unexamined beliefs when there are no standards for evaluation and no grounds for challenging the limitations of ideology, aside from political and institutional power. Human beings have an unsurpassed ability to avoid questioning themselves and objectively examining the consequences of their beliefs and actions on others. There is no need to discuss the effect of this in politics, because there are so many examples of destructive tribalism throughout the twentieth century, including recent tragedies in Europe, Asia, and many other parts of the world. But the impact of tribalism on design and the development of technology is unconscionable for individuals who have made creativity and innovation their life's work. The distinguished designer George Nelson has correctly pointed out that it is pretentious for design to take itself too seriously.[11] However, if designers do not take themselves seriously enough, even the limited influence that they do have will be wasted. At least as human beings, if not as designers and educators, we must think about the consequences of renewed factionalism and tribalism in the contemporary world. Where will our students find moral purpose to guide their work? Can anyone familiar with the events of the twentieth century seriously give their trust to personal sensitivity and good intentions in matters as complex as designers face today?

The danger of Branzi's first alternative – emphasis on personal codes and individual diversity – is a return to power and control as the central theme of design thinking, with the unintended but inevitable consequence of gradually squeezing out and eliminating diversity. When power and control are foremost, moral purpose is reduced to whatever is popular in the marketplace of ideas and commerce, rather than to what is right. This is the guiding principle of bad marketing and bad advertising, and it is also the guiding principle of bad design. Indeed, there is no reason to believe that design will have much power in

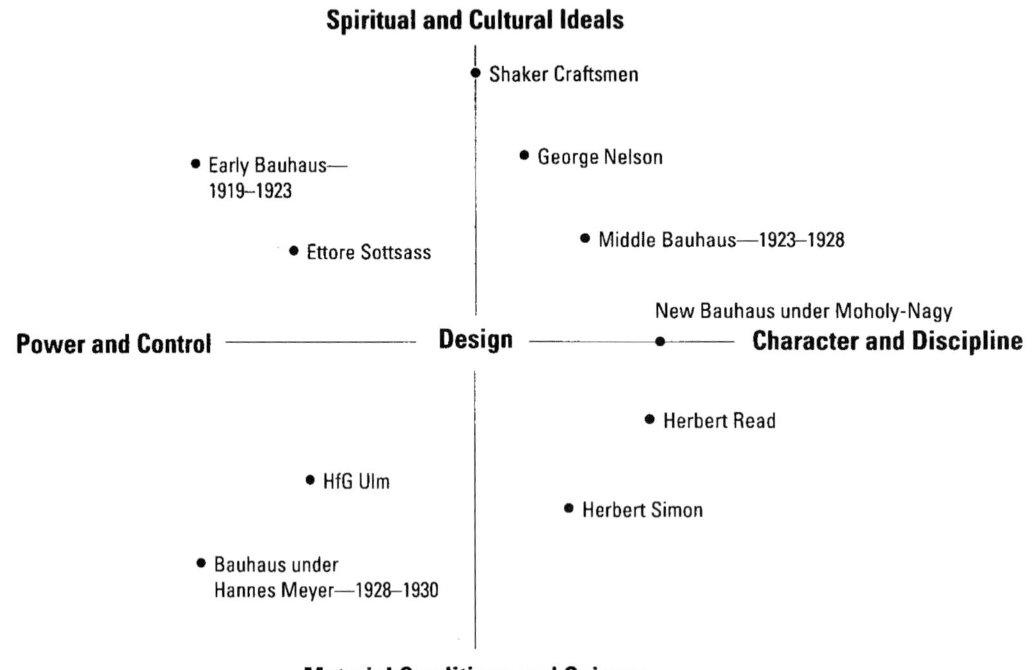

Figure 1.2 Perspectives on Design.

such a world, where engineering and the business professions have claimed dominance for so long as the ministers of merchant princes and corporations. We may posture about the ability of designers to shape the course of corporations, but this ability, to the degree that it may exist, comes from having good ideas that others must recognize because of objective and demonstrable worth. Of course, here we are again, back in Branzi's dilemma: how will we know if an idea has objective and demonstrable value if there is no shared vision among those who must make a choice among many alternatives?

DESIGN, DELIBERATION, AND ORGANIZATIONAL LEARNING

I began this essay by suggesting that a fundamental change is underway in design and that Branzi's dilemma is a useful way of characterizing one perspective on that change, focusing on the loss of a central ideology and the emergence of pluralism as a recognized feature of human circumstances. In the United States, this has led to what we call "culture wars." Skirmishes and battles are fought in a massive fog by diverse individuals and groups who believe, too often correctly, that they have been left out of earlier cultural debates. It is no surprise that design has been pulled into these culture wars, because design is an important tool of communication in popular culture.[12] Indeed, the images and objects created by designers in previous decades are often regarded as the symbols and instruments of oppression, serving the purposes and pleasures of an elite while quietly excluding other voices. Of course, this is a simplistic view of design. Designers have struggled and lost more often than they have won in trying to influence their clients and the general public. But it contains just enough truth so that many designers, particularly thoughtful young designers, are uncomfortable with their role in contemporary society.

In response, I would like to suggest that Branzi's interpretation of the change in contemporary culture is mistaken in its essential premise: the idea that culture is merely an ideology. By reducing culture to ideology, we neglect the original and more fundamental meaning of culture as cultivation. From this perspective, culture is not a state, expressed in an ideology or a body of doctrines. Rather, it is an activity. Culture is the activity of ordering, disordering, and reordering in the *search* for understanding and for values which guide action. Culture is the search for principles in the everyday engagements of life as well as in the special human engagements of science, art, politics, and design. In short, culture is what we do when we are alone or when we are together in such a pursuit.

What are the new circumstances of our culture? To properly characterize the philosophic engine of contemporary culture, we should examine two themes that echo quietly throughout our private conversations and public discourse. The first is the changed direction of deliberation in the twentieth century. Before this century, deliberation concerned *decisions about scarce means to be employed in particular circumstances to achieve generally desired and accepted ends.* We debated the means, but seldom the circumstances or the ends that we sought to achieve. However, in the twentieth century, through the advance of technology, the scarcity of means available for human use is no longer a fundamental problem; the problem lies in the potential consequences of our vast technological resources and in our moral purpose and commitment to develop technology in the service of being human. We are forced to ask what circumstances and ends we wish to pursue. We deliberate more about the circumstances and environments that we wish to create and the ends we wish to achieve than about the adequacy of means, except as a technical problem which is manageable, if there is sufficient political will.[13] Indeed, the debate about the incredible strain we are placing on planetary resources is framed precisely as a debate about ends and purposes in the human community, about our responsibility to others living and unborn.

For another example of the new direction of deliberation, consider the issue behind our current discussion. Pleasure and responsibility frame a discussion about the ends and purposes of design. Pleasure is set in opposition to responsibility in order to identify a place of public controversy and draw out contrasting views. In the course of discussion, we will find that some participants are comfortable with the distinction and will argue for an emphasis on one term or the other. Other participants, myself included, will not be comfortable with the distinction and will suggest a more complex relationship. For example, I prefer to argue that the creation of pleasure is one of the responsibilities of designers. However, I also argue that pleasure in design must be tempered and integrated with three other considerations that are essential for understanding the range of the designer's responsibilities: the good, the useful, and the just. The relation of these terms is represented in the matrix in Figure 1.3.

The ultimate purpose or function of design in society is to conceive products which express and, necessarily, reconcile human values concerning what is good, useful, just, and pleasurable. However, these terms no longer possess fixed and generally accepted meanings. Their meanings are the subject of our deliberations. They are *essentially contested* in society at large as well as in the complex processes of design and product development, although we seldom recognize the significance of the shift and are not well prepared to deal with it productively.

The shift in the direction of deliberation is inevitably perceived by some people as a weakening of culture, a sign of the loss of central vision and values, because vision and values are now an explicit subject of discussion. But it is a weakening only to the degree that we are frightened to have our values subjected to public examination, particularly if old ideologies are too rigid to allow for new expression – if they entrap our thinking in old solutions instead of helping us to find new ways of addressing the problems of ordering, disordering, and reordering as they are emerging in the circumstances of contemporary life. Instead, the new situation is potentially a strengthening of our culture, if culture is conceived as the type of activity that we described earlier: an active search for new principles or for new embodiments and expressions of trusted and traditional principles. However, the problem is to find new tools and disciplines to support the search for new principles or appropriate expressions of old principles. Our instrumentalities from earlier in the century are not adequate to the task, so we flounder in practical life and in design itself as we seek new approaches to culture and the conflict of competing values.

It should come as no surprise that in this new deliberative situation some designers have begun to shift their work away from images and physical objects, as such, and to place design explicitly in the context of strategic planning. They seek to place design at the earliest moment in the product development process, at the point where fundamental decisions are taken regarding the circumstances and ends to be pursued. This is a repositioning of design as a central agency of being human in contemporary culture. It is not the abandonment of the earlier disciplines of design, the disciplines of communication and construction, the creation of images and the fabrication of physical objects. Rather, it is an effort to place communication and construction in the context of action, with designers serving as collaborative agents in determining public, corporate, and private plans for action.[14]

The emergence of strategic planning as a discipline of design thinking may be illustrated in a matrix of commonplaces formed from the fundamental *abilities of designers* and the closely related *disciplines of design practice*. The premise behind this matrix is that the natural abilities of designers – the natural design abilities of all human beings, which we may identify as *invention*, *judgment*, *decision-making*, and *evaluation* – stand

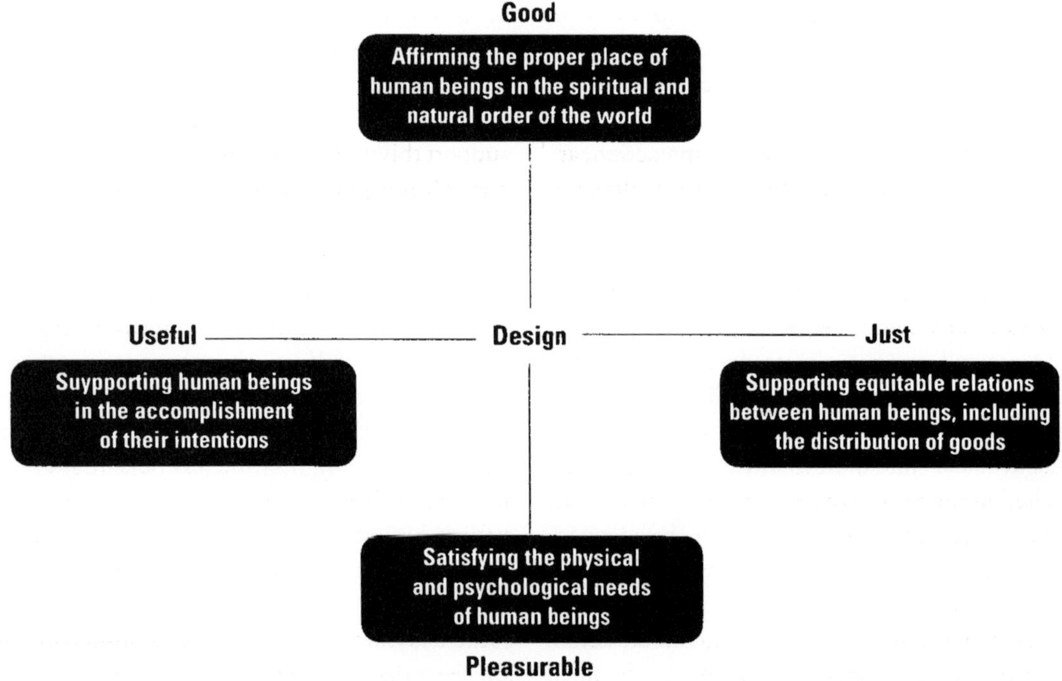

Figure 1.3 Relationships Among the Ends or Purposes of Design.

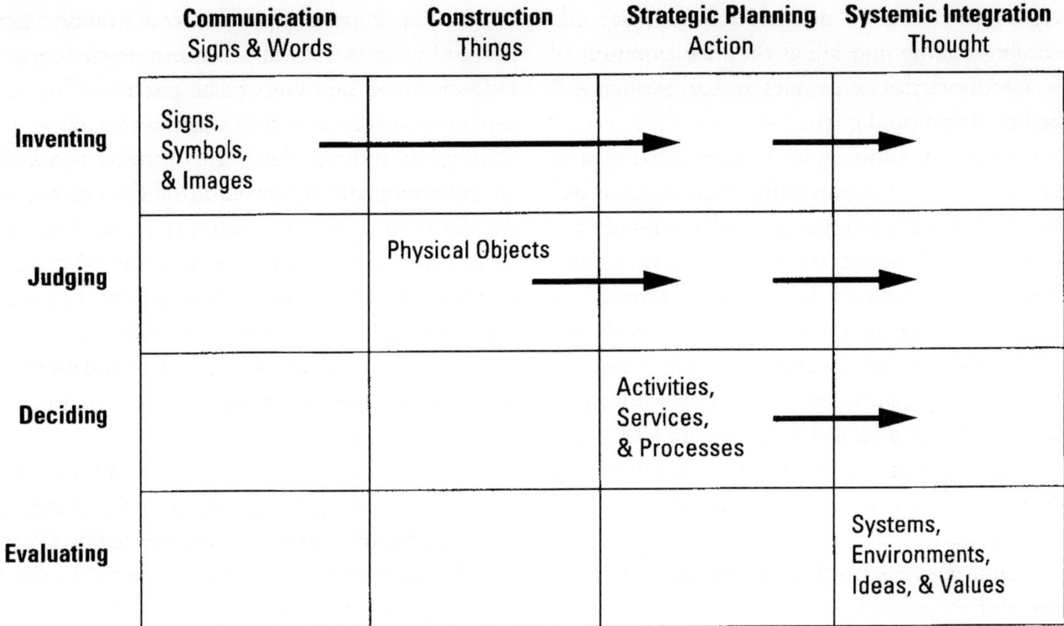

Figure 1.4 Human Abilities and Design Disciplines.

in need of disciplines or instrumentalities in order to become operative and effective in practice. In other words, disciplines are *enablers* of the natural abilities of human beings. Natural ability is not enough. The intellectual and moral character of designers is formed when natural ability is extended and supported by means of the arts and sciences, by the disciplines of thought, action, and production. In this sense, the history of design in the twentieth century is not merely the history of *products* or of *personal styles of expression* or even of *broad cultural ideas.* It is also the history of the *character and disciplines of design thinking as they are formed through encounters with new problems.*

The places of intersection between ability and discipline are illustrated in Figure 1.4. They represent the broad areas in which design is explored in the twentieth century; they are the areas where designers continue to focus and reinvent their professions to meet new opportunities and circumstances.

This matrix may serve as a heuristic device for investigating the shifting debate about design in the contemporary period. My argument is that many designers are engaged in rethinking the nature of products – communicative symbols and images *as well as* physical objects – in the context of action. Indeed, action itself – in the form of specific services, processes, and activities – has now become a recognized area of new products. And the broad discipline under development to support this rethinking in design is what I call *strategic planning* or *action-oriented design.* Emphasis on strategic planning leads to *third-order design* and *third-order design consultancies,* which expand the first and second orders of design that came to prominence in the early and middle decades of this century. Of course, there are many forms of strategic planning. The term is used in a narrow technical sense in business and in a broad common sense by many others, and the term is used explicitly by some designers and not at all by others. Nonetheless, the repositioning of design in the context of action and interaction is quite evident in contemporary work and requires little illustration. The issue is not decision-making, in the sense that designers have spoken of design as a problem-solving activity. The issue is how we find broader processes of deliberation that precede decision-making and allow the incorporation of diverse knowledge and values and an explicit discussion of ends and goals.

However, in addition to deliberation and strategic planning, I suggested that there is also a second theme quietly echoing through contemporary discourse. This is the theme of systems thinking or, as I prefer to call it, *systemic integration*. Emphasis on this theme leads to *fourth-order design* and *fourth-order design consultancies*. "Systems thinking" is not an elegant term. It does not strike the imagination with a vivid image. In fact, it can be quite misleading without a critical distinction between the early form of systems thinking that operated in the first decades of the twentieth century (and reached its clearest and perhaps most powerful expression in systems engineering in the 1950s) and the later form of systems thinking that is now emerging around concepts such as the networked enterprise, organizational learning, and the knowledge-based organization. The early form of systems thinking was fundamentally materialist and reductive in orientation, despite a concern for wholes. The wholes were material wholes – *things*, or information treated as a *thing* – such as one finds in systems engineering. This form of systems thinking was fundamentally concerned with the organization of means and offered only an anticipation of the deeper challenge of determining circumstances and ends.

Later forms of systems thinking began to emphasize the role of people in determining the course and results of systems and organizations. For example, the quality control movement began half a century ago as a form of high-end systems engineering, where statistical measures of manufacturing and performance provided concrete information on the successes and weaknesses of systems. However, the radical feature of this movement was not, as is sometimes suggested, a focus on statistical measures, but a rediscovery of collective human agency within organizations. Workers and managers began collaborating to discuss and evaluate problems of quality and to modify work processes. This was initially supported by statistical tools, but in essence it was a rediscovery of the value of dialogue and of the nature of rhetoric and dialectic as arts that are useful in shaping human affairs. This venture was both an extension and a relaxation of the traditional devices of dialectic, now separated from Marxist, Hegelian, or other philosophic ideologies which, in their academic and political forms, have too often limited the practical value of dialectic in the concrete circumstances and daily interactions of culture. Coupled with an ideology, dialectic is merely an art for interpreting things as they are and for promoting an ideology. However, separated from ideology, dialectic becomes a creative art for exploring opinions and knowledge, a form of cultural activity concerned with the exploration of ordering, disordering, and reordering in a search for understanding and for the human values which guide action.[15] Dialectic is, in fact, a powerful tool for collective deliberation about circumstances and ends, where a clarification and exploration of values and principles may be an essential condition for productive action.[16]

The potential of collaborative work was not achieved within the framework of quality control or total quality management. Although systems were expanded to include people and the focus became group planning and group execution, the orientation was still materialistic and quantitative. Indeed, in its worst form, total quality management remains a top-down approach, a tool of power and control within strongly hierarchical organizations. Nonetheless, the theme of systems thinking persists, focused on the collaborative nature of work and the need to integrate many kinds of knowledge in an effective enterprise, particularly when the enterprise is complex. This theme has found expression in the "learning organization" and the "knowledge-based organization," where dialogue is explicitly recognized as a new discipline of collaborative work.[17] The direction of this movement is illustrated in Figure 1.5 by means of another matrix. This matrix suggests the relationships among some of the management theories associated with systems thinking or systemic integration in the twentieth century.

The management approach known as "process reengineering," which speaks of reinventing and redesigning work processes, is located outside the discipline of systemic integration in this matrix, although it is parallel with systems engineering and total quality management. The growing dissatisfaction with the results of process reengineering – simple downsizing of organizations, without a redistribution of the creative energy and purpose of workers – may be traced to its separation from the cultural values of organizations and its emphasis on information technologies, detached from collective human agency. (Proponents of process reengineering have found it increasingly important to argue that the use of information technologies is not central to this management movement, although such technologies do provide a control mechanism as well as data for reengineering.) Recent literature on process reengineering seeks to address the problems of this approach by focusing on the motivation of managers. While this particular direction for rehabilitating process reengineering bears little resemblance to systemic integration, the turn toward people is a sure sign of the need to rethink process reengineering in the context of the cultural circumstances of an organization, not merely in the context of strategic business planning.[18]

The example of process reengineering is worth discussion here precisely because it suggests one of the boundary conditions of strategic planning itself: strategic planning breaks down when the larger cultural context is undergoing, or in need of, major transformation. Designers involved in strategic planning sometimes suggest that their approach does encompass broad cultural change within organizations. However, the evidence for this is not clear, and one may remain skeptical. The volatile period of transition may be led, managed, and facilitated by *fourth-order design thinking* that focuses on systemic integration, but it is not managed through the methods of strategic planning. The problems of transition are not problems of action but of reaching a new understanding of purposes and ends. Transition depends on discovering the core idea, values, and thought which organize a culture or system and propel it forward in a new search for expression in appropriate activities and products, often through a pluralism of individual initiatives that lead to creative debate. Strategic planning requires a community vision but it does not provide that vision; strategic plans

	Communication	**Construction**	**Strategic Planning**	**Systemic Integration**
Inventing				"Early Management Theories"--e.g. Mayo, McGregor, Barnard, & Selznick
Judging			"Process Reengineering"	"Systems Enginering" "Total Quality Management"
Deciding				"Networked Enterprises"
Evaluating				"Learning Organizations" and "Knowledge-Based Organizations"

Figure 1.5 Systematic Management Approaches.

may express core vision, but they are a poor and sometimes dangerous substitute for it.

Earlier, we observed that the design disciplines of communication and construction do not disappear in the new discipline of strategic design planning. Similarly, in the new circumstances of the learning organization and systemic integration the design disciplines of communication, construction, and strategic planning do not disappear. They are given new expression and development in the context of integration, where many kinds of knowledge and the participation of many people with different backgrounds and perspectives are required for effective product development.

However, it is not my goal in this paper to address the specific changes that are now underway in the design professions, design education, and some of the leading corporations and design consultancies in an effort to rethink the meaning of design in the new circumstances of organizational learning.[19] Rather, I want to explain the bearing of strategic planning and systemic integration on Branzi's dilemma, because these themes, operating in the philosophic engine of contemporary culture, suggest a third alternative which Branzi and others do not consider.

DESIGN, HUMANISM, AND THE PHILOSOPHY OF CULTURE

Branzi's dilemma presents two choices: the individual in the contemporary world may find identity and moral purpose either in individual vision, personal codes, pluralistic diversity, and tribalism or in a new general ideology – whatever that ideology may be – substituted for the old ideology of modernism. We have argued that both alternatives are distasteful and dangerous. Reliance on personal vision may easily lead not to productive pluralism but to relativism and a struggle for tribal power that ultimately suppresses alternative views. In turn, reliance on a new general ideology begs the question of what that ideology should be. We do not individually create a new cultural ideology; the candidates (such as Branzi's second modernity) are most likely to be no more than the projection of individual and tribal visions, *as if they had universal warrant and assent.*

The either/or form of the dilemma is characteristic of the style of argumentation in the impoverished two-term dialectic of most postmodernist theory. For example, some writers delight in the exercise of presenting two parallel columns of terms, with "modernist" terms on one side and opposing "postmodernist" terms on the other side, as if history or intelligence offered a clear choice between one term or the other. However, if we are correct in identifying deliberation and dialogue – dialogue as a new form of rhetoric and dialectic in community activity – as central themes in the new circumstances of the contemporary world, then a third alternative also exists, representing a more supple three-term dialectic suited to the needs of our complex situation. The third term is the mediated middle in any good discussion. It is the domain, not of dogmatically asserted truth on either side of an issue, but of honest uncertainty, hypothesis, and possibility. It is the domain of cooperation in common enterprise, despite differences of personal values or ideologies.

The key to this alternative lies in what we mean by culture and, subsequently, in a new relationship between culture and the individual. If culture is ideology, then there can be no single culture: no ideology achieves universal assent in the human community. Instead, there are many cultures, often in conflict and competition with each other on an ideological battlefield. Indeed, culture-as-ideology may be a tired and decadent stage in the development of culture, when conservative forces attempt to consolidate a particular philosophic, religious, or political position and close off further exploration, hastening a descent into tribalism. But if culture is an activity of ordering, disordering, and reordering in an ongoing search for principles and their expression, then the picture changes. Culture can be, in the words of philosopher Richard McKeon, "the framework within which many cultures are developed, interact, and communicate."[20] Instead of a new ideology shared by all in the contemporary world, there is the alternative of responsible discussion, deliberation, and collaborative decision-making on critical issues of action, where the participants recognize that there may be some truth in the arguments, beliefs, and perceptions of their opposing colleagues.

The hope for such an alternative may seem dim at the moment. We are moving through a difficult period where conflicting values often seem irreconcilable in practical affairs. Yet this is where design and the work of designers may offer an example of new ways of thinking and acting. By focusing on concrete problems and practical situations – on what designers call "the project" – design shifts attention away from ideology and theory as the ultimate goal of cooperative work and towards action and production. This does not lessen the value of theory, but it makes theory accountable in the objective results of what is done and what is made.

Perhaps the focus on the concrete and objective is one reason why design attracts increasing attention in the contemporary world and is given broader scope than at any time in the past: there is hope that design thinking, applied in many new areas, can serve as an alternative to the old forms of technocracy based on scientific specialization, where experts in narrow areas of learning once believed that they could improve and enrich life merely by applying technical knowledge to solve the problems of everyday life. In contrast with technocracy, design increasingly seeks to include in its processes of deliberation and decision-making all of those who will be affected by a new product. This is not a vague or sentimental gesture. The new disciplines of strategic design planning and systemic integration, as they are now explored by many designers, are providing the instrumentalities for inclusion in the group processes of product development. They are providing tools for addressing the conflict of competing values and directing attention towards agreement on what is possible.

The result of the new disciplines of design thinking is typically not agreement on an ideology that may stand behind a new product. Instead, the result is an agreement that this or that is what shall be done today, so that ideological disagreement may be suspended and production move forward with the support of all of those involved in the planning process. Such support – practical agreements reached through discussion – serves as the shared vision of a group and as the ground for objective evaluation and choice among competing alternatives in product development. The ground is a mediated middle of reasonable possibility and intentional operations, not a claim of universal infallibility or truth. It is a contribution to the search that we have described as culture. Instead of a new general ideology that is substituted for modernism, design can advance culture as a an ongoing search for values and understanding.[21]

There is an important parallel between this approach to contemporary culture and the earlier cultural revolution in man's relation to nature that occurred at the beginning of the twentieth century. Philosopher John Dewey explains the earlier revolution as a change in the center of the universe: from the mind seeking to understand a separate exterior material world to the mind as part of nature.

> The old center [of the universe] was the mind knowing by means of an equipment of powers complete within itself, and merely exercised upon an antecedent external material equally complete in itself. The new center is indefinite interactions taking place within a course of nature which is not fixed and complete, but which is capable of direction to new and different results through the mediation of intentional operations.[22]

In the new turn of the revolution that began in the early decades of the twentieth century, culture is not a fixed ideology existing outside the individual, something comparable to the old metaphysical idea of nature. We are all embedded in the course of a culture that is not fixed and complete. Culture is what we do individually and together through our intentional operations and projects.

In contrast to Branzi's dilemma, where individuality is threatened in either of the two alternatives – threatened by the power of tribes or submerged in an oppressive ideological order – the new philosophy of culture offers a suitable ground for defending the individual. Universality in the new philosophy of culture is not achieved through consensus in a general ideology. Rather, universality is an *expression of individuality placed in its context*. The emphasis is on the dynamic functional relations among individuals and groups, not on the old dichotomies of ideology which impede interaction. Paradoxically, collaborative work and the group processes which play an increasingly important role in the design and development of complex products are not a threat to individual vision. The task of the individual is to find his or her place in relation to others, and this is precisely what is at stake in exploring values in the context of what is good, just, useful, and pleasurable. Identity and moral purpose come from considering our relations with others, from learning to perceive what is true and valuable when the world is regarded from other perspectives. The pluralism of individual perspectives is essential to ensure that the exploration does not become entrapped in a single ideology. Design is the most vivid domain for this cultural activity in the contemporary world, because it deals with concrete and objective results whose consequences affect us all.

CONCLUSION: DESIGNING FOR THE INDIVIDUAL

There is one observation that has immediate bearing on the work of designers today. If the arguments we have advanced are valid and useful, the task is no longer to design for a universal audience, or national groups, or market segments, or even the ideological abstraction known as "the consumer." Despite the continuing role of mass production in many societies, the task is to design for the *individual placed in his or her immediate context*. Our products should support the individual in the effort to become an active participant in culture, searching for locally significant coherence and connection. Products should be personal pathways in the otherwise confusing ecology of culture.

Designing such pathways is a difficult challenge. However, there is some hope that designers are increasingly equipped for the task. Improvement of design education may help to make them more sensitive to the individual than they already are, while also increasing their awareness of the diverse kinds of knowledge that bear on design. There is no reason to be unhappy with the pluralism of design explorations in the contemporary world, so long as these explorations are not entrapped in ideology and each of us may pursue our own paths in design within the reasonable bounds of responsibility, based on informed discussions of what is good, just, useful, and pleasurable. We may be distressed by some of the work that we see in graphic and industrial design today and delighted by a wide range of other work. Design is very young and has far to go in the exploration of its role in culture. For many of us, this means better understanding of the disciplines of design thinking, not merely changes in style and surface treatment. Our hope is that the quality of discussion about design continues to improve and that designers do not become afraid of having their ideas and work subjected to wider and more insightful discussion than in the past. We all have much to learn about living together in a culture that is not fixed and changeless, and this is both our pleasure and our responsibility.

NOTES

First published in *Design Issues* 14 no. 1 (Spring 1998): 3–20.

1. Andrea Branzi, "We Are the Primitives," in *Design Discourse: History Theory Criticism*, ed. by V. Margolin (Chicago: University of Chicago Press, 1989), 37–42. This essay is reprinted from the Italian journal *Modo.*
2. Held at the University of Art and Design, Helsinki, Finland. June 1994.
3. Harold Rosenberg, *The Tradition of the New* (Chicago: University of Chicago Press, 1965).
4. Branzi, "We Are the Primitives," 37.
5. Andrea Branzi, *Learning from Milan: Design and the Second Modernity* (Cambridge, Massachusetts: MIT Press, 1988), 71.
6. Branzi, *Learning from Milan*, 73.
7. Branzi. "We Are the Primitives," 39.
8. Branzi, "We Are the Primitives," 39.
9. Branzi, "We Are the Primitives." 38.
10. Richard Buchanan, "Rhetoric, Humanism, and Design," in *Discovering Design: Explorations in Design Studies* (Chicago: University of Chicago Press, 1995), ed. by R. Buchanan and V. Margolin.
11. George Nelson, "What is Good Design For?" in *Problems of Design* (New York: Whitney Publications, 1965). For Nelson's view of the other side of the issue, see "Design as Communication" in the same volume.
12. Consider, for example, the recent dispute involving the Air and Space Museum of the Smithsonian Institution in Washington DC. Plans for an exhibition of the aircraft that dropped the first atomic bomb in World War II were scrapped because of extremely intense controversy among many groups about the exhibit's proposed interpretation and contextualization of the event. Exhibition design is now a dangerous political act.
13. For a discussion of this theme in the context of the twentieth-century metaphysics of communication, see Richard McKeon, "The Future of Metaphysics," in *The Future of Metaphysics,* ed. by Robert E. Wood (Chicago: Quadrangle Books, 1970), 306–7.
14. One of the dangers for consultancies that place an emphasis on strategic design planning is to believe that graphic and product design may be subcontracted after a strategic plan has been conceived. This is a new version of the old fallacy of linear product development, where plans are tossed over the wall from specialist to specialist. The plan may easily be lost in the details of execution.
15. For background on the changing nature of dialectic and dialogue, see Richard McKeon, "Dialectic and Political Thought and Action," *Ethics* 65 (1954), 1–31, and "Knowledge, Community, and Communication," in *A Center for National Goals and Alternatives: Collected Papers* (New York: National Industrial Conference Board, 1971), 245–72. Also, see Chaim Perelman, ed., *Dialectics/Dialectiques* (The Hague: Martinus Nijhoff, 1975). Elsewhere, I have suggested that systemic integration or dialectic may be regarded as the fourth art of rhetoric. See R. Buchanan, "Rhetoric, Humanism, and Design."
16. In addition to the work of Richard McKeon and Chaim Perelman, the work of Stephen Toulmin has also played an important role in the rediscovery of dialectic as a practical art of deliberation. See Stephen Toulmin, *The Uses of Argument* (London: Cambridge University Press, 1958).
17. Peter M. Senge, *The Fifth Discipline: The Art and Practice of the Learning Organization* (New York: Doubleday, 1990). See William N. Issacs, "Taking Flight: Dialogue, Collective Thinking, and Organizational Learning," and Edgar H. Schein, "On Dialogue, Culture, and Organizational Learning," *Organizational Dynamics*, 22, no. 2 (Autumn 1993).
18. See James Champy, *Reengineering Management: The Mandate for New Leadership* (New York: Harper Business, 1995).
19. Some aspects are discussed in Richard Buchanan and Craig M. Vogel, "Design in the Learning Organization: Educating for the New Culture of Product Development," *Design Management Journal*, 5, no.4 (Fall 1994).
20. Richard McKeon, "Fact and Value in the Philosophy of Culture," in *Akten des XIV Internationalen Kongresses für Philosophie, Wien, 2–9 September 1968* (Vienna: Herder, 1969) 4: 503–11.
21. McKeon, "Fact and Value in the Philosophy of Culture," 506. "Culture is the constitutive whole or regulative universal in which cultures have their being, their interrelations, and their communications; particular cultures are described and investigated as configurations, constellations, clusters, and transmutations of values. The objectivity of facts and values is not discovered or achieved in a structure of fixities but in an ongoing development of achievement and invention which is compounded of advancements of science, society, and art in the creation and establishment of truths and values."
22. John Dewey, *The Quest for Certainty: A Study in the Relation of Knowledge and Action* (New York: Capricorn, 1960), 290–91. For a discussion of the bearing of these ideas on design, see R. Buchanan, "Design and Technology in the Second Copernican Revolution," *Revue Sciences et techniques de la conception*, no. 1 (1992), 21–7.

2

DESIGNING THE ARTIFICIAL: AN INTERDISCIPLINARY STUDY

Massimo Negrotti

INTRODUCTION: BEYOND COMMON SENSE

Even in a scientific lexicon, some terms suffer from a sort of meaning inertness which seems to disappear only in actual use. Take, for instance, the adjective *artificial*: for almost everybody, it seems to designate something designed and produced by man, or anything that is not natural. In this way, "artificial" is a simple substitute for "technological," since all not-natural things, obviously, are made by means of some more or less refined human technology.

Scholars including Herbert Simon,[1] Jacques Monod,[2] and others have taken this position, neglecting the teleological difference between a cathode tube and an artificial heart. Actually, the *perspectiva artificialis* which Leonbattista Alberti and Piero della Francesca had in mind in the Renaissance was something quite different from this inertial meaning. In fact, everybody today also understands the expression "artificial kidney," while nobody would attach any meaning to the expression "artificial telephone."

The reflexion on technology has not yet come to a scientific theorization and, on the basis of illuministic or romantic attitudes, it confines itself to an analysis which deals with technological objects as something which man constructs, after Archimedes, as "secondary and pleasant applications" of the so-called pure sciences, such as mathematics or geometry.

But, as a matter of fact, since the dawn of civilization, man shows a great, twofold constructive ambition: one, the Prometheus syndrome, aims at *inventing* objects and machines able to dominate nature, grasping its laws and adapting itself to them; the other, in turn, the Icarus syndrome, aims at reproducing natural objects or processes through alternate strategies,[3] as compared to those nature follows. While the former may be called *conventional technology*, the latter should be called the *technology of the artificial*. From the wings of Icarus, attached by naive glue, to current techniques for replacing human organs, or to reproduce the capacities of the mind or the properties of life through ancient or recent automata, there emerges clearly a *continuum* worthy to be seriously considered as a man's specific turn, which today's and future technologies will greatly enhance.

A formula for defining the artificial may involve three logical points:

1. *A necessary condition*: the object or the process must be built by man;
2. *A sufficient condition*: the object or the process must be inspired by a natural one; and
3. *A methodological constraint*: the object or the process must be realized by means of materials and procedures different from those nature adopts.

Thanks to his extremely well-developed brain, man is an animal that not only adapts itself to the natural world, but tries to *know* it, to *control* it, and even to *reproduce* it. Furthermore, from a cultural point of view, many of us think that the ability to reproduce natural objects or processes exceeds our capability of knowing.[4] The rationale behind this is: if one is able to make an effective artificial organ, he cannot lack some deep knowledge of the natural organ. Nevertheless, what really happens very often is a different affair. As the history of artificial devices openly indicates, the reproduction of natural objects, or processes, frequently is an attempt to cope with nature "cost what it may." In other terms, under the pressure of some kind of urgency – curiosity or whatever – man has designed a wide range of devices, most often neglecting any accurate knowledge of the correspondent natural object. It is enough to think of artificial hair, teeth, arms, flavors, flowers (often and meaningfully defined as "feigned"), or even processes very far from each other, such as rain or intelligence, and taste or gravity.

On the other hand, what is it meant by an "accurate knowledge" of some natural object or process? This is a key point if one wants to understand the artificial and, on a different plane, science itself.

LOGIC OF THE ARTIFICIAL

In whatever field one chooses, in order to consider artificial objects or processes (bioengineering, substitutes for natural elements or substances, artificial intelligence, robotics, artificial life, remakings, etc.), we may say that man cannot but reproduce something – which we shall name the *exemplar* – he has experienced at some *observation level*.

He then attributes to the *exemplar* some peculiar structural or dynamical property, that is to say its *essential performance*. Both the selection of an *exemplar* and the attribution of an *essential performance* strongly depend upon the available knowledge (not necessarily the scientific one) and the selected *observation level*. In turn, the selection of an *observation level* depends upon certain attitudes which range from pure personal belief to established scientific paradigms.[5]

In considering a biological system, a tree for instance, as an *exemplar* to reproduce, it is clear that the selection of a mechanical observation level leads to some possible *essential performances* which are very different from the ones coming from the selection of electrochemical, physiological or, perhaps, aesthetical, symbolical, or even religious *observation levels*.

To sum up this point, if the current scientific community maintains that the *essential performance* of the kidney is that of filtering the blood according to certain modalities, it will decree the success of a reproduction attempt if it will consist of a machine able to generate that filtering function. On the other extreme – but in the same logic – if people think that the devil exists and has some features, then its reproduction in painting will be accepted – as it was in the Middle Ages for the one proposed by Coppo di Marcovaldo in the Florence Baptistery – if the painting exhibits those features.

Thus, one can answer our question ("What does an 'accurate knowledge' of some natural object or process mean?") first of all, only by indicating different *observation levels* in different units of time, and then by taking into account the more or less objective and shared models of that object or process as "seen" from the *observation level* he has selected.

The selecting role of the *observation levels* is very clear even in the seemingly simple activity of selecting an *exemplar*. Actually, in this case, man "decides" to bring something into the foreground, leaving the rest in the background. This is an observational strategy, consistent with our nature, which very often works fine. But it also is an intrinsically arbitrary strategy which, having to deal with the reproduction of natural objects, reveals all its critical aspects. While scientists may separate objects and processes for heuristic reasons – giving rise to ultra-specialized disciplines on the basis of more and more specialized *observation levels* – artificialists have to introduce separations for practical and concrete reasons, since they have to build up something, and not only to study it.

But which rules govern the selection of an *exemplar* from the perceptive background? As we know, the "ways of seeing" are, to some measure, imposed or prevented by the culture we live in. But there also is a more objective problem before us, namely, that of the boundaries that separate the *exemplar* from the background.

Speaking of an artificial heart, we all refer to a well-known and recognizable *exemplar*, which is, at least apparently, well distinguishable from all that is not a heart. Obviously, to an engineer, the question is much more complex: which organic parts, vessels, muscles, subsystems, define the "boundaries" of the heart?

Besides our awareness of heart valves, today there are devices which assume as *exemplar* the left ventricle (the so-called *left ventricular assist systems*) and which should collaborate with the natural heart of the patient, and others which reproduce both ventricles. Only recently, the total artificial heart, able to completely replace the natural heart, has been considered an achievable target, but many problems remain, and many of them may be conceived as problems concerning the fixing of boundaries.

As another example, if we want to reproduce a pond, how should we establish its boundaries? On a topological level, should we include in the pond even the geological structure of its bottom and of its sides? As far as the flora and fauna of the natural pond are concerned, which degree of likelihood should we reach, for instance, along the range that includes, on the one extreme, ducks and fishes and, on the other, microbiological creatures? It is quite clear that different answers to these questions will give rise to different models and concrete achievements, depending upon the essential performance we have in mind.

In the field of artificial intelligence, this is a well-known and very often debated problem: how may we fix the boundaries of human intelligence with respect to the other functions of mind, such as memory or intuition, and fantasy or curiosity?

In the extreme, we could consider the case of the *exemplars* drawn from the animal field, e.g., a *holothuria* ("cucumber of the sea") that lives symbiotically with the little fish *Fierasfer acus*: how could we separate these two entities, first of all in representational terms, and then in terms of design and of reproduction?

It seems clear enough to us, that the task of outlining an *exemplar* is a somewhat arbitrary operation by which one isolates an object or a process from a wider context, which includes it, or from an environment which hosts it.

Because of its philosophical and scientific tradition, Western civilization was highly capable of carrying out the analysis of the natural world, and gained great advantages from this operation. But analysis (significantly, the word derives from ancient Greek "to break down") surely is much more useful for scientific than for artificialistic purposes. Actually, while the knowledge we may get through analysis is always to be considered as a potentially valid one – at least in descriptive terms and, sometimes, even in predictive ones – the concrete reproduction of an *exemplar* which, in nature, behaves specifically could require the cooperation of many of its constituent parts. In turn, this will require more *observation levels*, and the analysis, with its usual isolation strategies, may not succeed in rendering observable all of the levels required.

The choice of an *exemplar* is a sort of literal "radication" of some region of nature, and this can happen, as we saw, both in terms of its concrete isolation in space, and of modeling its structure.

SCIENCE AND ARTIFICIALISM

Here, science and artificialism exhibit some discrepancy and some analogy. In fact, while science proceeds analytically, step by step, but without any hope of getting a definite knowledge at all possible levels, designers of an artificial device (let us call them "artificialists") have to construct something real. Therefore, they set up "pieces of reality" *as if* they would know all that is necessary for "replicating" the *exemplar*.

Nevertheless, what cannot be wholly known, cannot be wholly reproduced. Just as it is conceptually impossible for scientists to synthesize a natural object through a bottom-up strategy, which could put together all of the possible observation levels, artificialists cannot expect their devices to possess all of the possible performances exhibited by natural *exemplars*, just because they proceed through a multiple-selection process: *observation level*, *exemplar*, and *essential performance*. On the other hand, while a scientist can write a book with chapters that deal separately with the mechanical, electrochemical, and physiological aspects of a tree, an artificialist who wants to make an artificial tree cannot build four or five artificial trees and put them together in one and the same device. Perhaps he could do so, but, he thus would build a gadget or a toy, rather than a "replica" of the tree. The main reason is that the relationships among different *observation levels* would require new *observation levels*, in a sort of hopeless *petitio principii*.

Replicating something is an autopoietical enterprise reserved to nature (or to man in very special and unnatural cases, e.g., when he reproduces man-made objects like in mass production or in cloning pure informational systems), while making the artificial means to build something on the basis of some (more or less) refined model of the *exemplar* and of its *essential performances*, assuming some clear-cut "profile" or *observation level*. This is a matter of analytical strategy – which has no rational alternatives – which prevents science from capturing the synthetic "core" of the whole system and, therefore, prevents artificialists from reproducing it.

In fact, what we name the *essential performance* of a natural *exemplar* always is "essential" with reference to some specific *observation level*, and not in ontological terms.

The selected *essential performance* can be very complex, and it even can include several subperformances, but these must allow a manageable model because, otherwise, the problem of coordinating two or more *observation levels* would arise.

Since this is a rather general problem, empirical evidence can be drawn from several different fields. John Young, a biologist involved in the sixties in understanding some aspects of the sensorial functions of the *Nautilus*, wrote:

> Another fascinating problem is the relationship between visual and tactile learning ... Since the two systems overlap in the vertical lobe, maybe there is some kind of coordination between them. However, it has been demonstrated that the objects detected by sight are not recognized by touch.[6]

The attempt to reproduce in a bionic system the coordination between tactile and visual learning will imply the discovery of the whatever stuff it is based on, and, thus, a selection and even the creation of a third *observation level*. On the other hand, if we know the basis of the coordination performance, we have to make tactile and visual performances able to work according to its rules. This could introduce some additional problems which we did not face when we only had to reproduce the two performances as standalone functions.

If these additional problems can be solved, then the resulting artificial system will work well at the *observation level* described by the coordination performance if, and only if, its working is locally determined. That is to say if, and only if, the subsystem is a rather locally self-sufficient one which does not involve a linkage of any other subsystem with the coordination performance, and this is, of course, a very rare case. The basis on which the coordination works – as a truly new *essential performance* – could impose a complete redesigning of the two performances, visual and tactile learnings, in accordance to the needs of other systemic levels that govern the coordination as such.

THE ARTIFICIAL AT WORK: INHERITANCE AND TRANSFIGURATION

Artificialists deal with concrete materials – not only with concepts – which involve material complexity. Whatever material has to be conceived as a reality observable from an unlimited number of *observation levels*, and, therefore, nobody can claim that he or she knows them completely. Scientists and artificialists share the same human basic rational limits, and this means that both, when considering some material, select some observation level. Thus, artificialists will select the *observation level* most coherent with their reproduction goal.

At the start, the materials and the technologies which usually are adopted for an artificialistic enterprise are taken from current conventional technologies, exactly as they are available in their own area. We may refer to the enthusiasm of Jacques Vaucanson, who was involved, in the eighteenth century, in a project to reproduce the digestion process of a duck, when he heard of the new rubber materials coming from India. Also today's researchers in the field of the artificial are, of course, always looking for conventional materials suitable for their enterprise. For instance, "The life-saving heart surgery often relies on a polymer originally developed for women's fashions or a plastic meant for insulating electrical wires."[7] Thus, the search for application-specific improvements of the materials which have been originally taken from other applications, soon becomes a central concern in meeting the increasing pursuit of *essential performances*.

What should be clear is that the adoption of materials for replacing parts of a natural *exemplar*, or for getting some natural *essential performances* from the artificial device, may generate unforeseeable situations. The reason is that, very often, only one feature of the selected conventional material will overlap the properties of its correspondent material in the natural *exemplar*. But, as a principle, all of the features – known and unknown – of the material adopted will be unavoidably *inherited*. As a consequence, they will interact in an unpredictable way both with other parts of the artificial system, and with the hosting context (body, environment, landscape, etc.).

Surely, the most spectacular instance of this phenomenon is the bio-incompatibility which leads to the so-called "rejection" of allogeneic substances or elements in biological organisms.

Nevertheless, it is a matter of a much more general tendency, which characterizes whatever artificial device or process when it is concretely realized and put at work in whatever environment. Every artificial device, object, or process, (be it an artificial muscle or a flower, an intelligent software program or a robot, grass or rocks, or whatever else) works fine only within a rather narrow spectrum of internal and external configurations: the ones matching the situation in which it was designed and constructed. In other terms, the artificial can exhibit an acceptable approximation of the natural *essential performance* it wants to reproduce only if the original *observation level* is respected, and if no relevant side effects due to unpredicted material interactions arise. If we move even a little from that spectrum, then we get unpredictable behaviors or "sudden events" from the artificial, not belonging to the spectrum of performances normally exhibited by the natural *exemplar*.

To sum up, in an artificial device, the *transfiguration* of the natural *essential performance* may depend on four main reasons:

1. The "eradication" of the exemplar and, therefore, of its *essential performance* from the whole natural system, thanks to the unavoidable selection of a single *observation level*.
2. The interplay among the features inherited from the materials used in building the parts or components of the artificial device.
3. The interactions between these features and the host environment, and its features and requirements.
4. The growing amount of conventional technology which, as a rule, is needed to improve the

essential performance, or simply to control and minimize the side effects.

Thus, the unavoidable and paradoxical destiny of the artificial is that, starting from nature, it develops towards conventional technology while trying to preserve an *essential performance* which may be impoverished or, sometimes, even improved, but always is transfigured in comparison with the natural one. A growing amount of conventional technology means that the more an artificial device develops, the more its *essential performance* tends to represent a smaller proportion of the total amount of the performances exhibited, actually or potentially, by the device. By the way, this explains why artificialists often give up their original projects and start a new ones suggested just by the "novelties" coming from their development.

Our discussion is not only academic: it deals with well-known real problems in bioengineering, where, in order to avoid transfigurations, i.e., troubles coming from the interplay of different *observation levels*: "Until recently, most research in the field [of cell transplantation] has focused on minimizing biological fluid and tissue interactions with biomaterials in an effort to prevent fibrous encapsulation from foreign-body reaction or clotting in blood that has contact with artificial devices. In short, most biomaterials research has focused on making the material *invisible* to the body."[8]

The artificial results from the overlapping of nature with conventional technology. The arrow pointing to the right suggests that the artificial, in its concrete achievements, cannot but develop towards conventional technology, and this fact pulls it further and further away from nature.

On the other hand, the tacit ideal of artificialists to get, even in the distant future, a "replication" of the *exemplar* is prevented not only from a logical viewpoint – if something is replicated, then it is not artificial – but also, as we said, from the impossibility to take into account all of the observation levels of the reality. Once again, a bioengineer clarifies the situation saying that, "If we want to engineer a material that has the characteristics of soft composite biomaterials, we have to understand the interactions at all scales, from the molecules up to the cells, and up to the macroscopic properties of tissues."[9]

It should be added that, in this field, the most advanced research trend is now on active biomaterials and, therefore, on devices which begin to be named as bioartificial: those materials which, in other words, are able to interact in a controlled way with some specific aspects of the body, rather than remaining intentionally separated from it. This means that, if the items we have discussed have some likelihood, they will enter the scene very soon because it is very difficult to imagine a biocompatibility at all the possible *observation levels*. Really, this would be the image of a replica rather than of some artificial device.

THE INTRINSIC FICTION COMPONENT OF THE ARTIFICIAL

The "invisibility" of the artificial is a very general constraint. The artificial has always to be "defended" from what comes from the neglected *observation levels*, that is to say from all the possible *observation levels* of the environment apart from the one which was assumed for the reproduction enterprise.

This is why "realistic" landscapes built for contemporary zoos have to be carefully maintained, in order to avoid degenerations due to the interactions among their components and with the hosting environment. This also is true for the Japanese *domes,* the well-known and big remakings of European or American landscapes, where people can spend their time in virtual holidays, or for the famous Paul Getty's Roman villa (the Villa dei Papiri of Ercolano, buried by an eruption of Vesuvio) near the Pacific Ocean.

Surely, these problems were well known in the past. For instance by the Venetian doge Caprese who, in the twelfth century, asked the architect Nero Faggioli (founder of the Scuola di Lattuga from which some great masters including Filippo Brunelleschi and Lorenzo Ghiberti came) to build an artificial landscape with a mountain, a garden, a zoo, and even a stream moved by a pump which flowed down from the mountain.

But the same occurs in very different projects, such as artificial intelligence or robotics, where the *essential performances* can be obtained only within "paces of interactions" very carefully delimited by formal boundaries, concrete walls, and other controlling procedures which make artificial intelligence "purified" from all psychological and physical features which constitute it in humans.

In principle, an artificial device needs a sort of artificial environment, or, when this is impossible, it has to be "encapsulated" in such a way that, as said by twentieth-century artificialism pioneer Willem Kolff concerning the artificial heart, it can be perceived by the environment only in its main function, that is to say in its *essential performance*. Said differently, an artificial heart has to "cheat" the organism.[10]

Thus, we discover that even fiction and illusion play a central role in the growing history of the artificial.

Artificial cavities, or nests, for some animal species; artificial flavors or turves; flight simulators or artificial bodies for testing safety devices for cars, teaching or surgical techniques; artificial fertilizers, or gravity, and many other devices, are objects or processes which, like artificial organs, have to be "accepted" by their environments – users included – and this is possible only by some "illusory" strategy which is not, of course, a pure fiction game. Rather, artificialists try to force the environment or the hosting organism to orient itself only towards the same *observation level* taken in the design and in the building up of the artificial device.

Figure 2.1 Eighteenth-century automata.

When this strategy is possible, the artificial realizes the *essential performances* which, in the natural world, are generated in the global interplay of the reality levels. When this strategy is impossible, the artificial realizes *essential performances* which are, so to say, at the disposal of and open to the environment. In both cases, the artificial generates *essential performances* which transfigure the natural performances it has to reproduce.

The degree of transfiguration, both in terms of quantity and quality dimensions, strongly depends upon the disposition of the natural *exemplar* to be eradicated from its context without any significant loss of its *essential performance*. In turn, all this depends upon the amount of relationships which, in nature, make possible the *essential performance*, and, even more, upon the quantity of *observation levels* involved by these relationships.

This explains why two different artificial devices referring to two subsystems of a whole system, like the human body, each working acceptably on their own, cannot easily be made to work together, when they reproduce two different *exemplars*, according to two *essential performances*.

As a rule of thumb, while this remains an open question, one has to think that the more the two natural *exemplars* and *essential performances* are functionally close to each other, the greater the difficulty, and vice versa. On the other hand, the knowledge of the "functional distance" – and of the *observation levels* involved by it – between two or more subsystems of a natural system is not always available, and this poses the greatest challenge to the work of artificialists. Therefore, the work of the artificialists, in every area, is truly an exploratory one.

Many researchers, for instance, appear to be persuaded by strictly analytical strategies. On the contrary, others seem to follow the idea that, in many cases, the problems of the materials are secondary, because the real problem in reproducing natural *exemplars* or, rather, natural *essential performances* is to find the right organizational plan. This was a central point in the study of artificial intelligence in the eighties, and in artificial life in the following decade,[11] both founded on the doctrines of the so-called *emergence*, a term coined by G. H. Lewes in 1875. According to this doctrine, in many real systems, the high-level properties cannot be explained by the properties of lower levels.[12] In this approach, the main goal was the search for the "right organizational plan," neglecting the fact that a concrete artificial object or process, in contrast with pure informational systems, must adopt real materials and fit real environments.

More generally, these problems strongly emerge when we consider the possibility of combining and putting to work, in one and the same organism, two or more artificial devices. In this case, the inheritance of the materials adopted will explode exponentially, giving rise to a much more complex network of unpredictable interactions (on this point, see Negrotti, 1999).

CONCLUSIONS

However, as a final general rule, one can say that "something will always happen": no artificial device will work *only* according to its designer's intention. In other words, the reality of the artificial is not less rich in levels than any other real object. This means that, in the end, every artificial object or process will behave according to its complex interplay of levels, and not only according to its design. This is, of course, a rather general rule that could also apply to conventional technology objects or processes. But, when the target is the reproduction of some natural *exemplar* and of its *essential performance*, the transfiguration – i.e., performance degenerations, sudden events, and side effects – cannot but assume a special meaning, not always dangerous and not always promising, but always "new" as compared to what nature exhibits.

These kinds of intuitions have started to appear in several fields of the technology of the artificial. For instance, in his 1994 doctoral dissertation, T. W. Hall at the University of Michigan highlights the limits and the "transfigurations" of artificial gravity (needed for the space journeys) as compared to the natural ones. He maintains that, beyond the machine which generates gravity, the environment in which natural gravity works and human beings live also should be studied and designed. We should, in other words, design the artificial environment surrounding the artificial objects. Hall concludes:

> The goal of environmental design in artificial gravity is not to fool people into thinking they're on Earth but, rather, to help them orient themselves to the realities of their rotating environment.[13]

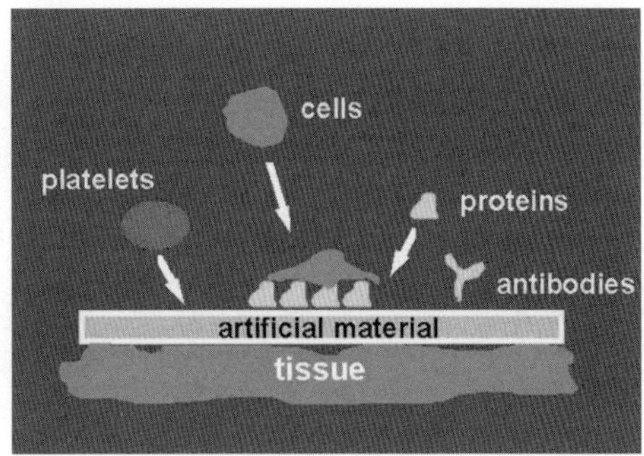

Figure 2.2 Mixing artificial and natural structures.

Figure 2.3 Japanese architectural remakings of landscape for leisure.

In this sense, the realm of the artificial truly consists in a "third" reality that lies between nature and conventional technology. It cannot but "swing" between these two realities, since it can overlap neither the former nor the latter unless it loses its peculiarity. It is a matter of a new reality, coming from very far in the history of human civilization, which is destined to grow a great deal in the near future. We cannot face it in terms of pure common-sense understanding or with a fragmented, nonunitary, conceptual frame.

NOTES

First published in *Design Issues* 17 no. 2 (Spring 2001): 4–16.

1. H.A. Simon, *The Sciences of the Artificial* (Cambridge, MA: MIT Press, 1969), tr. it. *Le scienze dell'artificiale* (Milano: ISEDI, 1970) 18–19.
2. J. Monod, *Il caso e la necessità* (Milano: Est Mondadori, 1972), 18.
3. R. Rosen, "Bionics Revisited" in H. Haken, A. Karlqvist and U. Svedin, eds., *The Machine as Metaphor and Tool* (Berlin and Heidelberg: Springer Verlag, 1993), 94–5.
4. R. Cordeschi, *La scoperta dell'artificiale* (Milano: Dunod, 1998).
5. C. Emmeche, S. Køppe, and F. Stjernfelt, "Emergence: Towards an Ontology of Levels," *Journal for General Philosophy of Science* 28 (1997): 83–119.
6. J.Z. Young, *A Model of the Brain* (Oxford: Oxford University Press, 1964), tr. it., *Un modello del cervello* (Torino: Einaudi, 1974), 278.
7. The Whitaker Foundation, *Annual Report: Tissue Engineering*, Internet Website (http://fairway.ecn.purdue.edu/bme/whitaker/95_annual_report/tissue95.html) (1995).
8. A.G. Mikos, R. Bizios, K.K. Wu, and M.J. Yaszemski, *Cell Transplantation,* The Rice Institute of Biosciences and Bioengineering, Internet Website (http://www.bioc.rice.edu/Institute/area6.html) (1996).
9. W. Hoffman, "Forging New Bonds" in *Inventing Tomorrow* (Minnesota: University of Minnesota Institute of Technology, Spring 1995).
10. Personal interview with W. Kolff, reported in M. Negrotti, *The Theory of the Artificial* (Exeter: Intellect Books, 1999). See also M. Negrotti, "From the Artificial to the Art: A Short Introduction to a Theory and Its Applications," *Leonardo* 32: 3 (1999): 183–9.
11. C.G. Langton, C. Taylor, J. D. Farmer, and S. Rasmussen, eds., *Artificial Life II,* Volume X of *SFI Studies in the Sciences of Complexity* (Redwood City, CA: Addison-Wesley, 1992), xiii–xviii.
12. C.L. Morgan, *Emergent Evolution* (London: Williams and Norgate, 1923). See also F.E. Yates, ed., *Self-Organizing Systems: The Emergence of Order* (New York: Plenum Press, 1987), *idem.*
13. T.W. Hall, "The Architecture of Artificial-Gravity Environments for Long-Duration Space Habitation" (doctoral dissertation, University of Michigan, 1994).

3

A SCENARIO FOR DESIGN

Wolfgang Jonas

Dedicated to V.M.

1 INTRODUCTION

This paper illustrates a functional framework (a scenario) for the design process comprised of epistemological, theoretical, and methodological aspects, and introducing the concept of scenario as a guiding idea.

A scenario is a design in itself. So the criteria for the appropriateness of the construction have no correlation to some reality "out there," but comprehensiveness, coherence of the different chunks of knowledge, and beauty of the design, as well as adaptability and flexibility. "Designing designing"[1] does not claim truth, but universality. I like to call it "neorational" in the sense that it is a rationalism that has passed post-rationalism/ modernism, and has evolved into "post-post-rationalism." It strives to bridge the gap between the "two cultures" of the humanities and the sciences. The starting point is science, using such concepts as autopoiesis, self-organization, and second-order cybernetics.

The scenario can be considered as an experimental stage set for design and planning practice, and a conceptual framework for disciplinary development.

2 SITUATION AND DISCIPLINARY DEFICITS

Design is developing from a craft and trade activity to a profession and, hopefully, towards an established academic discipline.[2,3] Krippendorff[4] examines the question, "What makes a discipline?" in detail, and describes the deficits of design, mainly concentrating on the disciplinary discourse yet to come. Owen[5] calls design a "slow learner" with regard to the establishment of a knowledge base. Jonas[6,7] describes the structure of these "learning pathologies," arguing that frequent crises in self-concept lead to the reactive adoption of stylish ideologies ("small theories"/"theory fashions") which focus on isolated aspects of the field. They postpone the crisis for a while. Theory fashions (functionalism, product semantics, eco design, and ethical design, for example), fiercely fighting each other, suddenly appear in close proximity.

On the other hand, there are the less spectacular, longer-term activities of theory-building that undergo considerable delays before showing any effect in practice. The last big effort of this kind, trying to enable design to deal with the increasing complexity of problem situations, took place in the 1960s, and ended in the early 1970s. There was little positive immediate effect. Some results were even negative, driving researchers including

Alexander[8] and Jones[9] to retreat from the field. Nonetheless, long-term influences have been produced.

Working on the basis of short-term theories has had the side effect of fundamental work increasingly being neglected. The disciplinary infrastructures to do this autonomously waste away or even disappear completely. Unlike medicine, another academic discipline aiming at practice, the necessity of continuous theory work is not widely acknowledged. This is a vicious circle, driving design into the poor role of an auxiliary profession of economy or marketing, not really responsible for its contributions to culture. Theory, mostly about design, is left to those reflecting disciplines as philosophy or cultural sciences, which normally do not care much about design's fitness for its crucial, everyday function of shaping our way of living. Figure 3.1 illustrates this "shifting-the-burden" pattern[10] in systemic language.

There still seems to be too little internal complexity to deal with increasing external complexity. The "critical mass" of coordinated efforts to produce reliable foundations has not yet been reached. This weakness of discourse and value system weakens design's ability to communicate with established disciplines such as economics or engineering on an equal basis. Other disciplines (including marketing) speak for design instead. Of course, there are a few individuals who are "Starck" enough to communicate according to their own rules, acting rather as a prima donna than as a partner.

3 WHAT IS SPECIAL ABOUT DESIGN?

The question is: How can design achieve autonomy? Design has not (yet?) reached the status of science, art, technology, and economics. Ongoing definitory attempts which revert to previously established areas include those of the Bauhaus, New Bauhaus, and Ulm schools. They might be useful, at best, as negations. Design is *not art* because it does not aim at individual expression, but instead to serve various stakeholders, even though there are all of those intuitive, creative, and individual components. Design is *not technology* because it deals with fuzzy, discursive criteria rather than objective criteria, even though design shares many functional objectives. Design is *not science* because it does not offer new explanatory models of reality, but changes reality more or less purposefully, and yet the experimental process of research resembles the design process. Obviously, design is something very special.

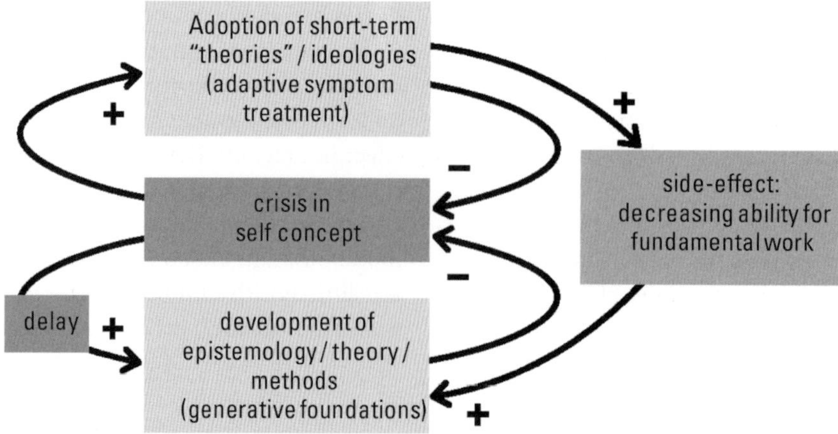

Figure 3.1 Creating generative foundations seems to be a necessary intervention for overcoming learning pathologies in design.

Table 3.1 Two Recent Attempts to Redefine Designing.

Reinterpretation	**Functional Definition**
Bonsiepe[12]	Jonas[13]
Design is a domain which can manifest itself in *every area of human knowledge and practice.*	
Design is oriented towards the *future.*	Design is *anticipative* (looking ahead, in different directions and time scales).
Design is related to *innovation*. The design act introduces something new into the world. Design is *generative* (aiming at the synthesis of material or immaterial artifacts and patterns of behavior).	
Design is tied to *body and space*, especially the retinal space.	
Design aims at *effective action.*	Design is *use-oriented* (taking quality of life as its criterion, without claiming to know what this is).
Design is fixed at *language* in the area of assessments.	Design *is illustrative* (creating wholes, contexts, narratives, aiming at agency and dissemination).
Design aims at the *interaction of user and artifact*, acting in the domain of the interface.	
	Design is *integrative* (neglecting disciplinary boundaries, moderating perspectives, and including its own).
	Design is *context sensitive* (being aware of and using social, cultural, technological interdependencies).

Glanville[11] uses the similarities in design and the research process to perform a complete "U-turn," arguing that design thinking should be the model for scientific research. Though very appealing, it really is not a solution since it shifts the burden of basic explanation to design, the weakest part of all. While design, in fact, is a cross-discipline and integrates various expert fields, it cannot be basic to everything else. Instead, it should be conceived as an expert discipline of a special kind: for integration, relation, and meaning. There have been numerous attempts to redefine design.

Theory-building has to consider that design, in aiming at "solutions," needs a theory for practice to deal with complex entities of different types (material, cognitive, and social) so that some kind of "systemic" concept seems inevitable. Design is future-oriented and, of course, serves people and social institutions. This is not to stress human-centered nature; there is nothing other than people to design for, with the possible exception of self-conscious machines. Yet it does emphasize that design, for the most part, is a matter of fuzzy, changing, cultural criteria as opposed to scientific criteria. There is ongoing negotiation between stakeholders of perspectives, with the goal of understanding each other's viewpoint. Design changes the world and, in turn, is changed by these changes.[14]

To derive the requirements for the framework, we should distinguish human operations by their orientation in time. They are either forward-oriented, aiming at purposeful action (called practice), or backward-oriented, aiming at reflection,

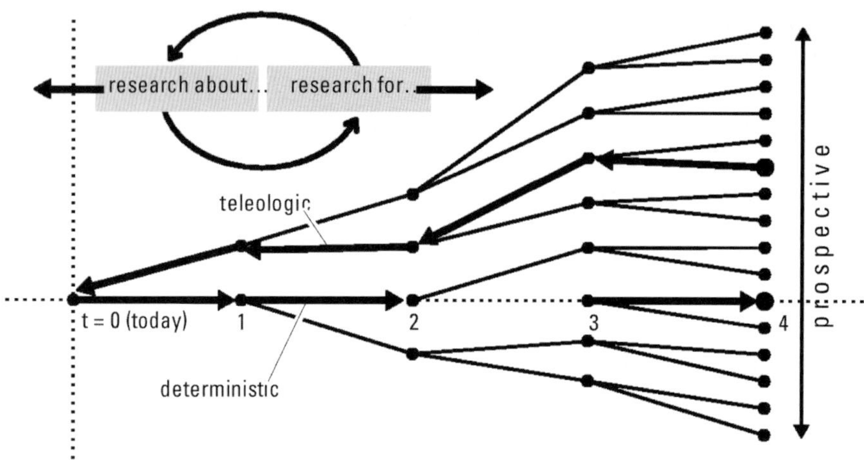

Figure 3.2 Design as a bifurcation process of decision-making.

interpretation, and causal reconstruction (called theory). A hypothetical abstract definition might describe design as a permanent sequence of decisions to reduce contingency at the individual, organizational, and social levels. The function of each decision is to define and, subsequently, to eliminate alternatives and absorb uncertainty in order to create novelty. In order to do this on a rational, meaningful basis, it is necessary to have feedback cycles established between theory and practice, and between the forward and the backward perspectives. This really is not new, but known as forecasting (deterministic), planning/backcasting (teleologic), scenario-building (prospective) or, more generally, learning (Figure 3.2).

Any claim as to the priority of either the humanities or the sciences in this endeavor is counterproductive, since it tends to broaden the cultural gap.[15] We should not hesitate to include everything into a general framework which seems to be useful (from pragmatic philosophy to chaos theory).

This approach implicitly covers the issue of values and ethics in the Aristotelian sense as deriving from good practice, and not vice versa.[16] To focus on ethics would make design a religious project.[17]

4 EPISTEMOLOGICAL CONSIDERATION

Epistemology concerns the basic assumptions of our way to gain knowledge of the world we are living in. Normally, the epistemological basis either is taken for granted in a scientific field or more or less arbitrarily chosen, depending on the researcher's intellectual biography, as in design. Nevertheless, the choice shapes the complete building.

Design theory deals with an inherently context-dependent and temporal subject matter. Recognizing change as an essential feature should not be considered as an uncritical adaptation to contexts, but rather an essential condition of any dynamically stable theory. There are two major problems: self-reference (leading to circularity) and paradox (leading to nothing or everything). Like linguistics, psychoanalysis, and other disciplines, design research is a reflexive project. The most awkward characteristic of the subjects mentioned is that they examine themselves in their own terms. The observer is, at the same time, part of the observed field and observing from outside of it. The same is true for theory. Design theory is part of its subject; and creating a theory changes the subject.

Any comprehensive theory or model of design should be able to explain its own emergence and change.

In the classical scientific paradigm, this situation is extremely critical. The thing talked about is on one level, and the thing in terms of which it is talked about must be on another (meta) level. Gödel proved in 1931 that it is impossible to describe something both completely and consistently in its own terms. But some subjects, such as design, do and must talk about themselves in their own terms – that is, their metalevels are the same as their levels. This leads to the flaw that they have to be considered as incomplete and/or inconsistent in terms of the classical paradigm.

Is there any way out? Glanville[18] argues that self-reference is obvious even in "hard sciences" and, therefore, must be accepted as basic. The problem thus arising (see the "U-turn," above) is to redesign the whole of scientific knowledge to encompass not only the classical view (possibly modified), but also those things which currently are excluded. Are there, then, any levels at all? If self-referential (living) systems are basic, then levels cannot exist. Glanville's explanation is based on the observation of the way in which scientific knowledge actually is produced, and on remembering how it is that levels come into being:

> Science (and how often we do forget this in our oversimplifications) is a corpus of knowledge, and a corpus of knowledge requires agents to know it. It is not constituted of cold facts, but of working hypotheses. The corpus of knowledge does not, a priori, exist; it is constructed. The relationships in it have to be made through the act of relating, and they have to be expressed linguistically, and stabilized through shared interpretation in shared language …

Glanville shows, in detail, that the sort of mechanisms that must be assumed for self-referential systems to be observable to others permit and require the making of such relationships and, thus, of levels. Without this assumption, there would be nothing left to talk about. This reinforces the concept of science as being a social endeavor. But it also provides the theoretical basis for the observer in any experiment – or the designer in any design – as being involved in a circular, feedback process in which the observer's description and the experimental arrangement's behavior interact and modify each other until they are in apparent agreement, allowing predictions to be made (inductively) without the need for any recourse to "truth."

This leads to the *autopoiesis theory* of living systems, and its further extension to mental and social systems. Maturana and Varela[19] argue that living organisms are autonomous, operationally closed, dissipative systems because they strive to maintain an identity by subordinating all changes to the maintenance of their own organization as a given set of relationships. They do so by engaging in circular operations. Thus, continuous patterns of interaction are established that are always self-referential, because a system cannot enter into interactions that are not specified in the pattern of relations that define its organization. The concept of operative closure already has been indicated by Schütz,[20] who clearly describes the irreconcilable gap between subjective meaning and alter ego's understanding:

> Intended meaning is essentially unapproachable, because it is constituted exclusively inside my own flow of consciousness.

For all these reasons, a constructivist approach seems to be appropriate. Luhmann[21] states:

> Constructivism is the consequence of some theoretical positions which focus on operational closure. This means that a system can only work within itself and not outside. A system can never operate in its environment … In cognitive science, this idea comes from brain research, as the brain is an operationally closed system. So, if we have to use our brains to make science, how can we get into the environment?

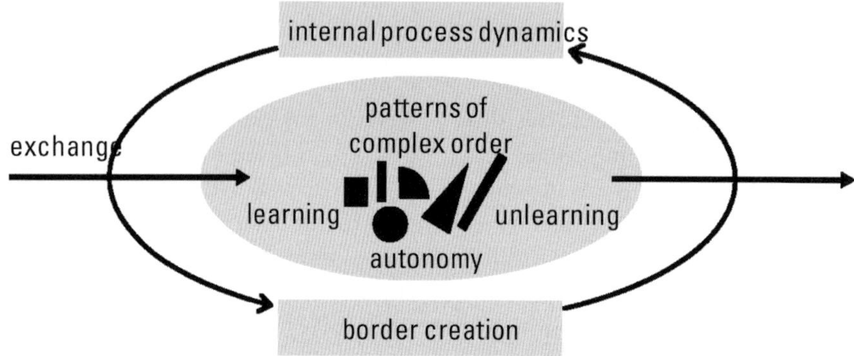

Figure 3.3 Dissipative systems (living, mental, and social) build internal complexity by autopoietic closure. This permits interaction with the environment, exertion of influence, evolution, and learning.

Luhmann's theory (see section 4) uses the concept of "observation," which is defined formally as an operation with a distinction in order to indicate one side and not the other side of the distinction. The initial distinction is, more or less, arbitrary but influences the rest of the construction. The theory does not refer to ontology, but to the basic distinction system/environment. Any observation is based on the dualism of self-reference and external reference. Both types of reference imply each other, so that no materialism (only external reference) and no idealism (only internal reference) are possible. What is stable is not the objective world, but *eigenvalues*, functions and structures which are the product of "second-order observation."[22] A shared world is constructed and continually tested out of second-order observations.

To sum up: there is a "real world" which we cannot perceive as it "really" is. Constructivism provides a consistent and comprehensive way to account for that. Due to its foundation in autopoiesis theory, constructivism is a contribution to the naturalization of epistemology.

5 SYSTEMS THEORY AS CORE AND GENERAL FRAMEWORK

The theory has to be comprehensive, highly abstract, and flexible in structure in order to integrate numerous subject theories on different levels of resolution. And it has to be adaptable to change, while keeping its basic character.

Every observation is a unity of a distinction and an indication.[23] Cognitive operations begin following the imperative: Make a distinction! This section started with a contingent (i.e., neither necessary nor impossible) decision to be stabilized through the coherence of the total approach: the adoption of sociological systems theory for theory-building and methodology, and the choice of the distinction system/environment as a starting point. The guiding idea is that design, if it intends to act generatively, has to become an autonomous system itself (theory). Other fields, if seen as subjects of intervention (methodology), have to be considered as autonomous systems.

5.1 OUTLINE OF SYSTEMS THEORY

The reception of social systems theory in design seems to end with Parsons, whose structural functionalism, concerned with the problem of conserving existing structures, is rightly considered too rigid and static.[24] The further differentiation of systems theory is widely neglected. One of its origins lies in first-order cybernetics,[25] dealing with observing an objective reality and the problem of control. Here, many designers still stop listening and turn away with horror. But there also is second-order cybernetics (developed at the

Biological Computing Lab at the University of Illinois, Urbana, by von Foerster et al., and at the Palo Alto Mental Research Institute by Bateson et al.), dealing with the problem of negotiation and argumentation, and the construction of a reality by observing observations. Whereas, first-order cybernetics deals with observed systems, considered open, and with the observer defining the system's purpose; second-order cybernetics deals with observing closed systems with the observer defining "his or her own purpose."

Luhmann's theory of social systems[26] is the most advanced model of modern society. He extends the autopoiesis concept of living systems to the description of mental and social systems since about 1980. Living systems act in the medium life, mental systems in consciousness, and social systems in communication. Both mental and social systems operate with language and meaning. Communication cannot take place without presupposing consciousness, and vice versa.

The theory asks for the function of systems. The purpose of system formation is, generally speaking, the creation of separated regions which allow the system to record and process the complexity of the world. Systems establish a difference between inside and outside, acting as a sense-making, symbolically mediated interface between delivered and processable complexity. Thus, a system defines, for itself, the boundary which allows it to create its own identity according to internally produced and processed rules, and to maintain it against an external reality.

No analysis of consciousness will ever reveal anything about communication and vice versa, just as no analysis of mental processes will reveal anything about brain processes, which are the domain of living systems. Autopoietic systems act in operative closure; mental and social systems being totally distinct. The construct of person is the structural coupling of mental and social systems, allowing both references to communication and consciousness.

Boundaries increase the level of "stabilizable improbability" (organized complexity), limiting meaning to the internally meaningful. Every kind of environment is perceived only with respect to the own difference schema. The kind of relationships possible with its environment depends on the mode of operation, which is determined by the system's internal structure. External control of autopoietic systems is impossible, except at the price of destroying their autopoietic quality and identity.

Functional subsystems are the products of ongoing differentiation. They increase their operational efficiency by using generalized media and codes (e.g., the economy operates in the medium money, science in the medium truth, politics in power, etc.). Subsystems are closed and create their own domains, allowing only certain operations. Though creating a shared orientation

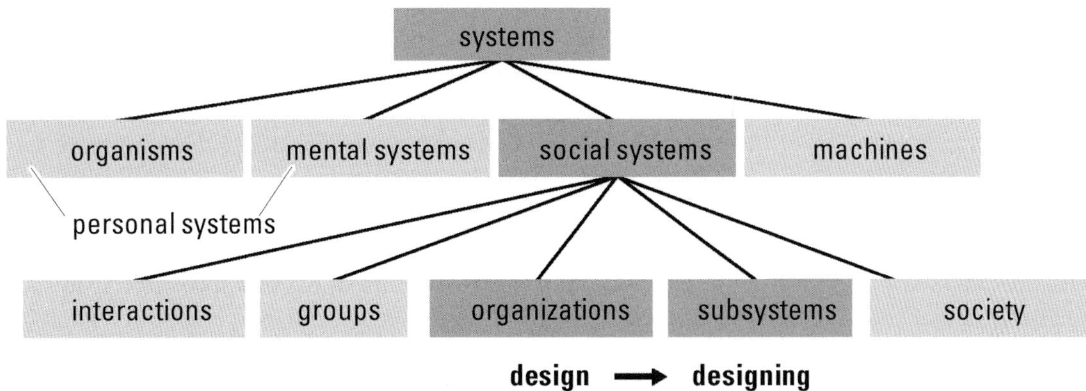

Figure 3.4 System classification.[27] Design can be conceived as a social system interacting with other social systems.

via their codes, they are not based on consensus but, rather, stabilize around conflict. Conflicts are productive, and allow for change and learning. Thus, no vantage point exists to observe society as a whole, and it is impossible to talk about what is rational for society or what will benefit society as a whole.

Jonas[28] elaborates on the concept for design by introducing three contextual and/or historical phases – satisfaction, creation, and reflection of need – three process steps (expanding the "problem-solving" process – see section 6), five process levels (from creative to cultural processes), and four reality levels (vision, structure, patterns, and events/objects). The hypothetical social subsystem designing (on the level of science, economy, etc., – see Figure 3.4) is introduced as a flexible, project-oriented and, thus, temporary framework that integrates engineers, designers, economists, social scientists, and futurologists, depending on the specific task at hand.

5.2 RELATED PARADIGM SHIFTS

From Adaptation to Generation One of the crucial questions in a theory of open systems, from evolution to organization or education, has been: How does a system adapt optimally to its environment? In a theory of closed systems, we ask: How does a closed system constitute and reconstruct itself in an overly complex, chaotic environment? Adaptation is not central, but rather the conditions of the possibility of establishing a complex order.

Meaning as a Formal Process Concept Meaning (*Sinn*) does not refer to a certain aspect of reality, but describes the formal order of human experience and action as a continuous process of selection, following internal criteria and based on the difference of the actual vs. the possible. The present core of actuality is unstable because it permanently needs new indications of possibilities. Meaning is a surplus of relationships to further possibilities of experience and action, so that what is in the center of attention is surrounded by a horizon of assumptions and references. The "automobility" of processing meaning, which sustains itself through self-referentially enabling its own reproduction, is autopoiesis par excellence.

From Aggregation to Emergent Qualities Social entities constitute realms of their own, emergent orders, irreducible to the characteristics of biological and mental systems. It is the *form of processing meaning* which makes the difference: mental systems are processing meaning in the form of thoughts and imagination, whereas social systems process meaning in the form of symbolically mediated communication. Communication is necessary for their formation and continued existence. The connectivity of communication is meaning in social systems.

From People to Communication One of the irritating consequences is that social systems consist of the processing of communication, not of human beings. There is no place and no need for the individual in the theory (there are simply too many of them). Man is a very diffuse idea, depending on who is observing and how. No supersystem encompasses living, mental, and social systems. In this perspective, the "members" belong to the environment because they are never, in total, only part of a system in some respects, with certain roles, motives, and attentions. Only a radical depersonalization of social systems enables us to understand their peculiarity and autonomy in a way that prevents them from being regarded as a mere collection of biological and psychic moments. "Intersubjectivity" does not solve this problem, because the neurobiologically founded assumption of the autopoietic quality of mental processes leads to the conclusion that every person possesses his or her own intersubjectivity.

From Purpose to the Function of Purpose The concept of intentional action has to be qualified in the systems context. Speaking of the "true" purpose of product development apparently is meaningless in the economic context. The point here, whether design likes it or not, is the magnitude of the flow of goods and capital. Thus, the key question is the function of purposes on whatever level. Purposes reduce the complexity inside the acting system and increase performance. They provide the neutralization of values needed to minimize irrelevant side effects; they serve for the operationalization (i.e., the formulation of clear instructions); and they justify the means. Purpose also is a means of drawing borders, establishing identity and, thus, system formation. Purposes do not denote the "nature" of an action (there is nothing of that kind); rather, they have important auxiliary functions.

From Action Theory to Systems Theory It therefore is necessary to transfer the concept of action from action theory to systems theory. The relationship of action and system can be broken down into various components mainly through the boundaries of action systems which, on different levels of generalization, produce different rationalities, features, and problems. *The level of individual action is sociologically irrelevant.* Even Schütz questions the seemingly clear and distinct category of action:[29]

> So it is left to the observer, be it a partner in social life or a sociologist, to fix high-handedly the start and end-point of alter ego's acting the meaning of which is to be explored. The objective course does not offer any criteria for the distinction of a "unified action."

From Means and Ends to Continuance/Viability Systems theory starts from the permanent problem of system continuance. The basis of this is not single purposes or simple chains of purposes and means, but "purpose programs." They transform permanent, insoluble problems into sequences of soluble problems. At the end of this multistage reduction are concrete design problems leading to design solutions. Purpose programs formulate and formalize the conditions on which a subsystem may handle the means of the supersystem's like own purposes and, therefore, become indifferent to effects that nonetheless may be relevant in the whole system. For example: "gute form" or "quality of life," as self-defined purposes of the subsystem (design team or school), are contingent on the supersystem (firm or economy) with its purpose program of securing continuance. Changing contextual conditions (satisfaction, creation, and reflection of need) produce crises and hectic reformulations of design purposes. These conflicts are more fruitless the less autonomous the subsystem is.

Design thus should make an effort to transform its simple, sometimes naive, contingent purposes, mainly of a reactive character, into generative purpose programs, including specific modes of interaction, codes, and values relative to the general context. More disciplinary autonomy might initiate a design evolution from a fuzzy subsystem towards a clear and distinct cosystem of economy.

6 SCENARIO-BASED METHODOLOGY

Methodology integrates and puts into operation the product development process. It has to be abstract and flexible enough to cover projects in firms, educational projects of any size, public development projects, and policy-making projects. And it has to leave room for individual approaches.

By emphasizing systemic description, providing intervention strategies, and methodological openness and interactivity, it takes account of the stakeholders' involvement in the process, and performs the intermediate step from first- to second-generation methods.

Though (or because) the methodology is directed at people, the concept of the individual as the center of design production and reception has to be abandoned. To illustrate, when designing an object (e.g., an ATM), we do *not* have to take into account the "whole person" (whatever that might be). But we do have to take care of the communicative/interactive needs of persons related to this specific situation, as far as these are recognizable. What is the whole person? Those who can observe it from the outside, cannot observe it from the inside, and those who can observe it from the inside, cannot observe it from the outside.

Everything else is, in my view, a misconceived and idealistic/romantic concept of "wholeness" which does not work. This means: don't care for individual people (they are inaccessible anyway). Instead, care for their communicative patterns of behavior. This should not be considered as anti-humanistic, but as methodological.

6.1 A PROCESS FRAMEWORK FOR REFLECTIVE INVOLVEMENT

Figure 3.5 shows the outline of a broadened concept of the design process covering such requirements as universality, future-orientation, reducing contingency, and providing feedback.

SYNTHESIS is the phase in the design process which, traditionally, is the focus of interest. An apparently clear and distinct "problem" is given/"thrown over the wall," and has to be solved. This step should not be neglected or disregarded (a common misunderstanding, sometimes fear, of traditional product designers concerned with this approach), but it is not the main interest here. In times of accelerated technological and social change, and globalized economies with saturated markets, the two preceding steps become increasingly important. It is not at all trivial to find an answer to the question: What is the problem? (ANALYSIS). And it is just as challenging to ask: How might the future environments look in which our solutions have to prove their worth? (PROJECTION). It becomes a design problem to define the design problem (see the concept of "problem design"[30]).

6.2 SCENARIO-BUILDING AS A CENTRAL CONCEPT

Scenarios are images of possible, probable, or preferable futures or futures to be avoided, and sometimes comprise the steps to achieve them. Early scenarios (except Utopias such as Bacon's *New Atlantis* or More's *Utopia* are, for example, those of Kahn.[31] Coming from the military field and public policy-making, they entered business planning (e.g., the Shell scenarios by Wack[32]).

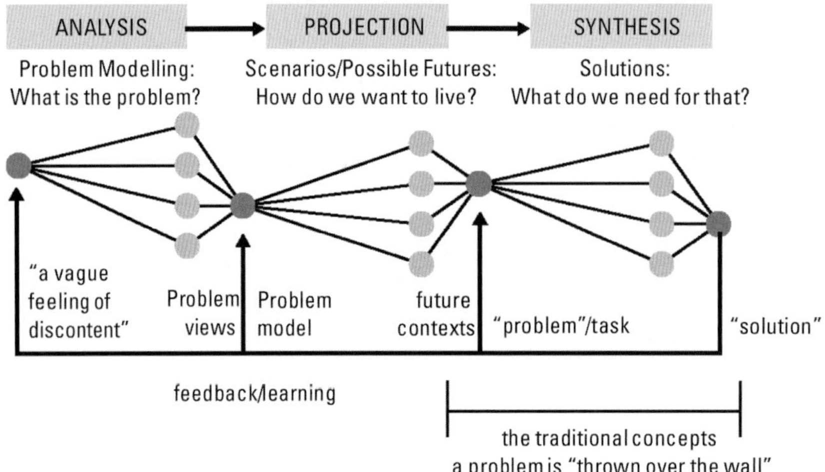

Figure 3.5 Broadened concept of design (designing).

The concept comprises a broad range from global models to user scenarios as already widely used (e.g., in HCI design). Scenario-building is a central concept in design, shifting the focus from the object to the process of communication and interaction, and covering all phases of the design process:

ANALYSIS: analytical scenarios (e.g., sensitivity modeling)
PROJECTION: context scenarios (possible futures, dealing with uncertainty)
SYNTHESIS: user scenarios (e.g., human-computer interaction).

Hasdogan[33] worked on user-oriented scenarios in design. The approach presented here combines analytical scenarios (for sensitivity modeling, see Simon[34] and Vester[35]), contextual scenarios (see Schwartz[36] and van der Heijden[37]), and user scenarios; and explores their usefulness in design projects.

Scenario-building is the process of reflected involvement. It invites open communication and participation in creating new information and knowledge. It can be performed only by participating persons/stakeholders/authors that influence and themselves are influenced in the process.

The following introduces the example of a context scenario which, in the concrete project, was related to analytic and to user scenarios.

Possible futures are determined by those external forces (variables) which have a "high impact" on the system and, at the same time, display "high uncertainty" in their future behavior. They can be determined intuitively or discursively (e.g., by consulting experts in the field or stakeholders involved in the process – see Schwartz[38]). It also may be possible to use the findings from cross-impact analysis and sensitivity modeling, especially the highly active (independent) and highly critical variables, for that purpose.[39,40]

"Quattro stagioni" is an approach, following Schwartz,[41] for the creation of four extreme contexts using those two variables with highest impact and highest uncertainty. Because of the uncertainty, it is possible to identify two extreme states of each variable (flip-flop). The combination of two extreme states of two variables each results in a frame of four scenarios. For example, the variables "communication patterns" (individualization – new communities) and "structural change" (stagnation – innovation) provide the scenario frame of Figure 3.7.

Fleshing out the four quadrants with characters and events yields four stage sets, contexts, or

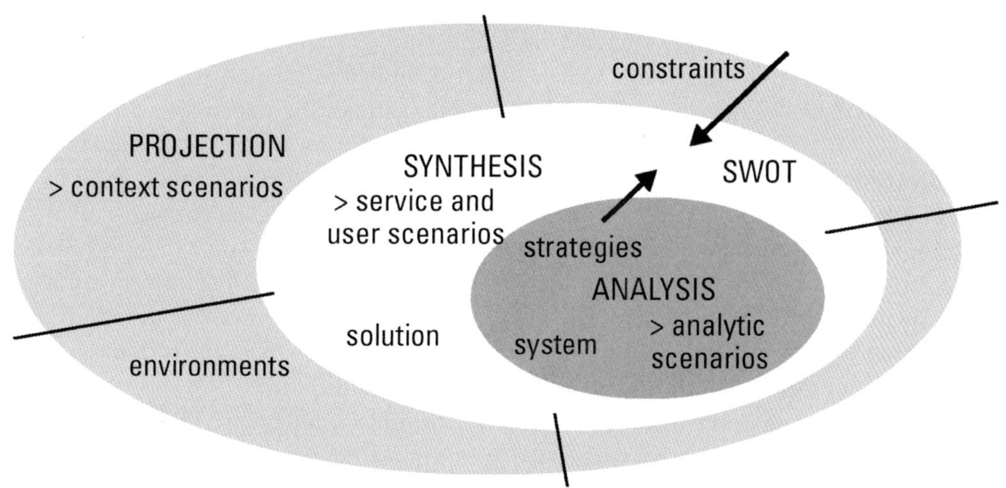

Figure 3.6 Design solution space between system and context. Design acting as an interface discipline.

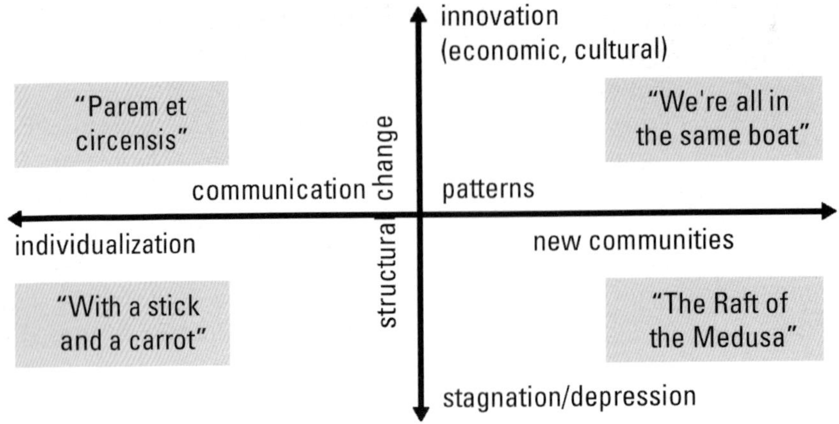

Figure 3.7 "Quattro stagioni": Frame of four scenarios derived from two variables, with two extreme states each.

testbeds for subsequent design activities. Figure 3.8 shows the above-defined frame illustrated with strong metaphoric images. The choice of concise titles and strong images is of utmost importance to the communicative function of the scenarios for their recognizability and for their function as focal point for design considerations, as well as for organizational learning. The four, related narratives are not given here.

Solutions emerge in the field of tension between the system (analytical scenario) and its environment (context scenario), as shown in Figure 3.6. On this level, service and user scenarios play an important role in developing solution concepts. Solutions have to take into account the strengths and weaknesses of the system, and the opportunities and threats of the contexts (SWOT analysis).

The matrix of decision options (Figure 3.9) is a tool to systematically test solution variants before the background of the different scenarios. How does the scenario act on the solution? What happens if the solution has to survive in this context? Viewing the options in one row will result in the robust options (i.e., those that are useful in all possible contexts). Considering the options in one column will lead to the range of competencies which will support optimum viability in one, specific scenario.

7 RESEARCH FIELDS AND DISCIPLINARY PERSPECTIVES

Design research has to be strengthened in order to stabilize the delicate dynamic balance between autonomy and context-dependency (Figure 3.3). Otherwise, we perpetuate the well-known practice of frequent "paradigm-shifts," starting from scratch every ten years or so, and claiming to finally have found out how it "really" is. If it is true that the process of intervention into complex autopoietic systems will be the design product of the future (see Krippendorff[42] and Willke[43]), then research has to focus on the *process of design.* Apparently, a circle of double-loop learning has to be established for that purpose.

This can best be accomplished by research *for* design, i.e., by researchers involved in the process, and in the disciplinary learning cycle in education and practice. Research *about* design, which is mainly backward-oriented (Figure 3.2), delivers essential contributions but can, in principle, at least, be done by anybody as distant as possible from the discipline (e.g., an art historian studying medieval architecture).

The project, as a more or less arbitrarily cut out piece of the continuous flow of time, delivers the experimental setting or framework for research. The form of a workshop might be a further

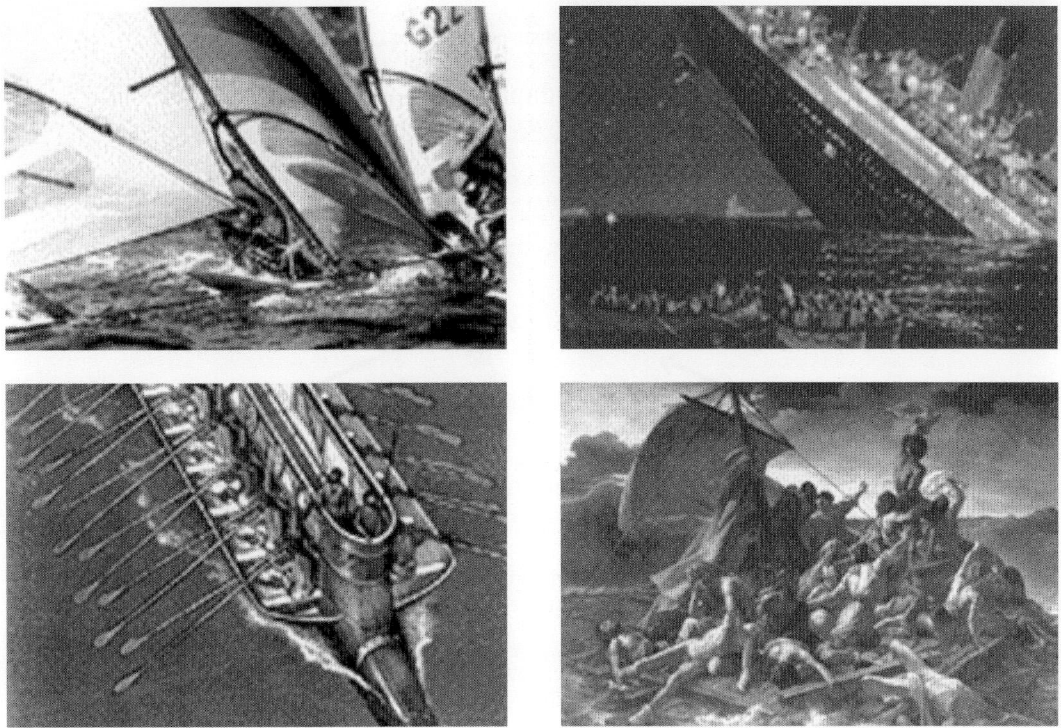

Figure 3.8 "Quattro stagioni": Scenario frame filled with strong metaphoric images.

refinement. A research program has to crystallize around the concept of project and projection activity as the main features of designing. Design research is project-oriented research, making the design process a subject of design. Research, as an inherent component of education, creates a strong link between theory and practice. The project, as subject matter, is the link.

It turns out that there is a strong interrelation between the process of design practice and the process of design research; sometimes the two are hard to distinguish. And there is a further

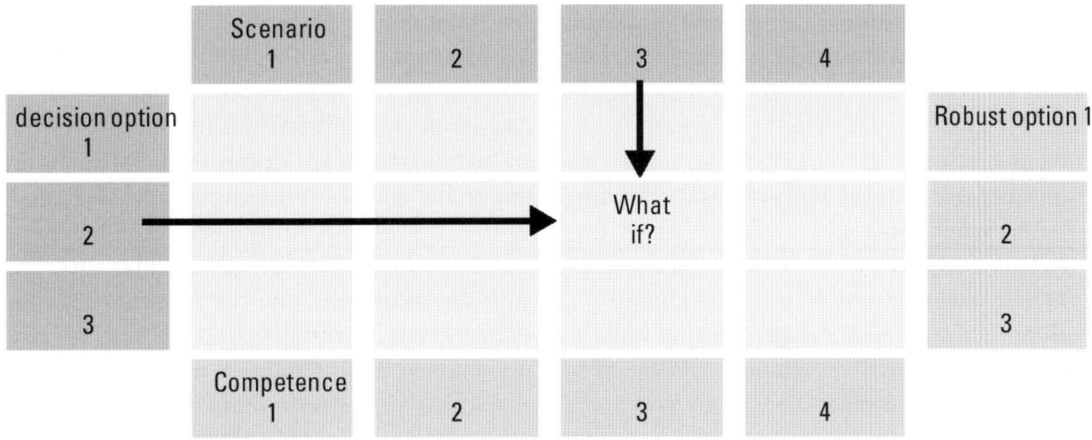

Figure 3.9 Matrix of decision options.

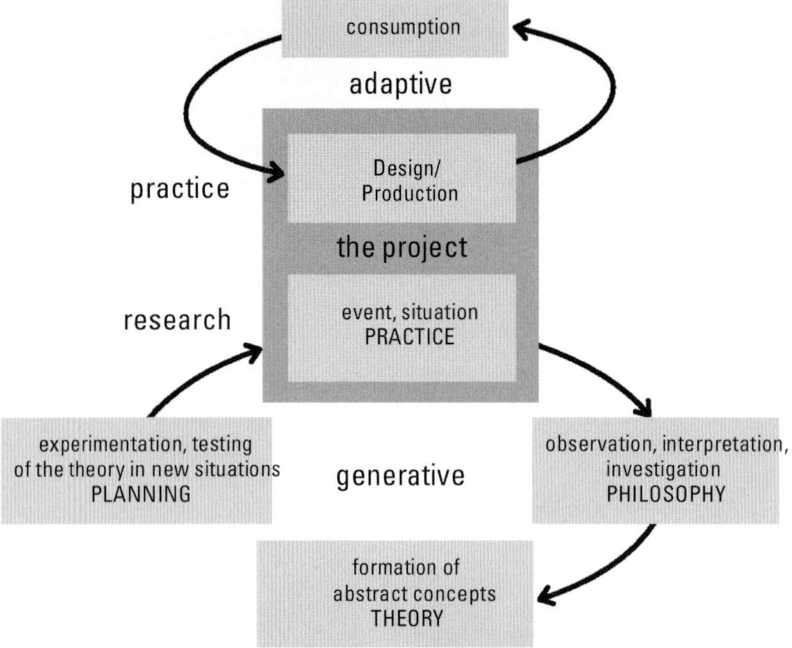

Figure 3.10 Double-loop learning in design.[44]

problem: neither practitioners nor most theoreticians like this connection. Practitioners want instant-to-apply recipes (if at all), while theoreticians prefer to stay in their protected niches because practice could spoil the purity of their preferred approaches. But this combined effort is necessary in order to become a discipline. And it is the only way providing the advance of education before practice.

Hasdogan[45] points out that *scenario-building* is the core activity in the design process. It can provide a thematic core for design research, because it:

- Deals with involvement (understanding understanding),
- Is a communicative process (organizational development),
- Is projective (linking design to futures studies),
- Is transdisciplinary (developing a language of autonomy – exchange), and,
- Generative (creating wholes which produce "solutions").

Design might become a respected autonomous partner in a hypercyclic network of future-shaping disciplines. Designing (Figure 3.4) might emerge as a functional subsystem of society, with its own language/code to allow increased internal complexity, and with its own disciplinary ethics, concerned with the quality of the decision-making process instead of individual ethics.

The general perspective can be described as the establishment of design thinking as the guiding paradigm, not only in product development, but also as a central concept in the process of decision-making in social life (organization, firm, and community). So "design as one of the most important and least recognized arts of human culture"[46] evolves towards a respected discipline which is not concerned with the necessary, but with the contingent, and the artificial.[47] Maybe, there now is a critical mass of researchers and practitioners to push things forward.

Perhaps in the very distant future, we could achieve Glanville's point, where design thinking is the paradigmatic model for scientific research, as opposed to the present practice, where design tries hard but vainly to be scientific according to well-established standards.

NOTES

First published in *Design Issues* 17 no. 2 (Spring 2001): 4–16.

1. John Christopher Jones, "Designing Designing" in *Essays in Design* (Chichester: John Wiley & Sons, 1984, originally, 1978).
2. Richard Buchanan, "Myth and Maturity: Toward a New Order in the Decade of Design" in *Design Issues* 6 no. 2 (Spring 1990): 70–80.
3. Richard Buchanan, "Education and Professional Practice in Design" in *Design Issues* 14 no. 2 (Summer 1998).
4. Klaus Krippendorff, "Redesigning Design. An Invitation to a Responsible Future" in Vihma Tahkokallio, ed., *Design – Pleasure or Responsibility?* (Helsinki: UIAH, 1994), 138–162.
5. Charles Owen, "Design Research: Building the Knowledge Base" in *Design Studies* 19:1 (January 1998): 9–20.
6. Wolfgang Jonas, *Design – System – Theorie. Überlegungen zu einem sy-stem-theoreti-schen Modell von Design-theorie* (Essen: Verlag Die Blaue Eule, 1994), 50–68.
7. Wolfgang Jonas, "Viable Structures and Generative Tools – An Approach Towards 'Designing Designing'", "Contextual Design – Design in Contexts" (European Academy of Design, Stockholm, April 23–25, 1997).
8. Christopher Alexander (interviewed by Max Jacobson), "The State of the Art in Design Methods" in *DMG Newsletter* 5:3 (1971): 3–7.
9. John Christopher Jones, "How My Thoughts About Design Methods Have Changed During the Years" in *Essays in Design* (Chichester: John Wiley & Sons, 1984, originally 1974).
10. Peter Senge, *The Fifth Discipline. The Art & Practice of the Learning Organization* (New York: Currency Doubleday, 1990).
11. Ranulph Glanville, "Why Design Research?" in R. Jacques and A. Powell, *Design: Science: Method* (Guildford: Westbury House, 1980).
12. Gui Bonsiepe, *Interface. Design neu begreifen* (Mannheim: Bollmann, 1996).
13. Wolfgang Jonas, "Research for the Learning Design School," *The New Academy* (Barcelona, October 1997).
14. Alain Findeli, "Theoretical, Methodological, and Ethical Foundations for a Renewal of Design Education and Research," *The New Academy* (Barcelona, October 1997).
15. Victor Margolin, "Design Research and Design Studies: Why We Need Both," a lecture given at the conference *"No Guru, No Method?"* (UIAH Helsinki, September 6, 1996).
16. Wolfgang Jonas, "Design und Ethik – brauchen wir eine Sondermoral für das Design?" 15. designwissenschaftliches Kolloquium *Design und Ethik* (Hochschule für Kunst und Design Halle, 1995).
17. Ezio Manzini, "Prometheus of the Everyday. The Ecology of the Artificial and the Designer's Responsibility" in Buchanan and Margolin, eds., *Discovering Design* (Chicago: The University of Chicago Press, 1995), 219–243.
18. Glanville, "Why Design Research?"
19. Humberto R. Maturana and Francisco Varela, *Der Baum der Erkenntnis. Die biologischen Wurzeln des menschlichen Erkennens* (Bern und München: Scherz, 1987).
20. Alfred Schütz, *Der sinnhafte Aufbau der sozialen Welt. Eine Einleitung in die verstehende Sozio-logie.* (Frankfurt: Suhrkamp, 1974, originally 1932), 140.
21. Ole Thyssen, "Some Basic Notions in the Systems Theory of Niklas Luhmann" and "Interview With Professor Niklas Luhmann, Oslo, April 2, 1995" in *Cybernetics & Human Knowing* 3:2 (1995): 3–22 and 23–26.
22. Heinz Von Foerster, *Sicht und Einsicht: Versuche zu einer operativen Erkenntnistheorie* (Vieweg: Braunschweig, 1985) – originally *Observing Systems* (Seaside, CA, 1981).
23. George Spencer Brown, *Laws of Form* (London: George Allen & Unwin, 1968).
24. Victor Margolin, "Design Research and Design Studies: Why We Need Both."
25. Norbert Wiener, *Cybernetics or Control and Communication in the Animal and the Machine*, 1948.
26. Niklas Luhmann, *Social Systems* (Stanford: Stanford University Press, 1995) – originally *So-ziale Systeme. Grundriß einer allgemeinen Theorie* (Frankfurt: Suhrkamp, 1984).
27. Niklas Luhmann, *Social Systems.*
28. Jonas, "Viable Structures and Generative Tools – An Approach Towards 'Designing Designing.' "
29. Schütz, *Der sinnhafte Aufbau der sozialen Welt. Eine Einleitung in die verstehende Sozio-logie*, 82.
30. Wolfgang Jonas, "Design as Problem-solving? Or: Here Is the Solution – What Was the Problem?" in *Design Studies* 14:2 (April 1993).

31. Herman Kahn, *The Year 2000: A Framework for Speculation on the Next Thirty-Three Years* (New York: MacMillian, 1967).
32. Pierre Wack, "Scenarios: Uncharted Waters Ahead" and "Scenarios: Shooting the Rapids" in *Harvard Business Review* (Sept./Oct. 1985): 73–89, and (Nov./Dec. 1985): 139–150.
33. Gülay Hasdogan, "The Role of User Models in Product Design for Assessment of User Needs," *Design Studies* 17:1 (January 1996): 19–33.
34. Herbert A. Simon, *The Sciences of the Artificial* (Cambridge, MA: MIT Press, 1996).
35. Frederic Vester, *Sensitivitätsmodell Prof. Vester. Ein computerunterstütztes Planungsin-strumen-tarium zur Erfassung und Bewertung komplexer Systeme* (München: Studiengruppe für Biologie und Umwelt GmbH, 1993).
36. Peter Schwartz, *The Art of the Long View* (New York: Currency Doubleday, 1991).
37. Kees Van der Heijden, *Scenarios: The Art of Strategic Conversation* (Chichester: John Wiley & Sons, 1996).
38. Schwartz, *The Art of the Long View*.
39. Van der Heijden, *Scenarios: The Art of Strategic Conversation*.
40. Michel Godet, *From Anticipation to Action. A Handbook of Strategic Perspective* (Paris: UNESCO Publishing, 1994, originally, 1991).
41. Schwartz, *The Art of the Long View*.
42. Krippendorff, "Redesigning Design. An Invitation to a Responsible Future."
43. Helmut Willke, *Systemtheorie II: Interventionstheorie. Grundzüge einer Theorie der Intervention in komplexe Systeme* (Stuttgart and Jena: Gustav Fischer Verlag, 1994).
44. Jonas, "Research for the Learning Design School."
45. Hasdogan, "The Role of User Models in Product Design for User Needs."
46. Buchanan, "Education and Professional Practice in Design."
47. Vester, *Sensitivitätsmodell Prof. Vester. Ein computer-unterstütztes Planungsinstrumentarium zur Erfassung und Bewertung komplexer Systeme*.

4

INFORMATION AND REALITY AT THE TURN OF THE CENTURY

Albert Borgmann

Our ability to command information grows every day. We wake up to the news on the radio, read the paper during breakfast, are immersed in signs and advertisements as we make our way to the office, sit down and fire up our computers – that really opens the floodgate of information – return home, turn on the television set and let waves of information wash over us until we go to bed.

Many people say they get much pleasure from cruising and surfing on this sea of information. But, at times, we feel like the sorcerer's apprentice, unable to contain the powers we have summoned, and afraid of drowning in the flood we have loosened. Where does all this information come from and what is it doing to reality?

In earlier times, information arose from the interplay of three factors, a messenger, a recipient, and a message. Paul Revere was the messenger, the Patriots were the recipients, and "The English are coming," was the message. The dove with the olive branch was the messenger, Noah the recipient, and the message was "The waters are receding." Even today, smoke is the messenger, the pilot of the spotter plane the recipient, and "There is a fire in section 36" is the message. A rock-lined cavity can be the messenger, a historian the recipient, and the message: "This is the root cellar of an abandoned homestead."

The general pattern is always *x informs y about z*. X is the messenger, but we also call x the sign, the signal, the symbol, or the vehicle. Y is the recipient or the receiver, the audience, the listener, the reader, the viewer, the spectator, or the investigator. And z is the message, the information, the news, the intelligence, the meaning, or the content conveyed by the messenger or the signal. This basic triad of factors had an engaging sturdiness and intelligibility. It incorporated distinctions that may have been grist for abstruse philosophical mills; but they were clear and serviceable enough for lay people.

We can call this the core meaning of information.[1] It is *information about reality*. In its simplest form, it is a natural phenomenon relevant to animals as well as to humans. A scent carried by the wind is information to a bear that carrion is to be found down by the creek. Information is a difficult phenomenon, not because its origin is mysterious, but because, throughout human history it has been evolving in tiny steps from something simple and natural to something exceedingly complex and technical.

The fire ring you left at a campsite a few years ago informs you, in a natural and incidental way, that this is a good spot to put up your tent. But if it took you a while to find it again and you want to avoid going in circles next time, you might pile up a few rocks where you have to leave the trail and head down to the creek. While the rocks around the fire ring compose an incidental and nearly natural sign, the rocks in the pile constitute an intentional and conventional sign.

The first conventional signs in human history were reminders, tallies on bones or sticks, and collections of pebbles or shells, to keep track of the phases of the moon or animal kills, or sheep, or goats. Pebbles were followed by clay tokens; these by incisions and impressions on clay tablets; and those, again, in succession by logographs, syllabaries and letters. These signs served, and some of them still serve, to set down information about the past. But they also can bring nearer what is distant in space, edicts from the king, reports of disasters, and news of life everlasting. Of course, information about things past and distant events does not literally convey those things and events to the here and now. A record of a bushel of grain delivered to the granary is not the same as the bushel of grain, itself. Nor is a royal edict the same as the majestic presence of the king. It takes comprehension to gather the message from the sign and to grasp the impact of the message on the here and now.

The ability to comprehend a message and integrate it into one's immediate world is, except for one's native language, an arduously acquired and ever incomplete skill. But once acquired, more or less, comprehension makes for an incomparably more comprehensive and comprehensible world. Reality no longer trails off rapidly in the mists of distance and past, but becomes perspicuous as far as information and comprehension can reach.

Information, however, not only can illuminate what is distant in time and space, but also what is remote in conception and imagination; and what would remain a distant possibility without the aid of conventional signs. Complex social arrangements, monumental buildings, and artful pieces of music would be inconceivable without the information laid down, e.g., in the texts of covenants, drawings of cathedrals, and scores of cantatas. This no longer is *information about reality* but *information for reality*; information for making a community, a building, or music. But here again, the steps from *information about* to *information for* reality and back are small. In the sketchbook of the medieval master mason, Villard de Honnecourt, plans that inform us about the existing cathedral of Laon are mingled with plans for churches that were never executed.[2] Gregorio Allegri wrote a score for the mass *Miserere,* to be performed in the Sistine Chapel only and, therefore, kept secret. But when the fourteen-year-old Mozart, on having heard the mass once, wrote down the score from memory, it was information about rather than for the performance of the music.

While *information about* reality chiefly requires comprehension and renders the world more perspicuous, *information for* reality calls for realization and makes for a more prosperous world. By realization, I mean the process of translating information into reality. To realize a covenant is to make it come alive in practices and celebrations. To realize a blueprint is to construct a building conforming to it. And to realize a musical score is to perform it.

Realization, too, requires the acquisition of demanding skills; the particular literacies of rabbis, artisans and musicians, among many others. But again, when these skills are mastered, the world becomes incomparably richer; adorned with festive customs, material structures and musical events that are intricate and magnificent beyond what human imagination, without information and notation, could have conceived and carried out.

Information about and for reality used to mediate between humanity and reality to produce a distinctive kind of world. The central feature of this world was a focal area of nearness that was understood against a comprehensible background of farness. Information about reality, even today, tells us of faraway things and events; but it does not transport them into our midst. They remain distant, yet they inform and illuminate what is present. If, on a hot and windy August afternoon in the Rockies, you see smoke billowing up like thunderheads behind the farthest ridge on the horizon; the smoke conveys information about a raging wildfire; but it does not carry the fire, itself, into your immediate world. The focal area of your life is still safe. The fire is distant though the fire danger is close.

Similarly, when you stumble upon a collapsed root cellar from early in this century, you learn of a way of life where perishables used to be entrusted to the coolness of the ground. Yet root cellars remain a thing of the past. They are part of the background that defines your way of life where food is stored in freezers and refrigerators. And so it is with letters from distant friends and colleagues; with journals and memoirs of homesteaders; and with tipi rings and cairns left by the Salish and Kootenai Indians. Information about reality keeps, or used to keep, the farness of space and time distinct from the nearness of those persons and things that make up the focal area of our lives. Yet information makes farness comprehensible, and provides an illuminating background for what is here and now.

While *information about reality* renders our world perspicuous in its order of nearness and farness, *information for reality* is the source of a distinctively prosperous culture. Such prosperity requires submission to a definite kind of discipline. Discipline is needed, first, to acquire the skills of reading texts, following plans, and playing musical scores; and then to submit continually to the text of a covenant, the specifications of a blueprint, and the notes of sheet music. The reward of such discipline is a franchise in a magnificent culture. If you are given the culture without being instructed in the requisite discipline, the culture is not truly yours. You are dependent on others for the realization of the founding information of the culture. But if you are skilled, you can fully and freely appropriate your inheritance.

In addition to discipline and competence, a world built on information for reality engenders a vigorous sense of continuity, community and intimacy. Jewish people trace their community back for some four thousand years. Their tradition would not be so astoundingly continuous and vigorous had it not been for a writer, now commonly called J, who set down the story of Abraham and Sarah a few hundred years later.[3] But to realize the promise God made to Abraham, one needs not only an unbroken tie to the founding event, but also a community of people with whom to enact the tradition.

Similarly, the music which Bach left us requires not only discipline and competence, but also fellow singers and players. And more is needed yet. Since information for reality is never more than an instruction or a recipe, we must gather from the tangible reality around us the materials and ingredients necessary for the realization of a text, a plan, or a score. To realize musical scores, we need instruments. To realize a blueprint, we need building materials. The realization of texts, particularly of poetry and fiction, is the most subtle. But it, too, calls for us to draw on our experiences with the tangible world. In any case, to realize information for reality, we have to be intimate with the visible, audible, palpable shapes of our immediate world; with the strings, mouthpieces and keys of instruments; with the stones and timbers of construction; and with the faces and gestures we recall when we read a poem.

Traditionally, information has been about and for reality. But through the technological developments of the past century and a half, information, though still about and for reality, also has begun to rival reality, itself; and has emerged virtually *as reality.* The culture of technology, in general, is animated by a pervasive and evident desire for more copious and refined consumption. Yet the implementation of this project looks more like bricolage than the execution of a grand design. Rather than follow the twists and turns of the transformation of information, I will trace the conceptual path that leads from information about and for reality to information as reality.

I begin with the landmark that has defined a crucial stretch of this path, viz., Claude Shannon's paper of 1948, "The Mathematical Theory of Communication," and Warren Weaver's comments of 1949.[4] Shannon's paper is strictly a technical accomplishment, but it was thought right away to be a cultural milestone. The excitement it generated is obvious in Weaver's remarks. Shannon's work served as a catalyst of powerful cultural elements that were ready to react.

Weaver's reaction, in particular, is emblematic in what it had to say about the rising cultural force of information.

The rise of this force has inundated and begun to wash out the structure of the world that was built on the traditional information about and for reality. The threat to its central feature, the focal area of nearness surrounded by a comprehensible background of farness, was signaled by Weaver when he erased the distance between nearness and farness. Nearness used to be marked by the immediate presence of things and persons, as opposed to the farness of distant things and persons that were represented through the information we had about them. But, for Weaver, our access to persons, at any rate, is always through information; whether a person is near or far.

"In oral speech," Weaver said, "the information source is the brain, and the transmitter is the voice mechanism producing the varying sound pressure (the signal) which is transmitted through the air (the channel)."[5] Was Weaver simply making a technical point which, as one critic has charged, was not technically warranted?[6] Roughly half a century later, Deborah Tannen tells us about her colleague, Ralph:

> E-mail deepened my friendship with Ralph. Though his office was next to mine, we rarely had extended conversations because he is shy. Face to face, he mumbled, so I could barely tell he was speaking. But when we both got on e-mail, I started receiving long, self-revealing messages; we poured our hearts out to each other.[7]

Tannen calls e-mail "a souped-up conversation." Apparently, it brings people closer to each other than a traditional f2f (face to face) conversation can. The contrast between nearness and farness has evaporated. It is an irrelevant circumstance that Ralph's and Deborah's offices are on the same floor. They might as well be on different continents.

Underlying this particular illustration is the general view that humans are in touch with the world through information, and through information only. The mountain peak across the valley is visual information; the wind in the trees is acoustic information; and a caress from your loved one is tactile information. In this sense, everything out there, all of reality, has always been information.[8]

Though this view is a powerful undercurrent in our culture, there also is a more particular connection between information and reality, where reality is simply not revealed or claimed to be information, but information arises as a rival and pretender to the throne of traditional reality. The rise of this particular pretension is closely bound up with a threat to the discipline and competence the world of traditional information used to require.

On this issue, Weaver is divided. Like Shannon, he holds to a distinction between the signal and the message; between the vehicle and the content of information.[9] That seems to make eminently good sense, since the two traditionally have been so disparate from one another. A thin plume of smoke curling up from the Rocky Mountains on a breezy August afternoon is, all by itself, a slight and innocent signal. But the message it conveys is awful: within a few hours there might be a roaring wildfire.

It is similar with the messages that are conveyed by conventional signs or signals. There is a huge disparity between the mere 20 column inches of print that a report of a forest fire occupies in a newspaper, and the many acres of incinerated grass and charred trees the report informs us about. As e-mail illustrates, the austere signals of the alphabet can carry weighty messages even today. As long as signal and message, or vehicle and content of information, remain distinct, the need to learn how to gather the message from the signal or the content from the vehicle, and achieve competence in appropriating one's cultural heritage, will persist. But the traditional discipline is in jeopardy.

Signal and message contrast much like quantity and quality. Message and quality are subjective and elusive, while signal and quantity are objective and measurable.[10] Some people believe that the life of the spirit is essentially, and will forever be, beyond quantification and objectification. But a more aggressive and confident view of the matter holds that quality is simply unanalyzed quantity; and that all qualities, when analyzed all the way down to their basic constituents, will turn out to be objective and measurable quantities.

The crucial contribution Shannon made to technological culture was his definitive underscoring of information as a quantity measurable in bits, by showing that the basic unit of information could be used to demonstrate interesting theorems about the coding and transmission of information. Weaver sensed that differences in the quality of information are superficial and ultimately irrelevant; and that it really doesn't matter "what kinds of symbols are being considered – whether written letters or words, or musical notes, or spoken words, or symphonic music, or pictures."[11] In this spirit, he might have proposed to erase the distinction between the message and the signal, or the content and the vehicle of information, by analyzing the message or content into just so many bits of information. But he might as well have offered a thimble to someone trying to drain a pond. At the time, the technology available could not command and control a sufficient number of bits.

Let me illustrate the problem as well as the solution that eventually emerged. Imagine I tell you the Baroque Consort will give a performance tonight and you ask, "What's the first piece on the program?" and I answer: "Bach's Cantata No. 10." The symbols I have strung together to reply carry about 175 bits of information, and so would the letters if I were to point silently to the first item on the program. "Bach's Cantata No. 10" is the signal or the vehicle. But what does it convey? In one sense, nothing less than an entire cantata of some 25 pages of sheet music and some 20 minutes of performance; a church cantata for four soloists, choir, trumpet, two oboes, basso continuo, and strings. But how many people could bring to mind Bach's music in all its details when they hear "Bach's Cantata No. 10"? Perhaps no more than a few dozen among the more than five billion people alive today. Of course, there is a gradation and division of competence when it comes to recalling music. To determine what "Bach's Cantata No. 10" should convey to an educated mind is a difficult and contentious task. E. D. Hirsch lists *Johann Sebastian Bach,* but not *cantata,* as an item literate Americans should know.[12] In any case, "Bach's Cantata No. 10" is an example both of the great disparity that is possible between signal and message; between an extremely austere vehicle of 175 bits and an abundantly rich content of baroque music; and of the inverse proportion between the magnitude of the signal and the magnitude of the competence needed fully to comprehend the message.

Now assume that, instead of pointing to an item on the program, I were to hand you the score and text of the cantata for you to peruse. This information comes to perhaps 164,000 bits, a vehicle richer than the entry on the program by a factor of about a thousand. The distance between signal and message has been decreased, and so have the demands on the competence needed to gather the content from the vehicle. All that is needed now are musical literacy and a command of German. But in contemporary culture, these are still forbidding requirements and, accordingly, the signal and message are still separated by a prohibitive abyss.

Moreover, even for competent readers of the score, there is a significant gap between it and the presence of the cantata in an actual performance. Much of that which still must be decided and filled in to have a performance is left blank in the score; including matters such as tempo, phrasing, pitch, the particular choice of instruments and singers, and more. How many bits would it take to have everything spelled out to the last detail? In a dubious but still enlightening sense, it would take about 1.2 billion bits, a signal about seven million times larger than the entry on the program, and seven thousand times larger than the score and text.[13]

You can find these billion-plus bits recorded in binary notation on a compact disk. Many would say that, at this level of richness, the signal has all but caught up with the message and perhaps even surpassed it. What you have on the disk is the music itself. And if the gap between vehicle and content has not shrunk to zero, the demands on the competence required to bring the music to life certainly have. It takes less than a minute to show someone how to use a CD player.

CDs not only suggest that, in contemporary culture, the line between information and reality has become questionable as Weaver had hinted; they demonstrate outright what Weaver had claimed explicitly, viz., that all information is fundamentally alike. The compact disk can contain all kinds of information indifferently; whether it consists, as Weaver has it, of "written letters or words, or musical notes, or spoken words, or symphonic music, or pictures." But this account still leaves us with a fuzzy picture of information as reality. Sound recordings, after all, have existed for more than a hundred years. Is it not a mere matter of technical convenience whether the sound is recorded in analog or digital form? The crucial point is that information in analog form, such as photographs, films, or vinyl records really isn't emancipated from reality and, like a satellite in low orbit, is in constant danger of falling back into reality. Moving analog information in and out of storage media is a relatively slow process; and it is irreversibly deteriorated as it moves through time and the mechanics of copying. Its internal structure is as viscous as honey, and difficult to manipulate and control.

Traditional writing and print, of course, are digital and therefore mobile, durable and crisp; where analog information is inert, corruptible and fuzzy. But writing also is an extremely austere vehicle of information. It was the wedding of binary digitality with electronics that, in time, provided the union of control and abundance of information.

A digitalized electronic recording of a cantata gives us a richer rendition of the music than an analog recording but, beyond that, digitalized electronic information can move at the speed of an electric current or of light. It retains its fidelity with immutable perfection from copy to copy; and, possessing a sharply articulated internal structure, it can easily and speedily be analyzed, sorted and modified any way you please. Digital electronic information has emancipated itself from the poverty of traditional digital information, and from the heaviness and caducity of reality. Thus, it hovers as an omnipresent and unblinking virtual reality above the slow and weary actual reality.

What has been the cultural effect of this new kind of information? Again, Weaver caught the rising wave of excitement. He underscored a phenomenon which is inherent in all information, but was not clearly grasped until the question of the amount of information was raised and answered in bits. In one sense, information signals behave like any normal vehicle or container. If you have two buckets, you can carry twice as much water as if you had one. On two pages, you can say twice as much as on one. But the vehicles or containers of information have the peculiarity that, when their capacity for amount is doubled, their capacity for variety is squared. So if on a page you can say a thousand different things, then on two pages you can say not just twice a thousand, (i.e., two thousand different things), but a thousand times a thousand (i.e., a million different things).

Weaver calls the availability of variety "freedom of choice" and, in his view, a steady increase in the vehicles of information leads to an explosive growth in freedom of choice.[14] Not very many people of the information age may be aware of this fine point of information theory. But the realization that the growth of information brings with it an explosion of possibilities is widespread. Of course, this development has simply benefited information about and for reality.

The Internet can serve as the emblem of the digital and electronic improvement of information about reality. By now, it is a truism that it furnishes us with information about persons and things that would be difficult to obtain without the net. Moreover, the Internet provides for the collective exchange of information by way of bulletin boards, lists, conferences, etc., that would be impossible without it. More generally, computers and databases furnish information that you would not think of looking for without them, e.g., information on how many places down you rank from the most frequently cited scholar in your field.

Less frivolous information, uniquely obtainable from computers, also is available. One example is information on precisely how air flow builds up drag around the pod of a jet engine, when the pod is placed under the wing or when it is ahead of the wing; and when it is round and when it is pear-shaped. Such information about airflow naturally becomes essential in the designing of an airplane.[15]

The Boeing 777 can serve as an emblem of the power of digital electronic information for reality. Supercomputers are playing a crucial role in its development. Computerized information has largely replaced blueprints and mockups, and it has suffused the very thing in its final shape. The 777 no longer is guided by Newtonian levers and wires, but by information relayed from the pilot or a computer to servomechanisms.[16]

Such achievements are, undoubtedly, occasions for admiration with regard to the virtuosity that has gone into the conception and construction of the information technology. As for the end use this technology is put to, there again are occasions for gratitude. But when it comes to the overall cultural effect of it, the result lies somewhere between the trivial and the troubling.

To begin with the Internet, most of what flows through it, as far as I can tell, is overwhelmingly flimsy. There is much throat clearing, half-hearted criticism, throwing out of suggestions, crashing obviousness, and instruction by the moderately knowledgeable of the totally ignorant. The tone oscillates between the obsequiously laudatory and the rudely offensive, with much blandness in between. The Internet, for the most part, is a dump of wasted time.

Wasting time is not a uniquely late twentieth-century phenomenon, of course. Does electronic information technology have a specific impact on culture? It does, and its influence flows from information as reality down to information about and for reality. Information as virtual reality has inherited the enormous pliability and preternatural perfection of digital electronic information. The norm of pliability and perfection that is enshrined in virtual reality has cast a shadow on information about and for reality, and thereby rendered persons less personable and reality less real.

To return to Deborah Tannen's colleague as an example, Ralph has not actually been cured of his shyness nor has Deborah actually learned how to "break the ice." Both have used the Internet to create versions of themselves virtually possessing the virtues they actually lack and no longer have any reason actually to acquire. One hears anecdotes of virtual beginnings having actually happy endings. But veterans of virtual reality, as David Bennahum has well put it, "are wary – they've been burned too often by net friendships that collapsed once the stuff of real life came in."[17]

As for the bearing that the norm of pliability and perfection has on information for the shaping of reality, consider once more the Boeing 777. What is striking in historical perspective is the slackening of the power to shape things over the last thirty or forty years. To a lay person, the manifest differences between the 777 and the 707 of a generation ago are slight. The same must be said of buildings, highways and cars. The crucial changes have not been in shape, but in sophistication.

The latter is astounding and admirable in its own right, to be sure, and, other things being equal, beneficial to humanity and ecology. In the case of the 777, the end result will be cheaper, quieter and more commodious flights. But notice the end effect of this result. The sense of passage from place to place will be further attenuated, and so will be the distinction between nearness and farness.

Information as virtual reality has its own and direct effects on culture. It serves utility in design, manufacturing, medicine, and science. But it serves consumption as well, and saps everyone's vigor in dealing with the actual world. It is no respecter of class or education. Some it traps with keyboards and texts; others with buttons and pictures.

To put the drift of information technology briefly and starkly, information at the turn of the century tends to enfeeble persons and attenuate things. Luddism, of course, is not the answer. Information cannot and should not be wished away. But it has to be counter-balanced. We must regain the actuality of people and the nearness of things, and turn from information as reality to information and reality.

NOTES

First published in *Design Issues* 11 no. 2 (Summer 1995): 21–30.

1. Fred I. Dretske, *Knowledge and the Flow of Information* (Cambridge: MIT Press, 1981), 41–47.
2. The Sketchbook of Villard de Honnecourt, ed. by Theordore Bowie (Westport, CT: Greenwood, 1982), 88–91, 106–7.
3. For background and a fanciful view of J. see Harold Bloom, *The Book of J* (New York: Grove Weidenfeld, 1990).
4. Claude E. Shannon and Warren Weaver, *The Mathematical Theory of Communication* (Urbana: University of Illinois Press, 1949).
5. Ibid., 98.
6. David Ritchie. "Shannon and Weaver: Unraveling the Paradox of Information." *Communication Research* 13 (1986): 283–7.
7. Deborah Tannen, "Gender Gap in Cyberspace," *Newsweek* (16 May 1994): 52.
8. See Robert Wright, *Three Scientists and Their Gods* (New York: Harper, 1988), 21–38.
9. Shannon, and Weaver, *Mathematical Theory*, 3 and 100. See also Seth Finn and Donald F. Roberts, "Source, Destination, and Eutropy: Reassessing the Role of Information Theory in Communication Research," *Communication Research* 11 (1984): 456.
10. Donald M. Mackay, *Information, Mechanism and Meaning* (Cambridge: MIT Press, 1969), 17.
11. Shannon and Weaver, 114.
12. E. D. Hirsch, *Cultural Literacy: What Every American Needs to Know* (Boston: Houghton, 1987).
13. There is no hard and fast way of measuring the amount of information of a given item in bits. For an alphanumeric test, I have followed ASCII. For Bach's musical notation, I have assumed 12 bits per note. For the CD, I have assumed 54 million bits per minute.
14. Shannon and Weaver, 100–1.
15. Albert M. Erisman and Kenneth W. Neves, "Advanced Computing for Manufacturing," *Scientific American* (October 1987), 163–64.
16. See the April 1994 issue of *Aviation Week and Space Technology*, devoted to the Boeing 777.
17. David Bennahum, "Fly me to the MOO: Adventures in Textual Reality," *Lingua Franca* (May/June 1994), 26.

5

THORSTEIN VEBLEN AT THE UNIVERSITY OF CHICAGO AND THE SOCIALIZATION OF AESTHETICS

Ellen Mazur Thomson

From the time of its publication in 1899, *The Theory of the Leisure Class* was hailed as outrageous and delightful and, at least by some, as unerringly accurate in describing American buccaneer capitalism.[1] Although it was to become a classic in economics and sociology, it has only been recognized intermittently as a key text in the analysis of material culture and as a dramatized account of design aesthetics. In his 1947 book on the history of fashion design, Quentin Bell wrote that the book was "undoubtedly the most valuable contribution yet made to the philosophy of clothes …," but he acknowledged, "it has been strangely neglected by our historians of fashion."[2]

Not only Veblen but other scholars at the University of Chicago at the turn of the century constructed philosophies of art that attempted to integrate the fine arts and design with the rest of human experience. During this period of industrialization and the development of a consumer economy, these men introduced a social dimension to the study of aesthetics. Their ideas represented an alternative view of aesthetic values and a new attitude to the high-low dichotomy in the arts, in contrast to philosophers and connoisseurs, such as Henry Rutgers Marshall and Bernard Berenson, who were content to work within the hierarchical canon of art as codified in the eighteenth century.[3] For design historians, they provide a different perspective of the time – in sharp contrast to both the contempt espoused by these guardians of high culture for machine-made products, as well as the anti-intellectualism of those who defended the applied and industrial arts.

The difficulty of such an undertaking is acknowledged by Jerry Palmer in his introduction to *Design and Aesthetics*: "We start from the commonplace recognition that 'an aesthetics of design' is always problematic insofar as 'design' and 'aesthetics' refer to divergent traditions of understanding creative activity – indeed to different traditions of such activity."[4] Aesthetics as a discipline has been closely related to metaphysics and spiritual experience, while design has been dealt with primarily through histories of technology and commerce. When it has been treated as part of the history of art, it is considered to be of lesser aesthetic value. The following essay is an examination of some of the earliest attempts, by academics who represented diverse disciplines and drew on an even wider array of ideas, to create a new aesthetic tradition.

Turn-of-the-century American art journals and philosophical treatises concentrated on defining art and explicating its relationship to nature and beauty in characterizing the aesthetic experience: was it in the eye of the beholder? Was it a question of perception or even an attribute of the art object itself? Essayists of the period explored questions of taste and the subjectivity of aesthetic judgment, and attempted to systematically define those qualities which gave certain objects or experiences an aesthetic value. A few philosophers, such as

Hugo Munsterburg at Harvard were inspired by the development of experimental psychology and undertook to measure aesthetic experience.

Despite evidence provided by anthropologists such as Lewis H. Morgan, E. B. Tylor, and Franz Boas, that other societies did not share Western cultural values, many writers sought to maintain the idea of a universal canon of art and beauty. Faced with new media and materials – products of the Industrial Revolution – critics struggled to find a basis for incorporating or excluding them. These issues took on weight in the graphic arts, for example, with the introduction of photography and the halftone process, the mechanization of typesetting and printing, and the increased commercialization epitomized by the advertising industry. "Is photography an art?" was a common obsession in popular and academic literature of the period. Aestheticians concentrated on fine arts, painting, sculpture, and limited edition prints and, with the notable exceptions of George Santayana and Charles Caffin, a disciple of William Morris, continued to treat them in isolation from other aspects of life.[5]

During the same period, a number of scholars began to apply new ideas taken from the sciences and the social sciences to their understanding of aesthetics. Evolutionary theory, experimental psychology, and anthropological studies, as well as a new approach to sociology and economics, provided the impetus. For the first time, academics began to look at the arts as an integral part of, and expression of, society and they focused their attention on the audience, often as consumers, as well as on the function of art objects as part of material culture.

Integrating academia into city life was an important aspect of its mission when the University of Chicago was founded in 1892. Faculty members as well as administrators considered academic research to be part of a reform movement, a means of solving the problems of industrial democracy and of ameliorating, if not ending, poverty and injustice.[6] The University created the Extension Division to carry out this mission. Between 1892 and 1902, it presented public lectures, sponsored classes outside the University, and offered correspondence courses; courses covered a wide variety of subjects and were hugely popular. In addition, faculty members volunteered at Jane Addams's Hull House, and took part in creating the new profession of social work. Chicago was a major center of William Morris's Arts and Crafts movement in America, and professors at the University of Chicago were active in the Chicago Arts and Crafts Society and the Industrial Art League.[7]

When J. Laurence Laughlin, Veblen's mentor at Cornell University, became head of the economics department at the University of Chicago in 1892, he brought Veblen with him. The faculty already included John Dewey, who was head of the Department of Philosophy (which included psychology), and the Department of Pedagogy from 1894 to 1904. Dewey served as a member of the board of trustees at Hull House. Oscar Lovell Triggs, a docent in the English department at the University, was a leader of the Chicago chapter of the Arts and Crafts Society, a founder of the Industrial Art League (1899–1904), and an ardent exponent of William Morris's ideas in an American idiom. James H. Tufts, Dewey's colleague and sometime coauthor, also taught in the philosophy department. Ira Woods Howerth, was a professor of sociology.[8] These scholars shared a common interest in evolutionary theory, the economics of industrialization and its production of a consumer-oriented culture, and a desire to reconcile these with the principles of a democratic society.

ORIGINS AND INFLUENCES

Darwin's theory of evolution, in a wide variety of permutations, pervaded all aspects of intellectual inquiry during this period. Many aesthetic theories of the time relied extensively on the work of Herbert Spencer (1820–1903), who constructed a history of art based on the theory of evolution. Spencer believed that, as art evolved, it became increasing complex and diverse, and that it was inextricably part of a larger social movement. Art, for Spencer, did not simply change, but progressed; from its beginnings in primitive cultures, it had developed into more intricate and superior modern forms. Spencer's conception is central to Veblen's understanding of the designed world, as well as economics and cultural evolution. Veblen, like his colleagues at Chicago, rejected the idea that society could be understood by discovering fundamental, unchanging laws. He maintained that economics should be studied as history, in its evolutionary dimension, that is, as a dynamic force shaped by advances in technology. The arts, like all human activity, not only change as society evolves but develop into higher forms.

The influence of contemporary anthropology was evident in the thinking of Veblen and his colleagues, even though they applied it in a loose and somewhat fanciful manner. Veblen identified four stages of economic evolution linked to comparable stages of social evolution: a golden age of "peaceable savagery," that was supplanted by an age of predatory barbarians in which warfare, property, and aggressive behavior were glorified. Leisure class attitudes originated during this period; labor gained "a character of irksomeness by virtue of the indignity imputed to it." Predatory barbarianism gave way to an age of handicraft economy and, finally, to the present age of the machine.[9]

The work of the anthropologist Franz Boas (1858–1942) also inspired several formulations of Veblen's ideas. Boas was curator of Chicago's Field Museum during this period, and already had published studies on the Kwakiutl Indians of British Columbia. He described the Kwakiutl potlatch ceremonies during which the host distributed gifts to guests to enhance his own prestige and status. The idea that objects do not simply have value in themselves, but take on value in their social context, and that their function in society confers extra-artistic worth, certainly shaped Veblen's concept of conspicuous consumption, status emulation, and waste.

Veblen's understanding of design and the industrial arts derives, in large measure, from his belief that history, by which he meant cultural evolution, is driven by technological advances. Technology remakes culture, but that does not necessarily mean that cultural institutions immediately change to accommodate it. In the short term, those with a stake in the status quo resist change, creating tension between new technologies and resisting institutions.[10] Eventually, technology prevails. Veblen considered that his own era exemplified such a time lag; social institutions and attitudes suited to an earlier, handicraft economy had yet to come to terms with industrialization and a class with ideas suited to medieval serfdom controlled manufacturing.

In his essay "The Instinct of Workmanship," Veblen addressed the ramifications of this struggle. He contrasted "the conventional aversion to labor" with "the ubiquitous human impulse to do the next thing." "All men," he asserted, "have this quasi-aesthetic sense of economic or industrial merit, and to this sense of economic merit futility and inefficiency are distasteful."[11] Members of the leisure class are not idle or indolent, but preindustrial in their idea that work is degrading. They aspire to a nonproductive consumption of time from a sense of the unworthiness of productive work, and as evidence of their ability to afford a life of idleness.[12]

In making the idea of work central to his argument, Veblen embraced the Arts and Crafts ideal of workmanship but rejected its celebration of handicraft. He repudiated the handicraft industry, the production of objects outside the dominant environment of machinery and machine technology, as "an inconsequential interloper."[13]

THE ARTS AND CRAFTS MOVEMENT

As Veblen celebrated the industrialization of manufacturing, much of his critique of the Arts and Crafts movement centered on its disdain for machine-produced goods. For Morrisonians, machine production is a necessary evil, "a perfunctory concession to facts rather than an integral element in the principles on which the advocates of the movement go about their work," wrote Veblen, and slyly noted that in later phases of the movement, "machine production is not condemned without qualification, except in practice." He accused members of the Arts and Craft societies of arguing sentimentally rather than logically, of championing a sophisticated form of nostalgia. Machine-produced goods are not only less costly, but often better made:

> Articles of daily consumption in modern industrial communities are commonly machine products; and the generic feature of the physiognomy of machine-made goods, as compared with the handwrought article is their greater perfection in workmanship and greater accuracy in the detail execution of the design.[14]

The cult of the handcrafted book, which he labeled the "exaltation of the detective," provoked one of Veblen's most inspired rants, displaying the slashing, vitriolic humor he used in criticizing leisure class values. He derided the hand-printed volumes of the Kelmscott Press, as well as its followers in the private press movement, for their cost and unwieldiness, their barely legible type, exaggerated margins, their use of archaic spelling, and their uncut pages, with "bindings of a painstaking crudeness and elaborate ineptitude."[15] "The special attractiveness of these book-products to the book-buyer of cultivated taste lies, of course, not in a conscious, naive recognition of their costliness and superior clumsiness."[16] By appealing to a nostalgia for a preindustrial, premachine aesthetic, the book acquires value. It may, indeed, be beautiful, but the designer has to fulfill additional requirements to make it valuable, the requirements of "the law of conspicuous waste": scarcity achieved by limiting the edition and the cachet of the handwrought with intentional awkwardness.[17]

When he helped to found the Industrial Arts Society, Oscar Lovell Triggs renounced his anti-machine stance. In reviewing Triggs's book on the Arts and Crafts movement, Veblen acknowledged Trigg's conversion and proclaimed his own sympathy with a great deal of the craftsman aesthetics, as well as his admiration for William Morris ("the Dreamer"):

> ... it does not follow from all this that the movement initiated by the Dreamer need be without salutary effect upon the working life of the workmen or the artistic value of their output of goods. Indirectly, these ideals, romantic or otherwise, have already had a large effect, and there is every reason to hope that the propaganda of taste carried on by organizations like the Industrial Art League and its congeners will count for much in checking the current ugliness of the apparatus of life.[18]

Like Veblen, Triggs integrated Morris's political views with his aesthetics. Taste and ideas of beauty are closely related to questions of economics and politics. Both men considered taste to be a question of class, and distinguished aristocratic culture from culture in a democracy.

Triggs called his ideas "industrial aesthetics." He based them on three principles: that art is a necessity of human life, that "beauty is a subjective effect and has to be defined in terms of pleasure," and that it can only be achieved by human labor. Triggs linked his industrial aesthetics to what he considered the scientifically based "evolutionary aesthetics" of Herbert Spencer, seeing it as another mode of reaffirming the importance of play and progress:

> When play came to be consciously regulated under some principle of order, and conducted to the satisfaction of higher instincts and the conveyance of the sense of spiritual significance in material things, the long process of art began.[19]

As art embraces more and more human experience, it improves as it expands. Classicism, he argued, was limited to "formalism," "that which was appropriately designed and ordered."[20] Like Veblen, Triggs constructed stages of human history to trace changes in aesthetics: from the "philosophic monism" of Greek aesthetics, to the "romantic dualism" of the Middle Ages, to "the spiritual monism" of the present. Here, in a social democracy, form and content are united and art takes on a great force: "The artistic outcome of the process is an art that does not aim primarily at a beautiful form, but at the most adequate expression of some particular content," or "Beauty comes into being when a significant content is duly expressed."[21]

According to Triggs, the distinction between the fine arts and the industrial arts was eroding:

> When the industrial artist works under the conditions of freedom and self-realization, he ceases to be a slave to commerce and production, is entitled to the name of the fine artist as well as to his rewards in joyous existence – the rewards that the divine artist gets, in his own creations. Not a perfect object but a perfected man, not a rigid definition but a fluid personality, is the end of socialistic art.[22]

Triggs did not dispute the existence of standards, but he argued that they must be universal and appeal to that "which stimulates, within the limits of pleasurable action, one or all of the faculties of being, the senses, the intellect, the emotions, the imagination, and the will."[23] Art was not merely concerned with beauty, but had to embrace all of human life. "The definition of art founded upon the current metaphysics of beauty is a class definition, and is intended to preserve the upper classes in their special privilege of culture and 'taste.' "[24]

Veblen, with his flair for concrete examples, vividly demonstrated how class interests are interjected into taste with a rousing feminist attack on fashion. There is nothing natural in our appreciation of a particular form of female beauty, Veblen argued; it is predicated on power and it is learned. Female beauty is defined so that upper-class males can advertise their economic success by reducing women of their class to nonproductive aesthetic objects. The Western ideal of the tiny female waist was achieved by wearing bone corsets that constricted breathing and limited movement. "The corset is, in economic theory, substantially a mutilation, undergone for the purpose of lowering the subject's vitality and rendering her permanently and obviously unfit for work." Similarly, the Chinese aristocrats' ideal of tiny feet, produced by foot binding, forced women to take short steps and constricted their movements. There is nothing immediately appealing in either of these practices. Veblen notes:

> Both of these are mutilations of unquestioned repulsiveness to the untrained sense. It requires room to question their attractiveness to men into whose scheme of life they fit as honorific items sanctioned by pecuniary and cultural beauty which have come to do duty as elements of the ideal of womanliness.[25]

If Veblen's attitude towards the Arts and Crafts movement was ambivalent, he ardently espoused the belief that beauty was born out of a function. Like Triggs, Veblen viewed the design of common objects as a subject of importance and, like him, insisted on the value of simplicity and fitness for use.

> So far as the economic interest enters into the constitution of beauty, it enters as a suggestion or expression of adequacy to a purpose, a manifest and readily inferable subservience to the life process. This expression of economic facility or economic serviceability in any object – what may be called the economic beauty of the object – is best served by neat and unambiguous suggestion of its office, and its efficiency for the material ends of life.[26]

Veblen contended that "the simple and unadorned article is aesthetically the best" but reminded his readers that it is opposed by the requirements of "the pecuniary canon of reputability," the need for affirming status by owning and displaying economically valuable goods.[27] Veblen contributed to Morrisonian functional analysis by adding the concept of latent functions, the informal or extra-formal use of objects. For example, the ostensible function of private press books, like all books, is to be read; their latent function, however, is to demonstrate or enhance the status of their owners.

ART AS A SOCIAL ACTIVITY

In a 1903 essay, University of Chicago philosopher James H. Tufts wrote:

> Art has its origins, almost without exception, in social relations; it has developed under social pressure; it has been fostered by social occasions; it has in turn served social ends in the struggle for existence. In consequence, the values attributed to aesthetic objects have social standards, and the aesthetic attitude will be determined largely by these social antecedents. Or, in other words, the explanation of the aesthetic categories is to be sought largely in social psychology.[28]

Tufts distinguished three aspects of aesthetics that set it apart from the ethical, logical, economic, or even "other pleasures."[29] First, although aesthetic judgment is subjective, it is felt to be objective – belonging to the object rather than the viewer's consciousness. Second, it gives immediate pleasure, characterized by inner unity, "a world apart" from usefulness. Finally, the aesthetic experience is distinguished by a sense of universality and disinterestedness. Tufts believed that aesthetic feelings relate first to art (manmade) as opposed to nature. He did not argue that aesthetic judgments are objective or universal, but only that they are felt to be.

Traditionally, aesthetics focused on the appreciation of beauty but Tufts also insisted that the creation of art involves many aspects of human experience. He contended:

> that art has its origin, not in any single impulse, much less in any desire to gratify an already existing aesthetic demand for beauty, but rather in response to many and varied demands, economic, protective, sexual, military, magical, ceremonial, religious, and intellectual.[30]

Significantly, he demonstrated this with examples from other cultures: American Indian drinking gourds he had seen at an exhibition at the Field Museum, as well as the more usual objects of Western art history: Assyrian reliefs, Egyptian tombs, and Greek temples. The extra-aesthetic impulse does not vitiate the aesthetic response. What may begin as the exigencies of construction or other requirements, stimulates and strengthens the purely aesthetic. Like Triggs, Tufts believed in the importance of "the play-factor," an idea based on research conducted by his contemporaries on children and animals at play.[31]

What is missing, or certainly not central in his discussion, was the concept of the driven genius, cut off from the rest of society, and inspired by demons or muses. Citing studies in art history, ethnography, and psychology, Tufts constructed his case to show that art-making is a social enterprise involving community activities and ideas. Art is social in origin, Tufts maintained, because art begins within a group. It requires sociability; it is not only a shared experience, but the group or community inspires and supports the art experience. Individual artists must be connected to the common culture of their group in order to express and communicate emotions or ideas effectively. Participation in the artistic experience reinforces social cohesion by creating "an emotional as well as ideational community of attitude." Ultimately, the arts encourage communication and reinforce community values. While not denying the individual's aesthetic experience, Tufts insisted on its existence within a particular time, place, and social structure.[32]

Veblen had argued that humans, because we are social animals, literally cannot perceive objects devoid of their social meanings, and that our sense of beauty and value is mediated by these accretions. Tufts, like Veblen, held that aesthetic appreciation is created by, and conditioned by, social values. Both scholars insisted on the previously ignored phenomenon that certain kinds of art objects confer status, and that their value is mediated by social values at least as much as by abstract aesthetics values. Veblen, however, regarded this as problematic.

"THEIR MEDIUM IS MATTER"

Could the new media and materials of the Industrial Revolution produce objects and images of value and beauty? Veblen was interested in how the monetary value of materials distorts aesthetic appreciation. He chose the spoon, that most ubiquitous tool, to demonstrate that our appreciation of a designed object is compromised by our recognition of its "pecuniary beauty." Veblen contrasted handwrought spoons made of silver with machine-made spoons of aluminum.[33] The machine product is more uniform, and in fact, may be more precisely constructed and stronger, but,

> the superior gratification derived from the use and contemplation of costly and supposedly beautiful products is, commonly, in great measure a gratification of our sense of costliness masquerading under the name of beauty. Our higher appreciation of the superior article is an appreciation of its superior honorific character, much more frequently than it is an unsophisticated appreciation of its beauty. The requirement of conspicuous wastefulness is not commonly present, consciously, in our canons of taste, but it is none the less present as a constraining norm selectively shaping and sustaining our sense of what is beautiful, and guiding our discrimination with respect to what may legitimately be approved as beautiful and what may not.[34]

No one actually decides to value one object more than another because of the price of its materials or because one's fellows look on it with esteem, but we do so because we are social animals, because we value things in addition to beauty, and because no one can "perceive" in isolation from the past or from our surroundings in the present. Veblen admits that the consumer is not aware of this distinction:

> The connection here indicated between the aesthetic value and the invidious pecuniary value of things is, of course, not present in the consciousness of the valuer.[35]

Our aesthetic is contingent upon our experience as part of a particular culture at a particular historical moment.

The question of how materials affect value was pursued by Ira Howerth of the University of Chicago's sociology department for quite another purpose – to revise the artistic canon. Borrowing heavily from Spencerian art theory, Howerth proposed a scheme in which the arts are redefined and analyzed in terms of the media they use, as well as their complexity. In his 1907 essay, "The Classification of the Arts," Howerth dismissed traditional categories as "unscientific" and, instead, called for "an evolutionary classification based on material phenomena," since, "All arts are alike in this – their medium is matter." His hierarchy would be logical in nature – classification by material, and scientific, follow evolutionary theory to achieve classification by complexity.[36]

In terms echoing Veblen and Tufts, Howerth asserted the traditional hierarchy of the arts simply reflected the past:

> It is the relative historical circumstances under which the respective arts originated and have been developed. The useful, mechanic, or industrial arts are allied to productive labor, and their history is the history of labor; while the liberal, polite, or fine arts have always been associated with leisure and culture.[37]

Howerth spelled out the political implications of these divisions:

> This, then, is the explanation of the long-accepted division of the arts into fine and useful: the monopolization of the fine arts by the leisure class, and the compulsory practise of the useful arts by the slave, the serf, and the wage laborer. It is a division based primarily upon a class distinction.[38]

Claiming to apply logic over historical accident, Howerth created a three-tiered hierarchy to account for all human endeavor: the "physical arts" at the bottom, the "vital arts" in a middle tier, and the "social arts" at the pinnacle. In concepts borrowed from Spencer, he categorized every human activity first by media – from simple to complex, and second – from inorganic to organic – and, ultimately, "superorganic." The resulting scheme inverted the traditional classifications of artistic hierarchy. (Figure 5.1.)

Within this scheme, Howerth placed the visual arts, including design and handicraft, on the bottom tier with the fine arts because they all employ nonliving matter. Paintings, sculpture, and drawings are created out of wood, stone, and minerals, which Howerth called "lifeless elements" and "passive material." They are, therefore, of less worth than the arts, "that deal with living things and arts that deal with organized groups of men, or societies." Even within the lowest category, however, the fine arts are at the bottom. Arts that use machines are more complex and are, by definition, higher. Graphics, photography, and machine-produced objects are in a more elevated plane than the "fine" arts:

> Now, the physical arts that minister to the vulgar wants, or needs, of mankind have reached a high degree of perfection. They are, today, the theater for the display of the highest reaches of inventive genius. A watch, a locomotive, a printing press, are marvels of ingenuity.

At present, however, Howerth believed that their value was tainted because "salability has been their main consideration."

"They have been the instruments of trade and gains, rather than the ministers of joy and life. They have, thus, been degraded …The repulsion which some profess to feel toward the machine arts is based upon a misconception. It is not these arts which should excite disdain: it is the purpose for which they are employed and the conditions under which they are practised."[39] Once man is freed from being "an appendage to profit-grinding" "… the machine arts will become fine arts." "Carving a statue to please the eye ought not to differentiate the 'artist' from the laborer who carves a chair … If the one act is accompanied by pleasure, and a manifestation of the beautiful, while the other is not, it is due to factitious circumstances."[40]

We should complete this description of Howerth's scheme by noting that his second tier encompassed "the vital arts": agriculture, horticulture, the domestication and breeding of animals, and the education of man. These are higher because they employ living matter as a medium. Howerth argued that it made empirical sense to

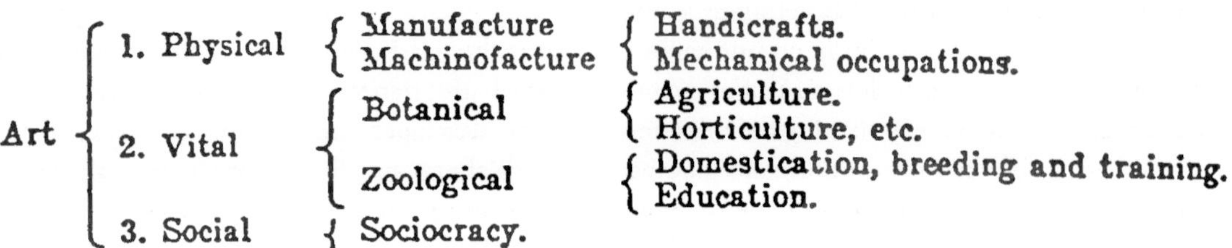

Figure 5.1 Ira W. Howerth, "The Classification of the Arts," *Popular Science* 70 (May 1907), 436.

place "farming above music, and gardening above painting" because they use "more complex forms of matter." Since "the ultimate end of all the arts is a perfected humanity," the third tier belongs to "the social arts" or "sociocracy," which he defined as "the scientific control of the social forces by the collective mind of society for its advantage." A fitting conclusion, no doubt, for Howerth, a sociologist.[41]

SOCIOLOGY AND AESTHETIC THEORY

Critics of a sociological analysis of art contend that it reduces aesthetic values to purely social and economic concerns. Certainly this criticism has been leveled at Veblen.[42] Yet, throughout *Theory of the Leisure Class*, there are passages showing that Veblen believed that beauty was more enduring than fashion and fad; it was in some sense, a basic component in human perception, unmediated by economics or politics, and irreducible to anything else. He wrote, "The canon of beauty requires expression of the generic," although his notions of "generic" or "intrinsic" beauty were never fully developed.[43] In discussing clothing fads, for example, he wrote:

> Our transient attachment to whatever happens to be the latest rests on other than aesthetic grounds, and lasts only until *our abiding aesthetic sense* has had time to assert itself and reject this latest indigestible contrivance. (Italics added.)[44]

What creates this abiding aesthetic sense? Veblen does not address it either in this study or later ones. Admittedly, he did not set out to create a systematic aesthetic, but evidently he did believe in some sort of "intrinsic beauty" with regard to the aesthetic. Veblen only briefly goes beyond concrete objects to a general statement about form, beauty, and the power of habit. In *Theory of the Leisure Class* he alludes to the concepts of perception as understood by psychologists of his day:

> Beauty of form seems to be a question of facility of apperception. The proposition could, perhaps, safely be made broader than this. If abstraction is made from association, suggestion, and "expression," classed as elements of beauty, then beauty in any perceived object means that the mind readily unfolds its apperceptive activity in the directions which the object in question affords.

He then is forced to suggest the evolution of some sort of basic instinct:

> So far as concerns the essential elements of beauty, this habituation is an habituation so close and long as to have induced not only a proclivity to the apperceptive form in question, but an adaptation of physiological structure and function as well.[45]

Beauty is linked to economics, but more as it relates to function than to monetary value: "So far as the economic interest enters into the constitution of beauty, it enters as a suggestion or expression of adequacy to a purpose ..." Here "adequacy to a purpose" would appear to come close to Arts and Crafts aesthetics.

CONCLUSION

These theories share the sense of the optimism, the belief in the benign potential of technology and the unstoppable expansion of democracy of their time. In their misapplication of Darwinism, apocryphal anthropology, and outdated psychological theories they surely are obsolete. Historian James T. Koppenberg summed up Veblen's place in American intellectual history as one that "connected the nineteenth-century utopian tradition to the empirical social sciences of the early 1900s."[46] This characterization may be equally applied to the other work described here.

Perhaps the greatest contribution that the Chicago-based scholars made to aesthetics was to show how the arts, including design, could be understood within the larger framework of culture. They explored the cultural meaning and social uses of the arts rather than glorifying individual artists or creating canons. Treating aesthetics as part of social history necessarily reduces the role of the individual designer/creator. Individual artifacts are seen as representing categories of work or approaches to problems rather than as entities to be analyzed as an end in themselves. This made it easier to redefine the arts to include applied and industrial design, and to explore its relationship within the artistic hierarchy, indeed, to expand the boundaries and destroy hierarchies. By defining aesthetics within culture, as the University of Chicago scholars did, they were able to identify the politics underlying hierarchical schemes that relegates design to a lesser position within the artistic canon.

These scholars shared a belief in the universal human need for beauty and art and revisioned the arts as an essential part of all humanity. Although several of them expressed a horror of crass commercialism, and blamed it for the failures of the designed world, none of them explained how this might be changed, except in semireligious, millennarian terms. In this sense they were at the end of a great tradition that envisaged a grand union between democratic ideals and artistic ones, and between economic justice and universal participation in the arts. At the same tune, their belief that art is shaped by divergent forces and cannot be understood apart from other aspects of culture, is not as easily dismissed. Though their work, in many ways, reflects the end of a tradition, it also was the foundation for a new paradigm John Dewey defined in *Art as Experience.*

NOTES

First published in *Design Issues* 15 no. 1 (Spring 1999): 3–15

1. Citations in this essay refer to the 1994 Penguin Book's edition, with an introduction by Robert Lekachman, hereafter *TLC.*
2. Quentin Bell, *On Human Finery* (London: The Hogarth Press, 1947), 11. Sociologist Chandra Mukerji used Veblen's ideas in analyzing the transformation of movies from industrial commodities to a medium for artistic expression in "Artwork: Collection and Contemporary Culture," *American Journal of Sociology* 84 (September 1978): 348–65. In the 1940s, the philosopher Theodor W. Adorno attacked Veblen's aesthetic theory as anti-intellectual and regressive in "Veblen's Attack on Culture," *Studies in Philosophy and Social Science* 9:3 (1941): 389–413. More recently, Rick Tilman described the Kantian foundations of Veblen's aesthetic theory in *The Intellectual Legacy of Thorstein Veblen* (Westport, CT: Greenwood Press, 1996). See especially "Kant, Veblen, and the Aesthetics of Heterodox Economics," 143–165.
3. Paul Oskar Kristeller, "The Modern System of the Arts: A Study in the History of Aesthetics," *Journal of the History of Ideas* (1951): 496–527; 13 (1952): 17–46. In this now classic essay, Kristeller traces the concept of "art" and the development of the concept of "fine art" in the eighteenth century.
4. Jerry Palmer and Mo Dodson, eds. *Design and Aesthetics* (London: Routledge, 1996), 3.
5. George Santayana's theory of aesthetics is expounded in *Sense of Beauty* (1896) and in the fourth volume of *Life of Reason,* titled, *Reason in Art,* published in 1905.
6. *The University and the City. A Centennial View of the University of Chicago,* ed. by Daniel Meyer (Chicago: University Library, 1992), 21–22; Horowitz, H. Lefkowitz, *Culture and The City* (Lexington: University Press of Kentucky, 1976), 157–59.
7. For a discussion of these groups, see Eileen Boris, *Art and Labor: Ruskin, Morris, and the Craftsman Ideal in America* (Philadelphia: Temple University Press), 46–51.
8. I have not discussed John Dewey's ideas, although he taught at the University of Chicago during the time frame of this essay. Dewey's major contribution to the subject, *Art as Experience,* was not published until 1934, but it draws on many of the ideas and attitudes from this period.
9. Joseph Dorfman, *Thorstein Veblen and His America* (New York: Viking Press, 1934), 248.
10. Lewis A. Coser, *Masters of Sociological Thought* 2nd ed. (New York: Harcourt, Brace and Jovanovich, 1977), 273.

11. Veblen, "The Instinct of Workmanship" in *Essays in Our Changing Order*, ed. Leon Ardzrooni (New York: Viking Press, 1954), 81.
12. *TLC*, 43.
13. Veblen, "Art and Crafts," *The Journal of Political Economy* 11 (December 1902); reprinted in *Essays in Our Changing Order* 195–7.
14. *TLC*, 161.
15. Ibid., 162–3.
16. Ibid., 164.
17. Ibid.
18. Oscar Lovell Triggs, *Chapters in the History of the Arts and Crafts Movement* (Chicago: The Bohemia Guild of the Industrial Art League, 1902); Veblen, "Arts and Crafts," 198.
19. Ibid., 422.
20. Ibid., 426.
21. Ibid., 427.
22. Oscar Lovell Triggs, "Democratic Criticism," *The Sewanee Reviewer* 6:4 (October 1898): 418–19.
23. Ibid., 431–2.
24. Triggs's *Chapters in the History*, 168–9.
25. *TLC*, 149, 172, and 149.
26. Ibid., 151–152.
27. Ibid.
28. James H. Tufts, "On the Genesis of the Aesthetic Categories," *The Philosophical Review* 12: 1 (no. 67) (January 1903): 1.
29. Ibid., 2–4.
30. Ibid., 7.
31. Ibid., 6–9.
32. Ibid., 11–13.
33. *TLC*, 126–8.
34. Ibid., 128.
35. Ibid., 149.
36. Ira W. Howerth, "The Classification of the Arts," *Popular Science* 70 (May 1907): 431. Howerth maintained that music and poetry, although ostensibly immaterial, in fact involve "writing and printing materials, musical instruments and sound waves."
37. Ibid., 429.
38. Ibid., 430.
39. Ibid., 432–3.
40. Ibid., 433.
41. Ibid., 434–6.
42. For example, the Frankfort school. See Adorno, "Veblen's Attack on Culture."
43. *TLC*, 153. Did Veblen then think that it was possible to strip pecuniary and other extra-artistic associations from aesthetics? Tilman, a sympathetic analyst of Veblen's ideas, argues Veblen's aesthetics were ultimately derived from his early study of Kant and the German tradition of idealism. See "Kant, Veblen and the Aesthetics of Heterodox Economics" in R. Tilman, *The Intellectual Legacy*, 143–165.
44. *TLC*, 178.
45. TLC, 151.
46. James T. Koppenberg, *Uncertain Victories* (New York: Oxford University Press, 1986), 14.

6

ADOLF LOOS AND THE APHORISTIC STYLE: RHETORICAL PRACTICE IN EARLY TWENTIETH-CENTURY DESIGN CRITICISM

John V. Maciuika

Adolf Loos has been described in the annals of architectural and design history as the individual most responsible for introducing the principles of abstract, austere, orthogonal design into numerous pre-World War I Viennese buildings.[1] His early commissions – the Steiner House of 1908, the Scheu House of 1910, and others – are generally interpreted as embodiments of the maxims contained in his most famous 1908 essay, "Ornament and Crime." As one of the most radical polemics of design criticism of the twentieth century, this essay gained Loos considerable notoriety in the way in which it violently denounced, and then claimed to close the door forever on, an "arbitrary" use of ornaments that had predominated in Viennese architecture and applied arts for decades. Employing a series of grand rhetorical gestures to denounce nineteenth-century historicism as well as newer styles being explored by the Austrian Secession, the Deutscher Werkbund, and the Wiener Werkstätte, Loos's written and built works generally are credited with inventing the forms that inspired countless modernist architects to embrace abstraction and the International Style of the 1920s.[2]

Succeeding generations of scholars and architects have treated Loos with varying degrees of sophistication, analyzing his buildings as expressions of his cultural polemics, connecting him loosely with other Viennese cultural innovators, or mining his writings for justifications of new directions in late twentieth-century architecture. Among the most illuminating analyses of Loos's complex, anti-systematic philosophy are those of architectural historian Stanford Anderson. Anderson has argued that Loos's critical breakthrough consisted of developing an awareness of how competing conventions and practices – drawing, photography, master craftsmanship and building, and the production of art – could constructively criticize one another from within respective, sovereign domains of praxis.[3] Instructive for understanding Loos's approach to the process of building and making, Anderson's work nevertheless leaves open the question of how Loos used language in particular ways to advance his ground-breaking design philosophy.

This article contrasts Loos's celebrated early design criticism with certain rhetorical practices in his writings, insofar as the field of rhetoric traditionally has concerned itself with "the way discourses are constructed in order to achieve certain effects." This definition of rhetoric, borrowed from Terry Eagleton, emphasizes rhetoric's long-standing interest in writing as a form of power-laden performance.[4] Arguing for a cultural and geographical specificity that has been omitted in many studies of the International Style, this article begins by examining the dependence of Loos's thought on his Viennese context. It then investigates the extent to which Loos's writings and his agenda for design and architecture followed radically different sets of rules. Not only did these rules conform to different conceptions of modern public and private domains, as Michael Hays and Beatriz Colomina have argued, but Loos's writings embraced a colorful, even ornamental style that assisted him in the construction of his celebrated theory of modern culture and identity.[5]

THEATRICALITY AND AUTHENTICITY IN *FIN-DE-SIÈCLE* VIENNESE CULTURE

Loos's early and formative writings give him a significant relationship to other major late nineteenth-century rhetorical masters who, together, make up a group known as the Viennese "language circle" because of their commitment to language as a tool of cultural reform. Intellectual historian William Johnston, author of *The Austrian Mind*, refers to Loos's associates such as the writer Karl Kraus as one of Vienna's "therapeutic nihilists," to the poet Peter Altenberg as an "expert at dissimulation," and to the philosopher of language Ludwig Wittgenstein, who designed his own house inspired by Loos's ideas, as "a Utopian and therapeutic nihilist at once."[6]

These figures shared a cultural and social matrix that has been characterized by an array of historians in Vienna as being highly "theatrical," and though the term is significant, it also is used very differently by different scholars. In works by Carl Schorske, Donald Olsen, and Allan Janik and Stephen Toulmin, for example, Viennese tendencies toward performance and theatricality could be seen spilling over into the journalism, café culture, and street life of the city.[7] Other historians, such as Michael Steinberg and Edward Timms, have interpreted tendencies toward Viennese theatricality much more darkly. To Michael Steinberg, theatricality denotes the settings and rituals of a centuries-old ideological technique with roots in Catholic baroque culture.[8] In Edward Timms's more nuanced view, theatricality permeated the structure of Viennese social, cultural, and political life as a form of performance and dissembling throughout the waning years of the Habsburg Empire. In a multinational entity struggling to preserve its dynastic structure through the early decades of the twentieth century, Timms argues, Austrian leaders and much of the rest of Viennese society exhibited an increasing tendency to embrace theatricality in cultural forms, as well as in behavior. As a form of dissembling, theatricality could be detected in society through the blurring of the lines between actors and the behavior of avid Viennese theatergoers, in the layers of pomp and historicist ornament self-consciously intermingled with products of modern manufacturing, and in laws, customs, and cultural practices that fundamentally conflicted but persisted side by side. These trends compensated for tensions building up within the Austrian Empire's increasingly anachronistic system. At the same time, they betrayed a hypocrisy that Timms locates at different levels of the Imperial government, the military, and the social hierarchy.[9] It is not surprising, therefore, that theatrical performance and social dissembling figured as central themes in works of contemporary literature by such *fin-de-siècle* literary figures as Arthur Schnitzler and Robert Musil.[10]

It was precisely such hypocrisies and seemingly decadent frills that gave rise to radical cultural critics like Adolf Loos. The architect's writings and buildings suggest that he knew his targets well. Largely an autodidact, he appeared poised from early in his career to articulate a vision for architectural and cultural change – his total of two semesters at Dresden Technical University notwithstanding.[11] Loos's work, however, cannot easily be separated from the very Viennese dissembling against which the architect claimed so forcefully to rebel. Exhibiting, in fact, a kind of anti-theatrical prejudice, Loos's crusade for an authenticity befitting the modern age led him to enact his own versions of Viennese theatricality.

As Jonas Barish has shown, upsurges of theatricality in Western cultures historically have been opposed by a "rage for authenticity" which, for many reformers, represents the reassertion of a reality seen as distorted or suppressed.[12] Loos's contributions to the nascent modern movement in architecture and design must thus be understood as the product of theatrical and anti-theatrical forces balanced in palpable tension. To the extent that his writings and architecture charted new cultural territory, on the one hand, they were not-so-subtly undermined by dissembling, performative, and highly theatrical conventions that the architect absorbed from his cultural context on the other. More than the achievement of an eccentric architect forming a new style before his time, Loos's work is particularly useful for understanding many features of modernism's own ambivalence.

In view of the numerous historical accounts of *fin-de-siècle* Viennese theatricality, it is easier to understand Adolf Loos's contemporary criticism of a culture that embraced so much historicist ornament in its architecture and design of everyday objects that it undermined the very idea of a modern culture. His designs for buildings, furniture, and everyday objects were, in part, a critique of an urbanity Loos regarded as intrusive and grossly out of step with the times. As other scholars have pointed out, Loos, Wittgenstein, and Karl Kraus thematized "the limits of language" by constructing an ethical critique of Viennese social practices.[13] Loos's relatively blank exteriors in architecture, the "silences" of Wittgenstein's language philosophy, and Kraus's denunciations of print media conventionalism in his one-man journal, *Die Fackel* (*The Torch*), sought collectively to purge superfluous elements from a culture seen as carnivalesque and debased.[14]

To Adolf Loos the writer, however, Viennese theatrical traditions left an indelible imprint on his ironic, aphoristic, and, at times, incendiary prose style. As the architectural historian Reyner Banham put it, Loos's writing typically consisted of "not a reasoned argument but a succession of fast-spieling double-takes and non-sequiturs holding together a precarious rally of clouds of witness – café Freudianism, café-anthropology, (and) café criminology."[15] To what can we attribute the difference between Loos's austere, even "silent" buildings, and the highly "ornamented" and theatrical quality of his writings? If there is a connection between aphorism and ornament, how should we understand the seeming contradiction between the writing style featured in Loos's design criticism and the outward sobriety of his architecture and furniture?

One can begin by pointing to Loos's fundamental distinction between the qualities of private and public life, an attitude usefully explored by Beatriz Colomina in her 1994 book, *Privacy and Publicity: Modern Architecture as Mass Media*. She recounts how Adolf Loos and Josef Hoffman, his Viennese counterpart and rival, developed radically different approaches to urban residential design. Hoffman understood the house as a social artifact: the architect's task was to design an elegant residence that reflected the owner's station to an outside world which, beholding a monument to taste, would elevate the house to the status of an artwork. This point is illustrated in one of his best-known works, the Palais Stoclet in Brussels, whose interior mural paintings were carried out by Gustav Klimt.[16]

Loos, on the other hand, renounced that aestheticization of building which confused utilitarian objects with art. He insisted on the use of architectural drawing not for the production of images, but as a tool for communicating constructional and technical ideas to the builder. Since humanity had evolved past the need for superfluous historicist ornaments, Loos reasoned, modern creativity lay in the development of a method of designing houses three-dimensionally, in section rather than in plan, and from the inside out. Presenting "masked" exteriors to the outside world, these houses were designed with an emphasis on spatial fluidity and adaptability, shielding the owner from the fast-paced modern metropolis. The most inventive spatial features of

Loos's architecture did not translate in the new technology of photography which, like drawing, was regarded by Loos as an "irreducible system" for the communication of form.[17]

CULTURAL REFORM AS DESIGN REFORM: LOOS'S RHETORICAL DEVICES

A different set of rules applied to the public realm, however. Loos's public persona was that of an outspoken cultural critic and mesmerizing lecturer who delighted as well as educated audiences through his performances.[18] Regarding the private and public realms of the modern city as radically discontinuous, Loos adopted such additional performative elements of Viennese theatrical culture as the feuilleton and an aphoristic writing style as his chosen means of public self-expression.

As a lecturer and through his tenure writing feuilletons for Vienna's best-known liberal newspaper, *Die Neue Freie Presse* (*The New Free Press*), Loos revealed himself to be a masterful writer and incisive cultural observer. The feuilleton consisted of an impressionistically written article, one that seized upon seemingly minor elements of behavior or material culture, and examined them with merciless wit. Introduced first in Paris around 1800 before making its way to Vienna in the decades that followed, the feuilleton, as the historian William Johnston has noted, was the literary correlate to the intellectual camaraderie of the coffee house. Carl Schorske has further demonstrated that the feuilleton was symptomatic of an expanding aesthetic strain running through late nineteenth-century Viennese culture, one which provided a competitive, educated bourgeoisie, or *Bildungsbürgertum*, access to aristocratic privilege via recognition in the arts and literature.[19] At their best, feuilletons cleverly expanded on small details of cultural life until they became, in the hands of skilled authors, virtual embodiments of the hypocrisies and afflictions of the culture at large. In *Wittgenstein's Vienna*, historians Allan Janik and Stephen Toulmin attest to Loos's talents through their observation that "to have an essay accepted by Theodor Herzl, the feuilleton editor of the *Neue Freie Presse*, was to have 'arrived' on the Austrian literary scene."[20]

In fact, Loos had "arrived" on this literary scene in 1897, after returning from three years in the United States.[21] Loos supported himself for several years in Vienna by publishing design criticism in various Viennese newspapers and journals. Many of Loos's early essays between 1897 and 1900 adhere to the style of the Viennese feuilleton, commonly appearing as a lead front-page piece of cultural commentary in Viennese dailies. Loos, however, went far beyond the limits of a mere disgruntled arbiter from the fashion pages. Instead, he published scathing, satirical reviews of Viennese society and cultural groups, diagnosing hypocrisy and cultural anachronism everywhere. A well-known early essay, for example, attacked the falseness of the facades of the famous Ringstrasse, the pride of late nineteenth-century bourgeois liberal Vienna. Calling the buildings part of a "Potemkin City," Loos likened the monumental Ringstrasse facades to the false building fronts erected in the Potemkin village of the Crimean peninsula by a conquering Russian military commander. The commander had hoped to impress the Russian ruler, Catherine II, by fabricating the appearance of a territory already developed when she passed through on inspection. But if a false stage had been put up in the rural Crimea, such pretense amounted, in Loos's estimation, to blasphemy in Central Europe's purported cultural capital.[22]

Loos's other feuilletons cleverly exploited seemingly minor details found in Viennese clothing, crafts, and other items of material culture. Through comparisons to these objects' counterparts in England and America, Loos inflated his interpretation of Viennese consumer products until they became a virtual index of Viennese backwardness and hopelessness – exhibits of a willful Viennese blindness to the challenge of living in the present. Loos interpreted the gaudy frills of outmoded Viennese clothing (compared to the smart, practical English suit), wallets and leather goods covered with Rococo ornamentation, and "tin bathtubs that aim to look as if they are marble" as part of a Viennese culture steeped in imitation. He identified quality in those objects that had escaped the ornamental applications of art and remained in the control of craftsmen, engineers, and trades workers (such as plumbers), the focus of whose attention had been on practicality and use.[23]

Loos did not shy away from finding direct institutional and personal targets for his attacks. His essay, "Poor Little Rich Man," lambasted the Secession movement's approach to design. Like his other feuilletons, "Poor Little Rich Man" performed the work of the knowing satirist: it took everyday life as the setting in which to tell the woeful tale of a successful man who was virtually strangled in the "total-work-of-art" (*Gesamtkunstwerk*) atmosphere of his house. Secession architects had designed furniture, wall coverings, and even clothing for the client in such excruciating detail that the simple act of living put the dweller in danger – either of injuring himself or of transgressing some ostensibly "artistic" principle governing the design of the house.[24] Loos penned equally aggressive essays with such titles as "The Superfluous Ones" and "Degenerate Art" to attack Hermann Muthesius, the whole Werkbund association, and the Wiener Werkstätte arts and crafts branch, led by Anton von Scala, for foolishly seeking to invent new styles truly "of their time."[25] Loos argued that such a search was pointless: abandoning artistic pretension, the English and the Americans already were introducing the world to a style for the times by using efficient production methods and by respecting older, evolved forms that did not have to be decorated or improved. The one contemporary Austrian for whom Loos reserved praise was Otto Wagner, the architect who had glorified practicality and efficiency as the principles of modern life in his expansion plan for Vienna of 1893, and who had published his ideas in an 1895 textbook for his students at the Vienna Academy of Fine Arts.[26]

Yet, if Loos's early essays contained exaggerated complaints about Viennese imitation in material objects, the essence of the architect's objections became clear in *Das Andere: Ein Blatt zur Einführung Abenländischer Kultur in Österreich* (*The Other: A Newspaper for the Introduction of Western Culture into Austria*), which Loos founded in part through the inspiration of Karl Kraus's radical journal of cultural criticism, *Die Fackel*. Loos's short-lived publication, with a run of two issues in 1903, furthered his polemic with such impressionistic articles as "Clothing," "The Home," "What We Read," "What We Print," and "How We Live."[27] In these pieces, Loos drew the crucial distinction between the culture of the Austrian countryside and the culture of the Austrian city – or, more accurately, the absence of authentic culture in the modern city. To Loos, the cultural authenticity of a people depended on cultural practices and production methods derived from their local context; thus geography as well as temporality figured into his notion of authentic culture. Since most city dwellers were immigrants from the countryside, it was much more difficult for urban centers to realize a culture that was truly their own. This, then, was the challenge of the city: to recognize that modern production methods represented an authentic cultural practice, just as traditional crafts generated the authentic products of rural culture. In a later essay Loos discussed authentic culture as "that balance of man's inner and outer being which alone guarantees rational thought and action." If the urban dweller could only unify his "inner being" with the outer practices being engendered in the modern city – something the Viennese had abjectly failed to do, in Loos's view – then there would exist an authentic urban culture as well.[28]

It was from this perspective that Loos glorified manufactured goods that had not received the beautifying attention of applied arts decorators. Loos rejected as inherently false any urban product that bore applied ornamentation. As long as the typical Viennese city dweller continued to accept outmoded Gothic script in the city's newspapers, along with masses of gaudy decorations from random historical periods on everyday consumer products, Loos argued, he or she was doomed to remain completely out of step with cultural progress.[29] Because Loos defined "progress" in terms of forward-looking Anglo-American accomplishments, Austria stood in need of Western culture's "introduction," as his journal title made plain. Until this happened, Loos's "blind burgher" would continue to buy inferior applied arts goods and "shake his head" at the English assertion that quality products were worth paying for; he also would continue to denigrate farmers and peasants – eighty percent of his country's population, as Loos pointed out – as second-class Austrians.[30]

This cleft between city and country especially bothered Loos. In all of their blindness, the Viennese failed to recognize the responsibility of their city to disseminate culture and civilization throughout the countryside in a process of cultural development. Idealizing the New World as a land unfettered by aristocratic traditions, the Austrian architect claimed to see fewer discrepancies between the American city and countryside. Instead, he perceived America as a place where modernization was dissolving unhealthy divisions between country and city in a process that was equal parts political, economic, and cultural. In short, Loos embraced a view, according to the historian Benedetto Gravagnuolo, that included "a necessary presupposition for a gradual breaking down of the historical discrepancy between town and country," a trajectory of history that Loos felt was being followed in the New World. As something of a wide-eyed traveler from the Old World, Loos idolized the efficiency and practicality of American culture, claiming to sense something Hellenic in its spirit. While leading American architects and engineers in Chicago tackled the new problems of the age – the design of new machine tools, tall buildings, electrical wiring and lighting, and fireproofing – they were availing themselves of the same spirit that enabled classical architects to meet and surpass the technical challenges of their own time.[31] But back in the Old World, Loos wrote in *Das Anderer*,

> When you travel for an hour on the railway and then go on foot for another hour and enter a peasant's house, you meet people who are stranger than those who live a thousand miles away across the sea. We have nothing in common with them … they dress differently, their clothes strike us in the same way as those in the Chinese restaurant of an international exhibition, and their celebration of festivities arouses the same curiosity in us as if we were watching a procession in Ceylon. This is a shameful situation. There are millions of people in Austria who are excluded from the benefits of civilization.[32]

In essence, the model for restoring authenticity was to be found in old Europe's "other," in the New World and its pragmatism. Through the idolization of selected features of American culture – filtered through his stance toward the Old World – Loos constructed a foil for the ornamented, theatrical culture of *fin-de-siècle* Vienna. Using the theatrical feuilleton and the articles in his own journal, he exhorted the Viennese to embrace the present, and to rejuvenate an authentic Austrian character embalmed in ornamental frills.

Yet Loos's conflicting attitudes toward rural culture reveal an ambivalence toward traditional and modern peoples characteristic of many features of early twentieth-century modernism. In some articles, Loos treated the farmer, rural builder, and craftsman as the untainted preserver of an unspoiled crafts tradition – the embodiment of Rousseau's primitive ideal.[33] In other essays, however (and most notably in "Ornament and Crime"), he denigrated peasants as primitive and backward, equating them with tribal peoples whom most Western contemporaries regarded as inferior. If Papuans were "savages" in essays such as "Ornament and Crime," in "Architecture," written two years later in 1910, Loos announced: "I am preparing a new lecture: 'Why the Papuans

Have a Culture While the Germans Do Not.'"[34] This sliding scale of cultural relativity depended on Loos's consideration of different criteria of social development and economic activity, making different cultures seem alternately more primitive or more advanced. Recent scholarship by Mitchell Schwarzer and Patricia Morton has traced connections between Loos's thought and the currents of the social Darwinism of Herbert Spencer, the criminology of Cesare Lombroso, and the teleological anthropology of John Lubbock and the philosopher Condorcet before him. These thinkers, including Loos or his Viennese contemporary, Sigmund Freud, contributed to models of individual and societal development that progressed linearly from primitive savagery to modern civilization. This view was linked to a deep-rooted tradition of modern social scientific thinking that rested upon problematic assumptions of Western superiority.[35]

ORNAMENT, APHORISM, AND CRIME

Loos carried many of the assumptions of modern social science into his design criticism. At the same time, he embellished these through the use of rhetorical techniques common among Viennese literary figures. Loos's criticism most frequently relied on the aphorism, a literary device closely allied with theatricality. As with the feuilleton and with the contours of Loos's thinking in general, the architect's aphoristic mode specifically locates him within a *fin-de-siècle* Viennese intellectual and cultural milieu. Once again the research of William Johnston on "The Vienna School of Aphorists" sheds light on the utility of a writing style known for removing the reader from his or her usual context – a precursor to the reconfiguring of the reader's reality through the arguments of the text.[36] Drawing on the biting wit of such contemporary Viennese authors as Arthur Schnitzler, Hugo von Hofmannsthal, and Karl Kraus, Loos exploited aphorisms as an ideal medium for radically dissembling, questioning, and reordering experience. They provide, moreover, a direct way of understanding his theory and criticism of culture.

A successful aphorism, in the view of students of this genre including William Johnston and J.A. Cuddon, expresses a kernel of wisdom in unconventional terms, addressing readers outside of their specific identities in the world. Aphorisms, in other words, reconfigure a reader's relationship to the commonplace or familiar. Aphorisms also tend to focus on moral rather than aesthetic considerations, furnishing the perfect technique for a writer intent on cultural reform. In commemorating Adolf Loos's death in 1933, architecture journals such as *Architectural Review* chose to publish a list of Loos's aphorisms as a provocative and entertaining "anthology" of the architect's outlook.[37] However, while Loos had observed many of the "chattier" conventions of judging taste in early feuilletons, he pushed the radical, perspective-altering potential of aphorisms to the limit in such essays as "Ornament and Crime" (1908) and "My School of Architecture" (1913).

Architectural theorist Beatriz Colomina has argued that Loos's writings participate in a storytelling tradition that, "like those of (Walter) Benjamin ... have an almost biblical structure." Colomina further asserts that Loos's approach engages in a Benjaminian resistance to that "replacement of [an] earlier storytelling tradition by information, of information by sensation, (which) reflects the increasing atrophy of experience."[38] In my view, however, Loos's rhetoric goes far beyond that of resistance, placing him squarely within a *fin-de-siècle* Viennese cultural milieu. Loos's aphoristic mode bears relatively little relation to the tradition of Benjaminian Marxism. It exhibits, in fact, a constitutive dimension whose building blocks are contained within the aphoristic style. With theatrical gestures and aphoristic flourishes, such Loos essays as "Ornament and Crime" ridicule and dismantle the usual structure of sense by which the reader might reasonably expect to relate to the world.[39]

> To illustrate briefly, Loos begins the following way: The human embryo in the womb passes through all the evolutionary stages of the animal kingdom. When man is born, his sensory impressions are like those of a newborn puppy. His childhood takes him through all the metamorphoses of human history. At two, he sees with the eyes of a Papuan, at four, with those of an ancient Teuton, at six, with those of Socrates, at eight, with those of Voltaire.

After offering similar comments on color theory, tattoos, and the erotic nature of art, Loos makes his point:

> I have made the following discovery and I pass it on to the world: *The evolution of culture is synonymous with the removal of ornament from utilitarian objects* [emphasis original].[40]

The rest of Loos's essay issues similar decrees even as it overreaches. But into the rhetorical space opened up by this performative style, Loos advances a fairly sophisticated theory of culture – though one admittedly riddled with the cultural biases identified by Schwarzer and Morton. With respect to the crafts, trades, and building, Loos's writing advocates a combination of a selective historical consciousness with a sensitivity to present circumstances, which, together, form the cornerstone of his program for Viennese cultural modernization. Influenced by Nietzsche, this program called, on the one hand, for the retention of the best that the ancients had achieved in their time; on the other hand, it called for the use of "new" practices made available by contemporary technological innovations. Truly modern practices, in Loos's view, were continuous with the "spirit" of the modern practices of past eras which had understood themselves as modern.[41]

As observed at the beginning of this article, Stanford Anderson has argued that Loos's achievement consisted of developing a critical awareness of how competing conventions and practice could constructively criticize one another.[42] Loos's writings, I would add, dismantle and reconstitute the reader's understanding within a dense narrative of aphorisms, hyperbole, and theatrical gestures. This writing style represents a radical abandonment of usual notions of narrative time. In so doing, this narrative structure bears some resemblance to Loos's program for simultaneous awareness of past and present in actual social practice. These rhetorical effects also could be said to embody elements of the same "highly differentiated subjectivity" which theorist K. Michael Hays points out has material analogues for Loos in the "insuperable partitions between languages of form." How this subjectivity translates into the everyday lives and practices of architects, designers, or users of buildings, however, is an issue that theorists including Hays still have to explain.[43]

The success of Loos's autonomous narrative logic, which I am suggesting embodied his theory of culture in form and content, derives in large part from the architect's participation in the Viennese milieu of theatricality. The leaders in this milieu formed a constellation of actors who assumed self-conscious roles for the express reason, it was felt, that dramatic personae could mount more effective attacks on Viennese culture. Thus, the wandering aphorist-poet and feuilletonist Peter Altenberg, one of Loos's closest friends, followed the motto "To live artistically," adapted from Nietzsche's *The Gay Science*. Altenberg's reputation and work has led the historian William Johnston to characterize the poet's café behavior, and live and written performances, as a "walking kaleidoscope of worldviews."[44] Karl Kraus, a complex figure who actually denigrated the feuilleton for its violation of his language-based ethics,[45] nevertheless admitted to writing his aphoristic journal, *Die Fackel*, "as an actor" whose utter conviction in the act of performing was meant to convert his masked persona into a "real identity."[46]

Adolf Loos clearly was part of this theatrical yet peculiarly sensitive Viennese culture. This was a culture in which, as William Johnston writes, "Experts at dissimulation, such as (Hermann)

Bahr and (Peter) Altenberg, professed to find no fixity beneath a flux of sensations, while positivists, like (Sigmund) Freud and (Ernst) Mach, ferreted out natural laws behind a welter of detail."[47] Into this matrix can be added the perspectivism of Adolf Loos, whose views were meant to "inoculate" his students of architecture against the mindless copying of classicism. Thus, to Loos, "The present constructs itself on the past just as the past constructed itself on the preceding past. It has never been another way – nor will it ever be any other way."[48]

To conclude, Carl Schorske's classic work on *fin-de-siècle* Vienna characterizes this city as an "infinite whirl of innovation" in which modern ideas appeared against the background of a fading Habsburg Empire.[49] Yet many Viennese innovations contained significant continuities with the past, for example, in the debt that aphorisms owe to the romantic tradition of what is known as the literary "fragment." One prominent theory of late eighteenth-century German romanticism goes so far as to maintain that:

> The motif of the unification of the Ancient and Modern, as it appears so often in the fragments, always refers to the necessity of bringing about a rebirth of ancient naiveté according to modern poetry.[50]

A critical modern awareness is evident here in these eighteenth-century roots of the German-speaking world's aphoristic style, containing a conception of historical simultaneity and perspective that resurfaces through figures such as Nietzsche to influence the literature of Kraus and the writings, and even the book titles, of Adolf Loos. Following a century of modernization and fragmentation in the Habsburg Empire of the nineteenth century, Adolf Loos re-tapped these romantic roots at the opening of the twentieth century. His theory of modern culture, in fact, is nicely encapsulated by historian Jonathan Crary's characterization of the nineteenth century as a whole. He writes: "The destructive dynamism of modernization [in the nineteenth century] was also a condition for a vision that would resist its effects, a revivifying perception of the present caught up in its own historical afterimages."[51] Bounded as he was by his particular historical and cultural context, the figure of Adolf Loos reminds us that, in our own era, among the most arresting visions of modernity are those that transfigure the fragmentation of the present into an intelligible pattern, a pattern somehow continuous with a meaningful past.

NOTES

First published in *Design Issues* 16 no. 2 (Summer 2000): 75–86.

1. This line of interpretation was inaugurated by Nicholas Pevsner in *Pioneers of the Modern Movement From William Morris to Walter Gropius* (London: Faber & Faber, 1936), 188–92.
2. For example, Loos is said to prefigure the International Style by at least eight years in Kenneth Frampton, *Modern Architecture: A Critical History* (New York: Thames and Hudson, 1980), 90–95.
3. Stanford Anderson, "Critical Conventionalism: Architecture," *Assemblage I* (1986): 6–23, quoted in Stanford Anderson, "Critical Conventionalism: The History of Architecture," *Midgard: Journal of Architectural Theory and Criticism,* 1: 1 (1990): 47. The architectural theorist Massimo Cacciari characterizes Loos's philosophy as "negative thought" that seeks to "give an order to the absence of synthesis." See Massimo Cacciari, *Architecture and Nihilism: On the Philosophy of Modern Architecture*, trans. by Steven Sartarelli (New Haven: Yale, 1993), 37.
4. Terry Eagleton, *Literary Theory: An Introduction* (Minneapolis: University of Minnesota Press, 1983), 205.
5. K. Michael Hays, *Modernism and the Posthumanist Subject: The Architecture of Hannes Meyer and Ludwig Hilbersheimer* (Cambridge, MA: MIT Press, 1992); Beatriz Colomina, *Privacy and Publicity: Modern Architecture as Mass Media* (Cambridge, MA: MIT Press, 1994). Both authors make this point but, as with many other examinations of Loos, these works do relatively little to examine the architect's theories in their specific relation – and in their debts – to Loos's Viennese cultural context.
6. William Johnston, *The Austrian Mind: An Intellectual and Social History 1848–1938* (Berkeley: UC Press,

1972), 207, 223, and 397. Paul Engelmann, a Loos disciple, forms a crucial link between Loos, Kraus, and Wittgenstein. As one-time personal secretary to Kraus, Engelmann also was assistant architect of record for Wittgenstein's own house in Vienna's Kundmanngasse, built between 1926 and 1928. See Paul Engelmann, *Letters from Ludwig Wittgenstein: With A Memoir* (Oxford: Blackwell, 1976). For another account, see Dagmar Barnouw, "Loos, Kraus, Wittgenstein, and the Problem of Authenticity" in Gerald Chapple and Hans H. Schulte, eds., *The Turn of the Century: German Literature and Art, 1890–1915*, The McMaster Colloquium on German Studies II (Bonn: Bouvier Verlag, 1981), 249–273.

7. Allan Janik and Stephen Toulmin, *Wittgenstein's Vienna* (New York: Simon & Schuster, 1973); Carl E. Schorske, *Fin-de-Siècle Vienna: Politics and Culture* (New York: Vintage, 1981); and Donald J. Olsen, *The City as a Work of Art: London, Paris, Vienna* (New Haven: Yale University Press, 1986), especially the chapter, "Vienna: Display and Self-Representation," 235–50. Also excellent on this period, though less specifically focused on theatricality, are Jacques Le Rider, *Modernity and Crises of Identity: Culture and Society in Fin-de-Siècle Vienna,* trans. by Rosemary Morris (New York: Continuum, 1993), and Hermann Broch, *Hugo von Hofmannsthal and His Time: The European Imagination, 1860–1920*, trans. by Michael P. Steinberg (Chicago: University of Chicago Press, 1984).
8. Michael P. Steinberg, *The Meaning of the Salzburg Festival: Austria as Theater and Ideology, 1890–1938* (Ithaca, NY: Cornell University Press, 1990).
9. Edward Timms, *Karl Kraus, Apocalyptic Satirist: Culture and Catastrophe in Habsburg Vienna* (New Haven: Yale University Press, 1986), 3–30. See also Kari Grimstad, *Masks of the Prophet: The Theatrical World of Karl Kraus* (Toronto: University of Toronto Press, 1982).
10. Typical treatments of these themes are Robert Musil, *Der Mann ohne Eigenschaften [The Man Without Qualities]* (Reinbeck bei Hamburg: Rohwolt, 1978); and Arthur Schnitzler, *Der Weg ins Freie [The Road Into the Open]* (Wien: Residenz Verlag, 1980).
11. See the discussion of Loos's education in Burkhardt Rukschcio's and Roland Schachel's unsurpassed, 700-page critical biography and catalog, *Adolf Loos: Leben und Werk* (Salzburg: Residenz Verlag, 1982), 14–21.
12. Jonas Barish, *The Anti-theatrical Prejudice* (Berkeley: University of California Press, 1981). See especially 451–69. This study explores the numerous complexities faced historically by Western playwrights, artists, writers, and philosophers who have grappled with the antagonism between theatricality and cultural authenticity.
13. Johnston, *The Austrian Mind*, 203–207.
14. Barnouw, "Loos, Kraus, Wittgenstein," 251–60; Schorske, *Fin-de-Siècle Vienna*, 339–40; Johnston, *The Austrian Mind,* 212–13.
15. Reyner Banham, "Ornament and Crime: The Decisive Contribution of Adolf Loos," *Architectural Review* (February 1957): 86.
16. Colomina, *Privacy and Publicity*, 38–43.
17. Ibid., 65.
18. See the reviews and description of Loos's "free, sparkling speeches" in "Vorträge: Karl Kraus und Adolf Loos," *Prager Tageblatt* Nr. 63 (March 5, 1913): 4; and "Ein reichbegabtes Brünner Kind," *Tagesbote aus Mähren und Schlesien: Feuilleton-Beilage* Nr. 7 (January 4, 1908): 1.
19. Johnston, *The Austrian Mind*, 115–27; and Schorske, *Fin-de-Siècle Vienna,* 7–21.
20. Janik and Toulmin, *Wittgenstein's Vienna*, 46.
21. On the journey to the U.S., see Rukschcio and Schachel, *Adolf Loos: Leben und Werk*, 21–32.
22. Loos, "Die potemkische stadt" (Juli 1898), *Sämtliche Schriften* (Wien: Verlag Herold, 1962), 153–56. All citations are from the German text, but Loos's early essays between 1897 and 1900 have been reprinted in an English translation in Adolf Loos, *Spoken Into The Void*, trans. by Jane O. Newman and John H. Smith (Cambridge, MA: MIT Press, 1982).
23. Loos, "Lederwaren und Gold- und Silberschmiedekunst," "Herrenmode," and "Die Plumber" (originally in *Die Neue Freie Presse*, May 15, May 22, and July 17, 1898 respectively) in *Sämtliche Schriften*:15–25; and 70–7.
24. Loos, "Von einem armen reichen manne" (April 26, 1900), *Sämtliche Schriften*: 201–7.
25. Loos, "Die Überflüssigen" and "Entartete Kunst" (1908) in *Sämtliche Schriften*: 267–75.
26. Loos, "Die Interieurs in der Rotunde," *Neue Freie Presse* (June 12, 1898); and "Das Sitzmöbel," *Neue Freie Presse* (June 19, 1898) in *Sämtliche Schriften*: 40–54. Also see the discussion of Loos and Wagner in Rukschcio and Schachel, *Adolf Loos: Leben und Werk*, 48–9.
27. Loos, *Das Andere: Ein Blatt zur Einführung Abendländischer Kultur in Österreich* 1: 2 (1903), reproduced in facsimile by Carlo Pirovano, ed. (Milan: Gruppo Editoriale Electa, 1982). Mark Wigley examines the relationships between clothing, dress, and the development of modern

architecture in *White Walls, Designer Dresses: The Fashioning of Modern Architecture* (Cambridge, MA: MIT Press, 1995).

28. Loos, "Architektur" (1910) in *Sämtliche Schriften*, 303.
29. In a 1921 foreword to his first book of essays written between 1897 and 1900, Loos enlisted the authority of the philologist-folklorist Jakob Grimm in order to criticize the Gothic "Fraktur" script, and to explain why he had not capitalized any of the common nouns in his early essays. Loos regarded this German convention as a degenerate, "distorted fashion" of writing that produced a "purposeless proliferation of capital letters." See "Vorwort," *Sämtliche Schriften*: 10.
30. Loos, "Abendländische Kultur," "Was man Verkauft," *Das Andere*, n.1 (1903), pp. 1–3.
31. Loos, "Wiener Architekturfragen" (*Reichspost Morgenblatt*, October 1, 1910), *Sämtliche Schriften*: 299–300.
32. Loos, *Das Andere*. The translated quote is from Benedetto Gravagnuolo, *Adolf Loos: Theory and Works* (New York: Rizzoli, 1982), 44.
33. Adolf Loos, "Architektur" (1910), *Sämtliche Schriften*: 302–18.
34. Ibid., 303.
35. Mitchell Schwarzer, "Ethnologies of the Primitive in Adolf Loos's Writings on Ornament," *Nineteenth-Century Contexts* 18 (1994): 225–47. For a useful discussion of Loos in the broader context of nineteenth-century German architectural theory, see Mitchell Schwarzer, *German Architectural Theory and the Search for Modern Identity* (New York: Cambridge University Press, 1995), especially 238–60; Patricia Morton, "Modern Architecture and Its Discontents: Loos and Le Corbusier on Ornament," (paper presented at the Annual Meeting of the College Art Association, Toronto, February 1998).
36. William Johnston, "The Vienna School of Aphorists, 1880–1930: Reflections on a Neglected Genre" in Chapple and Schulte, eds. (see note 6), 275–90.
37. "Adolf Loos Anthology: Basic Principles," *Architectural Review* 76 (October 1934): 151. J.A. Cuddon discusses the aphorism in *A Dictionary of Literary Terms* (Garden City, NJ: Doubleday, 1977), 376–7.
38. Colomina, "On Adolf Loos and Josef Hoffman: Architecture in the Age of Mechanical Reproduction" in Max Risselada, ed., *Raumplan Versus Plan Libre* (New York: Rizzoli, 1988), 74.
39. Loos's "Ornament and Crime," in which his earlier arguments reach a kind of rhetorical crescendo, is the best example of this practice. Quoted in Ulrich Conrads, *Programs and Manifestoes on 20th-Century Architecture* (Cambridge, MA: MIT Press, 1970), 19–20.
40. Loos in Conrads, 19–20.
41. Loos's debts and similarities to Nietzschean "historical perspectivism" are developed in Taisto H. Makela, "Modernity and the Historical Perspectivism of Nietzsche and Loos," *Journal of Architectural Education* 44: 3 (May 1991): 138–43. For a brief discussion of other German-speaking architects' reception of Nietzsche, see Steven E. Aschheim, *The Nietzsche Legacy in Germany, 1890–1990* (Berkeley: UC Press, 1992), 33–4, 48; and also Fritz Neumeyer, *The Artless Word: Mies van der Rohe on the Building Art*, trans. by Mark Jarzombek (Cambridge, MA: MIT Press, 1992), 53–61, 87–93.
42. Anderson, "Critical Conventionalism: The History of Architecture," *Midgard: Journal of Architectural Theory and Criticism* 1:1 (1990): 47.
43. K. Michael Hays, *Modernism and the Posthumanist Subject*, 62.
44. Edward Timms, *Karl Kraus: Apocalyptic Satirist*, 194. Johnston, *The Austrian Mind*, 123. For an in-depth documentary study of Altenberg, see Andrew Barker and Leo Lensing, *Peter Altenberg: Rezept die Welt zu Sehen* (Wien: Braumüller, 1995).
45. Johnston, *The Austrian Mind*, 122.
46. Edward Timms notes how much the aestheticized, conscious self-fashioning of Altenberg, Kraus, and (through Kraus) Loos owed to Oscar Wilde and Friedrich Nietzsche. Significantly for Loos's own crusade at the time, Kraus reprinted such Nietzschean aphorisms in a 1908 issue of *Die Fackel* in the definition of the artist as "a person for whom form is coextensive with content." This discussion of theatricality has benefited greatly from the analysis of Timms, 188–195.
47. Johnston, *The Austrian Mind*, 397.
48. Adolf Loos, "Meine Bauschule" (1913), in *Sämtliche Schriften*: 323.
49. Schorske, *Fin-de-Siècle Vienna*, xix.
50. Philippe Lacoue-Labarthe and Jean-Luc Nancy, *The Literary Absolute: The Theory of Literature in German Romanticism*, trans. by Philip Barnard and Cheryl Lester (Albany: SUNY Press, 1988), 49.
51. Jonathan Crary, *Techniques of the Observer: On Vision and Modernity in the Nineteenth Century* (Cambridge, MA: MIT Press, 1990), 21.

7

THE THINGS THAT MATTER

Peter-Paul Verbeek and Petran Kockelkoren

1 INTRODUCTION

Things have been rediscovered. Scholars who are studying the role of technology in our culture more and more come to the conclusion that it is not enough to look at ideas only. Philosophers of technology, who used to examine technology as a way of interpreting the world, and thus making technology a branch of philosophy, are increasingly interested in technological *artifacts*. And sociologists of technology, who used to study the social interaction out of which new technologies emerge, have come to the conclusion that this interaction cannot be studied without taking the role of *things* into account. This turn towards things brings science and technology studies closer to discussions within industrial design, where it is, after all, quite common to think about things.

In this article, we organize a confrontation between both. We will do this by discussing the way of "looking at things" of an interesting group of Dutch industrial designers, who joined under the name "Eternally Yours." Eternally Yours develops ideas about "cultural sustainability" or, better, "durability." It considers the currently most common approach to eco-design – Life Cycle Analysis – to be insufficient. Life Cycle Analysis may make it possible to design products that are friendlier to the environment, but leaves a fundamental problem unaddressed: the short lifetime of our products. We live in a throwaway culture. We discard products while they are still in good shape. It is not enough to make less polluting products, however important that may be, when they are replaced at high speed because people throw them away too soon. The environmental crisis is not only a technological problem, but a cultural problem as well. Therefore, according to Eternally Yours, we should not only strive for *sustainability*, but also for *durability*, by designing products in a way that stimulates longevity.

To be able to discuss the diagnosis and therapies of Eternally Yours, we will take a somewhat curious step backward. Something strange stands out when looking at the history of design. The discipline that consists of being occupied with matter, strangely enough seems to be trapped within a way of thinking that is the very counterpart of materialism. When designers discuss products, they almost always talk about them in terms of signs, functions, meanings, or styles. What they usually fail to do is to understand them as *material entities* that play a certain role in our lives and culture. Designers seem to be Platonists, considering objects to be only derivative "copies" of primordial ideas.

We believe this way of thinking cannot sufficiently meet the challenge of durability, as we will explain later. Against the dominant Platonism, we will propose an approach to our material culture that takes matter more seriously. We take our inspiration from the phenomenological work of the American philosophers Albert Borgmann[1] and Don Ihde.[2] Phenomenology always has wanted to return to "the things themselves" until it was frustrated in that by the "linguistic turn" of philosophy. We will try to formulate a phenomenological design approach that takes this linguistic turn seriously, without giving up the idea that matter matters.

2 ETERNALLY YOURS?

"It's time for a new generation of products that can age slowly and in a dignified way, become our partners in life, and support our memories." These famous words of Italian designer Ezio Manzini are on the letterhead of Eternally Yours. Eternally Yours was founded in 1995. It arose from worries about the ongoing stream of superficial products, designed to be discarded after only a short time no matter how well-functioning. Those worries do not only concern obvious throwaway products such as disposable teaspoons and cups. Research for the Dutch Ministry of Environmental Affairs has shown that a large proportion of objects for everyday use including hi-fi equipment, stoves, razors, and computers is discarded while still functional.[3] Even worse, some products do *not even reach the market*. Eternally Yours actually witnessed, at a recycling company, new computer hard disk drives being destroyed because they were already outdated before they could be sold.

If we want to design in a sustainable way, according to Eternally Yours, the most important thing is to extend the lifetime of products. This is no obvious solution. Eternally Yours discerns four possible directions within sustainable design. The first is shifting from products to services as much as possible. Extensive services involving products such as repairing, upgrading, and renting can result in a more intensive use of products. This will reduce production and, thus, pollution. A second direction is eco-design, already mentioned, which tries to minimize pollution in all stages of the lifetime of products. A third direction is recycling. Reusing parts of discarded products can reduce energy and material use. The fourth and least common direction is that of Eternally Yours: trying to elongate the lifespan of products.

Why are so many products prematurely discarded – before they are worn out or broken? Eternally Yours discerns three dimensions in the lifespan of products: the technical, the economical, and the psychological lifespan. Products are discarded because they simply are broken and cannot be repaired; because they are economically outdated, e.g., because new models have appeared on the market; or because they do not fit our preferences and lifestyle anymore. Eternally Yours believes the psychological lifespan is the most important. Often, products are discarded because their psychological time is over. Therefore, the significant question for sustainable design is: how can the psychological lifetime of products be prolonged?

Eternally Yours offers three answers to this question. First, under the header "Shape 'n' Surface," Eternally Yours searches for forms and materials that can create longevity. Materials are being tested that do not become unattractive while aging. Leather, for instance, may become more beautiful when it has been used for some time; whereas a shiny, polished chromium surface starts to look worn out with the first scratch. A second area of attention is "Sales 'n' Services," which examines how services connected with products can influence the length of their lifespans. Eternally Yours thinks it is important for companies to shift the focus of their attention from producing and selling products to maintaining relationships with customers. If these relationships have a durable character so will the products, because they are the focus of those relationships. Thirdly, under the header of "Signs 'n' Scripts," Eternally Yours investigates the way in which products function as symbols or icons for our lifestyles, and contain implicit prescriptions about how to use them ("scripts"). Stories involving products can give them more "character." Their iconological character makes them "fit" our lifestyle or not. A favorite Eternally Yours example of this is an old advertisement for Nikon cameras. It showed a camera that had been lying on the bottom of the ocean for ten years, but nevertheless still worked.

The product is not portrayed as the latest model with the newest features, but as a reliable product the owner can be proud of.[4]

3 THE PLATONISM OF DESIGN

However important and illuminating those strategies of Eternally Yours may be, in our opinion, they show a certain one-sidedness. Whereas their aim is to extend the "psychological lifespan" of products by creating a bond between users and products, the products themselves, as material objects, are hardly relevant anymore. In all three strategies, products are reduced to something nonmaterial: to signs, to actors in a story, to "character." Seemingly following Plato, the most primordial role is not given to matter but to ideas. In "Signs 'n' Scripts," the *stories* around products are central; and in "Sales 'n' Services," products are only relevant as *conversation pieces*. Only in "Shape 'n' Surface" products are seen as *objects*, but here the physical characteristics of products seem to be immediately translated into terms of attractiveness.

This implies that the bond that may arise between the user and the product will mainly concern the nonmaterial that is represented by the product, and not the material thing itself. And such a product could be replaced by any other product with the same nonmaterial quality. The attachment these products evoke does not concern the products *themselves*, but only the *ideas* they embody. To be sure, we do not want to deny that the initiatives of Eternally Yours can influence the lifetime of products in a positive way. But we think important opportunities are lost because of this bias towards the nonmaterial.

A SHORT HISTORY OF IDEAS

This Platonism is not unique in Eternally Yours, but is part of a long tradition. The Platonic reduction of matter to ideas has been a characteristic of the discipline of industrial design since its very beginnings.[5] The discipline came into being with the rise of mass production during the second half of the nineteenth century, since mass production explicitly demands that design and production are separated. At first, a romantic countermovement arose: the Arts and Crafts movement of the second half of the nineteenth century. Standardization and mechanization were considered dangerous, both aesthetically and socially. The Arts and Crafts movement tried to cope with these dangers by returning to medieval handicraft techniques, and by producing objects that were both useful and beautiful, according to William Morris "a thing of beauty and a joy forever." But, after the short transition period of Art Nouveau (*Jugendstil*) – which did not reject mass production but decorated products with organic forms, such as leaves and the female nude, which were supposed to refer to nature and thus to counterbalance the technological character of the production process – mechanization nevertheless took command.[6] Modernism got its way.

Instead of rejecting it, romantically, at the beginning of the twentieth century, the Modern Movement embraced the machine as a source of inspiration. Design should follow the rule of the machine in two respects. First, like a machine, products had to be *functional*. This functionalism can be considered the main characteristic of modernism. The slogan of modernist design clearly expresses this: *Form Follows Function*. Besides this, the machine ruled in a second way: the form of products was now dictated by the mechanical production process used to create them. The function that was followed was not only the function of the artifact produced, but also the functioning of the machine that produced the artifact. Modernism led to functional products with simple, geometric forms.

It should be noted that not all design of this period was of the "hard-core" modernist nature described above. In popular design, several "mild" variants of modernism developed, of which "streamlining" ("styling") in the USA and

Art Deco in France are good examples. These styles can be seen as "shallow functionalism," in that they applied the philosophy of modernism only to style and decoration. They did not really let form follow function, but developed forms that only *looked* functional because they reminded us of machines. Streamlined objects, e.g., those made to look like airplanes, and Art Deco used geometric shapes and electric flashes for decoration. Modernism thus was converted into a decorative style which is, of course, at odds with "hard-core" functionalism which eschewed decoration.

Modernism remained very influential until after World War II, although style gradually became more important. During the fifties, a new style emerged: Contemporary Style. New materials and production techniques were invented and used with great enthusiasm, which eventually led to the new style with its well-known hot-pink colors and its light furniture with thin, metal legs. The growing importance of style was the first indication that functionalism was gradually fading away. But it was only in the sixties that modernism was *fundamentally* challenged. Pop Design arose, which explicitly rejected the modernist obsession with functionality and durability. Opposed to this, it put the *consumer* at the center. Modernist design was considered not to fit the lifestyle of the rising youth culture. It was found that design had to be temporary instead of durable, and funny instead of functional. A new aesthetic arose: a throwaway aesthetic.[7] Design did not have to be functional anymore, but nice.

Pop Design paved the way for a definitive break with modernism. This break occurred in the seventies, when postmodern design was developed. Postmodern design explicitly rejects the modernist emphasis on functionality and durability. Products should not be conceived as machines. They are not only objects that fulfill functions, but also embodiments of *meaning*. People do not only use products as tools: products have become icons of their lifestyle and social status. And since culture had become pluralist, material culture should be as well. Therefore, postmodernism is not a name for a specific style, but for an explosion of styles. There are many subcultures and lifestyles in our culture, and all of these correspond to styles of products. The eclecticism of postmodern design turns away from the one-dimensional philosophy of modernism that had been dominating design for such a long time. *Form Follows Function* has been replaced by *Form Follows Fun*.

IDEAS IN MASS PRODUCTION

This short history shows that Platonism has been present in industrial design since its very beginnings. Modern as well as postmodern design considered products to be imprints in matter of something nonmaterial that was considered to be primordial.

The functionalist desire to design products that function well, are durable, and can be easily produced in large quantities reduced artifacts to the function they are supposed to fulfill. Of course, this functionality needs matter in which to be embodied but matter eventually is of secondary importance. It is not the object that counts, but the function it fulfills. Form follows function: it is necessary but derivative.

As the German philosopher Karl Jaspers already indicated in the early thirties, this stress on function results in a loss of attachment with products. When artifacts are designed mainly to fulfill a function, their individual characteristics become less important. Products, according to Jaspers, then develop toward ideal types that function well and can be produced easily but are not worth attention:

> When [the ideal type] has been realized, attachment to one specific exemplar indeed has no relevance anymore; one only loves the form, not the specific object. Despite all artificiality, one has a strange, new nearness to the objects, … namely to them in their function.[8]

From this perspective, the meaningfulness of products in postmodern design seems to be a giant improvement. Not the functional, but the symbolic character of artifacts has now become central in design. Jaspers's critique is outdated: his call for meaning has become irrelevant now that postmodern design has shown an explosion of meaning. Mass-produced objects can be obtained in so many styles that fear of a unification of material culture appears to be unnecessary.

But Jaspers's critique is not as outdated as it may seem. Indeed, retrospectively, we have to conclude that his critique, in fact, concerned functionalism and not "design" as such. But this historical contextualization does not make his observation of a lack of attachment to products irrelevant. This, after all, is exactly the same thing that troubles Eternally Yours. Postmodern design is trapped within another form of Platonism. It does not reduce products to their function, but to *meaning*. Postmodern products have become icons, symbols, or signs. They do not even need to be durable anymore, as they did for modernist design. The attachment such products evoke concerns their meaning and not themselves as material objects. They could, after all, be replaced by any other object with the same sign-value.

4 THINGS AS THINGS?

In short, industrial design has always been a Platonic discipline, concerned primarily with ideas and only in the second instance with things. The same goes for Eternally Yours. Attempts to realize "durable design" should not only focus on signs, shapes, surfaces, sales, and services. However important they are, all of these items – we deliberately did not mention "scripts," which will become clear later – fail to take the materiality of products into account. They understand products as elements of all kinds of *languages*: languages of form, of product meaning, and of relationships between company and customer. But when we strip all nonmaterial aspects of products, something remains that is more than language; more than symbol, meaning, function, or icon. What remains is the thing as *thing*. The deconstruction of the meaning of things hits something that is not reducible to language or meaning. But how can we do justice to this "thing as thing"?

The notion of a reality outside of language has become quite unpopular in philosophy, to say the least. The "linguistic turn" at the beginning of this century brought the insight that people never have access to reality immediately, but only mediated by language. Our interpretations determine what is "real" for us, and since interpretations take place within a language, the language in which we think determines what counts for us as "reality." People who refer to a reality outside of language, are termed "naive realists." What people call "reality" is, in fact, a construction of interpretations that could have been different. The task of the philosopher, therefore, is not to develop clarifying interpretations of the world, but to deconstruct the constructions we have come to see as "real."

And now do we come to report about the things themselves, the solid bottom we hit when we deconstruct them? It looks more dangerous than it really is. The mediated character of our access to things does not have to be denied if we, nevertheless, want to say something about them. Certainly, artifacts always are situated in a context and can be understood as constructions. But that does not mean it is impossible to think about the role these constructions play, concretely, in our culture. But how can we do this?

SCRIPTS

A new concept recently has been added to the toolkit of science and technology studies that seems to be helpful here. In her article, "The Description of Technical Objects,"[9] Madeleine Akrich developed the notion of the "script" of technical objects. A script, according to her, is the deposit in an object of the world-view of designers. Designers define users in terms of their taste, competence, motives, aspirations, and political prejudices. Such definitions then are "inscribed" into the technical contents of the object. Designers anticipate the use people will make of the product they are designing and, because of that, products contain implicit "manuals." Things co-shape the use that is made of them: they define relations between people, and distribute responsibilities between people and things. Technologies create a framework for action – even though it is never certain that they will be used in the way the designers intended.

This notion of "scripts" has become very popular in science and technology studies. Philosophers and sociologists have a warm interest in *things*. It is, by the way, quite remarkable that things got this attention only recently. In 1986, the American philosopher Langdon Winner wrote an article called "Do Artifacts Have Politics?"[10] – a question he answered, of course, affirmatively. Winner offered the example of bridges over a road to a beach in New York. Those bridges had been built so low that only cars can pass below them while buses can't. This implied that only people who could afford a car (read: white people) were able to reach the beach. But examples can be found closer to home as well. Most disabled people will not be amused by all this philosophical and sociological boast about "things" and their "scripts." They know the script of thresholds, stairs, and revolving doors all too well – and knew them before philosophers even had found words for it.

In our opinion, however, the concept of "script" does not escape the Platonic tradition of reducing things to language and interpretation. The first reason for this is that Akrich puts so much emphasis on the *origin* of scripts: she sees them as "inscribed visions" of designers. This way of looking at objects shifts attention again from the things themselves to the ideas they embody. In the context of this article, however, we are not so much interested in the *origin* of scripts as in the ways in which artifacts themselves are able to *give shape* to the practices around them. And also those practices are relevant that were not intended beforehand. The disabled will, after all, be even less amused with the suggestion that the practices around thresholds and revolving doors were explicitly intended by industrial designers. Those thresholds and doors should not be seen as nonhuman substitutes for guards who keep disabled people outside. They perform in a way we did not ask them to. To keep out the draft is the task we delegated to them, not to keep disabled people outside as well. Things do more than we tell them to do.

There is a second way in which the concept of "script" leaves open the door for Plato. It also can be used to describe how objects shape their environment as *signs* and not as *things*. Nelly Oudshoorn indicates, e.g., that "gender scripts" for her are "materialized definitions of gender." Part of such definitions is the technological competence of users. The script of certain technologies, according to her, defines women as technologically incompetent: "Razors, unlike ladyshavers, can be opened with a screwdriver, which offers men the opportunity to not only use but also repair the device."[11] The script that Oudshoorn reveals here is only partially the script of the razor as a *thing*. As a thing, it allows men to open and repair it, but Oudshoorn is not interested in this "reparability-script," but in the "gender-script" of the device. And this gender-script does not originate from the razor as *thing* but as *sign*. A product that can be opened *refers to* the technological competence of users. Since razors are designed for men, they define men as technologically competent. The ladyshaver, contrarily, which cannot be opened, defines women as technologically not competent. However important and illuminating it is to reveal scripts such as this, they do not concern artifacts as things but only as signs.

TECHNOLOGICAL INTENTIONALITY

We thus need a new concept to clarify the relation between people and products if we want to take products seriously *as things*. Such a concept can be found in Don Ihde's work *Technology and the Lifeworld*. He develops a perspective on technology that does justice to both the mediated character of people's relation to reality and the "own weight" of technical artifacts. Since Ihde is a phenomenologist, his analysis starts from the fundamental relatedness of people and their world.[12] "The" world does not exist for us; we can only access "our" world, which is the world as it is disclosed *by us*. From this perspective, it is impossible to speak about technology without taking into account the relationship people have with it. An artifact without people relating to it would be no more than a "piece of junk lying around." It becomes a technology only *in relation to people*. A technology is always a technology-to-..., and this "to-..." gives the artifact its identity. The telephone, e.g., originally was designed to assist the hearing impaired, but in the cultural context it entered it developed a much broader identity. What this technology "really" is cannot be determined. A technological artifact doesn't have an "essence," no identity "in itself." It is, as Ihde calls it, "multistable." It depends on the context in which a technology finds itself, what that technology "is."

But Ihde does not stop at this contextualization of technology. There is more to say about things than that they receive their identity only in a context. "Once technologies have received a (relative) identity," according to Ihde, "*within that relation* they nevertheless can have an own weight." Ihde calls this "own weight" *technological intentionality*. With this concept, he wants to indicate that technologies-in-use are no neutral objects, but that they themselves co-shape the use that is being made of them. Practices around technologies cannot be entirely reduced to human intentions.

Ihde, for instance, describes the difference in writing style that occurs when writing with a pen, a typewriter, and a word processor. When using a pen, people usually write rather slowly, which invites them to write longer, well-thought-out sentences. The speed of writing that a typewriter allows makes possible a style that comes close to spoken language. A word processor, in turn, invites careful layout and editing, and can be held responsible for the giant growth in the use of footnotes because it makes it so easy to place them. In all of these instances, no obligation is involved, but rather inclination: technologies invite certain ways of dealing with them. The use that is being made of technologies cannot be completely understood by looking at the human half of the human-technology pairing.

The concept of "technological intentionality" thus makes visible nonlingual aspects of the relation between people and things. It does not reduce artifacts to "signs" or "intentions of designers," but indicates the way in which they are present and help to shape their environment *as things*.

SCRIPTS VERSUS INTENTIONALITIES

The best way to illustrate that Ihde's phenomenological approach reveals other aspects of products than the "scripts" approach is to give an example. We take it from Cynthia Cockburn's and Susan Ormrod's book *Gender and Technology in the Making*.[13] In this book, the gender-loadedness of the microwave oven is analyzed as present in its design, production, sale, and use. We freely pick some elements from their story to illustrate our point.

Cockburn and Ormrod describe how the microwave oven originally was designed and marketed as a high-tech gadget. It entered a cooking practice which was not very hospitable to it, especially because it originally was not able to give our food the crispy crusts we like so much. Nevertheless, there was a market for it: it was sold in stores along with the hi-fi and TV sets as one of the "toys for the boys." Cooking with it was a real adventure, because you had to pre-program the thing to be able to cook with it: the intensity and duration of the radiation had to be set with the help of a lot of displays, handles, and buttons. But soon this market became saturated, and a new definition of the microwave oven had to be launched. Now, it no longer was portrayed as a high-tech gadget, but as a simple cooking instrument. As such, it was supposed to enter the domain of women. It was not sold as a "browngood" anymore, but as "whitegood." It found itself a place between the stoves and washing machines, and even got a white cover. The main change, however, was that it became much easier to operate. To operate a microwave, you do not even have to be able to read anymore: all handles have been replaced by buttons with pictograms on them. If you want to heat a cup of soup, you just push the button with a cup of soup on it. In this way, the supposed fear and incompetence of women concerning technology was met.

Although Cockburn and Ormrod do not speak about the microwave oven in terms of "scripts" we could say, in line with Oudshoorn, that the microwave oven clearly contains a gender script. Because of the places where it is sold, it is seen as a technology for women. And because of the way it now is operated, it stigmatizes those women as technologically incompetent. But, as was the case with Oudshoorn's analysis of the ladyshaver, this "gender-script" stems from the oven as a *sign* and not as a *thing* Operation by means of pictograms *stands for* technological incompetence.

As a *thing*, the microwave contains a quite different "script" or, better, intentionality. When looking at it as a thing, the question is relevant how it co-shapes the practices around it by its very *functioning*, instead of the qualities it *refers to*. Cockburn and Ormrod also offer examples of this. They show that the microwave, contrary to what one would expect, does not facilitate cooking at all. Indeed, it makes possible a much faster preparation of meals, but precisely because of that, it invites eaters to make individual menu demands. Sometimes, four dinners are prepared with it instead of one. Besides this, the microwave has dramatically decreased the frequency with which people eat together. Microwave ovens are particularly suited for instant meals, and those are preferably consumed individually.

In the latter two examples, the microwave oven is present as a thing, not as a sign. The effects of the introduction of the microwave cannot be understood as resulting from the intentions of designers, nor from its sign-character. It is because of the way it functions *as a thing*, that it co-shapes the cooking and eating practice around it. What it "is" within those practices, of course, cannot be *completely* reduced to the oven itself – it remains "multistable," – but it nevertheless has more "intentionality" than its designers gave it and its sign-character could accomplish.

It can be concluded that the concept of "intentionality" makes visible phenomena other than "scripts." And we believe *that it is precisely those intentionalities that are* of utmost importance for the designing practice, and for Eternally Yours. We will elaborate on this.

5 TOWARDS A MATERIALIST APPROACH

What does this turn towards the "things themselves" imply for the concrete practice of industrial design? What "materialist" alternative does it offer for the dominant Platonic approach toward things? In order to answer this question, we will discuss two forms of technological intentionality, inspired by the early work of Heidegger and the American philosopher Albert Borgmann. The intentionalities we will discuss concern ways in which products invite us to have a relationship with them as things, and not as signs. Under the header "transparent objects," we will take up Heidegger's notion of "readiness-to-hand," and under the header "engaging objects," Borgmann's concept of "engagement."

TRANSPARENT OBJECTS

Suppose you are listening to music on your Walkman, and the wire that connects your Walkman with the adapter it receives its current from breaks. You want to repair the wire but, when you try to, you discover the adapter is sealed. Repair is impossible: opening the adapter will only make things worse. The only thing you can do is to buy a new one.

Already in the twenties, people thought about inconveniences like this. Heidegger then analyzed, in *Sein und Zeit*, the relation between people and tools.[14] He concluded that there are two modes of this relationship. Use objects can be present-at-hand or ready-to-hand. When everything is working properly, they are ready-to-hand, absorbed into our everyday dealing with the world around us. Our involvement with the world takes place, as it were, *through* the object. When hammering, our attention is not directed towards the hammer but towards the nail we want to get into the wall. The hammer, in a certain sense, withdraws from our relationship with the world. But when something goes wrong, for instance when the hammer breaks in two (or the wire on your adapter breaks), it suddenly is not ready-to-hand anymore, but becomes present-at-hand. Our relationship with the object is transformed into a distanced attention to it. The familiarity is broken. We cannot embody the object anymore: it draws all attention towards itself and has to be repaired for the readiness-to-hand to be restored.

From this distinction between readiness-to-hand and presence-at-hand, two forms of technological intentionality can be derived which are important for a "materialist" approach within design. First: products must allow for a return from presence-at-hand to readiness-to-hand, if a durable relationship with their users is desired. Precisely, this was the problem with the adapter: once the readiness-to-hand was broken, our relationship with the product had to be ended. In order to allow for a return to readiness-to-hand, products have to be transparent in the sense that they allow us to reintegrate them in our action. The importance of this transparency does not only lie in the *repairability* that it results in: that would only enhance *physical* lifetime. Transparency enables people to sustain their *relationship* with the product, even when something goes wrong. And that relationship is what determines what Eternally Yours calls the "psychological lifetime" of products.

The second implication of the distinction between readiness-to-hand and presence-at-hand has farther-reaching consequences. From Heidegger's analysis also can be derived the fact that products must be transparent to be ready-to-hand at all. If no familiarity with a product can come about, and if all of our attention directed to the product itself and not to what we can do *with* it, the product will not be *used.* This seems a trivial statement, but it has implications which are not trivial at all.

When products are ready-to-hand, they permit engagement with the world "through" themselves. Don Ihde calls this, following Merleau-Ponty, the "embodiment" of objects. Objects can be, as it were, parts of our body. When using a pair of glasses, we do not look *at* our glasses, but *through* them to the world. Embodied or ready-to-hand objects thus play a *mediating* role: they help to shape our relationship with the world. And it is precisely in this mediation that artifact intentionality is at work. The intentionality of technological objects, as it were, enters the relationship between people and their world. Within the framework of this article, we are especially interested in *the role of the artifact* within this process of mediation. A closer analysis of this role, in the following paragraph, shows that there are two ways in which artifacts can withdraw from our involvement with the world: in an engaging way and a disengaged way. The latter hinders a durable relationship with products, whereas the former enables it.

ENGAGING OBJECTS

The example of the adapter again is a good starting point for an analysis of the different ways in which artifacts can "withdraw." An adapter withdraws from the praxis of listening to music in the sense that it is not noticed when we are listening. It does not ask for our attention, and yet it enables a praxis. Nonetheless, the *way in which* the adapter is ready-to-hand does not evoke a durable relationship with it. Not only because it does not allow for a return to readiness-to-hand when it breaks down, as we saw, but because its readiness-to-hand is of a purely *functional* nature. An adapter withdraws from our involvement with the world in such a way that we, in fact, do not have a relationship with it as an *object*, but only as something fulfilling a function. It works, and that's all.

Compare this to the way in which, e.g., a piano is ready-to-hand. A piano withdraws from our relationship with the world as well, in that it does not direct our attention towards itself but to the music we make with it. But the piano is not only functionally present here. Even though it's not the focal point of our attention, it nevertheless does form the focus around which the praxis of making music takes place. It withdraws, in a certain sense, but without ending our involvement with it. The reason for this is that it embroils us in its functioning: we have to *play* it. From its withdrawn position, it still asks for involvement.

We could call this phenomenon the *engaging capacity* of objects. The concept of "engagement" was introduced by the American philosopher Albert Borgmann. Borgmann's work concerns the role of technology in our everyday life. He developed a theory of technology which sheds more light on the mediating role of objects we are discussing here. According to Borgmann, the technological objects of our time differ from pre-technological ones in that they diminish people's engagement with each other and with the world around them. Technological products – "devices," as Borgmann calls them – can be seen as consisting of two elements. They are a "machinery" – the product as a physical object – which delivers a "commodity" when functioning. Our central heating system, for instance, is a device. Its tubes, radiators, thermostat, and heater are machinery and warmth the commodity. It is characteristic of modern technology that it shows an ever-growing commodification. Technology promises disburdenment and enrichment: we will get more for less. New products are being developed continuously with their major aim to deliver more commodities easily, quickly, ubiquitously, and safely.

In this process of increasing availability of commodities, the machinery of products necessarily withdraws to the background. Commodities, after all, can only be delivered easily, quickly, ubiquitously, and safely when the machinery demands as little attention as possible. The route towards commodities should be short, and preferably not even be noticeable. Devices only function satisfactorily if they do so with as little human involvement as possible – otherwise we would not need a device to do this for us. This withdrawal of the machinery of products diminishes our engagement with material culture. Devices are designed to leave us aside of their functioning: they do not ask for engagement, but for *consumption*.

This is not wrong per se. But the situation, according to Borgmann, would become problematic if *all* things that ask for engagement would be replaced by devices that procure their commodities instantaneously. That would reduce our existence to the immediate consumption of what is delivered to us whenever we wish, without any engagement with the world being required of us. To be clear, Borgmann does not reject technology – that would, after all, be a denial of the liberating and enriching character of technology. Borgmann only pleads for the preservation of spaces where engagement remains possible. This engagement, for him, has the form of "focal practices," centered around "focal things." Focal things, which also can be high-tech products, are things that ask for attention and involvement: they desire a practice that cannot be characterized by consumption but by "engagement."

One could also draw a different therapy from Borgmann's diagnosis – a therapy that is especially relevant for industrial design. Borgmann's analysis of material culture can imply a solution for the diminishing attachment with products that fits our materialist orientation. If we want our attachment to be directed toward objects and not only toward their meaning and the lifestyle they represent, it would be wise to design products from the perspective of their *engaging capacity*. This could be done by healing the split between machinery and commodity, thus creating a revaluation of the machinery of products. Product machinery should be freed from its withdrawal and be visible, accessible, and understandable again. Where possible, *dependent objects* should be created instead of *quasi-autonomous objects*. Accessible machineries which allow participation in their functioning, or in their recovery when they malfunction, could create a bond between people and products *as artifacts*.

The emphasis we put upon the functioning of products might raise the suspicion that we are secretly promoting a kind of neo-functionalism here. Functionalism, however, is quite the opposite of what we want to promote. Functionalist design would, indeed, focus on the functioning of products but, in doing so, it does not pay attention to the *involvement* of people in this functioning, but mainly to the *result* of it. Functionalist design does not result, therefore, in focal things, but in devices that procure commodities. Indeed, Riètveld designed chairs as "objects for sitting in," and Le Corbusier saw a house as "a machine for living in." Functionalism creates devices, whereas we are looking for engaging objects.

Possibly the example of the piano as an engaging product sounds a little too easy. After all, pianos are *intended* to engage people: who could imagine a piano that is not engaging. What could the notion of "engagement" imply for the design of objects that do not ask for engagement by definition? For instance, for the design of a central heating system, which is Borgmann's very example of a device that asks for consumption instead of engagement?

At Cranbrook Academy of the Arts, a heating device has been designed which is a fine example of an engaging object. It is a true *thing*, escaping the usual one-sided emphasis upon language and symbolism within contemporary industrial design. The heater consists of ceramic plates which have been bent to conic cylinders with different radii. The cylinders are placed concentrically, and can be adapted with the aid of an accessory, in order to radiate their heat in the correct direction. This heater is not only very beautiful, it is above all *engaging*. Users are involved in its functioning. It's not a device you hide under the windowsill: its proper place is in the middle of the room. When in use, the ceramic plates have to be rearranged from time to time. The heater evokes playful engagement, instead of disengaged consumption of heat. In the meanwhile, of course, it also heats the room: the engagement it asks for does not make it unusable. It functions, but is more than functional; it engages but, nevertheless, it can be ready-to-hand. With products such as this, our relationship does not end when we insert the plug into the socket. They are present *as things* – "eternally ours."

6 CONCLUSION

The "new generation of products" Manzini dreams of should be a generation of things, not only of ideas and signs. Durable products should be more than icons for our lifestyles, or "conversation pieces" between consumers and producers. A durable material culture is not only a matter of culture, but is first of all a matter of *matter*. All we wanted to say is: matter matters.

NOTES

First published in *Design Issues* 14 no. 3 (Autumn 1998): 28–42.

1. Albert Borgmann, *Technology and the Character of Contemporary Life* (London/Chicago: University of Chicago Press, 1984).
2. Don Ihde, *Technology and the Lifeworld* (Bloomington and Indianapolis: University of Indiana Press. 1990); *Postphenomenology: Essays in the Postmodern Context* (Evanston, Illinois: Northwestern University Press, 1993); *Philosophy of Technology: An Introduction* (New York: Paragon, 1995).

3. Eternally Yours. Lectures given during the Eternally Yours Congress 1997.
4. More information about Eternally Yours can be found at: http://www.ecomarket.net/EternallyYours.
5. The following historical speech on industrial design is based on, Penny Sparke, *Industriële vormgeving en cultuur in de 20e eeuw,* Cantecleer, De Bilt, 1989, translation of *An Introduction to Design & Culture in the Twentieth Century* (London: Allen & Unwin Ltd., 1986) and Catherine McDermott, *Essential Design* (London: Bloomsbury, 1992).
6. Siegfried Giedion, *Modernization Takes Command* (New York: Oxford University Press, 1948).
7. Reyner Banham, *Design by Choice* (London: Academy Editions, 1981).
8. Karl Jaspers, *Die Geistige Situation der Zeit* (Berlin: Göschen, 1931), 42.
9. Madeleine Akrich, "The De-Scription of Technical Objects," *Shaping Technology/Building Society*, W.E. Bijker and J. Law, eds. (Cambridge, MA: MIT Press, 1992).
10. Langdon Winner, "Do Artifacts Have Politics?" *The Whale and the Reactor* (Chicago: University of Chicago Press, 1986).
11. Nelly Oudshoorn, *Genderscripts in Technologie: Noodlot of Uitdaging?*, lecture, Universiteit Twente, Faculteit Wijsbegeerte en Maatschappijwetenschappen, 1996.
12. Peter-Paul Verbeek, "Don Ihde: de relatie tussen mensen en techniek," *Van stoom-machine tot cyborg – denken over techniek in de nieuwe wereld*, H.J. Achterhuis, eds. (Baarn: Ambo, 1997).
13. Cynthia Cockburn and Susan Ormrod, *Gender and Technology in the Making* (London: SAGE Publications, 1993).
14. Martin Heidegger, *Sein und Zeit* (Tübingen: Niemeyer, 1986). Original published in 1926.

8

DOMESTICATION OF EVERYDAY LIFE TECHNOLOGY: DYNAMIC VIEWS ON THE SOCIAL HISTORIES OF ARTIFACTS

Mika Pantzar

1 FROM SENSATIONAL FEELINGS TO ROUTINE USE

At the moment, social histories of technology are an expanding and interesting area for consumer research. However, standard consumer research, academic marketing studies, economics, or sociology have lacked general theories and perspectives historically integrating technology, needs, and human beings. Social development is seen unidirectly as determined by technology (i.e., technological determinism), or consumption is seen as resulting from human needs, and preferences (i.e., voluntarism).[1] This paper concentrates on the emerging perspectives integrating technology and human beings. Let us start with some observations from the history of technology.

In the beginning of this century, the automobile, like the bicycle, was a toy, a plaything for those who could afford to buy one. It was initially used mainly for recreation and sport, representing a new concept of personal mobility and taste for independent travel. In the United States, 4,192 automobiles were sold in 1900. Only ten years later, 485,377 automobiles were registered, and the automobile was perceived by Americans to be a necessity.[2] In comparison, automobiles were not perceived to be a necessity until the late 1960s in Finland. Nevertheless, the mental attributes related to the automobile have followed very similar lines across different cultures.

Whereas the first automobiles were sold because of the enjoyment and excitement they gave their owners, the first telephones, slightly more than a hundred years ago, were not meant to be used for enjoyment.[3] The telephone almost immediately was recognized as a marvelous invention, although how it actually might be used was not so obvious:

> Early users often discovered they had nothing to say. Even the enthusiastic were insufficiently imaginative. The problem was to figure out what the phone could be used for. According to an early enthusiastic prediction, "Why the telephone is so important, every city would need one!" The idea was that everyone could gather round the phone to hear the day's news.[4]

Trying to determine appropriate uses for the telephone continued for quite a while in the early days. The early telephone vendors often battled their residential customers over social conversations, labeling such calls "frivolous" and "unnecessary." For example, an 1881 announcement complained, "The fact that subscribers have been free to use the wires as they pleased without incurring additional expenses (i.e., flat rates) has led to the transmission of large numbers of communications of the most trivial character."[5] According to one local telephone manager of that time, about thirty percent of the calls were "purely idle gossip." The early telephone was introduced as a rational business tool. Nobody, except possibly Alexander Graham Bell, saw the future potential of the telephone. A hundred years ago, Bell's prediction that "One day, Mrs. Smith would spend and hour on the telephone with Mrs. Brown" was radical.[6]

Quite similar developments can be found in the history of popular mass media technology. Television, radio, movies, and recordings have witnessed a metamorphosis: from toy, through mirror, and toward art.[7] In the first stage, the fascination (need) of popular movies or television was their novelty as such (TOY). New media technologies gained first admittance into society as "Trojan horses, with their physical presence clearly visible, but their potentialities poorly understood."[8] Orvar Löfgren from Sweden calls this early period as a period of "happy experimentation and a multitude of Utopian schemes." He says, "People remember the solemn atmosphere and the intense concentration in early radio, or the ways in which you dressed up for a television evening, hushing both grandma and the kids."[9]

In time, however, playthings become transformed into practical technologies. At this stage, one can speak of emerging "functional needs." For instance, "The adoption of reality as film content distracted from the technology and artificiality of the film experience, directing attention to the nontechnological content – the events depicted on the screen – and, in turn, enchanting the believability of the content, i.e., that the events on the film were 'really' happening."[10] Technological media attained its second phase when it captured the useful role of MIRROR. In a social context, the media became routine and people learned how to "listen with half an ear, or have the television on as a background screen for conversation."[11]

In the third phase, mass media technology moved from retelling reality to refashioning reality, as ART does. To achieve the "artistic" jump, a medium must have the capacity not only to replicate reality, but to rearrange and edit it in imaginative way.

2 HOW TECHNOLOGY IS DOMESTICATED

> Motto: "Luxury, rather than necessity, is the mother of invention."[12]

Needs and practical functions arise and are transformed in use. On the basis of a sample of historical case studies, it could be maintained that, rarely is a new commodity a response to some basic need.[13] Either new commodities simply replace older products, e.g., in modern households margarine replaced butter;[14] or new commodities enter into the life of consumers as objects with almost no practical function. The latter applies to, say, the first automobiles at the end of the nineteenth century, early computers in the 1940s, and home computers in the 1980s, but also to the first refrigerators in the beginning of this century.[15]

The term "domestication of technology" suggests that there are interesting similarities between the ways technology enters our daily lives and the ways animals and crops were domesticated about 10,000 years ago: "Domestication: The process of hereditary reorganization of wild animals and plants into domestic and cultivated forms, according to the interests of people. In its strictest sense, it refers to the initial stage of human mastery of wild animals and plants. The fundamental distinction of domesticated animals and plants from their wild ancestors is that they were created by human labor to meet specific requirements, or whims, and are adapted to the conditions of continuous care and solicitude people maintain for them."[16]

The present paper focuses on the specific question of how artifacts, technologies, and social systems become stabilized and institutionalized into identifiable closures (e.g., lifestyles) within consumers' daily lives. I would argue that the ways commodities or consumption patterns are introduced, institutionalized, and expanded (i.e., domesticated) reflect quite general processes going on in modern market economies. Important generalizations can be explicated on the basis of

Table 8.1 Examples of changing determinants of consumer choice.

Sensation	Routine (e.g., car, bicycle)
Toy	Instrument (e.g., media technology)
Pleasure	Comfort (e.g., WC, piped water)
Luxury	Necessity (e.g., sugar, tea, coffee, tobacco)

the social history of technology. For instance, there seems to be a metamorphosis of novelties from "toys" to "instruments," from "luxuries" to "necessities," from "pleasure" to "comfort," or from "sensation" to "routine."[17] Motives and needs behind buying and using technology are transformed in use.

I would argue that these seemingly different and separate transformations become understandable when the perspective is shifted from single commodities and needs to systems of commodities, to the evolving networks – i.e., ecology of goods.[18] In time, commodities such as automobiles or televisions become embedded "as components" in larger systems of goods. When commodities are integrated with each other, e.g., within lifestyles, dwellings, neighborhoods, etc., there is less and less room for spontaneity. From the perspective of a single consumer, daily choices, of say, using cars, become increasingly dictated by situational factors, routines, and social norms, and less and less by individual preferences. In accordance with these tendencies, commodities seem to pass through different phases. Figure 8.1 gives a generalized picture of these transformations.[19]

The vertical axis refers to the mental states of consumers in a specific choice situation. It could be maintained that both standard economics (rational choice/upper left) and the sociology of consumption (upper right) deal with mental states

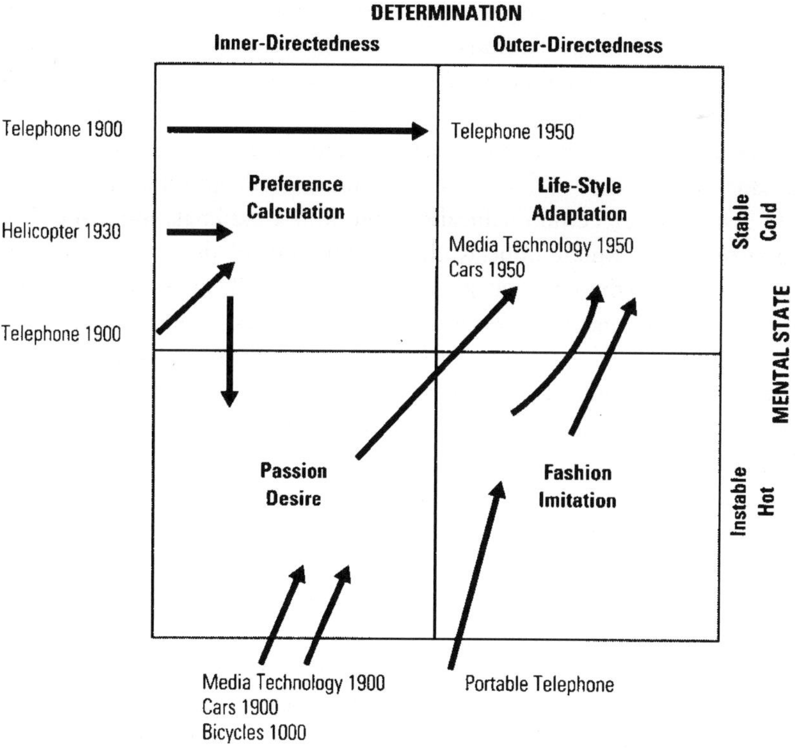

Figure 8.1 Domestication of Everyday Life Things

which are quite stable and durable. Standard economic theory suggests that consumers make their decisions and calculations on the basis of given preference order and beliefs subject to price and income constraints. In sociology, concepts such as lifestyle or way of life suggest that decisions are made on the basis of role-expectations and social norms. Fashion and passion are clearly different "reasons" behind individual choice behavior. These mental states are "hot," and less stable than those assumed in economic or standard sociology. Stability of lifestyle and everyday life i.e., "sphere of self-evident" – is reached through different socialization and routinization processes.

The horizontal axis refers to degree of inner- vs. other-directedness in choice behavior. It has been said that (neoclassical) economists operate with an atomized, "undersocialized" conception of human action, whereas sociologists tend to have an "oversocialized" conception of man.[20] Economists favor explanations with consumers as inner-directed (rational calculation), while sociologists' explanations emphasize other-directedness (adaptation, socialization). Passions are dominated mainly by "hot" internal states (desire, enthusiasm, excitedness) and emotions, whereas fashionable choices are dominated by others (conformism, imitation).

The fourfold table makes certain educated guesses about the channels through which radically new products have become rooted in our daily lives. Television, radio, and other forms of new media technology made their breakthrough in an initial phase of enthusiastic passionate experimentation, the boom, thereafter, being sustained by bandwagonism. Within only a few decades, radio and television became an accepted and inseparable part of our lifestyle. The story of the automobile and the bicycle proceeds along much the same lines. By sociohistorical accounts, the telephone, likewise, met few obstacles in its transition from a rational office tool to an indispensable household commodity.

Four groups of motives should be seen as an ideal type explanation with which consumer choice behavior and related motivations can be conceptualized in a historical setting. With this conceptualization, it is possible to elaborate consumer behavior in a multidisciplinary framework and relate different disciplines with each other.[21] When we are interested in questions of the entry of new commodities, or theories of rational choice, passion and fashion are relevant. When we are more interested in reasons why some commodities become a stabilized part of our everyday lives, sociological reasoning starts playing a major role.[22] In this context, the concept of consumption ritual is useful.

3 CONSUMPTION RITUALS

When a new product appears on the market, it elicits an initial response from the consumer – whether it be rational deliberation or the pursuit of pleasure or fashion. These reactions are fed by the continual influx of new commodities. The critical question is: why do certain new commodities but not others become *rooted* in our daily lifestyle, and what eventually forces them into *extinction*? The mechanisms which lead consumers to repeat and renew their earlier choices must be studied in the same depth as those which prompted the consumer to make that choice in the first place.

The repetition of certain choices, e.g., daily car use, is more than simply a matter of outer-directed influences such as advertising. Choices we make today will guide and restrict the choices we make in the future. The emergence and existence of routinous choices can be approached from the perspective of *consumption ritual*.[23]

By the term "consumption ritual," I wish to emphasize the self-perpetuating and self-transformative logic of consumer society. Choosing a certain form of transport can lead to a certain type of lifestyle which, in turn, increases the demand for the form of transport which originally shaped that lifestyle. Choices which trigger such chain reactions, and which increase (or decrease) the probability of the same choice being repeated, can be described as manifestations of "the Diderot effect."[24]

As the story goes, the renowned eighteenth-century French encyclopaedist Dennis Diderot received a brand-new burgundy-colored set of academic apparel as a gift. The only problem was that the new outfit seemed out of place in his stuffy old study. Diderot set about solving the problem by buying himself new bookshelves, chairs, and desks, and finally by repainting the whole room. By the time the room and outfit matched perfectly, Diderot himself began to seem out of place. This type of consumption cycle, in which commodities independently begin to make claims on one another, can have one of two possible outcomes: a harmonious and homogeneous lifestyle, or an irresolvable conflict as in Diderot's case.

According to Grant McCracken (1988), the Diderot effect represents both a process of change (the rejection of incompatible furnishings) and a dynamic of stability (an established entity/ensemble). So far, lifestyle analysis has failed to deliver its theoretical promises, since it has focused on systematizing empirical and fragmentary observations of attitudes, values, and background variables, rather than on elucidating broader theoretical entities. Lifestyle studies need fresh theoretical inroads, such as those offered by the Diderot effect.

Although the mechanisms which guide the invention, adoption, rejection, and domestication of a given commodity are widely diverse, there is a surprising degree of similarity in the way that different commodities become entrenched in our lifestyle. Consider, for example, the infiltration of the water pipe and the automobile. In the initial stages, both were viewed with a considerable degree of skepticism. Cars were thought to disturb the peace, and they were regarded as a general nuisance to horse-drawn traffic. Water pipes were dismissed as a superfluous luxury, and even as an outright health risk – particularly when the outdoor privy was replaced by the indoor lavatory. And surely piped-in water could never make better coffee than water drawn fresh from a well!

Despite these early misgivings, through a chain of thousands of infinitesimal choices, these two commodities – the automobile and the water pipe – have given rise to whole communities (as large as the entire Helsinki metropolitan area) which serve dual imperatives: mobility (the car) and stability (municipal water service). In retrospect, the progression towards motorization seems self-evident. Initially, however, it was difficult to predict what impact the automobile would have on the urban structure. Trains, airplanes, and cars were considered full equals until the 1950s. For instance, one architectural review of the Helsinki metropolitan area speculated forty years ago as to whether, in the future, flying would be the best choice for commuters traveling to the center of Helsinki.

In man–artifact relationship there appears to be a general trend toward ever broader consumer-commodity networks, with individual branches being cemented by interdependent commodity relationships (such as between the TV and the VCR), and the ties between man and commodity (e.g., the family unit and its chosen form of transport). The evolution of these commodity networks can be described with the following hypothesis: as commodities become increasingly widespread and firmly anchored in our lifestyle, human needs begin to take second place, and the priority shifts to "the mutual interdependency of the commodities in their own right." These networks become tighter and more solidly fixed. The inexorable standardization and routinization of both technology and everyday life offer a good illustration of this process.

It would generally be true to say that (systems of) goods either stabilize or disappear in time.[25] At the level of the individual household, this process can be described as the formation of a particular type of lifestyle. On a broader urban level, this process results in the formation of neighborhoods and communities. Each home "generates" demand for services and these services, in turn, uphold the community which created them in the first place.

4 TECHNOLOGY INTERACTS WITH HUMAN BEINGS – NEW PERSPECTIVES

> Motto: Unfortunately, we lack proper conceptualizations to analyze different organizing processes through which technology interacts with human beings.[26]

Indeed, modern consumer society, as a whole, beginning with Henry Ford's radical idea in his time that even laborers can be consumers, could be viewed as a vast metabolistic organism which perpetuates itself. A number of conceptual innovations are needed in both consumer theory and in broader social theory if we aim to study the changes and functions of the metabolic system of modern society.[27] Three alternative and complementary views on the dynamics of man–artifact interactions summarize in abstract terms much of what was said above: social shaping of technology, actor network theory, and the ecology of goods (replicative model of evolution). All of these perspectives focus on the interactions between human beings and technology, and the ways these interactions seem to either stabilize or disappear.

First, important developments in recent consumer research should be acknowledged. The term "biography of thing" refers to the new, emerging perspectives aiming to describe and understand the ways different commodities become integrated in the sphere of our daily lives, for instance, the ways meanings attached to specific goods are transformed from experience of uncontrolled chaos to ordered cosmos, and the ways anonymous commodities with objective exchange values are transformed into personal possessions. Compared to cultural critique typical to older sociology of consumption, new streams take their starting point more clearly from empirical evidence. Today, for anthropologists, historians, and sociologists, the meanings of things is an

Table 8.2 Perspectives on Human Being – Technology Interactions.

	Biography of Things	**Social Shaping of Technology**	**Actor Network**	**Ecology of Goods**
Unit of Analysis	Micro: Commodities and households	Meso: Technological systems	Meso: Socio-technic networks	Meso: Chains of commodities and consumers
Disciplines	Anthropology, sociology, consumer research	Sociology of science and technology	?	Institutional economics
Main Concepts	Domestication, appropriation, objectification, incorporation	Social construction, technological systems, and frames	Translation heterogeneous network	The origin, maintenance, and selection of variation
Representatives	James Carrie Igor Kopytoff Orvar Löfgren Daniel Miller Roger Silverstone[28]	Wiebe Bijker Thomas Hughes Trevor Pinch[29]	Michel Callon Bruno Latour John Law[30]	Kenneth Boulding Mika Pantzar Arie Rip Pier Paolo Saviotti[31]

empirical question.[32] In the following, however, I shall concentrate on the processes of domestication on a more general and theoretical level than the biography of things.

SOCIAL SHAPING OF TECHNOLOGY

The social shaping of technology perspective argues for the interpretative flexibility of scientific findings and technological inventions, and thus non-deterministic model of technological change.[33] It focuses on the legitimization processes and social mechanisms by which different commodities are constituted (e.g., social construction). The social shaping of technological systems view shares with the theories of path-dependent systems[34] a plea for seeing history as essentially open: there are multiple paths (equilibria) of technology. Non-optimality of technology is a distinct possibility, too. Often, complex technologies display increasing returns to adoption and network externalities (i.e., nonlinearity) in that, the more they are adopted, the more they will be adopted.

Thomas Hughes is one of the most influential authors in the field of the social shaping of technology. Hughes approaches man–technology relationships with the concept of "technological system."[35] Inventions such as the radio, the airplane, or the gasoline-driven automobile are embedded within technological systems. These systems are comprised of physical artifacts (e.g., turbogenerator), organizations (e.g., investment banks), and people – legislative artifacts (e.g., regulatory law), as well as communications, traffic and so on.

Hughes emphasizes that technological systems are both socially constructed and society shaping. Interactions between artifacts result in a "system goal": "An artifact – either physical or nonphysical – functioning as a component in a system interacts with other artifacts, all of which contribute directly or through other components to the common system goal."[36] Hughes's analysis of technological systems is largely acknowledged today. We are going, however, even further in our theorizing: it is not only that artifacts are embedded within systems which constrain human behavior, but that artifacts accomplish an agency.

ACTOR NETWORK THEORY

In recent years, important work has been going on which explicates the power of goods quite explicitly. Bruno Latour's and Michael Callon's theory of "actor networks," and Stewart Clegg's work on "power circuits," share notable commonalties with Hughes's technological systems.[37] However, in contrast, the primacy of human elements or any distinctions between the "technical" and the "social," is strongly rejected.

An "actor network" is suggested as consisting of very different kinds of actors: "The actor network is reducible neither to an actor, alone, nor to a network. Like a network, it is comprised of a series of heterogeneous elements, animate and inanimate, that have been linked to one another for a certain period of time ... The actor network thus can be distinguished from the traditional actors of sociology, a category generally excluding any nonhuman components and whose internal structure is rarely assimilated to that of a network."[38]

Latour and Callon emphasize correctly that it is impossible to separate social and technical: "... instead of asking 'is this social,' 'is this technical or scientific,' or asking 'are these techniques influenced by society,' or 'is this social relation influenced by techniques' we simply ask: has a human replaced a nonhuman? Has the competence of this actor been modified? Has this actor-human or nonhuman been replaced by another one? Has this chain of associations been extended or modified? Power is not a property of any one of these elements but a chain."[39] Stewart Clegg (1989) would call these kinds of chains "circuits of power."[40]

Theories of actor networks focus explicitly on organizational stabilization processes, i.e., the ways in which different networks (systems, circuits, etc.) either become stabilized or disappear.

The specific focus is on the association and dissociation processes of human beings, different organizations, and artifacts.

In sharp contrast to Hughes's technological systems view, actor network tradition is very critical about the standard environment-system distinction.[41] It focuses on emerging environments: as integration (of artifacts, ideas, and human beings) proceeds toward larger entities, single components relinquish their relative autonomy to the networks which they themselves comprise.

The concept of the actor network is used to explain both the first stages of the invention and the gradual institutionalization of the market: "It is applicable to the whole process, because it encompasses and describes not only alliances and interactions that occur at a given time, but also any changes and developments that occur subsequently."[42] Essentially, the term "actor network" refers to the reciprocity of different agents – in contrast to the mechanistic theories. Circuits, networks, and cycles tend to reproduce themselves. The emergence of these new conceptualizations might be a manifestation of a more general phenomenon. Clegg and Wilson, for instance, see a general cultural shift in perspective from a mechanical world-view (à la Hobbes) to a "circulatory" conception of power (à la Foucault, Machiavelli), and from modernist interest of control to a postmodernist interest of interpretation, empowerment, and participation.[43]

Actor network theory and the social shaping of technology tradition are not saying that there is no "logic" in the ways technology changes. There is. For instance, there is evidence that incorporation of new engineering knowledge into commercial products is related to the radicalness of invention, or that fundamental technical breakthroughs do not occur singly; instead, they tend to cluster. In time, designers' space for creativity diminishes and dominant designs emerge.[44] I would argue that these observations and generalizations could be approached in a context of general evolution.[45]

For the author, the main reason to approach the "life" of artifacts through the general evolution view is the possibility of generating relevant theoretical conjectures and new perspectives to the empirical realm. It might be that a biologist such as Stuart Kaufmann put it most clearly as to what is happening in the world of interdependent artifacts: An economy and single units within it, such as individual households, is a web of transformations of products and services among economic agents. New products and services entering the market for single households must "mesh together coherently to jointly fulfill a set of needed tasks."[46] The web of consumers, producers, and artifacts is transformed over time, driven by technological advances and economic opportunities.

TOWARD ECOLOGY OF GOODS – A REPLICATIVE VIEW ON SOCIAL DYNAMICS

The ecological perspective on goods takes as its starting point the following observations: Examining the various components of such entities, as cells, organisms, societies, it can be found that these entities exist, i.e., sustain, by self-maintenance or self-production, that is, by the continuous renewal of their own components. A Hungarian biologist and systems theorist, Vilmos Csanyi, has worked out a general model, the replicative model of evolution, based on these considerations. He maintains that self-organizing systems – both biological and social – exhibit a similar general tendency toward better replicative quality and integration with other systems.[47] Resulting systems are cyclic processes within processes, rather than given stable entities. The cycles reproduce themselves in a continuous resource exchange with their coactors and environment.

The components are associated and dissociated in various processes at the expense of a continuous energy and information flow going through the system. From the system's point of view, damaging components are wiped out, otherwise the system might disappear. This goal does not, however, mean that contradictory tendencies are absent but that, in time, these internal contradictions might be followed by reorientations required by the level of the system. A minimum requirement for a sustainable system is that its components, by their interactions, are not eroding the system. Quite clearly, this condition is not fulfilled in modern society. So far, as James Lovelock has pointed out in his "Planetary Medicine of Gaia," we know quite a little about different feedback effects influencing the sustainability of our planet.

The concern over emerging feedback mechanisms makes the living systems metaphor a suitable starting point for analyzing the relationship between consumption and production in mass consumption society. Whereas machine (mechanistic metaphors) is geared to the output of a specific product, a biological organism is primarily concerned with renewing itself. For instance, in the early period of economic activity in the automobile industry, there were only some minor feedback effects from the production of cars to the demand for cars, and there were some resources to start the evolutionary self-organizing process.[48] The latter could have been the Ford Motor Company's technological ability and economic resources to bring the Model T Ford to the market. The emerging cycle was related to the fact that, through Ford's original vision, even workers were able to buy a new Model T ("people's car"). Before this period, it could be maintained that the producers ("workers") and consumers ("idle class") were different people, and the feedback effect had a minor role. The emerging mass consumption society challenged this state of affairs. In modern mass consumption society, the behavior of each individual (artifacts, human beings, organizations, etc.) is bounded through reciprocation to the behavior of the others in an extensive way.

A group of commodities (e.g., a food system) must belong to an autocatalytic system of positive feedbacks in order to expand or exist. In brief, an autocatalytic feedback cycle is a concatenation of positive influences, in which one item in the chain catalyzes another. These causal loops are embedded within larger networks of causalities. In other words, if commodity A increases the probability of the genesis and maintenance of commodity B, and commodity B does the same to commodity A, then, in this autocatalytic cycle, the two commodities mutually enhance each other's rates of replication and gain an advantage over other commodities. Instead of commodities, we might talk about, say, product groups (e.g., TV sets) or groups of products (e.g., TV dinners), that are reproduced through participation in different autocatalytic cycles.[49]

These theoretical claims, or actually a very scattered picture of a general model, provide interesting insights and hypotheses to different routinization processes inherent in the life cycle of single commodities, too. On the level of the single consumer, we should examine connections between a consumer's first exposure to some new consumer item and his or her later contact with that item, and the resources which make this possible. For instance, in a way, an "accidental" exposure to pizza took place for many Finnish tourists in the 1960s in Italy. For some consumers, exposure to the new food item allowed processes to work to produce a more enduring, second-stage preference. This two-staged process of exposure-liking, might explain the emergence of a replicative cycle, and thus the continuity of new items in a single individual's life.[50]

Of course, there may be other kinds of linkages which affect the probability of repetition of, say, pizza intake. Another psychological cycle with similar effects is the pleasure-comfort cycle. Tibor Scitovsky has maintained that choices produce pleasure in the first stage but, in time, the pleasure fades away and is translated primarily into increasing comfort. Comfort, however, is like addiction: we become accustomed to it and soon take it for granted. Thus, once made, choices replicate themselves.[51] The two above-mentioned cycles are related to an agent's inner psychological structures. We can also imagine other kinds of, e.g., social or material, cycles. Consumer rituals?

It seems that the early phases of new commodities are dictated more by voluntary choices (enabling) and individualism. In time, however artifacts, when integrated with other goods, increasingly start playing the role of constraints (cf., network externalities). These evolutionary processes might be seen both on the most general level of mass consumption society,[52] and also on the level of single households.[53]

5 SOME CONCLUSIONS

It is not only that technology provides ways of satisfying human needs, but also that it creates novel needs and constraints for human behavior through its diffusion. Technologies have transforming potential which could be identified possibly only retrospectively.[54] In history, those businessmen have been the most successful who recognized the self-transformative power of new technology and a rising middle-class. In this respect, Henry Ford was an exceptional genius.[55] Today, "configuring the user" is one of the most debated topics in science and technology studies. It is increasingly recognized that the success of scientific and technological innovations depends upon the social relations between the producer and consumer, and on the mechanisms for communication between them.[56]

An important message of recent technology studies concerns the epistemology: in networks, there are no last instances and causes: "... POWER, whatever form it may take is recursively woven into the intricate dance that unites the social and the technical. What is the nature of the dance? Who or what has written the music? ... I think that the general answer would be non-reductionist. There are no 'last instances.' Rather, the authors detect emergent structural effects-properties of relationships between mutually constitutive socio-technical elements. So the object is not to offer simple explanations (for these will not be found), but rather to discern patterns in the 'networks-circuits' that tend to reproduce themselves, and so their various distributive effects."[57] Technological systems exist only "in and through" their reproduction in micro-social interactions. These interactions are, in turn, limited and modalized through the unintended consequences of previous social action.

Bruno Latour states this argument in other words: "The description of socio-technical networks often is opposed to their explanation, which is supposed to come afterwards. Critics of the sociology of science and technology often suggest that even the most meticulous description of a case-study would not suffice to give an explanation of its development. This kind of criticism borrows from epistemology the difference between the empirical and the theoretical, between 'how' and 'why,' between stamp-collecting – a contemptible occupation – and the search for causality – the only activity worthy of attention. Yet nothing proves that this kind of distinction is necessary. If we display a socio-technical network – defining trajectories by actants' association and substitution, defining actants by all the trajectories in which they enter, by following translations and, finally, by varying the observer's point of view – we have no need to look for any additional causes. The explanation emerges once the description is saturated."[58] This is an important epistemological point of view which resembles a lot of what evolutionary biologist[59] Stephen Jay Gould has so strongly emphasized: the scientific relevance of descriptions.

NOTES

First published in *Design Issues* 13 no. 3 (Autumn 1997): 52–65.

1. More encompassing perspectives integrating macro- and micro-level voluntarism and determinism have been proposed, e.g., in Russell Belk, "Possessions and the Extended Self," *Journal of Consumer Research* (June 13, 1988): 71–84; Ruth Schwartz Cowan, *More Work for Mother. The Ironies of Household Technology from the Open Hearth to the Microwave* (New York: Basic Books/Harper, 1983); Claude

S. Fischer, *America Calling: A Social History of the Telephone to 1940* (Berkeley: University of California Press, 1992); and Grant McCracken (1988), *Culture and Consumption. New Approaches to the Symbolic Character of Consumer Goods and Activities* (Bloomington: Indiana University Press, 1988).

2. For the details, see George Basalla, *The Evolution of Technology* (Cambridge: Cambridge University Press, 1988); Arnold Pacey, *The Maze of Ingenuity, Ideas, and Idealism in the Development of Technology* (Cambridge, MA: MIT Press, 1992); and Wolfgang Sachs, *For Love of the Automobile. Looking Back into the History of Our Desires* (Berkeley: University of California Press, 1994).
3. Fischer, *America Calling.*
4. Donald A. Norman, *Things that Make Us Smart: Defending Human Attributes in the Age of the Machine* (Reading: Addison-Wesley, 1993), 191.
5. Claude S. Fischer, " 'Touch Someone': The Telephone Industry Discovers Sociability" in *Technology and Choice, A Technology and Culture Reader*, Marcel C. Lafollette and Jeffrey K. Stine, eds. (Chicago: The University of Chicago Press, 1991), 103.
6. Fischer, "Touch Someone."
7. Paul Levinson, "Toy, Mirror, and Art: The Metamorphosis of Technological Culture," *Et cetera* (June 1977): 151–167.
8. Levinson, "Toy, Mirror, and Art," 154.
9. Orvar Löfgren, "Consuming Interests," in *Culture and History* (Copenhagen: Akademisk Forlag, 1990), 15.
10. Levinson, "Toy, Mirror, and Art," 156.
11. Löfgren, "Consuming Interests," 1.
12. Henry Petroski, *The Evolution of Useful Things* (New York: Alfred A. Knopf, 1993).
13. Basalla, *Evolution of Technology*; Mika Pantzar, *Domestication of Technology. From Science of Consumption to Art of Consumption* (Helsinki: Tammi Press, 1996); and Petroski, *The Evolution of Useful Things.*
14. Mika Pantzar, "Public Dialogue Between Butter and Margarine in Finland 1923–1992," *Journal of Consumer Studies and Home Economies* 19 (1995): 11–24.
15. See Basalla, *Evolution of Technology*, Paul Ceruzzi, "An Unforeseen Revolution: Computers and Expectations, 1935–1985" in *Imaging Tomorrow: History, Technology, and the American Future*, Joseph J. Corn, ed. (Cambridge, MA: MIT Press, 1986); and Cowan, *More Work for Mother.*
16. *Encyclopedia Britannica* (1990).
17. See Levinson, "Toy, Mirror and Art"; Mary Douglas and Brian Isherwood, *The World Goods* (Harmondsworth: Penguin Books, 1978); Tibor Scitovski, *The Joyless Economy* (NewYork: Oxford University Press, 1976); and Löfgren, "Consuming Interests."
18. The term "ecology of goods" has been elaborated by Kenneth Boulding, "Economics as an Ecology of Commodities," Lecture notes at George Mason University (November 1989); and Mika Pantzar, "Do Commodities Reproduce Themselves through Human Beings?" *World Futures, Journal of General Evolution* 38 (1993): 201–224. In design studies, a similar concept, the product milieu, has been coined by Victor Margolin, "The Product Milieu and Social Action" in *Discovering Design: Explorations in Design Studies*, Richard Buchanan and Victor Margolin, eds. (Chicago and London: The University Press of Chicago, 1995).
19. For the details, see Pantzar, *Domestication of Technology*, and cf. Douglas B. Holt, "How Consumers Consume: A Typology of Consumption Practices," *Journal of Consumer Research* 22 (June 1995): 1–16.
20. Mark Granovetter, "Economic Action and Social Structure: The Problem of Embeddedness," *American Journal of Sociology* 91 (Nov. 1985): 481–510.
21. On the basis of the conceptualization, conditions for "sustainable consumption" could be elaborated. For instance, we could ask whether we should influence:

    - The flow of new goods (inventions, innovations).
    - The ways novel products are received by the consumers (calculation, desire, imitation).
    - The ways novel products become stabilized into lifestyles.

    Or should we simply attack and destabilize daily routines? Should we recognize the water closet, cars, and televisions as luxuries and conscious choices rather than a daily necessity? In this perspective, there is nothing more wasteful than driving a car without deriving any pleasure from the speed, freedom, and independence it affords (Pantzar, *Domestication of Technology*).
22. Too little attention has been paid to the fact that most commodities disappear soon after introduction (e.g., the personal helicopter).
23. Grant McCracken, *Culture and Consumption.* The word "ritual" is understood in a broader and less specific sense than in the conventional (scientific) meaning of rituals. By referring to "consumer

rituals," I wish to emphasize the cultural and pragmatic conditions which sustain and reinforce certain consumer practices; and which may even lead to the consolidation of certain social or metabolic systems. Rituals sustain both micro-level traditions and macro-level technological paradigms. Catherine Bell, *Ritual Theory, Ritual Practice* (New York: Oxford University Press, 1992).

24. McCracken, *Culture and Consumption.*
25. Pantzar, "Do Commodities Reproduce Themselves." Trevor Pinch and Wiebe E. Bijker, "The Social Construction of Facts and Artifacts: Or How the Sociology of Science and the Sociology of Technology Might Benefit Each Other" in *The Social Construction of Technological Systems. New Directions in the Sociology and History of Technology*, W.E. Bijker, T. Hughes and T. Pinch, eds. (Cambridge, MA: MIT Press, 1987).
26. Bruno Latour, *We Have Never Been Modern* (New York: Harvester Wheatsheaf, 1993).
27. See Peter Baccini and Paul Brunner Baccini, *Metabolism of the Antroposphere* (Berlin: Springer-Verlag, 1989); and Eva Heiskanen and Mika Pantzar, "Sustainable Consumption – Two New Approaches" (mimeo, 1996).
28. See James C. Carrier, *Gifts and Commodities. Exchange and Western Capitalism* (London: Routledge, 1995); Igor Kopytoff, "The Cultural Biography of Things: Commodization as Process" in *The Social Life of Things, Commodities in Cultural Perspective*, Arjun Appadurai, ed. (London: Cambridge University Press, 1986) 64–91; Löfgren, "Consuming Interests"; Daniel Miller, *Material Culture and Mass Consumption* (Oxford: Basil Blackwell, 1987); and Roger Silverstone, *Television and Everyday Life* (London: Routledge, 1994).
29. See Wiebe Bijker, *Of Bicycles, Bakelites, and Bulbs* (Cambridge, MA: MIT Press, 1995); Thomas Hughes, *Networks of Power: Electrification in Western Society, 1880–1930* (Baltimore, MD: Johns Hopkins University Press, 1983); Thomas Hughes, *American Genesis: A Century of Invention and Technological Enthusiasm* (New York: Viking, 1989); and Wiebe Bijker and John Law, *Shaping Technology/ Building Society – Studies in Sociotechnical Change* (Cambridge, MA: MIT Press, 1992).
30. See Michael Callon, "Techno-economic Networks and Irreversibility" in John Law, ed., *A Sociology of Monsters: Essays on Power, Technology and Domination, Sociological Review Monograph 38* (London and New York: Routledge, 1991); Bruno Latour, "Technology Is Society Made Durable" in John Law, ed., *A Sociology of Monsters*; and John Law, "Introduction: Monsters, Machines, and Sociotechnical Relations" in John Law, ed., *A Sociology of Monsters.*
31. See Kenneth Boulding, "Economics as an Ecology of Commodities"; Mika Pantzar, "The Choreography of Everyday Life – A Missing Brick in the General Evolution Theory," *World Futures – The Journal of General Evolution* 27, nos. 2–4 (1989): 207–226; and Pantzar, "Do Commodities Reproduce Themselves." Some streams of evolutionary economics e.g., Pier Paolo Saviotti, "Variety, Economic, and Technological Development" in Yuichi Shionoya and Mark Perlman, eds., *Innovation in Technology, Industries and Institutions: Studies in Schumpeterian Perspectives* (Ann Arbor: University of Michigan Press, 1994), 27–48; and technology assessment e.g., Arie Rip, Thomas Misa, and Johan Schot, *Managing Technology in Society. The Approach of Constructive Technology Assessment* (London: Pinter Publisher, 1995) share many features in common with the ecology of goods.
32. See Daniel Miller, ed., *Acknowledging Consumption. A Review of New Studies* (London: Routledge, 1995). Certainly, the specific processes behind the incorporation of goods into our daily lives and consumer society have quite different manifestations (and theories), depending on the scale of incorporation. There is a difference if we study incorporation processes on the level of single transactions and commodities, or if we study emerging technologies. In Finland, for instance, roughly fifteen billion transactions take place every year.
33. Wiebe Bijker, Thomas Hughes and Trevor Pinch, eds., *The Social Construction of Technological Systems: New Directions in the Sociology and History of Technology* (Cambridge, MA: MIT Press, 1987).
34. See Brian Arthur, "Competing Technologies, Increasing Returns, and Lock-in by Historical Events," *Economic Journal* 99 (March 1989): 116–131 and Paul A. David, "Paradigm for Historical Economics: Path-Dependence and Predictability in Dynamic Systems with Local Network Externalities," High Technology Impact Program, Center for Economic Policy Research, Stanford University, 1989.
35. Thomas Hughes, *Networks of Power*, and American Genesis.
36. Thomas Hughes, "The Evolution of Large Technological Systems" in W. Bijker, T. Hughes, and T. Pinch, eds., *The Social Construction of Technological Systems: New Directions in the Sociology and History of Technology*, 51.

37. See Hughie Mackay and Gareth Gillespie, "Extending the Social Shaping of Technology Approach: Ideology and Appropriation," *Social Studies of Science* 22 (1992): 685–715.
38. Michael Callon, "Society in the Making: The Study of Technology as a Tool for Sociological Analysis" in W. Bijker, T. Hughes, and T. Pinch, eds., *The Social Construction of Technological Systems: New Directions in the Sociology and History of Technology*, 93.
39. Latour, "Technology is Society Made Durable," 110.
40. Stewart T. Clegg, *Framework of Power* (London: SAGE Publications, 1989).
41. Callon, "Society in the Making."
42. Ibid., 100.
43. Stewart T. Clegg and Fiona Wilson, "Power, Technology and Flexibility in Organizations, in John Law, ed., A *Sociology of Monsters* (1991).
44. See P. Anderson and Michael Tushman, "Technological Discontinuities and Dominant Design: A Cyclical Model of Technological Change," *Administrative Science Quarterly* 35 (1990): 604–633; Mika Pantzar, "The Growth of Product Variety – a Myth?" *Journal of Consumer Studies and Home Economics* 16 (1992): 345–362; and Devendra Sahal, "Invention, Innovation, and Economic Evolution," *Technological Forecasting and Social Change* (1983) 23: 213–235.
45. See Vilmos Csanyi, *Evolutionary Systems and Society, A General Theory* (Dufham: Duke University Press, 1989); Mika Pantzar, *A Replicative Perspective on Evolutionary Dynamics: The Organizing Process of the US Economy Elaborated through Biological Metaphor* (Labour Institute for Economic Research, Helsinki, Research Report 37/1991); and Mika Pantzar and Vilmos Csanyi, "Replicative Model of the Evolution of Business Organization," *Journal of Social and Biological Structures* 14, no. 2 (1991): 149–163.
46. Stuart Kauffman, "The Evolution of Economic Webs" in *The Economy as an Evolving Complex System*, Paul Anderson, Kenneth Arrow, and David Pines, eds. (Redwood City: Addison-Wesley, 1988), 126.
47. Vilmos Csanyi, *Evolutionary Systems and Society*.
48. Put more formally, the precondition for starting a self-organizing process here almost an unstructured consumer society at the beginning of the 19th century was the presence of a minimal set of components that could replicate and that fulfilled the criteria that it contained at least one cycle of component producing processes, and at least one of the components participating in this cycle could be excited by the resource flux flowing through the system.
49. Mika Pantzar, "The Choreography of Everyday Life" and "Do Commodities Reproduce Themselves."
50. Pantzar, "The Choreography of Everyday Life."
51. Scitovsky, *The Joyless Economy*.
52. Heiskanen and Pantzar, "Sustainable Consumption," and Pantzar, "Do Commodities Reproduce Themselves."
53. Pantzar, "The Choreography of Everyday Life."
54. See Jonathan Gershuny, "Postscript: Revolutionary Technologies and Technological Revolutions" in Roger Silverstone and Eric Hirsch, eds., *Consuming Technologies, Media and Information in Domestic Spaces* (London and New York: Routledge), 227–233; Victor Margolin, "Global Expansion or Global Equilibrium? Design and the World Situation," *Design Issues* 12 no. 2 (Summer 1996); Donald Norman (1993); and Nathan Rosenberg, "Why Technology Forecasts Often Fail," *The Futurist* (July–August 1995), 16–21.
55. The role of imagination (Pacey, *The Maze of Ingenuity, Ideas, and Idealism*) and the construction of markets seem to be important attributes of successful predictors (entrepreneurs): "Radically new products confront innovators with the problem of imaginatively constructing a market which does not yet exist … Determining the features of possible consumer markets at early stages of product development is, thus, a 'political' task. Not only does one's own company need to be persuaded of the viability of the proposed product: it is frequently necessary to build a wide 'constituency' behind the product," Ian Miles, Alan Cawson, and Leslie Haddon, "The Shape of Things to Consume," in Roger Silverstone and Eric Hirsch, eds. (1992), 72–73. A new market is always to be created (Callon, "Society in the Making").
56. Steve Woolgar, "Rethinking the Dissemination of Science and Technology," Crict Discussion Paper No. 44, May 1994.
57. Law, *A Sociology of Monsters*, 18.
58. Latour, "Technology is Society Made Durable," 129.
59. Stephen J. Gould, *Wonderful Life, The Burgess Shale and the Nature of History* (New York: W.W. Norton & Company, 1989).

9

ENVIRONMENTAL DESIGN AND INDUSTRIAL DESIGN: INTEGRATING KNOWLEDGE AROUND URGENT ISSUES

Medardo Chiapponi

My sincere thanks to Karen Yurkovich for her translation. Her questions and remarks gave me many reasons to rethink some relevant points of the article.

The connection between environmental design and industrial design is, by now, generally accepted.[1] Yet, when one considers the merits of the relationship, it becomes clear that there are certain aspects which require refinement and elaboration. This is particularly evident if one considers how disciplinary practices are currently defined within the separate fields. Actually, it is environmental design which requires further reflection as well as development of its contents, tasks, and methodological tools, and important work in this direction is being undertaken. The position of industrial design is, instead, better defined, in that it builds from the following cornerstones:

- A definition of the discipline formulated in 1961 by Tomás Maldonado; adopted that same year by ICSID, the International Council of Societies of Industrial Design, and still valid in its principal tenets;[2]
- The presence at an international level of a specific university education; and
- The existence of a profession – that practiced by industrial designers – which has an operational structure, fields of intervention, and well-defined operational methods.

Currently, we are witnessing changes in the field of concern of industrial design, in that diverse peripheral topics are gaining more importance, particularly those connected to environmental design. Yet the recognition of these changes does not mean to assert, as some do, that almost everything now falls within the field of industrial design, because such changes mean an irreversible dissolution of those aspects peculiar to the discipline.

It would be more productive to transfer to industrial design, with due care, the model of scientific research programs elaborated by Imre Lakatos.[3] The Hungarian-born philosopher of science has proposed a model that bases scientific research programs on two fundamental concepts: those of a "hard core" and of a "protective belt." The hard core consists of those stable elements which are essential to and characterize a program of research. The protective belt of a research program is, instead, more flexible and changeable in that its individual elements are subjected to experimental verification and must clarify their relationship to the hard core.

Remaining within this terminology, I would like to stress that, in examining the relationships between environmental design and industrial design, I will limit myself to considering only the hard core of industrial design. That is, I will concentrate on industrial design understood as the design of material products which are the result of industrial production and which are characterized by a plurality of features (formal, functional, performance-oriented, techno-economical, techno-productive, etc.).

Turning to environmental design, I believe it is necessary at this point to recall some of the essential characteristics of its subject – the concept of environment – and to mention some of their operational consequences.

1

The environment is a system. It is, therefore, characterized by the presence of diverse elements – physical, chemical, biological, sociocultural, techno-economic, etc. These elements are tied so closely together that they are very difficult to separate. This system is composed of both objective and measurable elements, such as the concentrations of various pollutants found in the atmosphere, as well as subjective and unmeasurable elements such as values, lifestyle choices, and individual and collective needs. Furthermore, an environment defined in this way can be structured upon the basis of four subsystems – the biosphere, the geosphere, the sociosphere, and the technosphere. Such a subdivision is, without doubt, conventional but its use has value in that it renders transparent the historical evolutionary process leading to the systemic notion of environment by making explicit the principal disciplines which have contributed to that process. Even more important is that such a subdivision stresses the basic character of environment, which is the indissoluble tie of anthropic (techno- and sociosphere) and nonanthropic (bio- and geosphere) elements. It then becomes superfluous, as well as improper, to qualify the term "environment" with such adjectives as natural or artificial, or to make a distinction between that which is noxious for human beings and that which is noxious for the environment. In fact, human needs, individual and social human behavior, the diverse forms of social organization, and technological production are constituent parts of the environment rather than independent and external variables. In some ways, the systemic notion of environment is in direct contrast to the notion of nature, notwithstanding the fact that they are considered synonymous, particularly in daily usage. This identification of one for the other is as much arbitrary as misleading. The concept of nature has, since ancient times, always been connected to the idea of a monolithic and immutable generative principle, which being outside and above human action has therefore determined it. Such a notion of nature has little cognitive value in that it refers to an uncontaminated and primordial world which in reality no longer exists, if it ever did.

Such an assumption is not at all lacking in actual consequences. Whether stated explicitly or not, it forms the ideological base of various movements such as Radical Environmentalism and Deep Ecology. These movements reject in concrete and even violent ways every and any intervention into "nature." This rejection is born of the firm conviction that even the smallest change in the original state of nature cannot but produce irreparable damage. This, however, compromises the mobilization of tools which are indispensable to plan and guide the inevitable transformation of the environment. The extreme consequences of such thinking would be the renunciation of even those actions directed toward the saving of the living elements of the environment.

2

Another relevant characteristic of the environment is that every problem within the field involves different scales of intervention. Let us consider, for example, a global problem such as the hole in the ozone. By now it can be stated with reasonable scientific certainty that the problem is caused by CFCs (chlorofluorocarbons), and that the solution would be the quick substitution of other chemical products for CFCs. But the characteristics of CFCs have allowed their pervasive use. They are odorless, tasteless, nontoxic, and inert in the lower levels of the atmosphere. They have significant power of thermal insulation, and are highly effective for use in refrigeration, as a propellant, and as a cleaning agent for microchips and other fine mechanical components. Therefore, it is not enough to forbid the use of CFCs to stop the thinning of the protective ozone layer. It is essential to rethink and redesign those products having to do with refrigeration and conservation, such as those used in the transportation of wholesale foods as well as the heating and cooling systems in buildings. More generally, it is indispensable to rethink our existing lifestyles.

This example, however summary, clearly shows the abstractness and, therefore, the inadequacy of those positions which aspire to deal with global environmental problems solely through the building of complex scenarios, through the establishing of international standards, or through the making of laws and regulations. These are obviously useful and necessary, but the more important game is played out on a more concrete and complex level where design action has greater opportunities for intervention. At this level, the relationships between environmental design, industrial design, and other design disciplines are not at all forced or arbitrary but, rather, they find indisputable justification in the types of problems that must be confronted.

3

The environment is certainly a system characterized by high complexity as much in a mechanistic as a holistic sense. More explicitly, the environment is a highly complex system because:

- it is composed of many and different components;
- each component has diverse functions within the system;
- the individual components and functions are both connected and, at times, contradictory; and,
- everything cannot be explained in terms of components, functional structures, and reciprocal relationships.

Moreover, that the environment would be characterized as a complex system is not only a statement of fact but also a value judgment. In many regards, complexity is a positive and even auspicious characteristic. This can be illustrated with a few examples. Biological diversity, a relevant part of the complexity of the biosphere, is a concept important enough to be protected by law. Concerning the sociosphere, we have learned from Emile Durkheim that complexity is a feature of an advanced society. In his doctoral thesis in 1893, he differentiated between the forms of aggregation of a mechanic society and an organic one.[4] The first form, characteristic of primitive societies, possesses a low level of complexity, as the process of socialization presupposes a drastic limitation of the individual's role in favor of cohesion to common, general principles. Emblematic of this are theocratic societies. On the contrary, the organic form of social aggregation typical of advanced societies, emphasizes the free interaction of individuals and groups, and therefore allows for a large increase in complexity.

Useful for a better determination of the objective of environmental design can also be the similarity between the characteristics of the environment and of Large Technical Systems (LTS). Large Technical Systems being the term used to designate, for example, systems of transportation, energy, and information. The concept, first introduced in the field of history of technology, has strongly influenced the more innovative trends of contemporary philosophy and sociology of technology. Significant contributions include those of Thomas P. Hughes of the University of Pennsylvania and Renate Mayntz of the Max-Planck-Institut in Köln.

The extension of the concept of LTS from the historical-analytical field to that of design seems particularly stimulating and promising. In fact, at the core of this theory is the thesis that technological innovations are not explainable in technocratic terms, but in systemic terms. Thomas P. Hughes states: Inventions such as the lightbulb, the radio, the airplane, and the gas-powered automobile are justified within the context of a technological system. Such systems, according to Hughes, are made up of much more than the so-called hardware, the equipment, machines, and networks of transportation, communication, and information individually connected. They also are made up of human beings and organizations. From our perspective, a conceptual and operational structure which consists of multiple factors (technical, scientific, organizational, and social, among others) and multiple scales (from technical products to networks) is very relevant.[5]

In the light of what has been said to this point, some questions become more significant.

1. Is it possible through design to confront environmental problems and, ultimately, legitimate and sensible to talk about environmental design, meaning the designing of the environment?
2. If the response to the first question is yes, what role can environmental design and industrial design play in this context?
3. How will industrial design change if, in the design of products environmental factors will have to be considered?
4. Does environmental design exist only as a more or less structured research sector, or rather as a real and legitimate discipline precisely located in the academic panorama, or does it also define a new profession?
5. If it is legitimate to recognize professional tasks for environmental design, what are its referents, and, finally but not less important, should new operational and design methods be developed specifically for this new profession or should those already codified be reconsidered.

In addition, the real meaning of the term "design" could be discussed at length, although this is not the point at which to develop such an important topic. We must be satisfied at this point with an extremely synthetic but workable definition in which the design process is seen as a two-way relationship between a reality to design (in our case the environment) and its model. The first phase of the process consists of the analysis, individuation, and delimiting of design problems. In this phase, one moves through a process of abstraction and formalization, from reality to a model which represents reality in a way coherent with the design objectives, methods, and techniques. The second phase consists of planning and implementation of design interventions. By working through simulations on the model and through directed actions built on specific, defined factors, this phase leads to a controlled modification of reality and to a solution to the problem.

In both these phases, simplicity plays a primary role. As every designer knows, the tools to formalize reality, the model, the simulation, and the interventions on reality must be as simple as possible. There exists an apparently unsolvable contradiction between the complexity of the environment regarded as system and the simplicity intrinsic to the design process. To confront this problem, the distinction between ontological and semiotic complexity introduced by Mario Bunge proves very interesting.[6] Seen in these terms, a distinction lies between the complexity of the environment and the complexity of the models, the theories, and the methodological tools used in the design of the environment. The reduction of the ontological complexity is as much impossible as illegitimate, and the simplification of the semiotic complexity is, instead, not only sensible but also indispensable.

Some disciplines already offer, if only partially, useful contributions to this notion. For example, systems research has developed formal methods to simplify the so-called large-scale systems. Similar procedures can and must be initiated for the design of complex systems which cannot be completely formalized, such as the environment.

In fact, intrinsic to design action is the determination of the limits of individual design problems and the choosing of those aspects to analyze and design. Put in other words, the determination of priorities and hierarchies is a fundamental characteristic of the design process. In this sense, we can talk about the relative complexity of the environment, meaning by this that the real level of complexity depends on the individual environmental problem considered, on the objectives and on the design methods. Pertinent to this is the example adopted by Ross W. Ashby: The brain has a very high complexity for a neurophysiologist. The same brain can be described by a butcher, who has to distinguish it from about thirty other cuts of meat, with not more than five bits.

Furthermore, the determination of priorities and hierarchies is a characteristic common to the design of the environment and to the design of industrial products. It is, therefore, an essential element in the relationship product-environment considered in design terms. If we wish to design environmentally sustainable industrial products, we are faced with a conceptual and methodological objective difficulty very similar to that dealt with earlier. One tries to achieve a higher environmental quality, that is, one seeks a solution which is holistic in character, being able to rely only on mechanistic methods and procedures. In fact, through design, we can influence only certain aspects of the quality of the environment, such as the energy needed during the phases of construction and use of the product, the materials needed and their quantity, the number of components, the ease or difficulty of disassembly, the reusability, and the durability of the product as a whole and of its individual components. We must therefore decide, on a case-by-case basis, if and how much the savings of energy, material, and water resources, or the reduction of waste from the outset, etc., are relevant.

From this perspective, it is worthwhile to look at the panorama of methodologies which have been put forth to evaluate and promote the environmental quality of products. Some methodologies, to overcome the above-mentioned apparent contradiction between objectives and methods, enlarge as much as possible the set of parameters. Among these methodologies, the most important and widespread is LCA – Life Cycle Assessment. LCA examines all the phases of the life cycle of a product (encompassing extracting and processing raw materials, manufacturing, transportation and distribution, use, reuse, maintenance, recycling, and final disposal), and then assesses the environmental impact of each of these phases based on a plurality of parameters (among which are the consumption of energy and raw materials, and the quantity and type of air, water, and ground emissions).

Confronted with the obvious difficulty of commanding rather complex tools and of finding necessary information, an idea which has made legitimate and opportune headway is that of proposing simplified methodologies of analysis and evaluation to support environmentally conscious product design. Such simplifications, however, are not without delicate passages. Put more explicitly, in a situation of inadequate scientific knowledge, it is not admissible to resort to a simplification which delegates to automatic procedures – computerized or not – those choices which fall within the area of responsibility of the designer. Such an approach would be only a short-lived delusion, against every indication to the contrary, about the knowledge that the industrial designer should possess in order to engage efficiently with other specialists.

Furthermore, a perspective of these problems which is excessively and inappropriately reduced can produce, notwithstanding good intentions, results which are opposite to those expected and pursued. For example, one of the most difficult problems to solve which demands the efforts of both environmental and industrial design is the preventive reduction of waste through the design of products which are easily reusable and recyclable. Many times though, this topic is banalized and reduced to that of the use of recyclable material, that is, of material for which there already exists recycling technology sufficiently tested and trustworthy, or at least presented as such. Certainly, the recycling technology is a necessary condition, but if we limit ourselves to this we go easily in the direction opposite to that desired. We cannot ignore the connections with the entire system of conditions which can ensure the reuse and recyclability of a product, such as the design of products easy to disassemble, a reduced number of components and materials used, the presence of an organization for the collection of recyclable material, the disassembly and reuse of the components of a product, and adequate norms or standards, etc. In fact, such misinformation leads to distorted buying behavior which, in turn, artificially increases the consumption of products which are recyclable only in the abstract, and which in reality are transformed only into garbage.

At this point, I would like to put forward some exploratory observations on the legitimacy and usefulness of interpreting design activity, in particular the areas of product and environmental design, as a collective decision-making process. In certain ways, it is self-evident that designing is a decision-making process. It is obvious that the design process involves a succession of decisions based on formal, technological, functional, performance-oriented, structural, and economic parameters. Already, we have recalled that the decisions concerning those aspects considered priorities fully belong to the design process. It is important now to note that such decisions are not undertaken individually or separately but, rather, collectively, that is, together with diverse social actors.

The complexity of the environmental system also means complexity of the system of actors involved in its design. The plurality of design aspects means that the designing of the environment is part of many and different discourses: from those of the discipline of design, to those of technology, social politics, economics, and still others. The design of the environment is, therefore, not a demiurgic intervention, in which a single designer with heroic gestures dispenses his or her own technocratic recipes. The plurality of social actors involved on each environmental subject makes environmental democracy almost ineluctable, in that no one is in a position, and not even wanting, to have his or her point of view prevail in any or whatever circumstances. Having said this, an issue of the first importance opens concerning which procedures and methods should be prepared to prevent a deadlock of democracy, where nothing is decided or done. In other words, it is necessary to avoid a situation of so-called non-decision-making and, on the contrary, to ensure that democracy also means efficiency.

A similar situation presents itself in industrial design. Not even the industrial designer lives and works in an ascetic ivory tower. He or she conducts his or her activity within a system of actors whose actual shape changes with each new situation. Belonging to this system are, among others, international industrial groups with their complex organizations, small and medium-size industries with their flexible structures; as well as government institutions, standard institutes, consultants for specialized topics, universities and research institutes, consumer associations, and environmental groups. Industrial designers must, therefore, construct on a case-by-case basis the most appropriate system of the actors and determine their own original contribution, without mimetic actions or role-playing. The designer should not, for example, assume the role of the industry marketing expert. Nor does this role-playing form part of industry's expectations. Since industry's job is the production of salable products, it is for that very reason that it has to cooperate with industrial designers who know how to present a true, autonomous vision of the problems, rather than conduct in a dilettante manner those operations which a business organization, with more professionalism and a complete knowledge of the field, know better how to face.

These topics could and certainly do require more development, which falls outside of the scope of this article. Nevertheless, it seems to me that the collective and social dimension of industrial design, particularly when it involves environmental aspects, is sufficiently clear. The relationship between environmental design and industrial design can be faced productively from this perspective.

In the light of what has been said, there should be no doubt about the fact that environmental design designates a solid and demanding research sector. There are important and urgent problems which fall unequivocally within this field, and there are sufficiently structured conceptual and methodological frames of reference. In my opinion, even more indisputable is the position of the discipline of environmental design in the academic context. In effect, the experience of the last few years has made the surpassing of the pioneer phase of the discipline incontestable. Environmental design, has in practice, demonstrated its capacity to integrate itself into many and different contexts of higher education. It should be stressed that inclusion into the university system has always represented an important step in the institutionalization of a discipline. It suffices to recall as an example the case of medicine, which took form as an autonomous discipline the moment it began to be taught at Salerno and Montpellier.

Certainly, we cannot ignore the difficulty that arises from the fact that environmental design is still in a formative phase. It can be described, to use an important distinction introduced by August Comte, in historical terms through the important events in its formative process, and not yet in dogmatic terms, that is, through its principles and methodology.[7] To make headway it would be fundamental to precisely delimit those subjects which belong to environmental design and underline its unique range of relevance, in other words, that which makes it autonomous from the other, more consolidated, disciplines to which it is related.

On the other hand, environmental design is only thinkable in relation to many other disciplines. In a certain sense, it could be addressed with considerations analogous to those which Herbert A. Simon directed toward cognitive science. In a recent interview, Simon affirmed that cognitive science is not yet really a discipline, but rather a conversation place, where various disciplines meet and converse.[8]

This position attempts to overcome an organization of knowledge based upon disciplines which are properly labeled and sorted in a rigid, taxonomic system. Parallel to knowledge organized by discipline (which, surely in many circumstances, plays a real role and with great efficiency) is emerging a notion of knowledge organized by problem. In this way, questions such as interdisciplinarity (or transdisciplinarity), or the dialectic relationship between specialization and generalization, can be put forth in new terms. From this perspective, interdisciplinarity is not an a priori choice, but rather a direct consequence of the problem being confronted. Specialization and generalization are no longer antithetical. Instead, they are two faces of the same coin, both of which are necessary to confront specific problems. Similarly, it becomes indispensable to develop that which could be defined as a "specialization of connections," which is the capacity to orchestrate diverse forms of knowledge, to make them meet and "converse" – to use Simon's terms – to resolve problems.

After all, the symptoms of the phenomenon of the more general transformation just described are diffuse and clearly perceptible. The "border" disciplines, which combine different thematic areas and examine them from diverse viewpoints, are always more numerous. Among these, environmental design certainly figures and, in this sense, its connections with other disciplines, particularly industrial design, must be recognized and dealt with.

Better articulated is the discourse concerning the existence of the specific professional profile of "environmental designer," and his or her relationship to the skills and tools of other professionals in the design field. We are living in a transition phase, and it is probably still premature to talk about outcomes with any certainty. Given the current state of things, it seems inopportune and untimely to hypothesize about an environmental designer who operates with methodological tools which are entirely new and completely distinct from those already used in the existing design professions. Such a hypothesis would underestimate the persistence of those methods profoundly rooted in praxis (master plans, regulatory plans, architectural projects, industrial design projects, etc.) and underestimate the advantages that routine offers from the point of view of procedure and from that of communication between social actors.

For the short term, we can envision an environmental designer who stands beside the more traditional figures of design and who, to a certain extent, renouncing the need to exert his or her autonomy, contributes to a revision of those methods already codified so that greater attention is paid to environmental topics. This apparently minor choice, though, already implies profound transformations in the modes of operation.

We have already touched upon some of the transformations in industrial design. Urban planning, to be able to be defined as environmentally sustainable, must occupy itself with themes such as the mobility of persons and goods, the reduction, management, and treatment of waste, clean technologies in the fields of production and of services, the organization of trade, the social equity in the distribution of risk, citizen's information, scientific popularization, and many others. Themes, therefore, which transgress traditional land planning, which is oriented toward the determination of ground use. From this perspective, the more or less ideological emphasis of a single aspect such as the provision of green space – the so-called sacredness of the green belt – is no longer sufficient.

We could continue with a similar analysis for every level of design, and it is easy to see that the results would be perfectly in line. That leaves us to foresee the direction which efforts should take in the near future, that being the predisposition toward tools and methods which are characterized primarily by their capacity to bring together different kinds of knowledge and to make these diverse kinds of knowledge dialogue, all of this working toward the solution of environmental problems.

NOTES

First published in *Design Issues* 14 no. 3 (Autumn 1998): 74–84.

1. Environmental design is in the English-speaking culture a concept with several different meanings depending on the disciplinary context in which it is used. There is, for example, an environmental design which is understood as the control of engineering-related aspects of the environment (air quality, thermal comfort, lighting, etc.) and an environmental design which is related to psychology and human behavior. To avoid possible misunderstandings, I would like to state from the beginning that I will use environmental design in the sense of a discipline concerned with designing a systemic environment as referred to later on in the article.
2. One aspect still valid in Maldonado's 1961 definition of industrial design is the idea that designing a product does not mean assigning to it an a priori form, but coordinating and integrating all of the factors that participate in the constitutive process of the form of the product, among others, functional, symbolic, cultural, technical, and economic factors.
3. Imre Lakatos, *The Methodology of Scientific Research Programmes* (Cambridge: Cambridge University Press, 1978).
4. Emile Durkheim, *De la division du travail social* (Paris: F. Alcan, 1893).
5. Thomas P. Hughes, *American Genesis. A Century of Invention and Technological Enthusiasm, 1870–1970* (New York: Viking Penguin, 1989).
6. Mario Bunge, *The Myth of Simplicity* (Englewood Cliffs: Prentice Hall, 1963).
7. Auguste Comte, *Philosophie première. Cours de philosophie positive, leçons 1 à 45* (Paris: Hermann, 1975).
8. Herbert A. Simon, "Technology Is Not the Problem" in Peter Baumgartner and Sabine Payr, eds., *Speaking Minds* (Princeton, NJ: Princeton University Press, 1995).

FURTHER READING FOR PART I

There is a growing literature of design theory and reflection on the concepts that shape our understanding of design emerging within the design disciplines as well as a wide range of other disciplines. See, for example, Richard Buchanan, "Thinking About Design: A Historical Perspective," in "The Philosophy of Engineering Design," *Philosophy of Technology and the Engineering Sciences*, ed. Anthonie Meijers, Vol. 9 of the *Handbook of the Philosophy of Science*, eds. Dov Gabbay, Paul Thagard, and John Woods (New York: Elsevier, 2009). This provides an overview and analysis of the major concepts and strategies of design and design research in the twentieth century. For many of the original papers of the Design Methods Movement, see Nigel Cross (ed.), *Developments in Design Methodology* (New York: John Wiley & Sons, 1984). One of the most important works of design theory is Herbert A. Simon, *Sciences of the Artificial*, 3rd Edition (Cambridge, MA: MIT Press, 1996). Research into product development has given important new ideas about design and user research. For example, Jonathan Cagan and Craig Vogel, *Creating Breakthrough Products* (Upper Saddle River, NJ: Prentice Hall, 2002). For a different perspective on concepts in design, see Donald A. Schön, *The Reflective Practitioner: How Professionals Think in Action* (New York: Basic Books, 1983). Works in the philosophy of technology have useful insight into the concepts of design. See, for example, Albert Borgmann, *Technology and the Character of Contemporary Life: A Philosophical Inquiry* (Chicago: University of Chicago Press, 1984) and Carl Mitcham, *Thinking Through Technology* (Chicago: University of Chicago Press, 1994). See also, Albert Borgmann, *Holding On To Reality: The Nature of Information at the Turn of the Millennium* (Chicago: University of Chicago Press, 1999). For a discussion of ethics in design, see Caroline Whitbeck, *Ethics in Engineering Practice and Research* (Cambridge: Cambridge University Press, 1998). For new concepts of design in the context of user research, management and organizational strategy, see Steve Diller, Nathan Shedroff, and Darrel Rhea, *Making Meaning: How Successful Businesses Deliver Meaningful Customer Experiences* (Berkeley: New Riders, 2006), Robert Verganti, *Design-Driven Innovation* (Boston: Harvard Business Press, 2009), and Richard J. Boland and Fred Collopy, *Managing As Designing* (Stanford: Stanford University Press, 2004).

PART II

FABRICATION

SECTION 1

INTRODUCTION TO SECTION 1: THE DESIGN PROCESS AND NEW DOMAINS OF PRACTICE

Any discussion of fabrication in design is complicated by two factors. One factor is that designing is not an established technique, like a craft, and consequently it changes according to the nature of what is to be designed. The other is that, despite historical narratives that attribute the design of a product to a single designer or a small design team, a product's realization requires a larger community of actors who contribute to its final form and methods of production and distribution.

Building on the orders of design that Richard Buchanan proposed in several earlier *Design Issues* essays, Tony Golsby-Smith lays out the parameters of a new design practice, which he chracterizes, following Buchanan, as "Fourth-Order Design."[1] Whereas Buchanan defined the four orders as "places of invention and discovery," Golsby-Smith equates their progression with what he calls "a widening *domain* for design." He uses as a case study the Tax Law Improvement Project of the Australian government's tax office. Whereas first- and second-order design involve images and objects and the third addresses their use, the fourth-order designer, he says, broadens the boundary of the task to encompass the organization whose aims and purposes the images and objects represent. Fourth-order design defines "the widest domain of discussion around a task," moving it into the realm of culture, where consideration of human customs and practices becomes part of the designer's brief.

Michael Punt describes the transformation of an object rather than an organization as he shows how the original ENIAC computer, which was invented during the Second World War as a scientific instrument, was transformed into a consumer product. He locates this transformation within a broad community that encompassed engineers as well as amateur inventors. His principal argument is that the computer's development was not directed by a small group of designers or engineers but rather happened as a result of many people's involvement. The principal point of his account, in fact, is that amateur groups played a significant role in the process. The history of the computer he recounts suggests that "the understandings that motivate commercial innovators might sometimes be vastly at odds with those of the consumer." Basing some of his history on the work of others, he nonetheless reinforces the point that amateurs, who provided an alternative to what the computer might be, contributed more to the personal device that it eventually became than the large established manufacturers who continued to see the machine as a technical object with computation as its specialty. The point of Punt's article is that the model of a design's development is not progressive and linear, nor is it necessarily controlled by an individual or single organization. Instead, he argues, "What a machine is must be negotiated within a complex network of different interpretations."

Tomiko Thiel's account of the Connection Machine, a supercomputer whose architecture was spearheaded by a young engineer, Danny Hillis, describes a search for the form of a machine that did not previously exist. As head of the team charged with creating a design that would communicate the supercomputer's function, Theil cooperated with the physicist Richard Feynman, who devised a series of hypercubes that eventually led to the computer's formal design. The key for Thiel was extending the traditional idea of function beyond the mechanical into the abstract realm. In her case study of the computer's design, she shows that the challenge of creating a new form was met by a collective effort involving participants from a number of different disciplines.

Barry Katz presents a case study of how the Office of Strategic Services, America's wartime intelligence agency, hired a group of well-known industrial designers to create a Situation Room whose purpose would be to visualize the progress of the war. They were brought together with Hollywood producers as well as economists and other academic experts with whom there were frequent disagreements about how data was to be presented. The Situation Room was never realized, but experts working in the OSS's Visual Presentation Branch produced numerous charts, graphs, and other forms that presented vital strategic information in a visual format. Following the war, the presentation techniques devised during wartime were adapted for the design of the courtroom, and the visual materials for the Nuremberg trials as well as for the graphics used at the conference in San Francisco where the United Nations was founded. Katz describes "presentation design" as a new type of practice, whose methods were developed during wartime and were subsequently offered commercially by a few of the OSS staff after the war.

Dennis Doordan describes a radical change in aquarium design, which was brought about by several factors, most notably the belief – based on a growing environmental consciousness – that no creature exists apart from its habitat. The possibility of fabricating large environments with acrylic panels facilitated the change from small tanks. Doordan shows how designers have increasingly played a role in creating a new kind of viewing space for fish and larger aquatic mammals, combining the enlarged habitats with additional displays of information. He notes that the new display strategy creates "a place of promiscuous vision where natural and enhanced forms of seeing are mingled."

Using the technique of discourse analysis, Peter Lloyd and Jerry Busby look at the ways engineers communicate during a design project. By recording the conversations of various engineers during a series of design meetings, the authors elucidate the informal exchange of ideas that engineers engage in during the design process. Their intent was to dispel the belief that "all engineering information is somehow scientifically based." One value of their study is to show that during the design process, engineers think and communicate in a language that can be shared by designers from other disciplines.

NOTE

1. See Richard Buchanan, "Wicked Problems in Design Thinking," in *Design Issues* 8 no. 2 (Spring 1992): 5–22 and Richard Buchanan, "Branzi's Dilemma; Design in Contemporary Culture," *Design Issues* 14 no. 1 (Spring 1998): 67–84.

10

SIMULATED SEAS: EXHIBITION DESIGN IN CONTEMPORARY AQUARIUMS

Dennis Doordan

In 1857, the British naturalist H. Noel Humphreys published *Ocean Gardens*, one of the first handbooks on aquarium care. In his opening chapter, Humphreys admonished his reader: "To appreciate Nature … the mind requires a special education, without which the eye and the ear perceive but little of the miracles passing before them … The wonders of the ocean floor do not reveal themselves to vulgar eyes."[1] Today, in an era of growing environmental awareness, Humphreys's call to develop our "vulgar eyes" is as important as it was almost 150 years ago. "It is the *seeing* that is everything," Humphreys told his readers.[2] What has changed in the intervening years are the means and opportunities available for the "special education" he considered imperative in order to appreciate nature. A visit to an aquarium (or related institutions such as marine parks, zoos, and natural history museums) is one form such education can assume. It is the character of contemporary *seeing* – in particular, the multiple forms of vision afforded visitors to public aquariums – that constitutes the subject of this essay.

The recent literature on aquariums is filled with journalistic hyperbole. The steady increase in attendance and the growth of new facilities have prompted writers to coin phrases such as the "Age of Aquariums" and "Aquatic Fever" to account for the popularity of what the *Wall Street Journal* labeled "the ultimate in environmentally correct family entertainment."[3] Attendance figures are impressive; for example, more than 80 percent of adult Americans have visited an aquarium.[4] In 1993, the number of visitors to major American aquariums reached 35.4 million, up from 23 million in 1989.[5] Aquarium visits are now so popular that new aquariums, or major additions to existing facilities, are projected or already under construction in dozens of cities. For those individuals charged with serving the growing numbers of visitors, the challenges inherent in aquarium design involve far more than solving the practical problems associated with circulation, lighting and life-support systems. The Age of Aquariums requires that curators, educators and exhibit designers consider the design problem of how to provide a built environment to accommodate plants, animals and experiences usually encountered in an unbuilt, natural environment.

Public aquariums are hardly new institutions (the New York City aquarium, for example, opened in 1896; and Detroit's Belle Isle Aquarium opened in 1904).[6] In recent decades, however, the way aquariums display their holdings has changed dramatically. Fresh approaches to environmental education, combined with advances in the manufacturing technology required to fabricate huge acrylic panels, have inspired aquarium staffs to replace the traditional arrangement of numerous small tanks holding individual species with exhibits conceived as the large-scale simulation of entire aquatic habitats. Since its opening in 1984, California's Monterey Bay Aquarium has been one of the leading institutions in developing new exhibition strategies.[7] The centerpiece of the Monterey facility is the re-creation of a kelp forest – one of the distinctive marine environments present in Monterey Bay. Visitors stand before a 335,000-gallon tank, 28 feet high, while divers explain the complex web of relationships that bind the plants and animals of a kelp forest together. Missing at Monterey, as well as at other new facilities, are the traditional zoological labels limited to the dry recitation of Latin names and data concerning the size, weight and global distribution of individual species. Contemporary gallery texts provide detailed habitat and behavioral information; employ inquiry-driven formats to challenge and engage the visitor; and make direct appeals to the aquarium visitor for support of scientific research projects and conservation efforts.

The new generation of aquarium exhibits are designed to reinforce the ecological axiom that no animal exists in isolation from its environment.[8] In addition, designers and educators argue that habitat simulation creates a richer, more stimulating learning environment for most aquarium visitors.[9] Reflecting on lessons learned from his experiences as the designer of major new aquariums in Europe, North America and Asia, the architect Peter Chermayeff recently wrote: "We find that visitors have the most rewarding opportunities for a sense of personal exploration and discovery when they see the wildlife in habitats of ecologically accurate detail."[10] In an effort to render principles of ecology and aquatic biology as vividly as possible, visitors are encouraged to imagine themselves immersed in the particular environment of the animals on display. Such exhibits, argues designer Jon Coe, "transcend the average range of stimulation" and, as a result, are far more likely to create a memorable experience for the visitor.[11]

The development, in the early 1980s, of new techniques for manufacturing acrylic panels allowed aquarium designers to intensify the sense of immersion in simulated habitats by altering the visual relationship between visitors and exhibits. In place of the small glass Windows typical of older aquariums, new facilities feature clear, wall-sized acrylic panels. Vision framed through an opening measuring only a few feet square in area reinforces the sense of separation between humans and animals. Considered in light of contemporary critical theory interpretations of the "commanding gaze" of modernism as an expression of power relationships,[12] the small windows typical of older marine facilities serve as the reification of the subject-object paradigm for humankind's relationship to the rest of nature. Behavioral-based designers, meanwhile, are quick to seize on the potential of enlarged openings, such as the 30 by 15-foot panels installed in New Orleans's Aquarium of the Americas, to project the viewer into the marine realm in a visceral manner that erodes the sense of distance and detachment of earlier designs, decenters the human visitor and undermines traditional stereotypes associated with animals in captivity.[13]

As an exhibit design strategy, habitat simulation has its critics. One critique of simulation involves physical design considerations. It often requires more space to exhibit fewer artifacts or animals than traditional exhibit design formats.[14] A second critique of simulation is a cultural critique, and is concerned with simulation's alleged subversion of authenticity as a cultural value. "The very definition of the real," Jean Baudrillard argues, "has become that of which it is possible to give an equivalent reproduction."[15] Simulations, critics warn, turn complex realities into controlled fantasies. It removes the unpredictability, hardships and ambiguities of authentic experience in favor of safe, easily accessible pseudo-experiences. Writing in the *New York Review of Books*, architectural critic Ada Louise Huxtable recently added her voice to the growing list of simulation critics: "But if these 're-creations' teach something … they also devalue what they teach; the intrinsic qualities of the real place are transformed and falsified."[16]

Critics, however, often ignore the full complexity of the settings and strategies they criticize. When one shifts from verbal criticism to visual

Figure 10.1 The Kelp Forest Exhibit, Monterey Bay Aquarium, Monterey California. The centerpiece of the Monterey Bay Aquarium is a 28-foot high tank displaying a typical kelp forest habitat. Photo: Monterey Bay Aquarium.

Figure 10.2 Inquiry Driven Graphics, Vancouver Public Aquarium, Vancouver, British Columbia. Questions and suggestions concerning animal behavior in the adjacent pools prompt visitors' attention in Vancouver.

experience, and begins to consider the actual environments characteristic of habitat simulations, a different perspective emerges. The contention that simulation strategies in exhibit design inevitably erode the distinction between the signifier and the signified appears exaggerated. For the recently completed Oceanarium at Chicago's John G. Shedd Aquarium, exhibit designers replicated a stretch of the Pacific Northwest coastline – a typical habitat for the marine mammals on display.[17] Despite the scale of the exhibit and the attention lavished on details of the "local" flora and fauna, no one confuses an afternoon visit to the Oceanarium in Chicago with an excursion to the Pacific Northwest coastline. The huge trusses spanning the Oceanarium's interior and the mullions of the great curtain wall framing exterior views are too unavoidably "present" to seduce the visitor into forgetting where he or she is. The effect is akin to that encountered in large conservatories and botanical exhibition halls: a distinctive blending of artifice and nature. Furthermore, many aquariums now reveal the artifice of their simulations, dispelling any illusions of displaying a natural environment devoid of human intervention. Special displays devoted to the facility's life support systems demonstrate the intricate web of relationships that bind the natural and the artificial – the animate and the mechanical – in the complex reality of the modern aquarium.

The creation of large-scale habitat simulations is one of the distinctive design strategies employed in new or refurbished aquariums, but it is not the only noteworthy approach to putting the natural world on display. Another significant aspect of contemporary aquarium exhibits is the diversity – the types and layers – of information curators and designers are able to present to visitors. In the Arctic Gallery of the Vancouver Aquarium, visitors observe Beluga and Killer whales through wall-sized acrylic panels, 24 feet long and 8 feet high. When visitors turn to face the opposite wall, they confront a different kind of display and a different way of "seeing" marine mammals. On this wall, curators have installed a series of exhibits detailing various aspects of cetacean biology, and profiling the aquarium's own marine mammal research programs. X-rays and models reveal the inner structure of the whales' bodies, and the biological mechanisms they have developed to cope with their aquatic environment.

Humans, as Stephen Jay Gould reminds us, are visual animals: "No other group of mammals relies so strongly on sight. Our attraction to images as a source of understanding is both primal and pervasive."[18] Two different ways of seeing whales are presented in the Vancouver exhibit. One – the direct confrontation with live specimens – involves the visitor's natural vision. The other way of seeing exploits what can be identified as forms of enhanced vision: human vision augmented and amplified through technology in order to reveal things not visible to the "naked" eye. Modern technologies have dramatically expanded the domain of information amenable to visual presentation. X-rays and CAT scans, for example, probe the inner structure of the body; color-coded satellite images describe major

Figure 10.3 Oceanarium, John G. Shedd Aquarium, Chicago, Illinois. A simulated habitat based on the Pacific Northwest coastline surrounds the Oceanarium's pool. Photo: Edward Lines, Jr., John G. Shedd Aquarium.

geological and oceanographic features; and sonograms transpose sounds into images. All of these forms of enhanced vision are working their way into aquarium exhibits, supplementing, enriching and expanding the range of information available to the visitor.[19]

The provocative juxtaposition of live animals, simulated habitats and multiple forms of enhanced vision typical of progressive aquariums presents exhibition designers charged with guiding visitors through these facilities with a considerable challenge. Unlike a formal classroom or studio environment, the amount of information and the order in which it is presented is difficult to control, even in aquariums with carefully choreographed and restricted circulation routes. Aquarium visitors often attend in family or mixed groups that include individuals of different ages and educational backgrounds. The amount of time individuals will spend reading gallery texts or observing animal behavior in a single exhibit varies considerably and the task of attracting and holding visitors' attention appears daunting.[20] But aquarium officials consistently promote their institutions as distinctive and unrivaled learning environments. According to David Lonsdale, assistant director of Chicago's Shedd Aquarium, aquariums (along with related facilities such as zoos and wildlife parks) possess what other educational venues lack: live animals.

"Natural history museums, conservation organizations, documentary filmmakers, and animal rights awareness groups all play a role in teaching the public about the living world … Zoos and aquariums, however, find themselves in a unique position. We have the magic – living, breathing animals – the real thing. No other institution can place reality before its visitors the way we can."[21]

One way to conceptualize the exhibit areas of a contemporary aquarium is as a place of promiscuous vision where natural and enhanced forms of seeing are mingled. Inspired by the presence of live animals, the visitor moves through an information-rich designed environment and selects from a variety of educational materials to construct his or her own experience. The role of designers is to assimilate and arrange discrete blocks of pertinent information, and to find ways to promote what Richard Buchanan has described as "the concrete interplay and interconnection of signs, things, actions, and thoughts."[22]

Navigating through an environment of promiscuous vision should provoke an exhilarating experience of discovery, learning and growth. Psychologist Mihaly Csikszentmihalyi has identified this condition as *flow*: a psychological state of optimal experience. His book of that title provides valuable suggestions for nurturing a state of flow.[23] Will visitors avail themselves of the learning opportunities surrounding them in the new aquariums? Can designers reasonably expect visitors to expend the effort necessary to learn? In a 1988 article, Csikszentmihalyi addressed the critical importance of motivation:

> Once they are motivated … how to present information becomes secondary because the learner will go out and find information no

Figure 10.4 The Marine Mammal Gallery, Monterey Bay Aquarium, Monterey California. Replicas of whales are suspended overhead while live marine mammals are on display in the two-level exhibit beyond. Photo: Monterey Bay Aquarium.

matter how difficult it is to get it. The question is how to get them to want to learn in the first place.[24]

In the case of aquariums, the answer to the question of motivation is rooted in the primal attraction humans feel for animals. People are drawn to other forms of life – an attraction the biologist E. O. Wilson labels "biophilia"[25] – and the "magic" of live animals provides the requisite incentive for people to create their own meaningful experiences. Aquariums bring humans into contact with some of the most foreign and exotic forms of life on earth. They do so in order to entertain, to educate and, ultimately, to inspire wonder and care for the natural world.

The importance of an experience charged with wonder, awe and mystery should not be overlooked. Many writers who deal with the issue of environmental consciousness have noted a pattern in the lives of leading environmental thinkers involving moments of epiphany that exercised a lasting impact on the their lives. In *The Idea of Wilderness*, Max Oelschlaeger noted: "The need for a personal relation to wild nature is often mentioned as prior to any environmentally oriented action or the ecological reform of society."[26] In his book *The Natural Alien*, Neil Evernden identifies such moments of epiphany with the term *radical astonishment* and observes:

Figure 10.5 The Touch Pool, Monterey Bay Aquarium, Monterey California. Aquarium guides assist visitors at this hands-on exhibit. Photo: Monterey Bay Aquarium.

> The well-known revelations which figure prominently in the making of an environmentalist may be understood as a triumph of experience over belief, of the concrete over the abstract ... In each case, wonder and reflection tell us of an intensity of presentness, of an integral unfolding of self-statement, clearly in excess of sensory data and neutral registration ... These events, minor though they may seem, were profoundly important to the individuals involved ... For it was the experience of a concrete reality that precipitated their rejection of societal convention and their advocacy of a different relationship with the natural world.[27]

Can a sense of wonder, of radical astonishment, corresponding in effect to the moments of epiphany experienced by wilderness philosophers like Henry David Thoreau, John Muir, and Aldo Leopold be provoked in the crafted and artificial environment of an aquarium? To affect, in an enduring manner, visitors' conceptions of their place in the world and their obligations to other forms of life may appear to be an overly ambitious goal for something that begins, more often than not, as a recreational outing or tourist activity. It is important to acknowledge, in this regard, the power of intentional acts – of design – not only to conceive and fabricate things but also to promote experiences that shape consciousness. Watching the sunlight filter down through the gently waving kelp forest at Monterey Bay Aquarium, or staring into the eyes of a Beluga whale in the Vancouver aquarium, is to realize the significance of H. Noel Humphreys's admonition: "It is the *seeing* that is everything."[28]

NOTES

First published in *Design Issues* 11 no. 2 (Summer 1995): 3–10.

1. H. Noel Humphreys, *Ocean Gardens* (London: Sampson Low & Sons, 1857), 3–9.
2. Humphreys, *Ocean Gardens*, 9.

3. Robert Frank, "Fishing for Business: Cities Hope if They Build an Aquarium, Crowds Will Come," *The Wall Street Journal* (October 27, 1994); also see: Elaine Underwood, "Aquatic Fever," *Adweek's Marketing Week* (February 10, 1992): 22.
4. Andrew J. Nelson, "Going Wild," *American Demographics* 12, no. 2 (February 1990): 36. Nelson reports that, between 1980 and 1987, attendance at aquariums increased by 50 percent and, in 1987, combined attendance figures for aquariums, zoos, and wildlife parks reached 103 million visitors.
5. Recent attendance figures for aquariums are reported in: Frank, "Fishing for Business."
6. For an account of the early history of aquariums, see: Leighton Taylor, *Aquariums: Windows to Nature* (New York: Prentice Hall, 1993).
7. There is an extensive bibliography for the Monterey Bay Aquarium. Three relevant citations are: Carleton Knight, III, "Purposeful Chaos on Cannery Row," *Architecture* 74 (June 1985): 50–59; Dana Cuff, *Architecture: The Story of Practice* (Cambridge, MA: MIT Press, 1991): 220–235; Judith L. Connor and Nora L. Deans, "David Packard and Julie Packard. Monterey Bay Profiles in Depth," *Oceanus* 36, no. 2 (Summer 1993): 74–79.
8. Dennis P. Doordan, "Nature on Display," *Design Quarterly* (Spring 1992): 34–36.
9. Stephen Bitgood, *The Role of Simulated Immersion in Exhibition*, Technical Report no. 90-20 (Jacksonville, AL: Center for Social Design, 1990).
10. Peter Chermayeff, "The Age of Aquariums," *World Monitor* 5, no. 8 (August 1992): 56.
11. Jon C. Coe, "Design and Perception: Making the Zoo Experience Real," *Zoo Biology* 4, no. 2 (1985): 199.
12. See, for example, Martin Jay, "Scopic Regimes of Modernity," in: *Vision and Visuality*, edited by Hal Foster (Seattle: Bay Press, 1988), 3–23.
13. Jon Coe, a principal in the design firm of Coe Lee Robinson Roesch, Inc., has worked and written extensively in the field of exhibition design in zoos and animal parks. In addition to the article cited in Note no. 12, see: Jon Coe, "Bringing It All Together: Integration of Context, Content, and Message in Zoo Exhibit Design," *AAZPA Proceedings* (1982): 268–274; Jon Coe and Terry Maples, "Approaching Eden: A Behavioral Basis for Great Ape Exhibits," *AAZPA Proceedings* (1984): 117–128.
14. This is a particularly contentious issue in natural history museums with limited space and extensive collections of ethnographic materials. For a discussion of this problem in connection with new exhibits at the Field Museum of Natural History in Chicago, see: William H. Honan, "Say Goodbye to the Stuffed Elephants," *The New York Times Magazine* (January 14, 1990): 34–38.
15. Baudrillard, *Simulations* (New York: Semiotext(e), 1983), 146.
16. Huxtable, "Inventing American Reality," *The New York Review of Books* 39 (December 3, 1992): 24.
17. Dennis P. Doordan, "Ocean by the Lake," *Inland Architect* (May/June 1991): 50–55.
18. Stephen Jay Gould, "A Tale of Three Pictures," in: *Eight Little Piggies: Reflections in Natural History* (New York: W. W. Norton, 1993), 427.
19. Enhanced forms of vision already constitute part of most Americans' daily visual fare. Think, for example, of radar and satellite images incorporated in the weather reports on television news programs.
20. There is extensive literature devoted to visitor studies. An excellent introduction to the field is John H. Falk and Lynn D. Dierking, *The Museum Experience* (Washington, DC: Whalesback Books, 1992). Of particular interest in the context of this essay is Robert L. Wolf and Barbara L. Tymitz, "Studying Visitor Perceptions of Zoo Environments: A Naturalistic View," *International Zoo Yearbook* 21 (London: Zoological Society of London, 1981), 49–53.
21. David Lonsdale, "The Magic Ingredient," *Zoo Life* (Summer 1991): 8.
22. Richard Buchanan, "Wicked Problems in Design Thinking," *Design Issues* 8 no. 2 (Spring 1992): 20. Given this line of thinking, it is possible to draw a parallel between the aquarium, as a place of promiscuous vision, and the hypertextuality of digitalized databases that allow the user to create distinctive experiences based on their own non-linear reading of texts.
23. Mihaly Csikszentmihalyi, *Flow. The Psychology of Optimal Experience* (New York: Harper Perennial, 1990). Also see Richard Buchanan's review of *Flow* in *Design Issues* 8 no. 1 (Fall 1991): 80–1.
24. Mihaly Csikszentmihalyi, "Human Behavior and the Science Center," *Science Learning in the Informal Setting* (Chicago: Chicago Academy of Science, 1988), 81.
25. Edward O. Wilson, *Biophilia* (Cambridge, MA: Harvard University Press, 1984).
26. Oelschlaeger, *The Idea of Wilderness*, 303.
27. Neil Evernden, *The Natural Alien* (2nd ed., 1993), 70–71.
28. Humphreys, *Ocean Gardens*, 9.

11

THE ARTS OF WAR: "VISUAL PRESENTATION" AND NATIONAL INTELLIGENCE

Barry Katz

A NOTE ON SOURCES

Unless otherwise indicated, sources for this article are the declassified records of the Office of Strategic Services R[ecord] G[roup] 226, US National Archives and Record Administration.

The great conflicts that have scarred the twentieth century are rightly called "total" wars, but the meaning of this term has shifted over time. In the most obvious sense, the geographic scope of World Wars I and II was unprecedented: never had the soldiers of so many nations taken up arms, never had so much of the earth been aflame at once. The wars of the twentieth century have been "total" in another sense, however. Although warfare has never left noncombatant populations unscathed, the logistics of permanent mobilization – the condition described by the French urbanist Paul Virilio as "pure war"[1] – have drawn upon industry, science, agriculture, education, medicine, and other spheres of civilian life to a wholly unprecedented degree. That war in the nuclear age threatens to be total in yet another sense is a truism that requires no elaboration.

This essay concerns the mobilization of the artistic community during World War II, not as expressed in the outraged imagery of a *Guernica* or a Heartfield montage, but through the direct recruitment of the applied arts – architecture, industrial design, and graphic design – by the Office of Strategic Services, America's wartime intelligence agency. The artists drawn into the "Presentation Branch" of OSS entered the secret war with boundless enthusiasm, a determination to support the antifascist campaign, and – like most other units of the fledgling intelligence service – no particular idea of how they were supposed to do it. Their early campaigns, accordingly, reveal the bravado of infinite possibilities. Gradually, as their ambitions became adjusted to reality, a series of theoretical principles evolved which enabled them to apply the *scienza nuova* of design to the ancient arts of war. Through their pioneering experiments in the visual display of information, in the propaganda war, in service of the War Crimes trials at Nuremberg and, finally, in the waning months of the organization, in preparation for the founding conference of the United Nations in San Francisco, they left a small but indelible mark on history. Armed with this extraordinary wartime experience, they went on to make a much larger mark on their respective professions.

The contentious history of the Presentation Branch offers a compelling insight into the politics of both art and intelligence. We begin by recalling the situation that prevailed at the beginning of the war.

1 THE OFFICE OF STRATEGIC SERVICES

Overtaken by events, the United States found itself at the onset of the Second World War wholly unprepared in the field of intelligence. The Army and Navy maintained their separate military intelligence branches, the FBI dutifully carried out domestic surveillance, and a dozen other agencies conducted information-gathering activities of various sorts. No centralized intelligence service existed, however, that was capable of operating on the same level of professionalism as the British SOE, the Soviet NKVD, or the German *Sicherheitsdienst.* This failure has been explained by the legacy of post-Wilsonian isolationism; by a populist fear of an invasive secret police apparatus; and even by the patrician etiquette, attributed to Secretary of State Henry L. Stimson, that dictated that "gentlemen do not read other people's mail."

Even before the attack on Pearl Harbor put an end to American innocence, President Roosevelt had taken the first steps to redress this deficiency. In mid-1940, he asked his friend, William J. Donovan, to undertake a series of overseas missions to assess the military situation and to evaluate American intelligence needs in what was shaping up to be a war of global proportions. On July 11, 1941, the President accepted Donovan's recommendation that a "Service of Strategic Information" be created, and designated him the nation's first Coordinator of Information.[2]

Donovan's charge, in the terms of the Executive Order that created the COI, was "to collect, analyze, and correlate information and data which may bear upon national security," and to make this information available to the President and the Joint Chiefs. Donovan accepted this mission with alacrity and in its first months the Coordinator's office grew rapidly, claiming for itself the functions not only of intelligence-gathering and analysis but of espionage, propaganda, subversion, and postwar planning. His expansive vision soon ran up against the claims of more established Washington bureaucracies and, after a year of bitter jurisdictional rivalries, the agency was surgically dismembered. The overt propaganda activities of the COI were reorganized as the Office of War Information, and its secret functions, restructured along regional and functional lines, became the Office of Strategic Services.[3] Although Americans had been engaged in clandestine operations from the time when Nathan Hale disguised himself as a schoolmaster and slipped behind British lines on Long Island, this may be considered the founding of the nation's intelligence establishment.

Having virtually no precedent on which to build, the early history of OSS is that of an organization inventing itself. With remarkable boldness, Donovan recruited New Deal economists from Washington, Marxist philosophers from the German refugee community, socialite adventurers from the Ivy League, and a motley assortment of American labor activists, European Social Democrats, White Russian monarchists, and some two hundred and fifty veterans of the Abraham Lincoln Brigade. "I'd put Stalin, himself, on the OSS payroll if I thought it would help defeat Hitler," quipped the Republican Donovan in an unguarded moment. His wildly unorthodox conception of modern warfare led him, finally, into the shadowy underworld of art, architecture and design.

2 "ONE PICTURE WORTH A THOUSAND WORDS"

Despite the legends that have engulfed him, Donovan was the first to admit, as he put it somewhat crudely after the war, that the real world of intelligence is not about the "seductive blonde" or the "phony mustache," but about *information*: its collection, evaluation, and – the final link in the intelligence chain – its timely presentation to the President and the Joint Chiefs of Staff. The torrent of raw data that flowed into Washington on a daily basis from all theaters of the war lent a particular urgency and complexity to this latter task.

Influenced by the slick persuasiveness of commercial advertising, Donovan had, in his civilian law practice, frequently supported his arguments with arresting visual devices. Behind the battle cry, "One picture is worth a thousand words," he vigorously promoted these practices in his new position as Coordinator of Information. Knowing that the President would be the focal point of an inconceivable volume of information, he allocated a remarkable 24.9 percent of his first annual budget toward the design of visual presentations. How might the latest techniques be applied so as to enable the President to absorb, in a one- or two-hour, multimedia briefing session, masses of intelligence data that, in written form, might take months to assimilate?

Responsibility for this program fell to Donovan's deputy director, Col. Atherton Richards, a Hawaiian pineapple magnate who had been impressed by the bravado of the industrial designers whose visual pyrotechnics he had seen at the New York World's Fair. By September 1941, Richards already was imagining some kind of "a semi-permanent exhibit, which would dramatize the elements involved in US national defense."[4] For creative energy, he enlisted the aid of Merian C. Cooper, one of the first Hollywood producers to experiment successfully with the documentary film, and who now was a captain attached to Army Intelligence.[5] Between them, an idea took shape for an autonomous "Visual Presentation" unit. One section of it would be made up of a detachment of Hollywood technicians that had been raised by filmmaker John Ford and secured intact by Donovan's organization. The other was to be a state-of-the-art facility, staffed by a team of artists, engineers, and design professionals, that would provide the President with "a panorama of concentrated information" at any hour of the day or night.[6]

Having had the opportunity to tour the British War Situation Room, Cooper proposed that a comparable installation be constructed under the White House. Outfitted with the latest electrical, mechanical and photographic gadgetry, and dominated by an immense illuminated globe on which could be projected everything from weather fronts and oil fields to the disposition of land, air and naval forces, the proposed Situation Room would present a flexible, comprehensive, and continually updated picture of the war. Within a few months, the idea had grown from a couple of rooms into a top-secret, windowless building that became known by the intimidating code name "Q-2." Donovan personally recruited a Technical Advisory Committee of prominent industrialists: "I cannot be very explicit by letter," he teased them, "but the invention and device of this room is of the utmost importance in the national effort."[7] That it also would assure him of a private channel to the President was never far from his mind.

This grandiose scheme set in motion an alliance, which was sustained throughout the war, between the infant intelligence profession and the only slightly older profession of industrial design. In search of "the inventive genius and the technical creativeness of the country's best engineers and industrial designers,"[8] negotiations were opened with the offices of Raymond Loewy, Walter Dorwin Teague, and Henry Dreyfuss who, flushed with their triumphs at the 1939 World's Fair, signed on as Expert Consultants in September. The visionary Norman Bel Geddes was taken on only when the job was fairly well defined "so that Geddes wouldn't start moving mountains."[9] They would be joined, at this early stage, by the inventive Buckminster Fuller, and architects Louis Kahn and Bertrand Goldberg, each of whom had been experimenting with prefabricated, mass-produced housing units.[10] Lewis Mumford, fresh from the anti-isolationist polemics of the day and anxious to play some part in the war, contributed his ideas, as did his friend, Lee Simonson, the theatrical designer, as well as the greatest visual communicator of them all, Walt Elias Disney. The language of theatricality – not surprisingly – pervaded their far-reaching discussions.[11]

In an unusual collaborative effort, Loewy, Teague and Dreyfuss worked out a complicated division of labor and, billing the government at only half the exorbitant rates usually charged to commercial clients, set their staffs to work on what was confidently expected to become "the hub of the Allied war effort."[12] By early November, sketches and a scale model of the wheelchair-accessible building were presented to the President, who gave his immediate and unqualified approval and allocated one million dollars from his special funds toward its realization. The place of the designers in the intelligence war seemed assured when a set of preliminary blueprints came to the attention of the Joint Chiefs of Staff, who eagerly ordered two such rooms outfitted for their own headquarters on Constitution Avenue.[13] Jolted by the attack on Pearl Harbor on December 8, 1941, the Bureau of the Budget authorized the remaining two million dollars to start construction on the building, and the concept of visual presentation was poised, in the words of one optimistic report, to achieve "a grandiose fulfillment."

The euphoria came to an abrupt halt with the reorganization that brought OSS under the jurisdiction of the Joint Chiefs, who decided that the facilities already designed for them would, in fact, be sufficient. The planned building – with its "epidiascopes" and "stereomotographs," its Variable-Speed Statistical Visualizer and three-dimensional terrain models, and its segmented semi-transparent screens and "projection animator" that could be blindered for top-secret screenings so that not even the projectionist could see what was being shown – was never built.[14] With the indefinite suspension of what was, in effect, its *raison d'être*, the Visual Presentation Branch, in the words of an internal memorandum, "fell apart like a shattered empire."[15]

3 TOWARD A PHILOSOPHY OF PRESENTATION

The collapse of the fantasy world of Q-2 was to have a sobering effect upon the designers but, far from undoing them, it was really during this period that a rigorous "philosophy of presentation" began to take shape within OSS. It was hammered out, amid a welter of political and methodological controversies, by an ambitious team of young design professionals who had converged upon to Washington from every quarter. Their advance to

Figure 11.1 Presidential War Situation Room as envisioned by the Visual Presentation Branch. The office of Henry Dreyfuss was primarily responsible for this fantastic plan.

the front lines of the intelligence war more than compensated for the retreat of the celebrities who had recruited them.

In *Never Leave Well Enough Alone*, that masterpiece of unabashed self-aggrandizement, Raymond Loewy recalled how, when the war broke out, he loaned Donovan "one of my most brilliant young men [who] became one of the top men in the Department of Visual Presentation."[16] Allowing for Loewy's preposterous claim that the Branch was "one of the most secret and important components in the strategical planning of the war," the offices of the celebrity designers were, indeed, among the most important channels by which artistic talent flowed into the emerging intelligence community.

The "brilliant young man" whom Loewy did not trouble to name was Oliver Lundquist, a prize-winning architecture student at NYU and Columbia who had been working for Loewy as a specialist in industrial and product design. Lundquist began to do consulting work for COI during the summer of 1941, and moved to Washington on a full-time basis in October. His first assignment was to design statistical charts reflecting Soviet economic capabilities. This seemingly mundane task proved to be a key element in the decision to continue the Lend-Lease program

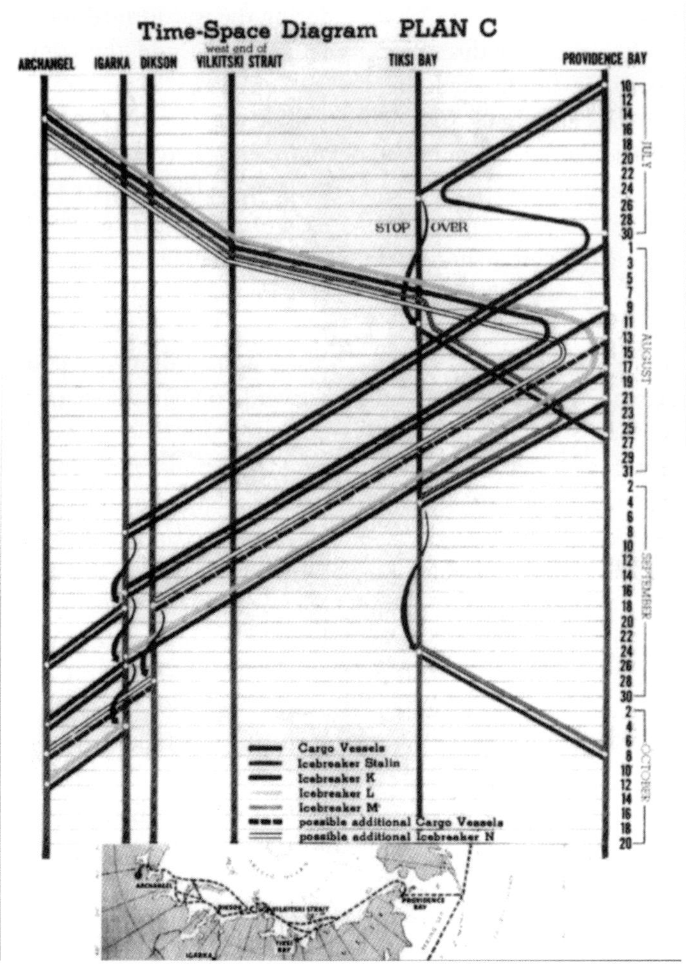

Figure 11.2 Time-Space diagram of supply routes to Russian ports, prepared by Oliver Lundquist. An example of the innovative graphics devised in the Visual Presentation Branch.

in the face of conventional military wisdom that held that a German victory in Russia was inevitable. It also suggests the imaginative approach that OSS applied to the new art of "envisioning information."[17]

Shortly thereafter, another architect, Donal McLaughlin, left the artful world of the New York designers for the more sober demands of a world at war. A product of NYU, the Beaux-Arts Institute and Yale, McLaughlin had worked with Teague on exhibits and dioramas for the 1939 World's Fair. He was doing shops and department store interiors at Loewy's when he was abruptly reassigned to the secret War Room project. In the spring of 1942, McLaughlin moved to Washington and became Chief of the Graphic Section of the Visual Presentation Branch. Over the next three years, he built up a team of artists who illustrated film reports, drew charts, graphs and maps, prepared technical illustrations of secret devices and weapons, made propaganda sketches, caricatures and forgeries, and more.

They were followed by a growing staff – 114 in all by the end of the war – of architects, industrial designers, artists, editors, illustrators, engineers, machinists, photographers, filmmakers, composers, economists, cartographers, psychologists, and even a historian. Eero Saarinen, already one of the most daring architects of his generation, had been smarting over the cancellation of a gigantic General Motors research center for which he had the contract – and from the arrival of his draft notice – when he received a call from his former Yale classmate, McLaughlin. In OSS, Saarinen became Chief of the Special Exhibits Division, with responsibility for all three-dimensional projects. Jo Mielziner, who by 1942 had designed more than 150 stage settings for New York theater, opera and ballet productions, became Chief of the Design Section. Walt Disney sent over a couple of animators and the editor of the Viking Press, David Zablodowsky, came on board to direct the Editorial Section.

Other people were drawn into the organization at early stages of careers that would blossom after the war, often on the basis of the multidisciplinary, multimedia hothouse experience of OSS. Edna Andrade moved from graphics work in OSS to a successful career in the Philadelphia art world, and Alice Provensen went on to become creator of the popular Golden Books series. Dan Kiley became one of the most celebrated figures in the modernist tradition of American landscape architecture. And Benjamin Thompson, who eventually would be awarded the coveted AIA Gold Medal for his campaigns to reinvigorate the urban life of Boston (Faneuil Hall), New York (Fulton Street Market), Baltimore (Harborplace), and Washington, DC (Union Station), acknowledged that the models and simulations he built during the war formed the basis of his later ideas about design and the communication of space and form.

Nor was this all. Georg Olden, who dropped out of art school to join the Presentation Branch, went on to become Art Director for CBS and is recognized as the first African-American to break through the color bar into the world of graphic design. Robert Konikow was drafted into OSS with a background in mathematics, but his experience in the Editorial Section redirected him into the world of communications and a distinguished career in the field of Exhibition Design. Paul Child was transferred from the Graphics Section in Washington to the OSS Outpost in Ceylon, where he prepared maps and other visual displays for the Far Eastern Theater. On the porch of a tea planter's bungalow he met – and later married – fellow OSS officer Julia McWilliams. Reassigned to the OSS outpost in Chunking, they acquired a taste for Chinese cuisine and, in postwar Paris, Paul and Julia Child mastered the art of French cooking.[18]

Overseeing this unruly gathering of creative energy were two economists, Hubert C. Barton and his deputy chief, Carl Marzani, who became the focus of some of the more scurrilous of the charges that were later directed against the agency. Barton's long-standing interest in the design of visual communications had evolved during his tenure as an economic statistician at the Federal Reserve Board. Economists had arrived in Washington only with the coming of the New Deal, and Barton soon recognized that a great deal of their work was being wasted for the simple reason of its unintelligibility outside their own charmed circle of professionals. By the beginning of the war, he had built a reputation around his campaign to bridge the gulf "between those who had the facts and knew their meaning, and those who needed the facts as a basis for decision and action."[19]

Barton's route into the COI/OSS was typical of the face-to-face network through which America's first intelligence service acquired its first generation of agents and analysts. His chief at the Federal Reserve had been Emile Despres, a theorist of acknowledged brilliance who moved to the COI in the summer of 1941, and immediately began to lure some of the nation's most gifted economists into the agency's Research and Analysis Branch (R&A). Barton – famous for his meticulous precision – was the obvious choice to serve as liaison between R&A and the proposed Visual Presentation project, and he spent much of his first year promoting his ideas for "constructive innovation" in the presentation of intelligence data.[20] In August 1942, this wily administrator became Chief of the "Presentation Division" of the newly reorganized OSS. Barton, together with his administrative assistant (and later wife), Marie Grammer, his deputy chief, Marzani, and the creative triumvirate of Lundquist, McLaughlin and Zablodowsky, formed the intellectual center of the division. Internally, it operated as "a congenial gang of brains, good humor and progressive orientation."[21] When dealing with the outer world, however, their heads were often "wreathed in clouds of polemic and dispute."[22]

4 THE POLITICS OF INFORMATION

Over the course of the war the OSS design team endured a series of administrative reorganizations. This would make for a tedious tale of bureaucratic intrigue were it not for the fact that each was occasioned by a substantive ideological controversy – some surprisingly bitter – over the nature of design and its role in the intelligence war. As in other theaters of operation, it was through the resolution of these conflicts that new and untested ideas were proposed, and theories took shape that would be conveyed into the postwar professional world. The theory of presentation took shape, in effect, in three chronological stages.

NOVEMBER 1941–JUNE 1942: VISUAL PRESENTATION UNDER THE COI

The Visual Presentation Branch was formally constituted in November 1941. Atherton Richards served as its first chief, and the documents of those halcyon days refer unabashedly to "the fun and adventure of adjusting oneself to unfamiliar and emergency conditions."[23] Still intoxicated by their newly won celebrity, the consultant designers spared neither effort nor expense in proposing extravagant futuristic displays, and Richards was advised to tread carefully so as not to disturb the "delicate balance of cooperation" that bound the artists to the generals in a common effort.

The first battle fought by the fledgling Visual Presentation Branch – and the one on which its survival ultimately depended – concerned the intellectual validity of nonverbal symbols in the communication of information. As commonplace as they may be today, the techniques proposed by the designers – illustrated reports, graphics, three-dimensional exhibits, animated motion pictures – represented an extreme departure from conventional reporting. Barton had campaigned for two years just to get the Federal Reserve Board to introduce *color* into its tables, and it was necessary now to establish the power of the image as a weapon of war.

Members of the agency's Research & Analysis Branch in particular – an outstanding unit whose academic dignitaries included five future presidents of the American Economic Association, seven future presidents of the American Historical Association, three founding members of the Frankfurt School, and a pair of Nobel laureates-in-waiting – were responsible for substantive analytical reporting, and often could not fathom the need for what they regarded as gratuitous visual embellishment. Drawing upon his professional training for a suitable metaphor, Oliver Lundquist characterized the dispute between the "academicians" of R&A and the "showmen" of the Presentation Branch in architectural terms: "On the one hand, the artist was trying to design and build a house without materials for a client who didn't particularly want one. On the other hand, the [academician] was trying to build a house for the same unreceptive client without hiring an architect."[24] It hardly mattered, however, as the designers continued their fearless march from World's Fair to World War.

AUGUST 1942–JULY 1943: THE PRESENTATION DIVISION UNDER R&A

On August 1, 1942, as part of the radical restructuring that created the streamlined Office of Strategic Services, an official order resolved the conflict between "showmen" and "academicians" by merging Presentation with the Research and Analysis Branch, the principal "intelligence" arm of OSS. This reorganization, necessitated by the sudden cancellation of the three-million-dollar "Q-2" building, put an end to the era of fantastic gadgetry and forced the unit to channel its resources into a rigorous theory of presentation.

The key figure in this program was certainly Hubert ("Hu") Barton, the first to recognize the potential for integrating visual devices into the process, and not merely the end product, of research. Barton inherited the remnants of the Presentation Branch and remained Chief, through its various reorganizations, for the duration of the war. His fundamental commitment was not to the use of graphics per se, but to the communication of *ideas*. Under his leadership a concept emerged: "Presentation is the selection, production and use of whatever medium or combination of media will transmit most effectively a particular body of facts to a particular audience."[25] That the essence of presentation was not primarily graphic or even visual, but *intellectual*, became evident in the second controversy to test the unit.

In pursuit of its mission (and of a clientele that would justify its existence), the Presentation Division ventured into the world of film and animation. Its first product was an experimental, one-reel motion picture report, consisting mostly of animated charts, on the status of *US Wartime Manpower*: How could the nation pull an estimated twelve million men out of the civilian workforce *and* increase production? The film – one of the first attempts ever to portray dynamic statistics by motion picture rather than by a static chart – was so successful in its rendering of complex demographic data that it came to the attention of Army Chief of Staff, General George Marshall. Marshall promptly commissioned the OSS to create a presentation on the structure of the US Army, which had grown from several hundred thousand to a fighting force of two million since the beginning of the war. At a meeting with Marshall's deputy chief, attended by Carl Marzani of OSS and Hollywood's Darryl F. Zanuck (then a well-tailored colonel in the Army Signal Corps), the Presentation Branch proposed a film format to include animation and live action. Zanuck scoffed that such a production would take the better part of a year, but *one month later* the five-reel film, *Organization of the Army*, was ready for its first screening. On the basis of its positive reception, Marshall ordered that it become the basic army orientation film shown to all new recruits, and the Presentation Branch – and, for that matter, OSS – were on the map.

The unexpected success of this naive foray into the movie business brought the Presentation Branch into a bitter confrontation with the professionals in John Ford's Field Photographic Unit.

On his own initiative, Ford had mobilized a unit of film technicians to undertake strategic reporting even before the outbreak of the war – the days, in the vintage Hollywood prose of one of his scriptwriters, when "Washington, the nodding head of a drowsing eagle, dozed fitfully."[26] With the dramatic success of his documentary, *The Battle of Midway*, only barely behind him, Ford clearly believed – as did the consultant designers – that his industry had a contribution to make to the war but on its own terms. When it came to making films, one of his closest associates acknowledged, Ford felt that "OSS was no different than Twentieth Century-Fox."[27]

To the Presentation Branch, however, Washington differed very much from Hollywood. According to the concept Barton and his colleagues were developing, the motion picture was not a privileged medium but one tool among many with which to represent ideas and information. A rapprochement might have been achieved, since the Field Photographic Branch tended to be concerned with newsreel-type combat footage whereas Presentation was interested in analytical films on problems of a more abstract nature. Unfortunately, Ford had brought a complete movie studio over which he exercised total control with him to Washington and his staff did not shrink from stealing its own equipment in order to deny access to his rivals. The standoff was resolved by administrative decree when the Presentation Division was unexpectedly transferred to Ford's Field Photographic Unit.

JULY 1943–MAY 1944: PRESENTATION UNDER FIELD PHOTOGRAPHIC

This arrangement actually worked only because of the mutual hostility that had grown up between the enthusiastic but cinematically inexperienced designers and the professional moviemakers, who had faint interest in problems of statistical analysis. Although committed to technically finished productions, the Presentation Division began with the premise that content was more important than form, that the media should be selected to suit the material in question, and that cinematographic techniques must never subordinate the basic idea the film was intended to convey: "We do not want or need to make 'great' motion pictures in the Hollywood sense of the word," one of Presentation's graphic artists observed pointedly. Even during the war Ford was receiving accolades from the Motion Picture Academy while, in Presentation, it was felt that the money and time expended by OSS in producing prize-winning films of the *Midway* and *December 7* variety "should have been put into analytical and official work which would have benefited OSS in the prosecution of the war."[28]

Ford, for his part, found the Presentation Division to be full of amateurs, interlopers and Communists, and a *modus vivendi* was achieved only when each group was given a clearly delimited terrain. It was, in fact, during this period that the designers did some of their most effective work. Having proven itself in the *Manpower* and *Army* films, Presentation found its services in constant demand, and productions followed on everything from the state of German morale to Edna Andrade's animations of the detonator mechanism for an explosive fountain pen to training manuals on underwater operations.

The event that pressed the Presentation team to begin to consolidate its various newfound specialties occurred in the fall of 1943. The War Department, concerned that the public not succumb to its own optimistic propaganda, announced a two-day conference to be held in the fifth floor auditorium of the new Pentagon building in which the urgency of the military situation would be presented to some two hundred and fifty leading representatives of industry, labor and the press. The OSS Presentation Division was asked to organize the event and, during the month of September, assumed responsibility for all of the two- and three-dimensional support: McLaughlin's Graphic Section created fifty-eight charts to illustrate the speeches of Generals

Marshall and Arnold; Saarinen's Exhibits team built a model Situation Room, and outfitted it with maps, terrain models and other displays; slides, animations and motion pictures were developed; and Lundquist took charge of "stage managing" the entire production, "since it became evident that not enough thought had been given to this very important element of successful presentation."[29] The War Department conference provided the Division with its first large-scale opportunity to realize Barton's theories in a single, coordinated presentation that utilized all visual media to facilitate the delivery of a vast body of technical information. The hugely successful conference was repeated to different audiences over the next several months – including a joint session of Congress – and the Presentation Division found itself swamped with requests.

5 VISUALIZING WAR AND PEACE

The successful implementation of the emergent theory of presentation seems, if anything, to have heightened tensions between the designers and the filmmakers, and ultimately it became necessary for General Donovan himself to intervene. Barton had from the beginning resisted all tendencies to have his iconoclastic unit pigeonholed: "To me," he appealed to Donovan, "presentation is a whole set of techniques (for movies, conferences, graphics, reports, speeches, situation rooms, brochures, etc.) focused on a single objective. The objective is to convey ideas … and [I] have built my staff accordingly."[30] Organizationally, this required the close collaboration of those who were presenting ideas with those who had ideas to present, and the unrestricted license to shift among all known media – verbal, visual and audio; two-dimensional and three – to convey the facts of a constantly changing situation as quickly and clearly as possible. The best means of achieving this integration of form and content seemed to be to disengage the designers both from the filmmakers and the academicians, and confer upon them the full status of "Branch," on a par with Research and Analysis, Secret Intelligence, or Special Operations. Thus, on May 9, 1944, on the eve of D-Day, American intelligence acquired its first dedicated division of designers.

In the final year of the war, the newly designated Presentation Branch expanded its range of materials and media, extended its clientele to the Departments of State and Treasury, and exported its designers to overseas bases in England, China and India. Increasingly, however, the concerns of the American intelligence community were shifting from war to peace, and the work of the Presentation Branch reflected this redirection. In January 1945, Secretary Stettinius wrote to his friend "Bill" Donovan that, "We are engaged in a number of very important projects which would be greatly facilitated by the use of presentation techniques," and requested that the services of the OSS designers be made available to the Department of State.[31] This overture led to a series of large-scale projects related to the design of the postwar world order.

Between August 21 and September 28, 1944, while the war still raged in Europe and the Pacific, delegates from thirty-nine governments met at the Dumbarton Oaks Center in Washington to lay the foundations of a postwar system of international security. On the basis of its proven record – their film version of the "War Department Report," narrated by Walter Huston, had by this time been seen by some ten million war workers across the country – the OSS Presentation Branch was asked to apply the techniques it had developed to a documentary film record of the proceedings.[32]

This assignment led directly to the first of two major postwar tasks undertaken by the designers of the OSS Presentation Branch. By the beginning of 1945, the Branch was at work on a series of projects relating to the forthcoming United Nations Conference in San Francisco – films, exhibits, publications, lecture materials, a full range of graphic services, and the behind-the-scenes tasks of "stage management" at which it had

Figure 11.3 *"Écrasez les trains Nazis!"* Zig-Zag papers containing instructions on how to derail German supply trains. A minor contribution of the Graphics Section to the Normandy campaign.

become so adept. "It looks as though we are going to be in on one of the great historic occasions of our time," wrote Donal McLaughlin to his colleague, Carl Marzani, by then stationed overseas in London: "At least we are going to do everything we can to make it historic."[33] Two weeks later, in pursuit of destiny, McLaughlin and thirty-two of his Presentation Branch colleagues – including Lundquist, Saarinen, Benjamin Thompson, and Georg Olden – boarded a special train for the four-day trip to San Francisco, where they set up shop in rooms in the old War Memorial Building.

The San Francisco conference ran for two months, during which the services of the Presentation Branch were in constant demand. Architect Benjamin Thompson developed a system of flexible charts that enabled Secretary of State Stettinius, Foreign Ministers Anthony Eden and Vyacheslav Molotov, and South African President Jan Smuts to visualize the shape of the emerging organization and the shifting political forces it reflected. Oliver Lundquist, serving as "Presentation Officer," together with Broadway theatrical director Jo Mielziner, designed the stage setting for the final signing ceremony. Working through the night, Graphics Chief McLaughlin created a lapel pin for the members of the national delegations, with an azimuthal equidistant world projection that so deftly met the political and aesthetic requirements of the occasion that it became (and remains) the official seal of the United Nations.

Such innocence as the designers still possessed was lost in San Francisco, as their graphical or stage designs met with storms of protest from delegates who perceived, better than they, that the placement of a chair, the choice of a color, or the positioning of a box on an organizational chart could have explosive ideological implications. Indeed, their attendance at virtually every committee meeting – innocuously hidden behind cameras or easels laden with diagrams and flow charts – finally put the designers of OSS in the position of true intelligence officers, as their copious notes were transformed into political reports by the Research and Analysis Branch.

The lessons learned in managing the historic San Francisco conference were applied with comparable effect to the trials of the Nazi leaders implicated in war crimes, crimes against humanity, and crimes against peace. In May 1945, as four occupying armies fanned out across a shattered Germany, the Office of the Chief Counsel circulated a memorandum to OSS outlining a comprehensive program "to demonstrate Nazi guilt clearly to the world."[34] The role of the Presentation Branch in this process would include the collection of evidence, the preparation of graphic materials for use in the trial briefs and during the proceedings, and the architectural planning and layout of the courtroom itself. Having won the propaganda war, and with the legitimacy of the tribunal at stake, the designers were now challenged to solve a barrage of technical problems in ways that did not compromise "its dignity, its dominance, or its authenticity."[35]

Concretely, this meant that supplementing the arguments of the American prosecutors would be a body of visual materials planned and executed by the Branch: detailed wall charts elucidated the political empire of Hermann Goering; photomontages exposed the functioning of concentration camps; exhibits represented the chain of accountability in the occupied countries; films were produced for use during the trials and as part of a coordinated program of public information. Justice Jackson's opening arguments were supported by a six and one-half by fifteen foot chart of the structure of the Nazi Party – "an intricate blueprint of the organization that wrecked Europe" – that was the product of six months of painstaking research by jurist Henry Kellerman of Research & Analysis and Cornelia Dodge, a twenty-four-year-old graphic designer in the Presentation Branch. In Nuremberg, Kellerman reviewed the chart in the course of his interrogation of Robert Ley, who since 1933 had been the NSDAP Chief of Party Organization. Ley, who once boasted that under Nazi rule "only sleep was still a private affair," verified the factual accuracy of their work but pointedly objected that its two-dimensional graphics had captured only the static structure and not the "soul" of the movement. Two days later, as if suddenly grasping the implications of his criticism, he committed suicide in his cell.[36]

For over a year, OSS had been closely involved in the preparations for the war crimes trials. At one point, it was expected that General Donovan himself – a skilled and flamboyant trial lawyer – would lead the prosecution. By the summer of 1945, the Presentation Branch had worked out the basic architectural logistics of the proceedings: the positioning of the judges, witnesses and defendants; apparatus for the presentation of evidence; facilities for a press corps expected to number in the hundreds; and the outfitting of offices, barracks and prison cells. There remained only the pressing problem of siting, which was resolved in July when an OSS surveying team, headed by the landscape architect Dan Kiley, began to close in on the medieval city of Nuremberg (Nürnberg). "I wanted the Nürnberg Opera House," Kiley recalled, "where we could have staged it in a very dramatic and thrilling way."[37] His dreams of a Wagnerian *Gotterdämmerung* were overruled, however, and the OSS designers began work on the repair and retrofitting of Nuremberg's imposing Palace of Justice.

Having been influenced by the teachings of Walter Gropius at Harvard, Kiley set out to solve a simple problem of functional design, consistent with his brief that "there should be no allowance in design and layout for purely decorative, propagandistic, or journalistic purposes."[38] As

Figure 11.4 Preliminary designs for the official UN lapel pin. Working within tight formal constraints and under an impossible deadline, Graphics Chief Donal McLaughlin created what is probably the most widely recognized product of the OSS.

the critique of the modernist project has by now long since demonstrated, however, there can be no design *degré zéro*, and in the highly charged environment of Nuremberg political symbolism was as much a part of "function" as were electrical outlets and a reliable public address system. This is most evident in the ultimate design of the courtroom, which placed the judges on high-backed, throne-like chairs, framed by their national flags, and towering over the twenty-one defendants seated directly across from them. On the side wall was mounted a large screen on which the record of Nazi criminality could be projected. A model was presented to Justice Jackson, head of the American delegation. "He instantly approved the plan," recalled exhibition designer Robert Konikow, "appreciating the drama inherent in the face-to-face positioning of the defendants and the judges," with the battling attorneys arrayed in a no-man's land in between.[39] With the physical site established, a team of Presentation specialists headed by David Zablodowsky was despatched to Nuremberg, where they designed everything from wall charts to press passes. By the time the historic trials opened in November, however, the Office of Strategic Services – its spies, its intelligence analysts, and its designers – had itself become history.

6 HISTORY BY DESIGN

On September 20, 1945, with the chill of autumn and the Cold War already perceptible in the Washington air, President Truman thanked General Donovan and his staff for their work, and abolished the Office of Strategic Services. The reasons for this decision were complex, but its reputation for sheltering people "of progressive orientation," as ex-Communist Carl Marzani discreetly put it, did not endear the OSS to other government agencies in the months when the shooting

Figure 11.5 Opening arguments on day three of the International Military Tribunal in Nuremberg. On the far wall is the Presentation Branch chart of the Nazi Party, "the organization that wrecked Europe."

war against German Fascism was hardening into a Cold War against Russian Communism. Heroic efforts were made to keep various units of the agency intact but, with the end of the war many individuals began to drift back to civilian law practices, unfinished academic manuscripts, or business careers. This pattern describes the Presentation Branch no less than Research and Analysis, or Special Operations.

By the time of the UN conference and the Nuremberg trials, the services of communications specialists – once tolerated as "an expendable luxury" – had come to seem indispensable in the policy process. The files of the Chief bulged with commendatory letters from high-ranking government officials, and Barton was asked to prepare a detailed proposal for the setting up of such an operation within the State Department. He seized this opportunity, once again, to elaborate the theory of presentation that had evolved during the war. It was not simply a matter of providing graphic services to random clients, he argued. Once the appropriate agencies had generated their basic facts and statistics, "Presentation performs the next stage in the process; that of selecting and producing the most effective means for transmitting the information to those responsible for ultimate review and decision."[40]

Matters were not to progress so straightforwardly, however. The end of the war saw the rapid demobilization of much of the intelligence community, and when the State Department authorized a staff of thirty-five as compared with the ninety Barton had proposed, he foresaw the dispersion of the extraordinary team he had so patiently assembled as Chief. Accordingly, the idea emerged that the Branch might, in effect, be "privatized" during this period of uncertainty, and the six ranked members put up $500 each, rented office space in a brownstone on "I" Street, and created the firm of "Presentation Associates." McLaughlin resigned from his government position to become its full-time Production Director.

In the first few months of its existence, the firm received an almost continuous flow of work, mostly from government agencies for whom its members had worked during the war. But in the spring of 1946, an extraordinary chain of events began to unfold. With the demobilization of the industrial workforce, the immediate postwar period witnessed a profound renegotiation of labor-management relations in the United States, manifest by a wave of militancy in the steel, automotive, communications, and electrical industries. A massive strike by the radical United Electrical Workers of America, violently suppressed by the Philadelphia police, had reignited the political passions of Carl Marzani, and he accepted with alacrity an offer from comrades in the UE/CIO to produce a film – *Deadline for Action*, it would be called – documenting the renewal of the class struggle.

Figure 11.6 Proposed State Department Presentation Room: a drawing by Eero Saarinen. "The general design of the room is intended to accommodate these [technical] facilities without loss of the traditional dignity of diplomatic surroundings."

Marzani's no-holds-barred film bore all the marks of his years with the OSS: animated graphics that had once traced the rise of the German Luftwaffe now exposed the rule of the American finance aristocracy; the montage techniques – using headlines, still photos, excerpts from speeches, and interviews – that had once summoned industrial workers to the antifascist war, now rallied them against the capitalist ruling class. Although he had thinly attempted to distance his project from Presentation Associates (by this time, at work on a documentary for the Federal Reserve!), the connection was readily made when Marzani was indicted for having lied on his Civil Service forms about his prior membership in the Communist Party. General Donovan – now back in his civilian law practice – declined to take the case; Marzani was sent to prison; Barton was fired on the spurious grounds of "maladministration;" and Presentation Associates was dealt a reeling but not fatal blow. The Cold War had begun, and it was a time of scoundrels.[41]

During these eventful years, however, "presentation design" had gone from a dubious and untested concept to become a vital link in a chain of intelligence, analysis and policy. Moreover, it had enabled designers to make one more critical step in their evolution toward professional identity and autonomy. Like the new sciences of atomic physics and cryptanalysis, design evolved under the exigencies of war, owing nothing to conventional academic categories and everything to the job that needed to be done. In this case, that job was to put intelligence data into forms that could be quickly assimilated and, just as quickly, translated into action.

The allied professions of design served during World War II as they have since: as a bridge – "a bridge between technicians and policy makers; a bridge between policy makers and those responsible for its execution; a bridge between those making and executing policy, and the public on whose understanding and agreement the success of policy depends."[42] The designers did not win the war, but neither, by themselves, did the generals, the diplomats, or the physicists. It was, in the truest sense, a united front in which the young design professions played an honorable and enduring role.

ACKNOWLEDGMENTS

I have greatly benefited from interviews and correspondence with the following "alumni" of the Presentation Branch, OSS, to whom I express my gratitude: Edna Andrade, Robert Konikow, Oliver Lundquist (dec.), Carl Marzani (dec.), Benjamin (and Jane) Thompson, and the tireless Donal McLaughlin. Thanks also are due the embattled National Endowment for the Humanities for research support, and the staff of the Military Records Division, National Archives and Records Administration.

NOTES

First published in *Design Issues* 12 no. 2 (Summer 1996): 3–21.

1. Paul Virilio and Sylvère Lotringer, *Pure War*, trans. by Polizzottti (New York: Semiotext(e) 1983); and Virilio, *War and Cinema. The Logistics of Perception*, trans. by Camiller (London: Verso, 1989).
2. The official documents pertaining to the creation of the COI and OSS – Donovan's "Memorandum of Establishment of Service of Strategic Information" (June 10, 1941); the Presidential Order "Designating a Coordinator of Information" (June 11, 1941); and the "Military Order of June 13, 1942" creating the Office of Strategic Services – are reproduced as Appendices B, C and E, respectively, to Thomas F. Troy, *Donovan and the CIA* (Frederick, MD: Aletheia 1981).
3. For general studies of the OSS, see also Bradley F. Smith, *The Shadow Warriors. OSS and the Origins of the CIA* (New York: Basic Books, 1983); Anthony Cave Brown, *The Last Hero. Wild Bill Donovan* (New York: Times Books, 1982); and Thomas F. Troy, *Donovan*. There is a vast literature on OSS overseas operations: for perspectives on the lesser-known Washington-based intelligence activities, see Barry M. Katz, *Foreign Intelligence. Research and Analysis*

in the Office of Strategic Services, 1942–1945 (Cambridge: Harvard University Press, 1989), and Robin Winks, *Cloak and Gown. Scholars in the Secret War, 1939–1961* (New York: The Harvill Press, 1987).

4. "The Rise and Fall of Q-2." R[ecord] G[roup] 226, Entry 99, Box 102, File 815, p. 105. See "A Note on Sources."
5. Cooper was something of an adventurer and OSS found him clearly in his element. His most famous documentaries were *Grass* (1925), filmed on location in the mountains of Persia; and *Chang* (1926), filmed in the jungles of Siam. His most celebrated feature was *King Kong* (1933).
6. "Presentation History," RG 226, Entry 99, Box 76, File 44a.
7. Donovan to Dr. Herben Kalmus [President, Technicolor Company], C. F. Kettering [Vice President, General Motors], O. G. Buckley [President, Bell Telephone Laboratories], and Dr. E. C. K. Meese [Vice President, Eastman Kodak]: RG 226, Entry 144, Box 48, File 364. The proposed building was to be erected on a sloping site adjoining OSS's existing "Q" Building – hence its name. A contemporary report, "The War in Pictures," appeared in the *New York Times*, October 8, 1941.
8. "The Rise and Fall of Q-2," loc. cit., p. 111.
9. Harry Sims Bent to Atherton Richards, "Services of the Designers" (April 29, 1942): RG 226, Entry 144, Box 49, File 369, and C. T. Coiner to Harry Batten (August 29, 1941): File 370.
10. See David Brownlee, et al., *Louis Kahn: In the Realm of Architecture* (Los Angeles: Rizzoli, 1991), 27–32; Michel Ragon, *Goldberg dans la ville* (Paris: Paris Art Center, 1985), 210–11; and Donald Albrecht, ed., *World War II and the American Dream* (Washington, DC: National Building Museum, 1995).
11. "History of Presentation in OSS" (Preliminary Draft), p. 1A: RG 226, Entry 99. Box 102, File 815. The documents from this period speak of "theatre rooms" in which "daily performances" would be "staged" for the President in order to "dramatize" the course of the war. A few documents pertaining to Lewis Mumford's consultancy, from June 2, 1942 to March 20, 1943, are included among the Mumford papers at the Van Pelt Library, University of Pennsylvania. Mr. Bertrand Goldberg provided additional information in the course of a stimulating interview in Chicago, on January 10, 1995.
12. [Assistant Chief] Armitage Watkins to the Bureau of the Budget (May 12, 1942): RG 226, Entry 144, Box 48, File 367. The arrangement is outlined in a memorandum from Henry Dreyfuss, Raymond Loewy and Walter Dorwin Teague to W. E. Reynolds, Commissioner of Public Buildings (n.d., but after mid-September 1941): RG 226, Entry 144, Box 49, File 370. Bauhaus designer Herbert Bayer also was considered at this time.
13. The facilities as actually constructed for the Joint Chiefs are described in a restricted pamphlet, "Some Facts about the Presentation Room in the Combined Chiefs of Staff Building" (Washington, DC, 1943): papers of Oliver Lundquist.
14. The Epidiascope was a device for projecting opaque originals onto a screen; the Statistical Visualizer indicated quantitative relationships through panels of vertical lights; and the Stereomotograph was a drum-type, automatic slide projector.
15. "The Rise and Fall of Q-2," p. 140; "Presentation History," RG 226, Entry 99, Box 76, File 44A. Most of the technical work on Q-2 was done by Henry Dreyfuss, whose office produced two sets of detailed blueprints preserved in the archives of the Cooper-Hewitt Museum (New York): uncatalogued microfilm. Henry Dreyfuss Collection.
16. Raymond Loewy, *Never Leave Well Enough Alone* (New York: Simon and Schuster, 1951), 150. Despite some genuinely important projects, Loewy seems to have regarded his enduring contribution to the war effort as being a swivel cardboard lipstick container designed without the use of critical war metals "to help maintain the morale of the American woman," and thus of their men: Loewy, *Industrial Design* (Woodstock, NY: Overlook, 1979), 52. See also Arthur Pulos, *The American Design Adventure* (Cambridge, MA: MIT Press, 1988), pp. 20–22.
17. The phrase belongs to Edward Tufte and his near-classic books, *The Visual Display of Quantitative Information* (Cheshire, CT: Graphics Press, 1983) and *Envisioning Information* (Cheshire, CT: Graphics Press, 1990).
18. Profiles of senior Presentation Branch officers are found in RG 226, Entry 85, Box 102, File 815. On Georg Olden, see the appreciation by Julie Lasky in *Print* (March–April, 1994): 21–4. Benjamin Thompson generously provided me with sections of his unfinished autobiographical memoir. Edna Andrade, Julia Child, Robert Konikow, Oliver Lundquist, and Donal McLaughlin contributed further details contained in this section.
19. Hubert C. Barton, "Response to State Department Accusations in February of 1947." I am grateful to Marie Barton for providing this transcript. It is useful to recall that economists entered the government in appreciable numbers only in the

1930s, and their theories and methods were still largely unknown.

20. H. C. Barton to [Edward] Mason and [Emile] Despres, "Plan for Visual Presentation of Economic Data" (November 26, 1941): RG 226, Entry 85, Box 18, File 333.
21. Carl Marzani, *The Education of a Reluctant Radical* IV: 111. Mr. Marzani generously permitted me to see this volume of his memoirs in typescript a few months before his death in 1994.
22. "The Rise and Fall of Q-2," loc. cit., p. 106.
23. Ibid., p. 118.
24. Oliver Lundquist to H. C. Barton (January 20, 1944): RG 226, Entry 85, Box 102, File 815.
25. "Proposed State Department Presentation Division" (February 1, 1945): RG 226, Entry 85, Box 25, File 413. It was at this juncture that the name of the unit was changed from "Visual Presentation" to "Presentation."
26. History of Field Photographic Branch: RG 226, Entry 99, Box 94, File 5. Ford's years with OSS are colorfully narrated by his grandson Dan Ford in *Pappy. The Life of John Ford* (New York: Prentice-Hall, 1979), 162–203. See also Andrew Sinclair, *John Ford* (New York: Dial Press, 1979), 106–125; and Tag Gallagher, *John Ford. The Man and his Films* (Berkeley: University of California Press 1986), 199–219.
27. Robert Parrish (Field Photographic Unit), quoted in Dan Ford, 164.
28. Oliver Lundquist to H. C. Barton (January 20, 1944): RG 226, Entry 85, Box 102, File 815.
29. "Official Program of the War Department Conference," Washington, DC, September 27–28, 1943: RG 226, Entry 85, box 10, File 208; Robert S. Patterson, Undersecretary of War, to General William J. Donovan (October 13, 1943).
30. Barton to Donovan (March 6, 1944): RG 226, Entry 99, Box 102, File 815.
31. [Secretary of State] "Ed" Stettinius to [Major General] "Bill" Donovan (January 10, 1945): RG 226, Entry 85, Box 25, File 413.
32. "Proposed State Department Film Report on the Dumbarton Oaks Conference" (n.d.): RG 226, Entry 85, Box 26, File 440.
33. Donal McLaughlin to Carl Marzani (April 3, 1945): RG 226, Entry 85, Box 45, File 746.
34. Lt. Gordon Dean, Office of Chief of Counsel (May 30, 1945): RG 226, Entry 85, Box 42, File 688; p. 6.
35. C. P. Kantianis to Lt. James Donovan: "Staging of Trials. The Courtroom of the International Tribunal" (June 12, 1945): RG 226, Entry 85, Box 42, File 687.
36. Draft memorandum to Lt. Gordon Dean, (n.d.): RG 226, Entry 85, Box 40, File 681. Telephone interview with Dr. Henry Kellerman, February 26, 1996.
37. Gordon Dean to General William Donovan, "Trial Site" (July 9, 1945): RG 226, Entry 85, Box 39, File 687. Kiley's rather inflated recollections of Nuremberg appear in the local Vermont publication *North by Northeast* 3, No. 3 (July 1988), pp. 6–9, 24, and are repeated by Calvin Tomkins in his appreciation, "The Garden Artists," *The New Yorker* (October 16, 1995). For another perspective on Kiley's contributions to American Modernism, cf. Gregg Bleam, "Modern and Classical Themes in the Work of Dan Kiley," in Marc Treib, ed., *Modern Landscape Architecture* (Cambridge, MA: MIT Press, 1993), 220–249.
38. "Problems Related to the Selection or Construction of the War Crimes Courtroom," Presentation Branch internal memorandum (n.d.): RG 226, Entry 85, Box 42, File 687.
39. From a private memoir graciously provided to the author by Mr. Robert Konikow: ch. 7, pp. 6–7.
40. "Proposed State Department Presentation Division" (February 1, 1945): RG 226 Entry 85, Box 25, File 413, 2.
41. Materials for the preceding section come from an interview with Carl Marzani (New York: August 4, 1994), from his memoir, "From Pentagon to Penitentiary," from Hubert Barton's "Response to State Department Accusations in February of 1947" (in the collection of Marie Barton), and from interviews with Donal McLaughlin.
42. "Proposed State Department Presentation Division" (February 1, 1945): RG 226 Entry 85, Box 25, File 413, 2.

12

"THIS IS MY BRAIN BOOK": DAY-TIMERS AND EXPEDIENT DESIGN[1]

Sara K. Schneider

Day-Timers manufactures and sells personal planners and organizers; the kind that indicate by their width and bulk how busy, organized, or just into leather you, your boss, your business prospect, or your competitor are. The Day-Timer is an object of veneration and status, like many other workaday icons: the door nameplate, the exquisitely tailored suit, and the corner office. What distinguishes the Day-Timer, however, from some of these other status symbols – as well as from its innumerable competitors – is its almost mercurial malleability; its seemingly infinite capacity to be customized to an individual user's time management and design needs. During the last ten years, the core of the Day-Timers system has changed from its relatively standard dated and time-segmented calendar sheets to what, since 1985, the company has termed the "Work Organizer," a corpus of modular add-in pages that order one's life, not by date, but by topic or project. The company sells preprinted and hole-punched customized sheets; including pages designed to take notes down from self-improvement audiotapes, keep track of frequent flier miles, record the names of spouses and children, and even note the hobbies of current sales prospects. One can also buy a three-copy, carbonless "One-Minute Memo" in a pad; sized and hole-punched to fit an existing Day-Timer; and need only check a box to indicate to a subordinate that one's aim in writing is, for example, to give him or her a one-minute, in-triplicate "praising." With this self-reflexive product, one can, of course, focus on practices with respect to time, itself; and track, on customized sheets, the intrusion of "Unscheduled Events"; with starting, stopping, and total elapsed (or wasted) time. There are time expenditure analysis forms that feature columns in which one can mark the time one would *ideally* spend on a given activity, and then track the time he or she is *actually* spending on it over weeks 1, 2, and 3. If the unseemly metaphor can be forgiven, the Day-Timer is every anal person's wildest fantasy become paper product; a kind of Charmin for the Type-A brain.

The company banks on its customers' enthusiasm for having the Day-Timer "their way" and, in fact, the manufacturer's own employees model their enthusiasm for the product they sell in much of their own behavior. The company's Customer Service employees are required to use a Day-Timer, in a format of their own choosing; and it doesn't appear to be a hardship on them. During my visits to the Allentown, Pennsylvania plant in the spring of 1994, employees typically asked me, with evident enthusiasm, how I had organized my own working Day-Timer system.[2] More than one asked to be able to handle and to page through it; to see how the pages were ordered; vowing, without my asking, not to read anything.

The Spring/Summer 1994 catalog presented employees as typical Day-Timers users, and featured photographs of them. These were captioned by testimonials attesting to the active role their

Day-Timers have played in their successes, both at work and in their personal lives. The designer of this catalog clearly placed employees' statements on pages featuring products with which there seemed to be some natural affinity. For example, on the pages featuring a new two-page, midnight-to-midnight appointment calendar, there appeared the endorsement of Barry Werley, the manufacturer's bindery manager, who explained how having a 24-hour-per-day page format allowed him to track printing done during all of the shifts.

Employees' involvement in the company is, at the very least, matched by that of its clientele. From a customer base of approximately four million, Day-Timers receives more than 100,000 letters of praise, suggestion, and complaint each year for its product and customer service. The company traditionally has sent a strong invitation to customers to provide any and all feedback. Early on, when the product was targeted primarily at lawyers and other professionals who billed for their fractions of hours, a 1963 newsletter gushed, "We love receiving orders but, honestly, we get more gratification and pleasure from your fan letters telling us how much comfort and help you get from 'Lawyer's Day' and our other products."[3] In fact, many customers explicitly mention in their letters their conviction that the company *wants* to hear from them. In addition to underscoring the kind of product continuity possible when 93 percent of its business is from repeat customers, Day-Timers' advertising plays on just how many new products actually have evolved out of such fan mail as this, and out of what it has termed its "dynamic relationship" with customers.[4] And, since 1986, each piece of correspondence has been answered personally and rather winsomely by a staff of three. A representative corporate response to a complaint letter read, in part:

> Our number one commitment is to customer service and satisfaction. We certainly missed the mark in this instance, Col. Meyers, and thank you for bringing it to our attention. We are glad to have input such as yours, because it helps us to focus our attention on areas that need improvement.[5]

Company policy regarding returns also fosters a feeling of accessibility, and an unusually cooperative relationship between manufacturer and customer. Every item it sells is unconditionally guaranteed well beyond the point of ordinary quality assurances: it is company policy, for example, that its leather binders be accepted back and replaced for up to *five years* after sale. Day-Timers even sends a Federal Express agent to the customer's door to pick up the offending item.

The stock of fan literature the company has amassed suggests a devotion, not merely to the leather and paper products that Day-Timers sells, but to the history of values that it promotes alongside its more palpable products; as well as an abiding admiration and even affection for the corporate culture, itself. Themes of survival, adventure, continuity from one generation to the next, and lifelong companionship between person and datebook are prevalent in the Day-Timers fan sagas; as is the message that, though life be fickle, the Day-Timer remains a faithful, abiding constant. Many of the letters are written with a remarkable degree of flair and energy. One customer enclosed a ten-year-old leather calendar cover that he wished the president of the company to inspect, share with his employees as a flag for their collective pride in their work, and then return for its sentimental value. He sang the praises of the product rather mellifluously:

> Often tossed into luggage and briefcases, left on rental car dashboards to bake in the searing sun, and even dropped in puddles while dashing in pouring rain from taxicabs to airline boarding gates; it has held up beautifully, showing only a beautiful patina for all this abuse. No torn or cracked leather; no broken or loose stitching; no flaws mar this product. Truly, this wallet embodies the real meaning of quality.[6]

The stories that people feel compelled to share with Day-Timers' staff often elevate the book to a status much beyond that of ordinary office equipment or personal gadget. Typically, fans admit that they refer to or think of their Day-Timers in such terms as: "my brain book," "my Bible," "my security blanket," "my lifesaver," and "my best friend." One writer testified:

> Besides having everything in one convenient place; which is a must for me since I have [the] mental handicap, from a close head injury, of not being able to pull information from my memory banks unless my mind is prompted. And this prompter is my Day-Timer! It works perfect[ly] to juggle personal memories and the so-important business dates and information. I've jokingly called it my "mind."
>
> And what an elegant and convenient place to keep one's mind.[7]

The adventuresome and lifesaving qualities of the Day-Timer can be physical as well as mental. A recurring theme of the fan mail is the death-defeating act the Day-Timer system and a faithful user can perform. One such customer wrote:

> My brother, Dick, a power plant manager, got me started on the Day-Timer system when I graduated from the State Police Academy in 1987. Recently, I was pulled from the wreckage of my flaming Troop car, leaving behind my Day-Timer to burn up with what was left of my vehicle. Shortly thereafter, my brother was kind enough to treat me to a brand new upgraded leather cover. The number of days I was without my Day-Timer system proved to me how much I depend on it throughout the day.[8]

Day-Timers makes a point of replacing those organizers that are lost in misfortunes such as muggings or the aftermath of Hurricane Andrew. And, in 1991, it made the shrewd marketing decision – given the tenor of its fan mail – to center a catalog around customer testimonials. Asking customers for releases on letters they'd already written, and sending them coupons to get their portraits taken at local Sears stores, the company began actively to collect those testimonials that told a colorful story or that gave Day-Timers use enhanced meaning. A Desert Storm tale became the leading story for the 1992–93 catalog. Major Rick Caniglia wrote in, enclosing a picture of himself seated with his open Day-Timer on a blanket in the desert:

> Dear Sir/Ms:
>
> Here is a photo from Desert Storm I thought might be of passing interest.
>
> I was Logistics Officer for a 1,650-soldier brigade. I was responsible for transportation, supply, and maintenance. My staff and I were confronted with details to boggle the mind, any one of which would bite us in more than the pocketbook if lost in the shuffle. Day-Timers' system worked.
>
> Later, when I commanded a combined arms task force, the notes in the Work Record allowed me to reconstruct details of the 300 Iraqi prisoners who "came to dinner" for the official records.
>
> Again, thanks for the system.[9]

The testimonial idea took off beyond the company's fondest hopes and, after the 1992–93 catalog appeared, the company was inundated with customers wanting their personal stories included in future catalogs. Day-Timers was able to be even more selective in the kinds of stories it used in the next catalog. Perhaps, in response to the plethora of planners that had been placed on the market during the 1980s, Day-Timers rode even harder the theme of the continuity of its product, as over and against its competitors. The company began to solicit testimonials from Day-Timers "families," boasting that: "In some cases, we've found three generations of customers in the same family."[10] One customer wrote after he awarded his daughter a Day-Timers system of her own, since she was going off to begin law school.

He reflected that he might never have been in the financial position to send her to law school at all, had he not begun using a Day-Timers system early in his own career.[11]

The indoctrination process can start quite young. A second-generation user, a nine-year-old girl named Lorian, wrote right after the New Year, 1993:

> Dear day-timers,
> I am 9 years old, and I got a day-Timer wallet (Style B22, Vinal, and colored Burgundy) and complete filler Box for Christmas. I use it every day to organize my schoolwork and free time. Both my mother and father have day-timers, and they use them all the time, too. I use the Notes & Memo Pages to write down things I plan to do that month that I don't have a date for yet. I use the 'calendar' pages in the Back to write down appointments (I don't have a lot, except Piano lessons) and things I Have to do (It's good to Be able to at a glance know what days are free for things). I use The dayly pages (2-a-day) To write down what I want to do, and what I accomplished. I also write down appointments for that day. (I use the "expense and reimbursement Record" to keep Track of how much I spend and how much I have). I use the Phone Book and work organizer to keep track of Phone numbers (Like my Piano teachers) and to put down my Ideas. I use every Bit of my day-timer Box and Wallet, and I expect to do so for many years.

Lorian's letter demonstrates how the company infuses a set of values into its customers as it initiates them in the use of its product. A Day-Timers user, almost by definition, lives the company credo: Plan ahead, follow-up, find a beauty and a virtue in efficiency, be loyal to us.

One hears in the customers' testimonials the curious duality that the company, itself, rides between its manufacture of a tangible product – the heritage of a company known in the 1940s as Dorney Printing – and its promotion, particularly during the 1980s, of ideas and terms that effectively downplayed the physical or manufacturing aspect of the company's work; that called *keeping a calendar* by the name "time management," and linked such an activity to personal success and self-mastery. A Day-Timers neophyte sounds as though he'll be prime testimonial material not too far down the pike; upon having received a "gift" of a three-months' sample of the Day-Timers system, one college student wrote to the company:

> You have enriched my life immensely by your generosity. The gift you have given me is much more than a simple planner; you have given me time itself.[12]

The influence of the original product on which the Day-Timer is based – called Lawyer's Day – remains strong in contemporary Day-Timers' corporate and fan cultures. The advertising for Lawyer's Day urged potential customers in the legal profession to keep careful tabs on billable hours in a centralized, customized-for-the-purpose location; and propounded an equation of time and money already embedded in postindustrial culture when it advertised: "Lawyers who keep time earn 42 percent more than non-time-keepers" and "Lawyer's Day earns its keep by helping you keep what you earn."[13] A spinoff product, Accountant's Day, was promoted with the line, "Time is money … Save it … Account for it … Charge for it!"[14] The postindustrial conflation of temporal and spatial modes of behavior control are seen nowhere more clearly, perhaps, than in the green-and-white lined pages, cordoned off by quarter-hours to show who must pay rent, or be called to account, for the amount of time spent in a professional person's brain.

The quality of fandom that these most energetic of Day-Timers' customers enjoy derives, at least in part, from the success with which what was originally a printing company has modeled itself as a center for training in personal development; and from its skill in linking its infinite array of customizable paper products with disembodied values cut loose from any necessary connection to pen and paper. As a portion of the mission statement reads, “We cater to individuals who are interested in organization, time management and personal achievement.”[15]

But I’d say that there is evidence as well that – despite the ephemerality of many of the ideas for which the company stands – its fan base is supremely wedded to the “thingness” of the product. The joy customers experience in handling, several times a day, a fine leather good; and in adjusting a physical notebook to reflect their personal mental “sets”; is largely what causes customers to lay out significant money, often more than $100, for a “system” in the first place.

During an all-day public training seminar the company offered in the spring of 1994, the morning session was devoted to inculcating the concepts of Day-Timers’ latest philosophy: that one must plan for team-playing to succeed at corporate ball. Right after lunch, each participant received a personal Day-Timers kit – leather binder and a seemingly endless stack of hole-punched pages, accompanied by an assortment of advertising materials and ordering forms. The next hour or so was spent teaching the group how to assemble their kits. The trainer carefully assured the participants that the leather binders might need to be handled for a while before they would become supple – staving off, I thought, any untoward questions about whether the “complimentary” binders were real leather at all. As we delightedly and somewhat blunderingly placed pages behind custom-printed binder tabs in the order specified, and noted all the different colors and formats, the trainer quipped that this part of the session is like “executive sandbox.”[16]

Executive sandbox. The phrase evokes images of out-of-scale children wearing tailored clothing, intent in their work simultaneously to make something of beauty and to “get it right” by the rule of some outside surveyor. The high level of ongoing excitement that Day-Timers fans evince in their letters may spring from the combination of two extremely self-affirming activities: that of making a physical thing that renders into objective form one’s attitudes toward time, and particularly futurity; and coming to believe that, in so doing, Day-Timers customers transcend such physical limitation: in Day-Timers’ words, “Free your mind for important decisions.”

These Day-Timers pen pals are fans not of a celebrity; nor of an oft-gazed-at sports team; but of a product, a corporate culture, and an evolving set of ideals about self-mastery. Consistent with recent discussions among scholars of fandom of the productive, rather than merely responsive capacities of fans, Day-Timers enthusiasts demand reciprocity and satisfaction, as well as the lead in communicating with the company, rejecting its attempts – in an increasingly competitive environment – to engage in cross-selling during phone sales encounters.

The sensuous component of the product is now giving way to computer software calendaring products that effectively make individual users desktop publishers of their own calendars. The Work Organizer is likely to fall by the wayside as Day-Timers makes what probably are necessary adjustments to remain competitive in an electronic age, and finds another way to market its image than as an icon of stability and longevity. Electronic culture has much of the bodilessness of existing Day-Timers culture – with no one person on whom to fix one’s enthusiasms. The thematic core of Day-Timers fan literature is hotly bound up with these themes of stability and longevity, and will likely change considerably as the product becomes increasingly bodiless in the electronic age. For a product some have come to call “my mind,” or “my brain-book,” a body – the kind that can rise phoenix-like out of a flaming car, or survive and master a Gulf War – may be the bottom line.

NOTES

First published in *Design Issues* 12 no. 2 (Summer 1996): 40–46.

1. This article owes much to the generous cooperation of Day-Timers staff, particularly Gwen Jones. Thanks also to the members of the American Anthropological Association, who heard and commented upon an earlier draft of these ideas presented at the annual conference in Atlanta in 1994. Unless otherwise noted, materials cited here are in the Day-Timers collection, Allentown, Pennsylvania.
2. The daughter of an inveterate weekend corporate pen pal, I am also an enthusiast about many of the products I use, the Day-Timer perhaps foremost among them.
3. Day-Timer Chats, 1963.
4. Day-Timer catalog, undated.
5. Letter to Col. Ed Meyers from Ann M. Koffel, Day-Timers' customer service coordinator, dated January 13, 1994.
6. Letter dated February 5, 1993 from Thomas C. Steidel.
7. Release Form for Testimonial from Elizabeth Hindman, dated February 2, 1993.
8. Testimonial Letter from John Shakeshaft, dated December 14, 1992.
9. Letter dated December 23, 1991 from Major Rick Caniglia.
10. Letter to Ken Janoski from L.J. Herman, Day-Timers' associate copy chief, dated October 15, 1993.
11. Undated letter from Jack Sebzda, Sr.
12. Undated letter from Michael Martines.
13. Undated Lawyer's Day brochures, ca. early 1960s.
14. Undated Accountant's Day brochure, ca. early 1960s.
15. *Operations Procedures* manual, November 1, 1992 version, page 1.
16. "4-D Time Management" seminar, held April 20, 1994 at Park Central Hotel, New York, NY; Tevilla Riddell, trainer.

13

THE DESIGN OF THE CONNECTION MACHINE

Tamiko Thiel

Looking towards the twenty-first century, scientists have made a list of "Grand Challenges" facing us today, tasks such as the mapping of genetic structures and the modeling of global climates. Whether of a macroscopic or microscopic scale, what these problems have in common is that, until recently, they were considered too complex to analyze. The revolutionary new research tools that make it possible to investigate these problems are the parallel supercomputers – machines with tens to thousands of multiple processors capable of performing simultaneously calculations that earlier supercomputers had to perform in sequence, one after the other.

One of the leading producers of parallel supercomputers is Thinking Machines Corporation. I was in charge of the mechanical and industrial design group that produced the package used for their first two supercomputers, the Connection Machine CM-1 and the subsequent enhanced version, the CM-2. Our desire to find a form for the machine that expressed its significance in the development of computer technology led us to re-examine the basic tenets of twentieth-century design philosophy.

The basis of this philosophy for almost a century, at least for design theorists, has been "form follows function." While both ordinary consumers, as well as acclaimed designers, have staged revolts against the asceticism this dictum seems to prescribe, no one has questioned the soundness of this "rule that shall admit of no exceptions."[1] We, too, took it as the basis for our design exploration, but quickly found that the standard interpretation of this dictum – whereby form is reduced to the utilitarian minimum necessary to fulfill structural and functional requirements – was inadequate to our purposes. This interpretation, appropriate to artifacts of the late nineteenth-century Machine Age, turned out to be inapplicable to the symbolic and abstract machines of our late twentieth-century Information Age.

We therefore began a search for a new paradigm for modern design, one that used form to express the functions of machines that manipulate signs and numbers, rather than physical objects. A second component of this paradigm, however, had to address the sterility that the modern movement has left in its wake. Although people have tired of the sublime ascetic purity of the early modern era, the gurus of "good taste" had instilled a permanent feeling of guilt that ornament, indeed anything that cannot be justified on strictly utilitarian grounds, is a "crime," a sign of cultural backwardness or degeneration.[2]

Steeped in the modern esthetic as we were, we could not simply paste decorations on a machine which, in the end, would have to prove its worth by raw technical performance in a fiercely competitive field. Nevertheless, we thought it important to express the emotional significance the machine had for us, and this led us away from what is considered "functional" design. Thinking that we had broken with the past, I discovered to my great surprise that we had, in fact, come full circle. We had fulfilled the original intent of "form follows function" as defined by the originator of the phrase, the American architect Louis Sullivan.

The following case study describes our search for this new paradigm and the solutions we found for the CM-1 and CM-2, solutions which have formed the basis of Thinking Machines' continuing design philosophy for all subsequent machines. Since the CM-2 was superseded in October 1991 by the next generation CM-5, this paper also serves as a valedictory for the original Connection Machine.

I THE FIRST OF A NEW GENERATION

Despite our ambitious goals for the appearance of the machine, Thinking Machines' concern was based on a pragmatic need: to communicate to people that this was the first of a new generation of computers, unlike any machine they had seen before.

Today, parallel processing is acknowledged as the leading edge of computer technology. In the mid-80s, however, when the first Connection Machine was introduced, it was a very radical design. At that time, all computers employed a single main processor that performed every calculation sequentially, one step after the other. Even supercomputers used this "sequential" processing, achieving faster speeds of computation largely by pushing electronic packaging technology to the extreme limits. Rumor had it that one company even hired midgets to do the wiring, as the cables formed such a dense snarl that people of average size could not service the machine.

What was true, in any case, was that supercomputers had reached nature's ultimate barrier: the speed of light, the absolute limit on the speed of signal transmission in wires. Theoretically, parallel machines could circumvent this barrier, gaining increased speed by having multiple processors execute calculations in parallel, but they seemed impossible to program and impossible to build. As a result they were either the object of scientific research or the target of skepticism and derision. For Danny Hillis, a student working on problems in human cognition at the Massachusetts Institute of Technology's Artificial Intelligence Laboratory in the late 70s, existing sequential supercomputers were simply inadequate for the problems that interested him. Even the fastest supercomputers were unable to recognize human faces, use language at the level of a five-year-old child, or perform other tasks that humans, equipped with brains much slower than any supercomputer, could solve with ease. He became convinced that it was necessary to design a parallel computer with a structure closer to that of a human brain.

In order to build the first of these new machines, Hillis helped found Thinking Machines Corporation in 1983, which introduced the CM-1 in 1986 and the higher performance version, the CM-2, in 1987. (Since the CM-2 quickly replaced the CM-1, being a faster version of the same computer architecture, as well as using the same external package, I will speak only of the CM-2 from now on.) These machines had 65,536 simple 1-bit processors that could simultaneously perform the same calculation, each on its own separate data set. For problems involving the separate but interrelated actions of many similar objects or units, such as movement of atoms, fluid flow, information retrieval, or computer graphics, this "data-parallel" structure brought tremendous increases in speed while also being easy to program. Many problems that seemed impossibly complex when analyzed with sequential logic fit naturally into a parallel data structure.[3]

This type of massively parallel architecture had been tried before, but what enabled the CM-2 to succeed where other designs had failed was an extremely flexible and fast communications network between the processors. Using the model of the human brain, Hillis's design placed importance not so much on the processors themselves, but rather on the nature and mutability of the connections between them, hence the name "Connection Machine."

Due to the highly controversial nature of the machine, Thinking Machines' top management, especially Danny Hillis and Sheryl Handler, the company's president, put a high priority on a package that would not only convince viewers of the machine's uniqueness, but would also explain the nature of its architecture, so that the appearance of the machine itself would communicate its function.

Challenged by a technically difficult packaging problem and the desire to find a unique form for the machine, Thinking Machines wanted to

Figure 13.1 This photograph of Richard Feynman, ©1986 Faustin Bray, is reproduced with the kind permission of Sound Photosynthesis, P.O. Box 2111, Mill Valley, CA, 94942. Impressed by Richard Feynman's open and creative mind, Sound Photosynthesis worked with him to make a series of videotaped lectures for laypeople on physics, computers – and just plain thinking – in the hope that they could pass on not just his ideas but also his unique way of thinking.

involve an industrial designer from the outset. Knowing that my background included industrial design as well as mechanical engineering, Danny Hillis asked me to oversee both the technical and esthetic aspects of the packaging design for the CM-2. The two functions have been split apart in subsequent design projects, but Thinking Machines maintains the policy of involving industrial designers at an early stage in the development of each new machine, so that the form of the machine can be influenced by esthetic, as well as by technical, considerations.

Far from deriding the esthetic aspects as unimportant, Dick Clayton, head of engineering at Thinking Machines, and Ted Bilodeau, the consulting mechanical engineer for the CM-2, fully supported the effort to produce a unique package for the machine and made it possible to implement an unusual design. Confronted with problems, they always found solutions instead of raising objections, and considerably enriched the design through their participation.

II THE ARCHITECTURE OF A NEW MACHINE

The search for a form had to start with bare practicalities: how do you physically organize a machine with 65,536 processors? Is it physically possible to build it like a "normal" machine, or would we have to wallpaper a room with boards, and weave a rat's nest of cables between them?

The processors were grouped 16 to a chip, making a total of 4,096 chips. These chips were to be wired together in a network having the shape of a 12-dimensional hypercube. The term "12-D," far from having to do with warp drives and extraterrestrials, had the mundane but complicated meaning that each computer chip would be directly wired to 12 other chips in such a way that any two chips – and thereby the 16 processors contained in each chip – could communicate with each other in 12 or less steps. This network would enable the rapid and flexible communication between processors that made the CM-2 so effective.[4]

Overwhelmed by the effort to visualize a 12-D connection scheme for 4,096 chips, I expressed my bemusement to Richard Feynman, the Nobel Prize-winning physicist who was helping us design the network. (His son Carl was working on the Connection Machine, and the project sounded so interesting that Richard asked if he could help too!) Feynman had the rare talent of being able to explain the most complicated things simply, and characteristically his reply to my complaint was, "Oh, that's easy!"

Feynman drew two chips and connected them to make a "1-D" cube. This is what we commonly call a "line." He then joined two 1-D cubes at their ends to make a "2-D" cube, what we commonly call a "square." Next he joined two 2-D cubes to make a "3-D" cube, which is the same as our usual understanding of a "cube." Then came the difficult step into the 4th dimension: he connected the two 3-D cubes at their ends, joining like corners to make a "4-D" cube, the first stage of what is called a hypercube, a cube with more than 3 dimensions.

Although this process can be repeated indefinitely, it becomes increasingly difficult to represent these multidimensional structures in a 2-D drawing. I finally resorted to a radical graphic simplification: I represented all dimensions greater than three as thick "hyperlines," and drew cubes as solid objects in order to visually simplify the resultant structures.

Using this simplification, it is easy to see that the structures always repeat themselves: a 4-D hypercube looks just like a 1-D line, except that it connects two cubes rather than two chips. A 5-D hypercube is a square of cubes, and a 6-D hypercube is a cube of cubes. Going further, a 9-D hypercube is a cube of 6-D hypercubes, and a 12-D hypercube is a cube of 9-D hypercubes. This is the structure used in the CM-2, a cube with 2 to the power 12 corners, or 4,096 chips, each connected to 12 other chips, each connection being one dimension of the cube.

This structure was repeated throughout every level of the machine, in the traces connecting processor chips, in the connectors between the printed circuit boards, and in the 1,000 feet of cable connecting the highest dimensions of the machine. Once we understood this basic organizational principle, we could start to build the machine. Ted Bilodeau, working on the mechanical side, and Dick Clayton, working on the electrical side, were able to reduce the machine's original proportions from room-sized to machine-sized, using only standard, off-the-shelf computer packaging technology.

III THE SEARCH FOR A DESIGN PARADIGM

Now we could turn our attention to the esthetic aspects of the Connection Machine: how did we view it, what did it mean to us, what did we want to say about it? We wanted a strong, simple form that had meaning, that expressed the essence of the machine – we wanted to let the machine speak for itself.

Our goal seemed to be clear: we wanted to show how the machine worked. The most obvious solution seemed to be to expose the interior of the computer, baring the boards and cables that made up the machine. But every computer had boards and cables – how could we show that this machine was quite different?

Just at this time Sidney Lawrence published an article called "Clean Machines at the Modern" in the magazine *Art in America.* Lawrence's article described the evolution of the idea of functionalism, showing how the Museum of Modern Art in New York had elevated the Bauhaus emphasis on "material and proportion rather than applied ornament"[5] to serve as the exclusive canon of good design and good taste. In MoMA's dictum I recognized the source of our own ideas on design: "it was precisely the inner workings of mechanical objects that offered an appropriate standard and inspiration for contemporary design … Functional design should expose and clarify function, not disguise it."[6]

Modern architects used this paradigm to lay bare the basic components of building: space, load-bearing members and building materials. Product designers dealing with exclusively mechanical products, where the physical form largely determines the function, could also implement this principle with ease. A mechanical device expresses its function in the visible world, it is graspable, and moves or physically affects its operators and their world. We, however, were working with a very different sort of product.

Our dilemma was succinctly described in the same article: "[electronic machines] are incomprehensible unless one knows about the existence of invisible forces … [they] do not visually explain themselves."[7] Indeed, both a simple text processor and a powerful supercomputer are composed of exactly the same elements – chips, printed circuit boards, and cables – and everyone except an electronics specialist will see a difference in quantity, but not quality, between these two extremes. As Lawrence concluded, "The jumbled appearances of a computer circuit, in fact, tell us nothing at all about its function."[8]

The MoMA design department has addressed itself to the esthetics of electronic components and has even exhibited the schematic beauty of integrated circuits and printed circuit boards. This fascination with the internal components of electronic devices gives no help, however, to the designer confronted with the task of developing the external appearance of a machine. Still, MoMA's design department gave us an important starting point with its characterization of the esthetics of electronics as "the dematerialization of finite shapes into diagrammatic relationships."[9]

It became clear to me that we had to extend the meaning of "function" beyond physical structure, beyond the purely mechanical into the abstract. Indeed, for people who work with computers, the image of the machine in their minds has nothing to do with boards and cables. Instead, they see the conceptual structure of the system, the

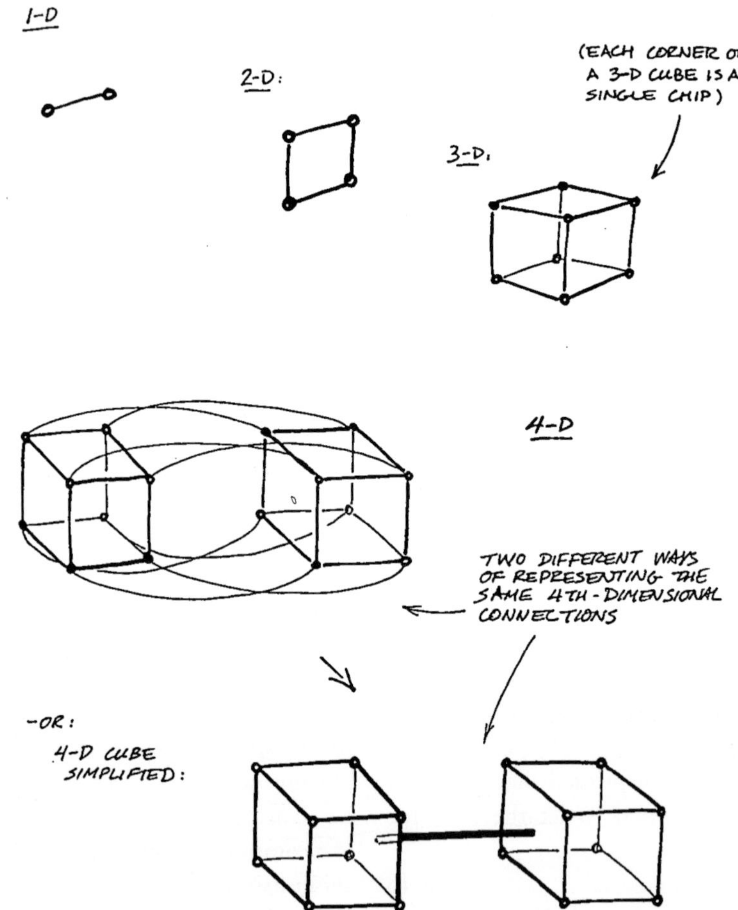

Figure 13.2a Development of a Hypercube.

"diagrammatic relationships" which can vary in function and detail in the same way that human habitation can vary from a rough, simple shelter to an ornate and complex palace. To truly understand the function of a computer one has to look at the schematic representations computer scientists use to talk about the architecture of a computer, the structure buried in microscopic layers of silicon and hidden in mazes of electronic circuitry.

This extension of the definition of "function" was our first departure from the tenet that mechanical machines should provide "a standard of reference for judging contemporary design."[10] The second departure was a rejection of the sterile, cold utilitarianism that the term "functionalism" has come to represent. We didn't want to build a computer that looked just like a refrigerator or a washing machine, even if that was the most "practical" and "functional" way to package it. We wanted the design to express the excitement we felt about the machine and about its potential to revolutionize computer architecture.

For many people, computers are bloodless beige boxes with incomprehensible electronic displays that never work anyway, especially when one is in a hurry. Scientists involved in computer research, on the other hand, see computers as the tools for building new worlds; they see themselves as pioneers and settlers in a wilderness conquered not by the plow and the rifle, nor by space ships and laser guns, but by mathematics and

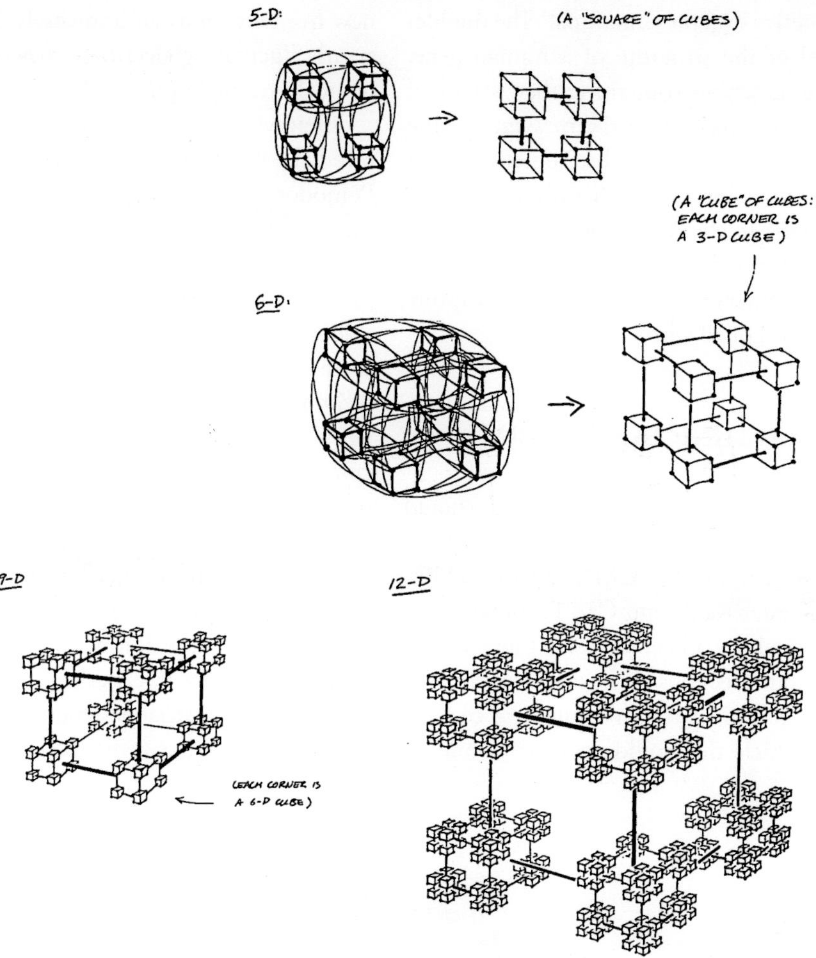

Figure 13.2b Development of a Hypercube (continued).

programs, by the brain and by abstract thought. In this community people often refer to acquaintances by their electronic mail addresses, and many friendships – and even marriages – have started on the worldwide communication network that instantly connects research labs in different cities into one great electronic watering hole.

We at Thinking Machines were all members of this electronic tribe. For us the "electronic village" eagerly awaited by preachers and gurus of the Information Age has long been a reality of daily life. The activities of this "daily life" are a semiotician's dream – or nightmare: the members of these tribes spend their time creating signs with no physical referents, systems of signs that mean exactly what their inventors wish them to mean, and worlds that function according to rules made up by their creators.

Artists and natural scientists also create intricate systems of signs or symbols, building worlds of their own that an outsider must study in order to understand. Why do lay people consider artists and natural scientists interesting, if slightly weird, while they view computer scientists as simply weird? The purpose of both art and science is to develop and communicate insights into the physical and spiritual world we all share. The systems of signs that computer scientists build, however, are actually schematic descriptions of the insides of machines and, as such, are self-referential rather than interpretive or representational. The double-helix model of the structure of a human gene, for instance, describes something that is part of each of us, but a diagram of the message-passing network of a computer describes something that is part of a machine in which only a specialist has an interest. In the design of the Connection Machine, we wanted to express the mystery of the world of computers in a way that would capture the imagination of all who saw it.

IV THE MACHINE TAKES FORM

The inspiration for the design, I believed, should come from the ideas of the computer scientists who were developing the CM-2. Danny Hillis, but also Brewster Kahle and Carl Feynman, with whom I shared an office, were all filled with a passionate and infectious enthusiasm for the machine. They talked of the machine as a cerebral starship, a vehicle that could open up boundless new frontiers, or as an immensely complex, constantly fluctuating electronic society – the image of an electronic brain.

Their visions of the machine evoked in my mind the sculptures of the Italian artist Arnaldo Pomodoro. His simple, smoothly polished geometric forms cut into or eroded away by deep surface incisions have always suggested strange planets or massive starships to me. Beneath the smooth and the serrated surfaces of his sculptures there seemed to be room for entire worlds, high-technology cultures, long-dead civilizations. His work communicated a sense of immense, seething complexity beneath the surface of a geometric, man-made object.

These were the feelings and images I wanted to capture in the physical form of the CM-2. Aware of the incestuous nature of our relationship to the Connection Machine, we looked for help from impartial, experienced outside viewers as well. The industrial designers Allen Hawthorne and Gordon Bruce, who had had many years

Figure 13.3 Arnaldo Pomodoro, *Cuba IV*, 1965–75 bronze, cm 130 × 130 × 130.

of experience designing computer products for IBM, agreed to help us with the detailed design of the machine. Additionally, to make sure we hadn't blinded ourselves to any possibilities, I asked the architect Tom Chytrowsky to spend some time helping me experiment with pure form, brainstorming whatever possible and impossible shapes the machine could take.

But if form should follow function, and function in a computer means the workings of the invisible processors hidden in the silicon chips, then the real function of the CM-2 lay in the way the processors communicated with each other, in the structure of the 12-D hypercube network. Hawthorne and Bruce were themselves convinced from the beginning that the cube-of-cubes was the right shape for the machine: the large cube built up out of 8 smaller cubes, which I had developed as a visual symbol of the CM-2 for internal use at Thinking Machines.

This symbol has been widely published on the Thinking Machines T-shirt worn by Richard Feynman on the cover of his popular book *"What Do You Care What Other People Think?"* The graphic of a 3-D hypercube represents the "hard" electrical connections of part of the 12-D network, but inside these hard rectangular boxes are the "fuzzy" software connections that can be changed independently of the physical wires and traces.

The hard physical wiring and the soft programmable connections were equally important aspects of the structure of the machine. How could we make something as abstract as a program – with the intangibility of a speech or a conversation – visible to the eye? Carl Feynman had described a fantasy of the CM-2 as a vast cloud of lights that flickered as they sent their electronic messages back and forth, like the firing of neurons in a brain. Status lights are commonly installed on printed circuit boards to provide visual monitors of the current state of components – indicating whether power is "on," or a chip is plugged in properly. Why not use these to make the intangible and unseen activity of the processors visible on the outside of the machine?

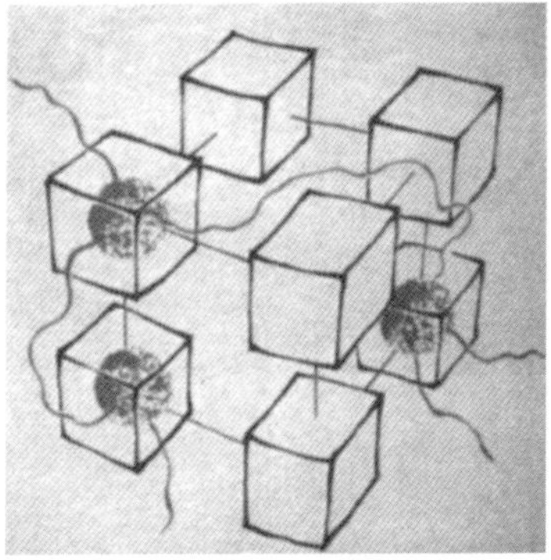

Figure 13.4 CM-1 T-shirt design, ©1983 Tamiko Thiel/Thinking Machines Corp.

Thus, we chose to depict the hardware structure of the machine in the external form of the CM-2 package, and depicted the software connections within this hardware structure using the status lights of the chips: eight cubes, each holding nine dimensions of the hypercube, are visually plugged together to form the cube-of-cubes, just as the internal electronic components are physically plugged together to form the highest level of the machine, the 12-D hypercube. Through the skin of the machine glow the lights from 4,096 chips, flickering on and off as the processors work in parallel, each one computing its own part of the data. The microscopic elements of the machine, as well as those buried in the confusion of traces and cables, thus become visible and let the machine speak for itself.

This would communicate to the viewer the immense complexity hidden beneath the surface of the machine. A massive electronic brain, 1.5 meters in height, it is connected with cables to the data drives that feed its processors information and to the workstations and monitors through which it communicates with its human users. A hard, geometric object, black (the non-color of sheer, static mass), it is filled with a soft, constantly changing cloud of lights, red (the color of life and energy). This would be a way to ornament without decorating, to express a symbolic aspect of the machine using raw form, size and proportion, color and material.

V A RETURN TO THE FUTURE

We had gone beyond the utilitarianism and sterility that "form follows function" seemed to require, defying the stricture that only structure is "good," and all else "evil." We wanted to go beyond the "necessary" to stress our vision of the CM-2 – the emotional meaning of this machine to us and our relationship to it. We saw it as a break from the past and from the strictures of the modern, but while researching this article I came to the realization that we had, on the contrary, come full circle.

Informal questioning of my architect and designer friends showed that most attributed the injunction "form follows function" to Louis Kahn or Mies van der Rohe, assigning the pronouncement to someone whose works fit our current idea of its meaning. In fact, its originator was Louis Sullivan, for whom it was the culmination of a lifelong search for a rule that "shall be so broad as to admit of no exception."[11] This came to me as quite a shock: Sullivan, a radical architect at the end of the nineteenth century, was celebrated for the power and invention of his ornament. He himself once said that "while the mass-composition [in an ornamented structure] is the more profound, the decorative ornamentation is the more intense."[12]

In Carl Condit's book *The Chicago School of Architecture*, I read: "The proper understanding of the word 'function' is the key to [Sullivan's] whole philosophy … These factors embrace not only the technical and utilitarian problems of building but also the aspirations, values, ideals and spiritual needs of human beings. Thus functionalism involved for him something far wider and deeper than utilitarian and structural considerations, as important as these are." In seeking to break away from the constraints of "form follows function," we had in fact come back to the broader intent that informed Sullivan's use of the celebrated phrase.[13]

Sullivan did seem to have set the course for the modern movement when he suggested in 1892 that "it would be greatly for our esthetic good if we should refrain entirely from the use of ornament for a period of years, in order that our thought might concentrate acutely upon the production of buildings well formed and comely in the nude."[14] This genteel formulation appeared in a much more vehement form in the writings of Adolf Loos some fifteen years later. His essay "Ornament and Crime" inveighed not only against the taste for the overly ornamented, but also against efforts to adapt ornament to fit the times, as in Art Nouveau and the products of the Wiener Werkbund.

Figure 13.5 Louis Sullivan and Dankmar Adler, Guaranty Building, Buffalo, N.Y., 1894. The Art Institute of Chicago, Ryerson Library, Burnham Library of Architecture.

Figure 13.6 Connection Machine® CM-1, Thinking Machines Corporation. (Photo: Steve Grohe.)

"Since ornament is no longer a natural product of our culture, but only a sign of backwardness or degeneration, the work of the ornamenter is no longer adequately compensated,"[15] he declared. Linking esthetic standards and social goals, he advocated the radical elimination of all ornament as the only morally permissible consequence. His was one of the most compelling voices calling for products to be manufactured to fulfill the demands of quality and durability rather than to satisfy the whim of fashion.

In a world of ever-shrinking resources and ever-mounting pollution and waste, Loos's goal has, if anything, gained validity. I believe, however, that his identification of the source of this evil was wrong. Despite his respect for native cultures, Loos saw "modern man" as being at a higher level of moral evolution than "primitive man."[16] Now, in an age that admires the aboriginal populations of the world as models of how to live in a forgotten harmony with the earth, we may also reject Loos's declaration that "Perceiving decoration as a merit means taking the standpoint of an Indian. We must overcome the Indian in us."[17] Perhaps we need to do exactly the opposite, and look at the so-called primitive or pre-industrial cultures to find out how they use ornament to increase the significance and worth of the objects they produce.

We in the industrial and post-industrial cultures have lost the tradition of ornament as an important carrier of symbolic meaning, and the "post-modernist" style of borrowing ornament from previous eras will not satisfy this need, because the symbols of the past bear no relation to the dreams, hopes, and fears that we harbor today. We cannot borrow from other cultures and other eras; we are confronted with a much harder task: we must relearn how to invest designed objects with a symbolic significance that can speak to the experience of living at the beginning of the third millennium. After years of just such an experiment as Sullivan had proposed, we must relearn the significance that ornament used to have, and what sort of human needs it used to fill.

We did not approach the CM-2 design with the idea that we must "ornament;" rather, we wanted to use the appearance of the machine as an expressive possibility to show how the machine worked. We had taken Sullivan's "form follows function," and nearly a century later adapted it to machines that he could not have dreamed of in his lifetime, machines that revolutionized the meaning of the word "machine" itself, with functions that are invisible, intangible, and abstract. We found that in a machine where structure can only be expressed through signs and diagrams, symbolism becomes a necessary tool to explicate function.

Sullivan, to whom symbolism and emotion were important aspects of a design, did not mean that designers should shy away from the emotional content of their designs. On the contrary, he celebrated human creativity as "the enormous power of man to build as a mirage, the fabric of his dreams, and with his wand of toil to make them real."[18] To us, building the Connection Machines CM-1 and CM-2, nearly a century after these words were written, no description of our efforts could ring more true.

NOTES

First published in *Design Issues* 10 no. 1 (Spring 1994): 5–18.

1. Carl W. Condit, *The Chicago School of Architecture* (University of Chicago Press, 1964), 35.
2. Adolf Loos, "Ornament und Verbrechen," from 1908, Sämtliche Schriften, ed. Franz Glück, (Wien: Verlag Herald, 1962), 27–71.
3. Daniel W. Hillis, "The Connection Machine," *Scientific American*, vol. 256 (June 1987), 108.
4. Hillis, "The Connection Machine," 111.
5. As quoted by Sidney Lawrence, "Clean Machines at the Modern," *Art in America* (Feb. 1984), 132.
6. Sidney Lawrence, "Clean Machines at the Modern," 135.
7. Sidney Lawrence, "Clean Machines at the Modern," 138–139.
8. Sidney Lawrence, "Clean Machines at the Modern," 166–167.
9. Sidney Lawrence, "Clean Machines at the Modern," 139.
10. Sidney Lawrence, "Clean Machines at the Modern," 167.
11. Louis Sullivan, *The Autobiography of an Idea* (New York: Dover Publications, 1956), 221.
12. Louis Sullivan, "Ornament in Architecture," *Kindergarten Chats* (New York: Dover Publications, 1979), 188.
13. Condit, *The Chicago School of Architecture*, 37.
14. Sullivan, "Ornament in Architecture," 187.
15. Loos, "Ornament und Verbrechen," 283.
16. Loos, "Ornament und Verbrechen," 277.
17. Loos, Adolf, "Das Luxusfahrwerk," from 3 July 1898, Sämtliche Schriften, 65.
18. Sullivan, Louis, *The Autobiography of an Idea*, 209.

14

ACCIDENTAL MACHINES: THE IMPACT OF POPULAR PARTICIPATION IN COMPUTER TECHNOLOGY

Michael Punt

This article is about computers, electronic communications, and how the current use of these technologies has been influenced by changes in the popular understanding of what they mean. It is about the role of ordinary users in defining the meaning of science and its products. It shows how, sometimes, this is a source of conflict between the narrow interests of the professional and the broader concerns of the amateur. Extrapolating from this premise, the article presents a history of the personal computer to suggest how the understandings that motivate commercial innovators might sometimes be vastly at odds with those of the consumer. It concludes by proposing that the type of historical method we use is important in explaining technology, and that this is a crucial problem to be addressed by all those with an interest in what the future of the computer industry and its products might be.

For most of us, the term "computer" has come to mean a small, inscrutable personal machine no bigger than the average television set, which sits on the desktop in the home and office, and has become an extension of our professional and recreational lives. Typically, it is used for a number of discrete operations such as word processing, spreadsheet analysis, publishing, multimedia applications, and telecommunications. This machine, commonly referred to as the PC, but more properly called a microcomputer, is the engineer's paradigm of a "black box." Few of us know how the apparatus works in detail, and there is little to be gained from the effort of understanding the finer points of the hardware and its operating system. This tendency has been nurtured by the imperative of "user friendliness," which suggests good computer/user interface design. Graphical user interfaces (GUIs) make it unnecessary for us to do more than decode the occasional acronym (ROM and RAM, for example) to which highly complex electronic modules known as "chips" have been reduced. The PC is one of the most technically complex and mysterious pieces of technology that we have to deal with on a daily basis, and it is not a coincidence that it is both a metaphor for the mind and the architecture for working models of human intelligence.

The history of the PC is the story of the transformation of a specialized piece of scientific equipment into a popular consumer product. After starting life as an ambitious laboratory project, the computer is now something that we switch on and use for either work or play, depending on circumstances. These machines, in utilitarian plastic cases, have insinuated themselves into private spaces, and provide an interface between the particular and esoteric concerns of professional science and the uncomprehending generality of the population. Increasingly, they eliminate personal relations because they are placed between one human resource and another – answering telephones, tracking accounts, and administering communities. Since personal computers are such incomprehensible and socially alienating things, it may seem willfully obtuse to want to insist that nonscientists were important in the invention of the computer, and that they continue to exert their influence on its current and future uses.

The popular response to new and complex technologies is a sensitive issue for the corporate concerns in the computer and television industries. It seems inevitable that the microcomputer will penetrate even further into professional and domestic life, and become the basis for all telecommunications in the future. Among commercial and industrial interests, there is considerable debate as to whether, in the next few years, the standard domestic entertainment and information platform will be cable television or some sort of hybrid Internet link using telephone lines and microcomputers. Some eminent commentators argue the case that television is on the point of expiring, and that the PC will take its place. Others see the apparent financial ineptness of the computer industry, and its inexperience at dealing with the entertainment world, as significant barriers to any shift away from the dominance of television as the main information and entertainment medium.

What is at stake in this question is the perception of the developers of "front end" products such as user interfaces, and even the hardware, which will make different forms of information and entertainment available. If designers can be persuaded to produce attractive products for one platform or the other (television or the PC), then the battle between the various corporate interests will be half won irrespective of the best technology. It is generally accepted now that, without the so-called "killer application" new technologies, however good, will not achieve market penetration. In the 1970s and 1980s, for example, the competition between the leading standards of VHS and Betamax in the VCR (domestic video recorder) market eventually was settled not by technical specifications, but by the widespread availability of videotapes of movies. The machine that is now most widespread (VHS) is technically inferior to its competitors, but the advantages of access to the huge back catalog of the Hollywood studios tipped the balance in favor of the VHS system.

New technology may be the beneficial fallout from science, which a thriving industrial economy and smart entrepreneurs can turn into profitable products, but when they reach the market, there are opportunities for new aesthetic forms. The impact that popular culture historically has had on the form and uses of technologies is often in competition with economic and institutional intentions. The VCR may be a successful product with high levels of market penetration, but its use as a home cinema stands as an indictment of the failure of broadcast television to produce new aesthetic forms in response to the opportunities that it offered. In their absence, the VCR resurrected the international film industry, television's most direct competitor, which was thought to be in terminal decline during the early 1970s. The interaction between technology and society is not a top-down relationship, but something much more complex in which there is a struggle for what inventions mean and how they will be used.

Something similar to the VCR story is already happening in popular telecommunications. The Internet is not only the consequence of certain technological developments, but also owes much to astute political maneuvers by the US government. It was expanded as an international public resource mainly by enthusiasts outside of the market system working long hours without payment. Not surprisingly, it has not fulfilled the corporate expectations of social cohesion as a computer-based Citizens' Band network, but has become a conduit for the exchange of radical politics and socially subversive material. Much of the traffic passing between subscribers is profoundly antitechnology, antiestablishment and, especially, anti-American. The current struggle is between those who see the network as an ideal forum for social criticism, and those who want to integrate it into the capitalist system. Although the odds always appear to be weighted in favor of large institutional bodies, as the case of the VCR shows, the users of a technology have some determining influence over its eventual meaning, and it is by no means certain that the Internet will indeed become the golden goose that many entrepreneurs and large corporations hope.

The determining influence of users on the eventual meaning of technology is not a particularly twentieth-century phenomenon. David Nye's account of the electrification of America has shown how the meaning of electricity was negotiated between the various constituencies who produced it, those who used it, and those who opposed it.[1] I have shown elsewhere how the very invention of the cinema in the closing years of the last century was, to some extent, the consequence of a crisis in the interpretation of the function of both the professional scientist and the amateur in the construction of new knowledge. The theme of this struggle has never disappeared from popular cinema, and remains in the foreground of many successful movies today. Hollywood producers currently appear to find the problem of technological change a compelling topic for major investments. The mainstream "blockbuster" movie may easily be dismissed as aesthetically bankrupt, manipulative, and cynically exploitative of ordinary people's anxieties; but often provides an archaeological trace of science and popular culture reaching satisfactory compromise through a mythical reinterpretation of technology. During the summer of 1996, cinema box office records were being broken by *Independence Day*, a film that showed the terrible consequences of letting technologists run the world. The annihilation of the human race by the superior intelligence of both the aliens and the scientists, with whom they had much in common, was ultimately overcome by cunning, physical prowess, and the common sense of the lay person. The success of *Independence Day* was closely followed by *Mission Impossible* and *Twister*, films that also pitched the cloistered abstractions of high science against a practical firsthand experience of the world. In each of these stories, it is, finally, an ordinary *man* in touch with *himself* and nature who saves the human race, and it is the professional scientists who are dispatched into oblivion.[2] The aftermath of the carnage in each case is a less scientific and a more humanly centered world. In these films, Hollywood, as usual, manages to resolve the pressing and intransigent problem of technology, which is both life-enhancing and dehumanizing, by providing us with a satisfactory imaginary solution.

Perhaps the movies are so good at articulating anxiety about science and technology because producers and filmmakers share some of the audience's ambivalence to them. During the early 1970s, it seemed that watching television had made going to the movies redundant. The film industry fell into deep economic depression and almost bankrupted itself, but somehow managed to revive. As Thomas Schatz has convincingly shown,

> Ensuing pronouncements of the "death of Hollywood" proved to be greatly exaggerated, however, the [movie] industry not only survived [television] but flourished in a media marketplace. Among the more remarkable developments in recent media history, in fact, is the staying power of the major studios (Paramount, MGM, Warners, et al.) and of the movie itself ...[3]

To even the most casual observer, the familiar logos at the end of prime time shows is evidence of the degree to which television production is now in the economic control of Hollywood.[4] One factor in this revival of fortunes is the new technologies for encoding and storing data. Computer techniques that reduce production costs and enhance the product, electronic distribution of both text and images, and high-definition television combined with cheap videocassette recorders (VCR) now make it possible for more people than ever before in the history of the world to watch movies. The proliferation of television channels, video entertainment, computer games, and cheap publishing has ensured that the film industry has never been more profitable, and yet the technologies that have made this possible – especially television and computers – are often demonized in the movies themselves. The films that Hollywood prefers to make are often stern reminders to the industry that the very inventions that appear to make life better can quite suddenly also make it worse. Inasmuch as moviemaking is now inextricably tied in with the electronic entertainment media, the ambivalence and anxieties of Hollywood are also not far below the confident exterior of the personal computer industry.

The uncertainties in the future of the entertainment industry, precipitated by new network technologies, were highlighted in the summer of 1996 with a number of well-publicized and contradictory predictions. Concurrent with the success of *Independence Day*, for example, Microsoft Corporation announced a new software development that would allow the home computer to become a terminal on the Internet. This software will allow users to not only access data but also store personal files remotely on servers which will appear on the PC desktop as icons and can be used in exactly the same way as if they were on the resident hard drive. Apple, too, has been working on a system called "Pippin" that will turn the home computer into a personalized unit similar in size to the Walkman.[5] These announcements herald the beginning of a new generation of personal computers which will dispense with the keyboard as an interface, and uses a standard television instead of a dedicated computer video display unit (VDU). Since this will reduce the cost of the PC (to around $400), it is hoped that they will be instrumental in the penetration of computer communications into a mass market through the entertainment opportunities of the Internet. Of course, this system will incur telephone connection charges but, increasingly, the economics of cable television distribution, based on selling consumers to advertisers, makes it attractive to offer cheap and sometimes free local telephone access.[6] There is a great deal at stake here since, if this does turn out to be the future of personal computing, then, as both Microsoft and Apple realize, seizing the initiative could significantly shift the balance of power between hardware and software producers, and this would have economic implications for the future of television (and Hollywood).

These two companies are, as ever, competitively responding to projected hardware trends with the software opportunities that public access to the Internet offers.[7] Phillips and The Interactive Digital Appliance Company, who are respectable players in the hardware side of the industry, are fighting back. They also see the future of the entertainment market in a convergence of television and computer technologies, and are developing their own products accordingly. By the end of 1996, Inteq promised a 27-inch entertainment machine which "... will be equipped with 'Zenith NetVision' capability based on [a] broad technology platform for information appliances. NetVision's capability will support a range of services including browsing the World Wide Web, accessing electronic mail, and future JAVA terminal applications." The NetVision set will include a fast telephone modem, "picture-in-picture" image (which allows the television to be viewed simultaneously with the Internet), and "Theater Surround Sound." It is expected to sell for around $1,000. The manufacturers do not intend to replace the PC, but instead allow the "home theater enthusiast" to "... combine channel surfing with Web surfing."[8] Zenith, too, is attempting to use the profit potential of the entertainment market to gain control of the technology through the convergence of consumer electronics and digital networks. "Net Vision," they claim, "will allow consumers for the first time to experience the Web without the expense or complexity of a PC."[9] These new products are based on the assumption that television will remain the dominant platform for home entertainment.

George Gilder, a prolific cultural commentator on the relationship between technology and electronics, on the other hand, forcibly suggests that, for technological, social, and economic reasons, the corporate preference for television technologies is a wrong turning. The combining of television and the computer is, in his view, a "convergence of corpses."[10] He argues that the electronic future lies with the PC, and supports his claim with an historical analysis of the market which shows that computer-centered technologies, which may not have the showbiz appeal of television, are nonetheless more successful than convergences. The PC market, Gilder points out, is expanding much faster than was expected, and certainly more than television. The current problem in the industry, as he sees it, is that much of the PC's power is diverted away from rapid data management to cope with compression protocols enforced by narrow bandwidths, and that this results in the poor video images that are currently tolerated in teleconferencing and on the Internet. This, he suggests, will be unimaginably transformed so that broadcast quality images will be the standard when broader bandwidths are introduced. In George Gilder's view, once this happens, multimedia will be a realizable goal rather than a rather sorry pastiche of other modes of entertainment such as television, the movies, and photography.

Most critically, however, Gilder recognizes that the active participation of a broad public, interacting with the formal properties of these new technologies, is important for their economic success. Television, he claims, cannot adequately deal with text and is inherently a "couch potato" device, principally because it consumes human capital. By this, he means that, whereas television (as an entertainment) is generally used as a distraction from business and careers, personal computing technology encourages personal growth. Even when the computer is used for recreation and entertainment, it tends to develop skills and intellectual competence that are productive in other domains. This asymmetry between the television and the PC will tip the balance in favor of the computer as the dominant entertainment platform. Gilder's further prediction is that, when this happens, the "PC age" will recuperate the lost cult of the amateur that preceded television, as people use it to advance particular interests. Moreover, it will stimulate an increase in book culture, which, in spite of competition from other media, is currently enjoying an enormous economic success.

Gilder's history and future of digital technology is influenced by the recent return to favor of so-called "supply side economics." The emergence of the PC coincided with some influential revision in the way that American, and some European, governments attempted to control inflation. It was felt that only by stimulating the movement of goods and services could the flagging economies of the industrialized nations be revived. Cutting taxes and government intervention, it was argued, stimulated investment and re-tooling which, in turn, would promote growth, increase revenues, and control inflation. The fashion for this policy stimulated a restructuring in some industries which had been built upon the early twentieth-century preference for vertical integration, in which all parts of the processes of manufacture, distribution, and retail were in the control of a single corporation. New horizontal structures were put in place which exploited and controlled the potential of network technologies. The largest corporations reorganized themselves more as financiers than manufacturers and distributors of products. In the process of this restructuring, limited opportunities for small-scale, low investment businesses opened up, to provide goods and services at prices and volumes which were controlled by the mechanics of a market economy. The pros and cons of supply side economics have been widely debated, but the extent to which George Gilder's case rests upon a quite specific idealization of the American economy is illustrated by Robert X. Cringely's equally compelling, although fundamentally different, aetiology of the PC and prognosis for its development.[11]

Since the early 1970s, Robert X. Cringely, a gossip columnist for *InfoWorld*, has assiduously followed the story of the impact of individual speculators on the development of the personal computer. His account of the PC industry is chronicled in *Accidental Empires*, which was first published in 1994 and revised in 1996. It describes the growth of the personal computer from an amateur obsession to the fourth most profitable industry in history (after automobiles, energy production, and illegal drugs).[12] Unlike George Gilder, who tells the story of computing from the point of view of the winners, Cringely provides a more symmetrical causality for the various changes in hardware and software technology by charting the realization of particular personal ambitions of some individuals associated with the industry, as well as the near misses of others. He shows how certain people with particular talents and similar social inhibitions, accidentally met others and were able to temporarily challenge the hegemony of the establishment (most notably the market leader – IBM) by developing an alternative view of the computer as a personal (rather than corporate) machine. With well-chosen examples of spectacular financial misjudgments by major players in the industry, he shows a gap between established powers in the industry and maverick entrepreneurs (such as the young Bill Gates) who were closely in touch with an alternative view of what computers and computing "meant." This interpretative group was a small, but obsessive, constituency of amateurs who were interested in computing relative to semirecreational uses. Once equipped with basic machines, many cemented their affiliation with the community of other enthusiasts by writing inventive software. Commercial exploitation was the obvious next step for the personally ambitious, and companies such as IBM, who were committed to the idea of computing as a hardware business, faced competition from unexpected quarters.

These competing interpretative groups – the hardware giants and the software-based enthusiasts – have, according to Cringely, reached some kind of consensus in the pattern of product development, and this accounts for the present characteristics of the industry. For example, he shows that hardware innovation is rapidly subsumed by software applications. His predictions for the future of computing as being dominated by software solutions from Microsoft are based on his personality-based overview of the past:

> The trend in information technologies is first to solve a problem with expensive, dedicated hardware, then with general purpose non-dedicated hardware, and finally with software. The first digital computers, after all, weren't really computers at all: they were custom-built machines for calculating artillery trajectories or simulating atomic bombs. The fact that they used digital circuits was almost immaterial, since the early machines could not be easily programmed. The next generation of computers still relied on custom hardware, but could not be programmed for many types of the jobs, and computers today often substitute software, in the form of emulators, for what was originally done in custom hardware.[13]

Cringely's approach suggests that understanding the historical causality of technologies is vital if expensive investment mistakes are to be avoided. As he observes, the errors of IBM are even now being repeated on a vaster scale by Pacific Rim speculators. "The hardware business is dying" he asserts, "Let it. The Japanese and Koreans are so eager to take over the PC hardware business that they are literally trying to buy the future. But they're only buying the past."[14] By implication, Cringely's history could teach them differently.

Hardware will, of course, change to some degree, and like many commentators, Cringely sees a convergence of television and the computer in a set-top device with a highly efficient processing chip to decode and decompress data. What will make this product successful in the domestic market is computing power that is both cheap and better than the average PC. Motorola is currently investing in this vision of the future with the Power PC 301 processor in the belief that the market for new personal computers has leveled off. New sales, based on a periodic replacement strategy, will be used as an opportunity to upgrade processing power (in much the same pattern as company car renewal). As Cringely points out: "The Power PC 301 yields a set-top device that has the graphics performance equivalent to a Silicon Graphics Indigo workstation, and yet will only cost users £250. Who is going to want to sit at their computer when they can find more computing power (and more network services) available on their TV?"[15] Motorola expects the demand for set-top devices to be one billion units in the next decade. Unlike Intel (the other leading player in chip production), which is going for ever higher specifications, they are structuring their research and development, as well as their marketing, to produce a cheap, fast chip. At the beginning of 1997, in line with Cringely's predictions, the Motorola Company announced that it intends to pull out of developing Power PC-based systems but added, nodding in the direction of convergence, they will, however, continue to work on Internet access devices using the chip.

Ultimately Robert Cringely's methodology, and his careful sifting of the evidence provides both a convincing explanation for the present and, as the recent announcement from Motorola illustrates, a credible forecasting tool. What distinguishes him from George Gilder is a belief that technology and culture do not function confrontationally, but rather more dialectically. Cringely maintains that technological innovation is shaped by both the possibilities of the hardware and the imagination of those who encounter them. In Cringely's history of the personal computer, he charts a transformation from the fixed, bulky machines, accessed by the professional elite, to ephemeral, simple, and cheap software that is, above all, popular. The causality, as far as he is concerned, is the interaction of a new kind of machine with "… disenfranchised nerds like Bill Gates who didn't meet the macho standards of American maleness and so looked for a way to create their own adult world, and through that creation, gain the admiration of their peers."[16] In a seductive homology, Cringely suggests that personal computers are the fallout from "nerds" replacing the heavy-duty muscle of the corporate hardware giants with "brainy" software.

Cringely is concerned with the power politics of Silicon Valley, his conceptual premise and methodology yield some brilliant insights, but the deficit in his account, at least for product designers working with multimedia, is what the personal computer might mean for "ordinary users" now. When new technologies meet ordinary people, they are sometimes transformed beyond recognition and, moreover, they can continue to change. It is now well understood by historians of early cinema, for example, that the basic apparatus became the foundation of a mass cultural experience because of the interaction of technological, economic, and social determinants.[17] Histories of the invention of the cinematographe, and the economic exploitation of the popular enthusiasm for moving pictures, cannot satisfactorily account for how the films looked. For this, we must turn to the audience's interpretation and expectations of the technology that were often (as they are today) confused and inconsistent. Early producers often were also exhibitors, and were able to adjust their films in response to popular reception. They changed topics and treatments (and even projection speeds) to suit the audience. In a similar way, Bill Gates and Paul Allen wrote operating systems for a constituency of amateurs with whom they were closely in touch. However, as the PC industry took off, the distribution arrangements for software and other products distanced the designers from the users. The seductive technological determinism (which suggests that culture is changed by technology) precipitated significant wrong turnings in much of the early design. People buying computers and software were often expected to follow the enthusiasms and agenda of the "disenfranchised nerds" now turned entrepreneurs. Some did, but the vast majority of the potential market had different ideas about what playing with computers meant.

Perhaps more remarkable than the rapid growth of the market is that the PC survived as a consumer product, given the gulf between the consumers and the producers' ideas about the machines. The uncritical technological determinism in the industry has inhibited the creative possibilities of what was possibly one of the most promising media to ever emerge from computer research and development – the CD-ROM. According to industry "vaporware," an interactive CD-ROM based on hypermedia architecture was going to transform education and popular entertainment in unbounded ways. This medium, it was predicted, would be used to store data in a great variety of forms (text, image, sound, graphics, movies), which would be accessed associatively to provide a powerful value-added learning tool.

CD-ROMs would transform libraries by eliminating the costly storage of volumes and providing different modalities of access to data, which would ultimately affect scholarship.[18] In short, it would be a new episteme. None of this seems to have happened, except in a number of highly specific applications, mostly concerning industrial training programs. Even there, according to some analysts, the changes are small. It has been noticed, for example, that trainees invariably make paper printouts of the contents of a whole disc (regardless of relevance) in order to be able to consult the material away from a machine.

The CD-ROM publishing business was thought to be worth around $5 billion in 1994, which for a world market is minute (consider, for example, US telecommunications predicted at a trillion dollars by 2000).[19] CD-ROMs, it appears, have been used to provide another format for the existing collections of computer games, the distribution of freeware (which works haphazardly), and pornography. Invariably, these do not exploit the nonlinear navigation, which is the true potential of the medium, but instead recirculate existing conventions for information retrieval disguised in vogue pop graphics.[20] Consequently, it has proved very difficult to market since, on the one hand, it was promoted as revolutionary while, in reality, it is more often than not simply an expensive, unwieldy and approximate copy of something that already exists. The products have failed to fulfill the imagination of the consumer, and retailers see little incentive in promoting them with large displays and shelf space. As the focus of attention has moved on to other promising forms, notably the Internet, the CD-ROM industry seems to have stabilized as a vanity publishing medium rather than any real alternative way of managing information.[21]

In the absence of any distinct advantage for using the CD-ROM as a medium, it has, consistent with Cringely's prognosis, been replaced by a software equivalent that we know as the Internet. Access to the Internet provides an associative database, and the storage and intelligent search engines that formed the basis of many of the earlier promises made for the emerging hardware medium of CD-ROM have been emulated. This is now achieved with a nonspecific piece of hardware called a modem that interfaces between the PC and the telephone system. If this trajectory is followed through, the immanent "convergence," using set-top devices to connect homes with cable companies, will be replaced by a programmed chip (presumably made by Motorola). In this case, the expected penetration of the personal computer into the domestic space will, quite possibly, be as a software product. Rather than innovative hardware, the application that is expected to support the popular uptake of home computing is a hypermedia graphical Web browser of which Netscape's Navigator and Microsoft's Internet Explorer are perhaps the most well known.[22]

Once again, however, industry "vaporware," advertising, newspaper copy, and particularly home computing magazines provide a dubious history. They tend to focus on the technological aspects of interactive hypermedia and give the impression that personal computers were always intended to be like this; all that was necessary was the appropriate advances in science. The Internet, however, has been around for a very long time (some suggest as early as 1969). It was the outcome of a rather specialized project to develop an associative database that could be accessed, and most important, added to, primarily by professionals in scientific research. It was never intended as a public access network and, consequently, most users were content to work with somewhat forbidding chopped-down machine codes rather than the friendly graphical interfaces we use today. However, in the early 1990s, a number of political decisions widened the constituency of the Internet to include amateurs, enthusiasts, and users without a specialist technical background. This group saw the Internet rather differently from the professionals, as a space for public access and universal connectedness. As this different interpretation has prevailed, more user-friendly interfaces have emerged, not through the insights and speculations of entrepreneurs, but from the creative resources of the new community of users. Graphical Web browsers are not so much *advances* in software design, but can be seen as both software emulators of existing hardware and responses to a popular engagement with the Internet which has produced new ideas about what personal computing means, in the context of a broader culture than that reflected by the industry's journalists.

Software emulations of existing hardware might mean that the PC could easily disappear from personal computing. This may be regarded as further evidence of a cultural slide towards the sort of virtuality that was foreshadowed by the cinema a century ago, when moving images were seen as substitutes for the realities that were represented. In this analysis, resistance to an increasingly vicarious existence is impossible, and keeping pace with a progressive dematerialization is almost an obligation for artists and designers. Another view of this is that nothing has changed, and that the personal computer (like the cinema) has always been a machine that had an imaginary dimension for both scientists and a lay public, and that its various incarnations since the Second World War are simply recirculations in a process of reinterpretation to which many technologies are subject.

The PC was not invented as a whole idea, nor was there any fixed, final objective to which its developers strove. As a piece of technical hardware, it emerged from applied scientific research and a community of enthusiastic amateurs. Each group had significantly different ideas about what the machine was and might do in the future. In this sense, it is an imaginary apparatus. It is an arrangement of smaller, discrete machines (chips, drives, keyboards, screens, etc.), a *dispositif* that can be regarded as a material response to imaginary scenarios about technology. The PC, as we now understand it (and this may just be a temporary interpretation), is a machine linked to telephone networks with a storage and retrieval system. It is, to use an engineering term, a kluge, or bricolage of a number of discrete components. These come together to produce an entirely new device, greater than the sum of its parts, that we recognize at different times as the personal computer (or perhaps, more accurately, a microcomputer). A closer examination of these parts, together with an account of how they were put together, may reveal something of the imaginaries of both scientist and enthusiast to show a different, less determinist causality.

One of these discrete components is the telephone. Its linkage with a computer in the mid-1980s gave us a new word, "telematics," which roughly means the confluence of telephone and computer technologies. One of its first manifestations in a consumer product was in 1981, when France Telecom introduced the Minitel. This was a small video display unit with a keyboard and telephone handset that was connected via the exchange to various providers, ranging from street directories to call girls. A critical mass of connected users was established by the free distribution of Minitel machines, as a replacement for the huge Paris telephone directory. Many subscribers found this apparatus compelling and, like some early Internet users, ran up crippling telephone bills. Minitel offered a reliable, compact, domestic version of prototypical networking devices that had been used by computer enthusiasts for some time. In these, data exchange with a host computer was made with a device called an acoustic coupler.

This was an electronic "black box" with a pair of rubber cups that engulfed the handset in a rather sinister manner. Since these devices used sound to transmit digital data (much like a fax), they were prone to error through "dirty" signals and extraneous noise. Moreover, the sheer bulk and inelegance of the apparatus made them unattractive products for the mass market. They remained an expensive item with a small constituency; but they did show that quite interesting things could be done with the telephone. This was not an obvious or natural extension of the computer, but the telephone became implicated, almost accidentally, because its network of wires and satellite relays was conveniently in place for professionals and amateurs exploring the possibilities of exchanging digital data. The diffusion of these pioneering efforts among like-minded enthusiasts had the effect of extending the imaginary dimension of the PC into the realms of social interaction. Business interests, and then domestic users, also began to take an interest in these telecommunications experiments. The ubiquitous modern modem, nowadays as chic as Reebok trainers, connect directly into the network to replace a clumsy piece of hardware with something smaller, more reliable, and stylish. They also now come as a standard component built into many small computers, and the next step is that this device, too, is likely to be replaced by something more technically elegant, such as an emulator chip inside the ordinary television set.

The subsequent development of the Internet as a popular medium has transformed the business plans of some of the largest companies in the world. The telephone companies initially became involved in network computing because their wires were already in place. This turned out to very lucrative but, as the market for telematic services has expanded, there is increasing competition from other connective systems. Microwave systems for portable phones, for example, are rapidly replacing wires in developed economies, and are becoming the start-up standard in Third World and Pacific Rim countries. Cable television also poses a competitive threat to the established networks, since delivering television signals is compatible with telephone communications. Established "phone companies" have responded with takeovers of digital networks and diversification into entertainment. Simply to survive in the changing market, the major telephone companies have become directly involved in show business, which is something for which they are barely equipped.[23] While this promises increased revenues, it is not without its problems because some of the largest corporations in the world are being forced to make vast and risky investments in unfamiliar territory. The imperative for this arises from the enthusiastic reception of the convergence of the telephone and the kluge we know as the PC. New products including those announced by Zenith, Phillips and The Interactive Digital Network Corporation are not technological inevitabilities (as George Gilder suggests), but responses to the current struggle for control of distribution networks precipitated by a new interpretation of the small computer by consumers.

The most visible and dynamic evidence of this response is the burgeoning Internet as a resource for recreational pleasure. Retrieving data from this network involves searching for the appropriate host and connecting with it to retrieve files. Early pioneers used arcane instruction codes. Since then, associative linking software, known as browsers, combined with "search engines" and Internet protocol management have provided one of the most widespread means of accessing the Internet. Most of these browsers are derivatives of hypertext programs that use "hot spots" (areas of the display which when clicked, access another file in the database). Like the telephone, hypertext was not a computer technology but, initially, a text-based microfilm system for keeping track of scientific publications called "MEMEX."[24] In 1932, Vannevar Bush began working on the problem of extending human memory. He was particularly concerned that scientific research might be stifled by the massive growth of professional literature.

Following a draft paper in 1939, his idea was finally published in 1945.[25] He proposed a system of "windows" which allowed comparative analysis of textual material from disparate sources and an input device that enabled the user to add notes and comments. A new profession of "trailblazers" (as he called them) would be formed of people able to bundle links together in a predetermined web, so that specialist scientists could follow their own threads, unencumbered by irrelevant material. Development was slow since it was essentially a research project and an in-house tool for scientists. A fully working version of the MEMEX was never built. The prototypes that were made, however, did provide a number of mechanisms that could model associative indexing. Using this device as evidence, Bush was able to show some deficits in contemporary ideas about human intelligence and thought processes.[26] For example, the MEMEX was able to illustrate how the parallel processing of serial data was possible with relatively small technical resources. Much later, his idea was used to form the basic architecture of hypermedia applications such as Netscape, but its immediate significance for artificial intelligence research ensured the continued support of the American government for thirty years until 1975.

One of the people who developed Bush's original idea was Doug Englebart. He is now most well known for inventing the mouse as a computer interface device. Quite coincidentally, it seems, he was inspired by the brief description of the MEMEX that he came across, at the end of the Second World War, in one of the many published profiles of Bush.[27] It remained with him as a generalized idea, but it was not until 1962 that he introduced it into data management and computing. Although both Bush and Englebart might be considered as pioneers of associative indexing, what neither of them anticipated was that a revolutionary idea for information management designed for specialist scientists subsequently would be crucial in the growth of a popular enthusiasm for personal computing. Nor did they envisage that it would become the preferred modality for the twentieth-century flaneur, surfing the virtual arcades of the "information super highway."

In the early 1960s, however, Ted Nelson, a media analyst, was able to make that conceptual leap. He saw in the concept of MEMEX the egalitarian ideal that was in tune with popular culture and the democratic aspirations of the times. Nelson is generally credited with the invention of the word "hypertext," and he proposed a particular use for Bush's original idea in a project he named (with characteristic ambition) Xanadu.[28] Whereas a professional like Vannevar Bush was concerned with maintaining the growth of scientific knowledge through narrowing access to relevant data, Nelson's project was concerned with wide public use of computer technology through associative linkage devices. His imaginative concept was to establish a worldwide network of information centers to provide interactive access to all of the scientific data and creative literature that could be encoded. At these centers, which would be as ubiquitous as Laundromats, hypertext interfaces would enable users to both retrieve data and add material of their own, which could then be accessed by others. The extent to which Xanadu was ever a realizable project, or simply a platform for visionary engagement with a new technology, is something of a question, but as it became a technical and economic possibility, it was increasingly hampered by issues of copyright and intellectual property. Details of the system of data verification and credit payments to authors overtook the vision of his proposal for an international information-rich culture. By the time it appeared that Xanadu might finally satisfy the lawyers and accountants, the political decision to enable wider public access to the Internet had already been taken. Ironically, the debate about intellectual property was sidelined by the enthusiasm and generosity of the surfing community, and his project was completely eclipsed. What remains of his (and Bush's) work, however, is a commitment to hypertext (and hypermedia) as a data management tool for ordinary people.

Hypertext is, as the name suggests, a system of accessing textual material associatively and originally was a microfilm technology. It was not immediately obvious that other kinds of information, such as pictures, sounds, and movies, might be managed in this way. The extension of Nelson's original idea to hypermedia, also was not computer-based technology, but a videodisc project developed in the Media Lab at MIT. By linking a computer-driven interface and a domestic laser disc player, images could be displayed at will on a screen at rates that provided the illusion of movement. One of the most developed experiments in this area was called "The Aspen Movie Map." In this project, photographs were "burned" onto a laser disc and, when interfaced with a simple PC, the material was accessed interactively so that an image map of the whole of the town of Aspen Colorado, including the interior of buildings, could be viewed. Rapid retrieval times, which are standard in laser disc technology, meant that, by using a joystick, the operator could travel through the landscape at speeds of 110 kilometers per hour. Like MEMEX, the "Aspen Movie Map" was intended as an in-house project at MIT. Interactive laser disc technology has hardly been exploited in the public domain, except as a superior playback device for television and in arcade games. Apart from one spectacular military use (at Entebbe airport) and a few pioneering attempts in education, little has developed in this area. But laser disc technology linked to a computer suggested possibilities for navigating and controlling different kinds of information. The diffusion of the idea that data could be stored in formats that were independent of the modality of representation introduced ideas to computing which appealed to amateur enthusiasts rather than large business organizations and government institutions.

In 1987, Macintosh responded to this new concept of computing and launched a simple hypermedia program called "HyperCard." In an inspired marketing coup, they "bundled" it free with their machines so that, in effect, it became public domain software. This turned out to be a brilliant strategy for launching a culture of "third party" (independent) Apple software developers. Small-scale speculative programmers with no more than a reasonable machine and creative flair "invented" uses for HyperCard ranging from address books and stock control packages to interactive interfaces for laser disc players. In proposing the visionary Xanadu project, Ted Nelson had correctly intuited a consensus around the idea of a shared intellectual property programming community, but Macintosh's HyperCard software provided a concrete resource to express this ideal in informal, low-capital software development. The enthusiasm for it confirmed the willingness of a global community, particularly the group most enthusiastic about electronics and computing, to sideline professional ambition in the pursuit of a vaguely articulated social imperative that computers would be good for democracy. For Macintosh, it meant that its machines and its operating system acquired a brand identity that became strongly identified with a creative community and a healthy suspicion of corporate exploitation. As a result of this effective low-cost research and development strategy, large software houses felt sufficiently confident in Macintosh's consumer base, and invested capital in ambitious projects to devise applications which commercial designers could use. Despite the failing fortunes of the company and its diminishing market share in recent years, this unorthodox approach to technological development has ensured that Macintosh still remains the preferred platform for desktop publishing (DTP), creative design, and multimedia uses. One consequence is that Hypermedia (as an associative cataloging tool) is currently the preferred standard for Internet data management, computer-based educational products including encyclopedias, and online catalogs in museums.

The facility with which computers can apparently cope with this form of storage and retrieval gives the impression of a certain technological inevitability. It is as though personal computing and hypermedia are somehow synonymous. However, but for a series of accidental meetings of scientists, the technological "excess" of rapid retrieval times in the domestic laser disc machine, and the brilliant marketing coup of placing HyperCard in the public domain, the design of microcomputer software, and the particular use of the machines, might be very different. There was not a single "big idea" that lead to hypermedia but, like many of the nineteenth-century achievements in the natural sciences, the development of computer software was the outcome of the steady accretion of the efforts of individuals and small groups of programmers, who were essentially working on an amateur basis (in the field of computer science at least), and who were willing to freely share their findings. This is contrary to the generally accepted "romance" histories that explain technological change in terms of the dedicated and visionary genius of individuals like Bill Gates.

The computer, like almost every invention, has an accepted "romance" history to account for its invention. Many authorities regard the nineteenth-century mathematician, Charles Babbage, as the father of computing, and his Analytical Engine as a mechanical progenitor of the machines we know today.[29] More teleological histories such as those by Vemon Pratt and John Cohen trace the ancestry of intelligent machines back to the abacus and further.[30] Together, such accounts lead to the impression that computers are the inevitable outcome of a long-established desire to build machines that could replicate human intelligence. One of the earliest realizations of the electronic computer, however, the ENIAC, was not thought of in such general terms, and its subsequent development was no less accidental than the convergence of the telephone and PC, the use of the Internet as a popular telematic technology, or Hypermedia as an international standard for data management.

The ENIAC was a calculating machine originally designed to meet a quite specific problem in producing firing tables for American naval gunnery during the Second World War. The task of compiling a complete set of data for each new gun was so time-consuming that it threatened to delay the strategic objectives of the war effort. The ENIAC (Electrical Numerical Integrator and Calculator), as the name suggests, was developed as a massive adding machine for the American military. The intention was that the multitude of repetitive calculations necessary to precisely predict the trajectory of a shell from each individual weapon under variable conditions could be undertaken with sufficient speed and accuracy to keep up with the output from the arsenals. It used a circuitry of vacuum tubes and relays to perform certain calculations and, although in principal it worked well, it was technically very vulnerable to component failure. J. Presper Eckert, a leading figure in the development team, suggested a practical solution based on an understanding of the ENIAC not as a single large machine, but as an accretion of small independent parts working together to execute a single complex task. He proposed the engineering concept of modular circuits that could be temporarily removed and repaired while the ENIAC was running, without necessarily affecting the work in hand. Some technical difficulties remained unresolved by the time of the armistice, but the logic of his design suggested that a perfected machine might be possible.[31] Although the cessation of hostilities made further development less pressing, the project was close to successful completion and represented a huge investment in time and intellectual energy. For these reasons alone, it was thought to be worth pursuing, but perhaps more important for what was to follow, the limited success of the ENIAC stimulated visions of what such technology meant for the conduct of civilian life in the postwar period.

Further development work on the ENIAC, however, required substantial financial support from public funds. Since the necessity of making calculations for firing tables had all but disappeared, and there was little popular enthusiasm for arithmetic, it was necessary to show the ENIAC as something more exciting than a "number cruncher." Illuminated ping-pong balls that flashed on and off were added to the casing to "show" it at work. These had no real function except to provide a simple analogy for the invisible electrical processes that made complex calculations possible. It was a brilliant publicity strategy that gave the illusion of a logical process going on in the otherwise inscrutable banks of vacuum tubes glowing lethargically. It also provided an enduring trope for machine intelligence that remains with us today. In both science fiction movies and contemporary product design small, light-emitting diodes (LEDs) have become almost mandatory features that often have no function other than to mark the willingness of a machine to cooperate with human efforts to make it work.

The task that the ENIAC was given for its public debut was equally inspired, and proved to have a lasting impact. To show its power to a lay audience, the computer was used to calculate the trajectory of a shell that took 30 seconds to reach its target. This calculation took only 20 seconds; in effect, the machine intelligence got to the target ten seconds before the real shell.[32] This demonstration suggested that a developed computer would not simply be a super-efficient calculator which analyzed data and confirmed empirical evidence, but could make evaluations of possible events faster than they had actually happened. Funding was forthcoming for the ENIAC project for a further five years, but yielded little other than stimulating the public's curiosity about computers. The imaginary possibilities of artificial life, at least as old as the Pygmalion myth, had acquired an added impetus by various nineteenth-century inventions (including the cinema). Suddenly, in the mid-twentieth century, these had a new objectification in the twinkling circuit-boards of the ENIAC. At its most fantastic the idea of an intelligent machine furnished both dystopian science fiction fantasies like those expressed in pulp fiction and Hollywood "B" pictures, and competing visions of Utopian idealism. In the latter, the drudgery of repetitive tasks, the last burden of nature, might be consigned to machines that could enhance human existence. At its most grounded, however, the particular collapse of time and space that the ENIAC demonstrated excited the creative imaginations of amateur scientists, artists, and business people who wanted to have access to the technology to explore its social and economic possibilities.

As a consequence of the visionary potential of computer technology, it became a focus for diverse interest groups that comprised unusual mixes of people. Philosophers, poets, and bankers – the traditional habitués of the nineteenth-century salon, formed the constituency of the many amateur computer science clubs that sprang up in the 1960s. At these clubs, the collective imperative of building a small computer for experimental purposes overrode individual ambition, and social and professional hierarchies. Students, professors, and technicians, as well as those who were "just interested," shared their experience and showed their latest achievements at the regular meetings. The most well known of these clubs is possibly the Homebrew Computer Club at Stanford University. It was at this club that Steve Wozniak modestly showed a prototype machine, the Apple I, as a contribution to the shared project of developing a small, personal computer. Its development as both a product and a computing concept was facilitated with the help and encouragement of the more flamboyant (but no less ingenious) Steve Jobs, whose chief interest was in computer games. Together, they eventually produced a machine and marketed it as the Apple II (including a color version) and, although it was by no means the first or only personal computer available, its design caught the mood of the amateur constituency of computer clubs and it found a market. The extraordinary popular enthusiasm for the Apple II not only laid the financial foundations of Apple Macintosh but also seemed to confirm that, aside from being a sophisticated calculating machine, in the hands of imaginative people, the computer could become something else (even if, in the late 1970s, no one was quite sure what that "something else" might be).

The Apple II and the many other amateur home computers that were built in the late 1970s and early 1980s were different from mainframes. They were not scaled-down models of the mainframe, in the sense that the Walkman is a miniature version of a tape recorder, but more like fellow travelers with different objectives and different applications. These small machines (known as microcomputers) shared the engineering concept of modularity, open architecture, and spirit of adventure which had turned ideas about computing into the ENIAC. Like the large-scale laboratory prototype, microcomputers were built from a bricolage of off-the-shelf and ad hoc electronic components put together in new combinations. But their appeal was to a constituency searching for new understandings of what computer technology meant. The Apple II was a machine for the computer enthusiast and the experimental programmer. It was built by and for people with open minds about the future use of computer technology. To broaden the constituency of users required the microcomputer to do something more than provide a platform for programming. Cringely suggests that the compelling application that achieved this for the Apple II was the spreadsheet software, invented by Dan Bricklin, called "VisiCalc."[33] The particular brilliance of the application was that the outcome of one changed accounting parameter in a project could be automatically processed and expressed in terms of profits or losses. Since this was a simple process that could be undertaken in relative privacy, there were no constraints on what financial fantasy might be modeled. It saved professional accountants and entrepreneurs hundreds of hours in the preparation of reports and business plans, and could run with very modest technical means. VisiCalc confirmed what the ENIAC debut had already suggested, that computers allowed imaginary scenarios to be played out as if they were real. It provided a hard-headed commercial justification for investing in a microcomputer without entirely disavowing the imaginative spirit of adventure that had launched these little machines.

The emergence of the personal computer from the collaborative atmosphere of campus clubs and the apparent ease with which committed and talented individuals could shape products, and even the future of the industry, gave rise to a carefree bohemian optimism vastly different to the corporate logic that dominated mainframe computing. The large corporate computers were invariably used as accounting and inventory machines. Individual access was on a grace and favor "downtime" basis after the main work of financial control had been done. Outputs were invariably sheets of printed textual and numerical data, which often were collected from a central printing resource (or even sent by post). The microcomputer, on the other hand, was available on demand to the individual, and processed text and high-quality images on a screen which could be manipulated, stored, and even distributed without ever being committed to paper. Furthermore, when hard copy was required, the screen display closely matched the final output. This feature alone transformed some publishing operations from a high-investment institutional base to a decentralized "cottage" industry. Since that time and the innovation of Hypermedia data management software (the poet's equivalent of VisiCalc), networking and games, the personal computer has become understood, at least in the popular domain, as a quite different machine from its corporate ancestors. Even though the production of microcomputers and software are virtually monopoly industries, some personal computers still retain a suggestion of a bohemian independence from large corporate institutions. To be sure, the personal computer was unthinkable without the scientific research that produced prototypes such as the ENIAC, but nothing could be further from the number crunching scientific and military machines than the personal microcomputer that is now so common in homes and offices.

The amateur enthusiasm for computing in the 1970s not only created a demand and a market for microcomputers, but also stimulated new scientific research. Miniaturization, for example, essential to the development of powerful domestic machines, eliminated the problem that the ENIAC was developed for. Nowadays, most ballistic missiles have onboard microcomputers that do the work of firing tables while they are in flight. In less applied research, low-power machines opened up projects in artificial intelligence to wider groups of scientists who refocused attention on more biological and quotidian models of the mind. In the 1980s, the previous predominance of linear processing solutions in artificial intelligence broke down under the weight of the burden of data that the human mind appears to cope with at any given moment. Parallel processing, or connectionist models, which had briefly been regarded as credible by scientists in the 1960s, were resurrected as a consequence of a new constituency of interest in the field.[34] According to Daniel Dennett and others, there were quite specific cultural determinants for this.[35] Among other things, he points out that in a period of relative freedom and hedonism, and a general preference among the younger generation for West Coast lifestyle (beach culture, surfing, and transcendental experiences), artificial intelligence research refocused attention onto the "wetware" of the brain. The connectionist models looked at simple organisms such as insects, whereas linear programming solutions had leaned towards "expert systems," (computer programs which could, in some sense, stand in for high-level professional expertise such as medical diagnosis). They developed small programs which processed data simultaneously though associative networks. This strand of artificial intelligence research has proved enduring, and has most recently been integrated with the earlier linear models. In these experiments, very basic instructions were shown to produce intelligent behavior in swarms of identically programmed robots. A host of simple prototypes, with single chips on board, responded to an imperative to avoid collision, for example, with intelligent wall-following behavior. This work has proved fruitful, and a new area of research known as "behavioral AI" has opened up.

In artificial intelligence, as in many fields of computer-based research, the various contributions of the professional and the amateur are hard to disentangle. This, however, is not the view of the computer industry nor many of the high-profile commentators. "Romance" histories of brilliant, gifted, and sometimes lucky individuals who are agents in the inevitable progress of technology tend to dominate the most visible accounts. The idea of an inevitable technological progress oversimplifies the complexity of the causality of technological change. It predisposes commentary to future-watching in which evidence is often difficult to disentangle from speculation. In popular literature, "hip" magazines with unconventional typography suggest that the changes in the technology are too overwhelming and too fast for ordinary people to understand.[36] Culture, they suggest, is changed by technology. For many theorists, this technological determinism is problematic since it renders the ordinary mortal ineffective in the construction of what is, after all, a shared culture. Furthermore, the resolution of difficult social problems requires no action on the part of the individual since he or she can be consigned to the pending file to await a new invention. Robert Cringely's *Accidental Empires*, alternatively, does define the limits of his methodology and, consequently, begins to offer an explanation for what might be happening based on a history of the major players in Silicon Valley over the last three decades. But both he and George Gilder provide a view of digital media that is selective in its historical evidence insofar as the mass of people who use these machines, and give them meaning, are rendered as passive consumers which, in view of the weight of evidence, is difficult to sustain. They overlook the creative exploration of the uses of particular technologies that the innovators have, for whatever reason, overlooked. Nor do they recognize the impact of reflective practitioners outside the business community whose interests and vision are informed by different cultural imperatives. This image of the consumer and designer as disenfranchised may be good for the rapid turnover of products necessary to sustain investment in research and development programs, but if, through repetition, it becomes uncritically accepted, the intellectual space for reflective practice and individual intervention in technology is significantly curtailed. In the long term (as we saw with the CD-ROM), the potential for new modes of expression and representation can simply atrophy.

The view of the history of the microcomputer set out in this article suggests that it was not inevitable that the ENIAC would eventually lead to the microcomputer, or that programming would yield a new profession, which fused many fundamental graphic design skills with computer science. Or even that the activity of software design would be concerned principally with the development of multimedia authoring programs which these new professionals could use. The histories of the telephone network, associative databases, and the microcomputer, outlined here, covers just some of the many little machines that have been brought together to form a particular information and entertainment apparatus that we now understand as the microcomputer. There are others such as the keyboard, the cathode ray tube, the microswitch, the electro-acoustic loudspeaker, and the numerical calculator whose accretion into a single machine was neither anticipated nor inevitable. Their convergence was not planned nor even intuited independently by gifted individuals. Rather, they were combined through a broad constituency of imaginative and social processes which did not cease with the innovation of a product. A crucial contribution to the development of the microcomputer was the active and insistent intervention of the enthusiast who challenged the professional interpretation of the machine. Had the technological development of the computer remained with scientists, corporate developers, and military strategists, it is possible that today it would still be understood as a centralized database and number cruncher for government institutions and multinational companies. Academic access and amateur use would possibly only extend to some form of grace and favor timeshare facility on a mainframe, or a public rental system, such as Ted Nelson envisaged with the Xanadu project, as a sort of information Laundromat. It also seems unlikely that the chief preoccupation in scientific projects concerning artificial intelligence and artificial life would be so committed to connectionist models based on biological models of the human being.

The computer industry may prefer to present itself as startlingly new and unprecedented, but many features of its emergence can be seen as a recirculation of another period in which inventions were enthusiastically received by amateurs who actively participated in the projects of the scientist. In the nineteenth century, many technologies that were the product of corporate and military ambitions such as the phonograph, the X-ray, and the movie camera were taken over by amateurs and demonstrators who developed not only new applications for these devices, but new inventions, and, above all, new scientific knowledge. The cultural framework of the first cinema, for example, was not one of unsophisticated awe and hysterical distraction. The audiences did not duck for cover as most histories would have it, but responded with curiosity and astonishment at the technology.[37] Its popular fascination was founded on intellectual goals that were shared between the audience, professional science, and an emerging class of technologists. The various meanings that were given to the cinema by its inventors, even the various permutations of the little machines which constitute the basic cinematic apparatus, emerged from the struggles between the conflicting interests of these groups.[38] On the one hand, a professional class attempted to control the discourse and meaning of scientific inquiry while, on the other, a lay public insisted on participation in the process. This polemical opposition was marked out as early as 1850 in *The Working Man's Friend and Family Instructor*, which offered the following thoughts about scientists and scientific inquiry:

> Every person must have right or wrong thoughts, and there is no reason why a hedger and ditcher, or a scavenger, should not have correct opinions and knowledge as a prince or nobleman. Working men and working women have naturally the same minds or souls as lords or ladies, or queens … if any one could have analyzed or cut to pieces the soul of Lord Bacon, or Sir Isaac Newton, and that of a chimney-sweeper, it would have been found that both were made of the same divine material.[39]

The critical tone of this comment is reflected in popular science journals throughout the rest of the century but, by the early 1900s, professional scientists established institutional frameworks that systematically excluded lay participation. Experimental practice progressively insisted on sophisticated instrumentation that eliminated the human observer. Some of these instruments, such as the phonograph, the X-ray, and the cinematograph, found their way into the public domain as spectacular entertainments at theaters and fairgrounds. Even then, they often were reinterpreted; the phonograph, which was designed as a business device, became a music machine, the X-ray was a huge attraction until the health risk became clear, and the cinematograph, which had its scientific origins in projects as diverse as the study of movement for military purposes and three-dimensional and color photography, was transformed into a mass entertainment.

The cinema, like personal computing, was not the inevitable outcome of a technology but the mediation of a scientific apparatus by audiences and producers negotiating economic and social imperatives. Exhibitors listened to the audiences as they left the seance, and bought films accordingly. Producers (who were sometimes also exhibitors) often came from scientific backgrounds and were sensitive to the tensions between professionals and amateurs in the ongoing struggle for the meaning of science and technology.[40] They often responded to a perceived appetite for the visualization of a popular criticism of science and technology by concentrating on the empirical reality of the appearance of the exotic. For the first decade of cinema, there were many fantasy films, but the majority were, by far, of a documentary nature (so-called actuality films) which showed the world as it appeared to ordinary people – and usually in color. Many showed scientific and surgical procedures with an awesome honesty and often, in their brutality, an implicit criticism. The appetite for such material provided the revenues to build cinemas as social institutions that provided audiences and protocols for yet another use for the cinematographe, that is the profoundly unscientific function of telling fantastic stories, many of which repeated the confrontation of the determinist world view of the professional scientist.

Even after a century of cinema, successful mainstream movies retain strong traces of this discourse engine in sci-fi movies, the mad scientist genres of the Cold War, as well as the contemporary Hollywood blockbuster movies such as *Terminator*, *Jurassic Park*, *Strange Days*, *Mission Impossible*, and *Independence Day*. And, of course, *Twister*, which rehearses the polemic that was aired one hundred and fifty years ago in *The Working Man's Friend and Family Instructor*. It depicts theoretical science as generally corrupt or corrupting, while field work, and especially the unassuming action of amateurs, is shown as honest and effective. In the film, relatively ordinary people are opposed by funded scientists supported by a fleet of vans packed with instruments. This is a movie by Steven Spielberg, a man who, evidently, knows the power of audiences better than most directors. *Twister* is a film about a science that was not possible until the advent of the VCR and domestic video camera. Before 1980, only a few films of tornadoes existed. Since then, knowledge of these meteorological events has grown exponentially as ordinary people filmed them with their home movie equipment. The film is a celebration of the power of ordinary people to control science, technology, and knowledge in an entertainment medium which has a long history of polemical opposition to scientific elitism.

If popular culture and blockbuster films can be admitted as evidence, then there is some suggestion that the market-led technological determinism, which is used to explain digital technologies, has a dubious currency. The current criteria for hardware development are photographic image quality, ever greater storage, and faster clock speeds. These impinge on the design concept of consumer products. Consequently, interactive CD titles, designed for the popular market, for example, must work at the leading edge of technology. Data transfer times, image quality, and screen refreshment rates have to match the latest microcomputers and the entertainment model of the cinema. They seldom work quite as well as they should. They are slow, and far too often, they do not work at all and "crash" the system. This means that, frequently, CD-ROMs have a provisional air to them, get bad word-of-mouth publicity, and sell few copies. In contrast, the network of networks which we call the Internet, is often frustrating and irregular, yet it has an enormous constituency of active participants trying to make it work in unscientific ways. It is a hit and miss technology that uses an ugly and burdensome language called HTML, slow screen refreshment rates, and low resolution, but it has captured a popular imagination in ways that have taken industry and dedicated media analysts such as Ted Nelson by surprise.

The Internet's origins are somewhat nineteenth century. It is a military technology that is appropriated by popular culture and transformed in ways that its inventors could not have envisaged. As with cinema in the early years, the Internet is an extraordinary heterogeneous collection of entertainment and information, determined, in part, by its audience. It provides a space for an imaginary interaction and nearly anything is possible. It is widely used for finding and retrieving specific information, but also as a vehicle for simply cruising through dataspace with the impulsive curiosity of the nineteenth-century flaneur. To surf the "Net" is to witness the amazing generosity of a large community of participants who are prepared to expend resources realizing personal imaginary worlds and making them freely available. There is currently little room for commercial production, nor does it seem likely that, without a major reinterpretation of the technology as a passive entertainment medium, there ever will be. Although much of the information that is available is banal and unreliable, the Internet challenges the authority of high science by recuperating it (perhaps sometimes crassly) into the public domain for pleasure. What may finally tip the balance in favor of convergence is not the issue of corporate strategy, the intellectual dissipation of television, or the usefulness of computing, but the interpretation of television and network computing as low-resolution representations that allow for a popular participation in its meaning.

A more sophisticated and representative understanding of how technologies acquire meaning needs to be investigated. The issue of whether there will be a convergence of television and the PC, or if indeed television is dead, will not finally be resolved by rhetoric and assertion alone. As seems clear in the history of both personal computing and the cinema (to take two examples), what a machine is must be negotiated within a complex network of different interpretations that includes those of the user.[41] The personal computer is a machine that has been developed in a culture which, in some respects, considers scientific knowledge to be the rightful domain of both the layman and professional. The recent growth of the ecology movement, forcibly claiming control of technological development, provides undeniable evidence of this. As a casual survey of Internet traffic shows, the meaning of the bricolage that we call the microcomputer is still volatile. Investors, designers, and media gurus might do well to remember that, when writing the history of popular computing, the user is made of the same divine material as Bill Gates.

The author would like to express gratitude to the editors of *Design Issues* for their help in the preparation of this article. In particular, he would like to thank Victor Margolin for his helpful comments in developing the paper and his stimulating responses to various drafts.

NOTES

First published in *Design Issues* 14 no. 1 (Spring 1998): 54–80.

1. David Nye, *Electrifying America, Social Meanings of a New Technology* (Cambridge, MA: MIT Press, 1990).
2. It is perhaps significant that women are not as active as men in these narratives. Often, women are allowed to help the men and, invariably, they embody nature and the winning of the woman assists in the understanding of nature.
3. Thomas Schatz, "The New Hollywood," *Film Theory Goes to The Movies*, Collins, J., Radner, H., Preacher Collins, A., editors (London: Routledge, 1993), 8.
4. Ibid., 12.
5. See George Gruman, *MacWorld* (August 1996): 45.
6. Where there is satellite and terrestrial competition available to consumers, cable companies often provide the incentive of cheap telephone connections in order to establish the presence of the service in the household. If the Internet becomes an established advertising medium, this could well become a standard provision rather than a short-term incentive to subscribers.
7. For an overview of the struggle for the control of the Internet, see Raymond Hammond, *Digital Business: Surviving & Thriving in an OnLine World* (London: Hodder and Stoughton, 1996).
8. Product information on *NetVison* can be found at http://www.diba.com.
9. Ibid.
10. George Gilder, *Life after Television: The Coming Transformation of Media and American Life* (London: Norton, 1994). For a discussion of broad bandwidth, see Bandwidth Tidal wave (http://www.forbes.com/asap/gilder/telescom10.html.
11. See, for example, Nigel Healey, *Supply Side Economics* (Oxford: Heinemann, 1996).
12. Robert X. Cringely, *Accidental Empires; How the Boys of Silicon Valley Make their Millions, Battle Foreign Competition, and Still Can't Get a Date* (London: Penguin, 1996), 316.
13. Ibid., 325.
14. Ibid., 316.
15. Ibid., 348.
16. Ibid., 8.
17. For an account of how the cinema developed in Britain, see Michael Channan, *The Dream That Kicks* (London: RKP, 1980).
18. For a brief discussion of this see Michael Punt, "English Poetry and Damp Mattresses," *Interact* (November 1994): 12–13.
19. For a development of this argument, see Michael Punt, "CD-ROM. Radical Nostalgia? Cinema History, Cinema Theory, and New Technology," *Leonardo* (September 1995): 387–394.
20. A spectacular exception is Broderbund's *Living Books* series which are notable not only for their good design but their "low-tech" use of the technology.
21. See McManus, N., "Forever Young: The CD-ROM Market Doesn't Want to Grow Up," *Digital Media Perspective* (December 1994). Available from (dmedia@netcom.com).
22. For a discussion of the "browser wars," see Raymond Hammond, *Digital Business: Surviving and Thriving in an OnLine World.*
23. For an account of this strategy, especially in relation to movies, see Judith Wasko, *Hollywood in the Information Age* (Oxford: Blackwell, 1994).
24. For a discussion of Hypertext, see Edward Barrett, ed., *Text, Context, and Hypertext, Hypermedia, and the Social Construction of Information* (Cambridge, MA: MIT Press, 1989). See also Benjamin Woolley, *Virtual Worlds*, (Oxford: Blackwell, 1992).
25. Vannevar Bush, "As We May Think," *Atlantic Monthly* (July 1945): 101–108.
26. A fuller explanation of Bush's intentions have been described by Nyce, J., and Kahn, P., "Innovation, Pragmatism, and Technological Continuity: Vannevar Bush's Memex," *Journal of the American Society For Information Science* (1989): 214–220.
27. There was a great deal of popular coverage for Bush's idea. *Time* ran an extensive article on him in 1945, as had *Life* earlier (November 1941): 112–124. It provided an artist's impression of what the machine might look like. It is suggested in a number of accounts, that quite by chance, Englebart came across one such article while waiting for a ship back from the Pacific.
28. Ted Nelson's seminal book, *Computer Lib/Dream Machines*, was self-published in 1974. The ideas behind his Xanadu project, set out in "Replacing the Printed Word: A Complete Literary System," was published in Livingston, S.H., ed., *Proc. IFIP Congress 1980* (IFIP: North Holland, 1980), 1013–1023.

29. This kind of account is generally favored in overview histories of technology, and is commonly in repeated in popular encyclopedias.
30. These long histories are detailed in Vernon Pratt, *Thinking Machines* (Oxford: Blackwell, 1987), and in John Cohen, *Human Robots in Myth and Science* (London: RKP, 1966).
31. The ENIAC was a very "provisional" machine intended to show the idea. Its vacuum tubes tended to burn out after two minutes, and it could only store 20 ten-digit numbers.
32. Programming ENIAC for this demonstration took nearly two days, but this was beside the point in as far as the apparatus on show was presented as a prototype.
33. Robert X. Cringely, 64.
34. This history is developed in Seymor Papert, "One Al or Many," *Daedalus*, 113 (1984): 1–19.
35. Daniel Dennett, "Computer Models and the Mind – a View From the East Pole," *Times Literary Supplement* (December 14, 1984): 1453–1454.
36. For a sense of this, see "George Gilder, Does He Really Think Scarcity is a Minor Obstacle on the Road to Techno-Utopia?" *HotWired* (http://www.hotwired.com/wired/4.03/features/gilder.html).
37. Time after time, histories of the first motion picture "seances" repeat the falsehood that audiences ducked for cover at the image of a train approaching. There is no historical evidence for this. See Tom Ginning, "The Aesthetics of Astonishment," *Art & Text*, 34 (1989): 31–45.
38. For a fuller discussion of these points, see Michael Punt. "Well, Who You Gonna Believe, Me or Your Own Eyes?: A Problem of Digital Photography," *The Velvet Light Trap* (Fall, 1995): 3–21.
39. Cited by Sheets – Pyenson, S., "Popular Science Periodicals in Paris and London: The Emergence of a Low Scientific Culture, 1820–1875," *Annals of Science*, 42 (1985): 553.
40. For a charming and readable account of an early film producer and exhibitor who was also a scientist and showman, see Cecil Hepworth, *Came the Dawn* (London: Phoenix House: 1951).
41. There is some significant work in the history of technology on these lines. See, for example, David Nye, *Electrifying America* (Cambridge, MA: MIT Press, 1990), and also Weibe Bijker and John Law, *Shaping Technology/Building Society* (Cambridge, MA: MIT Press, 1992).

15

TYPOGRAPHY AND THE SCREEN: A TECHNICAL CHRONOLOGY OF DIGITAL TYPOGRAPHY, 1984–1997

Loretta Staples

Digital technology radically influenced typographic design beginning in the early 1980s.[1] The computer enabled designers to create and manipulate letters in new ways, offering new options for crafting letterforms and "outputting" them – whether in the medium of toner particles on paper, or pixels on a screen. Digital tools, at first, necessitated (due to technical constraints), and later explicitly encouraged (due to technical advances) specific kinds of representations that would challenge their historical antecedents. Now, in the late 1990s, the mutation of letters continues. The spatial and temporal opportunities of cyberspace are resulting in even more radical depictions of letterforms that offer expanded formal and stylistic possibilities, while further challenging the norms of reading and writing.

This paper chronicles the technical developments responsible for the digital revolution in typography during the 1980s and 90s. It is an informal history based largely on my own observations as an early practitioner of "graphical user interface design" – one formally trained in graphic design and privileged to work at Apple Computer during the early 1990s. Because Apple was so instrumental in popularizing the technologies that stimulated typographic experimentation within the graphic design community during this period, my paper focuses on the Macintosh platform.

EARLY CONCEPTS AND TECHNICAL ADVANCES

The Apple Macintosh computer, introduced in 1984, popularized the key technologies and concepts that would herald a new typographic age. While many of these technologies and ideas originated elsewhere, their dissemination via the Macintosh introduced a broad public to WYSIWYG (an acronym for "what you see is what you get") and its associated technologies: bitmapped fonts and dot-matrix printing, which was quickly surpassed by laser printing.

In the 1970s, researchers at the Xerox Palo Alto Research Center (Xerox PARC) pioneered WYSIWYG and "direct manipulation," key concepts in graphical user interface design. Their efforts – based on earlier pre-Xerox research – culminated in the Xerox Star, a computer system introduced in 1981, and its successor, "ViewPoint" (Figure 15.1).[2] The Star utilized a high-resolution visual display consisting of windows, icons, and actual-size images of document pages that computer users could "handle" through a novel input device, the mouse, used to control a small pointer on the screen. Users manipulated these virtual objects by touching them with the pointer and then clicking with the mouse, an operation called "selection," used to isolate an object

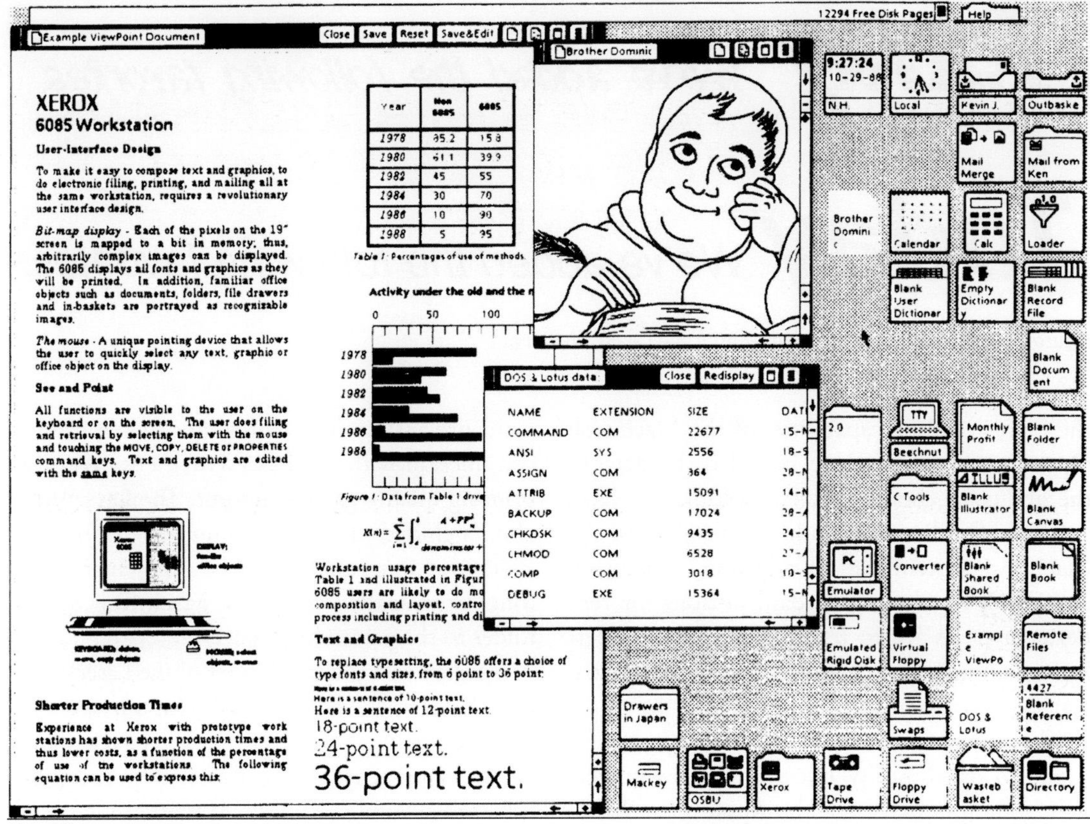

Figure 15.1 Xerox Viewpoint interface. From Jeff Johnson, et al., "The Xerox Star: A Retrospective," *IEEE Computer* 22:9 (September 1989), 11. Reprinted by permission of the Xerox Palo Alto Research Center.

and its corresponding range of possible actions. Once selected, users could further manipulate the object, performing actions such as moving and copying.

The document served as the seminal object in this scheme. While Xerox, a pioneer in photocopying technology, could not have desired a wholly paperless office, the company pursued office automation as a strategy for expanding its business markets. Electronic document production and storage promised new marketing opportunities based on computer systems designed for offices.

WYSIWYG employed the use of actual-size images of document pages on the computer screen and the corresponding ability to print them as they appeared. The Macintosh's 72 pixel-per-inch display corresponded closely to the number of dots used to print a Macintosh file on its companion product, the dot-matrix-based ImageWriter, making for a tight match between screen image and printed output.[3] While seemingly trivial now, in 1984, this innovation challenged the sterility of computerized word processing by presenting a graphically-enhanced environment for typing and visibly altering text through the specification of multiple fonts, sizes, and styles.

The tight coupling of image to output changed not only the way people created documents, but the way they thought about them. Computer users increasingly considered the text's appearance as central to the writing process. Early Macintosh users, discontent with impoverished "text entry," readily exploited typographic control through

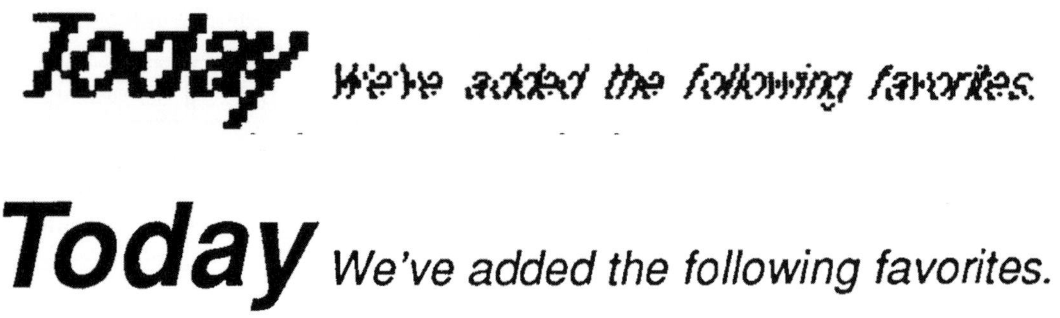

Figure 15.2 Comparison of ImageWriter (top) and LaserWriter output.

the built-in styling capabilities of the Macintosh Operating System.[4] These included, by default, the ability to choose among multiple typefaces and font families that could be installed in the Macintosh system file. In addition, Macintosh applications included standard options for rendering type as "plain text," bold, italic, underlined, outlined, and shadowed in a range of sizes, usually 10 to 24 points.

The coarseness of dot-matrix printing made for degraded visual quality, but this changed quickly with the introduction of the Apple LaserWriter printer in 1985. The LaserWriter enabled the Macintosh to rival offset printing through a technology that greatly enhanced the appearance of type and images (Figure 15.2). In moving to 300 dots-per-inch, the LaserWriter rendered letters considerably more smoothly, able to define subtler details in contour that would especially affect the appearance of serifs and smaller sizes of type.

While Apple's LaserWriter provided the hardware technology that would democratize typographic design through the rise of "desktop publishing," Adobe Systems provided the software innovation through PostScript, a "page description language" (PDL) built into the LaserWriter. PostScript made possible the printing of detailed page layouts, complete with images and text arranged and scaled to the designer's specifications.[5] Sophisticated graphic layouts previously requiring laborious manual composition now could be assembled with ease through software programs that made page layout almost as easy as word-processing. These programs, when used in conjunction with the LaserWriter, ensured offset printing quality graphic output. The LaserWriter also included a limited number of built-in PostScript fonts that could be supplemented by fonts downloaded from the Macintosh system folder to the printer's memory.

To showcase the capabilities of the LaserWriter and PostScript, Apple worked with selected software companies to develop page layout applications. Aldus's PageMaker, Boston Software Publishers' MacPublisher, and Manhattan Graphics's ReadySetGo provided programs ranging in price from roughly $150 to $500.[6] All supported the integration of text and images in multiple-column formats. While the documents produced with them could be sent to any Macintosh-compatible printer, they were especially impressive when transformed by the LaserWriter's PostScript software. Within a few years, desktop publishing supplanted professional typesetting and offset printing as the preferred low-end prepress and printing option.

THE DIGITAL CONSTRUCTION OF LETTERFORMS

In the late 1970s and early 80s, researchers and programmers, notably at MIT and Stanford, began developing new ways to describe and image letters digitally.[7] Philippe Coueignoux's CSD (Character Simulated Design) of 1975 decomposed the Roman alphabet into a set of primitives that could be recombined to form any letter.[8] Pijush Ghosh and Charles Bigelow attempted a similar strategy in 1983.[9] Donald Knuth's groundbreaking METAFONT provided a rich programming language for designing type through the algorithmic specification of geometrical relationships.[10] However, the mathematical expression it required was alien to most type designers, and METAFONT never caught on.[11] Digital typography embraced an ever-widening group of constituencies, from computer scientists such as Knuth to more traditional type designers including Charles Bigelow and Kris Holmes, who were to produce new innovations for the page and screen. Their typeface, Lucida, introduced in 1986, satisfied the multiple demands of page and screen through a comprehensive set of fonts suitable for printing and screen display (Figure 15.3).[12]

The cathode ray tube (CRT) used pixels ("picture elements") as the defining matrix for the construction and display of letters. The Macintosh of 1984 provided only two color options for their display: black and white. The Macintosh Operating System itself required different typefaces in order to communicate necessary textual information through the Macintosh interface. Chicago and Geneva, bitmapped typefaces designed to suit this need, typographically defined the Macintosh "look and feel" until 1997 (Figure 15.4). Chicago 12, used in pulldown menus and dialog boxes, employed a standard stroke width of two pixels, so that gray versions of usually black letters could be created by alternating black and white pixels. (Gray was required to signal the unavailability of various commands.) Geneva 9 appeared on the Macintosh "desktop" to label icons, and in list views of files and applications in the Finder.

While the typographic needs of the Macintosh interface posed one set of requirements, printed documents posed another: variety. The original Macintosh provided a number of bitmapped typeface options, most of them novel. A few classics emerged however – Helvetica, Times, and Palatino among them – with other options available from font vendors such as Adobe.

PostScript laser printers used economical descriptions of letterform outlines, as distinct from memory-intensive bitmaps, to form letters on printed pages. Thus, a given font family required two separate descriptions – one for screen display, and the other for printing. In fact, a third technology mediated between bitmap and outline during the Macintosh printing process: Apple's QuickDraw "drew" all images to the Macintosh screen. Printing from a Macintosh to a PostScript laser printer therefore required the translation of QuickDraw commands into PostScript, a task undertaken by the Macintosh Operating System's Print Manager in conjunction with the LaserWriter software driver.[13]

The NeXT computer, introduced in 1989, utilized PostScript for both screen display and printed output, eliminating any need for intermediate translation (Figure 15.5). In addition, the NeXT fully exploited grayscale technology in its user interface, an enhancement of the visual standard established by the Macintosh. The NeXT interface, through an expanded range of values from black to white, displayed icons and dialog boxes modeled with greater dimensionality, pushing the visual space of the graphical user interface from 2- to 3-D.

CORRESPONDING INNOVATIONS IN GRAPHIC DESIGN

Almost immediately upon the introduction of the Macintosh, a small handful of insightful graphic designers recognized the esthetic potential of computer-based typography. In 1985, Zuzana Licko designed three typefaces – Emperor, Oakland, and Emigre – that deliberately exploited the look of the pixel (Figure 15.6).[14] These typefaces soon redefined the look of an emerging publication, *Emigre*, founded by Licko's husband, Rudy VanderLans, with artist Marc Susan and screenwriter Menno Meyjes. It has since become

roman
ABCDEFGHIJKLMNOPQRSTUVWXYZ&
abcdefghijklmnopqrstuvwxyz .,:;!?‘“”
0123456789 #$%@+–=<>^~_()[]{}/|*

bold
ABCDEFGHIJKLMNOPQRSTUVWXYZ&
abcdefghijklmnopqrstuvwxyz .,:;!?‘“”
0123456789 #$%@+–=<>^~_()[]{}/|*

italic
ABCDEFGHIJKLMNOPQRSTUVWXYZ&
abcdefghijklmnopqrstuvwxyz .,:;!?‘“”
*0123456789 #$%@+–=<>^~_()[]{}/|**

bold italic
ABCDEFGHIJKLMNOPQRSTUVWXYZ&
abcdefghijklmnopqrstuvwxyz .,:;!?‘“”
0123456789 #$%@+–=<>^~_()[]{}/|*

sans
ABCDEFGHIJKLMNOPQRSTUVWXYZ&
abcdefghijklmnopqrstuvwxyz .,:;!?‘“”
0123456789 #$%@+–=<>^~_()[]{}/|*

sans bold
ABCDEFGHIJKLMNOPQRSTUVWXYZ&
abcdefghijklmnopqrstuvwxyz .,:;!?‘“”
0123456789 #$%@+–=<>^~_()[]{}/|*

sans italic
ABCDEFGHIJKLMNOPQRSTUVWXYZ&
abcdefghijklmnopqrstuvwxyz .,:;!?‘“”
*0123456789 #$%@+–=<>^~_()[]{}/|**

sans bold italic
ABCDEFGHIJKLMNOPQRSTUVWXYZ&
abcdefghijklmnopqrstuvwxyz .,:;!?‘“”
0123456789 #$%@+–=<>^~_()[]{}/|*

Figure 15.3 Lucida, by Charles Bigelow and Kris Holmes. From Richard Rubinstein, *Digital Typography: An Introduction to Type and Composition for Computer System Design* (Reading, MA: Addison Wesley, 1988), 216. Reprinted by permission of Addison Wesley Longman.

one of the most influential design publications of this century, serving as a primary vehicle for the dissemination of new critical typographic ideas. *Emigre* showcased typefaces designed by Licko and others, and served as a catalog for purchasing those very fonts. Licko and VanderLans lived and worked in the San Francisco Bay area, and their close proximity to Silicon Valley encouraged their exploration of its emerging technologies.

At the same time, in Los Angeles, April Greiman, a Swiss-trained graphic designer, began experimenting extensively with digital imaging

Chicago 12

Geneva 9

Figure 15.4 Macintosh system fonts Chicago 12 and Geneva 9.

and typography in her printed work. Like Licko and VanderLans, she used pixellated letterforms and pictures in posters and brochures, later incorporating video imagery as well (Figure 15.7).[15] By bringing the actual look of the screen – whether a computer display or television monitor – to paper, Greiman began to challenge the authority of the page as the official bearer of the word. Trained at Basel's Kunstgewerbeschule, Greiman had already garnered a reputation for combining the rigor of Swiss formalism with the irreverence of California pop to create an entirely new look and attitude in contemporary graphic design – "California Swiss." Silicon Valley's influence transformed her work even further by providing a new formal vocabulary explicitly shaped by digital technology.

While pixellation characterized the look of these early typographic experiments, blurring and antialiasing characterized the later look of digital typography.[16] "Aliasing" is a technical term used to describe the stairstep appearance ("jaggies") of curved edges of forms composed of pixels. In letterforms, aliasing is especially problematic because this stairstepping interferes with the smoothness of curvature required to define so many individual characters. The problem is compounded in

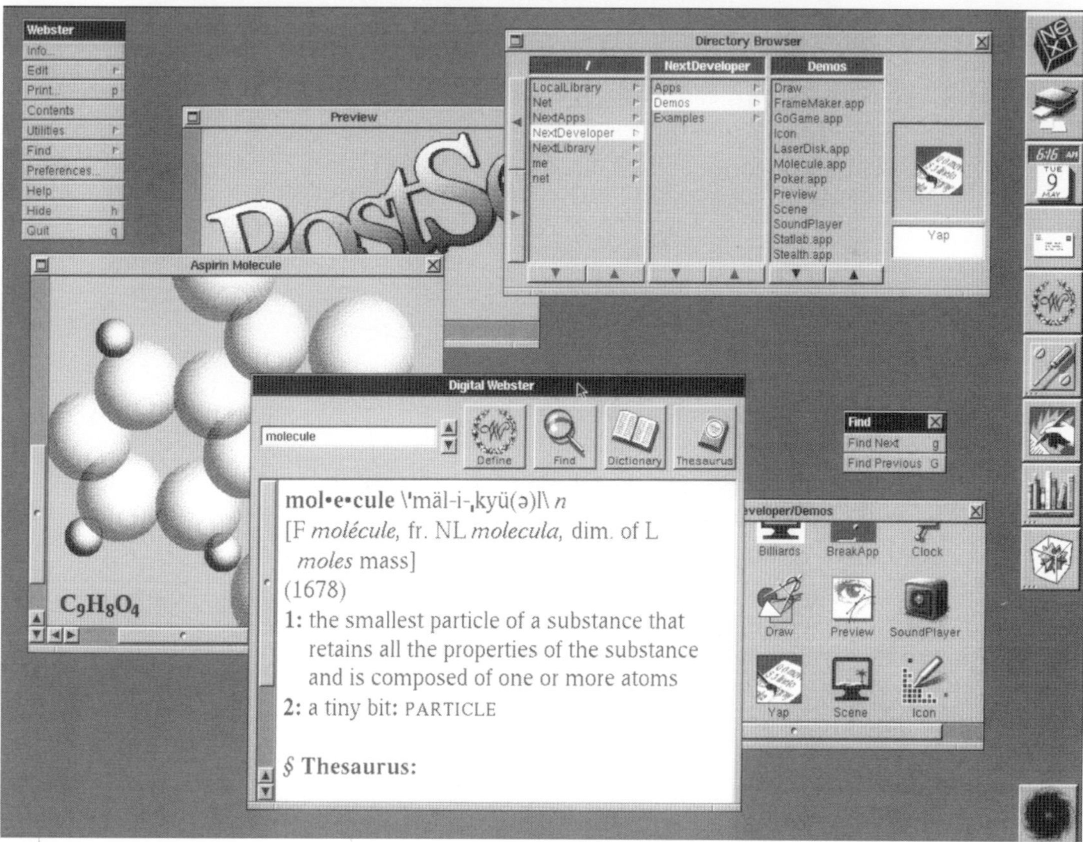

Figure 15.5 Display PostScript at work in the NeXT interface. From *Welcome to the NeXT Decade* (Palo Alto, CA: NeXT, 1988).

Emperor

Oakland

Emigre

Figure 15.6 (above) Emperor, Oakland, and Emigre, by Zuzana Licko.

typefaces with serifs and in type rendered in small sizes, since few pixels are available to create each letter.

Antialiasing solved this problem by blurring the edge of the letter into its background (Figure 15.8). For example, the edges of a black letter resting on a white background, when antialiased,

Figure 15.7 (right) Detail from 1986 issue of *Design Quarterly* by April Greiman, "Does It Make Sense?" Reprinted by permission of the Walker Art Center and MIT Press.

reveal the insertion of gray pixels along the contours of the letter. Only computer systems capable of displaying more than two colors (black and white) could support antialiasing. While antialiasing eliminates the jagged look of letters on the computer screen, it also diminishes their legibility by decreasing edge contrast. The loss of contrast between letter and background virtually obliterates smaller sizes of antialiased type.

Early Macintosh software programs for graphic editing did not include antialiasing. Until the introduction of the Macintosh II in 1987, the Macintosh computer supported only black and white displays. With grayscale technology, and then color, antialiasing became an obviously desirable feature and was later exploited in another innovative Adobe product, Photoshop, introduced in 1990.

Its developers originally intended Photoshop for use in high-end digital photo-retouching. As such, Photoshop presumed the existence of a workable image, in contrast with paint programs that provided a clean slate at the outset. Photoshop integrated a number of powerful yet relatively easy-to-use tools for editing images, and for adjusting and modifying color attributes. In addition, it provided a limited set of tools for creating and adding type to images – tools seized upon by graphic designers looking for new alternatives to standard typesetting in the desktop environment.

Adobe's earlier and equally influential product, Illustrator, had quickly become the preferred high-end drawing tool for digital designers. Behind its sophisticated interface, Illustrator automatically generated PostScript code during the drawing process. This code could be downloaded directly to any PostScript printer as a text file of PostScript code or saved as "encapsulated PostScript" (EPS), a format which retains a visual preview of the image created.

In contrast, Photoshop was a high-end bitmapped graphics program for editing pixels.[17] While this distinction may seem negligible, it is key. Photoshop provided designers with the technology for easily compositing photographic images and type within a single surface.[18] The unifying layer of pixels comprising them both, in essence, demoted letters to the status of pictures. This revolutionized typography by radically altering the way designers conceptualized and executed typographic (as opposed to image-based) work. Photographic space equally subsumed the two, undoing the descriptive or adjunct relationship usually borne by text to image. In a text-based culture already skeptical toward the visual, images had nothing left to lose, letters everything.[19] This blurry affiliation of letters and images became the new norm for graphic design.

In addition to its limited but significant phototypesetting capabilities, Photoshop's "filters"

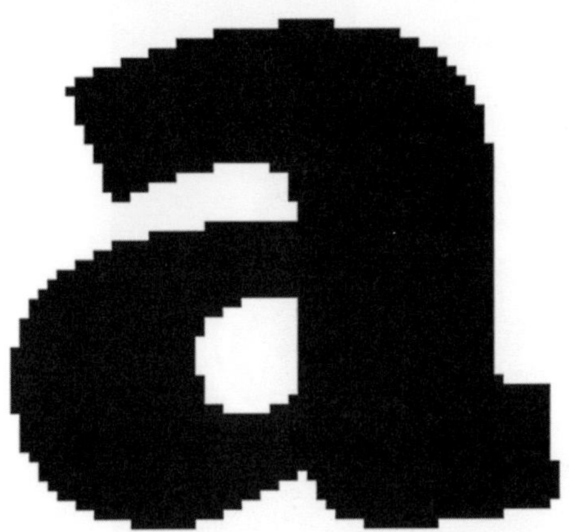

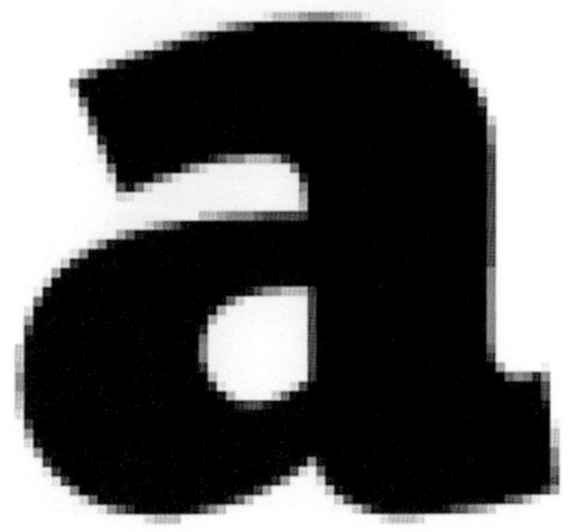

Figure 15.8 Aliased (left) and antialiased versions of the letter "a."

provided a readily available set of commands for applying sophisticated visual effects to an image at the touch of a button. England's Neville Brody began fusing images and type in 1992, designing provocative posters that would showcase Photoshop's photomanipulative powers.[20] He toyed extensively with ambient, blurred compositions, as did many others including P. Scott Makela at Cranbrook in the US (Figure 15.9).

The dissolution of the word continued as a major trend throughout the 1990s, with David Carson a major instigator. His pioneering sensibility, first at *Beach Culture* magazine and then *Ray Gun*, established new thresholds for type's

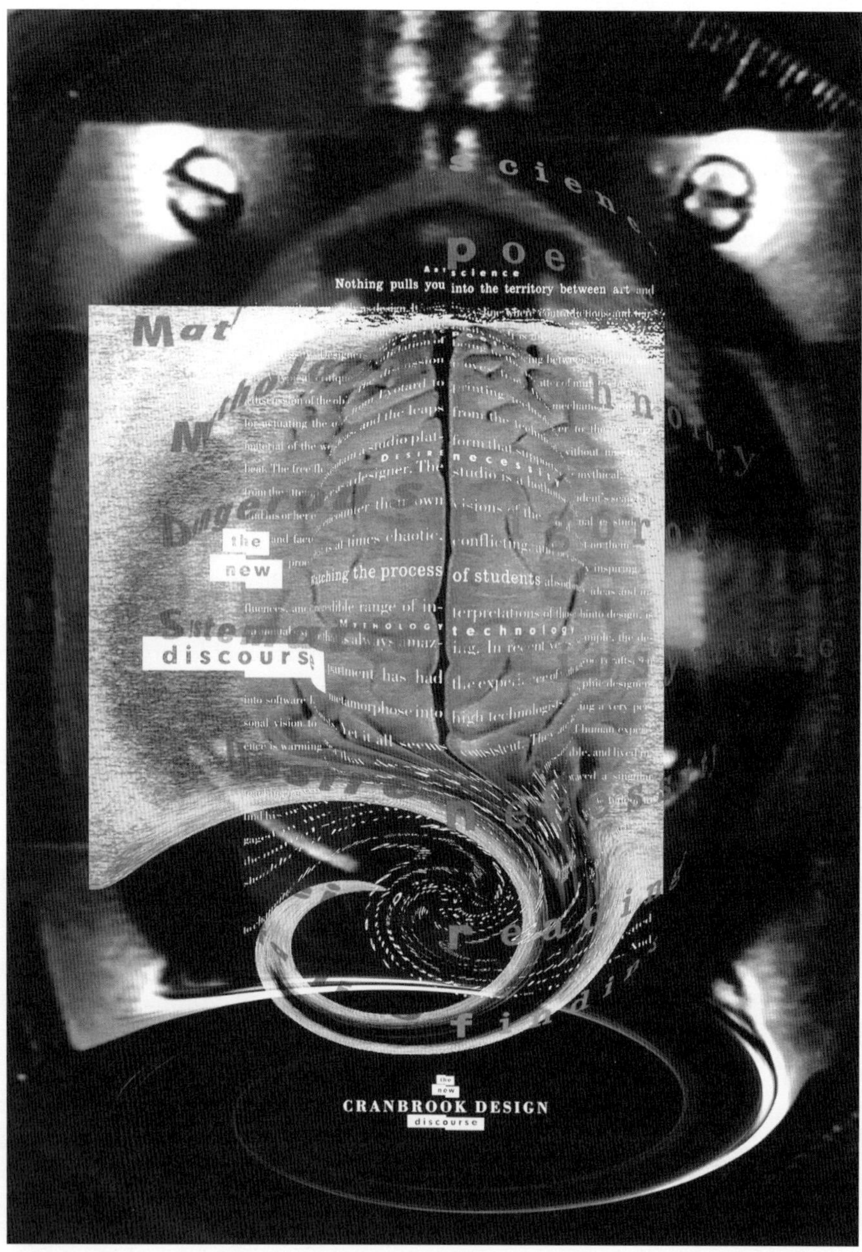

Figure 15.9 1993 poster by P. Scott Makela. Reprinted by permission of Laurie Haycock Makela.

legibility (or lack thereof). Often criticized, Carson's controversial work further threatened the authority of traditional typography through extensively distorted letterforms and erratic layouts (Figure 15.10). By offering an alternative to the more refined "production values" of TV, film, video, and advertising, Carson challenged the prevailing sensuous norms of mass media. As might be expected, however, the mainstream readily absorbed his once-radical esthetic.

PAPER VS. THE SCREEN

Digital typography's innovations through the early 1990s lay primarily in technologies and corresponding attitudes that revised the image of the printed word. Beginning in the late 1980s, however, a new medium emerged to force the issue of the screen to the forefront: the CD-ROM. Interactive multimedia created a new venue for displaying words, introducing new technical and esthetic issues. "Authoring" tools such as VideoWorks (later to become Macromedia Director) and Apple's HyperCard served as early development platforms for building interactive pieces destined for the screen, and included limited text-handling capabilities. The distinction between text and image persisted in these software development environments, with editing tools capable of creating letters either as "text," dynamically reeditable through the keyboard, or as "paint," static arrays of bitmaps that, once created, required the editing of their individual pixels.

Figure 15.10 Cover of *Ray Gun* by David Carson. Reprinted by permission of David Carson.

The suite of digital tools used to develop multimedia products supported numerous options for media creation and integration. Text (again, in multiple formats), still and motion graphics, video, and sound could be brought together within a single environment, and then orchestrated through built-in programming languages. Once "compiled," users could navigate these multimedia spaces freely, choosing from among preprogrammed options specified by the designer.

Despite the opportunities created by multimedia's screen requirements, typeface options remained limited. Among the hundreds of digital fonts available for use, most provided bitmaps not finely tuned for the screen but, rather, coarse counterparts to their corresponding outline files (again, these PostScript outlines were used in printing). Screen fonts remained of secondary importance despite the demands of the new medium.

A few insightful designers (Bigelow & Holmes already mentioned) recognized the needs of the screen, and worked to create more choices. Apple developed proprietary screen fonts, the Espy family, for use in its instructional products in 1993. Espy served as a legible alternative to Chicago and Geneva, which were too closely identified with the look of the Macintosh desktop. Matthew Carter, an experienced type designer who already had tackled numerous challenges in designing for various typesetting technologies, co-founded Bitstream to develop digital typefaces. Responsible for many print and screen-based innovations, in 1995, Carter designed Walker, a typeface commissioned by the Walker Art Center that featured interchangeable "snap-on" serifs.[21] He later worked with Microsoft to design proprietary screen fonts.

Adobe Systems had quickly emerged as the leading provider of digital fonts, but printing remained the company's priority given the fact that PostScript had never gained acceptance as a screen display technology. Nonetheless, many of their font families included well-drawn bitmaps used by early designers of electronic media. Adobe's 1990 product, Adobe Type Manager (ATM), contributed significantly to the quality of screen type in its ability to smooth and scale type to any size, using only a limited number of bitmaps along with the font's corresponding outline file, both stored in the Macintosh system folder.[22] With ATM, designers could generate type sizes beyond the 10–24 point bitmaps typically furnished by type publishers. While ATM improved the onscreen look of larger type sizes, small sizes proved a persistent problem. Designers wanting small sizes of type relied on the 10- and 12-point furnished bitmaps or the automatic scaling of the Macintosh system, which usually provided poor results.

Meanwhile, Apple began developing an alternative type format to rival Adobe's PostScript fonts. TrueType relied on auto-scaling to generate type sizes as needed, side-stepping PostScript. A "font war" ensued, with Apple and Adobe vying with each other to become or remain the industry standard. Eventually, both companies conceded. Adobe published its Type 1 standard to support the creation of non-Adobe PostScript fonts, and Apple supported Adobe Type 1 fonts in addition to its own TrueType format.[23]

Developers of authoring tools generally neglected typographic needs but, by 1996, Director included antialiasing as a feature of its built-in text editor. Designers now could create dynamically reeditable text, whose smooth appearance rivaled that created by an external graphics editor such as Photoshop.

TYPOGRAPHY AND THE WORLD WIDE WEB

An even more demanding and influential medium emerged in the mid-1990s to overtake the CD-ROM market, and bring the concerns of digital typography to a wider public. The World Wide Web presented the designer with even more complex typographic dilemmas by placing ultimate control of typographic appearance in the hands of the audience. Web browsers – software for viewing files (Web pages) stored on the array of servers that in essence comprise the Web – provided user-definable preferences for a number of design attributes including typeface, font size, and color. In addition, these browsers also provided, by necessity, predefined typographic specifications to ensure a minimally adequate display by default, should users choose not to specify their own preferences.

With users given the option to freely override the designer's specifications, most graphic designers made use of such tools as Photoshop to create text that could be set, antialiased, and saved as a graphic file. Despite the economy and efficiency of HTML[24] text, which requires no downloading time and remains dynamicaly reeditable, most graphic designers entering the arena of Web design chose (and continue to choose) "graphic text" as the means through which to ensure a stable typographic appearance on Web pages, reserving the use of HTML text for lengthy passages.

Graphic designers and clients alike considered the subversion of graphic identity by Web browsers a distinct problem. In an effort to enforce graphic identity, new companies including @ Home Network – founded to bring Web access to the home through the infrastructure of cable television – devised font strategies to override user preferences. @Home's proprietary browser automatically displayed HTML text in @Home's signature fonts (a default setting users could change, however). This strategy was in place by the time of the product launch in 1996. @Home's creative director, Roger Black, created the product's look

– as he had done success- fully for the *New York Times*, *Newsweek*, and a number of other popular magazines. The product strategy strengthened @ Home's overall look and feel, critical for a Web publication serving as a directory for the best on the Web. @Home's editorial identity offered a potential competitive advantage against search engines capable of directing users to specific Web pages and thus bypassing any intermediate editorial commentary that might urge or discourage visiting a given Website.

At the same time, Black's experience as a print designer limited his ability to recognize that the "magazine" served simply as a metaphor, and perhaps not the appropriate one for such an innovative medium. Black might have chosen television, film, or even architecture as the organizing metaphor for @Home's browser, breaking new ground in subverting the "pageness" of the Web. Other graphic designers would follow suit, bringing the limitations of page-oriented conceptual models to Web design.

In an effort to establish a standard that would unify digital type formats, an industry consortium proposed the OpenType format early in 1996. Through OpenType – a "common container format for TrueType and Type 1 fonts" – Adobe and Microsoft promised greater typographic control on the Web through the ability to embed fonts in HTML documents.[25] Other efforts, including TrueDoc, a joint initiative between Adobe and Bitstream, also ensured greater typographic control of Web documents.[26] On the whole, however, these efforts have been slow either in development, in gaining industry support, or in adoption as a standard.

TYPOGRAPHY AND COMPUTATION IN CYBERSPACE

While most graphic designers scrambled to take advantage of new opportunities posed by the Web in the mid-1990s, university and industry researchers pursued more innovative and radical approaches to type design in cyberspace as a result of their vast computing resources and funding to permit such exploration. MIT's Visible Language Workshop, under the direction of Muriel Cooper, produced prototypes of multidimensional information displays incorporating type. Using infinite zooming, along with various levels of transparency and opacity, VBL's designers – including David Small, Suguru Ishizaki, and Lisa Strausfeld – constructed maps, charts, and timelines that users could navigate as if in flight, a radical departure from the planar, frontal organization of most standard user interfaces (Figure 15.11). When VBL's work debuted at 1994's "TED5" conference, it created a stir among the graphic design community.

Since Muriel Cooper's death in 1994, the Visible Language Workshop has been supplanted by another Media Lab research group headed by Cooper's heir apparent, John Maeda. His Aesthetics & Computation Group explores the intersection between typography and programming to exploit computer processing power unconstrained by authoring tools. Maeda trained as a computer scientist, but his interest began shifting to graphic design while still a student. After completing undergraduate and graduate work at MIT, he earned a doctorate at Tsukuba University Institute of Art and Design in Japan. As an award-winning art director in Japan, he explored print and interactive design, and published whimsical electronic typographic works (Figure 15.12).[27] Maeda represents a new breed of designer – the programmer/typographer – destined to drive the future of graphic design innovation.

Outside the academy, J. Abbott Miller of the design studio Design/Writing/Research undertook innovative experiments in dimensional typography. Using high-end computer workstations, Miller and his colleagues created three-dimensional letterforms.[28] Lathing, extrusion, and texture-mapping defined new typefaces as well as novel interpretations of existing classics. While Miller himself acknowledged these studies as conceptual explorations, they already have proved

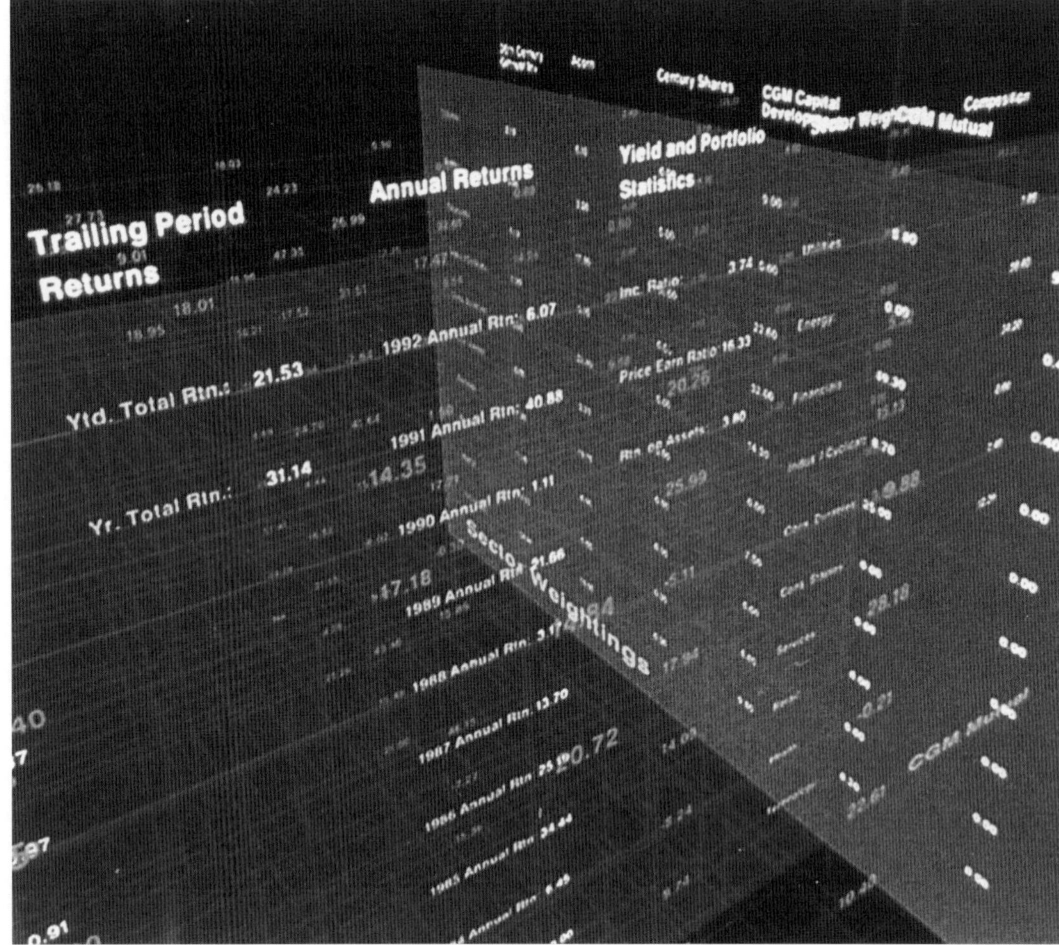

Figure 15.11 "Information landscape" by Lisa Strausfeld. From "Financial Viewpoints: Using point-of-view to enable understanding of information," http://www.acm.org/turing/sigs/sigchi/chi95/ Electronic/ACMcopyright.html (New York: Association for Computing Machinery, 1995). Reprinted by permission of the Association for Computing Machinery, Inc.

influential. Ji Byol Lee's lathed version of Univers and Univers Revolved (Figure 15.13) appeared in the pages of the *New York Times Magazine* of September 28, 1997, an issue on the impact of computing in contemporary life. The image of the letter in cyberspace has once again made its way back to the page.

CONCLUSION

The period from 1984 to 1997 saw the proliferation of key technologies that popularized digital design. New tools, including the Apple Macintosh computer and associated software, especially that from Adobe Systems, enabled designers to create, edit, and disseminate words and images in new ways. Initially, designers translated the onscreen image of pixellated letterforms into fonts for printing – a wry visual commentary on the play between page and screen. Numerous experiments followed that challenged typographic norms. Designers developed hybridized forms and ignored the traditional rules of legibility. Adobe Photoshop allowed designers to fuse text and image into a single pictorial layer, and stimulated the

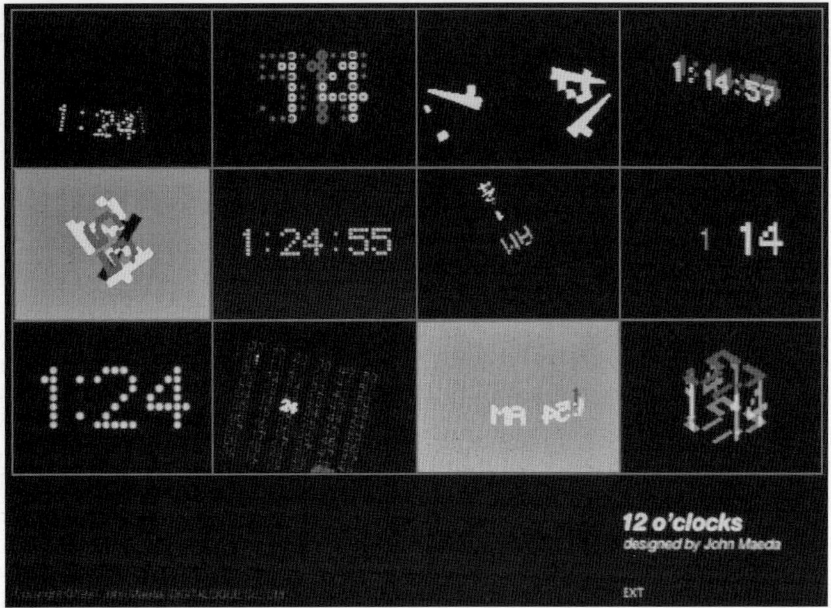

Figure 15.12 Screen from 12 o'clocks by John Maeda. Interactive clocks visually interpret the passage of time 12 different ways. Reprinted by permission of John Maeda.

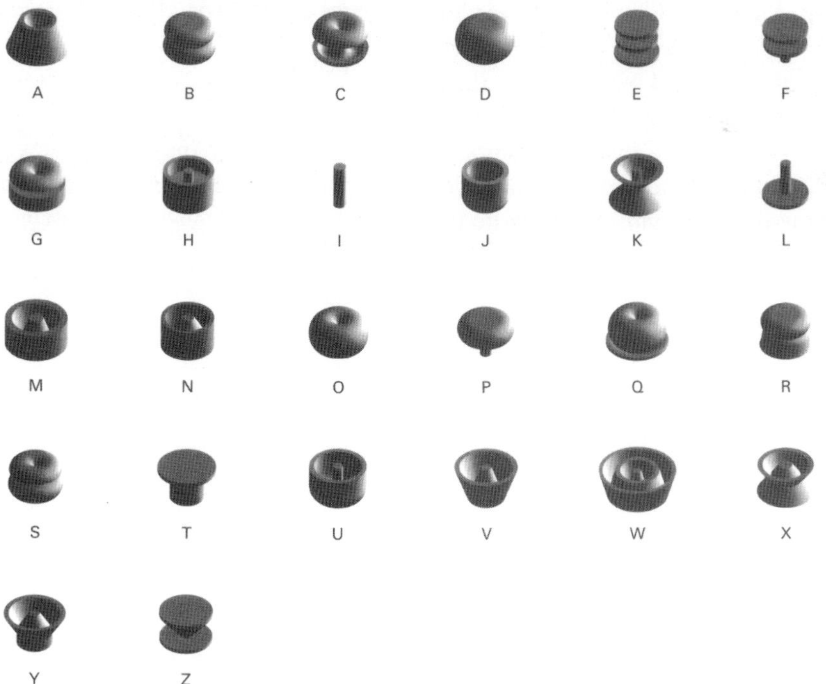

Figure 15.13 Univers Revolved by Ji Byol Lee. From J. Abbott Miller, *Dimensional Typography: Case Studies on the Shape of Letters in Virtual Environments* (New York: Princeton Architectural Press, 1996) pp. 24–25. Reprinted by permission of J. Abbott Miller.

rise of visual effects-driven typography in the early 1990s. The hyperplastic esthetic that developed in print design during this period migrated back to the screen through the World Wide Web in the mid-90s. Typographic innovation now continues in cyberspace through computer-modeled and algorithmically-driven typography.

By making it possible for designers to conceptualize and realize letters in new ways, digital technology has provided the platform through which words ultimately could be subsumed in the larger pictorial space of the image, leveling the relationship between the two. In so doing, digital technology revised the status of the written word in the late twentieth century.

ACKNOWLEDGMENTS

Much of the content of this article was originally presented as a lecture at the 1996 symposium organized in conjunction with the exhibition "Mixing Messages: Graphic Design and Contemporary Culture" at the Cooper-Hewitt National Design Museum. I would like to thank the curator of that exhibition, Ellen Lupton, for inviting me to participate in that symposium. In addition, I wish to thank the Radgale Foundation for granting me the space and time to write this piece.

NOTES

First published in *Design Issues* 16 no. 3 (Autumn 2000): 19–34.

1. In 1983, Charles Bigelow and Donald Day defined digital type as that "made up of discrete elements. These elements can be line strokes, pixels, colors, shades of gray, or any other graphic unit from which a letterform can be constructed. Hence, digital typography is not new: mosaic tiles, embroidered samplers, and arrays of lights on theater marquees have long represented alphabetic characters as relatively coarse discrete arrays." However, in focusing on the display device of the cathode ray tube (CRT), and the requisite "digital computer … needed to control the on-off pattern of the electron beam" that articulated letterforms on the screen, they defined it specifically in terms of computer technology. Charles Bigelow and Donald Day, "Digital Typography," *Scientific American* 249:2 (August 1983): 106.
2. Jeff Johnson, et al., "The Xerox Star: A Retrospective," *IEEE Computer* 22:9 (September 1989): 11–29.
3. The 72-pixel-per-inch display was designed to correspond with the point, since it was the standard unit of measurement for specifying type. Johnson, et al., "The Xerox Star: A Retrospective," 12.
4. Computerized word-processing's leading product at the time was WordStar, a program that supported limited WYSIWYG capabilities, but without extensive typographic control. Roger B. White, Jr., *WordStar With Style* (Reston, VA: Prentice Hall, Reston Publishing, 1983).
5. The PostScript PDL was not wedded to a particular output device, however. In being "device independent," PostScript document descriptions contain no specific information regarding output devices and, as such, will print at whatever level of resolution the given output device makes available. Frederic E. Davis, et al., *Desktop Publishing* (Homewood, IL: Dow Jones-Irwin, 1986), 167.
6. Ibid., 95–99.
7. See Richard Rubinstein, *Digital Typography: An Introduction to Type and Composition for Computer System Design* (Reading, MA: Addison Wesley, 1988) for a comprehensive description of digital typographic innovation from its inception through the late 1980s.
8. Ibid., 141.
9. Ibid., 141.
10. Donald E. Knuth, *Computer Modern Typefaces* (Reading, MA: Addison Wesley, 1986).
11. Rubinstein, *Digital Typography*, 141–145.
12. Charles Bigelow and Kris Holmes, "The Design of Lucida®: an Integrated Family of Types for Electronic Literacy" in J.C. van Vliet, *Text Processing and Document Manipulation, Proceedings of the International Conference, University of Nottingham, April 14–16, 1986* (Cambridge: Cambridge University Press, 1986), 1–17.
13. Jim Heid and Peter Norton, *Inside the Apple Macintosh* (New York: Simon & Shuster, Brady, 1989), 221.
14. Rudy VanderLans, Zuzana Licko, and Mary E. Gray, *Emigre: Graphic Design Into the Digital Realm* (New York: Van Nostrand Reinhold, 1993), 18–25.

15. April Greiman, *Hybrid Imagery: The Fusion of Technology and Graphic Design* (New York: Watson-Guptill Publications, 1990), 55–99.
16. For more on the technical aspects and esthetic and cultural implications of blurring in contemporary graphic design, see Loretta Staples, "What Happens When the Edges Dissolve?" *Eye* 5:18 (Autumn 1995): 6–7.
17. Graphics programs are bitmap- or vector-based. Vector-based programs rely on mathematical descriptions for describing geometrical forms. Their interfaces generate drawings consisting of curved or straight line segments, with "handles" used to conduct editing operations such as resizing, rotating, and skewing.
18. Photographic images and text were handled separately in manual mechanical production for offset printing. Text and line art were assembled together, while photographs underwent the intermediate process of halftoning (conversion from continuous tone to dots) prior to mechanical insertion. FPOs ("for position only"), low-resolution photo reproductions – were commonly used on mechanical boards as placeholders for the higher quality images that would replace them later during the film stripping process. Even within page layout programs, text and images remain separate due to their respective technical requirements for outputting.
19. Barbara Maria Stafford has written extensively about the status of the visual in contemporary culture, tracing its decline to the enlightenment, and elucidating biases toward the linguistic in contemporary thought. Barbara Maria Stafford, *Good Looking: Essays on the Virtue of Images* (Cambridge, MA: MIT Press, 1996).
20. Jon Wozencroft, *The Graphic Language of Neville Brody* (New York: Rizzoli, 1994), 16.
21. Ellen Lupton, *Mixing Messages: Graphic Design in Contemporary Culture* (New York: Princeton Architectural Press and Cooper-Hewitt, National Design Museum, Smithsonian Institution, 1996), 34.
22. ATM was not explicitly designed for this purpose, however. ATM allowed non-Postscript printers to print Adobe fonts, desirable because it strengthened Adobe's position as the premier digital type foundry. Improved screen appearance was a side benefit for print designers wanting improved screen previews. Gregory Wasson, "Adobe's Font Utility Isn't Perfect, but It's Still a Worthwhile Investment," *MacUser* 6:2 (February 1, 1990): 64–65.
23. Laurie Flynn, "Warnock Says Adobe Won't Make It Easy on Competitors," *InfoWorld* 11:41 (October 9, 1989): 6 and Jai Singh, "Apple Opens Door to Adobe Fonts – System 7 to Include Type 1 Fonts, Adobe Type Manager," *PC Week* 8:34 (August 26, 1991): 12.
24. HTML (Hypertext Markup Language) is the "tagging language" used to create Web pages. Tags placed before and after the words constituting the textual page content effect typographic attributes including styling and relative sizing.
25. Rebecca Gulick, "Interlocking Font Deals Find Center in Adobe," *MacWEEK* 10: 20 (March 20, 1996): 10–12.
26. John Clyman and Jonathan Matzkin, "The Font Forecast – Adobe and Bitstream Recast Type Design," *PC Magazine* 15:13 (July 1, 1996): 31.
27. John Maeda, *Flying Letters* (Tokyo: Naomi Enama, Digitalogue Co., Ltd., 1996) and *12 O'clocks* (Tokyo: Naomi Enama, Digitalogue Co., Ltd., 1997).
28. J. Abbott Miller, Dimensional *Typography: Case Studies on the Shape of Letters in Virtual Environments* (New York: Princeton Architectural Press, 1996), 24–25.

FURTHER READING FOR PART II, SECTION 1

A good discussion of presentation design can be found in Edward Tufte, *The Visual Display of Quantitative Information*, 2nd ed. (Cheshire, CT: Graphics Press, 2001). On aquariums, see Leighton Taylor, *Aquariums: Windows to Nature* (New York: Prentice-Hall, 1993) and on simulation, see Jean Baudrillard, *Simulations* (New York: Semiotext(e), 1983). On digital typography, see Richard Rubinstein, *Digital Typography: An Introduction to Type and Composition for Computer System Design* (Reading, MA: Addison-Wesley, 1988). Two books on designers associated with digital design are Rudy VanderLans, Susanna Licko, and Mary E. Gray, *Emigré: Graphic Design into the Digital Realm* (New York: Van Nostrand, 1993) and April Greiman, *Hybrid Imagery: The Fusion of Technology and Graphic Design* (New York: Watson-Guptill, 1990).

PART II

FABRICATION

SECTION 2

INTRODUCTION TO SECTION 2: THE DESIGN PROCESS AND THE SOCIAL MEANING OF THINGS

Once they are manufactured, designed objects, whether appliances, furniture, or digital typefaces, take on a life of their own. Consumers seek out these objects for their own reasons and use them according to their own purposes. The domain of use thus widens the context in which the fabrication of objects can be understood.

Design critic Reyner Banham, as Nigel Whiteley describes him, was more interested in the symbolic expression of objects and their use than he was in their style. Banham extended the range of design that was worthy of critical attention by writing about banknotes, neckties, and ice cream vans as well as more conventional objects. Whiteley discusses Banham's approach to design writing, noting that use for Banham was more about how design was consumed by different social groups than it was about the object's intended function. Banham's approach to design criticism departed from the strict modernist dictum that explained form in terms of its function, offering instead a more eclectic and sociological basis for discussing the way objects conveyed social meaning.

Conversely, Sara Schneider's article on the Day-Timer describes how the Day-Timers company sought to create a corporate culture that embedded one of its products in a system of ritualized use. The Day-Timer is a work organizer that fosters the efficient management of time. In its promotional material, Day-Timers featured accounts of how its own employees used the product, while it invited customers to provide comments on their experience with organizer. It then used the most positive of these in its future advertising.

In her article on the development of typography in the 1980s and 1990s, Loretta Staples looks at the fabrication of digital type, noting that: "The computer enabled designers to create and manipulate letters in new ways, offering new options for crafting letterforms and 'outputting' them – whether in the medium of toner particles on paper, or pixels on a screen." Similar to Michael Punt's account of the community that created the personal computer, Staples shows that numerous people were involved in developing the technology and design of digital type. Of significance is the fact that new technologies, such as Apple's LaserWriter, greatly enhanced opportunities for desktop publishing by individuals, while giving graphic designers more control over their final output. Digital technology also generated new aesthetic possibilities, beginning with fonts that exposed their bitmap construction and moving on to experiments with dimensional forms.

Giovanni Anceschi considers visibility to be an essential component of fabrication. He critiques the "excess of visual noise" that produces a "*civilization of blindness*" and looks to the graphic designer to reveal valuable information to the public. He likens the designer to a theater director or choreographer, who instead gives form, position, and behavior to graphic elements that are displayed as "representations of characters, graphics, and illustrations on the Flatland of the page." Anceschi treats graphic elements like physical entities and characterizes the designer's skill as knowing how to place them in relation to each other in order to produce meaning.

Raimonda Riccini addresses the issue of fabrication as a historian, by considering some of the different ways that designed objects can be interpreted. She claims persuasively that there is no single way to embed objects in historical narratives. One argument she makes is that the history of industrial design should be more closely related to the history of business, thus exposing the economic and manufacturing decisions and processes that generate objects. Wedgwood pottery, Thonet furniture, and Ford automobiles are products of distinct industrial cultures that need to be accounted for. At the same time, she recognizes that objects can be related to each other in a larger sense of forming typological chains that show the evolution of forms through multiple iterations. Besides the history *of* artifacts, Riccini is also concerned with history *through* artifacts, whereby objects contribute to the understanding of culture as a whole.

16

HISTORY FROM THINGS: NOTES ON THE HISTORY OF INDUSTRIAL DESIGN

Raimonda Riccini

A longer version of this essay was published in *Archivi e Imprese* 14 (July–December 1996): 231–58.

However paradoxical it may seem, the history of industrial design has, for a long time, been able to ignore business history, just as the history of enterprise has been able to avoid a real confrontation with the history of products. Far from being a sort of play on words, this opening statement deserves serious consideration and, at the same time, requires some explanation. For what reason, then, have the planes on which these two branches of history operate intersected so rarely? Why is it that two such closely interconnected worlds have generated two separate fields of study and of knowledge?

The history of enterprise is a recently formed discipline, and one which is trying to create its own identity, in part through the confrontation with other fields of study. At a congress on industrial design held at the Milan Politecnico,[1] Valerio Castronovo had addressed the question of the relationship between the history of industry and the history of industrial design. At the time, he had attributed the backward state of studies of the industrial system to the "low level of interest that business historians have shown so far in a subject like that of design." But the scarce interest shown by business historians has been matched by that of historians of industrial design. We can attempt to come up with some further explanations in order to sound out the problem. At least two points of my argument are of decisive importance to the reliability of the reasoning. The first concerns strictly disciplinary motivations, closely bound up with the way in which the history of industrial design has developed; the second refers to the marginal role given to artifacts, when they are not entirely absent, in the process of historical reconstruction.

I would like to commence, however, on the positive side by recalling that there have been significant exceptions in the historiography of both sectors. Thus, it is possible to cite important cases in which the history of an enterprise has been reconstructed around problems of industrial design, or on the basis of motivations or questions that arise directly from the study and the history of industrial design. Although they are very well known even to non-specialists, I would like to mention by way of example the meticulous reconstructions of the history of the British pottery industry and Josiah Wedgwood's factories at Etruria and of Thonet bentwood furniture and AEG, to stick to the phase of so-called proto-design.[2] The interest shown by historians in these enterprises stemmed largely from the fact that they were seen as the pioneers of a new industrial sector, bringing with them a high degree of innovation and representing a different way of manufacturing and marketing products. The entrepreneurs themselves are represented as emblematic figures, as in the case of Wedgwood.

In addition to his industrialization of the production of pottery, he is shown to have been capable of grasping that the manufacture of objects was part of a broader system comprising the phases of research, design, production, and, finally, marketing.[3] The same factors underpin the interest in figures such as Thomas Edison and, above all, the American automobile industry in the case of Ford and General Motors, as well as in the history of transportation in general. Moreover, the attention paid by scholars to some companies rather than others certainly is influenced by the presence of important designers, as in the well-known case of Peter Behrens and AEG.

However, while reconstructions of this kind provide a valid model, it is one that rarely has been taken up. Apart from a few emblematic cases, then, the attention given to economic and industrial factors in studies of the history of industrial design has all too often not extended beyond a few indispensable references to the context. The principal economic agents, though acknowledged to play a leading role in the fortunes of the company, have been characterized in an extremely vague fashion. And when it comes to systems of production, the relationship with the products, the role of design, and even quantitative analyses of the products themselves, little trace can be found.

As if to back up this attitude on the part of the vast majority of historical studies of industrial design, there has been – it seems to me – an underestimation of the problems connected with the final form of the product on the part of the companies themselves. In other words, historically, the enterprise as an economic entity has not always interpreted the role and function of design within its own organization in an appropriate manner. It is likely that things could have been otherwise, at least until such time as a model of organization based on the production process and its efficiency gave way to a model that concentrates more on the product and the market.[4] If to this we add the fact that, for many years, industrial design has been viewed as a "cosmetic" function,[5] then the fact that people have tended to think of the product as external or secondary to the production process becomes comprehensible.

If this is true, then we are dealing with a failing on two levels: on the one hand, the slowness of studies of the history of industrial design to realize that the enterprise offers an ideal vantage point from which to understand the history of products and of the profession of the industrial designer; on the other, the reluctance of the enterprise to see the overall identity of its products as a decisive part of its own identity.[6] As John Walker has suggested, the history of industrial design has studied enterprise in much the same spirit as the art historian has looked at patronage:[7] merely as the client for works of particular significance in the world of industrial products. In contrast, companies have sought, for the most part, to project an image of themselves through their successful products, presented in a linear sequence.[8]

Nonetheless, it is possible to identify a series of enterprises for which the products have represented, right from the start, a resource, even in terms of memory, that is indissolubly bound up with the way that the company has developed. Siemens provides an example of this. Some of the publications on the history of the company show a strong propensity to describe the evolution of its technology and production in terms of innovation and the characteristics of its products.[9] In addition, of course, to sales catalogs, which represent an invaluable but quite distinct source for the history of industrial design,[10] these publications are particularly revealing as they examine the stages in the development of the company and show us the products associated with them. Backed up by numerous pictures, sometimes assembled in true synoptic tables of images, this approach permits a comparative analysis of the models and, at the same time, offers a precise account of the stages in product innovation over the course of time.[11] The technological and functional characteristics of the products are clearly revealed (for instance, the appliances made in the twenties and thirties with systems for absorbing current at night), and sometimes even innovations in the production cycle are stressed (such as the rationalization of the plant for the assembly-line production of irons in 1924).[12]

In such a context, however, the contribution of design and the part played by the designer in the shaping of products are relegated to a secondary role, if not dismissed as totally irrelevant.[13] A simple comparison may serve to clarify this aspect. Anyone with even a nodding acquaintance with the history of German industry cannot fail to notice the different approach taken with a company such as AEG – contemporary with Siemens and operating in the same sector – and the different historical image that has grown up around this firm and Peter Behrens, as well as the famous electrical appliances that emerged from his work as a designer or which were produced under his supervision. In this case, one can even speak of an overexposure of Behrens's activity, with the result that an excessively homogeneous and consistent image has crystallized around a diverse and complex reality.

In addition to this illustrious precursor, there have been numerous other companies that have made industrial design a central element in their approach to the planning of products and even to the image of the company itself. There are some good examples of this in Italy, too, though on a different scale. It seems superfluous to look at Olivetti again, since it is one of the most widely studied and appreciated cases even at an international level. Instead, it is worth recalling a number of examples proposed by Mario Bellini, a designer who has been directly involved in many of these experiences:

> Another case that I would like to mention briefly is that of a smaller company, Brionvega, which, based in Milan, produces equipment for sound and music and television sets. Here, too, we see the involvement of design in the planning process. The technicians who are concerned with circuits and positions, with the innards of a television set, work with designers to produce a result that is, for example, a better television set; an object capable of entering into a relationship with our surroundings and with our sensibility. Here, too, the non-separation of function and ornament has, in my view, led to very interesting results, even though the product is aimed at an elite market ... Briefly, another experience, with Cassina. Here we are in a different situation: the product is not machinery but furniture. A machine is always made up of something that stays inside, a sort of mechanical, electronic, functioning intestine, and something that is outside: the activity of the designer is aimed at resolving this dualism in a synthetic manner. The piece of furniture on the other hand, apart from a few exceptions, is a unitary product ... in this youthful company we find a situation in which the moment of design is intrinsically essential to the very existence of a range of products and, therefore, to the industry that produces them.[14]

Bellini makes clear two of the questions that are central to our discussion. The first is the distinction between the design of machines and the design of other consumer goods such as furniture, to which I would like to add knickknacks, clothing, fashion accessories, and textiles. In other words, a distinction between the range of technical products that require the intervention of the designer to allow the user to operate and manipulate the object and that of products which establish a relationship of a functional type (sitting, wearing) that is, at the same time, perceptual, aesthetic, symbolic, and communicative. Which brings us to the second question, closely linked to the first: the theme of the relationship between the technical content of products and their covering, between the mechanism and the container.

From the early stages of the factory system, this point[15] has conditioned the role of design. Was the final form of the product a problem related to the entire process of production or could it be dealt with by the "external" intervention of a designer? Could the external form of the object be divorced from its mode of functioning? Just how great a degree of freedom could the designer have? These are questions that, in the end, bring us back to the old conflict, never completely resolved, between standardization and ornamentation, between creative freedom and technical constraints, around which the debate in Germany at the beginning of the twentieth century turned in particular.[16] But also to the idea that it is the production process that *de facto* determines the final form of the product and that it is, therefore, necessary to "incorporate" design into the process. Support for one or the other of these hypotheses has created a division between two ways of looking at industrial design, which go hand-in-hand with different ways of thinking about its history. In Italy, where designers have been involved chiefly (but not exclusively)[17] in the area of noninstrumental consumer goods, with a marked and much vaunted craft component, historians seem to be biased toward an approach based on individual creativity, on which much of the image of Italian design is founded.

HISTORIES OF INDUSTRIAL DESIGN

The alternative, necessarily outlined here only briefly, also constitutes one of the theoretical foundations of the discipline of industrial design, as a body of knowledge and as a working practice. As Victor Margolin reminds us, "designers, unlike architects, have not operated by following a series of principles and rules that specify the purpose of their work. Rather, they have invented the contents of their profession as they went along."[18] The relationship with architectural design (and even with technical design) is not just an abstract question, but also a powerful constraint on historiography. Perhaps precisely because of this relationship, industrial design was long relegated to the role of a younger brother, at least up until the time that it was recognized that the design of products for industry had broken architecture's monopoly of the field. Faced with such a wide range of products to be designed, the statute of the elder discipline proved inadequate: as Manlio Brusatin has shown, the architectural "vision" was too rigid for the design of objects and technical drawing incompatible with the cage of perspective.[19]

Nonetheless, the debate over industrial design has been very slow to separate itself from that of architecture.[20]

Anyone who has been involved with the historiography of industrial design will agree that the activity can be traced back to at least two cultural sources. On one side stands Nikolaus Pevsner,[21] with his pioneers of modern design and his accentuation of creative and individual aspects, but little interest in machinery and anonymous objects. On the other, Siegfried Giedion, with his investigation of the effects of the mechanization of objects in everyday use and emphasis on anonymous design.[22] Or, as Baudrillard has described it, his epic of the technical object.[23] These are two extreme and even antithetical viewpoints, between which there lies a wide variety of different lines of study, ranging from those relating to the history of the decorative and applied arts to those that make the practice of design the center of their interest. It is easy to see that the position of the products undergoes significant shifts in relation to the approach adopted, which also determines where the focus of the analysis is placed: on the products themselves, on the organization of production, or on the ideology and culture of industrial design.[24]

From the viewpoint of historical reconstruction, placing chronological limits on the analysis of a product is a decisive factor, which can even affect the analytical approach to the problem: we know that the division into periods is, in general, a decisive element since it implies taking a stand on the origin, contents, and ideology of the phenomenon under investigation. So it is that those who, following in the footsteps of Pevsner, have seen the Modem Movement as the key to the history of design, have ended up placing more emphasis on the designers than the products, on the ideas than the modes of production. It is clear that the question of origins conditions not just historical and narrative aspects, but also more strictly theoretical ones.

Similarly, the position assigned to products in historical reconstruction has an influence on the perspective taken by the research. Those who have stressed the anonymous object and the idea of utility are, in fact, led to extend the scope of the inquiry much further back in time than the industrial revolution: "Some studies (such as Herbert Read's old and classic work *Art and Industry* and Lindinger's extensive essay on *Designgeschichte*) err in their identification of the presumed historical origins of industrial design, tracing it back to the utensil, the pot, the beaker of antiquity, for the sole reason that these objects had a utilitarian purpose as well as an aesthetic one."[25] This line of analysis, which takes the functionality of artifacts as its key to interpretation, has played an important part in the history of industrial design. Hervin Schaefer has suggested that, in the nineteenth century, the functional form characterized both scientific and technical artifacts (means of transportation, sports equipment, musical instruments, machine tools, etc.) and anonymous, popular objects, especially for household use. Along the same lines, Schaefer himself and Clive Dilnot have pointed to the contributions made by Walter Dexel (*Deutsches Handwerksgut, eine Kultur-und-Formgeschichte des Hausgeräts*, 1939), by J. Kouwenhoven in the United States (*Made in America*, 1945, which investigates the contribution made by popular creativity in contrast to the cultured tradition) and by Herbert Lindinger (with a series of articles published in *Form* in 1963–64). For these authors, functionality is the point of equilibrium between technology and popular creativity.

Of course, as Gillo Dorfles had already pointed out, the risk of an approach based strongly on evolution is that it will find its legitimacy more in the history of technology than in that of industrial design: it is looking at the original archetypes, from which all the objects of our everyday life stem. "In their *Storia illustrata delle invenzioni*, Umberto Eco and Giovan Battista Zorzoli assert that 'all the instruments that we use are based on objects made at the dawn of prehistory.' And in his *Evolution of Technology*, George Basalla claims that 'any new object that appears in the world of artifacts is based on some object that already existed.' Such statements seem particularly true in the case of implements for eating."[26] Today, it is not uncommon to find analyses of products that rely on this type of genetic or evolutionary interpretation.[27]

Taking this line, Henry Petroski has recently studied the evolution of some of the simplest and most common artifacts that we use today: small utilitarian objects such as pencils and paperclips are made the core of an important reflection aimed at bringing the creative process of invention and design out of the realms of the unknowable.[28] In the *Evolution of Useful Things*, for instance, the birth and development of the can opener are examined in relationship not only to the emergence of new methods of preserving food, but also to the objects from which the can opener is directly descended (in part the bayonet, in part the sickle), to the production of metal alloys and to the evolution of containers: in other words, the technical and social circumstances of its design, production, and use.

This is, as far as I know, one of the few examples of exhaustive application of the methodology first introduced by Siegfried Giedion: the study of the birth and development of particular types of objects in common use, often the fruit of anonymous contributions,[29] as the culmination of a multitude of factors. This approach, if used solely to seek out the original genetic aspects, may seem of little use to a history of industrial products. Yet it can, in fact, be highly effective insofar as it places products at the center of a web of relationships of various kinds, in which those of production are far from secondary.

Naturally, other interpretations exist, such as the ones that look at the world of products from the morphological point of view.

This approach probably is very fruitful on the plane of the theory of design, and yet it seems to me to be less so where history is concerned. Assigning a leading role to the theme of form may lead to a classification of objects on the basis of a predetermined stylistic feature. In this way, the objects of a certain period will have characteristics consonant with the stylistic traits of the time, with a resultant emphasis on those that adhere most closely to them. This explains the critical appeal, for instance, of art deco furniture or jewelry, which have little or nothing to do with industrial production but which are genuine *objets d'art*. They are treated as elements representative of a "canon," the set of features that characterize a style. Siegfried Giedion tackled the problem as follows:

> The history of style deals with a theme by dividing it into horizontal sections, while typology divides it vertically. Both are necessary in order to see things in historical space ... The extent to which it is necessary to trace back the history of a type has to be decided case by case. There are no rules. It is the material that makes the decision, not the historian ... He reserves the right to make a scrupulous study of individual aspects and concepts and to let others go by unobserved. This leads to a similar lack of proportions to those found in contemporary painting, where a hand can fill the entire canvas, while the body remains fragmented and sketchy. This disproportion is equally indispensable if we are going to give the right value to the signification of the historical exposition as a whole.[30]

The idea of focusing the attention on a particular technology or product could have interesting consequences from the historical perspective, as has now been recognized where studies of material culture are concerned.[31] From this specific viewpoint, the product-artifact makes it possible to reclassify the entire system on the basis of the interrelationships between the technological and the social plane. To put it another way, as technology permeates the whole of human activity (and vice versa) through artifacts, concentrating the analysis on the artifact makes it possible to take in most aspects of the entire system: design, manufacture, distribution and use; use, perception, social organization and interaction with the artifact and its functions. This, in my view, is a conception very close to the idea of the artifact as an "interface" between the internal environment (the material from which the artifact is made and the methods used to do so) and the external environment (conditions in which the artifact operates) put forward, from another perspective, by Herbert Simon.[32]

Yet here we also find a whole series of conflicts with an approach to industrial design and its history that might be called "pluralistic." It is an approach that places other lines of investigation alongside that of the historical tradition of modern design, in order to take account of the multiplicity of factors that are involved in the "process of creating the form of the product."[33]

In such a theoretical context, it seems to me that the different roles played by the various protagonists in the formation of the industrial product, for example – and above all – the enterprise, can be given their full weight.

TRADITIONS IN RESEARCH AND ARTIFACTS

Nevertheless, to arrive at this type of proposition it has been necessary to draw on different traditions of research from those of industrial design: in the first place, material culture, in which the idea of artifact has been developed. Reference was made at the beginning to the fact that one of the reasons for the slowness of the historiography of industrial design to perceive and study objects in the guise of industrial products stems from the position of artifacts in historical research. A position that, at least up until just a few decades ago, was unquestionably marginal.

As is well known, artifacts have not had a good reputation in the history of our culture, as is perhaps testified by the pejorative meaning that the term has come to assume in several languages over the course of time. Simon has written: "It seems that our language reflects mankind's profound distrust of its products."[34] However, while the category of products immediately conjures up the mental image of a more or less broad range of physical objects, the category "artifact" needs more clarification, even from the linguistic viewpoint. In everyday language, the word *artifact* has a negative sense, not to mention the nuances of meaning attached to the term *artificial*, whose semantic range comprises the sense of contrived or affected.[35]

And so, while the production of artifacts has characterized human history from the outset, it is only in relatively recent times that the notion of artifact has entered the purview – and language – of certain disciplines. In anthropology, it was largely due to Bronislaw Malinowski that the notion of artifact became a systematic part of the fund of human culture. "Culture comprises the artifacts, goods, technical processes, ideas, habits, and values that are transmitted socially." In this way, the simultaneous presence of elements belonging to the "complex of reactions and activities that characterize the behavior of individuals"[36] is sanctioned. So the decisive importance of artifacts in defining the functioning and organization of a society, the patterns of behavior and distribution of roles of its members, and even its problems – in other words, in defining culture – has begun to be acknowledged. Yet, there still is a reluctance to give due weight to the concrete role that artifacts have played in society. Notwithstanding the explicit recognition of the material aspects of human culture, anthropology "has continued, for its part, to attribute a secondary importance to material phenomena in the proper sense"[37] in the conduct of its own researches, preferring to concentrate on the symbolic aspects of the material conditions of the society under investigation.

An approach of this kind may be explained by the attitude of anthropology to the investigation of so-called primitive societies. A different attitude has in a sense been imposed on it today by the fact that, orienting itself "toward the study of the various cultural realities that make up that vast, composite aggregate known as 'Western European culture' ... cultural anthropology has been unable to avoid looking at the world of industrial production which represents, when all is said and done, the supporting framework of our culture."[38]

Even those who, like Mary Douglas, have made the objects of contemporary society the focus of their investigation, place the emphasis on their representative value, as a means of access to the intelligibility of the world, to its coherence and stability.[39] Moreover, as Douglas herself has pointed out, any attempt to speak sensibly of an anthropology of consumption cannot ignore the assumption on which ethnography is based: the fact that all material goods are endowed with social significance, without which it would not be possible to go beyond mere descriptive archeology. The application of this assumption to contemporary society is certainly risky, but "if we do not make the attempt there will never be an anthropology of consumption."[40] As Raymond Eches reminds us, an ethnology of industrialized societies has emerged in the English-speaking countries and France.[41] Although still oriented chiefly toward patterns of social behavior, these studies have, in some cases, given rise to what has been called "ethnotechnology."

The work of the Centre de Recherche sur la Culture Technique (1979) is of particular significance to the history of industrial design, especially through the articles published in *Culture Technique*,[42] where the study of the typology of objects and machines has been developed by investigating "the technical culture of the consumer."[43] Despite its avowed concern with the social implications of technology, this magazine often contains typological investigations of great interest on such subjects as television and other means of communication or the washing machine, on which the author carries out a genuine "autopsy."[44]

In similar fashion, the sociological approach to the great questions raised by the study of mass society is distinguished by the attention paid to the communicative elements of artifacts. In this connection, it is necessary to bring in the theory of objects developed on the basis of research carried out in the sixties and seventies, in particular by Abraham Moles and Jean Baudrillard. Their goal was to analyze the different aspects of the world of objects in order to construct an approach based primarily on the theory of the social function and significance of the objects themselves.[45]

Finally, we should not forget the dual role that artifacts have always played in the artistic field. On the one hand, the history of art has always been founded on the analysis and criticism of special artifacts: not just paintings and sculptures, but also objects of the so-called minor arts. On the other hand, artifacts as objects have been ignored by representation for centuries, until 1900, except in marginal episodes or as fragments where what counted was the sacred or symbolic intention: objects that iconological research has taught us to interpret more as artifact-symbols than as artifact-utensils. The artistic boycott of objects, and especially machines, has been analyzed on several occasions in the context of the general attitude of contempt for technical matters shown by ancient and medieval Western culture.[46] "The basic outlook has not changed at all. We still find in both historical and theoretical work that disdain for the "mechanical arts" that (as Diderot wrote more than two centuries ago) "has filled the towns with presumptuous thinkers and the countryside with ignorant little tyrants."[47]

Moreover, in the past, artifacts have been interpreted in different ways even within the various disciplinary fields that are more or less directly concerned with the subject of industrial design: in particular, the history and theory of technology, the history and theory of architecture, and the history and theory of industrial design.

There certainly is no need to dwell on the importance that the history of technique and technology has assumed, even though only fairly recently. Technology as a means of production and its relationship with economic and industrial development has been examined by some eminent figures, and still is a subject of analysis by economists, historians, and historians of technology.

This can be explained by the fact that much of the history of technology has been built around the stages marked by the epoch-making inventions and discoveries of the last two centuries and their often devastating effects on economic and social life. This also is the reason behind the emergence and reinforcement of the positive image that our culture often still bestows on technology.[48] The difficulty which the very idea of technique and technology has had in gaining acceptance in Western culture has already been pointed out. It must be added, however, that, once established, it has quickly found some authoritative proponents. As has happened with many other types of history – history *tout court*, as well as the history of architecture, industrial design, etc. – the emphasis has been placed on "the pioneers of modern technology," both in the shape of the inventors, innovators, and entrepreneurs and in that of the archetypal machines: the mechanical loom, the steam engine, and the locomotive, which often has been accompanied by a genuine (and positive) *rhetoric* of technology.

Both faith in technological progress and apocalyptic Luddism normally refer to the technological system as a whole, in other words to an all-embracing concept that takes in all the factors that help to characterize our society as a technological society. The image of technology, on the other hand, does not appear so dramatic when the attention is shifted from large-scale systems to the technology of everyday life, to its real expression in the form of machines, instruments, products, appliances, and objects. "Technology, in fact, does not represent a problem for the forms of the civilization in which it is developed: it only takes on a contradictory dimension in the forms of culture."[49] So if the image of technology at closer quarters appears more blurred, the reason may lie in the fact that "the majority of classical sociologists make no careful *description* of techniques –

except in the field of study concerned with the impact of technology on society – and too many economists treat them like a black box."[50] Here, we are speaking of sociologists and economists but, paradoxically, some historians of technology could be added to their number. Indeed, they sometimes end up treating artifacts as little more than schematic abstractions of functional parts, or as complete individuals, *natural* products of the development of technology and manufacturing. A possible and plausible explanation for this may be found in the fact that the history of technology emerged within codified and accessible disciplines taught at schools of engineering.[51] It could even be said, as Mark Brutton has suggested, that mechanical engineering has become a great manufacturer of stereotypes.[52]

Starting from these premises, let us look at the position of artifacts in common use in some areas of the history, and the theory of technique and technology. Jean-Jacques Salomon has stated that the best treatments of the theory of technology come not from technologists, but from students of technology, historians, and ethnologists: the encyclopedists Beekman, Marx, d'Espinas, Reuleaux, Mumford and Gill, Usher and Bloch, Mauss and Leroi-Gourhan. This view can be shared but must be clarified by pointing out that each of these authors – and they are not the only ones – has introduced a hierarchy of artifacts stemming directly from the historical or theoretical model of interpretation adopted. "There are already (at least) two overlapping histories of technology …: the history of systems in which the relations between objects (and their invention) find their meaning; the history of objects that become complexes, that 'develop' into systems on the basis of a biological need and which is, in the end, guaranteed by the contribution of science."[53]

Yet, if the interest in the problems raised by technology from the theoretical viewpoint can be traced a fairly long way back in time, its treatment from the perspective of historical evolution was only given a systematic disciplinary endorsement around the middle of this century, with the foundation of the Society for the History of Technology (1958). Over the following years, the society's review published articles on the history of the family, office work, and household articles that are of great relevance to the history of industrial design.[54] One of the themes that stands out is that of the impact of technology on domestic life. Perhaps the most important study of this subject is the one Ruth Schwartz Cowan published in the magazine in 1976 ("The 'Industrial Revolution' in the Home"). This was followed by other weighty investigations of the "industrialization of domestic work,"[55] as well, more recently, as an analysis of products that in some ways comes close to the idea of a typological reconstruction of the history of artifacts and that falls within the recent tradition of studies of the social construction of technology.[56]

Among the disciplines that have made the greatest contribution to undermining the preeminence of written and visual documentation, a primary role undoubtedly must be given to industrial archeology: "manufactured articles of the ordinary kind, from toys to textile mills, which do not need to be 'stripped' of their symbolic attributes, may constitute the most authentic of all historical sources. In addition they, rather than written documents, bear witness to the life of the young, the old, women and the poor, in other words of those members of society who represent the mass of workers."[57]

Yet it would be naive to think, as some have done, that industrial relics are "a unique series not bound by historical conditioning, through which it is possible to analyze and verify numerous phenomena of the past."[58] And, therefore, in themselves, a privileged field of historical research, an area free of the ambiguities and uncertainties that all documents present to the observer. While hypothesizing that the product-document is "not bound by historical conditioning," in this case it is the interpreter who is even more strongly bound by various kinds of conditioning. These stem not just, as is obvious, from his or her prejudices and values.

They also derive from the multiplicity of meanings that accumulate around objects and from the different nature – not only of language but also of content – of the information that can be obtained from the object. It has been known for some time that the attitude interpreters adopt toward an artifact (as well as an image) is very different from the one they adopt toward a written document. Archaeologists and anthropologists are well aware of this. But even more so are students of architecture who, while usually dealing with concrete structures that are relatively stable in time, also are continually having to tackle aspects of the representation (sketches, plans, and drawings) and description (reports and photographs) of those structures in order to fully grasp their significance and value. Those who are most aware of this problem are the people who organize collections and museums.

It is precisely with regard to this question of historical research in relation to museums that the case of the Cooper-Hewitt Museum, a historic "bastion of the decorative arts"(set up in 1897)[59] and repository of collections of objects of decorative art dating from the sixteenth to nineteenth centuries, is particularly significant of the change in attitude toward the composite nature of the phenomenon of industrial design. In 1991, under its new direction, the museum organized the exhibition *The Cooper-Hewitt Collection: A Design Resource*, drawing on the 250,000 objects in its collection and commencing a transformation that would lead it to its becoming the National Museum of Design. Under the guidance of Dianne H. Pilgrim, who rejected the old museological structure of a museum of art, the museum launched a series of initiatives that have served to draw attention to the idea of design in its pluralistic sense.[60]

Returning to the problem of artifacts and their role in historical research, it seems possible to identify two main approaches. The first is that of the history of *artifacts* in which, on the model of the history of art, technology, and architecture, products are seen as the *subject* of historical research, and as elements to be studied, analyzed, and observed. A second approach is that of history *through artifacts* in which, following the example set by ethnology, anthropology, and archeology, products become *documents* of historical research, intermediaries for something else. It is my hypothesis that the history of industrial design represents an opportunity for an integration of these two approaches, an integration in which artifacts would be treated as both *subjects* and as *documents* of research.

This way of looking at things becomes even more meaningful if one considers that the history of a product often is reconstructed with a view to redesigning it. This is a question that chiefly concerns the teaching of industrial design, but it certainly touches on a delicate point in the planning and design of products within the companies themselves.

In this connection, I would like to mention a number of questions that might be raised, in a mutual exchange between the history of enterprise and the history of industrial design, by an analysis of such a commonly used product as the sewing machine. A very important product for the history of industrial design and for that of domestic sociology, it is, perhaps, the household article that has attracted the most thorough investigation from the historical viewpoint.[61] The reason for this interest is fairly obvious, if one considers the fact that the production of sewing machines was one of the first industrial sectors in which the American system of manufacturing was applied, and that the sewing machine was the first industrially produced "machine" to enter the home on a massive scale.[62] From the viewpoint of most interest to us here, the sewing machine provides an excellent illustration of a central point of our discussion: the attainment of a particular appearance on the part of an artifact and its stabilization.

This is, in more general terms, the theme of the typology of objects being fixed by industrial production and their crystallization in this form. But we know that the artifact which gains the upper hand is not the only possible solution, nor even, perhaps, the best one: it depends entirely on the contingent circumstances, including the interpretation of other artifacts. Indeed, for some authors, the artifact derives from the reinterpretation of similar artifacts in the light of particular problems and conditions.[63] In fact, the sewing machine appears to lend itself very well to this type of interpretation: the "prehistoric" analysis of a type is capable of setting it within the real processes of production that determined the definitive choice.[64]

After a period of disorganized research and a wide variety of proposals documented in an exorbitant number of patents, the sewing machine found a precise form that, once stability had been achieved on the market, would undergo no further substantial modifications. By the time Barthélemy Thimmonier patented his sewing machine on April 13, 1830, attempts to achieve the goal of mechanical sewing had been under way for many years. Tackled by British and German inventors ever since the middle of the eighteenth century, no satisfactory solution to the problem had been achieved due to an error of approach that was as banal as it has been common in the history of technological inventions. Thimmonier's predecessors had not been able to divorce the idea of mechanical sewing from that of sewing by hand, whose methods and techniques they strove to reproduce.

Thimmonier, the son of a tailor, had managed to overcome this impasse by resorting to another analogy, basing his insight on analysis of the chain stitch produced in crochet work, which made it possible, among other things, to use a continuous thread. Around the same time, a series of partial inventions and even brilliant attempts followed one another in both America and Europe, though without overcoming the stumbling blocks of continuous operation and industrial applicability on a large scale.

It is customary to identify the period between 1830 and 1845 as the one in which a series of results were achieved in the field of mechanical sewing, each of which made a contribution to the solution of a particular problem (continuity of stitching, transmission of movement and so on). Each of these results entailed a structural modification, and sometimes a major one. For this reason, there initially was a great deal of uncertainty over the appearance of the sewing machine. It suffices to look at the configuration of the model patented by Wheeler and Wilson in 1850, in which the position of the stitching mechanism is perpendicular to the operator. Even after the first Singer model appeared, inventors continued to patent machines with completely different characteristics to the prototype of 1851, which was the model adopted by industry and which already had all of the working parts, structure, and formal features of the modern sewing machine. The arm was horizontal, in a frontal position with respect to the operator, and parallel to the work surface; the needle was located on the left-hand side and in a vertical position; and on the opposite side was set the mechanism of cogs that transmitted the movement. This model was to remain more or less unchanged in spite of the continual improvements that progressively refined its performance and reduced the various drawbacks, such as breaking of the thread or the rigidity of the needle.

The appearance of sewing machines did not even change with the introduction of electricity. This brought a considerable improvement in the quality of the work, and the practicality and maneuverability of the machine. Ever since its birth, the sewing machine had had to cope with the problem of the transmission of movement to the needle. As early as 1852, Singer had introduced the pedal and belt drive which, with respect to the previous handwheel, offered the enormous advantage of leaving both of the operator's hands free. A second factor was the tension of the thread, and the precision and regularity of the stitches. As can easily be imagined, the introduction of electricity brought considerable advantages to both of these key elements of the mechanism. The first electric sewing machine was the 15K model brought out by Singer in 1889. The electric-powered motor was housed in the handwheel at the side, and was simply added to the existing body without altering its overall appearance. The handwheel was fairly large and had the air of a purely technological object, applied to a device that still retained, in the elegant softness of its lines and the gilded decorative patterns, the dignified tone typical of all early nineteenth-century exemplars. It made up for the impossibility of concealing all of the machine's mechanisms.

Notwithstanding the application of electricity, the older machine made of black cast-iron resisted any change up until the 1940s, when the introduction of materials such as light alloys and plastics and of new functions,[65] and the updating of the systems of production permitted another leap forward in quality. The motor and the illumination of the work surface were inserted into the body of the machine, which made it bulkier and reduced the room for maneuver. At the same time, the first portable machines began to appear, with a casing that opened up to form a work surface.[66] These years also saw the first interventions by the industrial designers who were to give the sewing machine its modern look.[67]

In the mid-seventies, Singer brought out their *Futura 1000* model, an electronically programmed sewing machine. This technological innovation supplemented the device's already high level of performance with some new and extremely sophisticated functions (programming of complicated stitches, embroidery, and the ability to move the needle in many directions and to different degrees, etc.). Yet the potential of electronics has not been fully realized, not even with the biggest innovation of all: complete automation of all of the operations; this may signify that a technological object which has struggled to find its formal and functional equilibrium will, once this has been achieved, put up greater resistance to change, even in the face of major technological innovations. More reasonably however, the factor that seems to have determined this stasis is the reluctance of the industrial system to modify a device that has attained a high degree of stability and popularity.

When we speak of the origins of the numerous artifacts that have acquired the appearance of useful objects over the course of time, we inevitably come up against a series of far-reaching themes that have attracted the attention of historians of technology and all those interested in the nineteenth-century adventure of industrialization and mass production. These include the discussion of inventions and patents, the role of technological innovations, the relationship of science to technology and the economy, and so on. Against this complex background, it is possible to cut out a limited series of figures, perceived to have simpler silhouettes than the others and, above all, to be better suited to throwing light on the question of the relationship between the history of industrial design, technological and economic history, and the history of enterprise.

The first of these figures could be defined as the theme of the *change of scale* which is, moreover, a highly topical one in view of the so-called miniaturization of objects brought about by electronic technology. Placed historically at the origins, this figure concerns the passage of a series of artifacts and devices from the realm of community services to that of the home.

The hypothesis – which can be advanced generically, but would certainly require a more targeted analysis of the historio-graphical type – is that the production of equipment for the home derives directly from the production of equipment for the community. That is to say, that a change of scale takes place that allows mass production of technologies and innovations that have already been tried out in the larger dimensions of the community. While this passage has not yet been empirically investigated by studies of individual companies, it is fairly evident, at least in the pioneering phase of inventions and patents. An example is provided by the cooking equipment developed for large welfare institutions during the eighteenth century, which was the organizational and typological forerunner of all subsequent kitchens. Or, again, by the history of refrigeration, which was first developed for the transportation of perishable foodstuffs and only later, and very slowly, applied in the domestic environment. Another example is one of the prototypes of the air conditioner developed by an American doctor who, in 1844, invented a device for cooling the air in the rooms in the hospital where he worked.[68] Or, finally, the mechanization of laundries specializing in washing for institutions, firms, and restaurants, which anticipated that of washing in the home by quite a few years.[69]

The priority of research aimed at resolving problems at the community level is comprehensible not just on the level of technology and production. It also derives its social logic from the fact that the problem of housing (in all its implications) and of the mass consumption of household appliances did not emerge until a later date.[70] Finally, the passage from the large to the small scale is still occurring today. Some authors do not exclude the possibility that automation, already highly advanced in various sectors of industrial production as well as in those of technological and scientific research, will have direct repercussions on household appliances. In other words, that devices derived from research and experimentation into large-scale industrial machinery may eventually come onto the market for household appliances: from the robots of the automated factory to domestic robots.[71]

A second figure that is central to an understanding of origins is that of the role played by the reconversion of industry, for example the transformation of wartime production into that of civil engineering, in the development of some household appliances. It is a role that historians have always admitted in general terms, but rarely demonstrated by detailed studies.[72] At the root of this phenomenon lies not just the availability of inventions or innovations, but the tendency toward mass production and the commercialization of products on an ever more open market.[73] It is through these elements that the possibilities of the American System of Manufactures were able to unfold, with its model of production based on interchangeable parts and the standardization of the manufacturing process. This is what happened with sewing machines, a sector in which the rivalry between Ford and General Motors was played out again as far as strategies of production were concerned, though with different results. "Singer and McCormick – the first relying on the quality of the product, the second on the frequent introduction of new models – also commenced the mass production of standard goods under the impetus of demand."[74]

Starting out from these presuppositions, people are beginning to carry out research into the history of industrial design that attempts to provide answers to the questions raised in this text.[75]

The road ahead is still a rocky one.

NOTES

First published in *Design Issues* 14 no. 3 (Autumn 1998): 43–64.

1. See V. Castronovo, "Storia dell'industria e storia del design," in *Design: storia e storiografia* (Bologna: Progetto Leonardo, 1995), 113–20, and cit. on 117.
2. Just a few titles of general reference. For Wedgwood, the reader is referred to the bibliography given in J. Fleming and H. Honour, *The Penguin Dictionary of Decorative Arts* (Harmondsworth: Penguin Books, 1977). For Thonet, see the catalogs of the exhibitions, *Form From the Process. The Thonet Chair* (Cambridge, MA: Harvard University Press, 1967), and *Bentwood Furniture. The Work of Michael Thonet* (London: Bethnal Green Museum, 1968). In addition, see G. Massobrio and P. Portoghesi, *Casa Thonet. Storia dei mobili in legno curvato* (Roma-Bari: Laterza, 1980). For AEG, see the impressive reconstruction of the relationship between the designer and the company on the basis of materials from the historical archives edited by T. Buddensieg, *Industriekultur. Peter Behrens und die Aeg. 1907–1914* (Berlin: Gebr. Mann Verlag, 1979).
3. I. Bignamini, "Gran Bretagna: primi passi verso il disegno industriale," *Storia del disegno industriale, 1: 1750–1850. L'età della rivoluzione industriale* (Milan: Electa, 1989), 130–47.
4. This shift, described here in an extremely simplified and generalized form, is crucial to the culture of design as well. On this point see, for example, the contributions made by M. Bellini, "Il designer e

l'industria" and T. Maldonado, untitled, in Camera del lavoro territoriale di Milano – CGIL, *Per chi lavora il designer. Il progetto, il prodotto, l'immagine e il mercato*, proceedings of the congress, Milan, January 20–21, 1983 (Rome: Ediesse, 1983): 21–6 and 138–41, respectively.

5. For a recent critique of the notion of design as "cosmetics" of the product, see G. Bonsiepe, *Dall'oggetto all'interfaccia. Mutazioni del design* (Milan: Feltrinelli, 1995), in particular the chapter "Le sette colonne del design," 17–27.
6. The idea that "corporate image" is created not just by a company's system of communication but by its products as well is a fairly recent one. "It is a question of inducing in the public a comprehensive set of favorable attitudes; a general appreciation not just of the individual product, but also of the line of products, the brand and the company itself. The theory of the 'brand image,' which has its roots in motivational psychology, would be developed by David Ogilvy: to the functional characteristics of the products have to be added emotional values, which will constitute the unitary personality of the brand," G. Anceschi, "Grafica, visual design, comunicazioni visive," in *Storia del disegno industriale, III: 1919–1990. Il dominio del design* (Milan: Electa, 1991), 74.
7. J. Walker, *Design History and the History of Design* (London: Pluto Press, 1989), 55–6.
8. Ibid., especially the chapter "Entrepreneurial and Company Histories," 55–8, on the limitations of company histories from the viewpoint of research into industrial design.
9. Among these, it is worth mentioning *Elektrogeräte für den Haushalt. Ihre Entwicklung im Hause Siemens* (Berlin-Munich: Siemens Elektrogeräte GmbH, 1966) and H. Warscho, *Chronik der Entwicklung elektrischer Hausgeräte. Siemens Haushalttechnik. Eine Dokumentation der Siemens-Elektrogeräte GmbH* (Munich: 1976). For the extensive documentation, including visual records, in the Historical Archives of the Siemens Museum in Munich, see W. Feldenkirchen. "L'Archivio storico Siemens," in *Archivi e Imprese* 7 (1993): 3–19.
10. In reality sales catalogs (and, more generally, mass and small-scale distribution and mail-order sales, as represented by Sears, Roebuck; Harrods; Marks & Spencer; and La Rinascente) are a fundamental resource and one that has still been very little explored by the historiography of design, except as an inexhaustible source of visual material. The Siemens 1938 catalog (Siemens Elektrische Hausgeräte, *Priesliste HK1 1938*, Siemens-Schuckertwerke Ag. October 1938) illustrates very well, from the technological detail to the domestic setting, the range of electric products available at that date. These are far more numerous than Werner von Siemens could have imagined in 1873, when he hoped to be able to distribute "the current, produced by imposing electric dynamos, to every house, just as gas and water are at present, to provide light and heat and to power other motor-driven appliances," *Elektrizität im Dienste der Industrie*, Berlin, January 12, 1873, Siemens-Archiv, quoted in *Elektrogeräte* ..., cit. 9. They included irons, kettles, lamps, radios, wall and table clocks, portable and ceiling-mounted fans, radiators, boilers, refrigerators, ovens, cooking ranges, and vacuum cleaners with the whole range of accessories, accurately illustrated with photographs and described largely in terms of the technology involved.
11. Typological history is one of the most controversial and interesting of methods, which was first applied to the history of architecture and then to that of design as well, in particular by Siegfried Giedion in his *Mechanization Takes Command: A Contribution to Anonymous Design* (New York: Oxford University Press, 1948). See Walker, 110–18.
12. H. Warscho, *Chronik der Entwicklung elektrischer Hausgeräte*, 40.
13. This does not mean that the concern was absent. See C. Kuehnel, *Chronik der Abteilung Elektromotorische*, 1954. Typescript, Siemens-Archiv, Munich, in which lengthy consideration is given to color as one of the means of encouraging the diffusion of electric appliances. It was, along with that of advertising and the name to be given to individual products, a central theme in the preoccupation of company executives.
14. M. Bellini, "Il designer e l'industria," in *Per chi lavora il designer...*, 25–26. Another example of a company built around research and design is that of B&B Italia. It is distinguished above all by the existence of a research center and the contribution of numerous designers. See P. Vidari, "Tra design e industria," in *Un'industria per il design. La ricerca, i designers, l'immagine B&B Italia* (Milan: Edizioni Lybra Immagine, n.d.), 35–41.
15. The relationship between container and mechanism once again has become highly topical due to the influence of microelectronics on the shape and size of products. For a historical view, see T. Maldonado, *Disegno industriale: un riesame* (Milan: Feltrinelli, 1991), 25–6 and 33, et seq.
16. For this debate, viewed in terms of a confrontation between the two souls of German culture during a

period in which the need for standardization and rationalization of products was emerging, see the collection of writings *Tecnica e cultura. Il dibattito tedesco fra Bismarck e Weimar* (Milan: Feltrinelli, 1979), edited by T. Maldonado, and in particular his introduction, 9–21.

17. T. Maldonado, *Disegno industriale...*, 81–6.
18. V. Margolin, "Design History or Design Studies: Subject Matter and Methods," *Design Issues* 11 no. 1 (Spring 1995): 4–15, cit. on 12.
19. M. Brusatin, "Disegno/progetto," in *Enciclopedia* (Turin: Einaudi, 1978).
20. V. Pasca, "Una terza via per il design," in Op. cit., 63 (May 1985): 15–23, id., "Design: storia e storiografia," *Design: storia e storiografia*, 17–50. In addition, Clive Dilnot, "The State of Design History. Part I: Mapping the Field," *Design Issues* 1 no. 1 (Spring 1984): 10.
21. N. Pevsner, *Pioneers of the Modern Movement. From William Morris to Walter Gropius* (London: Faber and Faber, 1936).
22. S. Giedion, *Mechanization Takes Command*. See H. Schaefer, *The Roots of Modern Design. Functional Tradition in the 19th Century* (London: Studio Vista, 1970), page 1 of the "Introduction." See also Clive Dilnot, *The State of Design History. Part I*, 4–23.
23. J. Baudrillard, *Le système des objets* (Paris: Denoël-Gontier, 1972), 6.
24. This lack of uniformity is clearly demonstrated by several Italian studies of the history of industrial design published in the eighties, and which still constitute the most substantial and significant discussion of this subject in that country: V. Gregotti, *Il disegno del prodotto industriale. Italia 1860–1980* (Milan: Electa, 1982), reprinted by the same publisher in a cut-price edition in 1986; E. Frateili, *Il disegno industriale italiano 1928–1981. (Quasi una storia ideologica)* (Turin: Celid, 1983), an expanded edition of which was brought out in 1990; R. De Fusco, *Storia del design* (Barín: Laterza, 1985).
25. G. Dorfles, *Introduzione al disegno industriale. Linguaggio e storia della produzione di serie* (Turin: Einaudi, 1972), 13.
26. Henry Petroski, *The Evolution of Useful Things* (New York: Alfred Knopf, 1993), 3–4.
27. For the evolutionary approach to the analysis of industrial products, see S. Pizzocaro's doctoral thesis *Approccio evolutivo all'analisi dei prodotti industriali* (Milan: Milan Politecnico, 1993). See also, M. Migliari, "Microscopi: da utensili a strumenti," *Area* 15 (September 1993): 82–93; "Radersi con la zappa: evoluzione del rasoio," *StileIndustria* 1 (1995); and M. Migliari and M. Millozza, "Macchine per il calcolo," *Area* 18 (June 1994): 66–77.
28. H. Petroski, *The Pencil. A History of Design and Circumstance* (New York: Alfred Knopf, 1992) and, by the same author, *The Evolution of Useful Things*.
29. See, for instance, various authors in *Sconosciuti e familiari. Oggetti di design "anonimo" prodotti in Svizzera dal 1920* (Milan: Hoepli, 1993).
30. S. Giedion, *Mechanization Takes Command*, 19–20.
31. See the essay by W.D. Kingery, "Technological Systems and Some Implications With Regard to Continuity and Change," in S. Lubar and W. David Kingery, eds., *History from Things* (Washington and London: Smithsonian Institution Press, 1993), 215–30.
32. H.A. Simon, *The Sciences of the Artificial* (Cambridge, MA: MIT Press, 1981), 29.
33. T. Maldonado, *Disegno industriale: un riesame*, 12.
34. H.A. Simon, *The Sciences of the Artificial*, 24.
35. See G. Anceschi, *Monogrammi e figure. Teoria e storie della progettazione di artefatti comunicativi* (Florence and Milan: La Casa Usher, 1981), 13. See also J.D. Prown, "The Truth of Material Culture: History or Fiction?," in S. Lubar and W.D. Kingery, eds., *History from Things*, 2.
36. P. Rossi, introduction to *Il concetto di cultura*, XII.
37. R. Bucaille and J.M. Pesez, "Cultura materiale," in *Enciclopedia* (Turin: Einaudi, 1978), 277.
38. T. Maldonado, *Il futuro della modernità* (Milan: Feltrinelli, 1987), 111. See also the entry by R. Eches, "L'anthropologie cognitive hier et demain. Vers une anthropologie industrielle?," in *Encyclopedie de la Pléiade, Histoire des Moeurs*, vol. II, *Modes et Modèles* (Paris: Gallimard, 1991), 1403–18.
39. See in particular the research that Douglas has carried out with B. Isherwood into *The World of Things: Objects, Values, Consumption* (New York, Basic Books, 1979).
40. Ibid., 63.
41. R. Eches, "L'anthropologie cognitive. Hier et demain. Vers une anthropologie industrielle?," in *Encyclopedie de la Pléiade, Histoire des Moeurs. Il Modes et modéles* (Paris: Gallimard, 1991), 1403–18.
42. See the monographic issues of *Machines au foyer* 3 (1980), *Design* 5 (1981), and the recent *Communications, Techniques et usages* 24 (1992).
43. J. de Noblet, editorial in the monographic issue *Machines au foyer* 5.
44. Y. Stourdéz, "Autopsie d'une machine à laver," *Culture Technique* 3 (1980): 29–42.

45. See the issue of *Communications* 13 (1969) devoted to *Les objets*, in particular the articles by Moles and Baudrillard. The latter had already put forward his arguments in *Le système des objets*. The tradition of interpretation of the representative value of artifacts and its relationship with the dynamics of consumption has of course many antecedents, among which one of the best known is that of Thorstein Veblen, *The Theory of the Leisure Class* (New York: New American Library, 1963, c. 1899).
46. See among others M. Le Bot, *Peinture et machinisme* (Paris: Klincksieck, 1973).
47. P. Rossi, introduction to the monographic issue of *Intersezioni* devoted to *La tecnica di fine millennio* XIII:2 (August 1993): 217.
48. M. Nacci, "Strumenti di servitù. Immagini della tecnica nella discussione contemporanea," 353–85.
49. F. Dal Co, *Abitare nel moderno* (Rome and Bari: Laterza 1982), 19.
50. B. Latour, "Dove sono le masse mancanti? Sociologia di alcuni oggetti quotidiani di uso comune," *Intersezioni* 223, note 2 (my italics).
51. W. D. Kingery, "Technological Systems and Some Implications With Regard to Continuity and Change," in S. Lubar and W. D. Kingery, eds., *History from Things*, 215–30.
52. M. Brutton, "Après le modernisme," *Culture Technique* 5 (April 1981): 63–71.
53. J.-C. Beaune, *La technologie introuvable* (Paris: Vrin, 1980), 23–4.
54. For an examination of the space given by *Technology and Culture* to the relationship between women and technology, and to female studies in general, see J. Rothschild's introduction "Why Machina ex Dea?" in *Feminist Perspectives on Technology* (New York: Pergamon Press, 1983), IX–XXIX. For a detailed analysis of the reviews of contributions to the history of technology, see J. Staudenmaier, *Technology's Storytellers* (Cambridge. MA: MIT Press, 1985).
55. R. Schwartz Cowan, *More Work for Mother. The Ironies of Household Technology From the Open Hearth to the Microwave* (New York: Basic Books, 1983).
56. See R. Schwartz Cowan, "The Consumption Junction: A Proposal for Research Strategies in the Sociology of Technology," in W.E. Bijker, T.P. Hughes and T.J. Pinch, *The Social Construction of Technological Systems* (Cambridge, MA: MIT Press, 1989), 261–280.
57. D. Newell, "Archeologia industriale e scienze umane," in A. Castellano, ed., *La macchina arrugginita. Materiali per un'archeologia dell'industria* (Milan: Feltrinelli, 1982), 18.
58. Ibid., 19.
59. S. Seller. "Mechanical Brides: The Exhibition." *Design Issues* 10 no. 2 (Summer 1994): 69–79.
60. For examples of the museum's activities, see E. Lupton and J. Abbott Miller, *The Bathroom, the Kitchen and the Aesthetics of Waste* (Cambridge, MA: MIT List Visual Center, 1992) and E. Lupton, *Mechanical Brides. Women and Machines from Home to Office* (New York: Princeton Architectural Press, 1993).
61. The historical and documentary data on this appliance are the fruit of intersecting lines of research deriving from different sources. See the chapter, "The Sewing Machine and the American System of Manufactures" in David A. Hounshell's volume *From the American System to Mass Production 1800–1930* (Baltimore and London: Johns Hopkins University Press, 1984). See also S. Piantanida ed., *La macchina per cucire* (Milan: Museo Nazionale della Scienza e della Tecnica, 1962), catalog of the exhibition of the same name; G. Cooper, *The Invention of the Sewing Machine* (Washington: Smithsonian Institution, 1968); and, with regard to aspects of product analysis related to design, H. Lindinger, "Näahmaschine 1962," *Form* 18 (1962): 32–43.
62. By 1890, less than forty years after the first Singer model had been patented, world production had risen to about two million units.
63. See J.R. Moore. "Science and Technology: Problems of Interpretation." in C. Chant, ed., *Science, Technology and Everyday Life 1870–1950* (London and New York: Routledge-Open University, 1989), 58–67.
64. In particular, D.A. Hounshell in *From the American System to Mass Production* has looked at the origins of the principal American manufacturers of sewing machines, 67–123.
65. In 1947, Necchi introduced a system for making zigzag stitches on a model dating from 1936. See D. Yarwood, *Five Hundred Years of Technology in the Home* (London: Batsford, 1983), 147.
66. In 1940, the "Elna" was introduced as the first portable sewing machine with a work surface powered by an electric motor and having a built-in light. See L. Schilder, "La macchina per cucire 'Elna' " in *Sconosciuti e familiari. Oggetti di design "anonimo" prodotti in Svisera dal 1920*, 56–63.
67. Some important results contributed to the success of Italian sewing machines on foreign markets.

Necchi, for example, turned to Marcello Nizzoli, Borletti to Marco Zanuso, and Salmoiraghi to Angelo Mangiarotti and Bruno Morassutti. Perhaps the most representative model remains Nizzoli's *Mirella* (Compasso d'oro, 1957). See G. Bosoni, "La macchina per cucire," in V. Gregotti, *Il disegno del prodotto industriale*, 306–7.

68. Cited in R. Thevenot, "La tecnologia del freddo compie 150 anni," *Il freddo* 38: 1 (January–February 1984): 18. See also O.E. Anderson, *Refrigeration in America. A History of New Technology and its Impacts* (Princeton: Princeton University Press, 1953), 74–6.
69. On this subject, see the lavish volume by P.E. Malcolmson, *English Laundresses. A Social History* (Urbana and Chicago: University of Chicago Press, 1986).
70. The text cited in the previous note also provides food for thought on the relationship between the development of mechanization in industry and in the home as contrasted in the United States and Great Britain.
71. This means those more or less anthropomorphic devices that might wholly or partly substitute for humans in housework.
72. The direct connection between wartime industry and other metallurgical industries in the United States has been clearly demonstrated by consumer products. See David A. Hounshell's *From the American System to Mass Production*. See also M. Roe Smith, "Social Processes and Technological Change: A View of the History of Technology in America," *Annali di storia dell'impresa* 2 (1986): 549–60.
73. It is a question of understanding how "innovations that originated in the antebellum American firearms industry spread to other technically related industries during the nineteenth century, and, with further elaborations and additions, eventually culminated in Henry Ford's system of mass production in 1913," ibidem 552–3.
74. See R. Giannetti, "Clio e la scatola nera: l'analisi del progresso tecnico tra storia e teoria economica," *Annali di storia dell'impresa* 3 (1987): 40.
74. See F. Ceccon and D. Fontana, *"Checucialei". La macchina per cucire*, research for the course Environment and Product, degree course in industrial design, acad. yr. 1995–96, Milan Politecnico. The authors have compared the technical, operative, and communicative aspects of domestic and industrial sewing machines manufactured by Rimoldi, a company founded in Milan in 1881, which makes special sewing machines for the garment industry. It may be possible to reconstruct the technical, functional and morphological relations between products on different scales.

17

OLYMPUS AND THE MARKETPLACE: REYNER BANHAM AND DESIGN CRITICISM

Nigel Whiteley

After his untimely death in 1988 at the age of 66, reviewers and obituarists assessed, *inter alia*, Peter Reyner Banham's contribution to the rapidly developing discipline of design studies – theory, history, and criticism. The clear consensus[1] was that Banham was a "pioneering figure," if not the "founding father," of design studies as it is now practiced, even if the discipline has undergone developments and changes since the time when Banham's influence was at its peak. Possibly over the last twenty years, and certainly during the last ten, Banham's reputation has entered a period of relatively low visibility. Principally, this paper[2] examines Banham's design criticism, its relationship to his more conventional academic writing, and its values, assumptions, and relevancy to the field today.

HISTORY VERSUS CRITICISM

If we were to take one of Banham's remarks literally, the significance he himself attached to his design criticism appears unambiguous: "… history is, of course, my academic discipline. Criticism is what I do for money."[3] This remark, uttered in a conference address in 1964, might lead us to suppose that Banham saw a distinct separation between his "serious" duties as a historian, and his relatively trivial activities as a critic. The supposition might be reinforced by Banham's "history" being published in hardback books and academic or professional journals, while his "criticism" sped in and out of sight via the transient vehicles of weekly magazines and, occasionally, Sunday newspaper supplements. Furthermore, the history writing was principally about architecture; the criticism usually dealt with design. When he did write about architecture as a critic, the ideas and observations tended to form a part of, and feed into, his "serious" architectural books and articles. Banham never wrote a book about design. Given his wholehearted enthusiasm for and interest in design, let alone his great influence on design studies and design history, this seems surprising, but would perhaps seem to confirm Banham's distinction between the importance of history and criticism.

However, just as his 1964 paper goes on to refute any significant difference between history and criticism, so Banham's underlying ideas and intentions need to be understood in order for us to appreciate the importance he ascribed to *both* hardback history *and* ephemeral criticism. Banham's design criticism, however enjoyable (as it undoubtedly was) and however apparently flippant (as it may appear), had a serious purpose.

His writing about design commenced in 1955 in publications such as *Design*. Regular design articles began in *New Statesman* in 1960, but it was with his contributions to the social science journal *New Society* from 1965 that design criticism became more central to Banham's output. *New Society* was typical of the decade in which it was founded[4] in that it was consistently left wing and "progressive" in most spheres, but unlike previous publications of that persuasion, at home with an inclusive view of culture that went beyond the conventional high/low hierarchy, Banham's contributions were perfectly suited to the journal, and he remained a regular author until his death in 1988. The design writing which has rightly made his reputation was published in *New Society* between 1965 and 1975 – more or less the period of his tenure as an academic at University College, London. Between those years, of the more than one hundred articles by him which appeared in the journal, over half were on design and/or popular culture. Banham's inclusive approach to design took in banknotes; local authority logos; paperback book covers; surf-boards; sunglasses; neckties; kitchen appliances; radios; cameras; furniture; pub interiors; potato chips; bicycles; cars; Argentinean buses; ice-cream vans; drag- and stock-car racing; Carnaby Street; cult programs and movies such as *Thunderbirds* and *Barbarella*; and movie monsters. The scope of these topics demonstrates a key aspect of Banham's contribution to contemporary design studies and cultural studies: his range of subjects was diverse, and his selection inclusive. Most important, all were treated as equal, and susceptible to analysis and deconstruction. This clearly separated him from earlier "high culture" critics who may have made occasional forays into popular culture, but who saw those subjects as either illustrative of aesthetic delinquency (and therefore "instructive"), or intrinsically trivial, minor, or light-hearted in contrast to their serious studies of Olympian subjects.

USE AND SYMBOLIC EXPRESSION

Banham explained his preference for writing about architecture and design rather than fine art in terms of their dealing with "the problem of use as well as, or parallel with, or on top of or underneath, the problem of symbolic expression, or whatever else you would like to call it."[5] The combination of "use" and "symbolic expression" holds the key to Banham's writing about design, yet it appears at first an unremarkable, and even conventional, pairing. Superficially, it might seem to echo modernist pronouncements of the 1920s. In 1923, Gropius was writing about the responsibility of the Bauhaus "to invent and create forms symbolizing that world."[6] This "symbolic expression" of the machine age, Gropius added, was to grow out of a concern with "use" "… one must first of all study [an object's] nature, for it must serve its purpose perfectly, that is, it must fulfill its function usefully …"[7]

But the modernist combination of use and symbolic expression was fundamentally different from Banham's version in the 1950s and beyond. For him, use was less a case of primary function, than of social context and meaning – the way in which design was used or consumed by particular groups. Use was a decidedly human aspect of design, not just a quasi-ergonomic one in which an object's "nature" – by which modernist designers tended to mean the graspability of a handle or pourability of a spout, for example – helped shape well-proportioned and handsome form. Whereas, for Banham, even as early as 1951, "aesthetic value is not inherent in any object, but in its human usage …[8] – a thoroughly postmodern claim.

The modernists' concern for the Phileban solids and classical aesthetics was invariably dismissed by Banham as "academic,"[9] by which he meant of interest only to academics. He defines academics as those whose "authority is in the past"[10] and, therefore, by definition, located in ivory towers, and wholly removed from the energy and excitement of life on the ground. The abstractness of modernist forms was also dismissed because Banham adjudged that "abstract is not enough."[11] Not only its abstractness, but the mathematical basis of classical aesthetics should not ever be deified as a worthwhile end in itself: "… it is not the ratio which matters, but the use which is made of it."[12]

Design for Banham and, as far as he was concerned, for the design critic, was a matter of the object in social use because that was the way in which one could assess its symbolic expression. Indeed, in Banham's preferred use of the terms, there was virtually no distinction – certainly not one of significance – between "use" and "symbolic expression." The two coalesced in what we might term "cultural usage" or "cultural signification," in which "use" could not be seen as something objective, factual, and ergonomic; but as something social, cultural, and meaningful. Hence, symbolic expression was part and parcel of the object's design and usage, and not something distinct and separate from it. This understanding of design resulted in a type of design criticism which has become an established postmodern discourse, and is widely practiced in design and cultural studies. However, Banham's own practice of this type of criticism is highly distinctive and, in some ways, as we shall see, significantly different from today's examples.

An example of Banham's criticism is the "Shades of Summer" *New Society* article of 1967[13] in which he discusses the design of contemporary fashion sunglasses. Banham starts by describing the appropriately named "Boywatcher" sunglasses, fashionable on the American west coast in 1965, which could "restrain the mandatory long, sun-bleached tresses of surf-girls-USA with a single, long inset strip of Polaroid, so that they could be dropped over the eyes when appropriate." A consumer magazine testing function might have found fundamental flaws in their design, but Banham's argument was that the demise of "Boywatchers" was due

> … not because there was anything wrong with the design functionally or the ergonomic analysis on which it was based. As it correctly presupposed, the prime function of sunglasses, statistically, was to keep the hair tidy, the secondary function was to conceal eye movement while studying form (hence the name) and, in extreme circumstances only, to shade the eyes from glare.

Here was "use" in the context of "symbolic expression," as opposed to use as the outcome of some supposedly objective and scientific primary functional analysis. "Boywatchers" failed, Banham suggests, because the market was not ready for a departure from separate lenses – the manufacturers of "Boywatchers" had quickly returned to the two-lens format the following season.

Banham's main attention in the article was focused on the current fad for the "blatant extremism" of granny specs, whose fashionability had been sealed by their being worn by members of the Byrds and the Lovin' Spoonful. With their metal frames and small oval or letter box lenses, granny specs "flout every utilitarian criterion the Consumers' Association will advance in its threatened *Which?* hunt on shades." Banham further noted that it is "*de rigueur* to wear them so far down the nose that they don't even conceal eye movement [which] underlines key aspects of the psychology and sociology of sunglasses." The history of the production of the glasses and their impact on the market was discussed, and the fact that "once you eliminate sundry small pockets of specialized, professional shade-wearers – skiers, airline pilots, Israeli infantrymen – the rest of a pretty large annual sale … is to a pure fashion market, putting increasingly expensive gear to increasingly frivolous use. And granny specs are the epitome of that frivolity, worn simply for show." The nonergonomic role of sunglasses, as worn by Garbo ("That's Garbo, being alone") and "cool jazz people, ostensibly to conceal the effect that the 'habit' was having on the pupils of your eyes," was described by Banham, who also commented on their current usage as "sinister disguise" in Harp lager advertisements and the "Man from UNCLE" television programs. This led him to perceive that:

> … by the time that you get to granny specs, all that is left of this disguise bit is a symbolic statement of the order 'I am disguised as a man wearing sunglasses.' When things have gone that far,

> the actual shape, form, or color of the shades hardly matters, as long as they can be recognized as sunglasses ... It's another way of manipulating your image, and quicker than having a body like Charles Atlas in ten days.

Sunglasses were being used as a fashionable part of the construction of identity, and Banham seemed to realize this was an integral part of the role of design in postmodern society. The nature of these symbolic statements, Banham noted, would mean that Thorstein Veblen-derived "trickle-down" theories of taste would have to be radically revised.

The "Shades of Summer" piece is not discussed here because it is Banham's best, and certainly not because it is his most "weighty," but because it demonstrates his understanding that design, embedded in popular culture, is part of a social language and cultural usage. Use and symbolic expression are not, for him, separate spheres, but integrally related ones. Written towards the end of the 1960s, "Shades" also upholds a number of other aspects of Banham's design criticism, albeit for the most part by implication. First and foremost is the acceptance of fashionability and concomitant change. The subject matter of Banham's design articles is, to a (usually) greater or lesser extent expendable, and this reflected the technological, fast-moving Second Machine Age so beloved by its author. Like "Boywatchers," consumer goodies aspired to "massive impact and small sustaining power,"[14] and so the particular product under discussion in any one article is less important than the condition of which it is a symptom.

Other aspects of Banham's design criticism, such as his rejection of the modernist idea of the type form, as well as the social and political values of design and its role in consumer, postmodern society, underlie his treatment of the subject matter in "Shades," but are not addressed as such; his informed and "knowing" attitude to the subject matter, the concentration on content as more important than form (in the modernist sense), as well as his style of writing, also have clear implications for what Banham saw as the role of the design critic; and it is some of these underlying values, ideas, and assumptions we need now to consider. In some of his earlier design articles, Banham addressed these more theoretical issues directly.

MODERNISM VERSUS THE MARKET

Banham discusses the issue of the type form in relation to change in his seminal "Machine Aesthetic" article in 1955, his first major published analysis of design. In that essay, Banham puts forward the argument that "The 'Machine Aesthetic" of the pioneer masters of the modern movement was ... selective and classicizing ... and it came nowhere near an acceptance of machines on their own terms or for their own sake."[15] Change, he regularly argued, was a fundamental aspect of the condition of technology in the twentieth century. Le Corbusier might have urged people to "scrap and re-equip," but he had turned away from that radical implication back to classical aesthetics. In the 1950s, aesthetic theory was still, regretted Banham, based on the timelessness of the classical aesthetic:

> we are still making do with Plato because in aesthetics, as in most other things, we still have no formulated intellectual attitudes for living in a throwaway economy. We eagerly consume noisy ephemeridae, here with a bang today, gone without a whimper tomorrow – movies, beachwear, pulp magazines, this morning's headlines and tomorrow's TV programmes – yet we insist on aesthetic and moral standards hitched to permanency, durability, and perennity.[16]

The "noisy ephemeridae" that Banham listed were typical products of postwar consumer society. All were items that were not only technologically produced, but were consumed within the market economy. Technology may have brought about continual change, but so too did the market. It followed that design in and for the market was not about the modernist quest for formal perfection, but about the satisfaction of the market's desires:

> To manufacturers, utility is a complex affair that, in certain products for certain markets, may require the addition of ornament for ostentation or social prestige. Similarly, the demands of economic production do not, as the authors of the model supposed, follow the laws of Nature, but those of economics, and in fields where the prime factor in costing is the length of the production-run, simplicity, such as would render a handicraft product cheaper, might render a mass-produced one more expensive if it were less saleable than a more complex form.[17]

The "demands of economic production" in a dynamic market were even greater than the demands of technological change. Rejecting the modernist propensity to think of the car as a version of the classical temple, Banham saw it as belonging to the realm of popular culture and, therefore, an "expendable, replaceable vehicle of popular desires."[18] Technical obsolescence for automobiles, Banham continued in another article of 1955, "is already acute after eight to ten years," but the average resale period – "the measure of social obsolescence" – is "only three to six years."[19] Furthermore, technological improvements may, in themselves, be relatively trivial compared to change for the sake of stimulating desire and increasing sales: "The technical history of the automobile in a free market is a rugged rat race of detail modifications and improvements, many of them irrelevant, but any of the essential ones lethal enough to kill off a manufacturer who misses it by more than a couple of years."[20] By making use of such ideas as "social obsolescence" and market appeal, Banham was not only declaring his own belief in the market, but attacking the holy cows of modernism and what he believed were its inevitable moralism and paternalism.

THE POLITICS OF DESIGN

Moralism and paternalism were often symptomatic of those whom Banham once memorably castigated for being "isolated from humanity by the Humanities"[21] – those whose rarefied and lofty Olympian interests prevented them from responding to, or even noticing, the live popular culture of contemporary society. Designers creating the glamorous dreams that money could buy were, of course, at the pulsating heart of the marketplace, and subject to its appealing whims and seductive fancies. The political implications of a market economy actually did trouble Banham because it left him, along with other members of the Independent Group,[22]

> ... in a very peculiar position ... because we had this American leaning and yet most of us are in some way Left-oriented, even protest-oriented ... It gives us a curious set of divided loyalties. We dig pop which is acceptance-culture, capitalistic, and yet in our formal politics, if I may use the phrase, most of us belong very firmly on the other side.[23]

This remained a profoundly contradictory issue for Banham, as it has for many design critics and cultural commentators since the 1950s who have had to come to terms with products' and images' role in individual expression and the construction of identities, and the political actualities of consumer capitalism and global colonization.

If the larger political issue remained, for Banham, unresolved (and perhaps remains so for many of us today), other issues such as paternalism could be dealt with straightforwardly. In modernism, paternalism had been linked to particular attitudes to the market. Modernists had an unshakable confidence in their higher purpose and superior taste that enabled them to dismiss popular taste as uneducated and beyond the pale. Banham most directly attacked this attitude, and the concept of moral improvement through design, in his address to the Aspen Design

Conference in 1966.[24] He categorically rejected those designers who subscribed to the "great progressive do-gooder complex of ideas based upon the proposition that the majority is always wrong, that the public must be led, cajoled, sticked, and carrotted onward and upward."[25] Even if the public had been unaware of the values of design in the 1920s,

> A lot of things have happened to people since the Bauhaus was young, things like junk sculpture, hand-held movies, Batman, action painting, the Hell's Angels, surrealism, custom car shows, Op art. Henry Moore, Cinerama, and the like. And, as a result, people have become sophisticated – remarkably so – and far less visually prejudiced.[26]

Banham's list reads like a collection of his *New Society* pieces, and indicates the inclusiveness of his cultural model, from the conventional high art of Henry Moore, to the shadowy world of the Hell's Angels. But his point was not just about his own cultural model, but about what he believed was a widespread cultural change which had resulted in a public no longer "dull and uncritical"[27] in design matters, but capable of distinguishing "stainless from spray chrome at fifty paces." With a design-conscious public, designers would be advised to realize that the "public might now be on your side and have stopped throwing rocks."[28]

We have a glimpse here of a criticism which can be leveled at Banham – that he did not adequately distinguish between what we might term "design-conscious" and "design aware." It is a criticism which may also be leveled at many cultural commentators today. A consumer who can recognize styles and decode street-level meanings is not necessarily the same as a citizen who understands the underlying economic and social conditions, and the political role of design in society. Under the conditions of an advanced capitalist society, glossing over this distinction is, I would argue, politically naive and inadequate. Banham chose to attack the relatively soft target of paternalism and what he termed the tradition of "art worry" which, he maintained, was not only condescending in its attitude, but wrongheaded in its notion of an inevitable relationship between worthiness and style. Accordingly,

> ... design theorists and worriers over the state of the art have insisted that style betrays the moral intention of the designers: Art Nouveau equals decadence ... white walls and flat roof equal care for functional performance ... chromium bright-work equals commercial swindle; and so forth.[29]

By denying any relationship between moral or social worth and visual style, Banham was not only countering modernist attitudes to popular culture, but confirming an agnostic or amoral attitude to the relationship in his own design criticism. However, in Banham's case, there is more than a suspicion that denying one type of relationship – moral worth and visual style – slides into denying another, more profound relationship between design and its political implications.

Banham's political ire was raised by those who dismissed popular culture as either trivial, debased, or exploitative – an affront to standards and, ultimately, an erosion of democracy. In 1962, he wrote:

> I have a crystal clear memory of myself, aged sixteen [1938], reading a copy of *Fantastic Stories* while waiting to go on in the school play, which was Fielding's *Tom Thumb the Great*, and deriving equal relish from the *recherché* literature I should shortly be performing, and the equally far out pulp in my hand. We returned to Pop in the early fifties ... back to our native literature, our native arts.[30]

Banham once described what he interpreted as the "revenge of the elementary school boys"[31] on the British public school-educated elite, who constituted the establishment of art and art history. When reflecting on his own contribution to art and design writing some time later, Banham concluded that he had "much to be modest about ... in a world that contains the likes of Nikolaus Pevsner, James Ackerman, Anthony Blunt or Vincent Scully, but I think I have been more assiduous than most of them in carrying their discipline down from Olympus into the market-place."[32] Not only was Banham equally at home with the high culture world of academic scholarship and the popular culture world of the marketplace, but he was claiming to be revising the approach to one by an acceptance of the values of the other.

VALUE SYSTEMS: HIGH AND POPULAR

However, it would be wrong to think of a one-way journey. The carrying of the discipline's cultural baggage may have been predominantly in one direction, but secure and well-loved bases were maintained in both locations. In other words, the "return" to popular culture and the marketplace was not made at the expense of high culture and its Olympian associations. This is something which distances Banham from most of today's design critics. The notion of discrete realms and, with them the idea of hierarchy has been comprehensively rejected by most contemporary critics who see an unstable and shifting network of signs to be explored. Banham may have been thoroughly committed to the Independent Group notion of "both/and" – the equal status and equal importance of high and popular culture, rather than a strict hierarchical ordering which saw the products of high culture as serious, and those of popular culture as trivial – but "both/and" assumed identifiable realms, each with concomitant value systems which permitted evaluation by the critic.

Indeed, Banham firmly believed that one of the key roles of the critic is to evaluate and judge. For example, in his "Machine Aesthetic" article of 1955, he commented on the "rapid evolution of an anti-purist but eye-catching vocabulary of car design – which we now call Borax."[33] Borax, he wrote, in the context of the "need to chase the market"[34] and in relation to the symbolism of speed, is "entirely proper" as a design vocabulary for cars, but this does *not*

> ... require a suspension of value judgments in front of it. There is plenty of bad Borax about, some of it as mean and skimpy as a great deal of contemporary architecture, and more of it is inflated and overblown than is any recent building. It is a design language which can be used badly or well ...[35]

It was the role of the critic to make those judgments, amongst other things, and to explain his or her reasoning for them, and not merely to detail iconography or *describe* a situation in sociological terms.

This view needs to be seen in the context of Banham's wider values, principal of which was the shift from design as a satellite of fine art to design as a social discourse. Thus, Banham's reference to Borax as a design *language* is significant, because it reflected his view that the emphasis in design criticism should not be the modernist one of an appreciation of abstract and disinterested form, but an examination of meaningful content. Writing in "Vehicles of Desire," Banham described how the "top body stylists" were handling the language of car design

> to give their creations qualities of apparent speed, power, brutalism, luxury, snob-appeal, exoticism, and plain common-or-garden sex. The means at their disposal are symbolic iconographies, whose ultimate power lies in their firm grounding in popular taste and the innate traditions of the product, while the actual symbols are drawn from Science Fiction, movies, earthmoving equipment, supersonic aircraft, racing cars, heraldry and certain deep-seated mental dispositions about the great outdoors and the kinship between technology and sex.[36]

The idea that designers were working with "symbolic iconographies" shifted design away from the modernist model of abstraction, with its "characteristic primary forms and colors," to a postmodernist model of "product semantics" with its culturally loaded, meaningful forms and images. The modernist designers may have thought their primary forms were "readily accessible to everyone," but Banham realized that accessibility was more likely to come through the application of specific cultural codes and conventions that, in view of the need for mass sales in the marketplace, would be based on symbols which had widespread public recognizability and appeal. The postmodern designer was also unlike the modernist designer in that the latter could remain aloof from popular taste, closeted in the academy: the former would need to understand popular culture and the "innate traditions" of the relevant products, and this would necessitate an immersion in popular culture.

THE ROLE OF THE CRITIC

If the designer was creating products from "symbolic iconographies," the critic's role was, in effect, to deconstruct them. The designer and the critic, Banham wrote, "must deal with a language of signs …"[37] – a very Barthian-sounding notion. Good criticism, he continues, depends "on the ability of design critics to master the workings of the popular art vocabulary which constitutes the aesthetics of expendability."[38] Because design was based on serial production and was consumed in the marketplace, design criticism was, therefore, fundamentally *unlike* art criticism: "The aesthetics of serial production must be the aesthetics of the popular arts, not of fine arts. To apply durable and time-bound aesthetic procedures to consumable and nontraditional products can only cheapen those procedures and – as in so much Victorian design – debases the fine arts without benefiting the expendable arts."[39] Art criticism would deal with form and iconography, whereas design criticism "depends on an analysis of content, an appreciation of superficial rather than abstract qualities, and an outward orientation that sees the history of the product as an interaction between the sources of the symbols and the consumer's understanding of them."

Banham's description of design criticism is fundamentally similar to the one that now predominates. The embedding of design in a social and cultural context – its "outward orientation" which calls on reception as much as creation – and an emphasis on its semantic meaning, characterizes a mode of analysis and understanding that we now expect from the critic. Banham's commitment to the critic as interpreter justifies his being termed the founding father of design criticism. He was aware of cultural shifts away from the modernist, formalist aesthetic, to what might be called a sociological aesthetic, and developed a criticism which dealt with culturally-derived meaning rather than "pure" form or even the "inward orientation" of conventional iconography. However, at the early stage of postmodernism when he was formulating his ideas, Banham did not perceive the magnitude and inclusiveness of the shift, and so drew a distinction between design criticism and art criticism, the latter of which he assumed would still be founded on conventional formal and iconographical analysis. While he was willing to see all aspects of design as open to the same critical treatment, he did not anticipate that art criticism, too, would come to be based on "a language of the sign" and an "outward orientation" which, socially and politically, embedded the artwork.

Probably the reason for this distinction was part of Banham's modernist-like differentiation between realms: design is one realm; art is another. Even his wholehearted enthusiasm for popular culture, and the seriousness he accorded it, did not eclipse his enjoyment of – and equal commitment to – conventional high culture, whether Le Corbusier's buildings or the Eames designs. The "both/and" mentality upheld by Banham may have signified a liberation of popular culture, but it did not, for him, result in either a *merging* of all aspects of culture, or the *replacement* of Olympus by the marketplace. High and popular culture may even have influenced one another, but distinctions still remained, and were upheld by Banham in his criticism. This, in part, accounts for Banham's attitude toward value judgments in criticism. Value judgments are unproblematic when terms of reference are commonly held, and when criteria are agreed upon. They become increasingly problematical once practices become no longer self-contained and self-referential, and when the role and function of the practice, itself, is fundamentally challenged from different critical positions.

Banham, as we have seen, argued for the critic both as an interpreter of meaning *and* as a judge of quality. Is it likely that, as Banham realized the extent of the opening up of postmodern practices, he would have retreated from value judgments towards the more descriptive, interpretative role of the critic? I think a retreat unlikely for two reasons. First, Banham maintained that value judgments would always be possible, in spite of the collapse of modernist absolutism, because a plurality of hierarchies – the legacy of Independent Group thinking – continued to operate.[40] There may be many hierarchies, but each could be addressed in terms of shared criteria, and so were open to *relative* evaluation. This is borne out by Banham's comments about good and bad Borax. Second, it was hardly Banham's personal style to be just descriptive and interpretative. There was too much of the proselytizer and polemicist in Banham for him to hold back his own judgments about the subject of his investigation. As several of his obituarists remarked, making judgments and arguing in an open and full-blooded way with others was what gave his work life and vitality, and prevented it from becoming "academic." Evaluation and subsequent dispute, he believed, moved a discipline forward: interpretation *and* judgment were inseparable parts of his critical project. It is this combination which is Banham's contribution and legacy, I would argue, to design criticism. The sort of evaluation practiced by Banham was undoubtedly problematic, but to turn away from it because of its intrinsic difficulties, or because judgment is – often simplistically or crudely – equated with elitism and colonization seems to me to be a loss of a type of vital contribution to an ongoing dialogue which, as Banham believed, invigorates and enlivens a discipline. Perhaps the loss of critical evaluation in much contemporary criticism tells us more about our preoccupations and prejudices – our fragile sensibilities and political reluctance to judge good from bad, however necessarily qualified – than about Banham and *his* preoccupations and prejudices. Perhaps, for all our pronouncements about diversity and difference, we are taking the easy way out as critics.

NOTES

First published in *Design Issues* 13 no. 2 (Summer 1997): 24–35.

1. See, for example, obituaries in *Design History Society Newsletter*, 38 (July 1988), 10–11; *Domus* (October 1988), 17–24; and *Journal of Design History*, 1, 2 (1988), 141–42.
2. This paper arises from research relating to my book, *Reyner Banham: Criticism and Design in the Second Machine Age*, to be published by Manchester University Press in 1998.
3. "Convenient Benches and Handy Hooks: Functional Considerations in the Criticism of the Art of Architecture" in Marcus Whiffen, ed., *The History, Theory and Criticism of Architecture: Papers from the 1964 AIA-ACSA Teacher Seminar* (Cambridge, MA: MIT Press, 1965), 91.
4. New Society started in 1962 and ran until 1988.
5. "Convenient Benches and Handy Hooks," 91.
6. Gropius, "The Theory and Organization of the Bauhaus" (1923), in Tim and Charlotte Benton with Dennis Sharp, *Form and Function* (London: Granada, 1980), 127.
7. Gropius, "Bauhaus Dessau – Principles of Bauhaus Production" (1926) in Ibid., 148.
8. "The Shape of Everything," *Art News and Review* (July 14, 1951): 2.
9. See, for example, "On Abstract Theory," *Art News and Review* (November 28, 1953): 3.

10. "Machine Aesthetic," *Architectural Review* (April 1955): 228.
11. "On Abstract Theory," 3.
12. Ibid.
13. "Shades of Summer," *New Society* (June 29, 1967): 959 (for all citations).
14. "Who is this 'Pop'?" *Motif* (Winter, 1962/63): 12.
15. "Machine Aesthetic," 225.
16. "Vehicles of Desire," *Art* (September 1, 1955): 3.
17. "Machine Aesthetic," 227.
18. "Vehicles of Desire," 3.
19. Ibid.
20. Ibid.
21. "Pop and the Body Critical," *New Society* (December 16, 1965): 25.
22. Banham was closely associated with the Independent Group, a loosely knit discussion group based in London in the early 1950s. The group seriously – and in opposition to contemporary British sympathies – addressed issues relating to technology and popular culture. See Anne Massey, *The Independent Group: Modernism and Mass Culture in Britain, 1945–59* (Manchester: Manchester University Press, 1995); and my *Pop Design: Modernism to Mod* (London: The Design Council, 1987), 45–74.
23. "The Atavism of the Short-Distance Mini-Cyclist," *Living Arts*, 3 (1964): 92.
24. "All that Glitters is not Stainless," *Architectural Design* (August 1967): 351.
25. Ibid., 352.
26. Ibid., 351.
27. Herbert Read speaking at the National Union of Teachers (NUT) Conference, 1960, on "Popular Culture and Personal Responsibility." Speech published in *NUT Verbatim Report of Proceedings* (London: NUT, 1960), 155.
28. "All that Glitters is not Stainless," 351.
29. Ibid.
30. "Who is this 'Pop'?" 13.
31. "Pop and the Body Critical," 25.
32. "Foreword" in Penny Sparke, ed., *Reyner Banham: Design By Choice* (London: Academy, 1981): 7.
33. "Machine Aesthetic," 228.
34. Ibid., 227–28.
35. Ibid., 228.
36. "Vehicles of Desire," 3.
37. "Space for Decoration: A Rejoinder," *Design* (July 1955): 24.
38. Ibid.
39. Ibid.
40. See Whiteley, *Pop Design*, 225–29.

18

VISIBILITY IN PROGRESS

Giovanni Anceschi

This article was originally presented as the ICOGRADA inaugural lecture at the PIRA/RSA Design Conference, London, April 1, 1992.

Translated by John Cullars with the author's assistance.

My theme is "visibility," a topic that happens to be close to the professional activity of visual design and the disciplinary field of visual communications. I intend to develop this theme in two stages: first, I'll try to consider how far visibility is present all over the world nowadays; then, I'll try to analyze how visibility is produced. The period we live in sometimes has been defined as a "civilization of the image"; and at other times as a "civilization of the written word." Some have spoken of a return to "the global village," a return to a civilization of a "second-degree orality"[1] promoted by electronic technologies. In any case, a very *visual* civilization, even if it is now also *audio-visual*, or more precisely *multisensoreal*, as is promised by so-called *virtual reality*. The general tendency is to emphasize the importance of the visual in our daily lives and in the scenario of our technological future.

In opposition to this kind of interpretation, some speak of the visual in a very critical way; they talk about a civilization of blindness, a "blackout" civilization. Paul Virilio, for instance, a French urbanist who defines himself as a "dromologist," which means a student of velocity, has become one of those critical voices by offering close-up observations of a series of phenomena in our society and technology.[2]

According to Virilio, the dissemination of technological innovations into our culture has prompted an acceleration of every single process and of all processes at the same time. This speeding up process alters the normal process of communication, which has a relatively slow rhythm, with an instantaneous kind of process that is called "switching" or "transducing." The time of transducing is governed by electronic devices; while the still, relatively slow, rhythm of communications is defined by the human organs and mind. Heavy stimulation can pass through the body of a person invaded by transducing processes, but it does not really interfere with the mind.

The surrounding world is then seen as a world of *dysphoria* – the contrary of *euphoria* – which means essentially the experience of a world of depression caused by a substantial impoverishment of communication and, even more, by a substantial deprivation of sensory pleasure. I recall, for instance, a very harsh indictment of the air travel industry by Virilio: velocity is achieved at the expense of treating passengers as bodies on stretchers, or even as corpses in the storage drawers of a morgue.

As to what more directly and specifically concerns *images*, it is increasingly less *figures* and more often *stimuli* that are activated to produce immediate reactions such as conditioned reflexes; "elements of diagrammatic efficiency" as Félix Guattari called it in a seminar held in Milan.[3] I feel that the act of piloting a warplane is becoming the model, the *allegorical key* of contemporary life, as in the new popular art of arcade games. With one's body imprisoned in the cockpit, indissolubly connected to the instrument panel as though it were a prosthesis, the problem of our survival becomes dependent on how prompt our reactions are, and on our capacity for dodging and taking the offensive. But, in fact, all the events already have been anticipated in the software.

Images appear to be losing their thickness, that is, the depth of their possible meanings. A single figure could be analyzed and interpreted for hours but, instead of that, images now are flattening out; becoming partially worked inert matter, refuse, and residue for a continuous superficial collage. Informatic devices and electronic technologies produce a global effect of unreality, generating the illusion of *dematerialization* Everything appears to happen as if by magic, in a flat space, or even in the depths of a *virtual* space. In any case, it is a space lacking *consistency* and *corporeality*.

This could be the description of a civilization of blindness due to a defect, but this same civilization in which we live also can be defined as a *civilization of blindness* due to excess; the excess of visual noise (aside from sonorous bedazzlements). I am thinking of "loud" road signs along some European highways on which everything is indicated at the maximum level of alarm; even information concerning normal driving. In the case of a genuine emergency, there remains no *expressive margin*; no possibility of an even greater contrast. A heavier typographical size cannot be used; and a more exciting blinking warning light cannot be produced. I am also thinking of urban traffic signs that simply destroy the magic of the historical ambiance of some Tuscan cities with their disorder and garish colors. In general, I'm considering all collective environments – environments of *transit*; environments that increase urban, suburban, national and international *mobility*; and environments such as airports, railway stations, and subway stations. In all of these, in response to our anxiety or nausea for information, we must endure visual and – in spite of the theory of the "silent airport" – auditory directions, as we are assaulted by excessive and even contradictory marketing messages.

Or one may consider *business* environments – the department store, the supermarket, the hypermarket, the commercial center – in which our appetites are inundated by a tide of seductive signals. Then there are certain *leisure* or spare time environments, such as stadiums, sports arenas, and most emblematically, dance clubs, in which our search for pleasure and heightened emotion is overwhelmed by a mixture of sensory impressions (lights, sounds, etc.) that are powerful enough to cross the threshold of pain. Blindness and numbness are this time the result of a generalized excess, the effect of which I call the *multisensory assault* of our civilization. In reality, the two kinds of blindness are complementary, since we are caught in a vicious circle. "Flashes" of sensual hyperstimulation are followed by "downers" of depression that drive us to seek a new din that is even more acute – a cycle of *hyperaesthesia* and *anaesthesia* from which there is practically no exit.

Within the media, the ferocious temporal scansion, and certainly the astronomical costs of every second of transmission, result in a deprivation of another order, the symbolic order. The search for a necessary simplification, rather than producing an elegant effect of shorthand, produces a vulgar caricature, a puppet, a buffoon, or a gladiator. Our civilization also is blind to other excesses: that's why there is too much information at our disposal. A glance at a palimpsest ends up serving as a substitute for direct experience. We no longer go to exhibitions, but read reviews of them instead. Rather than reading books, we rush through summaries, or even consult lists of "keywords."

Ours also is a culture of blackout because information is concealed. It isn't just intentional concealment. In fact, ours is a competitive culture of secrecy and of *confidential knowledge*. Information also is buried deep in those vast resting places known as libraries and archives. And it isn't just a technological problem of "information retrieval." It's the fact that, even after processing the information, these institutions try to make everything available to everyone. The fact is, they lack the means of organizing knowledge adequately for the human mind. What is lacking is a book of etiquette; a code of politeness that would allow us to communicate with the hypertextual structures.

Information also is concealed because of the great frameworks of social organization. Information is hidden behind and within the administrative structures of the state, region, and municipality. We're blind because we're denied access. Finally, information is concealed by the factual complexity of the totality of cultural structures – commercial, industrial, and social – and of their problematical administration. Consider science, which produces knowledge in secret, far from the public; and consider the fact that the same popularizing *mise-en-scène* of science often is accepted as an objective framework through its dissemination. For example, zoological documentation can become a particular kind of "fiction"; a kind of *porno-ecological*[4] entertainment, as the semiotician, Paolo Fabbri, calls it; a spectacle that satisfies our impulse to spy on animals, but has nothing to do with science. Here is the very excess that impoverishes what it seeks to elucidate. We live in an optical and visual world, but certainly not a visible one. Consider, in a very different sense, the phenomenon of technological miniaturization and the fact that, consequently, we can see ever more clearly *that* devices work but not *how* they work. Objects increasingly become "black boxes" – richer in functions but poorer in transparency.

Now I come to the designer's perspective vis-à-vis this situation, and wish to say immediately that I don't want design to take on the role of the Red Cross, arriving on the battlefield after the worst has taken place, as Wolfgang Fritz Haug said in the 1970s.[5] The professional field of communication design has been habitually defined by optical expressions such as "optical art" or "optical illusions." When we use these terms, we are referring to physical or physiological phenomena of sight; obviously to the physical sense of sight. Or we use the term "visual" (in the exact sense of "visual design" or of the "visual world"), and are then referring to perception; not to the passive, receptive component of vision; but, instead, to the active, selective, psychological aspects of seeing. We all understand, for instance, what Rudolf Arnheim meant by the fertile expression "visual thinking," or what Aldous Huxley meant by the "art of seeing."

In graphic design and in a great deal of professional thought that has circled around this and the field of visual communication, a great emphasis is placed on these two aspects of matter: reception and perception. Consider that the leading expert on "basic design," the American, William Huff, speaks on "geometrizing" and "perceptualizing" as the two principal operations that lead to configuration; "to the result of design." Or, in typography, think of the opposition between, as we say, the ergonomic laws of "legibility" and the aesthetic and perceptual laws of Dan Friedman's "readability."

These are very important questions, but I don't believe that the profession of visual design should limit itself to problems of how to "lubricate" the channel or, better yet, to guarantee the smooth passage of information. But we also should not confine ourselves solely to conferring "harmony" or *gute Gestalt* [good design] on the manner in which it is presented. In truth, another concept, that of the image, is floating around the discipline – in the sense, naturally, of "corporate image"; but especially of "imagery," of the *imaginaire*, as the French put it. This is an expression that calls to mind the illusionistic idea of representation; and of the historical and artistic categories of "genre," style, etc. In this regard, I don't feel that graphic design is dealing with a banal question of the stylistic use of images. Think of the tedious idiosyncratic rift between postmodern eclecticism and "International Style" mannerism, a topic which could justify another essay.

For graphic design, I affirm, it is a question of "visibility." It is curious that my attention to visibility has been reawakened by an encounter with the work of the Italian writer, Italo Calvino. I am speaking of his "American Lectures,"[6] in which he shows the subtlety of his experimental theories. In 1984, Calvino was invited to give the Charles Eliot Norton Poetry Lectures at Harvard University, a lecture series that would have been given in 1985/86 academic year, had he not died in the meantime. Calvino entitled the series "Six Memos for the Next Millennium", and decided to dedicate it to the following six values: lightness, quickness, exactitude, multiplicity, consistency, and visibility.

In October of 1991, a club of students at the University of Reggio Calabria in Italy organized a series of six lectures to be delivered by six authors in the Great Hall of the Faculty of Architecture, and I was assigned the theme of visibility. Thus, in a certain sense, visibility came looking for me. I reached the conclusion that the idea of visibility is genuinely central for designers insofar as the idea "to feel with the eyes" contains the idea of doing. If I say, "I want to make a thing optical" or "I want to make a thing visual," it doesn't make much sense. Now I understand why I've never had much sympathy with the expressions "visualizer" and "to visualize." When I say, "I am making a thing visible," that has a concrete meaning. A very precise example of the kind of thing I'm getting at is the title of a book by Richard Saul Wurman, *Making the City Observable*, which illustrates the possibility of making the city and its problems visible.[7]

Moreover, it seems to me that the question of visibility can unify a large number of sectors of the profession, and define the limits of the discipline. The illustrators of Diderot's and D'Alembert's *l'Encyclopédie* made the technical culture of the bourgeoisie visible; the Arab calligrapher, Massoudy, made Allah's word visible; any photographer makes what was latent in the photographic plate visible; a computer graphics artist generates, and thus makes, fractals visible; and the visualizer makes the ideas of the art director visible.

It seems to me that the expression "visibility" indicates a very specific area that is only marginally implied in other scientific disciplines. Visibility is not the topic for research in them, aside from semiotics, which concerns itself with everything having to do with meaning and communication, and of which a hypothetical theory of visibility could be a branch. Visibility, for example is not a research topic for physiological optics, even though the ocular capacity of focusing does relate to visibility. Nor is visibility a theme for the science of perception; and even the perceptual phenomenon of "borders without gradients," – as Gaetano Kanisza[8] states, is an extreme case of visibility; the visibility of something that is not physically present. Nor is it a topic for cognitive psychology, although visibility obviously is related to comprehension; nor to depth psychology, although there is current research stressing the importance of colors and other visible phenomena.[9] Nor is it studied in sociological aesthetics, although Walter Benjamin says that the multiple display of works of art – that is to say, visibility – causes the loss of their aesthetic aura;[10] nor in anthropology, in which it seems that the act of concealing and exhibiting is related to hierarchy and power. Visibility plays no part in technical and technological matters, although it is undeniable that research on resolution in video electronics or on anti-aliasing in computer graphics is connected to visibility.

In the past, the question of visibility was a question of art or skill; today, it is a question of design competencies. In a world such as I've described, a world of declining visibility, these competencies are acquiring a necessity and an urgency hitherto unknown. Designers cannot escape from this responsibility or, worse still, contribute merrily to this multisensory hubbub. It is clear that objective circumstances, so-called environmental conditions, are evolving with the speed of a viral culture. But design can't accept the role of a pure catalyst; an inert element that is favorable to unleashing a reaction. The designer must not be a "negligible quantity," as Gui Bonsiepe said a few years ago, but should behave as the representative of users at the project negotiators' table.

Today, clients see designers in two ways. Some see them as the long arm of the manager; as a kind of artificial joint that, possibly in real-time, makes the manager's visions tangible and visible; or commonly proposes a variety of versions from which to make their choice. Others, and not the least sagacious, see designers as critical consultants rather than as problem-solvers. This is the reason that a professional competence capable of predicting all possible solutions is the minimum requirement that should be offered. Then, in this case, designers are particularly requested to concentrate on doing what they can to make problems visible. The designer can assume responsibility in the bargaining space that this scenario opens between the two partners; between the power to make decisions and the knowledge of what is proposed. (However the topic of the designer's responsibility also would require an essay in itself.)

But why does the activity of realizing visibility, which is so important a value that it is worth entrusting to the next millennium, as Calvino said, seem to me to be the very heart of the discipline and profession? Visibility is definitely what the totality of capacity, skill, competencies, knowledge, tricks, artifices, and abilities that designers have at their disposal is moving toward. Visibility is the art of escape from the invisible. Basically, it is a magical art; the art of evocation; the art of conferring a particular form of existence on that which lacks it – not a factual existence, but the virtual existence of the simulation, of the conjecture, and of the prescription. It is an existence that allows for the manipulation of an object *in absentia*.

When we realize a sort of "close-copy at a distance" with a camera, through a field sketch, or with a monument drawing, we capture the object which we want to fix into memory, producing a second visibility beginning from an existing one. When using an instrument or prosthesis (a microscope, telescope, slow-motion camera, high-speed camera, Schlieren detector,[11] or X-ray apparatus), we transfer an object or phenomenon into the thickness of the perceptual present; we put the thing that interests us into the space and time available to our bodies. Then we are producing visibility, wresting it from the invisible. It's always a matter of making the invisible visible when, for instance, the scientist (or scientific illustrator) produces a figurative and structural hypothesis of a reality that hasn't yet seen the light of day; or generates a hypothesis that is altogether conceptual, such as the double helix of DNA, the planetary system, or the ecological cycle of a forest.[12]

On the other hand, this conjectural character of figures and plans, this behavior as a figurative hypothesis, is especially obvious with any design activity. Every single plan by an architect, every rendering by an industrial designer, and every rough sketch by a graphic designer is a document that puts forward a hypothesis, and makes a demand. In the first place, it says to designers, "This is how I'm made. Do I accurately describe reality? If yes, does the object that I represent solve all the inherent problems, etc.?" In the second place, it says to the client, "This is how I'm made. Is it worth the trouble to build, produce, promote, and market me?"

Basically, the designer's work consists of making things visible, that is, to "put into figure," as earlier painters such as Giotto did. But to "put into figure" also means to put significance into a system of notation, a code. A technical draft, for example, is a score which, instead of making strange gestures to gentlemen in evening clothes who are holding onto curious wood or brass objects, dictates precise gestures to other men in protective helmets and padded jackets, who clamber up ladders and scaffoldings; or to still other men, dressed in blue overalls, who push buttons and pull knobs; or, finally, to others in white shifts who use cutters, handle keyboards, or mix ink. This prescriptive character, this behavior as a true and proper order, is perfectly readable in the informatic term "command," particularly in computer-assisted manufacturing and robotics.

In the case of technical drafting methods, as with type design or pictogram design, we're dealing with a way of making things visible that is oriented to the storing of relevant data in the memory, rather than to recognition and the immediacy of recognition. Think of what we expect from a page of music and of what we expect from a photograph of a landscape. The problem isn't just that of acting on the world and manipulating it through the medium of a figure in the same way that our cave-dwelling hunting ancestors practiced propitiatory killing through effigies. It isn't simply a matter of producing handles to maneuver a world underneath, or indices to find one's bearings. It isn't simply a technical problem of knowledge and information.

The problem also is a social problem of communications. Designers don't just work for a receiver who must be put in a position to operate; they also work for an observer who can suddenly become a partner, or for a public whom they intend to (and must) persuade. This means that, once designers have made the invisible visible, their task consists of making a part still more visible in relation to the whole.

There is a general principle which unifies the infinite variations of the theme of rendering visible: Umberto Eco calls it "ostentation," and places it among the *mode of sign production*.[13] This semiotic procedure defines the act of isolating an object or a sign, and of lifting it into a more visible realm. This begins with the banal gesture of raising a bottle of beer in the direction of the bartender to have him fetch another. It could conclude with the raising of a sculpture over the base of a column in an art gallery. Or, transferring the principle from the field of exhibition design to typography and layout, we could begin with the yellow Magic Marker underlining that emphasizes a word in a photocopy and finish with the sophisticated hierarchy of headlines, column tops, headings, captions, and copy that leads the reader through the text of a page of the daily newspaper. It is the sacred gesture of the monstrance at the altar in the Catholic rite in which the Eucharist stands out from everything else and is exposed to the sight of the faithful. It is the functional gesture of every sign – street posters, directional arrows, the hands on a clockface, etc. It is the color contrast between geographic locations and topographical information on a tourist map; and it is the size contrast between street names of different importance.

Actually, the principle of ostentation comes into play in every case of representation, since every type of representation is a reduction, as Sartre said. The drawing of a rose has no scent. It is not possible to show the entirety of the object meant for representation. Whether we know it or not, and whether we intend it or not, a view is selected, and an appearance isolated. Every representation, even the most faithful (which means the most illusionistic) is a schema. Any representation will always be the presentation of a particular facet that must be judiciously selected. Every design is a bit of a caricature in that it selects and emphasizes some features at the expense of others. Every recognition emphasizes some parts, and excludes others, as Rudolf Arnheim said.

These ostentative manipulations are the designer's real tools. They tend to modify the behavior of the public and thus serve the interest of the client. Using the terminology of the art of discourse, these artifices could be called rhetorical figures.[14] In communication design, rhetorical figures are *figures of visibility*. Figures of visibility can be *visible metaphors*, the art of showing through resemblances and associations of ideas; whose ideal example can be indicated in the artistic movement, Surrealism, with its cutting and captivating possibilities of graphic humor and fantastic allusions. It also can be *visible synecdoche*, which is making the whole visible by showing only a part. This is a synthetic and concise art, pointing to clarity and economy of means. "Less is more," as Mies van der Rohe said.

Figures that are determined by the static disposition or dynamic movements of their elements may be called *figures of staging*.[15] In fact, we can envision this environment of maneuvers and manipulations needed to accentuate visibility as being like that of a stage set – a traditional set which is arranged for the disposition and movements of an ensemble of actors, putting them in poses and fundamentally regulating them so as to produce patterns and actions. A "visibility set" is likewise arranged for the movement of machines and variable optics, so as to determine points of view and groupings that are more or less advantageous. Such a set not only determines the apparatus that lights the scene and objects, for example, but also colors them and, in general, determines their *surface attributes,* as they are called in computer graphics terminology, so as to create the effects of the necessary differentiation.

We may particularly note that this model, which arises from the theatrical direction *mise-en-scène,* also is valid for the two-dimensional layout, the *mise-en-page.*[16] As already pointed out, this can be extended through the idea of choreography, and the management of scenic movements, to the theater and to cinematography; and even farther removed from the stage itself, to the "happening." In doing so, one may include, through the idea of programming, both the logic of the field of strategies that organize events and the field of communications.[17]

In other words, the profession of graphic design consists in giving form, position, and behavior to characters that could be persons as well as objects in the world of the designed, photographed, or kinetically represented. But the roles of the characters are played by graphs, illustrations, and typographical elements in the Flatland of the layout. Our characters can be either persons or objects in the world of designed, photographed, or cinematic representations. But, as previously pointed out, they are representations of characters, graphics, and illustrations on the Flatland of the page. The designer's skill consists in knowing how to place them opportunely, one in respect to the other. Placing one above the other, one below the other, or one to the side of the other means three very distinct things. Placing them with a lot or only a little surrounding space produces two radically different impressions.

The activity of visual design consists not only in putting things into a particular order to indicate a hierarchy of values, but also in knowing how to assign each element its proper dimension with respect to its importance in the whole. It consists of assigning the proper color scheme in order to direct or persuade the public (the photorealism of a cover girl), or guide and fix public knowledge (the symbolic red and blue coloration of the two systems of the circulation of blood). It consists in causing our element-characters to move in a meaningful way. The designer's work consists, finally, in knowing how to make things fall into place at the right moment; in not missing some significant appointments; in respecting certain successions of events; and in bringing about the convergence or condensation of other events. As with setting off fireworks, it consists in knowing when to set off the final explosion for maximum impact.

If rhetoric is the art of discourse, then visual communication is the art of composition, disposition, and modulation.[18] This art is a "sequential" one, as described by F. H. K. Henrion.[19] In other words, this art consists in orchestrating all the elements of form in space and time. The corporate image, or more precisely, the process of constructing a corporate identity, demonstrates this idea. Conferring significance to an institution or to a firm results from a planned sequence of *figures of staging* and events to produce a special kind of visibility; not only to be seen but to be remembered.

How we obtain this mode of being able to see will depend on a visibility that is really new or, better yet, fictitious in the case of those corporate images that are masks for faces which are completely different in reality. Or one may say that they bring to light or place in evidence authentic structural traits, even about the efficiency of the organization, that lie hidden. For each of the clients or partners, however, every encounter, every contact, every message received from the firm represents the addition of a characteristic; a subtle shading or a minute brush stroke to the sender's interior portrait that they are building in their minds.

At the beginning of this article, I painted a truly millenarian scenario. It had the somewhat sulfurous characteristics of the predictions made by monks approaching the year AD 1000. Curiously, circumstances seem to favor finding pleasure in amassing certain types of expectations and, especially, of preoccupations concerning specified dates and the end of epochs. Just as it is true that the change in millennia is upon us, it is equally true that this date is dawning surrounded by the problems that we've described. Or rather, if the analyses of the situation that we've shown have any basis in fact, the coming years represent a challenge to the designer of visibility; a challenge not without an element of risk.

The challenge isn't simply the need to counter the advance of opacity and blackout that, in the field of the production of visual messages, represents what is elsewhere known as pollution. It also is a pollution of impoverishment; a pollution producing asphyxia. The challenge is represented concretely in the requirements manifested in the manufacturing world. The challenge is represented by the great need for design in the new world of so-called immaterial production. It is evident enough that the information profession is currently linked to the communications industry, and is assuming a sustaining role in the industrial and commercial panorama.

Even material mobility, the physical transport of persons and things, is caught up in the competition for the transport of information. I don't mean by this that we're selling fewer automobiles because of the existence of faxes, and that the time of practical distribution by way of teleconferencing is approaching. The information industry intertwined with media systems represents the model for today's industrial culture just as, for example, industry of the 1950s drew on aeronautics, which was imitated even in the form of electric irons.

The numerous messages originating every day and the number of systems of presentation which must be invented every month of every year to nourish the media system are monstrous. The design of communications, which is, itself, graphic design, requires of its operators a continuous state of invention which has never previously existed. At this point, I feel that I can quote a brief passage from the "Charter of Graphic Design," a document born of the reflections of a group of Italian designers with whom I have the honor of collaborating. The charter says, "In the 1930s, architecture took the leading role in the design field. The shift in the '60s toward a consumer society meant that industrial design became the conceptual coordinator. In the '90s, however, it is graphic design that has taken on this strategic role."[20] For reasons of responsibility that I've pointed out, today's visual designer must grasp this opportunity. But I must add what we may call *the maieutics of visibility*, the unified field of knowledge and techniques to produce visibility;[21] as well as the knowledge accumulated by designers and by those who have preceded us working in communications and representations, needs a large program of research and theoretical foundations to face these problems.

NOTES

First published in *Design Issues* 12 no. 3 (Autumn 1996): 3–13.

1. First-degree and second-degree orality are terms used by Walter Ong in order to distinguish between the exclusively oral communication before the introduction of writing and the revival of orality induced by electronic technologies that is typical of today's culture. See Walter Ong, *Orality and Literacy: The Technologizing of the Word* (New York: Methuen, 1982).
2. Paul Virilio, *Speed and Politics: An Essay on Dromology* (New York: Semiotext(e), 1986).
3. Félix Guattari, *Lettere ecologie* (Turin: Sonda, 1991). The seminar "La ricerca sin crocevia: contaminare/tradurre" was held in Milan in 1990.
4. Paolo Fabbri, one of the best living semioticians; in the conference paper "Natura e comunicazione: i media farano male alia natura" (Milan, 1990), on

the question of scientific popularization; attacked the glossy, smart magazines that he claimed promote a hard pseudonaturalistic voyeurism, which he defined as *pornoecological*. Fabbri's concept is very similar to Otto Neurath's discussion of passéeist museums "die die Schaulust befriedigen und wenig auf den Willen einwirken" [that satisfy voyeurism and act very little on the will]. See Otto Neurath, *Gesammelte pädagogische Schriften* (Vienna: Verlag Hölder-Pichler-Tempsky, 1991).

5. Wolfgang Fritz Haug, "Stellung und Indienstnahme des Asthetischen im Verwertungsprozess des Kapitals" (1969. unpublished). See also "Waren-Asthetik und Kunst" and "Die Rolle des Asthetischen bei der Scheinlösung von Grundwidersprüchen der kapitalistischen Gesellschaft," *Das Argument* 1 (October, 1970) and 3 (June, 1971), respectively.
6. Italo Calvino, *Six Memos for the Next Millennium* (Cambridge, MA: Harvard University Press, 1988).
7. Richard Saul Wurman, *Making the City Observable* (Cambridge, MA: MIT Press, 1971).
8. Gaetano Kanisza, *Grammatica del Vedere* (Bologna: II Mulino, 1980).
9. See, for instance, Sergio Finzi, "Un uomo a striscie epifanie tra memoria e rimozione," *II piccolo Hans* 71 (autumn 1991).
10. Walter Benjamin, *L'opera d'arte nell'epoca delta sua riproducibilità tecnica* (Turin: Einaudi, 1966). In this work, Benjamin writes that the aura of a work of art comes up lacking in the epoch of technological reproductibility. For instance, he writes, "Certain images of the Madonna are kept invisible for almost the whole year" (p. 27) and "A portrait bust is more likely to be displayed, since it can be sent anywhere, than the statue of a god, which has a permanent place inside the temple" (p. 27).
11. The Schlieren apparatus is a very sensitive optical detector that can reveal refractions of a few millionths of a degree. It is used to determine changes in the very small layer of air that comes in contact with the skin and is modified by temperature, breathing, sweating, etc.
12. See Manfredo Massironi, *Vedere con il disegno* (Verona: Franco Muzzio, 1982), 119, *et passim* for the notion of *ipotetigrafia*. This is an area of increasingly promising features in computer graphics. I personally had the good fortune to participate in a research program for the Consiglio Nazionale delle Ricerche (CNR), the committee for mathematical and information sciences, called "Knowledge through Images." See Emilio Albino, Daniele Marini, Laura Moltedo, *Conoscenza per immagini* (Rome: II Rostro, 1989).
13. Umberto Eco, *Trattato di semiotica generate* (Milan: Bompiano, 1975). [American edition: *A Theory of Semiotics* (Bloomington IN: Indiana University, 1976).]
14. Studies of rhetoric in the field of communications virtually began with Roland Barthes, "Rhétorique de l'image," *Communications* 4(7), 1964; Gui Bonsiepe, "Verbal visuelle Rhetorik," *Ulm*, n. 14–16, 1965. Studies on visual rhetoric had begun in 1957 at the Hochschule für Gestaltung in Ulm with Tomás Maldonado. See *Avangardia e razionalitá* (Turin: Einaudi, 1974). See also Groupe M, *Rhétorique générale* (Paris: Larousse, 1979) and *Trois fragments pour une rhétorique de l'image* (Urbino: Centra Internazionale di Semiotica e Linguistica, 1979); René Lindekins, *Semiotica della fotografia* (Naples: il Laboratorio, 1980); Giovanni Anceschi, "Retorica verbo-figurale e registica visiva" in Umberto Eco et al., *Le ragioni della retorica* (Modena: Mucchi, 1986); Robin Kinross, "The Rhetoric of Neutrality" and Hanno E. Eshes, "Representing Macbeth: A Case Study in Visual Rhetoric" in Victor Margolin, ed., *Design Discourse: History, Theory, Criticism* (Chicago: The University of Chicago Press, 1989).
15. See Anceschi, "Retorica verbo-figurale e registica visiva," 1986.
16. See Gianfranco Bettetini's pioneering work, *Produzione di senso e messa in scena* (Milan: Bompiani, 1975). For the relationship *mise-en-page*/*mise-en-scène*, see Paul Fresnault-Deruelle, *Récit et discours par la bande* (Paris: Hachette, 1977), 98.
17. See Giovanni Anceschi, "Choreographia Universalis," in Anceschi's *L'oggetto della raffigurazione* (Milan: Etas Libri, 1992).
18. The term "art" is used in the sense of the ancient Greeks, for whom the *Kybernetes* [pilot] practiced an "art."
19. See *Sequential Design*, 14th ICOGRADA Student Seminar, February 8–9, 1988, London.
20. See "Charter of Graphic Design: Proposal for a Debate on Visual Communication Design," *Design Issues* 8 no. 1 (Fall 1991): 67–73.
21. For the idea of a *disciplinary unified field* of the *ostentative practices*, touching on activities and competencies of visual design and comics, advertising and fashion, illustration and photography, product design and furniture design, exhibition design and window dressing, architectural design and urban planning, see Giovanni Anceschi's "Scena eidomatica e basic design: il campo unificato della presentazione visiva," *Quaderni Dl* n. 8, 1981.

19

SOFTENING UP THE FACTS: ENGINEERS IN DESIGN MEETINGS

Peter Lloyd and Jerry Busby

1 ENGINEERING DESIGN IN THEORY AND PRACTICE

Engineering design is, perhaps, the most consistently complex of design processes – both in terms of the technical problem solving involved and the huge numbers of people having to communicate with each other in the average project. In a recent book describing the design and development of the Ford Taurus, for example, the author estimates 300 people were involved in producing a product with 30,000 parts.[1] It is self-evident, then, that engineering problems require both technical and social expertise. However, perceptions of engineering designers generally tend to simplify their character and role within a social and societal context. Although they often have a fine understanding of technical issues (allied with an uncanny ability to use computers effectively) this reasoning goes, they lack the social skills necessary for "good" communication, and tend to be reactionary or simply dull.

There is, however, a growing body of work recapturing something of the "humanity of engineering design," often by concentrating on the epistemology of practice,[2] but also by studying and documenting the highly specialized ways in which social interaction mediates technical problem-solving processes.[3] By refocusing on these aspects of engineering design *as it is experienced*, an identifiable constructivist approach has begun to emerge (drawing from, for example, the work of Donald Schön and Nelson Goodman[4]). This approach has arisen in opposition to rather Taylorist notions of "engineering design science,"[5] which holds that good engineering design is a result of following a normative set of scientifically determined procedures. Schön terms these notions pejoratively as "technical rationality."[6] They usually are voiced by stressing a way of working over the qualities of the people carrying out the work. The following quote provides an impression of a process "waiting to happen":

> By identifying and quantifying factors that affect critical element positions early in the configuration design stage, a design team is in a better position to specify a configuration that accommodates all the critical relationships necessary for function in a machine.[7]

The unnamed "design team" has only to execute this process correctly. There is a clear indication that the correctness of this method applies independently of the people who find themselves in this design process, and who are then bound either to be passive or to be wrong.[8]

This kind of "scientific" view contrasts very strongly with anyone familiar with the average engineering design meeting. The participants usually are anything but passive, often using a variety of means to get their point of view across. It is in these design meetings that one begins to observe very particular things: the past experiences, intuitions, and preferences of participants; the present subject in relation to the organizational history; the varying relationships between those present; the misunderstandings that occur; and even the surprisingly questionable and ephemeral nature of technical information. Most of all, one notices how these contingencies are expressed, interpreted, and re-expressed through language. One notices how words and phrases can refer to actual things, but also how they construct design opportunities and possible futures. In a previous paper,[9] the mechanism of "storytelling" was described in which individual narratives – often collapsed into a word or phrase – act as touchstones in social exchanges. The point here is that, in a very real sense, designers – engineering or otherwise – spend a great deal of time talking about something that, although slowly coming into existence, doesn't exist.

In a series of conversational vignettes, this paper will attempt to show just how far the process of engineering design is a process dependent on sketching out possible futures in words. It will conclude by suggesting that, if this "verbal sketching" ability indeed is a large part of being an experienced engineering designer, then, perhaps, courses promoting this skill, for example in rhetoric, should be explicitly taught at undergraduate level.

2 THE STUDY OF LANGUAGE IN THE DESIGN PROCESS

Studies of the design process through an analysis of language are becoming increasingly popular.[10] They often center around the idea that every design situation is unique, and that, in design conversations a kind of "world" is constructed with its own references, assumptions, symbol systems, and contributing experiences. With a close reading of these conversations, it has been possible to examine the construction of such a "world" and to identify mechanisms by which language functions in relation to a developing artifact. Elsewhere, cognitive studies have mentioned the idea of a particular "designerly" way of thinking,[11] and studies that focus on language seem to be asking a similar question: "Is there a designerly way of talking?"

David Fleming,[12] examining student/supervisor discussions in a graphic design project, finds a difference between what he terms "object-laden talk" and "language-laden talk." The former locates a design object in a discussion, "performing it" as Fleming refers to it, while the latter assumes the existence of certain design objects and concentrates on exploring their possibilities. This serves to: "position [them] in time, social relations, a system of values, etc.,"[13] and to make them real in some sense, rather that just conjecture. Peter Medway,[14] studying conversations in an architect's office over a two-day period, remarks on similar findings, noting in particular the "textual" nature of an architect's work; the interpretation of many interrelated types of media (drawings, faxes, legal documents, conversations, etc.).

For architects or industrial designers, one particular type of "text" dominates design discussions: the sketch. Sketches provide a common reference point to explore and explain a nascent design. The engineering design process, it might be argued, is a rather different affair. Although one still has the "textuality" of a design process, there would appear to be less visual thinking, less "reading" of sketches. Engineers are more adept at "reading" circuit diagrams, or layout schemes, or picking through software. Engineering design projects, often multidisciplinary in nature, lack the sketch "text" as a common means of expression. This multidisciplinary nature of engineering design is suggested by Bucciarelli to describe what he terms "object worlds" – "worlds of technical specializations; with their own dialects, systems of symbols, metaphors and models, instruments, and craft sensitivities."[15] With many disciplines negotiating during the course of an engineering design conversation, it makes more sense to talk about the existence of a number of discourses being conducted. Bucciarelli describes how the existence of different "object worlds" results in what he terms "constraining," "naming," and "deciding" discourses. It is in these episodes that we can begin to get a sense of language being used for very specific functions, as an essential part of the engineering design process.

3 THE DESIGN OF A TIRE ASSEMBLY MACHINE

It is the aim of this paper to try to relate some of the findings about the use of language in the design process to the present data set, using a discourse analytic method. The present data is constituted by five conversational segments, taken from transcriptions of a series of three engineering design meetings held over a six-week period in April–May 1998. The series of meetings concerned the design of a truck tire assembly machine for clients MB.[16] This is a machine that takes tires and wheel rims, and combines them into a completed wheel. This is the kind of operation that is carried out at "Kwik Fit," for example, but as a continuous process and at much greater speed. The enormous size of truck tires also presents considerable problems. The design project was planned to last from February to September in 1998 and contained a penalty clause. This meant that, if the company was late delivering the product, it would have to pay compensation for lost production to its client. Progress meetings were held every two weeks. The design content of the project was largely mechanical, but with electrical and software elements as well. Six designers were involved in the project, with approximately twenty-five people in total – including sales, manufacture, service, and management. An average of about eight people were present during the meetings that were recorded.

The company at which the meetings were held is called Chi-Tech.[16] It has approximately one hundred employees, and is situated on the outskirts of Birmingham in the United Kingdom. Chi-Tech produces test and assembly equipment mainly for the transportation industry. When a vehicle is being assembled on a production line, this sort of equipment helps to test whether it has been assembled correctly and is functioning properly. The total period of study at Chi-Tech was two months, during which time interviews, observation, the attendance at meetings, and the collection of documentation formed a complete data set.

Since tape-recording was not allowed by the organization during meetings, the transcripts were a combination of quickly taken notes together with the observer's recall, following the meeting, of what was said. Obviously, this means that small parts of the conversation may have been missed, but it is felt that the conversation segments retain much of their original sense and tone. Five segments were selected from the larger transcription of the meetings on the basis of two criteria. The first was coherence; each segment is about something fairly concrete and identifiable as a definite episode in the general flow of conversation. The second was variety; in total twelve segments were analyzed in detail, with the final five being chosen because they allowed a number of different subjects to be covered.

Underlying this approach to the data are two general analytical principles that should be made explicit. The first is that each segment should be a self-contained text with as little as possible reference to the wider context. This automatically ensures that it is the form of the language that is looked at, rather than the specifics of the design problem being solved. The second is that enough "text" should be given to allow alternative interpretations to be made by the reader. It often is the case in analyses of this sort that explanations are given without sufficient text as evidence for the explanation. (And a consequence of taking a discourse analytic approach is that there always are other explanations.) It is felt that enough evidence should be presented to allow (at least in principle) for the possibility of falsification.

4 FIVE SEGMENTS OF ENGINEERING DESIGN CONVERSATION

In the following sections, each conversational segment will be presented and then immediately followed by an interpretation of the exchange. Technical terms will be briefly explained in footnotes. The final discussion looks at the general form of the texts, and describes some of the discursive skills demonstrated by the engineering designers.

4.1 TEXT 1

Mark This weekend we had MB to visit to see about information ... We were successful about putting more pressure in the tire and we didn't damage the rim. We pointed out that, in production, the machine has to be spotlessly clean.

Steven How did you make the point? I mean, we really need to put it in writing.

Nad And also things like that should go into the manual.

Ian We shouldn't give them the idea that we've solved all the problems. Before we start writing letters, we should be sure to point out that it was a test on their machine ...

In Text 1, Mark introduces the subject of a number of "inflation" tests that have been carried out on an existing MB machine, looking at tire pressure in relation to wheel-rim damage. He notes that the tests were "successful" – a positive result. MB has been informed of these results, but with an important caveat: when the new machine is used in production, it has to be "spotlessly clean." Now, most production environments are not "spotlessly clean," so there is a rhetorical sense to the "success" reported to MB. The "success" will give MB confidence about the effectiveness of the continuing design process, but this doesn't guarantee that the machine will work well. For Chi-Tech's purposes Steven, Nad, and Ian are quick to play down the effects of this rhetoric of "success."

Steven asks how the comment of keeping the machine spotlessly clean in production was made, perhaps suspecting only a verbal instruction. He feels that the comment is important enough to be put in writing. Such a move would protect the company from a claim by MB in the event of a breakdown. There is a sense here that Steven doesn't quite trust the "success" that Mark reports; or at least, can see it as rhetoric. Nad adds to Steven's view by mentioning that "things like that should go in the manual." Again, there is a feeling here that problems lie ahead in the use of the machine in a production environment. By including in the manual specific instructions to keep the machine "spotless," Chi-Tech representatives again are covering themselves. By noting that "things like that should go into the manual," Nad's emphasis is, however, on the use of the machine in practice, as opposed to contractual agreements between the organizations. Ian cautions against giving MB the "wrong idea." This is a direct comment about the rhetoric of "success" and he clearly feels that too many unsolved problems exist for such impressions to work in their favor. Giving MB the wrong idea also implies that there is a "right" idea to give, assuming a more complex relationship between the actual process and the customers' perception of that process. Ian also notes that the tests were carried out on "their" (i.e., MB's) machine, preparing the way for the inference that if things do go wrong then it is partly "their" fault.

The specific results of the inflation tests that have been carried out initially are not questioned. Instead, the responses concentrate on either what needs to, should, or shouldn't happen as a consequence of the "successful" tests. Although the three responses are different from one another, they all suggest an understanding of the consequences that reporting such a "success" can bring. It would appear to be experience of similar situations that forms the basis for these imperatives; that is, experience of how one portrays what is happening in the design process to the customer.

There are, then, two things to note in this exchange. First, is the way that rhetoric is used as a continuation of well-defined tests that have been carried out during the course of the design process. Although the tests have yielded positive results – which the customer knows about – the discussion is about how to play down these results in the context of the possible future performance of the machine. The technical and objective results of the tests have been shaded into the wider discourse between design and client. Second is the conception driving this rhetoric, focusing on the differing representations of the design process between customer and manufacturer. The inference is that the manufacturer's representation of the design process is "the truth," while the customer's representation is an impression solely dependent on the information received from the manufacturer. This much is implied in the phrase "we shouldn't give them the idea that we've solved all the problems."

4.2 TEXT 2

Paul This project is going out one month after the TP project went out.[16] I thought we were further ahead at this stage, Mark disagrees, but TP was a repeat job. On this one, we haven't got the advantage of built-in knowledge …

Tony We said at the beginning of this project that we need extra time because of the size of the wheels …

Mark Well, if we work backwards … we've got seven weeks to make all the bits.
[Phil shakes his head.]

Tony We knew all this from the beginning, we sat down with Steven …

John It's very tight.

Tony It's more than very tight! On TP, people were virtually dead on their feet, and this is much heavier …

Ian But the positives are that we haven't got so many individual bits, just the sheer size, and that has got to mean more machining time. We've got to be mindful of the fact that we haven't done it before …

Tony It's going to take longer to put this together than TP just because of the sheer size …

The project is running late. The contract has a penalty clause associated with it, and this means that, if the machine is delivered late then Chi-Tech will have to pay compensation. Text 2 tries to establish how long the remainder of the project will take. Paul starts by saying that the TP project was "further ahead" in comparison.[17] The reason for this is that TP was a "repeat job"; itself a copy of a previous job. The difference with the present project is the lack of "built-in knowledge," the tacit knowledge acquired in the doing of something that speeds up the process of doing the same thing a second time. Paul is making the claim that the two projects cannot be compared in this respect. Tony doesn't contest Paul's reasons. Instead, he points out another reason for the difference: "the size of the wheels" to be fitted with tires. He then goes on to point out yet another difference: the present job is "much heavier" than the previous one, and that had been heavy enough ("people were virtually dead on their feet"). Ian stresses another difference between the two jobs, but it is a positive one. There are fewer components. However the "sheer size" of the components means "more machining time." Ian ends by echoing Paul, stressing that "we haven't done it before …" Tony reiterates Ian's comment about the "sheer size" of the new machine compared with the previous TP job.

Despite all of the reasons for considering the two jobs as different, the past job remains as a reference point in the discussion. The exchange reveals seven conceptions of how the speed of carrying out the present project will differ from the speed of carrying out the past project. Two refer to the lack of tacit knowledge ("we haven't got the advantage of built-in knowledge …," "we haven't done it before"); three mention the size of the new job ("size of the wheels," "sheer size," and "sheer size"); one mentions the weight ("much heavier"); and one mentions the smaller number of individual components ("haven't got so many individual bits"). The evidence suggesting a difference between the two jobs is overwhelming, and there is strong agreement about this between everyone.

Yet the past project, or at least the idea of it, is fulfilling a function here. The common experience – and the level of agreement suggests that it is common experience – is providing a rich means of discussing the present job. However, although there is agreement about the "facts" of the matter, there is not agreement about the suggested outcome. Tony, the manufacturing manager, is using "the facts" to argue for more time than originally was planned for. By using the pronoun plural "we," he is suggesting that the "extra time" he thinks is necessary for manufacture was agreed on at the start of the project. Others in Text 2, although acknowledging the truth of the facts, interpret them slightly differently. John simply says "it's very tight," suggesting that, although it will be difficult, the manufacturing department has enough time to complete the task. Tony has to persuade the others by attempting to exaggerate their common experience ("the facts"). He mentions that people were "virtually dead on their feet," and refers to the "sheer size" of the present project, both statements giving the impression of the present project's impossibility. In the exchange, what is of note is the agreement about certain "facts" and the corresponding differences in interpretation.

4.3 TEXT 3

Nad We need to move forward …

Mike It's only the circumstances of the drive that is holding me up …

Mark So how long before you start detailing and how long will it take?

Mike Eight weeks …

Mark Two weeks less then, on a heave?

Nad There will be a three-week slippage is my guess, based on experience …

Mark We need a month at the end of the job to get the thing working …

Nad We've got to bring that forward; we can't let it slip by three weeks: poor old Mr. Tarling is going to be testing the machine on the ship over to Germany!

Mark Well, we know what happened at TP, we were out there for weeks and weeks …

Mike Hopefully, it won't become a bottleneck, but it's happened on every job I've done …

In Text 3, Nad starts with the general feeling that project work "needs" to go further towards the final goal. Mike, being questioned as to how long it will take him to complete a set of concept drawings, answers that it is only external circumstances that are holding him up. Mark then asks Mike how long it will take him to start work on the detailed drawings. Mike is emphatic: "eight weeks." Mark, perhaps wanting a smaller figure and thinking that Mike's estimate has allowed for a large degree of error, suggests that, if he concentrated his efforts, the concept work might be completed sooner. Nad switches the focus to the work plan, commenting that there will be a "three-week slippage" – that the project will take three weeks longer than expected – given his experience with similar situations. Mark points out that a month will be needed "at the end of the job" – which means after the machine has been constructed – before it will be fully functioning.

A few seconds later Nad picks up on his thread again, possibly after having considered the consequences of what his experience tells him. He says that the project cannot afford to slip by three weeks, because that will leave very little time for testing. To support this view he provides a vivid image of the machine being tested on the ship on the way to Germany. Mark reinforces Nad's comment from his own experience ("at TP, we were out there for weeks and weeks") using "we," as Tony did in Text 2, to draw in the others present and appeal to some sort of common knowledge or experience. Mike brings the discussion back to the amount of time it will actually take to finish the concept drawings. He hopes that the delay will not prove to be a problem, but thinks that it might be if his experience is anything to go by.

Although the conversation is ostensibly about the time it is taking to finish the concept drawings, it turns into a conversation about the time it will take to finish the project as a whole, a subtle difference. Contrasts are made between planned time, desired time, actual time, and past time. There is the desire to "move forward" past problems that are "holding up" the project; to get through a "bottleneck." Then there is the estimation of how long it will take for the concept drawings to be finished. "Eight weeks" is the estimation, reduced to six on the assumption that what can be done in eight weeks at a certain pace can be done in six at a quicker pace. There might be a "three-week slippage," which has implications for the "month" needed to get the machine working at the end of the project. In previous projects, this task had taken weeks.

The impression given here is one of a malleable time. There is an original project plan, certainly, and a delivery date has been agreed by the customer; but within these "real" constraints, time is being managed and bargained for. Delays are explained as "bottlenecks," and time can be made up by "heaving." There is a feeling of elasticity, with negotiations between different perceptions of timescales in relation to certain tasks. Finally, there are intuitive feelings for how the time will go, accumulated, we might infer, from similar experiences on other projects (and different experiences on similar projects).

At the end of the exchange, it remains uncertain what has actually been decided. The plan appears to have remained the same. What then could be the purpose of such a discussion? There seems a deep relationship between time and experience in the exchange, encapsulated in personal heuristics ("eight weeks can be reduced to six on a heave," "a month is always needed for testing," or "concept drawings are always a problem"). The only way that time can be talked about is either in relation to the past, or in relation to an intuitive feeling about the present situation with respect to the project plan. Time here is not an absolute quantity, but a thing packaged with a particular task, past, or present. What happens in the exchange is that a number of possible scenarios are described. It would seem that the different scenarios illustrate to all present the sense of urgency that is needed. This is achieved not through any sense of control, but through a common understanding arrived at through different perceptions of possible outcomes. Some of these outcomes are baldly stated ("eight weeks"), while others are more creatively put ("poor old Mr. Tarling is going to be testing the machine on the ship"), but all give a sense of what possibilities lie ahead and it is also arguable that this also works to share responsibility between those present.

4.4 TEXT 4

John Basically we've got a chain conveyor on the walking loom.[18] It's going to be in the attention to detail …

Nad Is that sufficient for a 15-second cycle time?[19]

Brian I have my doubts about fitting it all in.

John We've got it down to 4.2 seconds on a small machine.[20]

Mark And the total machine time is 28 seconds.

John To get the time down, we've been looking at the rim grips; we used to use sixties technology to get the fitting head[21] to come down to find the rim, so it's got to come down slowly to sense the rim. With a servo motor, you can come down quickly.

Nad It's important to remember that, in everything we do, we don't forget the cycle time …

John Terry agrees that the fitting time is very tight. I personally can't see why you can't fit at increasing speeds …

Brian In theory I agree with you but, at increasing speeds, you might spin on the rim and leave the tire behind …

Text 4 is about the solution that has been used to converge on a key performance criterion: the cycle time. Initially, John describes the basic technology of the new machine ("a chain conveyor on the walking loom") suggesting that it simply needs refining to meet the key performance criteria: "it's in the attention to detail …" Nad questions whether this solution will meet the performance criteria, while Brian expresses stronger reservations ("I have my doubts about fitting it all in"). John replies by saying that the level of performance required has been reached on a previous, smaller machine which, together with the assumption that the big machine will behave in the same way as the small machine, suggests that the level of performance required can be reached. John then goes into more detail about specific refinements that have been made to the original level of technology, backing up his earlier "attention to detail" comment. He suggests that a servo motor will solve the problem. A little later, he reveals a slight difference in opinion about the proposed solution between himself and Terry (who is not present). John reiterates that he can see no problem fitting the tire at increasing speeds, while Terry obviously has told John how "tight" he thinks the tire fitting will be. Brian takes Terry's line and explains why the machine might not work at increasing speeds: "you might spin on the wheel."

Will the proposed solution work? No one says that it won't work, yet reservations are expressed about whether it will meet the "tight" performance criteria. The proposed solution is a refined and scaled-up version of solutions that have been used on previous projects. John sees no problem with this scaling up. Terry and Brian, however, are not so confident. During the exchange, John constructs a verbal "model" of this solution. All are agreed on this model – no one is directly disputing the solution principles – yet the consequences of this model, and the issue of whether or not it will meet the performance criteria, are the subject of a difference of opinion. The construction of this "verbal model" is possible only because of the familiarity everyone present has with both previous designs and the relevant technological principles, a common knowledge existing among those present. Out of these basic "materials," John is able to construct, in a few short utterances, a model of his proposed solution. He creates a common "object" for analysis.

Such a situation might seem highly specific. The design is at a very particular stage of development, and it is unlikely that it would be questioned in any fundamental sense. It could be argued that other participants may be keeping quiet about criticisms they may have. Yet the "method" of drawing on common experience to "sketch" a solution appears to be a familiar one. A way of quickly exploring a number of implications and consequences should a certain solution be adopted. There is a kind of tacit acceptance here, a suspension of disbelief among those conversing. There also is a sense in which the participants are "using" this "object," and commenting on its functioning. The key point is that the created conversational "object" is only a vehicle to explore decisions that have to be made. It is a hypothesis that will help to determine key indicators of success or failure.

4.5 TEXT 5

John Well, on the limit switches[22] MB was surprised that we suggested proximity switches. I said that they're standard at Chi-Tech. MB said proximity switches are expensive compared with reed switches, but I don't really mind …

Brian We've found reeds to be unreliable in the past …

David We changed a few on Tudor[23] because there were failures …

Brian They come loose and fall off, but there are applications where they can be used …

Ian My guiding principle has always been, where the machine is concerned, not to use proximity switches …

Mark Ninety percent at MB are reed switches, but they're not Festo ones.

Ian Festo[24] are cheap and cheerful.

John introduces the topic of limit switches in Text 5. He mentions that MB was surprised about the choice of limit switch ("proximity switches") because they thought that they were more expensive than reed switches. Although the "standard at Chi-Tech" is the proximity switch, he ends rather neutrally by saying that he doesn't really mind what they use. There then follows a series of comments about the performance and application of reed switches, as compared to proximity switches. Brain says he has found them "unreliable," David says that on a previous project, they failed. Brian remarks on the way that they usually fail: "they come loose and fall off," but also adds that there are some things which they can be used for. Ian mentions that his "guiding principle" is "not to use proximity switches where the machine is concerned." This puts an emphasis on not using one thing (proximity switches), rather than positively using another (reed switches). We then get the fact that ninety percent of the switches at MB are reed switches though, perhaps significantly, not Festo reed switches. Ian underlines the significance of this remark by stressing that Festo reed switches are "cheap and cheerful."

There is a basic taxonomy of types and instances in the conversation. First of all, there are the types of limit switch: proximity switches and reed switches. Then there is an instance of a type of reed switch: "Festo reed switches." The conversation circles around evaluations, opinions, and experiences of different types of detection mechanisms and products. Everyone (including MB) seems agreed that a decision has to be made between reed switches and proximity switches. To aid this decision-making process, the outstanding attributes of each switch are offered. Reeds are "unreliable," they have failed in the past, they "come loose and fall off," they "can be used" in some applications, and "ninety percent of switches at MB are reed switches." Proximity switches are: "expensive," they are "standard at Chi-Tech," there are intuitions – "guiding principles" – against using them, or in a similar vein, "surprise" at using them. Then there are the particular attributes of Festo reed switches. They are not used at MB, and they are "cheap and cheerful."

Text 5 is somewhat ironic in that it is concerned with deconstructing the capacities of existing technology in the process of constructing the capacities of new technology (i.e., the tire assembly machine). Such a discussion implies that the capacities of the new technology rely to some degree on associations with the perceived capacities of its components. "Cheap and cheerful" components might then result in the final product being perceived as "cheap and cheerful." The irony is that, in discussing a component's capacities, the people present are denying the possibility of that component having actual or objective capacities while simultaneously attempting to construct the actual or objective capacities of their own product. The decision to use a certain component, then, is a complicated act of judgment. There are objective elements involved, certainly: sizes, materials, and also functions; but there also is a large degree of personal (and hence in a group situation aggregated personal) preference. These preferences are formed through both particular experiences ("they come loose and fall off") as well as more nebulous "guiding principle." There is a case for considering these preferences as aesthetic judgments.

It is of note that the inquiry into the suitability of limit switches was triggered by the "surprise" of MB. This surprise has caused an explicit examination of the reasons for the preference of a particular component; preferences that would, we might assume, have remained unquestioned otherwise.

5 DISCUSSION AND CONCLUDING REMARKS

It is self-evident that the five conversational segments took place over a bedrock of common assumptions and experiences. This clearly enables the participants to forego lengthy explanations, and to talk quickly about the current situation. Common assumptions concentrate more on the technical properties of the design – often, in the text, it was clear that a particular way of solving the problem was not questioned – while common experiences focus more on the past as a means of exploring the present situation. This illustrates how much the current design process depends on the past experiences of those present, which also shows just how unique a situation it actually is. In all five texts, we have noted how past experiences have acted as touchstones during the course of the meeting. In effect, this situates the present design within a web of connections with past designs. In Text 2, for example, Tony remembers that: "on TP, people were virtually dead on their feet" while, in Text 3, Mike recalls: "it's happened on every job I've done." To those present, such touchstones are, in many ways, an objective reference for the situation in hand. That is to say, they are "objects," perhaps "discursive objects" might be a better phrase for interpretation and analysis. Fleming[12] notes two kinds of discourse in the design process. He observes: "object-laden" talk – situating objects within a discursive context; and "language-laden" talk – explaining the consequences of certain objects being the case. It is notable that, in this professional design situation, the talk seemed heavily biased toward the language-laden end of the spectrum.

Common assumptions and experiences ensure a large level of agreement but, in every text, there always was some level of disagreement. That is almost a prerequisite for a "discussion" taking place. This disagreement often was not, as one might have imagined in an engineering design context, over technical matters, but about the *consequences* of certain "facts" being the case. In Text 1, the discussion was about how to represent the ongoing design process to the client; and in Text 4, about how a certain solution would perform. In these discussions, the design engineers displayed a certain intuitive artfulness; their technical skill as designers playing second fiddle to their ability to make a convincing interpretation of the situation.

Such an ability is not one that usually is associated with engineering designers, and perhaps not even an ability they themselves are explicitly aware of. It is, nevertheless, an important ability as these texts show. The skill in constructing an effective argument from a few well-chosen words and references is one more akin to a politician than to an engineer. This is an important point. In the texts, the designers used several mechanisms to get their version of the consequences of a situation accepted by the meeting. One mechanism is the use of exaggeration and imagery. In Text 2, Tony mentions that, in the past project, similar to the current project, people were "virtually dead on their feet." In Text 3, Nad remarks on the limited time available by suggesting that the "poor old" test engineer "will be testing the machine on the boat on the way over to Germany." Both are effectively illustrating serious points. Another mechanism was the suggestive use of the pronoun plural "we." In Text 2, Tony states "we knew all this from the beginning" and, in Text 1, Mark remarks "we were successful." Both are trying to imply a *common* agreement about what has happened, in effect sustaining their "argument" for as long as possible. There also is an implied objectivity about past experience, something that is extremely difficult to refute directly. In Text 5, Ian cites his "guiding principle" as a reason for not using a certain component while Brian has found that certain components "come loose and fall off" In Text 3, Mike mentions that something has "happened on every job I've done." Such remarks have an important rhetorical function in putting an argument across to the others.

If all of these mechanisms add up to a kind of "rhetorical ability" of engineers in the current study, then there is one more distinct ability to note. That is the critical ability; the ability to recognize, analyze, interpret, and aesthetically judge an object. Such an ability was demonstrated in Text 5, in which the technological capacities of sensing equipment were constructed, together with the associations of meaning they held for the meeting. It is here that one gets the feeling that many decisions are made just as much on aesthetic grounds as on purely objective or technical grounds. Aesthetic is used here to refer to an individual expression of preference rather than anything solely visual in nature. This is a surprise given the supposed "objective" nature of engineering design (as illustrated by the quote at the beginning of the article[7]).

In design disciplines apart from engineering, graphical representations play a much larger "modeling" role in design discussions. In architecture, graphic design, or industrial design, a design is sketched, drawn, and modeled in a series of "physical" ways of expression. For these disciplines, it is easy to see how these physical objects can be "performed" in Fleming's terminology:[12] by pointing, gesture, and explanation. Once they have been accepted as valid objects for discourse, the consequences that derive from a performance then can be drawn out. It would seem as though engineering designers are achieving exactly this result, but by using words instead of graphical representations. That is to say that engineers use words to model and explore consequences. The words provide a sort of collective sketching function that is not possible in a graphical representation, simply because of the nature of the task. These words, these very particular words, can remain ambiguous while still suggesting possibilities – just as a quick sketch from an industrial designer might suggest a number of possible forms and hence, implications. And, just as industrial designers have a common sketching vocabulary, the engineer's words only properly function on a basis of common knowledge and experience. In other words, they provide a first level of prototyping.

Could it be that this kind of conversational function is found not only in engineering design and design in general, but also in other areas of professional practice? One of the essential aspects of design that we mentioned at the beginning was that design conversations are conversations about things that don't yet exist. It may well be that there are a number of possible parallels with other conversations concerning, for example, the future, or a future state of affairs. Schön[25] argues that design-like behavior forms a problem-solving prototype for much professional action, while Cross[11] has suggested that designing (and, we might infer, design talking) meets criteria to consider it as a separate kind of intelligence. This paper, however, has attempted to show how advanced this kind of talking is for engineering designers. This, we have proposed, might be because of the largely non-graphical nature of the task environment. It would appear that the typical analytical ability of the engineer – an ability that seems to be predicated on the idea of an individual "object world"[15] – also brings with it a skill in using and manipulating language – a strongly social ability.

There are educational implications here. If such a skill is something that experienced design engineers can perform without training, then explicitly nurturing that skill in students with a low level of experience might be worthwhile. The texts presented in this paper would point to both education in rhetoric and aesthetics as important areas of curriculum development in engineering design. It is highly likely that this knowledge could help engineers to become aware of the varying types of reasons, information, and experiences that design decisions are based on, and help to dispel the myth that all engineering information is somehow scientifically based.

ACKNOWLEDGMENTS

Funding for the work reported here came from a UK Engineering and Physical Science Research Council Grant (GR/L 40229). The authors would like to thank Chi-Tech for participating in the research.

NOTES

First published in *Design Issues* 17 no. 3 (Summer 2001): 67–82.

1. M. Walton, *Car: A Drama of the American Workplace* (New York: W.W. Norton & Company, 1997).
2. S. Florman, *The Existential Pleasures of Engineering Design* (2nd Edition) (New York: St. Martin's Press, 1996); E.S. Ferguson, *Engineering and the Mind's Eye* (Cambridge, MA: MIT Press, 1993); J.E. Holt, "The Designer's Judgment," *Design Studies* 18 (1997): 113–123; D.A. Schön, "Designing: Rules, Types, and Worlds," *Design Studies* 9 (1988): 181–190; W.G. Vincenti, *What Engineers Know and How They Know It: Analytical Studies From Aeronautical History* (Baltimore: Johns Hopkins University Press, 1990).
3. L.L. Bucciarelli, "An Ethnographic Perspective on Engineering Design," *Design Studies* 9 (1988): 159–168; L.L. Bucciarelli, *Designing Engineers* (Cambridge, MA: MIT Press, 1994); K. Grint and S. Woolgar, *The Machine at Work: Technology, Work, and Organization* (Cambridge, UK: Polity Press, 1997); T. Kidder, *The Soul of a New Machine* (Harmondsworth, UK: Penguin, 1981); S.L. Minneman, *The Social Construction of a Technical Reality: Empirical Studies of Group Engineering Design Practice* (Ph.D. thesis, Stanford University, 1991); and M. Walton, *Car: A Drama of the American Workplace.*
4. D.A. Schön, *The Reflective Practitioner* (London: Temple Smith, 1983); and N. Goodman, "Words, Works, Worlds" in *Ways of Worldmaking* (Indianapolis: Hackett Publishing Co., 1978), 17–29.
5. V. Hubka and W. Ernst Eder, "A Scientific Approach to Engineering Design," *Design Studies* 8 (1987): 123–137; and G. Pahland and W. Beitz, *Engineering Design* (London: The Design Council, 1984), 6.
6. D.A. Schön, *The Reflective Practitioner*, 21–69.
7. K. Harrison and C.C. Wilson, "Evaluating Configuration Complexity in Machines," *Journal of Engineering Design* 8 (1997): 165–174.
8. Larry Bucciarelli in *Design Engineers* describes a similar episode (152–159). At the beginning of a design meeting, a "performance specification" is set and those present try to choose between alternative design solutions as the method prescribes. However, no one can agree on just what constitutes a "performance specification." Bucciarelli comments that, although those present at the meeting felt it was a disaster, the conversation that occurred actually was useful. It helped to develop "shared meanings" and begin to construct the discursive "objects of design."
9. P. Lloyd, "Storytelling and the Development of Discourse in the Engineering Design Process," *Design Studies* (2000): 367–73.

10. L.L. Bucciarelli, *Design Engineers*, and D. Fleming, "Design Talk: Constructing the Object in Studio Conversations," *Design Issues* 14 (1998): 41–62; P. Lloyd, "Storytelling and the Development of Discourse in the Engineering Design Process"; and P. Medway, "Building With Words: Discourse in an Architect's Office" in *Carleton Papers in Applied Language Studies* (Vol. IX) (Ottawa: Carleton University, 1992), 1–32.
11. N. Cross, "Discovering Design Ability" in *Discovering Design: Explorations in Design Studies*, R. Buchanan and V. Margolin, eds. (Chicago: University of Chicago Press, 1995). Cross builds on the work of Howard Gardner which critiques the notion of a single human intelligence, instead suggesting a number of intelligences. Cross suggests the existence of a particular design intelligence.
12. Fleming, "Design Talk: Constructing the Object in Studio Conversations," 46.
13. Fleming, "Design Talk: Constructing the Object in Studio Conversations," 46.
14. Medway, "Building With Words: Discourse in an Architect's Office," 22–3.
15. Bucciarelli, *Design Engineers*, 62–64, and Bucciarelli, "An Ethnographic Perspective on Engineering Design," 162–163.
16. The names of organizations have been changed to ensure confidentiality.
17. The present machine is the same type of machine as the "TP project." They are both tire-assembly machines; however, the TP project was for car tires, which are much smaller than truck tires.
18. The chain conveyor and walking loom are a mechanical technology that allows a sequence of operations to be carried out through the tire-assembly machine. Wheels are metaphorically walked through the machine.
19. There are three times that figure in the dialogue. "Cycle time" is the rate at which the machine produces assembled wheels and tires. "Total machine time" is the time it takes a separate wheel and tire to become an assembled wheel and tire. "Fitting time" is a proportion of the total machine time, and is the time taken to complete the sub-task of fitting the tire to the rim.
20. The "small machine" refers to the previous TP project, which assembled car tires.
21. The "fitting head" is the part of the machine that fits the tires to the wheel rims. This is a piece of equipment that descends to complete the operation once a wheel rim is in place beneath it. It completes the operation by turning the rim so that the tire gradually works its way onto the rim.
22. Limit switches are a way of detecting whether a moving component has reached its intended destination. There are various ways to do this, but two well-known methods are: proximity switches which detect by magnetic induction, and reed switches, which detect by physical contact.
23. Tudor is another previous project.
24. Festo is a manufacturer of reed switches.
25. D.A. Schön, The Reflective Practitioner, 77.

20

FOURTH-ORDER DESIGN: A PRACTICAL PERSPECTIVE

Tony Golsby-Smith

The essence of design is the nature of thinking it entails. It is integrative, rather than merely analytical; visual rather than merely abstract; and humanistic rather than mechanistic. It is fundamentally about invention, not research. It begins with love and passion, rather than mere problems and puzzles. In the end, design is intuitive and irreducible to component steps, but still tantalizingly capable of description.

All people taste it; a few excel in it. This design thinking, rather than just the practice and products of design, will become increasingly intriguing and attractive to a wider audience than that which currently uses the services of the design industry. The design industry specifically is focused on very narrow portions of organizations, and on a narrow set of organizations. There are many organizations which have no idea what a "designer" offers, and have never used one; but for whom design thinking is looming as a coming dawn.

The so-called fourth order of design is taking design out of its narrow, original boundaries, and preparing it for wider application. In this essay, I intend to investigate the nature and the tendencies of this fourth order of design. My vantage point will be practical rather than theoretical.

THE ORIGINS OF DESIGN IN THE FIRST AND SECOND ORDERS

Richard Buchanan has described the changing places of design practice and thinking as moving through four orders of theory and practice.[1] While he presents the four orders as places of invention and discovery in design thinking, I would like to explore these places with regard to a widening *domain* for design (Figure 20.1). The widening "domain" is a widening of the influence of design outwards into the surrounding medium – the life of organizations in the modern world, or of governments and communities. This is a good typology of what happens as designers seek to exert wider and more energetic influence on the lives of organizations and communities.

This widening of domain could well be experienced quite practically in the work life of an individual designer who begins offering discrete skills but, as confidence and experience grow, and as he or she identifies wider needs, expands his or her range of offered services. Without knowing it, they could well be tracking through just the transitions that Buchanan describes.

The first domain is the "word or symbol" of graphic design: crafting bits of paper to elegantly

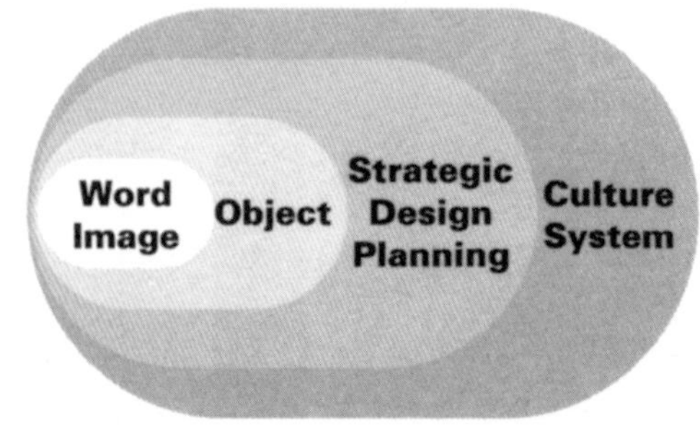

Figure 20.1.

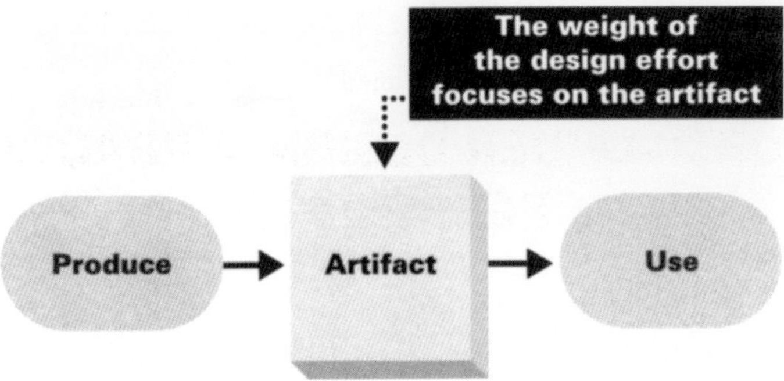

Figure 20.2.

represent some of the ways the technological community sees itself through brochures, pamphlets, icons, and manuals such as "Help us navigate our way through the zoo" or "Create a marketing symbol."

The second domain is the "object" of industrial design, which crafts *things* rather than words or images. These are elegant, functional and marketable things.

The graphic above (Figure 20.2) illustrates the point at which design adds value to a transaction. In domains one and two, the designer adds value to the artifact, itself. The weight of the design effort is to improve the shape of the product, and its fit with the world. It seeks to give better **expression** to the product concept. In the case of document design, for instance, this will mean, *inter alia*; adding elegance to the layout, clarity to the language, and balance to the distribution of the content within the document.

The designer assumes that the product boundaries (i.e., the concept and content) are stable and defined. The *form* of the product is, as yet, unstable and undefined. In these first and second domains, the concept of design is a proxy for "*shape*" or "*form*" – the value offered is, "You give me a product concept and I will 'shape' (i.e., design) it for you – it will be a better-*shaped* set of words, or a better-*shaped* object, as a result of my crafting it."

As for the *place* of work, the designer works within the scope of the artifact, chiseling and finessing it. A graphic designer will see his or her space of work as within the page – interacting with the text and the typography as a thing, with a sense that the designer's sphere of interest and of influence is in the thing. They will have passion for and opinions on the thing, itself; often expressing purist technical views ("this typeface never works as a heading"), and being dogmatic about them. This is proper, given the above model of their conception of how they add value. "Better" means better, according to technical and aesthetic criteria that the designer is privy to as a skilled artisan. They are hired for that technical expertise, and that is the boundary within which they are pleased to work.

This sense of place is exemplified by the work pattern of the centralized design studio, where everyone has neatly defined work stations; and where the account executive brings the jobs in and the design studio does the work according to those specifications.

THE MOVE TO THE THIRD ORDER

Both "words" and "things" live at the interface of two communities – a producer and its public. They function in a place of natural tension. Hence, they mediate the relationship between the two communities (Figure 20.3).

The upshot of this mediating tension is that there are natural magnets at work which will pull the designer's interest outside the scope of the artifact; for mediation cannot remain in an inert,

Figure 20.3.

static position. Therefore, the designer's interests and competencies are pulled out beyond the object to the interests and needs of the two communities (Figure 20.4).

Thus, the enlightened industrial designer researches the market and its needs, the producing company and its processes of manufacture, as well as its market aspirations. The designer is unwittingly undergoing a metamorphosis, since the interfacial role is shaping a wider set of competencies. To produce a fine object, the designer must go outside his or her craft (though not abandoning it); and manage *processes*, not just *products*.

These processes particularly are those of *strategic decision-making* leading to the product choice. This is quite a natural transition because things do not exist in a vacuum – they are *created* and *used*. They ride on the wave of processes and activities. Thus, it is only to be expected that some designers will wish to influence these wider process-related issues around the products they design (Figure 20.5).

In the case of document design, a third-order designer will move outside the document boundaries to the readers who will process the document: the designer will analyze readability, and take this into account in the document design.

But not only are documents read, they often are intended (however dimly) to be the source of action. The designer now sees the document not as dead information, but as the catalyst to reduce uncertainty in human activity. For instance, an investment policy document can be assessed for *readability*, but it also can be analyzed for *useability*. What behaviors does it seem to encourage; and what behaviors would we like it to encourage? (Figure 20.6).

The thinking process on the producer's side is a different matter. It is the process of actually determining the *content* of the product, rather than its use in the world. For instance, in the realm of documents, what are the processes by which ideas and data are generated, decided upon, and then included as content in the product? The third-domain designer will move explicitly into this area of the thinking process of composition, and will offer expertise in the planning of the document.

This expertise could include the skill to interview or to facilitate discussions from which product decisions are made.

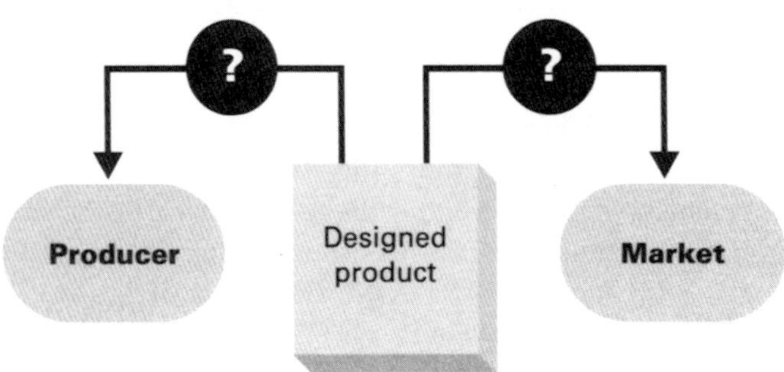

Figure 20.4.

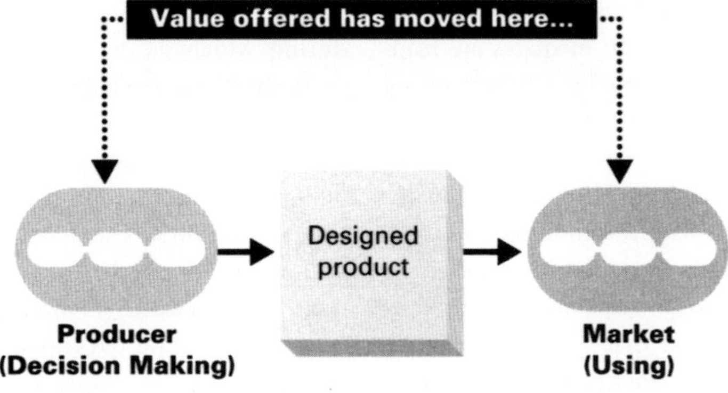

Figure 20.5.

CASE STUDY

The competencies of the third-order designer are well exemplified in a major project we are undertaking with the Australian Tax Office and the Australian Office of Parliamentary Counsel. Both these organizations are undertaking the largest project of legislative design ever attempted in Australia, and quite probably in the Western world – the rewriting of the Australian Income Tax Act. The Act is one of the largest in the world, comprising well over a million words, much of which is close to incomprehensible; and the structure of which is long buried under the barnacles of successive revisions, amendments and additions to the law. The project leader has aptly described the task as a kind of "urban renewal."

Second-order skills for this task would include skills of plain language, layout and document design. We have broadened the range of appropriate second-order skills by the explicit use of *schemata* and *models* to express aspects of the content. We believe that information is better considered as a two- or even three-dimensional space and, as such, is better characterized as models than merely as words. Words operate physically in a linear plane, but models operate in a two- or three-dimensional plane. As such, they are more able to represent subtleties of structure than words alone.

Hence, we view the act as an "information city," and the team's design efforts as a kind of "information architecture."

Since cities are made for people to live and move in, this realization paves the way for the

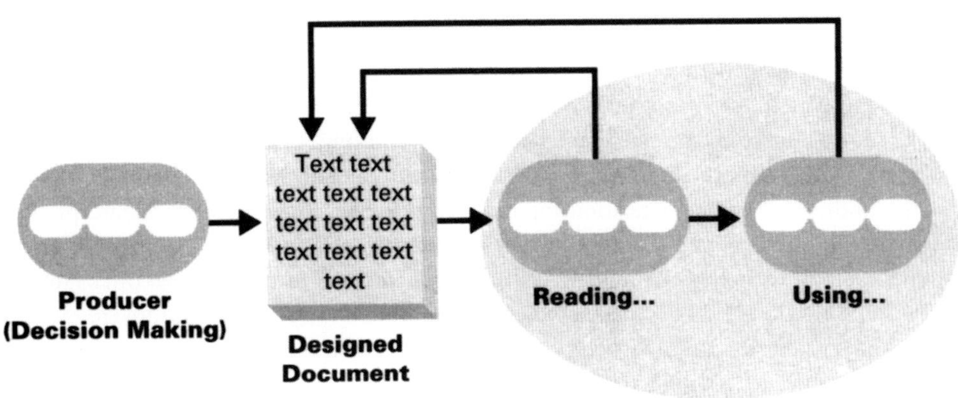

Figure 20.6.

move to the third order of design. The processes which a legislation document mediates are reading and writing. Most people have little sense of writing as a process, and are instinctively bound to the concreteness of the text as a "thing." This attitude makes the writing process very inefficient, because people have few tools to help them through the thinking and planning processes which will create the finished document. They also do not have a sense that they will *decide* to finish the document – rather people tend to harbor the notion that a document "preexists," and that the writing task is a matter of uncovering that preexistent document. They view the task of writing as the transfer of a defined body of content.

These unsophisticated views of the writing process are troublesome enough when one writes as an individual; but when the writing process is organization-wide, they become quite debilitating. Having little sense of process means that the status of a draft as a useful "in-process" tool simply is not appreciated; people insist on commenting on a draft as if it were a finished product. Whereas, in fact, the draft is often merely a useful externalization of early thoughts. Thus, commentary on drafts often is too sweeping and pedantic.

We reposition the writing task as a "product development" exercise. Thus, drafts can be viewed more like early prototypes than predictions of the finished product.

To reinforce this appreciation of process in the Tax Law Improvement Project, we introduced readability evaluations – not as final "inspection" testing, but as a key part of the conceptual design phase. Once the content[2] became stabilized, we generated several design devices to help communicate some of the more difficult concepts of the law. For instance, we used schemata and models, as mentioned above, to capture the relationship of the major sections of the bill, and also to model the four methods of deduction allowable in this section of the law. These graphic devices were quite revolutionary to use in such a formal context as the law; normally there would be quite some hesitancy to use such devices. But we framed their use as merely part of a conceptual design phase during which we were developing options. As such, they were reversible; this freed people to experiment with more vigor. They were assured that the evaluation would pick up devices that were failing, so we could afford to be adventurous. In fact, testing often encourages more adventurous options because designers become curious to see if options will actually work.

We then submitted the options to readability testing, using the "think aloud protocol" method.[3] The think aloud method was developed by cognitive psychologists to observe the process of comprehension as it happened clear of the filtering and forgetting that mars other measurements of comprehension. The results of the readability evaluation were then fed back into the final choices which were to be made about the document. One of the key findings of the evaluation was that the use of schemata was universally successful with the readers – including the sophisticated specialist whom we feared would treat them as condescending.

The exact nature of the think aloud method and the document design devices is not my key point here, though; the key point is that the client began to realize that this task was indeed a development process, and, as such, it could be separated into component processes that fed into each other. Thus, the process could be managed and guided with more precision than they had realized up to this point (Figure 20.7).

This emphasis on process is a hallmark of third-order thinking. Process is not a concept that people in organizations readily understand: they are more comfortable with structures and outputs. But the TQM movement and its later developments, such as Business Process Reengineering, have lifted the profile of the concept of process significantly, albeit their approach is rather a mechanistic and quantitative one. However, the processes that the TQM movement addresses are invariably very much more tangible that the writing process that I have been discussing. This makes the challenge of getting clients to realize the

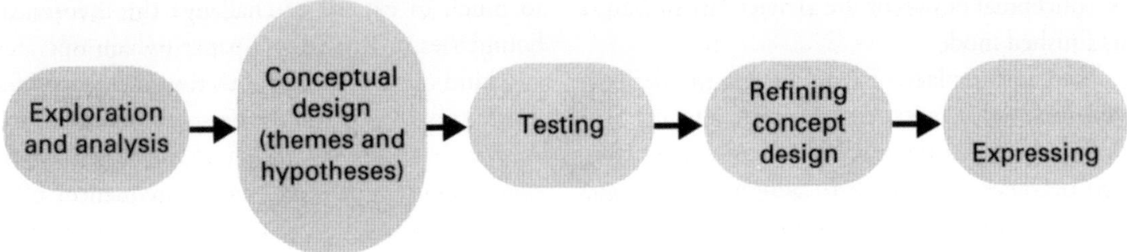

Figure 20.7.

process nature of the writing task doubly difficult. The point about this difficulty is that document designers and writers who aspire to work in the third order must develop a strong sense of what the writing process consists of; and they must be able to articulate that confidently to a client, and then adapt that process understanding to a client's context. This is where the study of rhetoric is potentially so powerful. Ancient though it is, the art of rhetoric is the writing art. The work to be done is to adapt it to modern organizational needs; to translate it into terms and concepts that are readily accessible to businesses and organizations.

TWO MODES OF SERVICE IN THE THIRD ORDER

In my experience, there are two main methods of working which occur in the third order of design. The first is when the designer intervenes in the decision-making process directly; the second is when the designer intervenes indirectly. The first occurs when the product is a one-off product – in the case of document design this could be a significant policy document, manual, or brochure. The point is that the product is produced once only, and the real need of the client is that this product really works. Hence, the focus is on the artifact, itself. The second occurs when the product is not one-time only, but is produced regularly – so the client does not want the designer perpetually designing all the products. They want the designer to demonstrate the product as a prototype, and then to describe the process in a way that makes it transferable to the client organization. The legislation project is of this latter kind. The client does not want us to write the entire law for them – it is too large, and the task is a perennial one since amendments come in every year. Therefore the value to be delivered in this third-order domain is ongoing capability to handle the designing process.

The second of these services (transfer of skills) will tend to the fourth order of design, because it begins to involve issues of people and cultural change quite explicitly.

The above case illustrates, in practical terms, the evolution of design services. It serves to show how wider in scope the third order of design is than the second order; but also how one does not obviate the other. The skills of the second order are just as relevant to underpin and give credibility to the skills of the third order. Nonetheless, they are quite discrete, and one could certainly offer one without the other to a client.

THIRD ORDER WIDENS ACCOUNTABILITY OF THE DESIGNER

In the third order, the designer decides that the client will benefit from an earlier intervention of design thinking, at a more strategic and crucial time. The value proposed by the designer becomes: "You will make a better product decision as a result of my leading you through the process of design."

The outcome of this intervention will still be in the artifact, but more properly in the specifications or conceptual design of the artifact rather than in its finished mode.

And so the place of working for the designer will shift, both metaphorically and literally. The designer now works much more with the client, and becomes *accountable* to design and manages the process of decision-making that will create the specifications. I use the word "accountable" deliberately. Everyone can have opinions on wider issues; it is a different matter to be accountable for them. If the designer is to claim accountability for managing process, he or she must formally propose that service. Too often, designers find themselves wandering into process management without formal recognition of their role: this means that the designer often is under-compensated and underappreciated.

Thus, the designer must have a sense of where to draw the new boundaries, or the client could expect more than the designer wishes to deliver. Similarly, the designer must have a strong sense of the competencies and experience necessary to deliver value in the third-order domain of process leadership.

It is important to note that, although the third-order designers have widened their accountability, they have not usurped the accountability for actually making the product decision. Should they do so, they would, in fact, become the client. They influence this decision, can provide options for it, can facilitate the process of getting to a decision; but, in the final analysis, the decision must be made by the client. Both client and designer must be clearly aware of this division of responsibilities.

FOURTH-ORDER DESIGN – CULTURE, SYSTEM AND INTEGRATION

What then of Buchanan's fourth order: Culture, system and integration?

Buchanan has set the context for this discussion of the fourth order in his paper, "Branzi's Dilemma."[4] My addition to this discussion is not so much to extend or challenge the theoretical boundaries of Buchanan's paper (which operates as a kind of hypothesis about the emergence of a fourth order) as to add the perspective of practical experience to the discussion of the fourth order, and to examine some of the consequences of it facing designers.

A key part of Buchanan's paper that is relevant to my discussion is his comment on *culture* as the distinguishing aspect of fourth-order design. He deftly redefines culture as a verb, not a noun; an activity, not a thing. Thus, "culturing" is an activity that we all can do. It is the art of seeking to find and express *identity* and *purpose*.

> Culture is not a state, expressed in an ideology or a body of doctrines. It is an activity. Culture is the activity of ordering, disordering and reordering in the search for understanding and for values which guide action.

This purpose is not necessarily a metaphysical absolute, but rather a practically useful sense of the shared significance of a task. Put simply, it is the widest domain of discussion around a task. It is a mode of thought that gravitates naturally and irrevocably to the question "Why?" It does so not in a metaphysical and absolute sense, as if a fourth-order designer is a philosopher or theologian or metaphysicist who is searching for any excuse to discuss dialectic issues; rather, the fourth-order designer recognizes that the issues of purpose and intention, of reason and passion, and of love and desire are a necessary and natural horizon for any task or problem confronting humans in their enterprises. To answer that question, we must address other related questions about values, perceptions and worldview.

Just as a product is not only a thing, but exists within a series of connected processes, so these processes do not live in a vacuum, but move through a *field* of less tangible factors such as values, beliefs and the wider context of other contingent processes. This area of the field is the concern of fourth-order designers. It is the set of

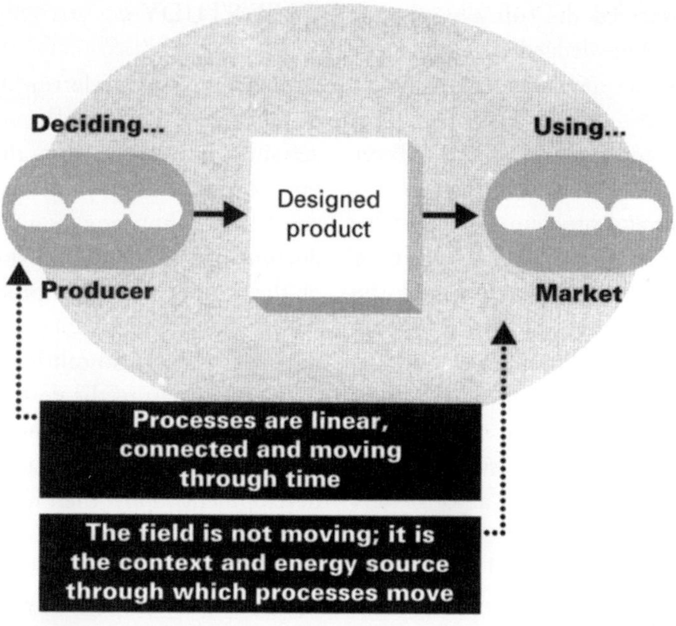

Figure 20.8.

organizational and personal values and purposes within which the processes and products live and move, and have their being. They only derive purpose and identity from the field: without it, they are merely exercises in time and motion, not meaning (Figure 20.8).

Thus fourth-order design pursues the realization of *purpose* and context around a task. But it also pursues coherence and *integration* around a task. The "field" includes other related processes that influence or are influenced by the task in question. It is within the scope of a fourth-order designer to understand and influence these connected processes – one of the passions and skills of the fourth-order designer is integration and pattern.

Integration and purpose are different, but connected, goals. Understanding purpose provides much of the momentum and energy which makes integration possible: integration is not just a rational process of fitting things together like a giant jigsaw puzzle. It also is a process of discovering the energy by which things cohere and fit together. Things don't fit only through either logic or aesthetics: this is a sterile and flat basis for integration. They fit because they make sense as a unit together to people – more sense together than apart. They fit primarily because they serve a shared purpose: hence, purpose not logic is the driving force behind integration.

Another key feature of the field is that it involves people or *communities*: it is not merely a mental place or a series of processes which might or might not involve people (some processes are almost entirely automated, and can be described and improved without any reference to people). It is a place of people and community.

The word "*system*" is useful to describe this aspect of the field of fourth-order concerns.[5] This word has a rich history; it has writhed its way through various, quite different incarnations. Its original use in the business context was to describe a mechanistic logic by which organizations ran – its proponents were engineers, and the word obeyed its masters. Of late, the word has been taken over by a "softer" set of intentions and has been used to describe ecological, holistic approaches to problems and the role of organizations. Peter

Checkland[6] has pioneered the soft systems approach, which has acknowledged that organizations and their processes include a vast factor of culture and worldview – system designers ignore these at their peril, according to Checkland. Peter Senge has popularized the notion of feedback and circularity in systems and problem-solving in his influential book, *The Fifth Discipline*.[7] Both of these authors have moved people right into the center of the systems debate, and seem to have humanized the previously mechanistic notion behind the word "system." Under the engineering domination of the word, one could achieve integration merely technically; leaving aside whatever disharmony there might have been among users and producers. Under the wider liberal umbrella described by Checkland, Senge and others, this is no longer possible. Integration must involve integration of purpose and people.

These attributes of purpose (culture), integration and system (community) provide the emerging subject matter for fourth-order design. Does this make a fourth-order designer a philosopher – one who habitually pursues high-order questions of meaning? If so, what practical use could they be in organizations? I am not arguing that fourth-order design pursues questions of purpose in the abstract and as philosophy; rather that, faced with any practical task, the fourth-order designer moves the boundary of the task out to encompass the issues of "Why are we doing this task?" and, in answering this question, "What does it tell us about our identity and value?" Similarly, the fourth-order designer also will move the scope of the task out to encompass connected systems and activities; to achieve integration so that the product does not operate as a fragment in the world, but within useful and viable patterns. Finally, the fourth-order designer widens the scope of this practical task to include the people involved in creating and using the product (i.e., the product decisions are not taken in isolation; nor are they driven primarily by the creative lone voice of the designer; but are developed in discussion with a sense of growing purpose and commitment).

CASE STUDY

Let me illustrate by referring again to the Tax Law Improvement Project. The scope of the project certainly has moved into the third domain of process and activity; primarily through an analysis of the reading process and its significance for document design; but also through the mapping of the legislative design process. Both of these widen the scope of design significantly beyond the artifact, and also call for new and additional skills on the part of the designer (e.g., knowledge of cognitive processes of comprehension as well as a knowledge of administrative process of policy development). How then might the scope of this task be stretched further into the field of the fourth domain?

First, we can do this by means of discussion of the fundamental question, "Why are we doing this task?" This question was, in fact, posed to the team by the Commissioner for Taxation. He asked, rhetorically, "Will you have done a good job if it is a shorter act, or a simpler act?" For his part, the answer was "No"[8]; the team had three objectives which were to increase the compliance of the community with their obligations; to reduce the cost to the community of that compliance; and to increase the fairness of the taxation law, and the perception of its fairness by the community. This gave a far wider sense of purpose to the project. In response to this challenge, the team built a model of evaluation that extends beyond readability into use and perception.

However, the question of evaluation is more complex than just building a model. Two factors threaten the efficiency and effectiveness of complex systems:

A They operate over such long time frames that cause and effect relations are very hard to trace.

B Their creation and administration spans more than one department, so no one person has accountability to understand and optimize the system.

These two factors make evaluation difficult; not only evaluation, but also invention because purpose has two children: evaluating and inventing. The creative designer uses a strong grasp of purpose as the energy and inspiration to invent bolder, more direct themes or design hypotheses; it provides new and wider boundaries for the inventive designer to pursue options. But that same sense of purpose also sets the boundaries for evaluation. It preserves a project from minimalist criteria that can narrow the vision.[9]

These factors for disintegration irritate a fourth-order designer intensely; they are a practical affront to the designer's yearning for "systemic integration." But the practical question remains – how do you evaluate a system's performance in the light of its wider purposes such as reducing the cost of compliance, improving compliance and increasing perceived fairness? In big systems, these are hard to measure.

One way of measuring the performance of large systems is to find "barometer" subsystems – activities which are de facto indicators of the health of the wider system. These activities are those which:

A Live and work at the interface between the producer and the user systems (i.e., they have regular communication with the host environment; they are "open" to that environment; and they are receptors of its messages).
B Are in a feedback mode (i.e., they are commissioned to listen to the host "environment).

One of these de facto barometer systems in the legislation environment is the departments which handle education, inquiries, or litigation. Their function is to explain or adjudicate on questions that the community raises about ambiguous or contentious aspects of the law. They offer their own interpretations of the law's meanings, and if that is contested in the courts, they sponsor the legal defense.

One of the problems with such groups is that their official role takes no account of such a wider learning brief; they are de facto barometer systems, but the organization does not recognize that role. This is another way of saying that they should be explicit participants in designing and redesigning the large systems under which they work. They need to be led by "systemic" thinkers who see beyond their immediate functions for education, answering inquiries, or litigation; and for any given ruling or contention, they must be aware of the costs to the community of ambiguity and legal battles. Without such leadership, wider learning is not feasible (Figure 20.9).

Systemic learning such as this often must span departments and authorities, lest the learning be too fragmented and narrow. To achieve integration means crossing organizational boundaries, spanning long time frames, and weaving together strands of opportunity and problems as they emerge. It is not a tidy or predictable process, and it takes some audacity. But it is very much motivated by a sense of sharing the wider purpose; of returning a sense of fairness and administrative efficiency to complicated and groaning systems.

Furthermore, this process of evaluation involves discussion as the key modus operandi. That is, it will operate in the community, not as a remote analytical exercise with a paper report at the end delivered to senior management (although such reports are necessary). By discussion, I mean facilitating cross-functional groups in carefully guiding explorations of their shared experiences; identifying and clarifying emerging key themes; and connecting these emerging themes to relevant tasks and applications. This is a key element of fourth-order design – Buchanan calls it "practical agreements reached through discussion."

CONVERSATION AS A KEY SKILL OF FOURTH ORDER

This last point raises another key practical skill of fourth-order design: the art of conversation. In order to demonstrate its importance we have to return to the subject of systems which is so

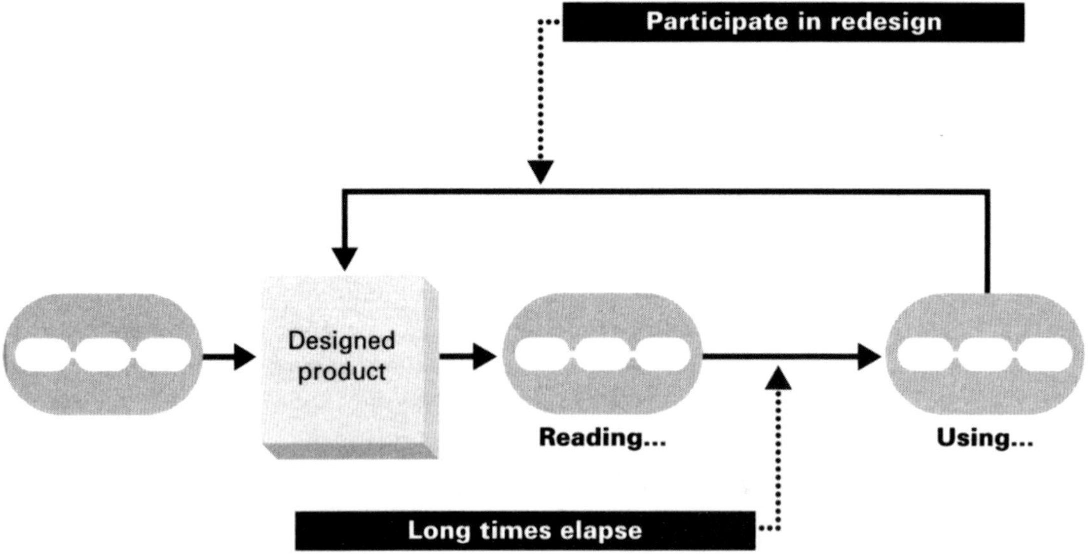

Figure 20.9.

characteristic of the fourth order. In my discussion of it above, I linked it with people and made the point that the word had been rescued in recent thinking from its more technical connotations, as recent writers humanized systems to include people and culture as key components.

A system is difficult to define because it is invisible and exists as a model in people's minds, which serves to describe organized sets of activities. Probably the most fundamental defining characteristic of the concept of a "system" is the input-output notion. A system receives inputs, processes them in a value-adding way, and creates outputs. This notion is useful, but there are some worrisome aspects to it. It suggests the mechanistic and functionary notions of systems engineering since it still only includes people indirectly and, indeed, does not need them at all. It is fundamentally tied to the concept of objectives and goals as the highest end or purpose statement about a set of activities. The input/output model of a system inevitably will lead to a purpose statement such as "We exist to produce output 'x'."

Confronted with these worries about the conceptualization of a system, we have sought alternatives to the biological model of a system and are exploring the model that a system is a "set of conversations around a shared purpose." This model sounds rather tenuous at first, but its practicality and utility grow on one. It preserves the primacy of purpose without immediately prostituting it to outputs. Conversations have "purposes," but these are *relational* as much as output oriented. Furthermore, a purpose works in a conversation to constrain and set its boundaries – another key aspect of the notion of system. Conversations are not strings of sentences, although they exist at that level as well. Rather, they are explorations of *themes*. Most appealing of all, conversations are not self-referencing ontologies, or things that exist in and of themselves. They exist to mediate relations between people.

So we are finding the concept of "system as conversation" increasingly useful as an analogy to understand what a system might be.[10] But the conversation model also appeals on the level of the representative and descriptive, as well as the level of analogy.[11] Most business systems literally are conversations around a common purpose, whether that conversation is mediated by documents, phone calls, electronically, or by physical products.

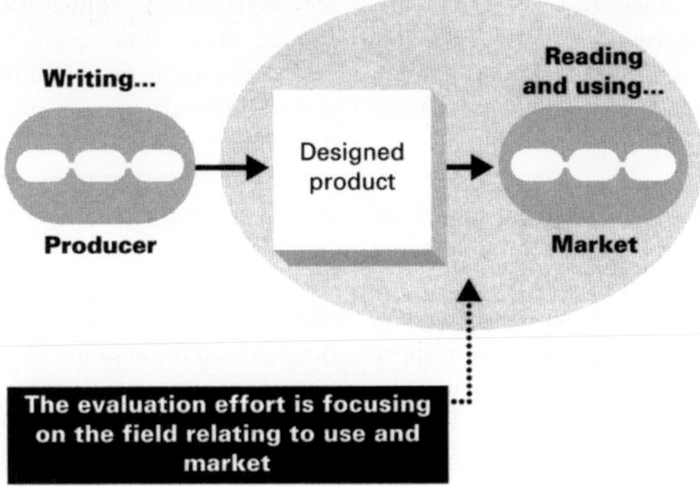

Figure 20.10.

If the concept of "conversation as system" is at all viable, then clearly one of the key arts of working with systems will be the art of orchestrating conversations. This art is beginning to receive significant attention in business literature, with one writer[12] claiming that the ability to understand and lead dialogue will be the key art in making successful organizations in the coming decade.

Certainly, it is the key art that we have begun to exercise whenever we work in a specifically fourth-order domain – the art of facilitating discussion and dialogue. This art is like a living composing process. It requires all the skills of composition that a good writer must master in the face of a complex topic. However, these skills are used in a live drama; in that you take the topic to a group of people rather than away to work on alone in the safety of the designer's cloister. You submit the topic to a group of people who care about it, but who probably do not all agree on their positions. Then you unfold the argument in real time with no predictability of outcomes.

This process is not as precarious as it might seem. The real purpose of the group is to search out shared purposes, so the outcome is less important than the process. It is this kind of conversation that we are facilitating as part of the learning/evaluation phase of the tax project. It includes a search for identity and purpose, as well as a search for better techniques.

The above discussion of fourth-order design concentrates on the *market* side of the designed product – the field of connected processes around the *usage* of the documents such as the law, and of their wider purposes (Figure 20.10).

WHAT OF THE UPSTREAM OR PRODUCER'S SIDE?

As I indicated earlier in my discussion of the third order, we have mapped the process of legislative design and produced a manual describing it. This exercise certainly widened the scope of our involvement out beyond the document, but it still falls short of true fourth-order activities. This is because the mapping process per se is characterized by linearity rather than integration, and by logic rather than people and community. Buchanan's circumscribing of the role of strategic planning is relevant here.

> The example of process reengineering is worth discussion here … strategic planning breaks down when the larger cultural context is undergoing major transformation … The volatile

> period of transition may be led, managed, and facilitated by fourth-order design thinking that focuses on systemic integration, but it is not managed through the methods of strategic planning.

Process reengineering involves mapping and rationalizing processes. It works in areas where the processes are defined and observable, and hence are capable of rationalization. Yet, in a new and emergent area which has never been mapped before and which also involves ambiguous tasks, it will prove inadequate. Our process was not just a rational description followed by a culling or rerouting of activities. Rather, it was a process of invention and participation. It involved much discussion of the nature of the tasks and of the best way to describe them. This description was not numerical but imaginative, with the frequent use of analogy to provide insight. Furthermore, the process described was very much a process of dialogue between different interest groups. The maps we drew were not just linear flowcharts, but more creative and idiosyncratic representations of action.

The participation also was a crucial element of our design efforts on the production side of the process. This task was not a cerebral exercise in analysis; but the opportunity for a group of people "in transition," as Buchanan states it, to discuss the nature of the task they have been given. This discussion is not trivial or peremptory; but explores difficult grounds such as the nature of the value they add, and the nature of the respective roles each person plays. Most organizational situations never fully allow such candor; identity and purpose are elided and assumed. The focus of organizational attention moves on to safer, more trivial matters of mechanisms and minor tasks. But when an organization sanctions the exploration of the nature of shared work, it becomes a culturing exercise as groups "order and reorder" their sense of purpose and value (Figure 20.11).

The key skills to support the delivery of value in this wider domain include the ability to design and lead discussion, and to develop strategies for appropriate methods for participation in the activity of writing the manual; inventiveness and the use of analogy as a mechanism to understand and describe the key themes that emerge; and a knowledge of systems thinking and complementary roles in tasks. Once the manual describing the legislative process is complete, the necessary skills can be applied to educational design, training and change management.

This extended discussion of the legislation project illustrates fourth-order design at work. Purpose, integration and systems (communities)

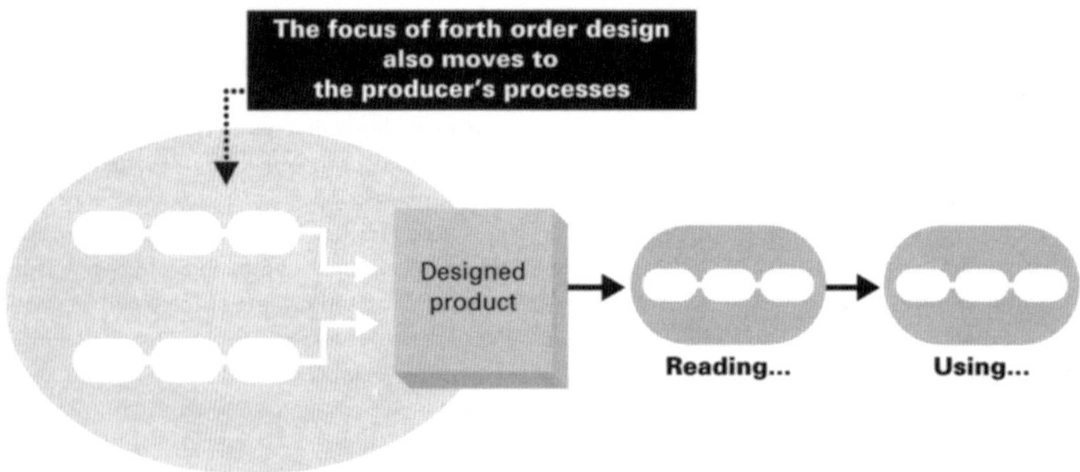

Figure 20.11.

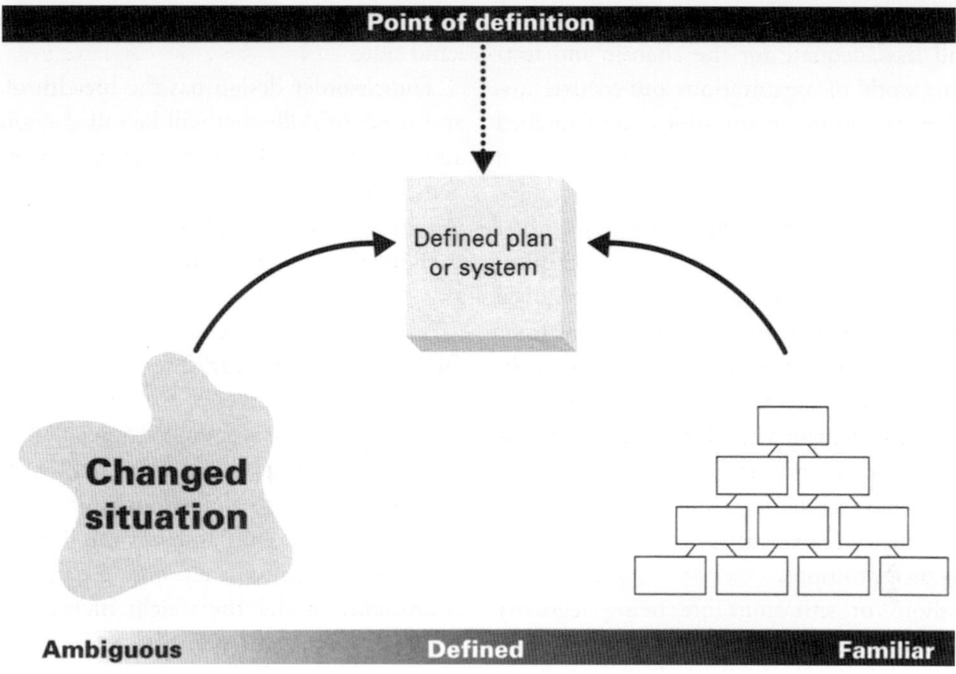

Figure 20.12.

are all vital subject areas in the project; but they are not approached abstractly. They are necessary extensions of the scope which began as document design. This case study illustrates the true nature of fourth-order design. It is not a tidy and predictable area, but relies on opportunism and alertness. More than that, it relies on eagerness and vision for change.

FURTHER BROADENING OF FOURTH ORDER

Thus far, I have characterized fourth-order design as the widening of task horizons beginning with an orthodox design task.

However, I predict that the scope of fourth-order design may well be broadened still further. As Buchanan argues in Branzi's Dilemma, "… designers (will) continue to focus and reinvent their professions to meet new opportunities and circumstances." The new opportunities I foresee arise from the nature of "traditional design tasks."

Design is the conceptualization and creation of products. As such, it is dealing in the area of the new and the uncertain: it is creative. In essence, it does not begin with a problem to be solved or a process to be refined or modified: it is not derivative thinking. It begins with a blank sheet of paper. The guiding impulses are love, intention and value. The words which will command the product to emerge.

Designers are all too familiar with this unstructured and ambiguous type of situation. It is the stuff of their professional lives. As such, it is in stark contrast to the pedigree of the management and engineering sciences that are so influential in organizations today. These disciplines fundamentally are not about invention so much as analysis. They rely on training to solve existing problems; at the most to discover by empirical testing and analysis; but certainly not to invent. In their sphere of analysis, "purpose" is reduced to the quantifiable and the numerical; it will be shrunken down to the level of objectives such as revenue, cost and productivity.

However, this structured training is becoming less and less adequate for the chaotic and fast-changing world of organizations and societies today. More and more organizations have watched as past beliefs, processes and products have been swept away in tides of (often unwelcome) change. Global competition has precipitated this. Another factor that is having a major impact on organizations is the environment, and the wider political and cultural situation. In the past, organizations have been able to steamroller their way ahead oblivious to the demands of these ecological factors. Those days have passed, and now organizations must be open and symbiotic. These external pressures are creating internal pressures for organizations, so that departments and groups have to reassess their positions.

In short, organizations are being regularly plunged into urgent deliberations about their purpose and their identity. As such, they are finding that they are in the *place* of design, as it were; in a de facto design process dealing with ambiguity; and dealing with a blank or illegible sheet of paper. In this place, the training of engineering, accountancy, law, and management science is not relevant preparation. Technocracy is, as it were, in decline as a viable system of governance. To whom will organizations turn? The art of design offers rhythms of thought, patterning skills, understanding of the defining role of love, intention and value in human agency, and the responsiveness to place and market – all key disciplines that are needed to be exercised in far wider applications than they have been in the past.

Imagine that we could map whole organizations and the systems within them along an ambiguity axis, with the most ambiguous on the left and the most defined on the right. In the middle is the point of definition and clarification.

More and more organizations are finding themselves being plunged onto the left-hand side of this diagram. *This is a crucial change of place* because the tools and management responses that suit an organization on the right do not suit an organization on the left. In fact, these right-hand tools are positively counterproductive on the left-hand side.

Fourth-order design has the breadth of scope and reach of skills that will be called upon more and more to help lead organizations. As this happens, it will not need a specific design task as the initiating factor. Design will be desirable for its thinking style, alone, without any artifact in view.

BRIEF CASE STUDIES

Let me illustrate this emerging demand for design thinking with other case studies. A resource company worries that its ability to take prospects from discovery to operating mines is too inefficient. A major government agency, only recently created, is burdened under the weight of extraordinary growth, public criticism of its performance, and a lack of training for its staff; while a nationwide suggestion scheme uncovers hundreds of suggestions but little that is new or promising. A significant research body feels the lack of creativity in its processes, and the lack of cultural skills to implement the outcome of its research in operating situations. Major computing projects are overburdened with downstream methodologies for writing software code, but feel exposed and uncertain about the early processes of creativity and invention.

These companies (all clients we are currently working for or have recently worked for, all major Australian organizations) all have a common theme. They have found themselves, in whole or in part, in de facto design situations. In these situations, they have responded with analytical management tools that have not proved adequate, partly because these tools are predicated on a more structured situation than they now confront. The symptoms that alert these organizations that something is wrong are major inefficiencies, or other dysfunctionalities.

All of these organizations are actively pursuing design thinking as a radical but promising alternative approach.

For the design community to meet these kinds of needs, one thing above all else will be necessary: the ability to articulate and to understand the art and disciplines of the design process. It has not been my purpose to explore these arts and disciplines in this article. Rather, my purpose has been to show that fourth-order design is a practical place and not just a theory. As a consequence of this practicality, I predict that fourth-order designers will find new applications and interests beyond traditional subject matter for design. The design community's best preparation is, first, to understand this widening context for design; and, second, to explore and articulate the art of design within it.

NOTES

First published in *Design Issues* 12 no. 1 (Spring 1996): 5–25.

1. Richard Buchanan, "Wicked Problems in Design Thinking," in *The Idea of Design*, Victor Margolin and Richard Buchanan, eds. (Cambridge, MA: MIT Press, 1995). Richard Buchanan, "Branzi's Dilemma: Design in Contemporary Culture," in *Design – Pleasure or Responsibility?*, Paivi Tahkokallio and Susan Vihma, eds. (Helsinki: University of Art and Design Helsinki, 1995), 10–29.
2. This work was done on the first section of the Income Tax Law to be rewritten. A short section of about 40 pages, it was deliberately used as a prototype to test communication ideas.
3. This evaluation was done by a joint team led by professors from the Design and English departments of Carnegie Mellon University.
4. Buchanan, "Branzi's Dilemma," 10–29.
5. Buchanan, "Branzi's Dilemma," 21.
6. Peter Checkland, *Soft Systems Methodology in Action* (New York: John Wiley, 1991).
7. Peter Senge, *The Fifth Discipline: The Art and Practice of the Learning Organization* (New York: Doubleday, 1990).
8. Although, of course, both of these remain immediate goals of the exercise.
9. One of the key skills of the fourth-order designer is not just to articulate purpose, but to sustain its presence on the task. Most people lose sight of purpose in the detail: fourth-order thinking regularly and intuitively returns to it for guidance and inspiration.
10. I am indebted to my colleagues, David Jones and Anne Deane, for much of these insights around conversation and systems.
11. Yet it is more metonymy than analogy.
12. William Issacs, "Taking Flight Dialogue, Collective Thinking and Organization Learning," in *Organizational Dynamics* 22, 2 (Autumn 1993).

FURTHER READING FOR PART II, SECTION 2

Examples of Reyner Banham's design criticism have been collected in two volumes: Penny Sparke (ed.), *Design by Choice* (New York: Rizzoli, 1981) and *A Critic Writes: Essays by Reyner Banham*, selected by Mary Banham (Berkeley: University of California Press, 1996). Nigel Whiteley has written an extensive study of Banham as a critic: *Reyner Banham: Historian of the Immediate Future* (Cambridge, MA: MIT Press, 2002). On visibility, see Richard Saul Wurman, *Making the City Observable* (Cambridge, MA: MIT Press, 1971). On the history of objects, see John Walker: *Design History and the History of Design* (London: Pluto Press, 1989) and Siegfried Giedion, *Mechanization Takes Command: A Contribution to Anonymous Design* (New York: Oxford University Press, 1948). Louis Bucciarelli writes about engineers as designers in *Designing Engineers* (Cambridge, MA: MIT Press, 1994). See also Donald Schön, *The Reflective Practitioner: How Professionals Think in Action* (New York: Basic Books, 1983) and Janet McDonnell and Peter Lloyd, *About Designing: Analysing Design Meetings* (London: Routledge, 2009). As background material for Tony Golsby-Smith's conception of fourth-order design, see Richard Buchanan, "Wicked Problems in Design Thinking," in *The Idea of Design*, eds. Victor Margolin and Richard Buchanan (Cambridge, MA: MIT Press, 1995) and Richard Buchanan, "Branzi's Dilemma: Design in Contemporary Culture," in *Design Pleasure or Responsibility*? eds. Paivi Tahkokallio and Susan Vihma (Helsinki: University of Art and Design, 1995).

PART III

EVALUATION

INTRODUCTION

The theory of value has a long history in philosophy, and only in recent years has it been applied to design. Traditionally associated with ideas of what is good, value theory includes the study of ethics and aesthetics, which are included within the sub-field of philosophy known as axiology. In the 1960s, Bruce Archer, one of the early design theorists, included design axiology as one of the ten branches of investigation that he proposed for the emerging field of design research.[1] Within philosophy, value theory considers how humans make judgments about what is good and bad. Value is considered in several senses. *Instrumental value* is the value placed on things, activities, or anything that serves as a means of attaining or achieving something that is said to have *intrinsic value* or value in and of itself. We can also mention quantitative value, which assigns a measurable quantity such as money to goods or labor, for example, in order to maintain a system of exchange as in an economic system where both are exchanged for money. Qualitative value is less tangible. It is associated with the good in terms of benefits to humans as in "quality of life." Recently, qualitative value has been central to definitions of design as a means to foster human well-being.

Value in design can be considered at different stages of the design process. Before designing begins, discussions of value can address questions of what should be designed and why. Current debates about sustainability may address specific products as in design for disassembly (DfD), but they are also concerned with broader questions of how design as a general practice fits into a sustainable world.

Other debates that precede actual designing relate to design education. Early programs in commercial art and industrial design were more concerned with the transmission of skills than with questions of design's values. In the 1920s and 1930s, when such programs were inaugurated, especially in the United States, the value of design was instrumental. It was recognized as a means to enhance the qualitative value of products, which in turn would increase their quantitative value as objects for the market. In Europe, design education was more idealistic, particularly at the Bauhaus, where Walter Gropius characterized the aim of the Bauhaus metaphorically as contributing to the construction of a great cathedral of socialism. Discussions of value may also take place during the design process as designers assess and reassess the quality of what they are doing. Where graphic and product designers once moved directly from their concepts into production, today designing involves considerably more feedback during the design process, particularly in what is called user-centered design. Techniques of ethnography, focus groups, beta testing, and user trials all provide feedback to designers before completion of a final product, thus incorporating evaluation into the design process itself.

And finally, products – whether objects or graphic designs – can be evaluated after they are completed and introduced to the public. These evaluations are of different types. They may be done by social scientists who look at a product or product group in terms of its effect on large numbers of people; or evaluations may take the form of design criticism, whereby a critic exercises his or her personal judgment about a product's quality, whether functional, esthetic, or social. In recent years, there has been a proliferation of design criticism, particularly on the Internet, where bloggers sustain a running commentary about new products, whether iPhones, posters, typefaces, or urban plans.

The articles in this section represent evaluation in two of the three possible locations – before designing begins and after it is completed. Four of the articles are concerned with the environment and the question of how design can fit into a sustainable world. Pauline Madge shows how the 1980s notion of "green design" expanded in the 1990s into "ecological design," and subsequently deepened to become "sustainable design." She describes how the media, notably in Great Britain, picked up the idea of "green" from the Green parties and how a general environmental concern emerged, although she demonstrates how so-called "green" products were easily incorporated into marketing strategies that promised modest environmental changes but did not address the larger issues related to the growing environmental problems. As Madge states in her conclusion, "It has become increasingly evident that the radical nature of an ecological approach to design implies a new design critique."

One of the leaders in mounting such a critique is Ezio Manzini, a professor of industrial design at the Politecnico di Milano, who has been actively promoting a vision of sustainable design since the 1980s. Manzini's books and articles have, in fact, been essential in stimulating debates within the design community about sustainability. At the beginning of the 1990s, Manzini was talking about an "ecology of the artificial" that needed to be studied in all its complexity in order to understand its diverse components. As one consequence of studying the artificial ecology systematically, Manzini concluded that: "We must now pass from a culture that considers itself to be part of a dynamics of unlimited development to a culture capable of thinking for itself of possible changes caused by limitations."[2]

In the article included in this section, Manzini calls for a radical model of development to replace the "normalized" adoption of eco-design in the 1980s, which led to a new environmental quality in the market but did not challenge the fundamental global structure that was the cause of so many environmental problems. Among the specific changes he proposed was a shift from goods to services and the development of related scenarios that would induce large numbers of people to change their behavior.

John Hirst's article is a direct response to Manzini's call for a shift from " '*existenzminimum*' (minimum existence) to quality maximum." Hirst is essentially in agreement with Manzini about the required changes, which he characterizes as "a vision of design that goes beyond the designing of artifacts, or even systems of artifacts, to the design of culture or at least aspects of culture." He focuses, however, on the question of values. To achieve the results Manzini advocates, Hirst says, it will be necessary to adopt a new logic based on the idea of a qualitative balance that is derived from a biological model. He then calls for a widespread adoption of values that lead to a more convivial form of life. Designers, he says, have a special talent for "identifying the balances that achieve conviviality in the domain of material culture."

Ideas that Manzini put forth in an early article, "Prometheus of the Everyday," serve as a stimulus for the article by David Stairs, who addresses Manzini's comparison of the natural and artificial environments. Stairs begins with a discussion of biologist Edward O. Wilson's concept of "biophilia," which Wilson believes establishes a genetic relation between humans and the natural world. Stairs rightly acknowledges that the relation between nature and culture has been insufficiently addressed by design theorists, and he seeks to define a balance between the two. He is highly critical of technological determinism, which he sees as casting "a two-century-long shadow across our society," and believes that "the future role of design will be to create culture as a sustainable part of the natural world." It is noteworthy that Manzini, Hirst, and Stairs each call for radical changes in the idea of culture. Manzini wants a new paradigm of development, which reduces the consumption of resources. Hirst desires a value system based on a more convivial style of life, while Stairs seeks to redress the balance between nature and culture. All relate to contemporary discussions of the need for new values to redirect the practice of design.

In his discussion of the intense debate within the Hochschule für Gestaltung, Ulm, Paul Betts takes us back to the early postwar years in Germany, when a desire to restore an acceptable material lifestyle after the devastation of the Second World War dominated German culture. The Hochschule für Gestaltung, Ulm, was originally conceived as an institute devoted to "contemporary and political education" but developed into a new design school when the Swiss designer and former Bauhaus student, Max Bill, was brought in as the director. Bill's agenda to recreate the Bauhaus in a more contemporary form was hotly contested by others on the faculty, especially the Argentine art critic Tomás Maldonado, who wanted the curriculum to represent the new theoretical and technical tendencies of postwar industrial culture. The debate centered on the question of what should be designed and how design should be done in the postwar world. Eventually, the faction that opposed Bill won and he left the school. By emphasizing the intellectual claims of the protagonists, Betts forcefully demonstrates the impact that design theory can play in shaping the identity and role of design in modern life.

Findeli, too, is concerned with design theory and its relation to design education, but in his article he does not focus on a particular educational institution as Betts does. Instead, he proposes a multidimensional model of design's impact on the spheres of nature and culture from which he deduces the principles of an ethical design practice. Findeli's thinking is informed in part by the extensive research he did on the New Bauhaus in Chicago, which was the subject of his doctoral dissertation as well as a subsequent book and various journal articles. László Moholy-Nagy, in particular, was the model of an ethical designer and educator whose influence Findeli surely felt as he developed his argument. Like Stairs, he is concerned with the effects of technology, adopting the term "technoethics" to address the conflicts resulting from rapid technological developments. Findeli adopts an especially broad view of design although he then focuses on "those professionals who are called on to design *material* objects …" Ethics and aesthetics must also be more closely related to the design curriculum and not introduced through special courses that are not connected to the basic pedagogy of design education.

Ann Tyler's article focuses on a magazine, *Colors*, that was launched by the Benetton Group in 1991 and is still published today. *Colors* is predominantly a pictorial magazine and the text is kept to a minimum. Tyler limits her critique to the first nine issues, which were published under the editorship of the late Tibor Kalman, who sought to make the magazine a vehicle for social change.

Tyler characterizes Kalman's intent to "communicate a fundamental similarity between people, and then point out the interesting differentiations that distinguish these groups and cultures." As a critic, she employs the methodology of rhetoric whereby she considers *Colors* as the purveyor of an argument rather than as simply a formal arrangement of images and text. Kalman claimed to propound a "rhetoric of amelioration" that characterized differences between the various represented groups or tribes as a positive force in a world where everyone can get along, but Tyler argues that the editorial strategy of *Colors* glosses over real differences between the groups that might actually set them apart from each other. She claims that *Colors* seeks to minimize conflicts and reduce threats by normalizing difference and establishing a safe relationship between its imagined audience and the content. Tyler raises questions about the magazine's authorial voice and reinforces the idea that graphic design is first and foremost about communication rather than form.

NOTES

1. Bruce Archer, "A View of the Nature of Design Research," in *Design: Science: Method*, eds. Robin Jacques and James A. Powell (Guildford: Westbury House, 1981), 33.
2. Ezio Manzini, "Prometheus of the Everyday: The Ecology of the Artificial and the Designer's Responsibility," in Richard Buchanan and Victor Margolin, *Discovering Design: Explorations in Design Studies* (Chicago and London: University of Chicago Press, 1995), 230. The essay was originally delivered in Canada in 1990, then published in *Design Issues* before it appeared in the book.

21

IT'S A NICE WORLD AFTER ALL: THE VISION OF "DIFFERENCE" IN *COLORS*

Ann Tyler

Figure 21.1 *Colors* No. 4, Spring/Summer 1994, cover (race attitudes).

All photos courtesy of *Colors* magazine.

Colors: A Magazine About the Rest of the World, though funded by Benetton, was conceived of as an autonomous publication[1] with ambitious and noble goals: "to change the world."[2] *Colors* states on the editorial page of its first issue: "This is a magazine about an idea." That idea? "Diversity is good." And, further, that "your culture (whoever you are) is as important as our culture (whoever we are)." The editors aver that we (authors and audience together) can read and hear about the problems everywhere else – in the world, in newspapers, and on TV. Instead, *Colors* will bring us "positive ideas," "positive change," and "people who are doing things right." In addition, technology, including communications, is erasing difference; while *Colors* brings us together in a celebration of difference.[3] An appreciation of the visible differences among people, cultures, and subcultures, as well as the realization that these are apparently the only differences, will effect harmony in the world.

In attempting to be a voice for change, the editors of *Colors* represent topics and individuals through the magazine that are rarely (sometimes never) made visible in the mass media.[4] Representation, or who and what is shown, in communication is an essential part of reinforcing, creating, and transforming an audience's vision of the world. However, communication/design is an argument comprised of not only the subject, but the implications based on that subject; as well as an authorial voice or voices; and an implied audience. All these aspects construct arguments and convey beliefs. While communicating diversity through a focus on alternative topics from a liberal perspective, many times the methods of representation, the authorial voice, and the implied audience[5] projected in *Colors* reflect a more traditional point of view that denies diversity. Thus, the arguments made in *Colors* often subvert the editors' intended goals. It is especially important in attempts to use design as a means of social change that these efforts receive close, serious criticism. Criticism can, hopefully, be one means of evaluating the implications and ramifications of particular strategies in the hope that design can become a vehicle for understanding a complex world, rather than a means of simplifying the world in order to "explain" it.

I examined the first nine issues produced from 1991 to 1995, all of which were edited by the graphic designer, Tibor Kalman. The structure of *Colors* is designed to first communicate a fundamental similarity between people, and then point out the interesting differentiations that distinguish these groups and cultures. *Colors* repeats overall categories across various magazine issues, and applies the topics to many countries and cultures. The topics, including heroes, tribes, food, and ecology, repeat as theme and variation uniting diverse peoples from around the world. The pages are a visual pastiche, with verbal text kept, in general, to single paragraphs; thus creating a caption-like appearance. Images are photographic rather than illustrated, and are presented as recordings of the world. Though criticism of political leaders as well as of certain organized groups and behaviors is expressed within the magazine, the primary focus is on individuals and their "positive difference."[6] *Colors*, like Edward Steichen's 1955 exhibition, "The Family of Man," is "dominated by a rhetoric of amelioration: things would get better if people celebrated each other."[7] Also paralleling Steichen's vision, *Colors* asserts not only a fundamental similarity between people, but, further, creates visual connections between viewer and subjects that infers an ease to cross-cultural relationships. Cultural context is treated as a sense of place rather than beliefs or values. People are located geographically, and often differentiated and grouped by their visual similarities – clothing and/or skin color. The context also remains in the present: history is absent and unnecessary in our understanding of culture and subculture. Since it is a magazine that its editors use as an attempt to extend acceptance of different cultures and subcultures, I approached *Colors* expecting to connect to it on the basis of my own identity – not as a designer, but as a lesbian. But instead, *Colors* homogenizes the very individuals and groups it is attempting to celebrate, denies important aspects of cultural identity, and reinforces an all too common, simplistic approach to social and cultural dynamics.

ACCENTUATE THE POSITIVE. ELIMINATE THE NEGATIVE

Communicating the acceptability of people who are "different" is *Colors*' means of accomplishing one of its main goals: persuading the audience that diversity is good. Acceptability of individuals and groups is achieved through photography and text that emphasize the positive, "naturalize" the shocking, diminish the threatening, and fail to represent anger and pain. Ironically, it is this vision of a fundamental similarity of people that is used in *Colors* to communicate that difference is positive. Differences among subjects or between subjects and audience are represented as merely stylistic or surface variations so they do not become points of conflict that disturb an image of unity. In utilizing this approach to representation, *Colors* often ignores and effectively eliminates the context and belief systems of the subjects.

"Tribes" is a category used to depict countries, cities, cultures, and then subcultures around the world. New York tribes in *Colors 1* (Figures 21.1a, 21.1b, and 21.1c) and Moscow tribes in *Colors* 2 (Figures 21.2a and 21.2b) are brought together by photographing every group in a similar manner. All of the pictures show members of each group lined up and looking out directly at the camera/viewer. And though the photographs are different sizes in their outside dimensions, the internal arrangement is the same: people in a line, centered left to right in the frame, with space on each end serving to define the group and not the setting. This parallel representation is reinforced in the text with captions of approximately the same length, despite the size of the photograph. The dominant difference that remains visible and is emphasized through this type of representation is *clothing*. Each group coalesces within its particular photograph through the subjects' clothes, which become an identifying uniform. The headlines for every image are abbreviated labels identifying a basis for the group's formation, and further defining their respective "uniforms" for the audience.

Developing images of similarity across cultures seems to be an attempt to unify a diverse world, and to create a notion of acceptance of that diversity on the part of the audience. Within contexts

Figure 21.1a *Colors* No. 1, Fall/Winter 1991, 6–7 (NY tribes).

black girls' coalition

wilfred beauty academy

555-soul

spike's joint

Figure 21.1b *Colors* No. 1, Fall/Winter 1991, 8–9 (NY tribes)

queen of the night and her court

korean golf academy

Figure 21.1c *Colors* No. 1, Fall/Winter 1991, 10–1 (NY tribes).

outside of *Colors*, many of the groups represented are perceived as shocking or threatening by some segments of the population. Drag queens, gay and lesbian police, and interracial, mixed gender groups often are seen as oddities and/or met with hostility in the United States. The smiling figures photographed in a professional studio setting become "normalized" within an innocuous setting, and through their similarities, with other "tribes." Within this "normalization" process, the audience is placed in a voyeuristic and safe relationship to the groups. The audience stands in the same position as the camera or editors – watching the scene. We look upon subjects who meet our gaze with friendly or nonaggressive and engaging faces[8] (Figure 21.1). The potentially shocking drag outfits (Figure 21.1c) are "naturalized" by becoming part of a visual spectrum that also includes "kids of the 90s"[9] clothes (Figure 21.1b) and New York City police uniforms (Figure 21.1a). *Colors* both focuses on the differences and then attempts to eliminate or deny any possible conflict over difference.

In an attempt to communicate a positive vision, and thereby prevent the audience from any *disagreement* with the subject, the editors avoid exploring negative experiences or belief systems. Unfortunately, this provides a very simplistic vision of people and culture; it can deny their cultural experience; and it avoids the basis of a great deal of conflict. Unlike this vision portrayed in *Colors*, many people hold beliefs that are in fundamental conflict with the beliefs of the subjects represented. And some of the subjects shown most likely hold conflicting beliefs with each other. *Colors* often strains to minimize or ignore conflict, and remove any threat. For example, in the "Musical Bodybuilders" (Figure 21.2a), the attempt at a positive representation never quite overcomes the visual and verbal implications of violence or intimidation. The men stand in stiff postures and stare out at the viewer with grim faces. Many members of the group are dressed in the brown shirts and high, black, military-style boots associated with fascism. "They are bodybuilders from … an area known for nurturing reactionaries and anti-intellectuals. The group's 'heroes' are those who battled the Bolsheviks …"[10] If one is aware of context, a logical assumption is that this is very possibly a right-wing, tsarist, anti-Semitic group. But the portrayal of tribes is about positivity so "*Still* (my emphasis) the band wants to be liked: 'We got a prize from an ecology newspaper for our song …' "[11] Clearly, there is some editorial ambivalence here, but not enough to alter the strategy of argument.

Accentuating only the positive in the subject also results in a failure to represent the anger and pain of that subculture. The Gay Officers Action League (GOAL) (Figure 21.1a) is portrayed briefly and positively in *Colors*, while the societal hatred that homosexuals experience is absent. Social hatred is ignored in order to "normalize" the lesbians and gay men. The argument made is that these are people, just like other (i.e., heterosexual) police officers, who are simply doing their jobs. But violence against homosexuals, contemporary and historical, is an important context for understanding the significance of gays and lesbians working on the police force. These are members of a group that is attacked and often unprotected by the justice system. One means by which the lesbian and gay community can secure basic protections in US society is to have homosexuals working in law enforcement. And it is also *for this reason* that many people *oppose* gay men and lesbians in these positions. Simply "normalizing" a group through their outfits, and presenting visually nonthreatening images, does not make one group acceptable to another.

Creating an appearance of agreement/sameness/unity is the strategy of argument employed throughout *Colors*. The representation of sameness in Figures 21.1 and 21.2 communicates a sense of harmony or agreement among the tribes – the subjects. But these notions of agreement extend beyond the subject into the domain of the author and the audience. While the devices in Figures 21.1 and 21.2 make the subjects "acceptable"; and also may be intended to unify subject,

Figure 21.2a *Colors* No. 2, Spring/Summer 1992, 10–11 (Moscow tribes).

Figure 21.2b *Colors* No. 2, Spring/Summer 1992, 16 (Moscow tribes).

author, and audience, they actually *separate* the audience from the subject by placing the audience in a voyeuristic relationship with the image and using an anonymous, reporting voice in the text. As seen in these examples, when the subject is an individual or a group of people, it often is *presented to* the audience or viewer in the style of documentary portraiture: facing or slightly turned from the viewer, and looking directly out of the picture plane to make eye contact with the viewer. While the subjects build a bridge out to the viewer, the viewer also is made aware of the act of looking, thus creating an awareness of the picture plane surface. An invisible "wall" is articulated between audience and subject.

The observer (the audience) occupies a distant, distinct, and different frame. The audience views the subjects from the same position as the camera, which is the eye of the author. Authorial position and audience inhabit the same space, effectively providing the audience and author with the same point of view. By joining the author and audience, the argument assumes that the audience takes on not only the spatial perspective of the author, but the ideological perspective as well. This strategy of argument is effective in attempting to persuade the audience of an editorial position. At the same time, a serious problematic occurs precisely because of the audience's separation from the subject and its unification with the author.

THE COST OF "NORMALIZATION"

The members of the Gay Officers Action League are represented as friendly, confident women and men; wearing crisp uniforms and standing at attention. The image communicates their professionalism and competence. Their facial expressions are calm and serious, although their half-smiles project this seriousness as a nonthreatening attitude. They are professionals, friendly but not too friendly. The image shows people we see everyday – people that some readers may assume are all heterosexuals. So, if the idea of gay police officers is surprising or shocking to a viewer, this representation presents an image of acceptability through the visual treatment that also is reinforced within the calm, removed (and therefore objective), matter-of-fact, authorial voice within the verbal text. The caption-like manner of reporting, limited in length and utilizing an omniscient, anonymous voice, is phrased to give a noninterpretive impression which also communicates objectivity.

In representing the gay officers, the authorial voice is positioned outside of that group and represents the group's views through direct quotes. The anonymous, authorial voice is heard through very straightforward prose, such as "he says" or "says GOAL Executive Director Sam Ciccone."[12] The impression of anonymity and absence within the authorial voice both reinforces the distance between author and subject (established through the voyeuristic relationship) and defines the author as someone other than the subject (i.e., not a gay or lesbian police officer). If the authorial voice was actually absent within the text, Sam Ciccone could speak for himself without an intermediary presenter. Or, if the author were within the subject group, the language would be more connected and inclusive. It is not just subjects that are defined within communication, but audiences and authors as well. Actual audiences and actual editors often are very different from *implied* audiences and *implied* authors. Through the authorial voice, the identity of the author is defined. The actual writers, photographers, and/or editors may very likely include lesbians or gay men; but the authorial voice used in the description of the gay officers defines the author/(s) as not homosexual and, therefore, as heterosexual.

How, in turn, does this strategy define the audience's identity? We look *upon* the subject as the authorial voice looks *upon* the subject. We stand on the outside and assume the same vision as the implied author. If the actual audience is heterosexual or not members of the police, then their position as outsiders is confirmed. But as a lesbian, *my own* identity is denied within this strategy of argument. My implied identity is heterosexual, thus folding me into the dominant culture. In attempting to raise up diversity in one arena – the subject, the strategy of argument employed in *Colors*, effectively erases and denies diversity in another arena – the audience.

WHOEVER ARE YOU? WHOEVER AM I?

In the previous figures, author and audience unite in appreciation of the subject. A sequence demonstrating the risk of HIV infection in *Colors*' AIDS issue attempted to inform or teach the audience through the authorial voice. This goal was achieved through a strategy of argument that sought to create agreement in the form of audience identification with the subject. The sequence was developed over eight pages as a personalized report of risk until the last page, when the authorial voice directly addressed the audience through text.

The first two pages contain a single photo of a woman on the left page and a man on the right

Figure 21.3a *Colors* No. 7, June 1994, 48–49 (AIDS issue).

page, accompanied by the text: "Last night Sara and Miguel slept together."[13] The following pages are diagrams with increasing numbers of photographs illustrating the number of sexual contacts: "Last year, they each slept with three other people"[14] (Figure 21.3a); "Each year before that those people each slept with three other people. Over four years, Sara and Miguel will have slept with people who slept with a total of 80 people"[15]; and, finally, "Over 7 years, these people will have slept with 1,460 people. And over 12 years, those people will have slept with 531,441 people. (It would take another 728 pages to show you all their pictures.) … By the way, in Paris, where Sara and Miguel live, one in 100 people is HIV positive … You might want to use a condom"[16] (Figure 21.3b).

All of the people are represented with snapshot-like photographic images: faces looking at the camera/viewer; heads centered in the frames; often smiling; and backgrounds subordinated through out-of-focus shapes, indeterminacy, or fragmentation. The sexual contact is indicated through connections made by bright, yellow arrows with a hand-drawn quality. These are the pictures of friends with friendly, cheery connections – just nice people enjoying life. The subordinated backgrounds also help to generalize time and space, thus contributing to a sense of the individuals as "anyone." The language, the positive images, and the representational quality of the arrows define the sexual contacts in a positive way, without negative moral judgment.

This representation of risk very effectively counters many stereotypes and rationalizations that contribute to an individual denying risk: the emphasis is on heterosexual rather than homosexual contacts; each person is limited to only three sexual contacts; and the individuals could be any "clean-cut," middle-class young person. The use of photographic imagery retains a sense of the personal, even when the photos fill the page

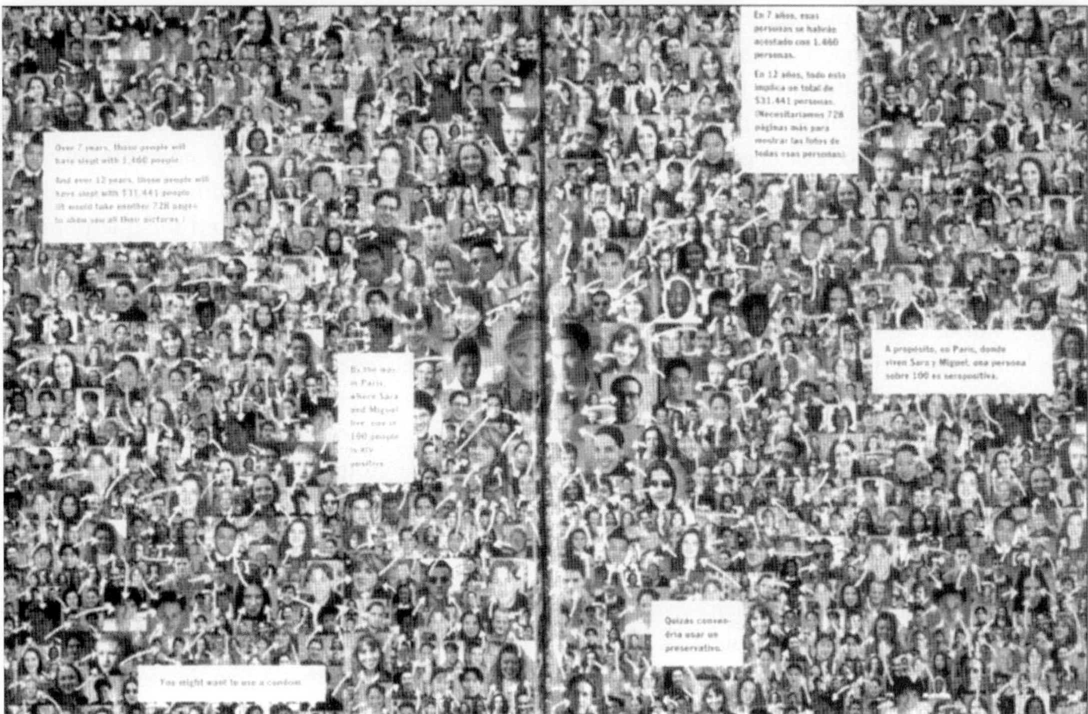

Figure 21.3b *Colors* No. 7, June 1994, 52–53 (AIDS issue).

and are reduced in scale. The viewer also can carry over the perception or sense of personality gained from the larger photos into this mass of smaller images.

It is on the final page: "*You* (my emphasis) might want to use a condom"[17] that it is made clear that the audience is to identify with the sequence. This identification is established not only by a very effective visualization of the massive risk of exposure through a small number of sexual contacts, but by the representations of the individuals photographed. These people are "anyone," as defined by the dominant culture. They are "nice" people who would be "undeserving" of AIDS. If these people can get AIDS – anyone can. The sexual contacts or pairings suggested by the arrows are heterosexual in the first two page spreads. When a few same-gender pairings are indicated in the third spread, the overall number of pairs has increased dramatically from 3 to 80 and, therefore, the size of each face also is much smaller. Differentiating opposite and same-sex pairings becomes difficult. The entire sequence first defines the heterosexual pairs as "nice" and "normal," and then tries to expand the societal definition to include homosexuals. Strategies of argument based on "sameness" often are based on the dominant culture's view of who or what is "normal." Homosexuals with HIV are made acceptable by being incorporated within representations of middle-class heterosexuality. While this is an attempt to transform the belief that homosexuals stand outside of "normal," the argument also reinforces oppressive class and cultural beliefs that narrowly define "normalcy" (i.e., acceptability).[18]

The authorial voice retains the objective, factual tone of the previous examples. Then, after providing the audience with the risk "information," the voice suggests that "You [the audience] *might* [my emphasis] want to use a condom."[19] The argument connects the audience to the subject in an attempt to influence behavior. It is implied that the audience can see themselves in this picture. If this *is* me, then who am I? It seems that I am a Benetton person in a Benetton world. It is striking how the individuals in Figure 21.3b could have made their way out of one of the Benetton clothing ads onto these pages. The people form a strikingly homogeneous impression. Diversity is characterized as skin color (which doesn't, however, make any difference) in a happy, middle-class, imaged world. *Colors* homogenizes the subject and then homogenizes the audience by suggesting that we are somehow reflected in these images.[20] Once again, viewers are assumed to match the profile of the implied audience. Or, if a particular viewer is not being addressed by this generic "you," then he or she is excluded from the audience. Either way, the argument alienates certain segments of the audience who do not see themselves within this imagery. Of course, every topic does not have to be addressed to every viewer. But *Colors* suggests that it is addressing every viewer through the combination of the individuals' gazes in the photos and first-person text speaking directly to the audience. Without differentiating between multiple audiences, every viewer is defined according to the argument.

US AND THEM. SOMETHING WE CAN AGREE ON

The authorial voice unites with the audience in appreciation of the subjects in Figures 21.1 and 21.2, while other arguments in *Colors* unite author and audience against the subject. In addition to celebrating the "good" in the world, *Colors* presents the "bad" from environmental destruction to political despots to hate groups. The religion issue, *Colors* 8, provides examples of very critical editorial positions. Within the "Cult" section of the magazine, an interesting change occurs in the authorial voice as a means of conveying this criticism. Rather than appearing absent or anonymous, the voice is made visible by creating a "conversation" between the author and the audience in the text. Questions are posed in first person, as if from the audience: "Do I get to drive the condom-mobile?"[21]; "What if *I* don't like red either?"[22]; and "*I* forgot to ask how many followers he has"[23] (my emphases). (If the authorial voice were speaking, the phrasing might be: Would *you* know one if *you* saw one?) And the questions are answered by the author in a conversational tone, thus establishing a "dialogue."

This strategy of argument is employed in the article on the Aryan Nation (Figure 21.4), a white supremacist group. The text and the photograph position the Aryan Nation as "other." The text portrays the group as on the outside, and not to be trusted: "How long have they been *around?*"[24] (my emphasis). The beliefs of the subject are treated pejoratively: "Who listens to this *stuff?*"[25] (again, my emphasis). The photographic treatment of the image supports this stance by showing the leader of the Aryan Nation, Reverend Richard Girnt Butler, in a pose in which he does not engage the viewer through eye contact. He is contained by his environment, but unlike the previous figures, he is dwarfed by the surroundings and the flags and insignia which are the symbols of his beliefs. He begins to merge with his physical context as the red color of the flags tinges his skin color, and the angle and blurriness of the photo cause his eyes almost to disappear. Because a bridge to the audience's world is not established through his gaze, he remains totally within this foreign context.

The "dialogue" between the authorial voice and the audience assumes agreement between the two. The author is merely providing the audience with *additional* information to reinforce this agreement: "It's not as simple as you [the audience] *might* [my emphasis] think."[26] Audience knowledge and belief is *presupposed* within the argument. This strategy, when applied to this subject matter, can accomplish certain goals within particular audiences. In previous examples, the voice spoke for the subject. Here, the voice speaks to the audience about the subject and, in this way, very clearly dissociates the author from the subject. There is no question and no confusion that the editors condemn the Aryan Nation. And by communicating an assumption of agreement between the audience and the editorial position, there also is no question that the audience condemns a group advocating racist, anti-Semitic, sexist, and homophobic beliefs. The argument creates a unified, self-satisfied, disgusted us (audience and author) and a distasteful, ludicrous them (the Aryan Nation).

The characterization of the Aryan Nation and Rev. Butler both ridicules and alienates them from the author-to-audience chat. The group is distinguished by how they look; and how they look is related to their beliefs. Not only does the visual representation of Butler diminish this leader, but we are told that we can recognize people who hold these racist and anti-Semitic views by what they wear.[27] [Q:] "Would I know one if I *saw* one? [A:] The Aryan Nation *uniform* is a nondescript blue. The only distinctive thing about it is the arm patch …You may *spot* one sticking anti-Semitic flyers on telephone poles …"[28] (my emphases, throughout). The idea that we can see beliefs is dangerously misleading, and also the same basis for some of the beliefs found in traditional hate groups – that is, color or non-European clothing is used to identify and attack people.[29] "You may *spot* one"[30] connotes bird-watching, bringing to mind furtive yet visually identifiable creatures. Not only are certain people and their beliefs diminished, but, in addition, these images when combined with the chatty "dialogue" make the group non-threatening. Members of the Aryan Nation are made laughable in their absurdity, and the informality of the chatty "dialogue" implies that a mainstream culture need not take them seriously. The very real dangers right-wing, extremist groups pose to the objects of their hate and to a democratic nation also is diminished, despite listing their crimes, which include murder.

E se non mi piace nemmeno il rosso?

CHI? LA FAMIGLIA DELL'UNICO AMORE

Who? ONE LOVE FAMILY

What if I don't like red either?

Who? THE CHURCH OF JESUS CHRIST CHRISTIAN, THE ARYAN NATIONS

Can Christians be terrorists?

I cristiani possono fare i terroristi?

CHI? LA CHIESA DI GESÙ CRISTO CRISTIANO, LE NAZIONI ARIANE

Figure 21.4 *Colors* No. 8, September 1994, 60–61 (religion issue, cult section).

Colors' model constructs the world as a place where "we can all get along," but has difficulty accommodating the obstacles to this vision. Beliefs the editors find objectionable are either glossed over, as in the "Musical Bodybuilders," or ostracized as with the Aryan Nation – avoidance or exclusion. Avoidance seems to be a convenient method used when the goal of a particular article/ section is to communicate harmony. Exclusion of a group such as the Aryan Nation means that the editors don't have to determine how individuals or groups holding objectionable or conflicting beliefs relate to the "positive" world. Characterizing these excluded groups as absurd also eliminates a perceived *need* to address this problem, because *Colors* is not dismissing a real threat.

THE GOOD AUDIENCE

The nine issues of *Colors* I examined cover a broad range of territory – geographically and thematically. Throughout these pages, the audience is assumed within the argument to accept, share, and, at least, openly consider the beliefs put forward by the editors. The audience is interested, engaged, and understanding; it agrees with or is sympathetic to the beliefs advocated. The audience is good.

When attempting to persuade an audience, communicating a receptive and accepting attitude on the audience's part is an effective strategy. This same strategy can be found throughout the mass media. It also is another form of positivity. An assumption of "goodness" may well help people to *be* good. But how do we learn to be good, if we don't understand the spectrum of ways in which undesirable behaviors are manifested? This assumption of audience "goodness" prevents any connection between the audience and oppressive beliefs. The audience escapes responsibility – it is not culpable.

One of the goals of the HIV risk sequence is to persuade the audience to use a condom; and another, related goal is to counter stereotypes of who is at risk and the idea that anyone is to blame. In this context, it would run counter to the goals and beliefs advocated to create audience culpability. The strategy sidesteps the issue of responsibility within relationships, while attempting to achieve it. One could argue that this is the intention in all of *Colors*: to avoid producing guilt in the audience, in the belief that guilt is not an effective or desirable vehicle for change.[31] Unfortunately, this is an approach that prevents an investigation of the variety of ways in which beliefs are manifested, and the relationship between degrees of manifestation.

The Aryan Nation article is an easy condemnation of white supremacy. The oppositionalism and the portrayal of the Aryan Nation's leader as alien disconnects this tradition of hate from contemporary and historical society in the United States, and the audience remains free from culpability; whereas the beliefs of groups such as the Aryan Nation are endemic to and supported by mainstream North American institutions and culture.[32] Characterizing the members of an audience as blameless may make them more open to an argument, but it also denies their responsibility within the social dynamic. White supremacy is an extreme position that attempts to maintain white privilege. But mainstream white institutions and individuals also are attempting to maintain, and certainly not divest themselves of, white privilege: from accepting superior employment opportunities; to not giving up city services in order to achieve neighborhood equalization; to not advocating an even distribution of monies across all school districts. In addition to maintaining white privilege, there is the wide range of individual behaviors that manifest racism in a racialized society: from the Aryan Nation's assertion of mud-people; to a white person's fear of black men; to assuming *first* a racial basis to any conflict in an interracial situation. Extremism is an exaggeration; not an isolated, social phenomenon. Helping an audience acquire more of an understanding or awareness of these complexities can provide them with tools for change.

Colors makes it look easy. For a better world, we don't have to give up anything. All we have to do is be willing to accept most people. All we have to do is change how we see other people – the change is outward toward the subject, and will not affect our own lives. But same-sex relationships *do* threaten the *primacy* of heterosexual and patriarchal beliefs in the United States. People of color in positions of authority do threaten white supremacy. If certain beliefs gain a measure of safety and legitimacy, they *will* effect change in the dominant culture. To think that oppression simply is the result of a misguided perception of people is to ignore and underestimate the ideological development of the right wing. American neoconservatives certainly understand that culture is political, and have developed their strategies accordingly.

DEFINING CULTURES

There are many ways to view cultures, and *Colors* seeks to bring its audience and subjects together in a visual appreciation of the world. It is true that the visual can be a flashpoint for hatred and violence – sometimes, what people look like is the basis of another person's hatred. But, sometimes, what people look like is a reflection or representation of their own belief systems; and a violent response (overt or covert) on the part of the perpetrator may be based on real or perceived conflicting belief systems. If *Colors* asks the audience to accept the subjects, what are we being asked to accept? What people look like? Are we really all the same, but different? Are we like a collection of Benetton sweaters – one large batch, just dyed different colors?

Acceptance of individuals or groups by the audience occurs in *Colors* through a realization of sameness: "they" are basically like "us." This realization by the audience creates an acceptance, and thus leads to a tolerant world. In this way, acceptance and tolerance are conjoined in the argument to achieve conflict resolution. Certainly tolerance has been a goal not only of *Colors*, but of many constituencies in a variety of human rights movements. And the strategy for creating a tolerant society often has been to present the minority or oppressed group as nonthreatening and homogenized. The group is portrayed as *deserving* fairness. Unfortunately, this strategy implies that those who are discriminated against must earn their rights, and tolerance is made to hinge on acceptability. "At its best, tolerance provides … 'annihilation by blandness.' At its worst, tolerance 'serves the cause of oppression.' "[33] *Colors* presents individuals and subcultures as *deserving* of the audience's approval. Through this argument, the conferring and the withholding of rights lies with the audience and the dominant culture in society. As Herbert Marcuse wrote on the repressive nature of tolerance in the 1950s: "… all contesting opinions must be submitted to 'the people' for its deliberation and choice."[34] Never is this assumption questioned through *Colors*' editorial stances – it is, rather, continually reinforced. Certainly, there must be a position between accepting others' beliefs and feeling or committing violence toward that group, otherwise resolving conflict is impossible. But, by hiding conflict as *Colors* does, this fundamental issue of opposing belief systems is ignored; leaving the audience without the resources to understand the conflict, let alone to negotiate that conflict within itself.

Defining a culture in "positive" terms – positive according to *Colors* – is not only a simplistic notion of conflict resolution, it also is a representation that denies an important aspect of a group's identity. Pain and oppression by no means fully define individuals or cultures. However, these experiences are embedded in the individual and the collective conscience of a people. A history reflecting violence against people also is a history of the belief systems of the dominant culture, that may be transformed in contemporary society but may not have disappeared. Proposing that people can "move on" to a level of unity if we just start from some imaginary beginning historically has been a position promoted by dominant political, social, and cultural groups. And though I believe the creators of *Colors* are not advocates of such a position, the argument constructed within the magazine lends support to this view. It is an argument that invokes the question "Why can't we all just get along?" Spoken by Rodney King this question is a painful lament that reveals the sordid history of the United States. But as a voice from the dominant culture, it becomes an argument that oppressed groups cannot afford to buy.

CONCLUSION

Colors is designed to reinforce an image of difference: from one issue to the next, it changes in size, overall topic, and subcultures depicted. But these differences remain stylistic rather than substantive. This visual and topical activity seems to be a substitute for any exploration of the complex nature of social issues, and masks the rigidity of argument. An argument is made and then remade, with another individual or culture as the subject. This simple replacement gives *Colors* its consistency, and communicates the fundamental "sameness" of people. The strategy also constitutes culture as clothing – just so much interchangeable color.

Attempting to present a vision apart from the mainstream involves more than representing people usually not shown in the mass media. For example, after people of color, or lesbians and gays, finally were pictured on television, it became clear that these groups still are not represented from their own cultural view. They are cast either as stereotypes of the dominant culture, or they are defined as "white" or asexual, respectively. The vision put forward by the dominant culture through the mass media is a vision that reflects itself. This mirror image is created not only through people and topics, but through authorial voices, belief systems, and strategies of argument. *Colors* presents cultures and subcultures that we usually don't see in a commercially funded publication, as if this will guarantee a different vision. But "it is impossible to subvert the present cultural framework within the discourses that define it."[35] Using design to question representation and provide alternative views, it is necessary to also explore alternative dynamics within arguments, and thus alternative strategies.

NOTES

First published in *Design Issues* 12 no. 3 (Autumn 1996): 60–76.

1. Henry A. Giroux, " 'World Without Borders': Buying Social Change," *The Subversive Imagination: Artists, Society, & Social Responsibility*, ed. Carol Becker (New York: Routledge, 1994) and Kate Jennings and Veronique Vienne, "Ad Campaigns (Benetton)," *Metropolis* (September 1992) discuss the motivations and implications of using photojournalism/news in a commercial context. While the editors of *Colors* insist on their separation from Benetton advertising, these writings provide valuable insight into this contemporary vision of making money and "doing good." These analyses also have remained within the arena defined by Benetton – culture as fashion. In this essay, I examine not only how the subjects (cultures) are represented but the ways in which audience and authors also are defined through the argument.
2. Tibor Kalman quoted by Steven Heller in "Benetton's Vivid Colors," "A Cold Eye" column, *Print* 47 (July/August 1993): 264–5.
3. *Colors 1* (Fall/Winter 1991): 63.
4. The heroes category in *Colors* includes groups that range from street children who are surviving in every part of the globe, to antiracist community activists in Germany, to an organization that removes the leftovers of war (i.e., land mines that kill civilians).
5. It is important to recognize that designers/editors are not the same as the authorial voice created, and actual audiences are not necessarily the same as implied audiences. The creation of an authorial voice, consciously or unconsciously, in part allows designers or writers to develop arguments that reflect views other than their own; whether or not they are those of a client or the subject represented. Design and communication often imply an audience that does not reflect everyone who actually views the representation. My focus in the essay is on these aspects of argument, rather than who is or is not designing, writing, or reading *Colors*.

6. *Colors* 1 (Fall/Winter 1991): 63.
7. Eric J. Sandeen, *Picturing an Exhibition: The Family of Man and 1950s America* (Albuquerque: University of New Mexico Press, 1995): 159. During my final revision, I came upon Sandeen's critique of Steichen's "Family of Man" exhibition, and I was struck by the number of parallels with my critique of *Colors*. The two do have "structural" similarities in that they both rely on the conventions of photojournalism and both were "underwritten with a large sum from a major source that blurred the distinction between family (culture) and corporation.
8. In *Picturing an Exhibition,* Eric Sandeen contrasts Edward Steichen's use of the gaze (connecting viewer and subject) with Robert Frank; who "did not encourage viewers to create bonds among the subjects within the picture," and he "did not allow his viewer to maintain the illusion that entering these compartments carried no cost ..." Ibid., 7.
9. *Colors 1* (Fall/Winter 1991): 8.
10. *Colors 2* (Spring/Summer 1992): 11.
11. Ibid., 11.
12. *Colors 1* (Fall/Winter 1991): 6.
13. *Colors 7* (June 1994): 46–47.
14. Ibid., 48–49.
15. Ibid., 50–51.
16. Ibid., 52–53.
17. Ibid., 52–53.
18. William Eric Perkins, "The Distorted Colors of Benetton," "A Cold Eye" column, *Print* 46 (July/August 1992): 268–9, critiques Oliviero Toscani's (photographer and art director of Benetton "advertorials") attempts to invoke racist images in Benetton advertisements as a means of exposing racial stereotypes. Perkins asserts that, rather than eliminating stereotypes, Toscani's images serve to reinforce racist beliefs. In the ads, Toscani begins with a stereotype, in an effort to alter it; in the HIV sequence, *Colors'* editors begin with a stereotype (i.e., the social definition of "normal") in an effort to expand it.
19. *Colors 7* (June 1994): 52–53.
20. The homogenization of subject and audience also parallels Benetton's notion of the market: interchangeable colorful people and interchangeable colorful clothing.
21. *Colors 8* (September 1994): 58.
22. Ibid., 60.
23. Ibid., 60.
24. Ibid., 60.
25. Ibid., 61.
26. Ibid., 61.
27. A relationship is built across Benetton clothing ads, Benetton "advertorials," and *Colors* Magazine. Benetton represents itself as a *visibly* "moral" company; the audience, the Benetton consumer, can be *seen* as moral; and "others" can be seen as immoral.
28. *Colors 8* (September 1994): 61.
29. Ibid., 61.
30. Ibid., 61.
31. *Colors* attempts to achieve change within the context of making the audience feel good. This is an interesting parallel to the requirements of consumption, that is, having to make consumers feel good so they will purchase products.
32. June Jordan, "In the Land of White Supremacy," and Loretta Ross, "White Supremacy in the 1990s," *Eyes Right! Challenging the Right Wing Backlash*, ed. Chip Berlet (Boston: South End Press, 1995).
33. Thomas Paine, quoted by James Darsey in "Die Non"; *Queer Words, Queer Images*, ed. R. Jeffrey Ringer (New York: New York University Press, 1994), 67.
34. Herbert Marcuse, "Repressive Tolerance," quoted by James Darsey in "Die Non," 67.
35. Steven Heller describes the changes in format as "unique." Although magazines don't change size from issue to issue, *Colors* does rely on tradition – the traditional methods and their associated beliefs of journalism and photojournalism. Steven Heller, "Benetton's Vivid *Colors*," "A Cold Eye" column, *Print* 47 (July/August 1993): 264–5.

22

DESIGN, ENVIRONMENT AND SOCIAL QUALITY: FROM *EXISTENZMINIMUM* TO "QUALITY MAXIMUM"

Ezio Manzini

The environmental issue has a lengthy history. In almost thirty years it has progressed from the agitated argumentation of a few scientists and environmentally conscious groups to become a theme which permeates the entire society, influencing the orientation of both generalized trends and everyday decisions.

During the course of this history at least two decisive changes in perspective have become necessary. The first concerned the passage of the question of the environment from a minority critique to a problem formally acknowledged and made a part of the agenda of all actors in the society. The second shift in perspective, which must take place today, is one which should lead to a vision of the environmental issue as an integral part of a larger phenomenon: the across-the-board crisis of the development model which has been dominant until today.

Beginning with this new perspective, the following contribution will advocate the necessity for a more radical approach in dealing with the interaction of design and sustainability, and presents proposals for this necessity.

THE 1980s: "NORMALIZED" ECOLOGICAL DESIGN

During the 1980s the environmental issue penetrated the mature industrial societies effecting, in different ways, their various social actors, leading to new policies, becoming a part of corporate programs, introducing a new demand for environmental quality in the marketplace. Thus an "ecological reorientation" of the system of production and consumption became a widely discussed and accepted theme. Nevertheless, it should be noted that this debate has taken place within a context (that of the 1980s in the industrialized society) in which the world appeared to be wealthy, healthy, and satisfied. The environmental reorientation of the system was imagined as a series of operations to be effected within a substantially stable social and industrial framework – a reorientation that would not require difficult changes in lifestyles nor, in any case, changes in the overall development model.

Within the cultural and economic atmosphere of the 1980s the environmental issue tended to be "normalized." In other words, it became a political, economic, and engineering theme to be treated in a substantially technical manner through an appropriate "redesigning of the extant." For example, CFC was removed from spray cans, park benches were made of recycled plastic, automobile bumpers were designed so that they could be removed and recycled.

All of this is important, and its significance should not be underestimated. The fact that it has become "normal" to think that the extant should be redesigned in order to render it less harmful to the environment is a noteworthy achievement, and all possible efforts should be made to ensure that theory be translated into coherent practice to the fullest extent. Nevertheless, at the same time the inadequacy of this "normalized" way of dealing with the environmental question is becoming increasingly evident today.

THE 1990s: FROM "NORMALIZATION" TO A "NEW RADICALISM"

Today the melding of environmental issues with other themes which are emerging during the 1990s and which, in turn, present us, at an international level, with an interweaving of social, economic, political, and ethnic questions, has led to the widespread sensation, even in the most industrialized nations, that what is taking place today is actually a structural crisis, and that the global model of development is the true issue under discussion.

I do not intend to develop this theme as a whole, on this occasion. Nevertheless, I am convinced that this general background outline is necessary, because it is the starting point from which it is possible to view the environmental question and its relationship to design in a new light.

Faced with the evidence of the interconnectedness of the environmental, economic and sociocultural crises, it becomes increasingly clear that the scenario of the "redesign of what exists" is not sufficient for the discovery of true solutions. And this is not true only because of the fact that such a path will lead to a system of production and consumption which is less polluting than the present one, but which cannot be considered sustainable over the long term (something which is becoming increasingly obvious to those who work closely on environmental questions).

It is also true because the "extant" is inevitably destined to change due to the other crises impacting it (and this is a conviction which is emerging among observers of reality who study the situation from many points of view, not just from that of the environment). In other words: a recyclable motorcar is better than a traditional one, but it makes no contribution to resolving the problem of urban mobility, nor the problem of unemployment, nor the conflicts between the North and South of the globe.

Thus what is required today is to imagine innovative solutions with a high level of radicalness (containing some kind of hypothetical response to the problems at hand), proposing alternative paths to those of the past and present. This objective might (justifiably) appear rather ambitious. But the aim is not to find "the solution" for all questions: the idea, more modestly, is to propose solutions which contain some spark of innovation, meaning a new way of behaving or of viewing the world.

In fact the new model of development will not be born on a drawing board or around a conference table as a perfectly complete theorem, but it will emerge from dialogue and conflict among a multiplicity of ideas, visions, and proposals. It will come into being thanks to a widespread atmosphere of innovation involving all social actors. Designers will indubitably play a part in the process.

ENVIRONMENTAL POLICY: TACTICS AND STRATEGY

From the entire problematic scenario described in the preceding section, let us now consider the parts most closely linked to the activities of the designer: products, services and, in wider terms, the criteria of quality and value with which we evaluate the artificial environment.

Considering this theme from the point of view of environmental sustainability it becomes obvious that, definitively, the objective to be pursued can only be that of a society in which lifestyles are based as little as possible upon the consumption of energy or materials (to which we must also add other resources such as land, air, and water). It is equally evident that this objective can take on a variety of meanings, and can be pursued with different environmental policies in keeping with different possible interpretations.

We are aware of the fact that environmental impact (I) is a result of the population (P) which represents a "demand for results" (R), thanks to the specific environmental impact of the technologies employed (T) to achieve those results. In a synthetic form this equation can be expressed as follows: I = P x R x T. We can consider an environmental policy as "tactical" when the following occurs: if (R) cannot be modified, one attempts to improve the technical eco-efficiency (tE) of the system by improving the technologies (T) employed to achieve the results (tE = R/T). Following this path, changes in lifestyle are not required and the role of design is that of introducing a technical redesign to the extant conditions.

On the other hand, it is possible to consider an environmental policy with a "strategic" effect which, placing the social demand for results in discussion, seeks to achieve a higher social eco-efficiency (sE). In other terms, an improved relationship between the individuals to be satisfied (P) and their demands for results in relation to the available technologies (sE = P / R x T). To make a strategic environmental policy practical it is necessary that significant changes in lifestyles take place, along with a sociocultural innovation leading to new "consumption scenarios."

CONSUMPTION SCENARIOS

Within the context of improved social eco-efficiency, differing but complementary proposals for "consumption scenarios" are possible. Although complementary, the following "consumption scenarios" are based on different degrees of transformation with respect to today's dominant "culture of consumption." In synthesis, they can be described as follows:

1. FROM CONSUMPTION TO CARE

This scenario implies going beyond the misunderstood notion of "functional" which has led to the acceleration of consumption and to the world of "disposable" objects. Here design will have to develop products with both the technical and cultural capacity to survive over time: products which require care, with which the user can establish an emotional relationship.

2. FROM CONSUMPTION OF PRODUCTS TO UTILIZATION OF SERVICES

This scenario implies going beyond the notion of possession (and, therefore, of personal consumption) of products, reaching a concept of "utilization," or in other words, of a "non-destructive" and "non-individual" consumption of product-services. This is a scenario in which a higher level of social eco-efficiency can be achieved by orienting the "demand for results" towards new services that offer more efficient use of resources. The task of the designer then will be to develop product-services with high environmental potential and, at the same time, a high level of social approval/attraction.

3 FROM CONSUMPTION TO NON-CONSUMPTION

This scenario is obviously the most radical, and that in which the operation can only take place at a cultural level.

Again in this context design, if viewed as the "culture of products and services," can play an important role. It can generate scenarios, criteria of quality and value judgments in which the "reduction of needs" can be experienced as an "increase in social quality."

CULTURES OF "REDUCTION"

All this may remind us of certain experiences of the past: the pursuit of an *existenzminimum*[1] during the first decades of this century in Europe, or the "anti-consumption" episodes of the 1960s in Europe and the United States. Undoubtedly links of continuity do exist with these movements. Here, for the sake of succinctness, it is more useful to point out the differences: in different forms, the two movements mentioned above sprang from motivations of an ethical nature in order to reach proposals which were in opposition to a model of production and consumption which was in an early phase of development (in the case of *existenzminimum*) or at a high point in its development (in the case of the anti-consumption of the 1960s).

The ethical force of my proposal, on the other hand, has a more concrete and tangible basis in the environmental issues and challenges to a model of consumption that is clearly destined to change because it is based on a model of development which is deeply in crisis.

If we examine the situation from the point of view of the designer, the problem is not so much one of evoking an ethical principle based on an environmental necessity, as of proposing solutions that appear to be better than those presently in use. Today's *existenzminimum* must be translated into proposals that can appear to increasingly large segments of the population as opportunities to achieve a higher level of social quality (a term which in an initial approximation we can equate with "quality of life;" but in doing so we must eliminate the individualistic, hedonistic connotations which have been attached to this expression). A possible slogan: *existenzminimum* as maximum quality.

EXISTENZMINIMUM? MAXIMUM QUALITY!

The problem for designers can be summed up as follows: how to propose an *existenzminimum* which will appear attractive and will thus be freely chosen in the midst of a variety of alternative proposals. First of all, in order to be attractive the proposal must not correspond to a scenario of deprivation. It must not correspond to a notion of life within the same values and criteria of quality as those of the past, offering a little bit less of everything (a world in which the expectations of quality remain the same, but which instead offers fewer automobiles, less lighting, fewer disposable products, fewer strawberries in December, etc.). Such a world could come into being as a necessary response to some sort of catastrophic event, but it is unthinkable as a product of free choice. Fewer automobiles, fewer disposable products, less exotic fruit are situations that can not only become acceptable, even attractive, but only within the framework of a new cultural scenario: a scenario in which cars are no longer as necessary because there are other, better ways of moving about; a scenario in which to rediscover the value of care for material things and the quality of things to be cared for, in which to appreciate the sense of the passage of time, the changing of the seasons which is communicated by the variations in the fruit available for consumption.

Design can play a fundamental role in the definition of this scenario or, better, of many such scenarios which, in a complementary or competitive way, lead in this direction. In order to do so, however, design will have to re-examine the very basis of its culture. It should not be forgotten that design was born and developed within the context of the development model in crisis today.

Likewise, fundamental concepts such as form, function, client, user, and market must be revisited. The same is true for the role of technology, aesthetics and design itself.

Here, in conclusion, are some brief considerations on these three last issues:

TECHNOLOGY: TOOLS FOR NEW TYPES OF BEHAVIOR

Over the years technology has been a powerful force for change. Not only because of the emerging evidence of the environmental problems caused by its employment, but also because of its destabilizing influence at both the social and cultural level: from the concept of space and time (changed by telecommunications) to that of matter (changed by new materials), from the notion of work (changed by automation) to those of reality (changed by the advent of virtual realities) and of life (in relation to the possibilities of genetic engineering). Therefore the theme today is how to direct the power of technology towards a sustainable society (and a coherent model of development). The sustainable society requires products and services that make use of new technologies for the care of things, for intelligent participation, for a new social quality. But the problem is also that of understanding how to transform this technical apparatus while being aware that it has already transformed us, and has transformed what we think of as "our environment."

AESTHETICS: GIVING FORM TO SUSTAINABILITY

Every era has its own ethics and aesthetics. Aesthetics represents the way in which a historical period and the values it contains "take form." During the first part of the century design played a decisive role in giving form to modernity. During the 1980s, for better or worse, design was the protagonist of an aestheticization (as superficial as it was widespread) of things: an aestheticization which, on the whole, has proven incapable of countering the more generalized aesthetic decay of the world. Today, the perspective of a sustainable society has not yet "taken form" and an aesthetic of sustainability has yet to be born.

This theme of aesthetics must be considered seriously: as it has become commonplace to view the aesthetic dimension as secondary, an "extra" to be added when the rest has been resolved, a luxury for those who have everything. This leads to the impression of a sort of contradiction between ethics (with its presumed rigor) and aesthetics (with its presumed frivolity). This opposition is typical of the 1980s and of the cultural confusion of the period. In reality, aesthetics is connected to ethics in the sense that no true, profound aesthetic renewal can occur without being based on a value system. Moreover, in a phase of transition such as that of the present this aesthetic dimension becomes a fundamental factor for change. It becomes a "social attractor," in the sense that it orients the choices of a multiplicity of individuals. It becomes a way of expressing a synthetic, and therefore intelligible form, the complexity of a proposal. In summary, in the present moment we can state that the perspective of the sustainable society has a great need for an aesthetic of sustainability.

DESIGN: GIVING FORM AND OFFERING OPPORTUNITY

Design certainly cannot change the world nor can it design lifestyles (imposing ways of acting on people in keeping with its intentions). But design can "give form" to a changing world, and "offer opportunities" for new types of behavior.

"To give form" means to operate within a more general cultural context: by amplifying and rendering visible the "weak signs" expressed by society (in terms of new types of demand and behavior), proposing consistent criteria of quality in a perspective of sustainability, and designing overall scenarios which, again, "give form" to the sustainable society. "To offer opportunity" means acting in the field of direct intervention, proposing products and services that make possibilities concrete, which in turn "offer opportunities" for new types of behavior and new lifestyles in keeping with a new notion of social quality.

These are the areas in which design can play a significant role in the social dynamics of the period to come. These are the limits of its action, but they are also its possibilities and responsibilities. The themes discussed herein will constitute the terrain upon which the hopes for the achievement of a new, sustainable society will rest, not by necessity or imposition, but through a "free choice" of solutions judged to be improvements. And, among all of the forms which the aftermath of the present model of development may assume, that which is the result of a free choice of solutions evaluated and understood to be better is certainly the most auspicious.

NOTES

First published in *Design Issues* 10 no. 1 (Spring 1994): 37–43.

1. The German term *Existenzminimum* was devised in the late 1920s to denote the minimum spatial requirements of an individual or family within a rationally planned large-scale housing project.

23

VALUES IN DESIGN: *EXISTENZMINIMUM*, "MAXIMUM QUALITY," AND "OPTIMAL BALANCE"

John Hirst

This paper seeks to contribute to the discussion of values that design activity could begin to realize in the coming years. It takes as its inspiration and starting point the article "Design, Environment and Social Quality: From *Existenzminimum* to "Quality Maximum" by Ezio Manzini.[1] Manzini argues that current design is based on a model of consumption that is going to change in response to the crisis in the model of economic and social development that has spread worldwide since the Second World War. The threat of global disaster at the level of the environment is the most compelling of a series of severe difficulties that beset the modern and modernizing nations, and implicate design. Manzini contends that "design will have to reexamine the very basis of its culture." He puts particular emphasis on the significance of the role of values in designing: "The problem is not so much one of evoking an ethical principle based on environmental necessity, as of proposing solutions that appear better than those presently in use." He proposes that the concept of *existenzminimum* must come to be identified with the realization of a higher level of social quality. He asserts the need for an aesthetic to be based upon a value system, and emphasizes the important role that an aesthetic of sustainability would play in the transition to a new economic and social order. This, he envisages to involve design "... proposing consistent criteria of quality in a perspective of sustainability, and designing overall scenarios ... proposing products and services that make possibilities concrete ... for new types of behavior and new lifestyles in keeping with a new notion of social quality."

We can see here a vision of design that goes beyond the designing of artifacts, or even systems of artifacts, to the design of culture or at least aspects of culture. It is arguable that design and the technological changes that it expresses have always been forces to reshape culture, even where this has taken place unconsciously or unintentionally. Hence, we may see the present time and the issues of environmentalism as offering an opening for a deeper cultural consciousness. In this regard, I wish to raise some general points about values; how we construe and interpret them in respect of material culture; and how we might reconstrue them. The ways we think about and act on our values are of crucial importance, since they give shape to society. Our very notions of what is a "problem" and what counts as a "solution" are bound up inextricably with what is "best," "right," "important," and "desirable." The way values are construed has to be clear to give us intellectual freedom of movement. While I do not propose to outline here a system of values for design in a sustainable society, I do intend that the points raised will advance the development of such a system.

SCALAR VALUES AND MATERIAL CULTURE

The economic system of the market places a monetary value on every commodity that is exchanged in a contemporary society, at each point of transaction. The monetary value is expressed as a numerical value of a currency. Conceptually, this system of signs deploys the arithmetic properties of the natural numbers so that it is possible to think that a commodity may increase or decrease in value; that it may be more or less valuable than another commodity; and that it may be affordable or unaffordable. This is one very clear instance of "scalar thinking" in relation to value. By "scalar thinking," I mean conceptualization that embodies a system of signs which are commonly understood to form a scale (i.e., a system of graded steps wherein the grading generates a sense of direction – upwards or downwards – with respect to the qualities of something). Scalar thinking is a stage beyond, but draws upon semantics of comparison as embodied in the "normal," "comparative" and "superlative" forms of adjectives (e.g., "large," "larger," "largest").

Scalar thinking in relation to values prompts us to see value comparatively, and to seek it in the superlative. One of its expressions to emerge early in the industrial era was the "principle of utility." This is the proposition that the "good" in any context is that which gives rise to the greatest happiness of the greatest number of people. In a more sophisticated form, it appears in cost/benefit analysis, seeking within social planning to determine what course of action gives the greatest benefit for the least cost.

The idea that there is a minimum level of physical resources required to sustain the survival of a human being has arisen in many contexts in this century. It has been an underpinning for the specification of nutrition schedules and for the setting of welfare payments, as well as the provision of living space in housing schemes. For implementation, any such minimalist program relies upon measurements of relevant elements (grams of protein, costs of essential commodities). Presumably for *existenzminimum* design in the context of a program of environmentally sustainable development, we might be concerned with the quantities of energy and raw materials used to produce particular designs, or to sustain particular lifestyles. Thus, designers might systematically seek to innovate to reduce those requirements. In this case, perhaps some extensions of the principles of value engineering would be appropriate. It could certainly progress the search for lower resource usage.

Ezio Manzini also states, "The problem for designers can be summed up as follows: how to propose an *existenzminimum* which will appear attractive and will thus be freely chosen in the midst of a variety of alternative proposals. First of all, in order to be attractive, the proposal must not correspond to a scenario of deprivation." Hence, there is the need for this version of *existenzminimum* design to be concerned not just with the notion of "adequacy" but, rather, with that of "maximum quality." European culture has derived much of its concept of the quality of material things from the era of aristocracy, in which the conspicuous consumption of materials and energy marked out those with status and power. Hence, the best materials are, characteristically, the rarest; and suppliers will control supply to keep them rare; and the most valuable products embody the most labor (e.g., the relationship between the price of a carpet and the number of knots per square centimeter). These visions of quality are kept very much alive by advertising and the business system that supports it, even though it is at odds with the logic of mass production. Hence, we inhabit a prodigious and all-embracing material culture; most of which, in its own terms, is rendered relatively undesirable. Scalar thinking in respect to values comes in with equal force with regard to both *existenzminimum* and "quality maximum." What seems clear is that Manzini leaves us with a paradox. If something is minimalist in its use of resources, it can't be maximum quality, and vice versa. Our scalar conceptions of value set these concerns at opposite poles on just about any scales you can imagine.

A CURVILINEAR LOGIC OF NEED-VALUE

What I wish to suggest is that, in order to get anything like the results that Ezio Manzini quite rightly sees as necessary, we have to find a different logic of value to replace the scalar logic. We have to reinvent the ways we construe our "blessings." As a first step, we might go back to how we relate "value" to the concept of "need." If we start with a physiological need such as that of the maintenance of the body temperature, then we could, perhaps, agree that our physical circumstances, in principle, fall into one of three categories which we could designate as "too cold," "comfortable" and "too hot." If we take a range of air temperatures between 5°C and 55°C, and plot them against a subjective scale of sensed physical comfort for a naked human subject; then we would produce a curved graph with the high area, probably around 30°C, representing an optimal point, with the degree of sensed comfort declining as the physical temperature increases or decreases outside of a small range. The comfort zone falls around the peak of a curvilinear rather than a scalar form. The comfort zone constitutes a physiologically grounded value.

It is not at all surprising that our environmental temperature preferences should work in this fashion, since our body temperature is the outcome of a built-in homeostatic process that keeps us at an optimum operating temperature. Our need to maintain our body temperature is not usefully understood in terms of minima or maxima (i.e., in scalar terms) but, rather, in terms of "optimal" value thinking, which is what comes from viewing the situation according to a "curvilinear" logic of value.

In how many contexts can this logic be applied? The answer to this question is not altogether clear at present, but I suspect that it can be extended a good deal further than the maintenance of the temperature of the human body.

CHINESE MEDICINE AND "OPTIMAL BALANCE" VALUES

Homeostatic processes in the human body are a familiar theme in the science of physiology. However, the theme of optimal balance value is much more evident in the theory of Chinese medicine. A contrast between the perspectives on health in scientific medicine and Chinese medicine brings this out clearly. Western scientific medicine construes the human body as a biochemical machine that is healthy so long as it does not malfunction. Its malfunctions are attributable to specific, naturally arising, organic disorders; tissue damage through accident; disruption through infection; genetically motivated deterioration or poisoning from the environment; or combinations of these.

Diagnosis relates to the categorization of symptoms and to the identification of the probable causes, whether internal or external. Treatment comprises the enactment of a sequence of steps to eliminate the cause of malfunction, or to remove or replace the malfunctioning element where restoration of the benign condition of the body tissue is no longer possible. Western medicine also has a concept of "fitness," which means that a body is able to undertake sustained strenuous activity of some sort without undue fatigue or damage. Keeping fit is commonly believed to be a way to stay healthy, although fit people are known to have suffered heart attacks. Generally, though, concepts of preventive health care are weak except where some clear correlations have been established between behaviors and various morbid physical conditions (e.g., smoking and lung disease). Lastly, there is a fairly sharp distinction in the culture between food and medicine. These are sold in different shops, packaged very differently, marketed on very different premises, and interpreted within very different conceptual frames. Food is multivalent; it should be tasty, attractive and nutritious. Its consumption is an essential component of daily life. It forms a major element in social life. It can be used to define self, status, gender, and culture. Medicine, on the other hand, is instrumental. It may be palatable if you are lucky. You shouldn't take it unless there is something "wrong" with you. It may have "side effects" which may be unwanted, or, themselves, a "symptom" of ill health. The taking of medicine usually is discreet, if not private, and may be construed as a sign of invalidity and, therefore, of weakness. Other things being equal, a sick person does not have the standing of a well one.

Chinese medical theory conceives things differently. The healthy person is in a state of dynamic equilibrium between the various balancing and interdependent forces, and energies that course through, generate and maintain him or her.[2] If there is an imbalance or disharmony, then it may be detected by recognizing subtle changes in surface features of the body: the pulse, the eyes, the skin, the tongue, etc., and measures can be taken to correct it. The body has its own system to restore and maintain its balances, and the role of the corrective measures is to support this system's efforts to restore itself. Everything that is ingested into the body can affect these balances, so that there is no sharp division between foods and medicines. All foods have medicinal impact, and all medicines have nutritive implications. Moreover, the benefit of any substance to the body is radically relativistic. Nothing is essentially poisonous nor essentially health-enhancing, in itself. Vitamin C, for example, seen as a universally beneficial item by westerners, is viewed as damaging for some conditions of chi-deficiency in Chinese medical theory. Seasonal changes, diet, lifestyle, and emotional conditions are seen as major factors in shaping health; and infectious diseases are given less prominence. The latter can get hold of a person's body only if the systems of the body become imbalanced. Therefore, there is a premium on a preventive approach to disease. The doctor counsels diet and lifestyle changes as much as prescribing specific remedies. Thus, in the system of Chinese medical theory, the notion of "optimal balance" of the body is the basis for determining all action.

OPTIMAL BALANCES IN THE BIOSPHERE

Environmental concern is based upon the insights of ecology and the systems sciences, such as meteorology and oceanography, that interpret the biosphere. These sciences also reveal the significance of optimal balances in the operation of the systems that support all life on earth, such as those regulating the proportion of oxygen against other gases in the atmosphere, the level of salinity in the oceans, and the balance between the assimilation and loss of heat between the earth's surface and space. If life on the planet is to continue as we know it, then these and other balances must be preserved.[3]

The concept of "carrying capacity," as applied to the biosphere or to an ecosystem within it, is very much a balance-related concept; as is the equation that within an ecosystem waste is equivalent to food.

Both the body and the biosphere have their own optimal balances. The world of human culture, of societies, organizations, and artifacts exists between the two. It incorporates the body and is lodged in the biosphere. If a culture that embodies an industrial ecology is to be possible, it must be able to situate itself in a balanced mediation of the microcosm of the body and the macrocosm of the biosphere. This requires a different vision of the role of culture than that which is common today; where it is seen as marking out a particular group on the basis of beliefs, values and customs. It calls for a critical approach to all practices and technologies supported by the different belief systems and modes of living that have evolved in human societies worldwide, with respect to their sustainability and their capability to promote balance in the physical bodies of members of those societies. It also calls for a search for the dynamics and optimal balances in the humanly designed and constructed world.

GIVING A SENSE TO THE CONCEPT OF OPTIMAL BALANCE IN THE DESIGNED WORLD

The anthropologist, E. T. Hall, has identified all elements of culture as being types of extensions of the human being.[4] This ability to develop bodily extensions and to change these rather than the physical body, itself, has given the human species an enormous evolutionary advantage, according to Hall. Humanity is not dependent on any particular environment or ecological niche, but can thrive in many contexts by modifying the immediate impacts of the environment. If it is a useful metaphor to see cultural products as extensions of the human being; then it may be an equally useful venture to explore whether the metaphor of "optimal balance" that occurs with respect to the physiological processes of the body does not also have its analogues in the cultural extensions of the body.

The idea that there may be balances that cultures either achieve or fail to achieve also is suggested in *Laws of Media*,[5] the last work of Marshall McLuhan with his son, Eric. Their vision is of a human culture as a dynamic field in which the change in a cultural element, be it a material artifact, a concept, a technology, or any other type of element, follows four law-like principles. These may be expressed as follows:

1. For every cultural artifact, there is something that it enhances or advances.
2. For every cultural artifact, there is something that it displaces, obsolesces, or pushes into the periphery.
3. For every cultural artifact, there is some aspect of a previously existing condition that it retrieves or brings out from the periphery.
4. For every cultural artifact, when it is pushed or extended to the limits of its potential, it will take on a form that reverses what had been its original characteristics.

This tetrad of effects is present simultaneously in all cultural elements.

If we take the private car as an example, then we can say that it enhances personal mobility and speed of travel. It has displaced rail travel (in Western societies). It retrieves the freedom of movement given to the individual traveler by the horse drawn carriage. As the number of cars multiplies, the characteristic of gridlock is approached and the reverse of enhanced mobility is produced.

This structure of change is a very close match to the process of change expressed in the Taoist symbol, where the contrary and complementary principles of yin and yang are shown as merging into each other, with each containing a part of the other. The contraries move in an eternal dialectic that constitutes the whole.

These ways of conceiving a situation invite the thought that there is a point or zone of balance before the process generates more contrary than intended effects, and that this zone is the ground to hold and around which to institute change. McLuhan's model of change suggests a system which inevitably is swinging back and forth between extremes, and where innovation in cultural elements is motivated by the lurch of the activity into its reversed side. The vested interest that a business corporation has in its current technologies and their outputs, and the system of the market, can operate as an obstacle to restraints. Returning to the issues surrounding the private car, a current development illustrates this. In Hong Kong at the present time, the government has proposed limiting the number of new cars allowed on the roads by introducing a quota system. The reaction of the automobile retail business and the motoring associations has been very hostile. The government has been accused of proposing something that is an infringement of human rights. This is in a society that does not have an automobile industry.

In the case of the private car and its impacts on society, most of the expressed concerns are about a balance of one type or another. In the Hong Kong case, it is about the ratio of cars to available road space. There also are concerns about the speed at which cars go on motorways relative to the control the drivers have over them to stop them to prevent accidents. There are concerns about the fact that the fuel consumed by cars is nonrenewable and is, therefore, not being replaced. There is concern in many cities about the buildup of aerial pollution from motor vehicles at a rate that is faster than the natural air flows can disperse it. There is concern over the amount of space within a city given over the cars, and the road systems that they require.

It might be argued that each of the above concerns argues for our having an intuitive sense for there being a balance of benefits in one form or another. The balance between the number of cars and available road space is, perhaps, the most obvious; while the balance between the space for cars and the space for other things in the city may be more contestable. But most people's commonsense probably would agree that a mode of transport should serve the interests of a city and its residents, and that there was a point at which redevelopment for urban expressways and multi-storey car parks was reversing that relationship.

Clearly, here is the issue of means and ends. The quality of life in the city is the end and the transport system a means to its achievement. When the speed of the transport system is put before the quality of the urban environment, then a clear view of that relationship has been lost. It is equally obvious that, in many cities, this has happened.

For city councils, as for national governments, the concern to increase the wealth of the community as measured in scalar terms is perceived as the predominant value. Road networks create jobs in their building, and the "improved communications" make the city more commercially competitive. But because the need-based values of citizens are not reflected in any simple relationship to the scalar values of the community's monetary income, life gets worse while the city gets richer. The "quality of life" seems to dissolve into a confusion of conflict between different constituencies and interest groups. The monetary measure of the city's increased trade becomes the only yardstick for its quality.

There is, of course, a vicious circle here. People form conflicting interest groups because they see their values as differently realized in the same situation. They see these values differently realized because they see themselves as participating differently in the situation. But this conflict is exacerbated if the people involved are seeing their potential benefits in terms of scalar values.

To take note of signs of deterioration in a dimension of urban life and to take preventive steps before the situation becomes a fully-fledged urban problem requires an orientation toward social and material culture that is analogous to the preventive approach of Chinese medicine to diseases of the body. If we sought to envisage such an orientation, then we might come to devise strategies to deal with urban problems and also reduce consumption; both of which would reduce environmental problems.

"CONVIVIALITY" AS AN OPTIMAL BALANCE VALUE

In *Tools for Conviviality*,[6] Ivan Illich critiques industrial society on the grounds that industrial tools are too efficient at upsetting balances between the human being and the environment. He introduced the term "conviviality," which he defined as the "... autonomous and creative intercourse among persons and the intercourse of persons with their environment: and this in contrast to the demands made upon them by others, and by a manmade environment."[7] His argument is that both technologies and organizations in the modern industrial state have displaced human power and autonomy to such an extent that they bring disutilities to society as a whole, and that further extensions of industrial capability will only make things worse.

Conviviality is a quality of technologies and institutions that increase human power and autonomy in a total sense. A favorite example is the bicycle, which increases a person's mobility without decreasing that of anyone else. The car, on the other hand, requires extensive roads which constrict the use of space by non-motorists and is, therefore, not convivial.

In Illich's view, industrial tools per se are inherently damaging, and continued expansion of their use will lead to a major catastrophe in the industrial system, itself, perhaps along the lines outlined in *The Limits to Growth*.[8] The only alternative he envisions is some type of industrially managed ecologically oriented society that would be even more repressive than growth-driven capitalism. Therefore, it is necessary to give up industrial tools entirely, and to begin what he terms "convivial reconstruction."

Illich's analysis is penetrating and still very pertinent to understanding what we are experiencing at the present time. Nevertheless, it seems to make more sense to construe the notion of conviviality as a concept to mark the point at which a tool is operating in a zone of optimal balance of its benefits within a society, rather than as an inherent quality of some tools and not others. Albeit there may be some technologies that are just never convivial, given the nature of life on earth (e.g., nuclear power), in the same way that some substances never can be ingested to benefit the human body.

If this idea is acceptable, then we might seek to extend and further define Illich's notion of conviviality in a range of contexts of human social life, and to establish scales and dimensions of interaction that could shape the constraints on the design of material culture.

GREEN POLITICS AND INDUSTRIAL ECOLOGY

A response to the environmental crisis from scientists in the early 1970s was *Blueprint for Survival*.[9] The direction for planning and design it outlined, and which has been followed in much green writing since, has been to take the constraints of the ecosystem and to work backwards from these to determine what is environmentally sustainable in terms of the structure of our material culture. Now, while an information-gathering program on the carrying capacities of different parts of the ecosystem in relation to different forms of technology and resource use would be an invaluable contribution to the setting of parameters, it might be seen as repressive if the concern with optimal human conditions were not central. In a similar way, industrial ecology orchestrates the operations of government and industry at the various levels, but does not deal with the relationship of these institutions to the individuals in the society. Unless there is a shift in values on the part of people, generally, there will not be widespread support for these changes, and politicians and legislators will continue to seek compromises with vested interests.

SOCIAL VALUE CHANGE AND THE ROLE OF DESIGNERS

What is proposed in this paper is that, as an international community, we must reappraise the way we construe what is valuable in our use of the material world and ask what gives us the most convivial form of life, instead of seeking to stockpile or consume as much as we can of what we have been led to believe is good for us. This requires a widespread change of values. Such a widespread change can take place as opinion leaders change their views and influence others. Designers are in a special position in this context. On the basis of their experience, they can contribute to identifying the balances that achieve conviviality in the domain of material culture. On the basis of their role, they have access to those who make decisions about how resources are deployed and to a variety of other professionals who have more specialized concerns. They are well placed to influence professional opinion.

Popular opinion is less entrenched than professional opinion on matters of value, I suspect. Also, among people in Western societies, there is a growth of opinion in favor of things that manifest the kind of approach to value outlined here. There is the interest in alternative medical therapies; most of which advocate a preventive approach to disease and, therefore, a concern with the balances of inputs to the individual. Psychotherapy and counseling encourage an attitude of honesty with respect to the recognition of needs, and of what is satisfying. If the ethos of the pursuit of balanced satisfactions were taken up more widely in other professions and disseminated through the media in place of the present encouragement to consume, a value change could occur quite quickly.

I do not contend that a misconstrued notion of value in scalar terms (to the exclusion of recognizing the significance of optimal balance) is the only factor in the overgrowth of material culture in industrial societies. There also is the displacement of needs from emotional and spiritual contexts to material ones. This is more complex, and worthy of a separate paper. However, awareness of the logic of physiological need is a useful starting point. If it is true of the demand for a material product that "The more you have, the more you want," then it is not meeting a physiological need or its extension in a functional need; but the need is construed materially from some other source. If there is not then a physiological or functional need, why try to satisfy it with a product of material culture?

Ezio Manzini calls for tools for new types of behavior. What is essential for innovations of all types now is that they do not initiate the global society into yet another form of material excess.

NOTES

First published in *Design Issues* 12 no. 1 (Spring 1996): 38–47.

1. Ezio Manzini, "Design, Environment and Social Quality: From *Existenzminimum* to 'Quality Maximum,' " *Design Issues* 10 no. 1 (Spring 1994): 37–43.
2. Ted J. Kaptchuk, *The Web That Has No Weaver: Understanding Chinese Medicine* (New York: Congdon & Weed, 1983).
3. James E. Lovelock, *Gaia: A New Look at Life on Earth* (Oxford: Oxford University Press, 1987).
4. Edward T. Hall, *Beyond Culture*, Chapter 2, "Man as Extension" (New York: Anchor Books, 1989).
5. Marshall McLuhan and Eric McLuhan, *Laws of Media: The New Science* (Toronto: Toronto University Press, 1988).
6. Ivan Illich, *Tools for Conviviality* (London: Fontana, 1973).
7. Op. cit., 24.
8. Donella H. Meadows, Dennis L. Meadows, Jorgen Randers, and William W. Behrens III, *The Limits to Growth* (London: Earth Island, 1972).
9. Editors of *The Ecologist*, *A Blueprint for Survival* (Harmondsworth: Penguin, 1972).

24

SCIENCE, SEMIOTICS, AND SOCIETY: THE ULM HOCHSCHULE FÜR GESTALTUNG IN RETROSPECT

Paul Betts

Perhaps nothing better reflects the contemporary crisis of architecture and design than its radical estrangement from science. For if nothing else, postmodernism has made us acutely aware of the extent to which the post-Renaissance theology of scientific rationality had furnished modernism with its guiding visual vocabulary, chiliastic visions and undeterred self-confidence. This is, of course, hardly new in itself, given the fact that the denunciation of right-angle messianism and its accompanying celebration of ornament and historicist pastiche (be it the Baroque, art deco, or Las Vegas pop) has itself become a vigorous transatlantic academic industry ever since the late 1960s. Less well known, however, is that the evident collapse of science as modernism's master narrative has recently given rise to a new historical interest in the conceptual foundation (if less the specific forms) of this oft-maligned "Enlightenment project," much of which pivoted upon the political desire to recast modern society in the image of scientific reason. Not to say that postmodernists have suddenly lost sight of the dark legacy of what Horkheimer and Adorno once called the "dialectic of Enlightenment." But at a time when the *fin-de-millénaire* oracles about the "end of history" and the "death of the city" have thus far provoked precious little design daring and/or architectural imagination, many long-condemned modernist programs and Utopian projects have started to win renewed attention.

In this climate, it is no coincidence that designers and design critics have become more and more curious about lost "futures past" resting at the former intersection of architecture and science. The colorful story of the highly influential Ulm Institute of Design, which was founded in 1955 as West Germany's "New Bauhaus" and later closed amid the upheaval of 1968, is a compelling case study of these not-so-long-ago modernist hopes and dreams. More than simply a story of Bauhaus redux, the school's history effectively marked modernism's last real attempt to unite industrial design and genuine social reform, to preserve in particular the redemptive pathos of the design object from the corrosive effects of Nazi irrationalism and American commercialism. The Ulm Institute thus occupies a special place in post-1945 cultural history in the way that it boldly tried to rehabilitate the damaged authority of science and rationality as the only true models of engaged design education and praxis. At issue here is to show how the school's changing ideal of the industrial designer – as seen in the pedagogic theories of Max Bill, Tomás Maldonado and Max Bense – revealed Ulm's ongoing effort to conjoin design, science, and cultural renewal.

From the very beginning, the Ulm project was shaped by a larger vision of post-fascist cultural regeneration and political reform. Leaving aside the complex history of the school's early years,[1] it is worth recalling that the idea of the Ulm

Institute originally was inspired by Inge Scholl, who wanted to establish a new school of democratic education in honor of her brother and sister, Hans and Sophie Scholl, both of whom were killed in 1943 as members of the anti-Nazi "White Rose" resistance group.[2] Together with fellow Nazi resister and graphic artist Otl Aicher, Scholl founded a new community college in the small south German town of Ulm in 1946 in an effort to preserve the resistance spirit of her slain siblings. Aicher and Scholl envisioned the school as a center of "true democracy" intent on eradicating the legacy of German militant nationalism and to provide postwar youth with badly needed cultural ideals and moral direction.[3] Its primary pedagogic task, however, was not simply to resuscitate the humanities, but rather to reconcile what they perceived as the fateful historical antagonism of "technical civilization" and German *Kultur*. In the spring of 1949, Scholl and Aicher busied themselves with drafting proposals for a new "Scholl Siblings Institute" devoted to "contemporary and political reeducation."[4] For this, they proposed a "universal education" that encompassed both general media studies (politics, sociology, journalism, radio, and film) and art instruction (photography, advertising, painting, and industrial design) as a tonic against the dangers of instrumental reason and cultural irresponsibility.[5] Above all, Scholl and Aicher hoped to create a new "crystallization point for a better Germany," where the "spirit of peace and freedom" would help rehabilitate and cultivate antifascist European culture.[6]

Even so, the subsequent appointment of the well-known Swiss sculptor, painter, and designer, Max Bill, as school director radically changed the Institute's tone and outlook. As a former Bauhaus student and acting president of the Swiss Werkbund, Bill set out to subordinate formal political education to the more practical teaching of architecture and design. For him, the guiding objective should be to produce design work in accordance with the "spiritual substance" of contemporary modern art,[7] one which privileged a more art-oriented design instruction over the studies of sociology, cultural theory, and politics. Like most Werkbund members, Bill believed that genuine social and cultural reform began not with forced political training, but rather with reconstituting the very forms of the social environment, i.e., city planning, architecture, and the design of everyday objects. Proper design practice, then, was a kind of political reform and moral reeducation for the simple reason that everyday spaces and objects presented an affective pathos to their users.[8] Bill, moreover, insisted that the school should drop the Scholl name on the grounds that it was both overly "sentimental" and too closely associated with a past devoid of any "positive impetus,"[9] suggesting instead that the school be renamed the Institute of Design (Hochschule für Gestaltung) in homage to the Dessau Bauhaus and its pioneering design program. After some deliberation, Scholl and Aicher reluctantly agreed, but only on the condition that painting and sculpture were removed from the school curriculum and that courses in sociology, politics, psychology, philosophy, and contemporary history would be included as a buffer against what they felt to be the Bauhaus's anti-historical millenialism. They clearly wanted to make sure that the "social effects and cultural meaning" of even technical design work would be firmly grounded in social awareness and informed political practice.[10] The original curriculum reflected this compromise, as the school's individual departments were arranged into the following four groups: "Information," which included the study and analysis of literary media; "Architecture and City Planning;" "Visual Design," which covered instruction in film, photography and graphics; and "Product Form," which comprised the industrial design of everyday household objects, furniture, and industrial equipment.

It was with this vision of design education that the Ulm Institute of Design was christened the "New Bauhaus" in 1955. No doubt, the opening served as a key spectacle of West German modernism. Not only did the institute's noble pedigree of both antifascist resistance and international style modernism assist West Germany's larger campaign to establish the 1920s as its authentic (and admittedly sanitized) cultural heritage, it also underlined the extent to which rebaptizing the Bauhaus served as a valuable Cold War symbol of a newly minted transatlantic cultural partnership between the Federal Republic and the United States.[11] However, the importance of the small design institute exceeded this Cold War conversion of design into diplomacy. It also was infused with a grand vision of social reform, one based on the reconciliation of art and life, morality, and material culture. Consider, for example, Bill's remarks at Ulm's 1955 inauguration:

> Nowhere in the world is there an institution dedicated to the same tasks as the Institute of Design. Above all, the school hopes to create simple useful everyday objects for a general everyday culture, especially since most designers and manufacturers neglect the importance of these commonplace things as cultural factors of great consequence ... We are of the opinion that culture is not the special domain of "high art," but rather must be present in everyday living and in all things of form; indeed, every form is an expression of function and purpose. Yet we are not interested in producing cheap arts and crafts (*Kunstgewerbe*), but rather genuine objects that people need ... in short, practical things which should improve and beautify life ...[12]

Here Bill captured the school's original mission, not only to extend the domain of culture beyond the exclusive world of fine arts, but also to target industrial technology and mass-produced goods as the very site of cultural intervention and reform. To this end, the Ulm Institute was initially dedicated to bridging postwar art and industry, serving as what one observer called a new "mediator between *Kultur* and *Zivilization*."[13]

At first, this cultural idealism may seem somewhat naive or simply a pale imitation of modernist ideology from the Weimar Republic. But it is crucial to recall that this Ulm project to forge a new post-fascist *Industriekultur* diverged markedly from the more widespread post-Nazi pessimism toward the potentially redemptive powers of science and industrial technology. It is not difficult to understand that much of this postwar sentiment was a response to the Nazi legacy of industrialized death and destruction, whereafter the West German right and left joined hands in disavowing Germany's prewar liberation theology of technology as a central element of this so-called "German catastrophe." After 1945, technology often was treated by West German and other intellectuals as the stigma of evil and danger. It was variably condemned as the instrument of cultural slavery (F.J. Jünger), the harbinger of violence and death (Giedion), the symbol of existential alienation (Heidegger), and/or the dialectical expression of instrumental reason and unfreedom (Horkheimer and Adorno).[14] Regardless of whether the Third Reich and/or Hiroshima functioned as the narrative resolution of these analyses, the point was that the historical faith in the benevolent marriage of technology and *Kultur* as well as science and society did not survive the war.[15] That technology no longer served as the central trope of (West) German liberation was nowhere more evident than in the fact that West German engineers never recouped their pre-1945 authority as anointed cultural heroes.[16]

In this light, the Ulm Institute was quite alone in designating industrial technology as the necessary locus of cultural reconstruction. Yet there was more at stake than simply confronting West Germany's intellectual antipathy toward science and technology. The Ulmers worried that this antimodern aversion would only reinforce the prewar split between humanism and efficiency. Postwar cultural developments only confirmed this fear. On the one hand, West German art schools celebrated artistic individualism and creative freedom as post-fascist and anticommunist cultural therapy; on the other, postwar engineering schools jettisoned their former discourse/practice of social engineering (since this was supposedly a species of illiberalism) in the name of mechanical learning and technical achievement. The irony of this of course was that this sociological separation of culture and technology was largely a reaction to the former fusion of these spheres during the Third Reich. The Ulmers thereby were attempting to rescue the concept of *Industriekultur* from Nazi corruption by regrounding it within the humanist tradition of social responsibility and moral education. Advancing the cause of the "Ulm idea" was viewed as all the more urgent given that the West German cultural elite was turning its back on technology precisely at the moment when its country was undergoing febrile modernization. The widespread postwar enthusiasm for automobiles, kitchen appliances, cleaning machines, radios, and television only underscored the extent to which West German popular culture was completely smitten by consumer technology and its capacity to liberate and comfort.[17] So the Ulm project to help heal the rift between society and technology was inseparable from the desire not to abandon West German modernity to narrow-minded technocrats, commercial designers, and advertising agents.

For a variety of reasons, science played a decisive role in the Ulm Institute's larger conception of redemptive modernization. First, the recuperation of scientific rationality was regarded by the school's founders as the best means of countering the dark patrimony of Nazi irrationalism. For them, Nazism was primarily characterized by an anti-intellectual emotionalism and monumentalist pathos. In part, this is why the Ulmers – perhaps best illustrated by the school's hyper-rationalist architecture, which one observer at the time called a "Cartesian cloister"[18] – saw the rehabilitation of the so-called "Enlightenment tradition" of improving society through reason and science as badly needed post-Nazi reform.[19] Secondly, the primacy of scientific rationality also was embraced as a needed defense against the worrisome commercialization of postwar design. What is often overlooked is that the Ulmers expressed an evident aversion toward liberal capitalism and the commodity culture of the "economic miracle."[20] In fact, the thorny issue of how to devise a scientifically based design education uncompromised by commercial motivations effectively accounted for the school's sound and fury during the late 1950s and early 1960s.

To better understand this, it pays to recount the changing image of the industrial designer at Ulm. Significantly, the original image of the Ulm designer was one which combined art, science, and design. In the mid-1950s, Bill developed this new occupational model in response to what he perceived as the pernicious influence of American streamline styling. Like other European designers of his generation, Bill strongly protested the international popularity of American star designer Raymond Loewy and especially the 1951 publication of his how-to-succeed autobiography, *Never Leave Well Enough Alone*. Bill condemned Loewy and his "spurious surface simplification known as streamlining" for abandoning the ethical foundation of all design (e.g., the fulfillment of genuine human needs) in the interests of stimulating consumer sales. For him, it was bad enough that this "sweet but dishonest" commercial ornamentation denigrated the lofty moral office of industrial designer; worse, however, was that it augured the "collapse of culture" (*Kulturverfall*) by severing aesthetics from moral idealism and cultural reform. Bill, in turn, envisioned the new Ulm Institute as a renewed Bauhaus dedicated to fighting this sinister cultural "perversion" (*Unsinn*) in the name of "the good, the beautiful, and the practical."[21] In his first public statement as director of the Institute, he elevated the importance of art this way:

> The founders of the school believe art to be the highest expression of human life and, therefore, their aim is to help in turning life into a work of art. In the words of that memorable challenge thrown down by Henry van de Velde over 50 years ago, we mean "to wage war on ugliness," and ugliness can only be combated with what is intrinsically good – good because at once beautiful and practical … If we intend to go further at Ulm than they did at Dessau, this is

> because postwar requirements clearly postulate the necessity for certain additions to the curriculum. For instance, we mean to give still greater prominence to the design of ordinary things in everyday use; to foster the widest possible development of town and regional planning; and to bring visual design up to the standard which the latest technical advances have now made possible.[22]

This passage makes it clear that Bill viewed the school as essentially dedicated to the task of re-enchanting the forms of everyday life in a kind of grandiose *Gesamtkunstwerk* which recognized no difference between fine arts and regional planning. In his grand aestheticizing project to "turn life into a work of art," Bill collapsed the distinction among moral renewal, aesthetic production, and social reform, gathering them all into the lofty idealism of "good form" design.

Yet Bill's design philosophy also posited a certain reconciliation of art and science as the bedrock of engaged design praxis. To safeguard design from degenerating into Loewy-esque aesthetic fancy, Bill strove to develop the theoretical insights of his former Bauhaus teachers – Paul Klee and Wassily Kandinsky – in combining spiritual artistic creativity with scientific logic.[23] For him, grounding art and design in mathematics by no means excluded individual artistic expression; rather, it served as the necessary bridge linking artistic endeavor, logical principles and industrial production. On this, point he maintained a classic 1920s modernist stance in arguing that function must determine form, and not vice versa; that function is the ground of all aesthetics; and that the sole objective of design remained the liberation of human needs.[24] But while defending the necessity of unadorned, non-expressionist "neutral form" as the best remedy against "personality design" and commercial styling, Bill was certainly not willing to hand over the mantle of design to the technical engineer. Indeed, he never surrendered his faith in the elevated cultural role and authority of the "responsible, true artist" to redeem the industrial design object as something more than cheap commodity or technical instrument. In the end, Bill insisted that only the engaged artist as "true creator" could properly address the complex technical, cultural, and moral issues inherent in modern design, precisely because only "free art" (*freie Kunst*) could transcend fleeting fashion trends and technical engineering imperatives.[25]

Yet Bill's elevation of the artist-designer as social engineer was more than simply residual popular front ideology. Rather, the reason that he valued the role of the artist in industrial design was because he believed that these everyday industrial design objects were first and foremost "cultural artifacts" (*Kulturgüter*). This is why he ultimately disqualified the commercial stylist and engineer as legitimate designers, for both in effect "de-cultured" these objects by reducing them to saleable commodities and/or technical equipment. The achievement of "good form" was reconstituting the industrial object as a "culture good." Only the engaged noncommercial artist-designer, so Bill reasoned, could thus be entrusted with re-enchanting the object with the "surplus value" of *Kultur* irrespective of strict commercial and/or technical import. In other words, the objective of industrial design education was not "to make square what yesterday was round," but rather "to view these objects of human need as cultural factors which decisively influence our form of life. Spoon and machine, traffic sign, and housing have, in this respect, the same meaning."[26] This was what Bill meant when he remarked that the design institute was primarily concerned with "bringing civilization and culture into harmony."[27] Elevating the importance of artistic production in industrial design training was the best way of pursuing Scholl's original 1949 task, namely to keep the dangerous forces of modern civilization and technology under cultural control.

With time, however, Bill's lofty vision of the industrial designer faced mounting criticism from other faculty members who wanted to shift the focus of design education from art to science. Dissatisfaction was first leveled by Tomás Maldonado, an Argentine artist and art journal editor who joined the Ulm faculty in 1954. While sharing the desire to train socially responsible designers instead of commercial artists, Maldonado rejected Bill's Werkbund-Bauhaus idealism in favor of a more scientific conception of industrial design. He first proposed a radically different model of modern design education during his well-known speech delivered at the 1958 Brussels World's Fair. Whereas most of the international representatives at the fair's design conference concurred with Bill that the cultural menace of kitsch and bad design could best be remedied through more design education and the popularization of "good form," Maldonado boldly asserted that "aesthetic considerations have ceased to be a solid conceptual basis for industrial design."[28] To this, he added that the rise of modern design as a new profession was really a child of the Depression, where designers were recruited by business to help aestheticize everyday commodities in order to reinvigorate flagging consumption. He continued by saying that most contemporary design (e.g., American streamline and/or West German *Nierentisch* forms) was ultimately less Industrial Age folk art than shrewd marketing stratagem to exploit human needs and desires.[29] But Maldonado's condemnation of this "pathological cult of differentiation" characterizing modern consumer capitalism did not prompt him to embrace Bill's idea of the uncorrupted artist-designer and his romantic "spoon to city" *Gesamtkunstwerk* project. On the contrary, he felt that Bill's totalizing artistic program was useless for training designers as future partners of industry. Maldonado criticized Bill for recasting the designer as a "Grand Inquisitor" who "graciously administers justice in the world of design according to the motto: 'the designer commands, the engineer obeys,' " for it assumed and necessitated the artist-designer's sociocultural removal from the processes of industrial society.[30] Maldonado regarded the artist-designer's cultured distance from industry as completely untenable, not the least because Bill's venerated "good form" itself become just another design style among many. To move beyond this danger, Maldonado insisted that "industrial design is not an art, nor is the designer necessarily an artist"[31] insofar as the cunning of capitalism had ironically transformed the moral idealism of "good form" into highbrow product advertising. As a result, Maldonado lumped together both commercial design and Bill's notion of the artist-designer as twin symptoms of the same outdated misconception about the role and meaning of engaged industrial design.

But if industrial design was to be divorced from artistic production, then what served as its new basis? To answer this question, Maldonado contended that both industrial design and the designer were on the threshold of historical transformation. Whereas rationalized mass production (Fordism) foregrounded the designer as inventor-planner in the first stage of design history, followed in the second stage by the rise of the artist-designer as a function of the 1929 Crash, Maldonado characterized the third and final phase as the historical emergence of the designer as "coordinator" who must "coordinate, in close collaboration with a large number of specialists, the most varied requirements of product fabrication and usage" so as to ensure "maximum productivity, material efficiency, and the cultural satisfaction of the user."[32] This new designer was no ordinary industrial technocrat, however. What had happened was that the engaged designer's adversarial ethos had been transferred from object styling into the production process itself. Bill's autonomous artist-designer had been replaced by the designer as active partner of industry. Unlike Bill's distant designer, this new designer was "to operate at the nerve centers of our industrial civilization," where "the most important decisions for our daily life are made," and "where those interests meet which are most opposed and often most difficult to reconcile." No longer a "mystical and indefinable apparition," the new industrial designer would now be trained as a specialist in the laws of mass production and industrial automation in order to help demystify and coordinate "our objective and communicative world."[33] The success of the new designer largely depended on "the breadth of his scientific and technical knowledge, as well as on his capacity of interpreting the most secret and most subtle processes of our culture."[34] Consequently, this critical design praxis – what Maldonado called "scientific operationalism" – could only begin once design had been divorced from aesthetics, once the mysterious "cultural good" had been superseded by a new conception of the design object as nothing but material information and production coordination. Rather than a cultural category of moral idealism and artistic production, design had been reconfigured as a more scientifically based sociological operation of product management and systems analysis. By integrating the designer into the industrial process itself, Maldonado had secularized the designer by transferring his/her sphere of operation from the lofty heights of *Kultur* to the workaday world of industrial *Zivilisation*.

This rejection of the art-based heritage of design education inevitably forced the school to reevaluate its Bauhaus legacy. On this point, Maldonado asserted that the Bauhaus could no longer serve as the model of industrial design education, since its "learning by doing" pedagogy ignored new scientific research and offered students very little preparation for the complicated world of postwar industrial relations. While acknowledging that it was an important break from the ossified academic culture of *fin-de-siècle* German art education, he maintained that the Bauhaus's effort to cleanse students of any prior academic training so as to restore the "free personality" based on a "lost psycho-biological unity" ultimately hindered modern students from assuming important positions in industrial society.[35] However exaggerated this may at first appear, Maldonado's critique that the Bauhaus heritage had never fully cast off its early expressionistic tendencies was not that outlandish. For example, Walter Gropius himself confirmed this image at the 1955 opening of the Ulm Institute. In his inauguration speech, Gropius completely ignored the fact that the Ulm Institute had effectively updated the Weimar Bauhaus program by means of removing the primacy of arts and crafts from its industrial design curriculum. Not only did Gropius underscore the Cold War importance of providing the "Bauhaus idea" with a "new German home" as a sign of "progressive democracy," he intoned that genuine cultural reform first began with training "artistic people" as cultural engineers since the "spiritual direction of human development is always distinctively influenced by thinkers and artists whose works transcend logical functionalism."[36] Like Bill, Gropius defended the unimpeachable authority of both art and artist as the primary means of cultural and political regeneration; he even concluded by saying that individual intuition, emotion and artistic sensibility – not scientific rationality – remained the mainsprings of authentic design work. The Ulmers could even find evidence of the expressionist Bauhaus within the school itself. The presence of Johannes Itten, the Mazdaznan guru who was largely responsible for shaping the famous Bauhaus *Vorkurs* in Weimar from 1919–1923, provided more grist for the mill. Even if Itten had long abandoned his monkish robes by the time he arrived in Ulm, he still tried to bring students closer to the mysteries of Eastern philosophy through collective meditation and even pre-class calisthenics. This is not to say that they were the only referents of the Bauhaus tradition after the war. The point, however, is that the Bauhaus legacy had been reworked after 1945 to suit the larger Cold War project to draw the Weimar Republic and the Federal Republic into the same elective liberal lineage, while at the same time conjoining West German and American cultural modernism. During the 1950s, the West German popular image of the Bauhaus – and Gropius and Itten contributed to this – had shifted from a hotbed of leftist architecture to a bold yet innocent school of fine arts, where it enjoyed a marked renaissance (as seen in decorative interiors, furniture styling, poster art, and graphic design) within mainstream West German culture.[37]

But rather than simply jettisoning Bauhaus history altogether, the young faculty at Ulm strove to resuscitate the one forgotten figure most responsible for radically shaping industrial design education at the Bauhaus, Hannes Meyer. As Gropius's successor at the Dessau Bauhaus, Meyer supervised Bauhaus activities from 1927 to 1930, devoting his energies to changing the Bauhaus's image and upper-crust clientele by instituting a more leftist program based on "the needs of the people instead of luxury needs" (*Volksbedarf statt Luxusbedarf*), as well as bringing the school's workshops in closer contact with trade unions and the workers' movement. Moreover, he transformed Bauhaus pedagogy by cleansing it of any lingering artisan ethos and/or expressionist mysticism in favor of a more "secularized" design philosophy grounded in the scientific principles of rational production.[38] For many at the Ulm Institute, Meyer's tenure in Dessau represented the Bauhaus's most fruitful period in terms of both work and design theory. In fact, Meyer's dictum that "How many mysterious things one tries to explain through art, when in fact they are things which have to do with science" served as the guiding pedagogical principle among Ulm's younger faculty members. Hence, Meyer enjoyed a preeminent status at Ulm as the original theorist of a scientifically based design education, whereby his tenure and not Gropius's Weimar directorship was reclaimed as Ulm's authentic Bauhaus heritage.

The fruitfulness of this new design philosophy was perhaps best illustrated in the Ulm Institute's well-known collaboration with the West German consumer electronics firm of Braun. Founded as a radio electronics parts firm by Max Braun in 1921, Braun enjoyed international success through the 1930s as one of Germany's leading manufacturers of radio consoles. Like most of its competitors, Braun console designs were initially conceived of as small furniture pieces wherein the radio equipment was housed in a dark wood encasing to complement the *gemütlich* petit bourgeois styling of 1930s homes. After the war, however, the firm sought to update its product forms and corporate image; Braun recruited Ulm design instructor Hans Gugelot to help the firm devise a new design aesthetic. Among the innovations was the highly acclaimed "SK-4" stereo console design by Gugelot and in-house Braun designer Dieter Rams, which immediately catapulted Braun into the public spotlight. What is most important is that the designers did not approach the consumer radio unit as a heavy piece of representational domestic furniture, but rather as a mobile machine engineered according to technical function. Not only was the stereo unit shorn of all conventional accessories such as big gold buttons and fine front-panel texturing, the color palette was reduced to neutral gray and white in response to the postwar penchant toward flashy and inessential styling. The collaboration with Braun illustrated the extent to which Ulm designers strove to modernize the "housing" of consumer goods along new functional lines just as 1920s architects had radically redesigned the German home and interior along *Neue Sachlichkeit* principles.[39] It marked the school's overarching interest in moving away from homey design styling to working closely with production teams to develop new high-tech industrial wares and public design projects (e.g., placards, photography, film, transportation systems, and even software programs) based on rational analysis and technical knowledge.[40]

With time, however, the simmering feud between Bill and Maldonado intensified and eventually divided the school over the proper conception of design education. Leaving aside the rich courtlife of the school intrigue during this crisis, it is enough to say that Maldonado's vision of the scientifically oriented designer eventually won out at Ulm. In fact, Bill soon thereafter resigned as school director in response to what he called the "technoid degeneration of its once good idea."[41] His departure signaled the end of the school's art-based design education, after which the Institute devoted its full attention to refining its bold conception of modern design and the modern designer freed from the historical baggage of aesthetics, *Kultur*, and artistic production. The increasing "scientization" of Ulm's design program was especially noticeable in the 1958 revised curriculum. In it, the instruction in colors was completely dropped from the course list; Gugelot and Walter Zeischegg were encouraged to expand the place of the engineering sciences; and more courses on scientific theory were now introduced, including mathematical operations analysis, perception theory, ergonomics, and epistemology. The Building Department under Konrad Wachsmann and Herbert Ohl discarded its metaphysical baggage as well, shifting its emphasis from the poetics of architecture to the rationalization of prefabricated housing components. Even instruction in the "Cultural Integration" Department, whose program of philosophy, history, psychology, and political science had been formalized as a corrective against both the anti-historical thrust of the original Bauhaus program and the dangers of overspecialization, had given way to the larger task of more "specialized training."

One particularly revealing aspect of the school's ongoing scientization of its curriculum could be seen in the primacy of semiotics. This stemmed in large measure from the larger attempt to decouple design from the trappings of *Kultur*, namely, morality, taste, and aesthetics. Here, Maldonado again led the way, though he drew heavily from the work of Charles Sanders Peirce, Charles Morris, Anatol Rapoport,[42] and especially the long-forgotten West German philosopher and Ulm lecturer, Max Bense. Bense was a philosophy professor at the University of Stuttgart who had published numerous books on the philosophy of mathematics before 1945 and was recruited by Bill to help shore up Ulm's "Cultural Integration" department, for which he offered courses on mathematical theory and semiotic analysis from 1954–1958. Having published a range of Heideggerian texts during the thirties and forties devoted to exploring the metaphysical linkage of space and the phenomenology of being, Bense shifted his interest after 1945 to focus upon the relationship between aesthetics and technology. Much of his work pivoted upon the idea that the once critical hermeneutics of *Kultur* no longer existed, since both nature and culture had forfeited their relevance as interpretative models for understanding the emergence of what he called "technical civilization." But rather than joining the chorus of West German critics who invariably greeted this "death of culture" as an irredeemable sociological scourge, Bense accepted this brave new world as simply modern reality. Indeed, his project to develop a philosophical system of "technical consciousness" was less some sort of engineer's fantasy about the wonders of a fully technologized world than an attempt to emancipate the social sciences and especially aesthetics from their outworn humanist framework.

Bense's effort to reconceptualize aesthetic production beyond the ken of *Kultur* carried profound implications for both design theory and the status of the aesthetic object. In one 1956 speech, for instance, Bense made the bold claim that in an age characterized by mass reproduction and the destruction of the precious cultural artifact, the age-old epistemological assumption that the art-object and by association the artist were the exclusive sites of aesthetic production was no longer historically valid. Certainly, Bense realized that the "end of aura" was in itself nothing new, having characterized modern life ever since the manufacture of imitation products.[43] The difference, however, lay in its totalizing effect in an era of unbridled postwar consumerism in which all culture goods could be and were immediately commodified, imitated, and reproduced. The historical disappearance of the autonomous cultural artifact therefore produced two decisive effects: first, it meant that the object's cultural status as an ontological category had been altogether undermined insofar as its "unique" attributes could be easily copied and reproduced; secondly, aesthetics itself, had been liberated from the "denatured" precious object and diffused throughout the social terrain, i.e., advertising, industrial design, and the advent of "lifestyle." For Bense, this social development followed the logic of both modern science (e.g., quantum physics) and modern abstract art (above all, Kandinsky) which, long ago, had jettisoned its nineteenth-century grounding in the representational world of palpable objects, whether it be the concepts of substance, impulse, and regular circuits for the modern physicist, or painterly naturalism for the modernist artist.[44] The modern philosopher/sociologist, so Bense argued, should follow the lead of the modern physicist who studies the "objective world" not by analyzing its objects but rather its interactive semiotic effects.[45] Of particular relevance is that, from this, he claimed that industrial design enjoyed a privileged position in the modern world in that it emerged at the very crossroads of "technical civilization" and the industrialization of aesthetics. Industrial modernity had unwittingly liberated aesthetics from the object and from the domain of *Kultur* as well, which meant that aesthetics had now become the exclusive property of *Zivilisation*. So more than just a new union of art and technology, industrial design represented the first aesthetic practice of "technical civilization," the first formalist strategy theoretically undetermined by the (elitist) rituals and reception strategies of *Kultur*.

During the late 1950s, Bense's semiotic theory of aesthetics exerted considerable influence on the Institute's younger faculty members. His highly analytical argumentation and untiring effort to demystify the social function of aesthetics in everyday life appealed to Maldonado's own project to replace cultural judgment (taste, beauty, morality) with more scientific evaluative criteria. What is often forgotten, however, is that the Ulm Institute's project to develop a new science of everyday objects was also motivated by a particular ethical compulsion. In fact, the effort to train new designers who – like natural scientists studying the behavior of physical objects in the natural world – could analyze social "communicative products" (consumer goods and media information) according to Weberian "value-free" scientific principles,[46] was less naive rationalism than an attempt to combat the postwar's reigning science of material culture, namely market research. By the early 1960s, market research had become a highly developed business science in its own right, replacing industrial psychology as the guiding postwar epistemology dedicated to addressing the relationship between people and (consumable) things. Not only could this be seen in the post-1945 merger of commerce and culture, but also in the rise of a new academic industry surrounding the romance of sales and psychology. In response, the Ulmers hoped to stem the ongoing commercialization of social science by developing a more ethically based "critical semiotics." The pioneering work of Ulmers' Horst Rittel and Hanno Resting to mathematize aesthetics, together with the effort by French sociologist and Ulm docent Abraham Moles to establish a theory about the semiotic laws of motion determining consumer culture,[47] were good examples of this larger campaign to develop a critical theory of modern consumer culture untainted by Madison Avenue machinations.

To preserve the adversarial ethos of design in the face of its ever-increasing co-option by industrial capital, Maldonado insisted upon the connection between design studies and the liberation of human needs. What was now evident was that the school was finding it more and more difficult to conceptualize a design form – since even the supposedly anti-aesthetic ethos of functionalism had become just another supermarket style, as the Braun design story attested – that would not be immediately corrupted by market capitalism. In this atmosphere, the young docents at Ulm began to turn away from product design altogether, gravitating instead toward more rarefied design theory. Not to say that their efforts to devise a non-market-driven "theory of needs" based on a "more systematic study of the most subtle aspects of consumption" was only idle philosophizing. For them, the issue was nothing less than the preservation of freedom itself. As Maldonado remarked, the "aesthetics of manipulation" informing West Germany's prosperous consumer culture was inextricably linked to (and even partly responsible for) the larger political problem in which the ideal of democratic freedom was ironically being undermined by the "limited real possibility of realizing this freedom." Semiotics – and by association, scientific rationality – were then considered as needed remedies against consumer alienation and what Ulmer Gui Bonsiepe called uncritical "instrumental intelligence," serving at once as intellectual and political liberation insomuch as it revealed the "conditions which make the manipulation possible and necessary."[48] The ethical imperative to confront the "pseudo-science" of market research was, thus, the determining factor in the Institute's "scientific operationalism," where the designer (unlike the more passive natural scientist) was obliged to intervene and help protect modern industrial culture from the whims of technocrats and advertising agents.

Unfortunately the development of this new science of society soon ran into problems. For one thing, the regional government of Baden-Württemberg was less and less willing to subsidize Ulm's theoretical experimentation and disinclination toward product design, thus throwing the school into perennial financial crisis. Worse, this new "scientization" of the curriculum encountered increasing resistance from faculty and students alike, many of whom felt that the school's faith in science and rationality had become polemic and excessive. Closely connected with this development was the fact that design rationalism itself began to lose its cultural authority over the course of the 1960s. The period witnessed a pronounced "crisis of functionalism" within West German architecture and design circles. For many West Germans, the 1920s belief in the therapeutic powers of functionalist building and city planning was transformed into a post-1945 nightmare, as its once soaring social(ist) rhetoric had been emptied of any Utopian promise and/or cultural redemption. And even if the banalization of functionalism had consistently served as a hated sign of a misguided West German culture for postwar conservatives, this new mid-1960s critique found its most prominent voices from those on the left who had formerly championed its cause during the Weimar Republic. Such notable figures as Theodor Adorno, Ernst Bloch, and Alexander Mitscherlich helped direct attention to the cultural dangers of "scientific" functionalism.[49] By 1968, the critique of functionalism had become synonymous with the critique of science, instrumental reason, and the perceived "uninhabitability" of West German cities, where the "tyranny of functionalism" was understood to symbolize the postwar loss of individual identity, the destruction of the environment, and the commodification of West German cultural life.[50] Once a passionate watchword of social democracy and the demystification of *Kultur*, functionalism was now demonized on all sides as the very expression of the miscarried dreams of postwar reform and renewal.

By this time, however, the school was in deep crisis. On the one hand, the regional government continued to exert more pressure on the school to behave like other design schools, even to the point of threatening to close the institute if a more practical design curriculum was not implemented. On the other, the Ulmers were more and more at a loss in how to reconcile industrial design and industrial capitalism, form, and freedom. They had realized that this was the inexorable paradox of industrial culture, insofar as aesthetics itself – once the liberation from the "constraints of necessity" – had been "pressed into the service of repression."[51] So, unlike the other 1968ers, the Ulmers did not embrace more whimsical individualistic design as post-functionalist emotional compensation.[52] Their continued affirmation of functionalism as the last anti-capitalist industrial aesthetic now lacked any former optimism about the social promise of scientific design philosophy. This loss of faith in the enlightenment-inspired marriage of science and society was perhaps best expressed in the fact that the Ulmers turned all of their energies toward design theory as the last uncorrupted refuge of activity. The once passionate hope in reconstituting the design object as the site of social reform and political liberation had all but collapsed. It was in this 1968 crisis atmosphere that the much-divided Ulm faculty, unable to maintain the Institute's cherished independence before the regional government's directive to reorganize the design center as a state-run engineering college, ultimately voted to disband itself as a last gesture of solidarity and defiance.

The closing of the school did not signal the end of the postwar reign of scientific functionalism. No doubt, much of (West) German industrial design from the 1970s on owes a considerable debt to the Ulm legacy. Nevertheless, the former project of reuniting science and society in a grand vision of cultural engagement and political liberation never survived the upheavals of 1968. After that, the focus of design shifted from aestheticizing the relationship between people and objects/machines (interior decoration, advertising, ergonomics, and cybernetics) to that between people and the environment (ecology movement, park design, and urban renewal), as space reemerged as a new politicized social category in the 1970s. Still, Ulm represented the postwar's most sustained attempt to rethink the role of social science and political engagement in a post-*Kultur* world of overproduction, hyper-consumerism and instant commodification. Even if its enlightenment faith in the redemptive powers of reason and science may date the school as modernist, it nonetheless serves as a valuable case study in the cultural contradictions of material affluence. For nowhere else in West Germany were the problems associated with trying to combine industry and enlightenment, aesthetics and liberation, as well as technology and culture so passionately explored and debated. In the end, it marked West Germany's last real effort to fight the historical elision of industrial culture and the culture industry. And in light of postmodernism's notorious ideological impasse regarding exactly this issue, the "Ulm experiment" may perhaps deserve another hearing.

NOTES

First published in *Design Issues* 14 no. 2 (Summer 1998): 67–82.

1. A good discussion of the school's early years can be found in Eva von Seckendorff, *Die Hochschule für Gestaltung in Ulm* (Marburg: Jonas, 1989).
2. Inge Scholl, *The White Rose*, trans. Arthur Schultz (Middletown: Wesleyan University Press, [1952] 1983) and *Die Weiße Rose und das Erbe des deutschen Widerstandes*, no author attributed (Munich: Beck, 1993).
3. Otl Aicher, "Fangen wir an," MS, June 16, 1948, Stadtarchiv, Ulm.
4. "Expose zur Gründung einer Geschwister-Scholl-Hochschule," MS, undated and unpaginated, Stadtarchiv, Ulm.
5. "Vorbereitung zum Prospekt: Geschwister-Scholl Hochschule," 1949, unpaginated, and "GSH-Programm," 1949, 19. Stadtarchiv, Ulm.
6. "Expose über das Forschungsinstitut für Produktform und die Hochschule für Gestaltung," undated and unpaginated, quoted in Hartmut Seeling, "Geschichte der HfG Ulm, 1953–1968," Ph.D. Diss., Universität Köln, 1985, 20–21.
7. Max Bill, *Form: A Balance-Sheet of Mid-Twentieth Century Trends in Design* (Basel: Karl Werner, 1952), unpaginated.
8. Bill, *Form*, unpaginated.
9. Quoted in Seckendorff, 41.
10. "HfG-Programm," 1951, unpaginated.
11. Walter Dirks, "Das Bauhaus und die Weiße Rose," *Frankfurter Hefte* 10:11 (November, 1955): 769–773.
12. Quoted in Wend Fischer, "Tägliche Kultur, nicht Extrakultur," *Werk und Zeit* 4:10 (October, 1955): 4.
13. Paula Andersen, "Vermittler zwischen Zivilisation und Kultur," *Frankfurter Allgemeine Zeitung*, October 4, 1955.
14. Friedrich Georg Jünger, *Die Perfektion der Technik* (Frankfurt: V. Klostermann, 1947); Sigfried Giedion, *Mechanization Takes Command* (New York: Oxford University Press, 1948); Martin Heidegger, *Die Technik und die Kehre* (Pfullingen: Neske, 1962); Max Horkheimer and Theodor Adorno, *Dialectic of Enlightenment*, trans. John Cummings (New York: Seabury Press, 1972 [1944]). See also William Kuhns, *The Post-Industrial Prophets: Interpretations of Technology* (New York: Weybright & Talley, 1973).

15. Andreas Schüler, *Erfindergeist und Technikkritik: Der Beitrag Amerikas zur Modernisierung und die Technikdebatte seit 1900* (Stuttgart: Franz Steiner, 1990), esp. 138–177. Even the social sciences – including history, sociology. and psychology – were badly damaged by Nazi association. *Wissenschaft in geteilten Deutschland*, eds. Walter Pehle and Peter Sillem (Frankfurt: Fischer, 1992).
16. Joachim Radkau, " 'Wirtschaftswunder' ohne technologische Innovation? Technische Modernität in den 50er Jahren" in *Modernisierung im Wiederaufbau*, ed. Axel Schildt (Bonn: JHW Dietz, 1993), 129–153. For a discussion of the elevated cultural status of the German engineer during the 1920s and 1930s, see Jeffrey Herf, *Reactionary Modernism* (Cambridge: Cambridge University Press, 1984), 152–188.
17. Hans-Peter Schwarz, *Die Ära Adenauer* (Stuttgart: Deutsche Verlagsanstalt, 1981–83), 383–388.
18. Bernhard Rübenbach, *Der Rechte Winkel von Ulm* (Darmstadt: G. Buechner, 1987), 33.
19. *Ulm Design: The Morality of Objects*, ed. Herbert Lindinger (Cambridge, MA: MIT Press, 1990), 77.
20. Inge Scholl, "Eine neue Gründerzeit und ihre Gebrauchskunst" in *Der Bestandsaufnahme*, ed. Hans Werner Richter (Munich: Kurt Desch, 1962), 421–427.
21. Bill, *Form*, unpaginated.
22. "The Bauhaus Idea from Weimar to Ulm," *Architects' Yearbook* 5, ed. Morton Shand (London: Elek Books, 1953), 29–32 [translation modified]. The turn-of-the-century educational ideas are addressed in *Kunstschulreform, 1900–1930*, ed. Hans Wingler (Berlin: Gebr. Mann, 1977).
23. Bill, "Die mathematische Denkweise in der Kunst unserer Zeit," *Das Werk* 36:3 (March, 1949): 86–90.
24. Bill, "Grundlage und Ziel der Aesthetik im Maschinenzeitalter," *Baukunst und Werkform* 9 (1955), 558–561.
25. Bill, "Grundlage," 560.
26. "HfG-Prospekt," 1956, quoted in Seckendorff, 48.
27. "HfG-Programm," 1956, unpaginated.
28. Tomás Maldonado, "New Developments in Industry and the Training of Designers," *Architects' Yearbook* 9 (1960): 174–180.
29. *Ulm* 2 (October, 1958), 30.
30. Maldonado, "Two Views on Architectural Education," *Architectural Education* 29:4 (April, 1959): 153–154.
31. Maldonado, "New Developments," 176.
32. Maldonado, "New Developments," 33–34.
33. Maldonado. "Two Views," 154.
34. Maldonado, "New Developments," 180.
35. Maldonado, "Is the Bauhaus Relevant Today?" *Ulm* 8/9 (September, 1963): 5–13.
36. Walter Gropius, "Eröffnung der neuen Gebäude der HfG," Ulm, September 1955, Bauhaus-Archiv, Berlin.
37. Paul Betts, "The Bauhaus as Cold War Legend: West German Modernism Revisited," *German Politics and Society* 14:12 (Summer 1996): 75–100.
38. K. Michael Hays, *Modernism and the Posthumanist Subject: The Architecture of Hannes Meyer and Ludwig Hilberseimer* (Cambridge, MA: MIT Press, 1992) and *Hannes Meyer: Bauten, Projekte und Schriften*, ed. Claude Schnaidt (Teufen: A. Niggli, 1965).
39. The connection between Le Corbusier's architectural work and Braun design is suggestively explored by Rüdiger Joppien, "Weniger ist Mehr: oder die Leere ist Fülle" in *Mehr oder Weniger: Braun im Vergleich*, no author attributed (Hamburg: Museum für Kunst und Gewerbe, 1990), 9–17.
40. A good discussion of how the school's photography department worked to expunge product photos of any subjectivistic pathos and emotionalism can be found in *Objekt + Objektiv = Objektivität? Fotographie an der HfG Ulm, 1953–1968*, ed. Christiane Wachsmann (Ulm: Stadtarchiv, 1991).
41. Max Bill, "Der Modelfall Ulm," *Form* 6 (1959): 32–33. The long and, at times, ugly infighting among the faculty on the eve of Bill's departure is recounted in Seckendorff, 162–166.
42. Kenneth Frampton, "Apropos Ulm: Curriculum and Critical Theory," *Oppositions* 3 (May, 1974): 17–37.
43. Oddly enough, Bense never mentioned the pioneering essay by Walter Benjamin, "Art in the Age of Mechanical Reproduction," in *Illuminations*, ed. Hannah Arendt (New York: Schocken, 1968), 217–252.
44. Bense, "Kunst in der künstlichen Welt," *Werk und Zeit* 5:11 (November, 1956): 3–4.
45. Bense, *Aesthetica II* (Baden-Baden: Agis, 1956), 14. Hence, it was no surprise that Bense identified Hegel as the prophet of this kind of semiotic analysis of aesthetics, since he was the first theoretician to divorce aesthetic judgment from the substance of the object, approaching aesthetic understanding instead as a series of affects or attributes in the world. *Aesthetics*, 196–203.
46. Maldonado, *Beiträge zur Terminologie der Semiotik* (Ulm: J. Ebner, 1961). Note as well his earlier "Communication and Semiotics," *Ulm* 5 (July, 1959): 70–75.

47. Abraham Moles, "Products: Their Functional and Structural Complexity," *Ulm* 6 (1962): 4–12.
48. Maldonado, "Notes on Communication," in *Uppercase* 5, ed. Theo Crosby (London: Whitefriar Press, 1963), 5–10.
49. Both Adorno and Bloch were invited guest lecturers at the German Werkbund's 1965 "Bildung durch Gestalt" Conference, where they delivered their famous "Funktionalismus Heute" and "Bildung, Ingenieurform, Ornament" speeches, respectively. See the special issue of *Werk und Zeit* 14: 11/12 (November–December, 1965). Mitscherlich's *Die Unwirtlichkeit unserer Städte: Anstiftung zum Unfrieden* (Frankfurt: Suhrkamp, 1965) served as the key text on the deleterious effects of functionalism.
50. Heide Berndt et al., *Architektur als Ideologie* (Frankfurt: Suhrkamp, 1968) and *Umwelt aus Beton oder Unsere unmenschliche Städte*, ed. Uwe Schultz (Hamburg: Rowohlt, 1971).
51. Gui Bonsiepe, "Comunication und Power," *Ulm* 21 (1968): 16.
52. Abraham Moles, "Functionalism in Crisis," *Ulm* 19/20 (August, 1967): 24.

25

ECOLOGICAL DESIGN: A NEW CRITIQUE

Pauline Madge

The author would like to thank Gui Bonsiepe, Tony Fry, Philip Goggin and especially, Harry Sutcliffe for their help on the preparation of this article.

Ecological design has come of age. It is now about a decade since the first wave of green design emerged as a significant new factor in product and graphic design. Though it is, by no means, fully developed and accepted, and only just beginning to be implemented in design education, for example, there is a broad consensus that environmental issues can no longer be ignored by designers and critics. There has been a significant change in recent years, from the days when it was just a matter of getting the environment onto the agenda, and establishing the broad parameters of a green design practice – the inevitable process of reappraisal and differentiation as a movement begins to acquire a history and a polemics. Already, a second or third wave of ecodesign practice and criticism has emerged which is concerned with a more subtle analysis of meaning and methodology.

As it has developed over the last decade, ecodesign has constantly borrowed ideas and terminology from ecology and environmentalism, though rarely is this explicitly acknowledged. It seems important, therefore, to evaluate the changing course of ecodesign since the mid-1980s within the framework of the broader development of ecological ideas. One notable feature is a change in terminology: the original term "green design" is rarely used today and, although it was the buzzword the late 1980s, it is already passé. Instead, ecologically or environmentally sensitive or affirmative design, or more generally ecodesign, has become the most widely accepted term. In the last year or so, this has, in turn, given way to "sustainable design." These terms are fairly interchangeable, and perhaps the importance of such substitution of words should not be exaggerated, but they are one indication of shifting attitudes.

The transition from "green" to "eco-" to "sustainable" in the design field represents a steady broadening of scope in theory and practice, and to a certain extent, an increasingly critical perspective on ecology and design. Here, use of terms seems to indicate an attempt to wrestle with the complexities and implications of an ecological approach to design – going beyond the rather simplistic notions of design and the environment in the previous decade.

In this essay, which is part history and part analysis of ecodesign criticism, I use these three terms as keywords to explore different facets of ecological design, and to contextualize them within particular phases of the environmental movement in the last decade. I have emphasized the more radical theories to emerge within both design and environmental thinking in order to demonstrate what this might imply for a new ecological design criticism. What will emerge is that this is not necessarily a cohesive or unified phenomenon – there are many shades of green and different ecological perspectives, reflecting political distinctions within the environmentalism and differences within ecological theory and practice. Although ecodesign in the last decade has been dominated by a concern for the mechanisms of putting policy into practice, a fundamental recognition has emerged that what is at stake is a new view of the world and a choice of possible futures, and it is this which has the most interesting implications for design criticism.

GREEN DESIGN

"Green" became the buzzword of the 1980s. As public awareness of environmental problems spread and green parties became more prominent throughout Europe, there was a sudden profusion of greenery within the media and in advertising in the mid- to late '80s. Because "green" encapsulated green politics, current environmental concerns, and identified them with a specific color, in an unprecedented way, green design arrived with a ready-made symbolism: green products, green packaging, and numerous books on "how to be green" in green book jackets. The "lead" nations, within Europe, in environmental terms, such as Germany and the Netherlands, began research into design and the environment in the early 1980s. Evelyn Möller coined the phrase "ecological functionalism" in 1982, and devised an ecological checklist for product designers and manufacturers which formed the basis of a working group on ecology and design in the *Verband Deutscher Industrie-Designer*.[1]

In the UK, the Design Council took the lead with an exhibition called "The Green Designer" in 1986, organized by Paul Burall, Design Council publicity officer, and John Elkington, environmental consultant. Despite the fact that the term "green" was borrowed from politics, the approach in this exhibition was largely apolitical, taking place as it did in the design culture of the mid-'80s, when the idea of "winning by design" or "profit by design," as the Design Council called it, was paramount. In fact, the exhibition was the Design Council's contribution to Industry Year in 1986, and it was mainly concerned with demonstrating that green design was not "anti-industry," and that the "the greening of industry had gone further than most people imagined." John Elkington argued that the problems had now been largely overcome because green markets and the emergence of the environmental industry meant that there was no longer a conflict between a green approach to design and business success.[2] The exhibition focused on examples of specific products, and devised "10 Questions for the Green Designer" related to energy use, durability, recyclabilty, and acceptability in the marketplace. Five years later, a similar exhibition was held at the Design Centre called "More From Less" which also included "Cradle to Grave Guidelines for Design." A number of books on green design appeared around this date to answer the need for basic information on environmental issues for designers, adopting the same basic approach as the Design Council.[3]

In political terms, all of these exhibitions and publications can be classified as "light green," as opposed to "dark green," terms that were being used by the mid-'80s to designate different tendencies within the green movement. To distinguish itself from the red/blue, left/right of traditional politics, the green movement referred to a spectrum from gray to green, with the deeper shades of green being the more radical. In the late '80s, the terms were somewhat trivialized to refer to light and dark green consumers, but they reflected a deep division within the environmental movement between those who advocated a radical rejection of the status quo, a critique of the paradigm of modern industrial society (whether capitalist or socialist), and the lighter green idea of modifying existing institutions and practices. This ideological division goes back to the historic roots of the environmental movement in the late 1960s and early '70s (and beyond), but it acquired a new urgency in the 1980s as the green movement came into the mainstream.

One very influential way of designating these different strands within the environmental movement which still seems relevant to the green or ecodesign movement today, is Timothy O'Riordan's classification of "technocentric" and "ecocentric." He used these terms to represent two fundamentally different outlooks on the world. The ecocentric attitude is based on bioethics and a deep reverence for nature. It is in favor of low-impact technology, and is concerned with the environmental impact of rampant economic growth and large-scale industrial development; emphasizing, instead, morally and ecologically sound alternatives. Conversely, the technocentric mode is characterized by an unswerving belief in the ability of human science and high technology to manage the environment for the benefit of present and future generations and is based on an ideology of progress, efficiency, rationality, and control, viewing discussions about the wider political, social or ethical dimensions of the environment with suspicion.[4] In the 1970s and 1980s, these different attitudes also came to be described in terms of "shallow" and "deep" ecology, the latter, like ecocentrism, emphasizing harmony with nature and the intrinsic worth of all forms of life, as well as simplifying material needs so as to reduce human impact on planetary ecology.[5]

In the mid- to late '80s, the predominate form of green design represented a light green, technocentric, or shallow ecological approach, but it is possible to identify darker green or deeper ecological design, too; for example, the range of products and services listed in John Button's *Green Pages*, with its emphasis on consuming less;[6] or the German *Baubiologie* movement which believes that "living with less is better than saving energy," and that it is possible to do without many existing products through the improved design of buildings and changes in lifestyles.[7] This raises the whole question of alternative or green lifestyles, which have long been part of the green movement but which came to the fore in the debate over green consumerism in the late '80s.

Green consumerism arrived in 1988 with the publication of the best-selling *Green Consumer Guide*, by John Elkington and Julia Hailes. It was timed to coincide with "Green Consumer Week," organized by Friends of the Earth in September 1988. In the next year or so, there was frenzied activity on the green marketing front with some major claims being made for the new green products. This led to certain misgivings on the part of environmental groups and, while supporting green consumerism in principle, Friends of the Earth, for example, warned of a "green con," and argued for the need to go *Beyond Green Consumerism*.[8] An essential conflict appeared to exist between what could be called a dark green approach to design and consumption, and the values of advertising and marketing:

> Notions such as durability, reduced or shared consumption, or substituting nonmaterial pleasures for the use of objects, conflict with requirements of mass marketing. Advertising is tied to an expanding economy, the one thing that we living on a finite planet, must avoid.[9]

Here was a danger that:

> efforts to promote a demand for consumer goods that are environmentally benign will simply result in strengthening the growth of consumerism.[10]

As a response to this two new consumer magazines emerged in 1989. *Ethical Consumer* and *New Consumer* attempted to promote the use of "consumer power for positive economic, social, and environmental change."[11] There was an essential contrast between this approach and the more mainstream studies such as *Green, Greener, Greenest* by Michael Peters, an investigation into whether green consumerism was a significant marketing trend in Europe.[12]

Although these issues were not explicitly discussed within green design circles at the time, and there was never any question that a dark green approach would be on the agenda, there were occasional nods toward darker shades of green. For example, the title of a conference at the Design Museum in 1990, "Green Design: Beyond the Bandwagon," reflected a similar concern over green con to that expressed by Friends of the

Earth, and concentrated on *genuine* green products and graphics. Alongside speakers from design and industry, Richard Adams of *New Consumer* broadened the debate.

In the next few years, the practicalities of greening products and industry came to the fore. The Design Research Society, for example, organized a conference called "The Greening of Design" in Manchester in 1992 which concentrated on environmental factors in new product development and business from a design management point of view. There was considerable overlap between this and attempts to introduce business ethics and green management into industry on the part of the New Economics Foundation and the New Consumer. But the latter adopted a more radical, watchdog role:

> The vital issues of the coming decades will revolve around the nature of global consumption and distribution. Fundamental choices will have to be made about lifestyles, patterns of production and consumer priorities. Planet-sustaining decisions must be based on extensive and wide ranging information about the nature of our consumer society and those who service it.[13]

In the next few years, such ideas were to be taken on board by green designers who, as a kind of recognition of a wider frame of reference, began increasingly to refer to their work as "ecological design."

ECOLOGICAL DESIGN

The adoption of the term "ecological" to refer to anything vaguely to do with the environment dates back to the beginning of the environmental movement in the late 1960s and '70s. In 1988, John Button referred to about ninety sightings of the prefix "eco" including ecocity, ecomanagement, ecotechnics, and eco(logical archi) tecture; but not at that time, ecodesign.[14] The term came into prominence a few years later, but one early use was by the Ecological Design Association, formed by 1989, whose journal was called *Ecodesign*. The EDA chose "ecological" rather than "green" because it was thought, quite rightly, that "green" would soon be an outdated term. This also reflected a broad understanding of ecological design, including radical notions of deep ecology:

> The design of materials and products, projects and systems environments communities which are friendly to living species and planetary ecology.[15]

Although, by 1990, ecodesign was most advanced in European countries, there were some new initiatives in the early '90s in Australia. In 1990, the EcoDesign Foundation in Sydney was set up, "dedicated to the promotion of ecological sustainability through industrial re-creation."[16] There, Tony Fry and Ann-Marie Willis focused on both the immediate task of greening products and the longer-term goals of redefining design and industrial practice – what Chris Ryan of the Centre for Design at the Royal Melbourne Institute of Technology has recently referred to as "EcoRedesign" and "Ecodesign," respectively.[17] An international EcoDesign conference was held at RMIT in October 1991 which, according to Anne-Marie Willis, reflected "the unchoate nature of ecodesign":

> … for many this simply meant the "adding in" of environmental criteria to the design process. Yet ecodesign has the potential to be more than the reform of existing design, for if taken seriously, it can establish a new foundation for design that could bring economic and ecological needs into a new union …[18]

In the Netherlands an international gathering of designers met in March 1991 to discuss ecodesign, focusing on principles and methods as well as prevention by design.[19] This was a working group of the European Union's Eureka program, set up to provide the forum for the concept of environmentally sound product design. It was organized under the auspices of the Dutch Ministry of Economic Affairs. This was one example of many government-sponsored initiatives in the early '90s. UNEP (the United Nations Environment Program) had identified fifty of these by 1994[20] – a sign that ecodesign was beginning to be incorporated into national policies. Joint research was undertaken by academic institutions and industry, too, in the Netherlands[21] and the UK.[22]

Much of this research in the UK and elsewhere focused on the minutiae of ecodesign practice, adopting a systems approach either to the individual product or product system, or to industry as a whole. This included life cycle models which charted energy and material flow through a product system from "cradle to grave" or "womb to tomb," and there was a proliferation of flowcharts and circular diagrams. This was related to the new interdisciplinary subject of industrial ecology, "a framework for conceptualizing environmental and technical issues" which could help to inform the implementation of ecodesign or DFE (Design for the Environment).[23] Industrial ecology, like LCA, is closely modeled on ecological systems:

> Industrial ecology is meant as a conceptual tool emulating models derived from natural ecosystems, aimed at developing fundamentally new approaches to the industrial system reorganization.[24]

This attempt to draw upon ecological models to analyze product or industrial systems has proven very useful, since it is a way of containing the complexities of an environmental approach to design within limits by defining the boundaries of a system. But it does present some problems. It tends to be technocentric in that it embodies a belief in objective, value-free, scientific evidence; whereas, like EIA (Environmental Impact Assessment) or COBA (Cost Benefit Analysis), it clearly involves value judgments. Only by "scoping," that is concentrating on key areas of environmental impact, can LCA, for example, be at all manageable. Otherwise, the detailed analysis would include a huge amount of data and take years to complete. Selectivity inevitably introduces an element of bias, and what is excluded from the debate may be as important as what is included. A recent study of 132 LCA schemes found that they did not share a common methodology, and that they tended to support the views of the company which sponsored them.[25] A more fundamental issue is that certain kinds of ecological models are being borrowed from ecological science as if they were absolutes, whereas, in fact, a closer look at the history and development of ecology reveals a range of methods, approaches, and philosophies.

There is no real consensus on whether ecology is a science or a philosophy, even though the term "ecology" was coined in the mid-nineteenth century by Ernst Haeckel to refer to a new subbranch of biology concerned with the relationship between living organisms and their surroundings. For him, it had social and political implications, too.[26] In the twentieth century, ecological science can be roughly divided into two main phases. In the period up to about 1960, it was based on the idea of homeostasis and ecological balance. The concept of the ecosystem was developed by Tansley, Odum, and others. This has been described as the "ecology of the machine age," and is still based largely on the mechanistic beliefs of nineteenth-century science.[27] By contrast, the new ecology which developed from the 1970s onwards rejected the idea of nature as a balanced system, and emphasized instead the disequilibrium of natural systems. Linked as it was with chaos and complexity theory, it revolutionized the concept of nature which was now seen to consist of unpredictable, dynamic, evolving, self-adaptive systems.[28]

In many respects, the ecodesign studies referred to above are based more on the first kind of ecology than on the second, and reflect a mechanistic view of the world. The new ecology of chaos and complexity throws the whole basis of the inquiry into dispute. In a pragmatic sense, designing systems or products based on a mechanistic mode would be doomed to failure if the real world does not, in fact, work like that. The old dogma that the modeling of ecosystems is an exact science appears to have been shattered.[29] This raises the problem of the nature of the evidence culled from ecological science. Not only does the long-term nature of ecological research make it difficult to produce the hard and fast evidence called for by environmentalists, policymakers – and now designers – but recent ecology presents a dynamic picture of unpredictable chaos-like successions which contradict the classical models of stability and homeostasis.[30] The implication of chaos and complexity theory for ecodesign are not yet clear, but it does seem to suggest that an incremental approach is difficult because small changes can trigger gigantic impacts. The study of complex adaptive systems also implies a new model of design, one that is more modest and relational.[31]

There is a further implication of recent ecological thinking for design. Edward Goldsmith contrasts an ecological world-view with the modernist world-view of industrial society, which is:

> … methodically substituting the technosphere or the surrogate world of human artifacts for the biosphere – or the *real* world of living things – from which the former derives its resources and to which it consigns its waste products …

This suggests a different version of ecological design because to reverse this process means rethinking priorities and changing fundamental attitudes including phasing out unnecessary products, reversing the process whereby luxuries are turned into needs, living with less, and working with the natural system.[32] Under the impact of such thinking, and that of the Gaia Hypothesis[33] and the Permaculture Movement,[34] a new model of a radical, dark green, sustainable lifestyle has begun to emerge but this has, so far, been only partially reflected in ecodesign – in the EDA, for instance. There are some signs that such ideas are beginning to have an impact on more mainstream ecodesign. In 1993, the O2 Group, for example, held a conference call "Striking Visions" to create visions of sustainable lifestyles, taking a long-term view of the changes in attitudes needed to bring this about, and how design can make a new consumerless world palatable and even enjoyable.[35] This was reflected in a shift in the discussion about ecological design and a move toward the idea of "sustainable" or "global" design.

SUSTAINABLE DESIGN

Sustainability is not a new concept. It is an ecological term that has been used since the early 1970s to mean: "the capacity of a system to maintain a continuous flow of whatever each part of that system needs for a healthy existence,"[36] and when applied to ecosystems containing human beings refers to the limitations imposed by the ability of the biosphere to absorb the effects of human activities. The term "sustainable development" was first used in the early '80s, but was popularized by the Brundtland Report of 1987.[37] "Sustainable" has become the buzzword of the '90s in the same way "green" was in the '80s, and is equally open to different interpretations and misuse. The Brundtland Report adopted a global perspective on the consumption of energy and resources, and emphasized the imbalance between rich and poor parts of the world, arguing that: "Sustainable development requires that those who are more affluent adopt lifestyles within the planet's ecological means."[38] However, because the report also argued that economic growth or development is still possible as long as it is *green* growth, this has been interpreted by many to endorse a "business as usual" approach, with just a nod in the direction of environmental protection. This ignores the real meaning of sustainable development, which is enshrined in the widely quoted concept of "futurity": … "meeting the needs of the present without compromising the ability of future generations to meet their own needs."[39]

When applied to design, this not only introduces – or reintroduces – the ideas of ethical and social responsibility, but also the notion of time and timescale. Thinking about the life cycle of products through time, and considerations about design for recycling, have led to the concept of DfD – Design for Disassembly – followed by the idea of going *Beyond Recycling*[40] towards the design of long-life, durable products. These two concepts are not as contradictory as they sound, as Victor Papanek has recently remarked: "To design durable goods for eventual disassembly may sound like an oxymoron, yet it is profoundly important in a sustainable world."[41]

The term "sustainable design" has begun to be used in the last year or so to refer to a broader, longer-term vision of ecodesign. At the Centre for Sustainable Design, established at the Surrey Institute of Art and Design in July 1995, sustainable design means "analyzing and changing the 'systems' in which we make, use, and dispose of products," as opposed to more limited, short-term DFE.[42] The ECO2 group makes a similar distinction between "green design, project-based, single issue and relatively short-term; and 'sustainable' design, which is system-based, long-term" ethical design.[43] Emma Dewberry and Phillip Goggin have also explored the distinctions between ecodesign and sustainable design; arguing that, whereas ecodesign can be applied to all products and used as a suitable guide for designing at product level: "The concept of sustainable design, however, is much more complex and moves the interface of design outwards toward societal conditions, development, and ethics ...[44] This suggests changes in design and the role of design, including an inevitable move from a product to a systems-based approach, from hardware to software, from ownership to service, and will involve concepts such as dematerialization and "a general shift from physiological to psychological needs." Finally, they emphasize the extent to which consumption patterns must change, and refer to the inequality between developed and developing nations, the fact that 20 percent of the world's population consumes 80 percent of the world's resources and conclude that ecodesign does fit into a global move toward sustainability, but has many limitations in this context.[45] This is the point made by Gui Bonsiepe, who has expressed the fear that ecological design will remain the luxury of the affluent countries while "the cost of environmental standards would be shifted onto the shoulders of the Third World."[46]

This raises the other dimensions of sustainable development: "Equity," meeting the needs of all, and "Participation," effective citizen involvement in decision-making, without which global sustainable growth would be impossible – except by an unacceptable form of "ecofascism." These issues are only just being raised in design circles, but were explored in detail recently by the WorldWatch Institute in reports on global resources and consumption patterns. In *How Much is Enough? The Consumer Society and the Future of the Earth*, Alan Durning divides the world population into three consumption classes and analyzes their consumption of food, transport, and goods, concluding that environmental destruction results from the overconsumption of the top one-fifth of the world's population and from the poverty of the bottom one-fifth. He asks if there is a level of sufficiency for all the world's population, a level above poverty and subsistence but below the affluent consumer lifestyle that is sustainable. The answer is a shift from the "cultivation of needs" to "a culture of permanence": "substituting local foods for grain-fed meat and packaged fare, switching from cars to bikes and buses, and replacing throwaways with durable goods."[47] This obviously implies a new agenda for design, and this is beginning to be discussed in the UNEP Working Group on Sustainable Product Development which was started in January 1994 as a follow-up initiative to the Rio Conference of 1992. It is a network of 360 people in 40 countries all over the world, including 18 from developing and transitional countries. The Research Program is based on the principles of sustainable development:

> The very concept of "sustainability" underlies our fear for the next generation's future, and forces the question; is a harmonious balance between their product demands and the earth's ecology possible and how can it be sustained?[48]

Products are redefined in terms of categories such as "service" (transport "pool," rented products); "dematerialization" (virtual libraries, teleworking systems), as well as life cycle design and longevity. But perhaps even more interesting is the focus on "Products, Services and Systems that Meet Human Needs," and which can lead to an improvement in living and working conditions. Areas of "need" to be explored include transportation, communication, heating, cooling, clothing and textiles, and the use of water by the end-consumer.[49] This shift of emphasis from the products to the needs reintroduces an important theme from the 1970s, that of "Design for Need,"[50] and, in many ways, sustainable design has come back full circle to some of the radical design theories of the 1970s.

CONCLUSION

Thus, ecological design, as it has developed over the last decade, has reinvented some old ideas and produced some new ones. It has gone through a process of maturity, moving toward a deepening of understanding of environmental issues and a darker shade of green. It has become increasingly evident that the radical nature of an ecological approach to design implies a new design critique. In the 1980s, this was not necessarily apparent when green was the flavor, or rather the color, of the month and it seemed that green design would comfortably settle down into the mainstream of design industrial practice. In the 1990s, the oppositional nature of ecological design is more apparent, since even fairly pragmatic attempts to apply ecological principles to design seem to inevitably challenge existing practices and ideologies.

Designers and design critics are increasingly emphasizing the actual or, potentially, radical nature of an ecological approach to design which implies a new critique – a recognition of the fact that to adopt an ecological approach to design is, by definition, to question and oppose the status quo. Ezio Manzini, for example, has described this as a shift from the "normalized ecological design" of the 1980s and the "new radicalism" of the '90s, which increasingly recognizes that ecological design necessitates changes in lifestyles that challenge the current global model of development.[51] In a similar way, Tony Fry argues that ecodesign is the means by which industrial culture can be remade, and that the need to change basic values can only be achieved "by design so long as design itself is redesigned." He is critical of existing ecodesign theory and practice, but postulates a potentially radical ecodesign which could create a new direction for design.[52] From a different perspective, Gui Bonsiepe has also recently critically evaluated ecodesign. Although a new environmental ethic implies a new design ethic, he says, ecodesign, in theory and practice, has not yet developed enough to have created a new paradigm for industrial design. However:

> The unquestionable merit of ecodesign consists in having articulated concerns which put into question paradigms of design and industrial production and consumption that we took for granted.[53]

These issues may be new to design in the 1990s but, within the environmental literature, there has been a constant discussion since the 1960s of the extent to which an ecological world-view represents a new paradigm requiring a fundamental challenge to industrial society, or merely a minor modification of existing values and practices, and a debate over the degree of change required to overcome the current ecological crisis. That such issues are now being taken seriously within the design field – more so than the 1970s – suggests a shift in attitudes which will have far-reaching consequences for design criticism. During the last few decades, design criticism has followed design practice and has been dominated by a nonecological approach, tending to view consumerism as having positive economic and social value, and thereby endorsing the kind of industrial culture under attack by Greens. Only now, in the wake of discussions of ecological design theory and practice, is an ecological design criticism beginning to emerge.

NOTES

First published in *Design Issues* 13 no. 2 (Summer 1997): 44–54.

1. Evelyn Möller, "Design-Philosophie der 80er Jahre(2). Kommit mit dem Ende der Wegwerf-Ideologie ein Ökologischer Funktionalismus? *Form* 98 (1982) and *Unternehmen Pro Umwelt. Ansätze ganzheitlichen Denkens in Politik und Wirtschaft, Architektur, Produktenentwicklung und Design* (Munich: Lexika, 1989). In the Netherlands at this time, 1984–5, the Advisory Council for Research on Nature and the Environment was promoting research into product design: J. C. Van Weenen, C. A. Bakker, and I. V. de Keijser, *Eco-design: An Exploration of the Environment* (Milieukunde: Universiteit van Amsterdam, 1991).
2. *The Green Designer* (London: Design Council, 1986), 4.
3. For example, Paul Burall, *Green Design* (London: Green Council, 1990) and Dorothy Mackenzie, *Green Design, Design for the Environment* (London: Lawrence King, 1991).
4. T. O'Riordan, *Environmentalism* (London: Pion Ltd., 1976).
5. Deep ecology was first developed by the Norwegian philosopher Arne Naess in the early 1970s. See Arne Naess, "The Shallow and the Deep, Long-range Ecology Movement. A Summary," *Inquiry* 16 (1973) and special issue of *The Ecologist* on Deep Ecology: "Rethinking Man and Nature: Towards an Ecological Worldview" 188, no. 415 (1988).
6. John Button, *Green Pages: A Directory of Natural Products, Services, Resources and Ideas* (London: Optima, 1988).
7. Keystone Architects, statement at the EDA exhibition, London Ecology Centre, 1990. Hartwin Busch, "Building Biology: Towards a New Era of Healthy Building," *Caduceus* 7 (1989).
8. Sandy Irvine, *Beyond Green Consumerism* (London: Friends of the Earth, 1989).
9. Sandy Irvine and Alec Ponton, *A Green Manifesto: Politics for a Green Future* (London: Optima, 1989).
10. James Robertson, *Future Wealth: A New Economics for the 21st Century* (London: Cassell, 1989), 9.
11. *New Consumer Review* (Newcastle, England: New Consumer, 1991).
12. Michael Peters Brand Development Division and Diagnostic Market Research Ltd., *Green, Greener, Greenest: The Green Consumer in the UK, Netherlands and Germany* (September 1989).
13. Richard Adams, Jane Carruthers, and Sean Hamil, *Changing Corporate Values: A Guide to Social and Environmental Policy and Practice in Britain's Top Companies* (Newcastle: Kogan Page, 1990), x.
14. John Button, *A Dictionary of Green Ideas: Vocabulary for a Sane and Sustainable Future* (London: Routledge, 1988), 139–142.
15. EDA leaflet (London 1990).
16. EcoDesign Foundation, *NewsLines* 1 (Sept. 1991): 4.
17. Chris Ryan, "From EcoREdesign to Ecodesign," *Ecodesign* IV, no. 1 (1996).
18. Anne-Marie Willis, "Echoes of EcoDesign 1," EcoDesign Foundation Newsletter (Sydney, Dec. 1991): 2.
19. J. C. Van Weenen, C. A. Bakker, and I. V. de Keijser, *Eco-Design: An Exploration of the Environment* (Milieukunde, the Netherlands: Universiteit van Amsterdam, 1991). Delegates included Dorothy Mackenzie, Ezio Manzini, and Chris Ryan.
20. "Eco-design Initiatives Gather Momentum," *ENDS Report* 231 (April 1994): 29.
21. In the Netherlands, there was discussion of a formal system to put products through a green filter and a team of designers and environmental experts at the TNO Product Centre. Delft Technical University studied eight product systems in terms of material and energy use, and suggested ways in which manufacturers could improve them. Harry te Riele and Albert Zweers, *Eco-design: Acht vorbeelden van milieugerichte produktontwikkeling* (Delft: Delft Technical University, 1994).
22. In the UK, a Eureka ecodesign seminar was organized by the Royal Society of Arts in March 1994 on the telecommunications industry. This provided a forum for all those researching into ecodesign, LCA, innovation, and the strategy of firms, notably at the Institute for Advanced Studies, Manchester Metropolitan University and the Design Innovation Group at the Open University.

23. Brad Allenby (AT&T), "Sustainable Development, Industrial Ecology, and Design for the Environment," White paper no. 10 (June 1993).
24. Silvia Pizzocaro, "Theoretical Approaches to Industrial Ecology: Status and Perspectives," international seminar "The Scenario of Sustainability: The Systemic Context" (Milan, April 1994): 1.
25. "Critical Review of LCA Practice," *ENDS Report* 219 (April 1994).
26. Anna Bramewell, *Ecology in the Twentieth Century: A History* (New Haven: Yale University Press, 1989). A good example of the word "ecology" being used in a general philosophical or political sense.
27. Daniel B. Botkin, *Discordant Harmonies: A New Ecology of the 21st Century* (New York: OUP, 1990).
28. See Donald Worster, *Nature's Economy: A History of Ecological Ideas*, 2nd edition (Cambridge: Cambridge University Press, 1994) and Richard Huggett, "Nature's Design: The Ecologist's View," a paper originally intended to be given at the "Eco Design" conference held in the Department of Philosophy, University of Manchester in October 1995. I would like to acknowledge how much this interesting, interdisciplinary conference has influenced my recent thinking on ecology and ecodesign, especially papers by John Wood, James Cullen, and Richard Huggett (whose paper was circulated to delegates afterward).
29. See, for example, John Harte, "Ecosystem Stability and Diversity" in Stephen H. Schneider and Penelope J. Boston, eds., *Scientists on Gaia* (Cambridge, MA: MIT Press, 1991).
30. I. G. Simmons, *Interpreting Nature: Cultural Constructions of the Environment* (London: Routledge, 1993).
31. A point made by John Wood at the Eco Design conference in Manchester, October 1995. The Santa Fe Institute in the USA, home of complexity theory, began to look at global sustainability in the early '90s, and suggested that the study of complex adaptive systems implied a new model. Sustainable human society is an interconnected system in which economic, social, and political forces are deeply intertwined and mutually dependent on each other. Thus, a sustainable human society cannot be achieved by rational methods and technical fixes, but only by the transformation of traditional attitudes and appetites. M. Mitchell Waldrop, *Complexity: The Emerging Science at the Edge of Order & Chaos* (New York: Viking, 1992).
32. Edward Goldsmith, *The Ecologist* 188, no. 415 (1988): 118, and *The Way: An Ecological World View*, 2nd edition (London: Green Books, 1996); *De-Industrializing Society* (London: *The Ecologist*, 1988).
33. Gaia, the earth-goddess, is the name given by scientist James Lovelock to his hypothesis that the earth is like a super, self-regulating organism. Gaia has become a potent symbol in the last few years because it provides a planetary perspective on the current ecological crisis. See James Lovelock, *Gaia: A New Look at Life on Earth* (Oxford and New York: OUP, 1987) and *The Ages of Gaia: A Biography of Our Living Earth*, 2nd Edition (Oxford and New York: OUP, 1995).
34. Permaculture (*perma*nent agri*culture* or *perma*nent *culture*) is a total design system based on the functional zoning of a site in a series of concentric circles according to frequency of use, and brings together the design of dwellings, animal husbandry and edible landscaping, and community building. There is little reference to the contents of the innermost zone, the dwelling, but permaculture implies a radical rethinking of products and services, too. Permaculture has been one of the fastest growing organizations within the green movement in the 1980s and '90s – it is the equivalent of the alternative technology movement of the '70s. See Mollison, *Permaculture: A Designer's Manual* (Tagari: Tyalgum, Australia: 1988).
35. "Striking Visions," 02 Event (Netherlands, Nov. 1993) organized by the Dutch 02 group. 02 was founded by the Danish designer Niels Peter Flint as an international organization of environmentally aware industrial designers.
36. John Button, *Dictionary of Green Ideas*, 446.
37. World Commission on Environment and Development, *Our Common Future* (Oxford: OUP, 1987).
38. Ibid., 9.
39. Ibid., 8.
40. Tim Cooper, *Beyond Recycling: The Longer Life Option* (London: New Economics Foundation, 1994).
41. Victor Papanek, "Eco-logic," *Ecodesign* III, no. I (1994): 10. Discussed in his recent book, *The Green Imperative: Ecology and Ethic in Design and Architecture* (London: Thames & Hudson, 1995).
42. Anne Chick, "MA in Sustainable Design," Centre for Sustainable Design leaflet, 1995.
43. ECO2 group, "Hierarchy of EcoProducts in Strategies," workshop on defining ecodesign, Nov. 1994.
44. Emma Dewberry and Phillip Goggin, "Ecodesign & Beyond: Steps Towards 'Sustainability' " (Open University and Nottingham Trent University, Nov. 1994): 7–8; and Emma Dewberry, "Ecodesign Strategies," *EcoDesign* IV. no. 1 (1996), in which she

distinguishes between green design, ecodesign, and global design approaches and company initiatives.

45. Dewberry and Goggin, "Ecodesign & Beyond."
46. Gui Bonsiepe, "North/South: Environment/ Design," *Inca* 14. Gui Bonsiepe, formerly of the *Hochschule für Gestaltung*, Ulm, until recently has been living and working in Latin America since the 1970s, and so he is in a good position to view the situation from a "south" perspective.
47. Alan Thein Durning, *How Much is Enough? The Consumer Society and the Future of the Earth* (London: Earthscan, 1992), 109. See also John E. Young and Aaron Sachs, *The Next Efficiency Revolution: Creating a Sustainable Materials Economy* (Worldwatch Paper 121, 1994). Peter Harper of the Centre for Alternative Technology, Wales, has been working along the same lines, and has made an interesting analysis of the acceptability of putative "eco-technology" and lifestyle changes. He has classified possible response from light to dark green in "The L-Word: A.T. and Lifestyles," *Proceedings of AT2000: A Conference on Alternative Technology for the 21st Century* (Milton Keynes: Open University, 1994).
48. United Nations Working Group on Sustainable Product Design News Fax (August 11, 1965); 1.
49. Ibid., 2, 3. See also Yorick Benjamin, senior researcher, "Sustainable Product Development," *EcoDesign* IV, no. 196.
50. "Design for Need" was the name of an ICSID (International Council for Societies of Industrial Design) conference held at the Royal College of Art in 1976. See J. Bicknell and L. McQuiston, eds., *Design for Need: The Social Contribution of Design* (Oxford: Pergamon Press, 1977).
51. Ezio Manzini, "Prometheus of the Everyday: The Ecology of the Artificial and the Designer's Responsibility," *Design Issues* 9 no. 11 (Fall 1992): 5 and "Design, Environment and Social Quality: From *'Existenzminimum'* to Quality Maximum," *Design Issues* 10 no. 1 (Spring 1994).
52. Tony Fry, *Remakings: Ecology, Design, Philosophy.* (Sydney: Envirobook, 1994), 9, 11–12.
53. Gui Bonsiepe, "North/South Environment/ Design," *Inca*, a publication of the San Francisco Chapter of the Industrial Designer's Society of America (August 1992).

26

BIOPHILIA AND TECHNOPHILIA: EXAMINING THE NATURE/CULTURE SPLIT IN DESIGN THEORY

David Stairs

In most cases the designer wants to set and solve problems for human use, but in most cases he feels obliged to set and solve problems for human abuse. This is, without doubt, the problem of all problems.[1]

Tomás Maldonado, speaking at IDCA, 1961

1

In 1984, Harvard biologist Edward O. Wilson published a modest volume in which he proposed the existence of a genetic basis for the human predilection towards the natural world. This concept, which Wilson called "biophilia," is loosely suggested by certain affinities and aversions which occur in societies widely separated by geography and ritual. For example, when asked to choose between photos of urban or rural settings, most people indicate a preference for the latter, implying an ancestral connection to our roots as hunter/gatherers. Biophilia was an unproved theory, but either because of its elegance or its timeliness, it struck a chord in the intellectual community.

Nearly a decade later, in 1993, an anthology of essays inspired by Wilson's idea appeared. Entitled *The Biophilia Hypothesis*, it presented authors from a variety of disciplines who grappled with the relation of civilization to the natural world. Some of the essays in *The Biophilia Hypothesis* sought to describe our influence on nature through plant and animal husbandry, others detailed nature's reciprocal influence on our language and mythology. Not all of these commentators were optimistic about the effects of human technology upon species diversity. David W. Orr chastised the failure of our economics, our politics, and our science to comprehend the enormity of the threat to the environment.

Other contributors took an opposing viewpoint. Dorion Sagan and Lynn Margulis went so far as to challenge the assumption that the planet is sick. They proposed that loss of biodiversity might be balanced by a gain in technodiversity, "… a trade-off that may ultimately enhance the longevity of the biosphere."[2] Madhav Gadgil's essay argued the coevolutionary basis of artifacts in the human evolutionary process, at one point comparing the worldwide building mass to the worldwide woody plant mass. This notion echoes Wilson's own sociobiological argument for "gene-culture coevolution" as "… a plausible explanation for the origins of biophilia."[3]

Not surprising, many of these points have been touched upon by design writers. In *Design for Human Scale*, Victor Papanek cites H.J. Eysenck in an effort to locate the evolutionary basis for aesthetic experience in associational memories which "… derive from the immemorial terrestrial environment of humans."[4] Yi-Fu Tuan writes: "The physical environment itself has an effect on perception. People who live in a 'carpentered' world are susceptible to different kinds of illusion

Figure 26.1 (a and b) Love of forests may have as much to do with a genetic disposition to the natural world as with the higher oxygen levels. This old growth stand at Terwiliger Hot Springs, on the western perimeter of Oregon's Three Sisters Wilderness, has been a human gathering spot for centuries.

from those who live in an environment lacking orthogonality."[5]

In "Prometheus of the Everyday," Ezio Manzini takes the comparison of nature and the built environment further. He invokes Bateson's idea of an ecology of the artificial to underline the difference between nature's nonpurposive evolution and culture's purposive change. Manzini recognizes the illusion which equates well-being with increased production and suggests that "... the question of rethinking the relation between the human race and the environment must be asked in a radical manner."[6] Manzini's admonition to reexamine our place in nature is not original; the canon of the environmental movement is now decades long. What makes Manzini's exhortations noteworthy is their relative rarity among design writers.

In a later essay, Manzini's tenor assumes the more radical tone he calls for: "Faced with the evidence of the inteconnectedness of the environmental, economic, and sociocultural crises, it becomes increasingly clear that the scenario of the 'redesign of what exists' is not sufficient for the discovery of true solutions."[7] Whether this is a

Figure 26.2 (a and b) Nature is not even referenced in certain man-made interior spaces. The United Airlines terminal at Chicago's O'Hare International Airport, a completely self-contained artificial environment right down to the recycled atmosphere, is no place for a claustrophobe.

recantation of his earlier enthusiasm for balanced satisfactions attainable through "ecotechnological equilibrium" remains unclear. That such an equilibrium would be compatible with the tenets of a conservationist ethic is uncertain. Harmony, unity, and interdependence are classic ecological concepts, and it is questionable that Bateson's "artificial ecology" means anything outside a natural construct. But Manzini's hypothesizing still raises the tantalizing question of how an empathic, enlightened, self-regulating design culture would affect the natural picture.

2

Design discourse is very preoccupied with the process of self-delineation. In this, it has followed the well-worn lead of art, literary, and social criticism in its focus on visual and material culture. The basis for this discussion has ranged from the venerable theorizings of the Frankfurt School through the macabre semiotic exegeses of deconstructionism. Although this may seem like a broad spectrum, it is often constrained by the current fashions of academia. And until recently, the environment has not been one of them.

Herbert Simon is a theorist who has thought seriously about design's relation to both nature and science. He considers design a science rather than an applied art. He also differentiates design's purpose, synthesis, from the analytical purposes of science. In characterizing the human brain as a symbol-producing artifact, Simon has ventured further than any writer in his attempts to define design as the "science of the artificial." He writes: "The artificial world is centered on (an) interface between the inner and outer environments; it is concerned with attaining goals by adapting the former to the latter."[8] As a working definition of why design arises, this is an intriguing suggestion. It proposes culture as the mediator between the natural world and the world of ideas. But in his efforts to resolve the pesky paradox of our apparent nature/culture schizophrenia, Simon conjures a slew of other insidious dichotomies, including the mind/body duality. Such either/or hypotheses, so prevalent in an era of information theory, are disturbing.

Even more troubling are the remarks of Paul Rabinow as quoted by Allucquere Stone. Stone cites Rabinow's description of "biosociality" as it relates to genetic research:

> … in biosociality, nature will be modeled on culture understood as practice; it will be known and remade through technique; nature will finally become artificial, just as culture becomes natural. The objectivism of social factors is now giving way to … the beginnings of a redefinition and eventual operationalization of nature.[9]

This chilling anthropocentric inversion, a veritable Frankenstein Unbound, overlooks the relative brevity of culture when compared to the magnificence of biological evolution. As one friend visualized it for me, if the deep history of natural evolution is a tabletop, culture is a dust mote on that table.[10] Wilson reminds us that "… the brain evolved in a biocentric world, not a machine regulated world." The biophilia hypothesis "… suggests that when human beings remove themselves from the natural environment, the biophilic learning rules are not replaced by modern versions equally well-adapted to artifacts."[11] In other words, the fear of snakes and high places has yet to be superseded by the fear of motor vehicles and firearms.

Human culture is rapidly evolving and, as some suggest, may well be an advanced manifestation of nature. But culture has attained nowhere near the level of complexity of the natural world it is in danger of unbalancing.

3

The technophilic stance taken by Rabinow, Simon, Sagan, and others is understandable. In a civilization still dominated by a mechanistic paradigm, such attitudes are bred in the intellectual bone. Cultural historian Leo Marx writes, "The idea of history as a record of progress driven by the application of science-based knowledge was not simply another idea among many. Rather it was a figurative concept lodged at the center of what became, sometime after 1750, the dominant secular world-picture of Western culture."[12] The breathlessness surrounding technological advancements was bound to influence design analysts. The idea that technology cannot be an anodyne for all of society's ills is a relatively recent development. In the heyday of what Leo Marx calls "technocratic utopianism," it was only the countercultural crank who provided a reality check for the prevailing ideology. Thoreau was one such person, and in our era, Lewis Mumford was another. But in a century in which "progress is our most important product," such voices often have been drowned out by the percussive din of metaphoric drop forges.

That technology, like life, is developmental, gives small solace in the face of accelerating technological change. The spectre of technological determinism casts a two-century-long shadow across our society, but the spectre is personified not so much by Prometheus as by Faust. In the appendices to his *Critique of Commodity Aesthetics*, Wolfgang Haug likens the function of design under capitalism to that of the Red Cross in wartime, boosting morale yet complicit in the slaughter. When queried about how best to design for the human environment, he responded, "… environment is the world over which we have no say and through which we should move like animals in the jungle …"[13]

Haug's pessimism is palpable, but the reasons for despair are obvious. This is the same anxiety voiced by Manzini and Wilson. Yet, as densely ironic as Haug's answer to the International Design Center is, it points to a recognition of the contrived split between nature and culture.

4

Design literature abounds with definitions of environment, from Victor Margolin's "product milieu" to Carl Mitchum's "techno life-world." As we've seen with Rabinow and Simon, most of these definitions, of necessity, assume a technophilic bias. Arnold Berleant, a phenomenologist who claims to dislike the word "environment," defines it as "… a dynamic perceptual/cultural system that assimilates person and place."[14]

Critics of modern industrial society such as Charles Reich have pointed to its damaging effects on the spirit of human community. In *The Greening of America*, Reich refers to the institutional and occupational communities which serve the corporation's ends at the individual's expense as "false communities." He indicts the "corporate state" as the instrument which imposes centripetal routine on the family unit in the name of group consumption.

Berleant's analysis is more sophisticated. He recognizes individuality and self-sufficiency as false ideals. He cites an ethic of care as the feminist alternative to the theory of rights. He describes four modes of community: the rational, the moral, the organic, and the aesthetic, dismissing the first three because they fail to develop "… a unity of individual and social in which neither dimension dominates but each enhances the possibilities of the other." Berleant feels this condition is limited to the aesthetic community, a realm of inherent relationship and mutual reciprocity ruled by an ethos of interdependence.

Berleant likens the aesthetic community to the sense of closeness one experiences in erotic intimacy.[15] He considers aesthetic continuity to be a continuum of self, environment, and conscious awareness and, consequently, situates the continuity of our relation to nature in the aesthetic field. He argues that "… an aesthetic community recognizes the social dimension of environment and the aesthetic conditions of human fulfillment."[16] This unity of experience, replacing false dichotomies, is at the source of the aesthetic community. In so saying, Berleant frees culture and, by association, design from their antipodal relationship to nature. Hypothetically, the mutual reciprocity of culture and nature, Manzini's "eco-technological equilibrium," becomes supportable.

5

In his introductory essay for *The Biophilia Hypothesis*, Edward Wilson locates the ultimate answer to the clash between nature and human civilization in the word "spirit." He sees a deeper understanding of life on earth, not the colonization of inhospitable space, as the frontier of future exploration.[17] In his call for a "... more powerful and intellectually convincing environmental ethic," he is joined, in word and spirit, by Berleant, Manzini, and many others.

Words such as "sharing," "engagement," and "community" have trickled down into the common critical parlance of the reenchanted '90s. Victor Papanek's latest book, *The Green Imperative*, has a chapter entitled "The New Aesthetic: Making the Future Work" in which he argues for the spiritual basis of design practice. In placing sustainability at the top of his list of imperatives, Papanek urges an ethical design practice which is environmentally responsible and human in scale.

It is misleading to dichotomize the material and the spiritual; the genetic imperative of biophilia and the creative imperative of technophilia. Such division is a seventeenth-century construct whose time has passed. The future, like the past, will be determined by biology, and culture will continue to conform to the inherent dictates of nature. Designers and design theorists cannot afford to be mere adjuncts of the theory of unlimited growth, functioning in advocacy of an obsolete economic model.

The purpose of an enlightened design discourse must be to hasten the inevitable rapprochement between nature and culture. The pejorative effects of our technology cannot be ameliorated by bigger and better machines, but must be examined through the development of a meta-technological discourse. A good example could be made of indigenous people, such as the Inuit. Papanek has called them "the best designers in the world"; their handicraft technology enables them to survive in the harshest climate on earth without compromising their link to actuality. The future role of design will be to create culture as a sustainable part of the natural world.

Industry's apologists will recoil from these suggestions. But they are not so much a retreat into environmental determinism as a call for us to admit and accept our limitations. If at first it seems absurd to speak of comparing our industrial technology to preindustrial handicraft, perhaps we should recall the humility that comes from being mortal creatures in a finite natural universe. Low or no-growth, steady-state economics and the tenets of ecofeminism are proven alternatives.[18] We must rediscover Mumford's biotechnic, or life-centered technology, and apply it to design thinking. And we must never equate entropic or closed models with creatures for whom evolution is the only acceptable model. The development of monolithic, hierarchical technologies in which virtuality is the ideal goal should be recognized as inimical to our humanity.

In the end, it will be as futile to ask us to stop designing as it is to ask us to renounce our dependence upon nature. In a moment of probity Simon writes:

> One of the charges sometimes laid against modern science and technology is that, if we know how to do something, we cannot resist doing it. While one can think of counterexamples, the claim has some measure of truth. One can envisage a future, however, in which our main interest in both science and design will lie in

what they teach us about the world and not what they allow us to do to the world. Design, like science, is a tool for understanding as well as for acting.[19]

The argument for the genetic basis of biophilia is compelling. It does not diminish the fact that designing is one of our primary functions in this world, but it should give us pause to reflect. We must accept that our future resides not in the psychotic vision of unending cultural, technological, and economic progress, but in working to preserve the community of all earthly life.

NOTES

First published in *Design Issues* 13 no. 3 (Autumn 1997): 37–44.

1. Tomás Maldonado, "The Problem of All Problems," *The Aspen Papers*, Reyner Banham, ed. (New York: Praeger, 1974), 125.
2. Dorion Sagan and Lynn Margulis, "God, Gaia, and Biophilia," *The Biophilia Hypothesis*, Stephen R. Kellert and E.O. Wilson, eds. (Washington: Island Press, 1993), 362.
3. E.O. Wilson, "Biophilia and the Conservation Ethic," *The Biophilia Hypothesis*, 32.
4. Victor Papanek, *Design for Human Scale* (New York: Van Nostrand Reinhold, 1983), 137.
5. Yi-Fu Tuan, *Topophilia* (New York: Prentice-Hall, 1974), 111.
6. Ezio Manzini, "Prometheus of the Everyday. The Ecology of the Artificial and the Designer's Responsibility," *Discovering Design*, Richard Buchanan and Victor Margolin, eds. (Chicago: University of Chicago Press, 1995), 224–228.
7. Manzini, "Design, Environment and Social Quality: From "*Existenzminimum*" to "Quality Maximum," *Design Issues* 10 no. 1, (Spring) 1994: 38.
8. Herbert Simon, *The Sciences of the Artificial* (Cambridge, MA: MIT Press, 1969; rpt. 1981), 132.
9. Allucquere Rosanne Stone, *The War of Desire and Technology at the Close of the Mechanical Age* (Cambridge, MA: MIT Press, 1995), 38.
10. I am indebted to George Gessert for this analogy.
11. Wilson, 31–32.
12. Leo Marx, "The Idea of 'Technology' and Postmodern Pessimism," *Does Technology Drive History?*, Merritt Roe Smith and Leo Marx, eds. (Cambridge, MA: MIT Press, 1994), 250.
13. Wolfgang Haug, *Critique of Commodity Aesthetics* (Minneapolis: University of Minneapolis Press, 1986), 136–137.
14. Arnold Berleant, "Aesthetics and Community," *The Journal of Value Enquiry* 28 (1994): 257–272.
15. Ibid., 266.
16. Ibid., 271.
17. In referring to the *Star Trek* television series, Leo Marx describes space travel as "… the quintessential fantasy of a technocratic paradise."
18. An interesting discussion of these topics occurs in *Radical Ecology* by Carolyn Merchant.
19. Simon, 188.

27

ETHICS, AESTHETICS, AND DESIGN

Alain Findeli

"… For in the final analysis it is spirit alone that animates technology."

Goethe

This is a slightly shortened version of a paper first read at a conference entitled "Savoirs et éthiques de l'ingénieur … " *held at the National Institute of Applied Sciences at Lyon (France) in December 1992. The text has been adapted and updated according to new research developments.*

Translated from the French by John Cullars and revised by the author. All sketches by Vincent Bédard.

When Goethe wrote the phrase that serves as an epigraph for this essay, he was thinking about artistic practice. But its truth seems to fit our present context so obviously that I don't hesitate to hazard an analogy, in itself always a delicate maneuver. Moreover, during the course of this paper, I will turn to the originality of Goethe's vision once again, this time to evoke certain specific points of his epistemology and methodology. But for the moment, it is the relations of humankind to technology that engages us, more precisely, the ethical questions arising from the unprecedented technological developments in the Western world over the past few decades. To that general problematic, concerning which some philosophers of technology have coined the neologism "technoethics," is associated another of a practical kind: many professions – medicine, law, engineering, journalism, etc. – are currently caught in unprecedented conflicts for the most part also the result of accelerated technological development, which their respective professional code of ethics didn't foresee and are unable to resolve. This is the case with design as well.

The two questions that I just raised were the topic of a collective research project called, "Prométhé Eclairé (or Prometheus Enlightened): Ethics, Technology and Professional Responsibility in Design," carried out at the School of Industrial Design at the University of Montreal. The project was part of a vast program, devoted to applied ethics, designated as "strategic" by the Canadian Council for Research in the Human Sciences.[1] We set ourselves the task of establishing **the general problematic of design ethics**, in the broad context of technological ethics or "technoethics," and examining in this light the manner in which the responsibility of designers can be reevaluated. This paper presents some partial conclusions that I believed were worth drawing. They most directly concern design theory, the practice and teaching of design, but in some respects they touch equally on aesthetics. But before presenting these conclusions, I wish to make two clarifications on the use of the words "technoethics" and "design."

The term "technoethics" was coined by analogy with "bioethics."[2] It designates that portion of ethics which deals with questions arising from technological development and activities. More precisely, technoethics deals with moral questions governing or resulting from the conception, production, distribution and the use of artifacts or technological systems. In this sense it then embraces bioethics, insofar as the emergence of the latter results from decisive technological innovations that have enlarged the range of medical practice and possibilities and consequently of the traditional medical codes of ethics. Technoethics deals with all professional acts mediated by ever more complex, powerful and sophisticated artifacts, tools, and techniques. One thinks immediately of computer science and the way in which it is altering teaching and pedagogy, the management of business and local communities, or the practice of law. Technoethics just as greatly challenges all professionals who plan and make these artifacts and tools and, more generally, all our built environment, the "technosphere": engineers, designers, architects, manufacturers, artists, etc. Finally, since the proliferation of these artifacts modifies, sometimes radically, our daily activities, including our relationships with others (affective, communicational, etc.) it is readily understood that technoethics finds ample cause to reflect on these matters also. The least one can say is that the range of application of technoethics understood in this extended sense is quite vast. For this reason, I will limit myself to the field of product design.

In the most restricted current sense that we're familiar with, the word "design" refers to that more or less well-identified category of specialists who claim to improve the quality of the everyday objects that surround us: furniture, clothing, domestic and leisure appliances, various vehicles, advertising images, all the way to the most apparently useless gadgets. While it is generally the aesthetic appearance and the novelty of products that capture the attention of the public, one associates their "practical" properties with the intervention of designers (anthropometry, ergonomy, maneuverability, and safety). Whenever possible, designers strive to dispel this reductive vision of their profession, deploring the perception of the public and, worse, of manufacturers and engineers, who fail to grasp the complexity and specificity of their tasks. The recognition and acceptance they so much desire could well come to them by other routes, through a much more general definition of the word "design," which is current in the disciplines of artificial intelligence and expert systems and designates the processes inherent in any activity of conception or project making. "Conceptual sciences," "sciences of the artificial," "design sciences," "praxeology": how many synonyms for a new discipline appeared in the '60s![3] In this sense, design encompasses the set of operations organized so as to fill the objectives of a project, and is no longer just concerned with the above listed professionals and objects but with most professions: architects, urban planners, engineers, lawyers, doctors, politicians, corporate leaders, etc. One could even widen this definition to include all the specifically human operations that we carry out intentionally on a daily basis. It then becomes somewhat analogous to the Greek metis, so well analyzed by Marcel Detienne and Jean-Pierre Vernant, who note that it is embodied in "the principal types of individuals in Greek society, from the coachman to the politician, passing through the fisherman, the blacksmith, the orator, the weaver, the pilot, the hunter, the sophist, the carpenter and the strategist."[4] Just as previously with technoethics, we notice that our field of investigation has widened considerably. I'll limit myself for the time being to considering, in the field of design, only those professionals who are called on to design *material* objects, that is, principally industrial and product designers, architects, engineers, artists, artisans, and manufacturers.

Finally, a few general words on the methodology that has guided us throughout this study. It was in a *multidisciplinary* perspective that the preparatory deliberations were made toward the construction of a problematic of design ethics. For this final stage, however, we strove to reach *transdisciplinarity* and thus to give as general a validity as possible to the resulting concepts and hypotheses.[5] Moreover, and parallel to the theoretical reflection, we explored the possibility of introducing ethical reflection into the teaching of design. Many initiatives originated at the School of Industrial Design in Montreal: the creation of a course on design ethics; the organization of a studio on applied ethics in design focusing on the topic of money and banking; design projects with a strong ethical component (the evaluation of products, eco-products, the social impact of new products, "intelligent" products and ethics); ethics and project oriented teaching. An intensive seminar had also been held at the École Nationale Supérieure de Création Industrielle in Paris based on the notion of scenario as exposed by Ezio Manzini in his writings, and its possible integration with ethics. These pedagogical experiments led me to test a number of hypotheses and models derived from earlier analyses and, in return, to better tackle the most important issues. As such, they acted as a permanent interactive lab within the main research project.

THREE PROVISIONAL CONCLUSIONS

The perspectives opened by the project Prométhée Eclairé have such vast consequences that it is hard to grasp all aspects, given the present state of our reflection. They equally concern design theory, design methodology, assessment of products and of their impact, as well as professional codes of ethics (urbanism, architecture, industrial design, graphic design, engineering). Rather than with definitive conclusions, we ended up with a program of inquiry into some specific questions. Such a result conforms, after all, to the very idea of what a general problematic is. For this reason, this paper takes the form of a research note, and should be considered as a work-in-progress rather than a set of definitive results. The three questions that I sketch out here have been intentionally chosen for their bearing on the teaching and pedagogy of design. This choice is justified in the current context where many engineering and design schools are seeking a thorough reform of their own curricula.[6]

1 THE UNIFICATION OF THE DESIGN FIELD THROUGH THE MAPPING OUT OF THE WORLD OF ARTIFACTS

From the user's point of view, the space of artifacts stretches between two distinct poles. One may use an object for its strictly instrumental or utilitarian or "functional" qualities. There are numerous situations of this nature every day. On the other hand, one may just as well use objects for their symbolic, ritual or sumptuary qualities. These occasions also mark our everyday lives.[7] It even happens occasionally that the same object answers now, for one, now for the other purpose, but more frequently it is difficult to clearly distinguish between these two functions that analytical reason has separated. So, at first sight, it seems possible to arrange all technological objects along a line stretching between a "purely instrumental" pole and a "purely symbolic" pole.[8] Most tools, specialized instruments (for instance used in surgery or measuring), machines, weapons, etc., tend toward the first pole whereas works of art or cult objects tend toward the second (Figure 27.1). However, in order to take into account the previous observations i.e., the existence of artifacts being both functional and symbolic, it is necessary to move from one-dimensional space (the segment) to two-dimensional space (the plane), thus moving from a polarity of an exclusive type to a possible complementarity. The principal advantage of so simple a model is that it represents the world of objects as a continuous space, thus suggesting the possibility of describing it by means of a unified theory. Such a scheme allows the consideration of objects that have both a great symbolic and instrumental value as well as banal objects, lacking any significant symbolic or instrumental value, but nonetheless necessary. This "cartography" makes clearer why, historically, designers have believed themselves

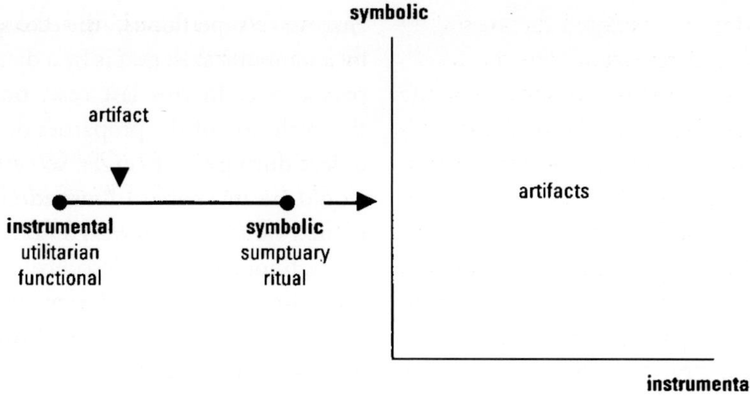

Figure 27.1 The instrumental/symbolic polarity: from an excluding opposition (left) toward the space of artifacts (right).

assigned the mission of reconciling those two poles that the Western mind stubbornly continues to oppose to one another, both conceptually (in philosophy, for example with the oppositions rational/irrational, matter/mind, etc.) and practically (the oppositions theory/practice, architect/engineer, etc.). The most noteworthy historical example of this is the Bauhaus, which, four years after its founding and upon the occasion of its first important public exhibition in 1923, adopted as its motto: "Art and technology, a new unity."

It is appropriate to mention here that the space created in this way is not as ideal and isotropic as Cartesian space. In fact, the two poles are not "commensurable," in that the instrumental quality of an object results mainly in *internal* technological logic, while its symbolic quality is assigned to it by *external* human representations (i.e., the object is only the signifier of a signified). This kind of space is, however, currently used in the humanities and social sciences (factorial analysis), which justifies my recourse to it here.

Pursuing the analysis allows us to better investigate and interpret this space. To do so, let's plunge it into the field of the techno-economical rationality of the designers of these objects. Each time one turns to a designer, it is specifically to confer a symbolic and/or instrumental value upon an object, to avoid the trap of banality or uselessness, to make the object safe and aesthetic. Moreover, we've seen that it is practically difficult, if not impossible, to clearly separate the two principal functions of objects, in other words, to isolate a purely symbolic or instrumental object. These considerations may be translated in the following way: in order for the designed and manufactured object to have a certain meaning for its users, the product of its utilitarian value and symbolic value must be greater than a certain limit, the "threshold of significance" (curve S). To this first condition is added a second well-known condition resulting from the fact that the manufacture of any artifact is effected within the framework of budgetary and technological constraints that vary according to the project. This may be viewed in the following manner: in order for an artifact to be viable, it is necessary that the sum of the investment of money and means of developmental research, design, manufacture and distribution necessary to guarantee the users its expected instrumental and symbolic values be less than a limit called "the budgetary ceiling" (straight line B).

If we reproduce these conditions in our previous space, we get the following figure, in which three distinct areas appear (Figure 27.2).

Finally, recalling remarks made earlier, we notice that it is easy to represent, in this space, the diverse practices and professions responsible for the conception and production of artifacts (Figure 27.3).

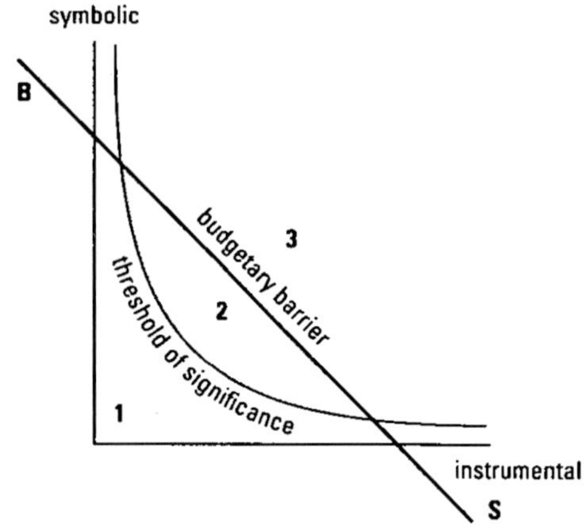

Figure 27.2 The space of artifacts: 1. meaningless, banal, or inefficient objects; 2. existing artifacts; 3. utopian artifacts or projects "on paper."

This space has many remarkable topological properties, whose pedagogical value must not go unnoted. Thus, the relative positions of curve S and line D result from conditions peculiar to each individual project i.e., from specific design criteria; the range of actually existing or possible objects (area 2) can increase, shrink, or even disappear depending on circumstances.

It would be possible to make this simple model more complex by adding supplementary dimensions. Thus the moral dimension could be introduced by a third axis deployed along the polarity "necessary/superfluous," the ecological dimension by a temporal axis, that is by a dynamic or genetic perspective. In this last case, one could follow the evolution of the properties or functions of an object during its life cycle; so certain trajectories would be inevitable (diminution of the instrumental value through wear and tear, deterioration or technological obsolescence), others possible (a utilitarian object becoming symbolic, such as a souvenir), and others still improbable (a banal object becoming useful).

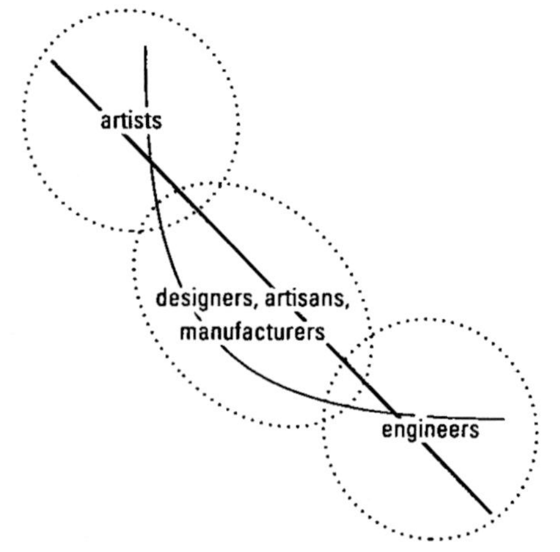

Figure 27.3 How professionals share the space of artifacts.

This space has also a fractal structure. Figure 27.2 is indeed valid whatever scale we consider within the space. The above schemata use the very largest scale, one which allows us to take in at a glance the complete set of objects. But one could as well, with a moderately sized scale, consider only a single class or type of object, such as books, pictures, clothes, or buildings. Let's consider chairs, for example: at the top on the left, we find a sovereign's throne, a chairman's chair, or a chair by Joseph Beuys; at the bottom to the right, we find an airline pilot's seat, a dentist's chair, or a wheelchair; in the upper center are located living or dining room chairs; at the lower center, workplace chairs (office, cashier, etc.) One could wonder where the electric chair, the barber's chair, or some chairs by postmodern designers fit. Using a still smaller scale, the topological properties of this space are applied to an individual object; thus, a secretary's chair has at the same time instrumental and symbolic value (aesthetic, affective, etc.). This last scale is that of the design project in general, the one designers are most familiar with.

Finally, note that the technical impossibility of representing or **making images** of a space of more than three dimensions (four, if one considers cinematographical, video, theatrical, and choreographic techniques) should not prevent us from **imagining** such spaces. Likewise, the extreme simplification of the reality of the world of objects affected in the above model must not keep us from considering an important consequence: the possibility of unifying, conceptually, at least, the space of artifacts. Actually, it is the design process underlying all artifacts that makes this unification possible and plausible. It is, in other words, what should allow an engineer and a composer, for example, to hold a fundamental dialogue on their respective experiences of creation, and to enrich, by so doing, the field of design theory.

A final remark: nothing a priori prevents us from extending the model to immaterial objects and acts, i.e., "political" objects such as a garbage collecting system or a film festival. This perspective would lead us to consider design as a "generalized rhetoric," a hypothesis already considered by some authors.[9]

2 THE ARTIFACT AS MEDIATOR. CONSEQUENCES FOR DESIGN METHODOLOGY

After having considered the artifact per se, it is appropriate to examine it from the standpoint of its relations with the environment (the latter in the phenomenological sense of the German concept, *Umwelt*). It is convenient, in this regard, to divide this environment into different "worlds," cosmos, systems, or spheres. Each sphere could be characterized according to the terminology of systems theory, i.e., according to its structure, organization, morphology, mode of operation, function, purpose, etc. In the present framework I propose to distinguish four worlds: the technocosm, the biocosm, the sociocosm, and the semiocosm. The first is the world of artifacts that we just examined, i.e., the built environment. The second is the natural environment, that of ecologists; it includes the world of physical geography (mountains, rivers, seas, clouds, etc.) and the plant and animal worlds. The third is that of human geography, of ethnology and sociology, i.e., the whole of human collectivities. The fourth includes the symbolic world, that of meanings, i.e., the world of culture in the broad sense, or, more precisely, the religious world in the most secular sense of the term.[10] One easily understands that any production of a new artifact (a cellular phone, for example) will disturb each of these worlds. It is precisely these disturbances that must be taken into account within the design process. Some of them are wanted (they are part of the design criteria), others unwanted (the designer tries then to minimize them). Within the framework of the current ecological crisis, an increasingly large consensus seems to have formed on this very general model, if not in practice at least in principle. However, its actual operational and pedagogical application conceals difficulties that have yet to be overcome.

As such, this model is still lacking, for it propagates the most deep-rooted prejudice of the "natural philosophy" of positivism and its underlying theory of knowledge: the separation of subject/object and, implicitly, the existence of a universal and perfectly "objective" knowing subject. This paradigm that has characterized modernism since at least the seventeenth century is now being challenged in the name of a "new paradigm," for which many qualifiers are being proposed: holistic, constructionist, systemic, postmodern, etc. I prefer to call it "relativist," a qualification that is at the same time more descriptive and closer to the scientific tradition that imposed it: twentieth-century physics. What this relativism implies, among other things, is that the observer's point of view is no longer exterior to the system, but is an essential component of the total system; in other words, that the opposition subject/object is neither possible nor acceptable, epistemologically speaking. As will be seen, this very fundamental principle applies not only to the theory of knowledge, but also to ethics and aesthetics.

Among the various possible viewpoints, two are essential for our purpose: that of the user, on the one hand, and of the designer, on the other. (Figure 27.4 illustrates the general model.)

In order to extend its validity, I found it necessary to distinguish, **at the interior** of each individual, several "worlds," spheres or centers that are analogous to those of the environment, so that the observer can be viewed as a kind of mirror-image of the environment, a microcosm within the macrocosm. A fundamental anthropology (or

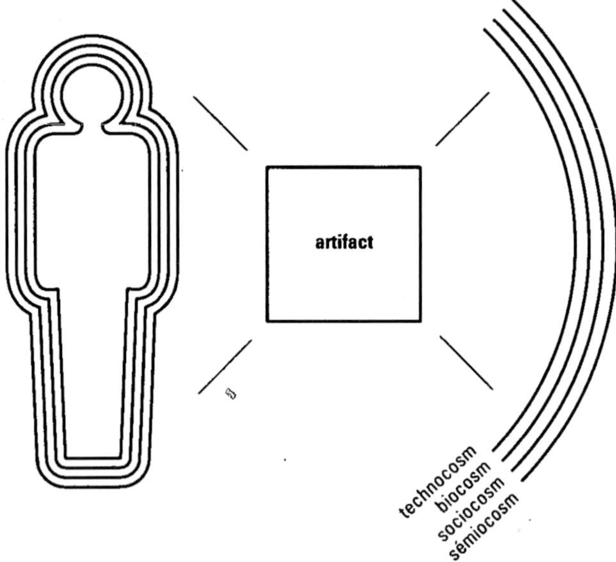

Figure 27.4 The relationship between the individual (user, designer, etc.) and the environment, mediated through the artifact, form the general system of the design project.

ontology) is sketched out here, as an answer to the claims of many contemporary ethicists and philosophers of technology. The development of such an anthropology, that is, the detailed description of the nature of the human technocosm, biocosm, sociocosm, and semiocosm, substantially goes beyond the scope of this essay. To guide one's own thoughts, I suggest that it is a matter of recognizing the ways in which the essence of the human being participates simultaneously in the mineral, vegetal, animal and spiritual aspects of existence.[11] The study of the relationships between the object, the environment and the four human spheres calls on several disciplines: anthropology, ergonomy, semiotics, mythology, sociology, epistemology, technology, psychology, etc.; it is an absolute necessity to bring these disciplines together in the perspective of a general science of design. From the viewpoint of such a science, it is the disturbances of the global system which embrace the user/object/environment which must be considered in priority; those are usually expressed in terms of needs, desires, aspirations, intentions. This point of view results from a fundamental humanist position, which considers technological production as a means to increase human well-being; I am aware here of touching on one of the most crucial problems of philosophy – and of ideology – of design, which will necessitate an in-depth revision of the notion of "needs."[12] Given the present state of this research, I can neither further refine the model presented here nor propose a general theory of needs. This study is currently part of a further research project.

The considerations discussed above have important consequences for the methodology of design. As presented in numerous theoretical writings and practical works in design, the "traditional" view, reviewed and corrected in the light of an often confused systemic paradigm, is the following: one considers the system formed by the interactions between one or several individuals and their environment, the latter being frequently reduced to the built environment; any disturbance of the system, usually identified by the term "need," is a potential problem for the designer; the intervention of the latter consists of proposing a "solution" to the problem, thus reestablishing the equilibrium of the system according to the following interventionist diagram:

Problem > intervention > end of problem (solution)

To correct the perspective shown above i.e. design viewed as a problem-solving activity, it is necessary to modify radically the diagram thus:

state 1 of the system > intervention > state 2 of the system

This new manner of seeing has considerable theoretical and methodological consequences. It implies that:

- we abandon the ideal of a system in equilibrium in favor of a dynamic conception of systems;
- we radically revise our current notion of needs (see above);
- we modify our "interventionist" model of design, replacing it by a "regulator" vision.

These conditions fulfilled, it then becomes possible to complete the model to take account of the distinctions discussed above (the four worlds). Although it is still too early to draw concrete results from such a new point of view, Ezio Manzini's hypothesis proposing that the designer become a "conceiver of scenarios" (and not just of products) was explored with some degree of success at an intensive workshop held at the l'École Nationale de Création Industrielle in Paris titled, "The Design System: Theoretical Aspects."[13] Ultimately, this model implies that we imagine the possibility of a technology that greatly goes beyond the materialist viewpoint inherited from the nineteenth century (as a guideline, think of the technique or art of gardens, the art of bringing up children, all the "techniques" that address themselves to living and human beings, such as they are).

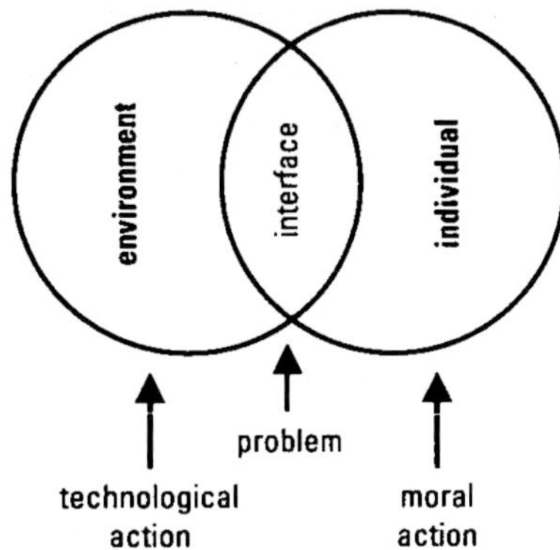

Figure 27.5 Conceptual scheme for the human/environment system: problem (disturbance of interface) and possible actions.

3 COMPARATIVE PHENOMENOLOGY OF THE TECHNOLOGICAL ACT AND THE ETHICAL DECISION

Here we touch on one of the most critical points of our conclusions. Let's recall first of all the most common position concerning the relations of technology to ethics: the former is supposed to be concerned exclusively with means, leaving the definition of ends to the second. In other words, an engineer or designer doesn't have to be preoccupied with the moral or political ends assigned to the usage of the objects that they are commissioned to design. Their skills restrict them to the technological domain and their responsibilities are defined by the professional code of ethics. Now let us take up, regardless of its imperfections, one of the small models described above, which is laid out in the manner shown in Figure 27.5.

This is how it reads: a problem arises whenever a disturbance occurs in the global system or at the interface of the human/environment system (strictly speaking, the individual really should be placed inside the environment). As was seen, a designer intervenes to set this state of affairs right, acting upon the built environment (or technocosm) to modify or to restore it, generally by introducing a new artifact into the interface. Acting on the individual (or group of individuals) is virtually never considered in design since such action does not inhere in the designer's prerogatives and abilities (but rather in those of law or of politics, etc.).

If we now consider the question from the viewpoint of the user facing a problem, two "solutions" are equally possible: either to use an artifact to "solve" the problem, or to change one's own behavior to "dissolve" the problem. The first alternative relies on technology, the second on morality (in the sense that it derives from manners, morals, and customs). Let's illustrate this by taking some examples:

(a) Two alternatives are conceivable for the prevention of AIDS: to use condoms (the technological solution) or to modify one's sexual behavior (the moral solution). Only in the first case is a designer requested.

(b) The increasing number of meetings, appointments and engagements assailing us pose a problem of organization and planning of daily, weekly, monthly and annual activities; several possibilities are available: to use an electronic engagement-book (the technological solution); to increase one's memory by training (the moral solution); or to diminish the activities by setting a hierarchy of priorities (another moral solution).

(c) A small city in the United States was having trouble with garbage collection. Rather than enlarging its dumping grounds or constructing a treatment facility (technological solutions), the city chose to require that its citizens dispose of their household garbage in only standard garbage bags sold at $3 a piece (twenty times more than conventional bags of the same size) color-coded by the municipal authorities. The conventional bags were no longer accepted by the garbage collectors (the moral, i.e., political solution). The amount of domestic waste diminished by half during the first week of operations (modification of behavior).

These examples invite us to consider what we use to call "the technological solution" as a particular **attitude** to a problem that we contrast to another attitude, the moral one. This implies that **choosing the technological mediation is a matter of ethics,** not technology; in other words, designing an artifact is acting in the field of ethics, not of technology alone. In classical philosophical terms, one would say that technology is not associated with **doing** (poiesis) but with acting (praxis).[14] Let's note that unlike the polarity instrumental/symbolic discussed earlier, the polarity evoked here seems to be of an exclusive nature: choosing the technological way excludes the moral way, just as the exercise of the moral way exempts one from activating the technological way. In the first case, one decides to resolve the problem under the pretext that it arose from an expressed or identified technological need; in the other, one accepts the fact that in some way the need isn't really a need or extends the notion of need. Thus one understands why a theory of need is so necessary.

According to this model there is a great temptation to suggest the image of a scale in which each half represents one of the two possible "solutions." When one rises, the other descends. More prosaically still, we could claim that one "solution" always hides another. That image helps us also to understand why technology, which solves a problem in its own sphere, can readily create new ones outside its own limited domain. The increasingly generalized public debates about decisions bearing on urbanism only confirm this model. If this apparent antinomy between the two poles eventually finds a solution as far as the user is concerned, as the above examples suggest, this is not the case with designers, who experience a sense of powerlessness in that the problem has gone beyond their professional capabilities. My own experience with students has confronted me with numerous examples of this situation. As such, the model was empirically confirmed within the framework of a design workshop organized around the theme of design ethics. After inviting a group of students to propose a prioritized list of pressing contemporary problems, I proposed that they suggest ways in which industrial design could contribute to remedying these problems. The group thus found itself facing the dilemma noted above: in most cases, the solution to the problems didn't, they admitted, belong to technology, i.e., address their professional competence. Nonetheless, and it is revealing and encouraging for those of us who subscribe to a widened and unified science of design, the group affirmed, intuitively, that the method practiced habitually in design was quite appropriate to explore vaster questions.

That last observation led me to examine in a comparative manner the usual methods of exploring a design problem, on the one hand, and a problem of applied ethics, on the other. Many texts on methodology, both in design and in ethics, deal with these questions, and the first thing to strike the reader, is the formal and structural analogy of the graphical models and diagrams used to illustrate the approach. The process usually follows the standard cycle: setting the problem > analysis > proposed solution > evaluation. In the most complex cases the process needs to be reiterated and resumed several times before deciding on a final decision. Even taking account of the numerous variations proposed and of the sometimes very complex methods required by the various phases of the process (especially concerning analysis and evaluation), this elementary structure seems to turn up everywhere. This might seem to lead to the conclusion that ethical deliberation is not very different from any other decision-making process. If, structurally speaking, this appears to be true, a more fundamental analysis reveals that it differs from others on one fundamental point: the way or the rhetoric in which the final decision is legitimated. Contrary to the technological decision which always rests on "scientific" reasoning – at least, this is what is required from technology on theoretical grounds – and thus upon a whole complex of norms universally shared by the actors and exterior to them, the ethical decision always requires total moral engagement on the actor's part. In epistemological terms, as we have seen, the former rests on the postulate of a radical separation between the subject and the object of the deliberation while the latter requires the involvement of the subject in its object.[15] The main consequence is that the ethical decision must begin anew for each individual case (there is no universal truth, each case is particular, subjectivity is constitutive and necessary), while similar conditions authorize similar decisions in the technological domain, so that objectivity constitutes its ideal horizon. Furthermore, practitioners of ethics recommend that the final decision be publicly justified, in front of all who are concerned by it, by a thorough reasoning "toward the goal of reaching a collective final solution."[16]

As all practitioners know from daily experience, the epistemological crux of the entire design process is located at the moment of passing from a descriptive to a normative procedure, that is, at the moment of decision-making. All efforts of design methodology and design theory tend to let us believe that there exists between the two distinct phases a logical sequence and implies the search for it. Ever since Poincaré, we have known that nothing authorizes us to establish such a link.[17] We are entitled to state that, in any case, it is absolutely impossible to explain such a course analytically (and, for example, to simulate it on a computer). Thus, it is an illusion to even wish to require the objectivity characteristic of rationalism or positivism in this matter. More simply stated, the criteria for choice in design do not arise, as in science, from truth: a solution is never true or false; it is more or less appropriate, more or less acceptable, correct, satisfactory and thus depends on an evaluative judgment of an essentially qualitative or rhetorical type. For their part, the principles of ethical deliberation show that subjectivity, that is, the deliberate involvement of the subject into the object, which rationalism considers as its major epistemological obstacle, should be accepted as the key for the course of action mentioned above. It is that attitude alone which permits the overcoming of the aporia and dilemmas that confront all decision-making after the initial period of analysis has correctly posed options for action. Now we can more clearly understand the usefulness, from the designer's point of view, of the anthropological model of four worlds presented in Figure 27.4. For when I mention the "total" involvement of the subject this means not only an intellectual involvement, but an involvement on all four levels of the anthropological structure:

"mineral," "vegetal," "animal," and "spiritual." It is noteworthy that the so-called "multicriteria" approach in design currently considered as the ultimate in design methodology aims to go beyond the incommensurability and incompatibility of the numerous contradictory objectives that condition decision-making by the use of interactive methods based on communication among the several intervening actors of a design project, namely, by a **moral** action.[18] In conclusion, I suggest that the different stages of moral deliberation, as described, for instance, in the book by Louis Racine et al. (see note 16), the formulation of the problem, the identification and classification of the values at stake, the setting up of a hierarchy of values, the making of a decision, the justification and explanation of the position adopted, the search for a collective solution, serve as a paradigm for the technological decision and thus for the design process.

These observations on the intimate nature of ethical deliberation raise difficult pedagogical questions, and here is why. Similar to the cognitive or logical development, a child's moral development also seems to pass through a number of stages, each of which is characterized by a specific level of structural complexity, as has been shown by studies of Jean Piaget and Lawrence Kohlberg.[19] Since our primary and secondary education centers principally, if not exclusively, on logical and rational development, there is a strong chance that most adults are partially "illiterate" from the moral point of view. This would be true for aesthetics as well. According to Lawrence Kohlberg, who identified six stages of moral development, most adults don't reach beyond the third stage, and only a very small minority ever achieve the final two stages. Considering the results, the quality of ethical decisions that we are led to make in our daily lives and professions dispenses with commentaries. That's why all the textbooks on applied professional ethics insist that the teachers operate on two levels: that of general morality (macroethics) and that of the ethics specific to the profession being considered (microethics). All the above general observations tend to discredit, to a considerable degree, the thesis of a possible "technicization" of the ethical decision (for example, by artificial intelligence or expert systems) and moreover justify the fears expressed by some authors at the general use of the term "technoethics."

SOME PEDAGOGICAL CONSEQUENCES

By reason of the principle of non-separability that has guided us through this text, we understand that some of the following recommendations, which are inspired by considerations discussed above in the field of design, are addressed to professional teaching in general, i.e., to medicine, law, architecture, design, engineering, business, etc. Nevertheless, given the framework of this essay, it is design education that I will address specifically.

1. My first conclusion led us to consider a continuous space of artifacts. A general theory of artifacts then should be possible in such a space. As far as the design of objects is concerned, it is necessary to reexamine the functionalist bias arising from rationalism, not necessarily to reject it as the postmodernists wish, but rather to widen its scope.[20] This means we reach beyond the materialistic and mechanistic definition of "function" and of "functionalism" to extend it to the symbolic realm. The notion of usefulness, which is endowed with a clearer moral connotation than that of function, should thus be reconsidered and altered just as radically as that of need. If a degree of consensus on these points seems to be attained nowadays, their practical adoption runs up against the difficulty of measuring these new variables, a necessary operation in order to treat them with conventional methods (i.e. cost-benefit, multicriteria, etc.).

In the design studio these theoretical considerations will be usefully supported by practical exercises of the exploration of the space of artifacts, conducted both analytically (case studies) and in actual design projects, so as to reach a phenomenological apprehension of that space and of its continuous character. It is only upon the completion of such exercises that one may eventually introduce fundamental concepts of semiotics, for example, while not losing sight of the two complementary viewpoints to be considered, that of reception (the user's point of view) and that of conception (the designer's point of view).

2. In my second conclusion, I considered the impact of the artifacts on the various worlds constituting its environment, as well as its interaction with the corresponding human worlds, whether at the moment of use or of design. The complexity of the relationships thus manifested encourages us to broach these questions on theoretical and methodological levels by a systemic approach.[21] The more than abundant literature devoted to this topic over the past decade should at least exempt me from supplementary commentaries. Nonetheless, at the risk of pedantry, I wish to make some observations whose importance was confirmed by numerous pedagogical experiences. All treatises on systemics approach their subject **analytically** (of necessity, given the nature of language), which is in fundamental contradiction with one of the founding principles of systemics. In the strictest sense, the systemic apprehension of a complex reality arises from **intuition**. Now it is well known that this word suffers from disfavor and confusion, especially in design education. Moreover, this prejudice is quite understandable when we consider how intuition is most often defined, in spite of the rigorous studies devoted to it by philosophers and scholars of epistemology (Dilthey, Weber, Bergson, Poincaré, Bachelard, etc.). Intuition is no more a given than is analytical reasoning and, as with the latter, it is necessary to train it. I believe that an aesthetic education is most apt to develop intuition in a rigorous, progressive manner, provided the nature of this education is well defined.[22]

Most design schools offer one or more courses with purely artistic content. Though those can be considered as a kind of aesthetic practice, it is rarely a matter of aesthetic **education**. In this realm, as with logic and reason or mathematics, one must start with extremely simple problems before very gradually increasing their complexity. In this regard, the apparently simplest works by abstract painters (like Malevich, Mondrian, Moholy-Nagy) are already extremely complex for the aesthetic illiterates that most of us are. With aesthetics as with logic, it is necessary to begin with composition assignments of very simple forms, and to make them more complex, either by variation of shapes or color; then, in order to stimulate the students' sensitivities, various tools, materials, and techniques will be suggested (painting, photography, sculpture, etc.). This is the very principle of the basic design workshop that the Bauhaus systematically elaborated. That type of education was in part discredited with the advent of postmodernism, which criticized its rationalism and formalism; that is quite right, since in most cases, that is really what is happening, for the original pedagogical goal (the formation of intuitive thought) has been lost with time. Composition in color, in particular, is a remarkably effective way to grasp intuitively and then understand the notion of system, for the juxtaposition of two colors modifies the nature of each seen individually, that is, the global equilibrium of the whole. Any painting by Mondrian can be considered as a particular problem of systemic coherence that has to be resolved within the framework of particular constraints (the limited number of colors and forms available, the perpendicular orientation of the whole picture, the limits of the picture frame). Significantly, in 1928, at the Bauhaus, Moholy-Nagy had already thought of extending that basic instruction (*Grundlehre*) to all professional schools (law, medicine, engineering, etc.) with the precise goal of developing the intuition and judgment of the students, all necessary and irreplaceable qualities.[23]

The theoretical familiarization with systemic complexity will gain, as seen above, when it builds upon a practical experience. To achieve this, I recommend generalizing John Dewey's project-oriented pedagogy. In the studio one should, however, avoid proposing exclusively "real" projects, like commissions by local corporations, which most design school practice. These projects have the disadvantage of taking place in a world subject to the constraints of technoeconomical rationality, which often reduces their potential pedagogical fecundity. "Fictive" projects, which are designed according to the pedagogical goals proceeding from the models proposed above, are often preferable. The realm of games and toys, for example, offers possibilities of a richness that defies the imagination.

3. Let us now take up the delicate question of the teaching of professional ethics. All writers and specialists agree to discourage a priori any effort at teaching of the theoretical, magisterial, or deductive types in this matter. "[That type of] knowledge is inseparable from a **conversion**," asserts Rose-Marie Mossé-Bastide, who writes further: "In no way is reflection upon ethics separable from experienced ethics."[24] So it is, once again, an active project-oriented pedagogy that is needed here. For this, it is appropriate to differentiate between two main orientations:

- One, which can be called microethics, concerns itself with problems of strictly professional ethics, i.e., occasions for conflict arising during daily professional practice like, for instance, conflicts of interest, public safety, professional integrity and competence, confidentiality, unfair competition. For this purpose I cannot but recommend to readers the book *Ethique et ingénierie* (see note 16), which presents, in addition to a general method with which to approach all these problems, several cases of the kind, real or imaginary. Experience has shown that the switch from engineering to design doesn't pose any major methodological problem.
- The other, which can be called macroethics, where the goal should be to have the students develop a **general attitude** vis-à-vis the problems entrusted to them. That attitude is characterized by an openness to the values underlying all technological alternatives, a sensitivity to the complexity of problems, a heightened consciousness of the impact of their "solutions" on the technological, ecological, social and spiritual levels, a care to systematically include an evaluation process into their projects. On a practical methodological level, this means that the phase of problem-setting, as opposed to problem-solving, of the project be extended. On the ethical level, it will lead students to reach beyond simple professional **competence** toward global professional **responsibility**.

I would like to point out that the macroethical level isn't completely absent from current codes of ethics. As an example, clause 2.01 of the moral code of ethics for engineering in Quebec stipulates that "in all aspects of work, engineers must respect obligations toward human beings and take into account the consequences of the execution of their works upon the environment and upon the life, health and property of all individuals." The code of the Association of Industrial Designers of Quebec requires that "an industrial designer has the professional obligation of ameliorating the social and aesthetic norms of the community." The first clause of the code of ethics of the Order of Architects of Quebec requires that "in the exercise of his profession, the architect should take into account obligations toward human beings and the environment." All these clauses, which find their equivalents in many other countries, arise from good intentions, but are somewhat tautological; their excessively large generality obviates all efficacity, a fact borne out by a review of the grievances made against members of these professional corporations.[25] The extremely general nature of these clauses perhaps indicates that it would be difficult, if not unwise, to go into more detail about the resolutions that they contain. It is all the more reason, since they must be interpreted and not blindly applied, to encourage students to develop a general critical attitude, recalling in this way Moholy-Nagy's famous phrase, "Designing is not a profession, but an attitude."[26]

In this respect, I suggest we return to the model presented above (Figure 27.5), in which was noticed the apparent exclusive opposition between the two poles (technological and moral), in order to envision the possibility of a **continuous** space, marked by two axes corresponding to the two poles (analogous to the instrumental/symbolic space of Figure 27.2). The modalities of setting such a space remain to be defined. To do this, let's begin with an observation made above: the sense of powerlessness and paralysis felt by students (and, by extension, by designers) when confronted with the moral dilemma illustrated by the model. A scientific analogy can help clarify this feeling: the search for first causes in science is an infinite process that can only be interrupted by some expedient that lies beyond in the epistemological canon (postulates, axioms). In ethics, the actor is concerned with the determination of ends, that is, final causes; but here still, the process has no end and is only halted by an arbitrary expedient (a priori principles, the categorical imperative, etc.). To set up the space referred to above, to envision a continuity between the technological act and the moral act, amounts to interrupting the infinite process toward the identification of final causes. This implies that we take into account the values that control our rationality and our acts and intentionality and that we consciously choose to set them in a hierarchy, giving sufficient attention to the conditions peculiar to each case, fully aware that this choice will have to be justified eventually. This is precisely what is meant by assuming responsibility for one's actions and having confidence in one's moral judgment.

These important remarks lead us back to aesthetics. The fact that ethics and aesthetics both deal with values is another reason to build a bridge between these two seemingly foreign realms. We have seen that ethical deliberation requires the total involvement of the subject at the moment of decision-making. The latter happens when the subject has the intimate conviction and deep-seated feeling that his or her act and its ideal representation coincide. This feeling of coincidence is actually of the aesthetic order: it is the apprehension of harmony, the sentiment of unity.[27] Therefore, aesthetic judgment and moral judgment act as a pair and, consequently, the training of an adequate aesthetic judgment will be a guarantee for reliable moral reasoning.

One final remark: increasing the sensitivity of student designers to the ethical dimensions of their practice is usually effected through the introduction of a sociology course into the curriculum ("introducing the social dimension," is the unfortunate hallowed phrase). That practice, praiseworthy in theory, nonetheless can offer several disadvantages depending on the fashion in which this "social dimension" is introduced. First, as with ethics, the educational approach of a magisterial or theoretical type doesn't fit this purpose disregarding the fact that it seldom encourages the enthusiasm and interest of students. A situational, "learning-by-doing" approach is invariably preferable. In this case, it is very probable – and desirable – that students be introduced to the methodology of sociology, so that it will be difficult to avoid mentioning the methodological conflict existing within that discipline between advocates of quantitative methods and advocates of qualitative methods. If, for the most part, the technical-methodological disputes exchanged by the two camps may be understood and even endorsed (questions of internal and external validity, reliability, precision), it is no longer the same if we transfer the debate to the ethical plane. A number of these methods rely upon axioms – most often implicit – that are contrary to one of the central tenets of ethics: to respect the dignity of persons, i.e., the fact of considering all persons as ends in themselves. The use of quantitative (statistical) methods requires that, of individuals and groups of individuals, one consider only the most "mineral" (to use my terminology), the most "mechanical," predictable, deterministic, conditioned aspects. This is exactly the reproach that has been made against the behavioristic methodologies practiced in psychology and psycho-sociology, which are used for numerous opinion polls, market studies, product evaluations, etc. effected by "applied" sociology. In other words, to rely on conventional marketing studies in order to justify the design of a new product, or on polls to determine the wishes of "consumers," or even on classical ergonomy to design a machine raises ethical principles that are hard to defend. All the same, to avail oneself of the market, that is, users, to test the technological and symbolic performance of a product is indefensible. These remarks invite us to be cautious when we consider "introducing the social dimension" into a design or engineering curriculum.

GENERAL CONCLUSION

In its original form, the research presented here lent itself very naturally to an investigation and a revision of the codes of ethics of the design professions. This endeavor is on the agenda of several professional associations and corporations, and one understands the difficulties and hesitations they face. Although this was a major goal of the original project as described, we were led progressively and quite naturally to transfer our priorities to design education and pedagogy instead of design practice. Indeed, I became convinced that in heading upstream, the project would achieve much greater generality and better efficacy at the risk of losing some of its technical efficiency.

Orienting the general problematic in this way toward pedagogical goals allowed us to center the research on very specific issues in regard to the following topics: a topography of the global set of artifacts; the determination of the phases of the design process corresponding to the setting of the problem and to the evaluation of the "solutions"; the stage of decision-making in design within the framework of a global ethical attitude in relation to the strictly technological project. I pointed out that because of the structural analogies that exist between the two processes, it was not necessary to leave the field of design in order to construct a general problematic of design ethics, provided that one expands the currently accepted definition of "design." Finally I wish to insist on the fact that the proposals introduced here could only be validated and clarified within the framework of a methodological position borrowed from the design process, which requires that theoretical speculation must constantly be checked against a pedagogical and practical test of the models being worked out. It is likely that this pragmatic position is responsible for the fact that I haven't come out with a "theoretical" model describing "the general system of design ethics" or with any other speculative product of the kind, but that I have limited myself to making some recommendations and partial conclusions instead. Does this mean that in the "applied" disciplines, i.e., in the normative – as opposed to the descriptive – realm, all theoretical reflection is necessarily of a methodological order? In other words, that a design theory, the search for which appears to be mounted on all fronts, is of necessity a methodology?

Be that as it may, it is thus for their educational value above all else that it is fitting to evaluate the models presented here. In view of these goals, some will surely reproach them for being a bit simplistic. But that is to forget that they will reveal their heuristic potential only upon being systematically tested in practical situations. Still other observations need to be made. I willingly concede that presenting the space of artifacts as I have done has serious drawbacks, especially since it tends to isolate these objects from the human and social context in which they operate; this objection I strove to compensate for in the second model (Figure 27.4). In its present state, the latter is still no more than a sketch; specifically, there is yet the matter of detailing the various components of the proposed anthropological structure (the four "worlds") and their relationships with the four subsystems of the environment, through the mediation of the artifact. Such a task will most likely reveal some important aspects of the general act of design that are currently neglected or forgotten. As for the third model (Figure 27.5), though it has the advantage of presenting alternatives in a clear and radical fashion, it, however, has the disadvantage of being difficult or uneasy to use, given its present form, for practical decision-making. I feel that this disadvantage is largely compensated for by the considerable opening that it makes into the field of design, which is still overly confined to its strictly technological and material aspects. Finally, I believe that the idea of establishing a relationship between ethics and aesthetics will give the latter a very necessary impetus, for it is doubtless one of the areas of design philosophy that has been least understood during the twentieth century and which calls for a serious fundamental reconsideration.

NOTES

First published in *Design Issues* 10 no. 2 (Summer 1994): 49–68.

1. This research project has given rise to numerous endeavors and publications. Thus, 4 special numbers of the journal *Informel* were devoted to the theme of the project 3 no. 2 (Summer 1990); 4 nos. 1–2 (Winter and Summer 1991); 5 no. 1 (Winter 1992). These papers constituted preparatory documents for a colloquium that was held May 8–11, 1991 at the University of Montreal and whose proceedings have been edited by the author under the title: *Prométhée éclairé. Ethique, technique et responsabilité professionnelle en design*, Montreal, Ed. *Informel*, 1993. The application of the conclusions to architecture and engineering were also examined by the author.
2. The use of the term "technoethics" is strongly resisted by some writers. Gilbert Hottois prefers the "ethics of technology" because of the risk of possible semantic slippages; according to him, "technoethics" could be understood to mean an ethics of a technological character, that is, subject to a technoscientific rationality. See his argument in "Vérité objective, puissance et systeme, solidarité. D'une éthique pour l'age technoscientifique," *Informel* 3 (2, Summer 1990): 16–29, note 7. In his work *Contre la peur* (Paris: Hachette, 1990), Dominique Lecourt, commenting on Jurgen Habermas, raises the same fear: "Nevertheless, the illusion is spread that 'practical' questions – those that arise from law and from morality – can be treated, posed, and solved technologically" (p. 138).
3. Some classic works are cited below: Tadeusz Kotarbinski, *Praxiology: An Introduction to the Science of Efficient Action* (Oxford: Pergamon Press, 1965); Herbert A. Simon, *The Sciences of the Artificial* (Cambridge, MA: MIT Press, 1969); Donald A. Schon, *The Reflective Practitioner* (New York: Basic Books, 1983); Wojciech Gasparski, *Understanding Design: The Praxiological-Systemic Perspective* (Seaside: Intersystem, 1984); Philippe Boudon, *Sur l'espace architectural: essai d'epistémologie de l'architecture* (Paris: Dunod, 1971); J. L. Le Moigne, *La théorie du système général: Théorie de la modélisation* (Paris: Presses Universitaires de France, 1977; 1990).
4. Marcel Detienne and Jean-Pierre Vernant, *Les ruses de l'intelligence: La métis des Grecs* (Paris: Flammarion, 1974), 295.
5. Gilbert Hottois's *Le paradigme bioéthique* (Brussels: De Boeck/Université, 1992) offers such transdisciplinary effort.
6. In support of this observation, one may cite the following documents: *Introduction du Design dans l'Enseignement Supérieur*. Proceedings of the colloquium organized by CEFI under the aegis of the Ministry of Industry and Exterior Commerce, Paris, 1990; *A Proposal for the Renewal of Engineering Education and its Infrastructure*, edited by ECSEL (Engineering Coalition of Schools for Excellence in Education and Leadership), Washington DC, 1990; Ron Levy and Alain Findeli, *An Evaluative Review of the School of Industrial Design, Minority Report* (University of Montreal, December 18, 1990); *The Science Technology Society Program at Eindhoven University of Technology* (Eindhoven, 1992); *Department of Design: Proposal for a Revised Undergraduate Curriculum Plan* (Pittsburgh: Carnegie Mellon University, 1992). Oddly, parallel to this movement to extend the realm of design, one finds in several institutions a contrary movement toward "straight and pure" professionalism which is sustained mainly by economic and corporate motivations and by professionals who, to borrow Condorcet's phrase concerning jurists, "are more concerned with maintaining their power than with

honoring it."

7. Remember that we refer to a "technological object" or "artifact," as opposed to a natural object, as any object invested with a human intention. Thus, to take a limited case, a dead limb in the woods is no longer a natural object as soon as a child plays with it, all the more so if the child begins to trim and shape it with a penknife to make a sword or a cane. In their study of the relations that members of a family have with various domestic objects. Mihaly Csikszentmihalyi and Eugene Rochberg-Halton itemized 37 categories or types of person/object relations, the "utilitarian" class being among them; the other classes are lined up along the pole that we called "symbolic" in this study. See *The Meaning of Things: Domestic Symbols and the Self* (Cambridge: Cambridge University Press, 1981), 57 and Appendix C, 270–274.
8. The model presented here can be found, explicitly or implicitly, in numerous works by anthropologists, historians of technology, etc. To our knowledge, it was Abraham Moles, who presented it most explicitly in his works, beginning with *Théorie des objets* (Paris: Ed. Universitaires, 1972). In his presentation at the symposium "Prométhée éclairé," he used the polarity useful/useless (in French he liked the play of words "utile/futile") to map out the world of objects. One also finds the model in Yves Deforge's evocatively titled *L'oeuvre et le produit* (Seyssel: Champ Vallon, 1990). Moreover, in his presentation at the symposium "Prométhée éclairé," Gilbert Hottois reflected on C. P. Snow's *The Two Cultures* in the light of an analogous opposition reminiscent of the title of his book *Le Signe et la technique* (Paris: Aubier-Montaigne, 1984).
9. One must mention here Richard Buchanan's noteworthy approach, a work in progress, whose premises are presented in "Declaration by Design: Rhetoric, Argument, and Demonstration in Design Practice," *Design Issues* 2 no. 1 (Spring 1985): 4–22.
10. As an example, this sense of "religious" is used by Fritz Oser, Paul Gmunder, and Louis Ridez in *L'homme, son développement religieux* (Paris: Cerf, 1991), also by Paul Tillich in his work. The term "semiocosm" is borrowed from Ezio Manzini. The definition proposed by Csikszentmihalyi and Rochberg-Halton of the word "religion" is similar to the one I have used here (see note 7 above, pp. 42–43).
11. One finds comparable anthropological models with various philosophers throughout history; thus Aristotle differentiated in human beings the vegetative soul, the sensitive soul, and the intellective soul. Under the influence of Plato, Renaissance philosophers developed several analogical models of the macrocosm and microcosm. The early Christian division into body, soul, and spirit was taken up, sometimes in a misunderstood or mutilated form, by modern philosophers and psychologists.
12. Other writers have been aware of the problem and proposed trains of thought that I do not necessarily share. See, for instance, Tomás Maldonado, "The Idea of Comfort," *Design Issues* 8 no. 1 (Fall 1991): 35–43; Tony Fry, "Against an Essentialist Theory of 'Need,' " *Design Issues* 8 no. 2 (Spring 1992): 41–54.
13. Ezio Manzini presented his hypothesis during a presentation at the symposium "Prométhée éclairé," a summing-up of his work *Artefatti: verso una nuova ecologia dell'ambiente artificiale* (Milan: Edizioni DA, 1990). He took it up in "Prométhée au quotidien: Ecologie de l'artificiel et responsabilité du designer," *Informel* 4 no. 2 (Summer 1991): 21–29 and he finally completed his reflections in "Prometheus of the Everyday: The Ecology of the Artificial and the Designer's Responsibility," *Design Issues* 9 no. 1 (Fall 1992): 5–20.
14. Here we borrow a classic distinction, established by Plato in *Charmides* (163 b–d) and especially by Aristotle in the *Nicomachean Ethics*, book 6, chapter 4, amply discussed by G. Even-Granboulan in *Action et Raison* (Paris: Meridiens Klincksieck, 1986).
15. During an international conference Margaret Sommerville, the director of the Center for Medicine, Ethics and Law at McGill University, recently declared in relation to caring for the terminally ill, "Those who unconditionally support the right to euthanasia and those who oppose it formally argue from a **logical** base ... They are seeking **technological** means to regulate a question concerning emotions, intuition, and spirituality."
16. My discussion of the ethical deliberation largely draws upon a recent work that synthesized many models, principally North American, and of pragmatic orientation; see Louis Racine, Georges Legault, and Luc Begin, *Ethique et ingénierie* (Montreal: McGraw-Hill, 1991).
17. Henri Poincaré, "La morale et la science" in *Dernieres pensées* (Paris: Flammarion, 1924), 225.
18. The so-called "aids to multicriteria decisions" methods are currently raising high hopes in design and in environmental evaluation. For an introduction without too much mathematical material, see A. Scharlig, *Décider sur plusieurs criteres* (Lausanne: Presses Polytechniques Romandes, 1985).

19. Jean Piaget, *Le jugement moral chez l'enfant* (Paris: Presses Universitaires de France, 1957); Lawrence Kohlberg, *Essays on Moral Development* (San Francisco: Harper & Row, 1981).
20. Abraham Moles suggests a move in this direction in his article, "Pour un néofonctionnalisme," *Informel* 4 no. 1 (Winter 1991): 28–37. In order to be comprehensive the revision of the concept of functionalism that I am proposing would need more than these few lines. If enlarging the notion of function is a necessary step, it is certainly not enough. Considering, as Moles proposes, not just the object, but the object in context, that is the act of use itself, would definitely be more comprehensive and discriminate than a mere list of specifications and design criteria that is too technical and reductive. But such a revision should tackle the very methodological foundations of functionalism and its epistemological premises, which arise from rationalism, atomism and economics. As to the implicit ethical foundations of functionalism, they have been discussed in terms of utilitarianism by A. McIntyre in "Utilitariansim and the Presuppositions of Cost-Benefit Analysis: An Essay on the Relevance of Moral Philosophy to the Theory of Bureaucracy" in Martin Wachs, ed., *Ethics in Planning* (Rutgers: The State University of New Jersey, 1985), 216–131 and by Barry Commoner in "Comparing Apples to Oranges" in Pablo Iannone, ed., *Contemporary Moral Controversies in Technology* (New York: Oxford University Press, 1984), 64–65.
21. A clear definition – a rarity in itself – of "systemic" was proposed by Bernard Paulré in a book he edited, *Perspectives systémiques* (Limonest: L'interdisciplinaire, 1989), 8–11.
22. I define intuition as the capacity to instantly grasp the structure of the relations that lend coherence to an organism or system, to seize its **form** (in the Aristotelian sense). Intuition then perceives something that is invisible to the "eyes of flesh": it sees the physiognomy ("le regard/the glance") of phenomena. This concept is central to the epistemology of Goethe, who called it "*anschauende Urteilskraft*" (contemplative judgment), thus affirming its close relation to aesthetics.
23. Names such as Kandinsky, Itten, Albers, Moholy-Nagy, Klee continue to be associated with this type of education. The most systematic and accessible introduction to this method is László Moholy-Nagy's in *Von Material zu Architektur* (Mayence: Florian Kupferberg, 1988, a reprint of the 1929 edition), and *Vision in Motion* (Chicago: Paul Theobald, 1947). See also Gyorgy Kepes, *Language of Vision* (Chicago: Paul Theobald, 1944), or any other good treatise on basic design intended for architecture or design schools. Moholy-Nagy had also foreseen and remarkably well analyzed the ethical problems that we're facing today. In regard to this, the introductory chapters of his testament *Vision in Motion* remain of greatest interest and remarkably up to date.
24. Rose-Marie Mossé-Bastide, *Genese de l'éthique* (Geneva: Patino, 1986), 227.
25. During this short research I found that no suit had been filed in ten years against an architect in the title of the clause cited. See Alain Findeli, "Architecture et technoéthique," "Contribution a une éthique de l'architecture," in Alberto Pérez-Gómez, ed., *Architecture, Ethics and Technology* (Toronto: McGill Queen's University Press, 1993): 163–185. For numerous examples of codes of ethics, see the report edited by Carl Mitcham, *Engineering Ethics throughout the World* (University Park: STS Press, Pennsylvania State University, 1992).
26. László Moholy-Nagy, *Vision in Motion*, 42.
27. Poincaré noted that, as far as he was concerned, the final choice of a theoretical model among several arose from aesthetic judgments. As indicated above, Goethean epistemology, which prefigured the phenomenology of the twentieth century, rests completely on a specific-aesthetic-way of apprehending phenomena: the contemplative judgment (*Anschauende Urteilskraft*).

FURTHER READING FOR PART III

There is considerable literature on the analysis of images. See, for example, Roland Barthes, *Image, Music, Text*, edited and translated by Stephen Heath (New York: Hill and Wang, 1977); and Gunther Kress and Theo van Leeuwen, *Reading Images: The Grammar of Visual Design* (New York: Routledge, 1996). On design criticism, see the special issue, "A Critical Condition: Design and Its Criticism" *Design Issues* 13 no. 2 (Summer 1997). Among the many books on sustainability and its relation to design, see Victor Papanek, *The Green Imperative: Natural Design for the Real World* (New York: Thames and Hudson, 1995); Janis Birkeland, *Design for Sustainability: A Sourcebook of Integrated Ecological Solutions* (London: Earthscan, 2002); Jonathan Chapman, *Emotionally Durable Design: Objects, Experiences and Empathy* (London: Earthscan, 2005); Tony Fry, *Design Futuring: Sustainability, Ethics and New Practice* (Oxford and New York: Berg, 2009); and Barbara Predan and Cvetka Požar (eds.), *Sustainable Alternatives in Design: It's High Time We Start Losing Time* (Ljubljana: The Architectural Museum of Ljubljana, 2009). See also Carlo Vezzoli and Ezio Manzini, *Design for Environmental Sustainability* (London: Springer Verlag, 2008); and Ezio Manzini and François Jegou, *Sustainable Everyday: Scenarios of Urban Life* (Milan: Ambiente, 2003). On the Hochschule für Gestaltung, Ulm, see Herbert Lindinger, *Ulm Design: The Morality of Objects, Hochschule für Gestaltung, Ulm, 1953–1968* (Cambridge, MA: MIT Press, 1991); and René Spitz, *hfg Ulm: The View Behind the Foreground: The Political History of the Ulm School of Design, 1953–1968* (Stuttgart: Edition Axel Menges, 2002). On design ethics, see Clive Dilnot, *Ethics? Design?*, The Archeworks Papers 1:2 (Chicago: Archeworks, 2005).

GENERAL BIBLIOGRAPHY

Aicher, Otl (1994). *The World as Design.* Berlin: Ernst & Sohn.

Alexiou, Katerina, Jeffrey Johnson, and Theodore Zamenopoulos (2009). *Embracing Complexity in Design.* London and New York: Routledge.

Bierut, Michael, William Drentel, Steven Heller, and D.K. Holland (1994). *Looking Closer: Critical Writings on Graphic Design.* Introduction by Steven Heller. New York: Allworth Press.

Bierut, Michael, William Drentel, Steven Heller, and D.K. Holland (1994). *Looking Closer 2: Critical Writings on Graphic Design.* Introduction by Steven Heller. New York: Allworth Press.

Bierut, Michael, William Drentel, and Steven Heller (2002). *Looking Closer 4: Critical Writings on Graphic Design.* Introduction by Steven Heller. New York: Allworth Press.

Beirut, Michael, William Drentel, and Steven Heller (2006). *Looking Closer 5: Critical Writings on Graphic Design.* New York: Allworth Press.

Bierut, Michael, Jessica Helfand, Steven Heller, and Rick Poynor (1994). *Looking Closer 3: Classic Writings on Graphic Design.* Introductions by Steven Heller and Rick Poynor. New York: Allworth Press.

Buchanan, Richard and Victor Margolin (1995). *Discovering Design: Explorations in Design Studies.* Chicago and London: University of Chicago Press.

Bürdek, Bernhard E. (2005). *Design: The History, Theory and Practice of Product Design.* Boston: Birkhauser.

Clark, Hazel and David Brody (eds.) (2009). *Design Studies: A Reader.* Oxford and New York: Berg.

Conway, Hazel (1987). *Design History: A Student's Handbook.* London and New York: Routledge.

Cross, Nigel (2006). *Designerly Ways of Knowing.* London: Springer Verlag.

Design Issues 24 no. 1 (2008). Special issue on *Design + Organizational Change.*

Doordan, Dennis (ed.) (1995). *Design History: An Anthology.* Cambridge, MA: MIT Press.

Doorst, Kees (2003). *Understanding Design.* Amsterdam: BIS Publishers.

Flusser, Vilém (1999). *The Shape of Things: A Philosophy of Design.* London: Reaktion Books.

Fry, Tony (1994). *Remakings: Ecology, Design, Philosophy.* Sydney, Envirobook.

Fry, Tony (1999). *A New Design Philosophy: An Introduction to Defuturing.* Sydney: UNSW Press.

Fry, Tony (2008). *Design Futuring: Sustainability, Ethics and New Practice.* New York and Oxford: Berg.

Gorman, Carma (ed.) (2003). *The Industrial Design Reader.* New York: Allworth Press.

Helfand, Jessica (2001). *Screen: Essays on Graphic Design, New Media, and Visual Culture.* New York: Princeton Architectural Press.

Heskett, John (2002). *Toothpicks and Logos: Design in Everyday Life.* Oxford and New York: Oxford University Press.

Highmore, Ben (ed.) (2009). *The Design Culture Reader.* London and New York: Routledge.

Julier, Guy (2008). *The Culture of Design.* Los Angeles and London: Sage.

Laurel, Brenda (ed.) (2003). *Design Research: Methods and Perspectives.* Cambridge, MA and London: MIT Press.

Löwgren, Jonas and Erik Stolterman (2004). *Thoughtful Interaction Design: A Design Perspective on Information Technology.* Cambridge, MA: MIT Press.

Maldonado, Tomás (1972). *Design, Nature, and Revolution: Toward a Critical Ecology.* Translated from the Italian by Mario Domandi. New York: Harper & Row.

Manzini, Ezio (1989). *The Materials of Invention: Materials and Design.* Cambridge and London: MIT Press.

Margolin, Victor (2002). *The Politics of the Artificial: Essays on Design and Design Studies.* Chicago and London: University of Chicago Press.

Margolin, Victor (2004). *Healing the World.* (The Archeworks Papers 1:1.) Chicago: Archeworks.

Margolin, Victor (ed.) (1989). *Design Discourse: History, Theory, Criticism.* Chicago and London: University of Chicago Press.

Margolin, Victor and Richard Buchanan (eds.) (1995). *The Idea of Design*. Cambridge, MA: MIT Press.

Simon, Herbert (1970). *The Sciences of the Artificial*. Cambridge, MA: MIT Press.

Suchman, Lucille (1987). *Plans and Situated Actions: The Problem of Human-Machine Communication*. Cambridge and New York: Cambridge University Press.

Thackera, John (2005). *In the Bubble: Design in a Complex World*. Cambridge, MA: MIT Press.

Whiteley, Nigel (1993). *Design for Society*. London: Reaktion Books.

Woodham, Jonathan (1997). *Twentieth-Century Design*. (Oxford History of Art.) Oxford and New York: Oxford University Press.

Woodham, Jonathan (2004). *A Dictionary of Modern Design*. Oxford: Oxford University Press.

INDEX